Fodor's 2015

NEW YORK CITY

W9-AYN-560

WELCOME TO NEW YORK CITY

From Wall Street's skyscrapers to the neon of Times Square to Central Park's leafy paths, New York City pulses with an irrepressible energy. History meets hipness in this global center of entertainment, fashion, media, and finance. World-class museums like MoMA and unforgettable icons like the Statue of Liberty beckon, but discovering the subtler strains of New York's vast ambition is equally rewarding: ethnic enclaves and shops, historic streets of dignified brownstones, and trendy bars and eateries all add to the urban buzz.

TOP REASONS TO GO

★ **Landmarks:** With towering edifices and awe-inspiring bridges, the skyline says it all.

★ **Shopping:** Whether you're in the market for top designers or inexpensive souvenirs.

★ **Food:** Dim sum to pizza and everything in between, NYC has what you're craving.

★ **Museums:** Art is it, with museums like the Guggenheim and galleries all over town.

★ **The Dazzle:** From the lights of Broadway to celebrity sightings, NYC is full of stars.

★ **Brooklyn and Elsewhere:** Cool neighborhoods and restaurants are a subway ride away.

Fodor's NEW YORK CITY 2015

Publisher: Amanda D'Acierno, *Senior Vice President*

Editorial: Arabella Bowen, *Editor in Chief*; Linda Cabasin, *Editorial Director*

Design: Fabrizio La Rocca, *Vice President, Creative Director*; Tina Malaney, *Associate Art Director*; Chie Ushio, *Senior Designer*; Ann McBride, *Production Designer*

Photography: Melanie Marin, *Associate Director of Photography*; Jessica Parkhill and Jennifer Romains, *Researchers*

Maps: Rebecca Baer, *Senior Map Editor*; Mark Stroud (Moon Street Cartography), David Lindroth *Cartographers*

Production: Linda Schmidt, *Managing Editor*; Evangelos Vasilakis, *Associate Managing Editor*; Angela L. McLean, *Senior Production Manager*

Sales: Jacqueline Lebow, *Sales Director*

Marketing & Publicity: Heather Dalton, *Marketing Director*; Katherine Punia, *Senior Publicist*

Business & Operations: Susan Livingston, *Vice President, Strategic Business Planning*; Sue Daulton, *Vice President, Operations*

Fodors.com: Megan Bell, *Executive Director, Revenue & Business Development*; Yasmin Marinaro, *Senior Director, Marketing & Partnerships*

Copyright © 2015 by Fodor's Travel, a division of Random House LLC

Editorial Contributors: Jessica Colley, David Farley, Anuja Madar, Jacinta O'Halloran, Michael Hornburg, John Rambow, Josh Rogol, Christina Valhouli

Lead Editor: Caroline Trefler

Editor: Joanna G. Cantor

Production Editor: Jennifer DePrima

ISBN 978-0-8041-4254-0

ISSN 0736-9395

SPECIAL SALES

This book is available at special discounts for bulk purchases for sales promotions or premiums. For more information, e-mail specialmarkets@randomhouse.com

PRINTED IN THE UNITED STATES OF AMERICA

10 9 8 7 6 5 4 3 2 1

CONTENTS

MAPS

ABOUT THIS GUIDE

Fodor's Recommendations

Everything in this guide is worth doing—we don't cover what isn't—but exceptional sights, hotels, and restaurants are recognized with additional accolades. **Fodor's Choice★** indicates our top recommendations; and **Best Bets** call attention to notable hotels and restaurants in various categories. Care to nominate a new place? Visit Fodors.com/contact-us.

Trip Costs

We list prices wherever possible to help you budget well. Hotel and restaurant price categories from **$** to **$$$$** are noted alongside each recommendation. For hotels, we include the lowest cost of a standard double room in high season. For restaurants, we cite the average price of a main course at dinner or, if dinner isn't served, at lunch. For attractions, we always list adult admission fees; discounts are usually available for children, students, and senior citizens.

Hotels

Our local writers vet every hotel to recommend the best overnights in each price category, from budget to expensive. Unless otherwise specified, you can expect private bath, phone, and TV in your room. For expanded hotel reviews, facilities, and deals visit Fodors.com.

Restaurants

Unless we state otherwise, restaurants are open for lunch and dinner daily. We mention dress code only when there's a specific requirement and reservations only when they're essential or not accepted. To make restaurant reservations, visit Fodors.com.

Credit Cards

The hotels and restaurants in this guide typically accept credit cards. If not, we'll say so.

Top Picks
★ Fodor's Choice

Listings
⊠ Address
⊠ Branch address
☎ Telephone
🖷 Fax
⊕ Website
✉ E-mail
🎟 Admission fee
🕙 Open/closed times
Ⓜ Subway
✢ Directions or Map coordinates

Hotels & Restaurants
🏨 Hotel
🛏 Number of rooms
🍽 Meal plans
✗ Restaurant
🍷 Reservations
👔 Dress code
⊟ No credit cards
⑤ Price

Other
⇨ See also
☞ Take note
🏌 Golf facilities

EXPERIENCE
NEW YORK CITY

NEW YORK CITY TODAY

The phrase "in a New York minute" is clichéd for a reason: in this frenetic city, things really do change in a flash. These days, foodies are still salivating about "farm to table," "artisanal," and "Brooklyn," but the buzzword on every New Yorker's lips for 2014—and surely well into 2015—is "new." New Mayor, new waterfront developments, new hotels, new locations for the Brooklyn's Smorgasburg, and a new definition of "library" (if plans for New York Public Library don't get old before they finally get underway). Some newly completed projects that will bring closure to old wounds—and new life to a part of the city under cover since 9/11—are the 1,776 foot tall One World Trade Center and the long-delayed National September 11 Memorial & Museum.

Politics
After three terms and 12 years of Mayor Michael Bloomberg, the big story in New York City politics will, no doubt, be the city's new mayor, Bill de Blasio. With top priorities that include reigning in the police force's controversial "stop and frisk" practices (random street searches of minority New Yorkers) and the replacement of the city's iconic—and controversial—horse-drawn carriages with electric antique cars, the new mayor's first years in office will be of great interest to locals and visitors alike.

Economy
A few quick positive economic indicators: New York is experiencing its biggest hotel expansion in a generation, attracting a host of new brands—from high-end boutiques to budget chains—all across the city. The city has 143 hotels in the pipeline to open by 2016, with 43 of these properties slated for the outer boroughs—a key indicator of recent visitor trends to visit, and stay, in boroughs beyond Manhattan. And tourists keep on coming: 2013 had a record number of visitors—around 54 million, up from the previous year's 52 million, and the city is projecting 55 million visitors by the end of 2014.

Sports
If there's something the quintessential New Yorker can't get enough of, it's sports, so if you're looking to make small talk with a local, just pick a team. Basketball fans can support the trendy Brooklyn Nets (Jay Z is a part owner) in their new digs at the Barclays Center in Brooklyn or the New York Knicks

WHAT'S NEW?

"SuperPier," the Pier 57 development at West 15th Street in Hudson River Park, originally earned its *super* status in 1952 when it opened as a shipping terminal. But the name applies just as easily to the 2015 pier, which will reopen with a riverfront spa, a beach club, restaurants, a food bazaar, retail stores housed in repurposed shipping containers, a rock climbing wall, and more.

The South Street Seaport took a battering from 2012's Hurricane Sandy but plans—and shovels—are finally underway to rescue the area, replacing the existing complex at Pier 17 with a new $200 million glass retail complex, including new restaurants and stores. Planned reopening is late 2015.

Governor's Island, a favorite summer escape, reopened in 2014 with 30 acres of new parkland, new ball fields, and

(Spike Lee is practically the team mascot) at Madison Square Garden. In late 2015, the New York Islanders hockey team will move from their suburban Long Island stadium to their new home at Barclays Center. The Islanders haven't won a Stanley Cup since the early 1980s and the hope is that Brooklyn will help them get their mojo back. The Islanders compete with the New York Rangers for the hearts, and tickets, of New York hockey fans. Baseball lovers can choose between the New York Yankees (Yankee Stadium in the Bronx) or the New York Mets (Citi Field in Queens). New York football fans declare their loyalties to either the New York Giants or the New York Jets—both teams play at MetLife Stadium in New Jersey. Soccer fans can choose between the New York Red Bulls, the newly revived New York Cosmos and the newly formed New York City Football Club (who plan to sway NY fans with a new stadium just south of Yankee Stadium in the Bronx). If you can't pick a team, pick a less-contentious sport, like tennis; the U.S. Open brings the best in tennis to the USTA Billie Jean King National Tennis Center in Queens at the end of every summer.

The Arts

Some of the biggest movers and shakers in the New York art scene will be moving and/or shaking off dust after renovations in 2015, perhaps suggesting that the art world will be more focused on exhibition spaces than the exhibitions themselves. One big move is the Whitney's relocation to its state-of-the-art new space in the Meatpacking District in late 2015. Before it air kisses the Upper East Side good-bye, the museum will depart its Marcel-Breuer designed old home with a museum-wide retrospective of Jeff Koons's work—the first time a single artist has ever taken over almost the entire museum. But why move when you can just eat up real estate around you? In 2014, the Museum of Modern Art (MoMA) will begin work on a controversial plan to raze its neighbor, the critically acclaimed former home of the American Folk Art Museum, to create more gallery space.

an open lawn. Transformation of the site will continue into 2015 with features including "the Hills," made of recycled construction and fill material, which will have breathtaking panoramas of the Statue of Liberty, New York Harbor, and the Lower Manhattan skyline.

Coney Island's New York Aquarium will reopen in 2016, after a $150-million renovation, with exciting new features like a roof deck overlooking the ocean and a walk-through coral tunnel with sharks swimming overhead.

Staten Island is hoping to become a destination, and not just a pit stop on the Staten Island ferry, as it redevelops the waterfront to include a mall, a giant Ferris wheel, restaurants, and a hotel. Construction is scheduled for completion in 2016.

PLANNER

When to Go

New York City weather, like its people, is a study in extremes. Much of winter brings bone-chilling winds and an occasional traffic-snarling snowfall, but you're just as likely to experience mild afternoons sandwiched by cool temperatures.

In late spring and early summer, streets fill with parades and street fairs, and Central Park has free performances. Late August temperatures sometimes claw skyward, bringing subway station temperatures over 100°F (no wonder the Hamptons are so crowded). This is why September brings palpable excitement, with stunning yellow-and-bronze foliage complementing the dawn of a new cultural season. Between October and May, museums mount major exhibitions, most Broadway shows open, and formal opera, ballet, and concert seasons begin.

Getting Around

On Foot. The best way to explore New York is on foot. No matter what neighborhood you're headed to, you'll get a better sense of it by wandering around; you can check out the architecture, pop into cool-looking shops and cafés, and observe the walk-and-talk of the locals. And if you get lost, New Yorkers are surprisingly helpful with directions.

By Bike. Since Citi Bike's bike sharing program rolled out in 2013, there have been glitches but ridership has been steadily increasing and New York City's program now boasts the largest fleet of bikes in the nation. The city is slowly acclimating (its bike lanes and attitudes) to the popular new mode of transportation but it's no Copenhagen . . . yet. Ride off-peak if possible, stay out of midtown, and stay alert!

By Public Transportation. New York's subway system is probably the most efficient and cost-effective way to get around, and it runs 24 hours a day. The subway is safe, but be smart; try to avoid riding alone—especially late at night, and avoid riding in empty cars. Rush hour is crazy crowded, train floors can be sticky, stations are sweltering in summer, and platforms are grimy year-round, but this all just adds to the "charm" of riding on a system that is more than 100 years old.

If you prefer to stay above ground, and—unlike everyone else in New York—you're not in a rush, consider taking a bus. They're especially good if you need to travel cross-town—between the East and West sides of the city. What a city bus lacks in efficiency (especially at rush hour), it makes up for in people-watching and city views.

By Taxi. If you'd rather be comfy than thrifty, hail a yellow cab (the new apple-green "Boro Taxis" serve the outer boroughs and won't make pickups south of East 96th Street or West 110th). A taxi is available if the center panel of the roof light is lit and the side panels are dark. It's best to give your destination address using cross streets: ask to be taken to "55th and Madison" rather than "545 Madison." Avoid trying to hail a cab between 4 and 4:30 pm, when drivers change shifts. And remember that the subway is often faster than a cab, especially during rush hour.

For more information, check out the Travel Smart chapter.

A Guide to the Grid

The map of Manhattan is, for the most part, easy to follow: north of 14th Street, streets are laid out in a numbered grid pattern. Numbered streets run east and west (crosstown), and broad avenues, most of them also numbered, run north (uptown) and south (downtown). The main exception is Broadway, which runs the entire length of Manhattan on a diagonal. Below 14th Street, street patterns get chaotic. In the West Village, West 4th Street intersects West 11th Street, Greenwich Street runs roughly parallel to Greenwich Avenue, and Leroy Street turns into St. Luke's Place for one block and then becomes Leroy again. There's an East Broadway and a West Broadway, both of which run north–south, and neither of which is an extension of Broadway, leaving even locals scratching their heads.

Street Smarts

Avoid deserted blocks in unfamiliar neighborhoods. A brisk, purposeful pace helps deter trouble wherever you go. New York City is a safe city, but it's still a city, so keep jewelry out of sight on the street; better yet, leave valuables in your hotel safe.

Of course, you want to capture every "New York minute," but instead of parading your camera—and your tourist status—consider securing it in a nondescript cross-body bag.

When in bars or restaurants, don't hang your purse or bag on the back of a chair.

Expect to have yourself and your possessions inspected thoroughly in such places as airports, sports stadiums, museums, and top attractions. Police officers stationed by subway-token booths also reserve the right to check your bags before you pass through the turnstile to enter the platform.

We suggest politely ignoring panhandlers on the streets and subways, people who offer to hail you a cab, and limousine and gypsy-cab drivers who (illegally) offer rides.

Opening Hours

Subways and buses run around the clock, as do plenty of restaurants. Some shops and services have more extensive hours than you'll find elsewhere in the United States, so you can get groceries, or get your hair and nails done, at 11 pm. In general, though, you can safely assume that most shops are open seven days a week, from about 10 to 7 Monday to Saturday, and from noon to 6 on Sunday. Bars generally close at 4 am, though some after-hours clubs are open later.

Money-Saving Tips

Consider buying a CityPass, a group of tickets to six top-notch attractions in New York: the Empire State Building, the Guggenheim Museum or Top of the Rock, the American Museum of Natural History, the Museum of Modern Art, the Metropolitan Museum of Art (including the Cloisters), and Circle Line Cruises or admission to Liberty and Ellis islands. The $106 pass, which saves you almost half the cost of each individual ticket (and all that time on ticket lines), is good for nine days from first use.

Sign up for social discount shopping sites like Groupon, Gilt City, Bloomspot, and LivingSocial a month before your visit to New York to score discounts on everything from trendy restaurants and clubs to beauty treatments and attractions.

WHAT'S WHERE

Numbers refer to chapters.

2 Lower Manhattan.
The Financial District, NY Harbor, and TriBeCa. Heavy-duty landmarks anchor the southern tip of Manhattan, including Wall Street and the waterfront parks of Battery Park City. The ferry terminals dispatch boats to Ellis Island and the Statue of Liberty. The evolving construction site at Ground Zero is also down here.

3 SoHo, NoLIta, Little Italy, and Chinatown. Luxe shops dominate in SoHo these days, while NoLIta, to the east, has lots of boutiques and restaurants. Little Italy is a shrinking zone of touristy red-sauce eateries. Farther south, Chinatown teems with street vendors selling knockoff handbags and side streets with Chinese herb shops and noodle joints.

4 The East Village and the Lower East Side.
Once an edgy neighborhood of artists and punks, the East Village is now a melting pot of students, artists, and professionals. The once seedy, now trendy Lower East Side has live-music clubs, independent clothing shops, and wine bars.

5 Greenwich Village and the West Village. Artists with rent-controlled apartments, out-and-proud gays, and university students still live in the Village but because those townhouses have become so expensive, residents also include wealthy media moguls, celebrities, and socialites. From 14th Street south to Houston and from the Hudson River east to 5th Avenue, the blocks are a jumble of jazz clubs, restaurants, former speakeasies, and rainbow flags.

6 Chelsea and the Meatpacking District.
Chelsea has supplanted the Village as the center of gay life in the city. To the south, the Meatpacking District has evolved into a swanky clubbing and restaurant scene by night and—with the High Line and high-end boutiques—a shopping and strolling destination by day.

7 Union Square, the Flatiron District, and Gramercy Park. Bustling Union Square Park hosts the city's best greenmarket. On the 14th Street edge are broad steps where break dancers and other performers busk for onlookers. Nearby, private Gramercy Park is surrounded by storied mansions and town houses.

WHAT'S WHERE

8 Midtown East and Murray Hill. Midtown from 5th Avenue to the East River is the refined big sister of flashy Midtown West, with grand hotels, grand shopping, the Chrysler Building, and Grand Central Terminal. Murray Hill is a mix of quiet tree-and-town house–lined streets and attractions like the Empire State Building and the Morgan Library.

9 Midtown West. Head to 42nd Street to see Times Square in all its neon and massive-TV-screen glory. Towering office buildings line Broadway up to Columbus Circle at the edge of Central Park. At Rockefeller Center are the famous ice rink and tree (in season), and nearby are swank shops like Saks and Bergdorf Goodman.

10 The Upper East Side. The Upper East Side is home to more millionaires than any other part of the city. Tucked into this stretch of 5th Avenue are the Museum Mile and Madison Avenue's haute boutiques.

11 Central Park. Fredrick Law Olmstead's ode to the pastoral in the heart of New York, Central Park is the place to escape the bustle of the city. There's a small zoo, a boathouse, and activities as diverse as rock climbing, softball, and Frisbee.

12 The Upper West Side with the Cloisters. Wide sidewalks and ornate prewar buildings set the tone, and the American Museum of Natural History and Lincoln Center are big draws. Farther north is the Cloisters, a branch of the Metropolitan Museum of Art housing medieval works in a reconstructed monastery.

13 Harlem. A hotbed of African American and Hispanic American culture for almost a century, Harlem still sizzles. The brownstone-lined blocks are being refurbished, boutiques and restaurants are popping up, and music venues from the 1920s and '30s are still in full swing.

14 Brooklyn. Manhattan's largest borough counts among its stars Coney Island, Prospect Park, and the Brooklyn Botanic Gardens. Its distinct neighborhoods include Williamsburg, Fort Greene, and Brighton Beach.

15 Queens, the Bronx, and Staten Island. Queens is known for its ethnic communities and Citi Field. The Bronx may be best known for Yankee Stadium, but the New York Botanical Garden and the Bronx Zoo also score home runs. Staten Island's most compelling feature might be the ferry, but there are reasons to stick around.

NEW YORK CITY TOP ATTRACTIONS

Metropolitan Museum of Art

(A) The largest art museum in the Western Hemisphere, the Met is a mecca for art lovers of all stripes. Treasures from all over the world and every era of human creativity make up its expansive collection. If you need a breather, you can always retire to the Temple of Dendur or the rooftop café.

Times Square

(B) Times Square is the most frenetic part of New York City: a cacophony of languages and flashing lights, outré street performers, shoulder-to-shoulder crowds, and back-to-back billboards. These days it's also a pedestrian-friendly zone, so you won't have to take your eyes off the excitement to watch for traffic.

Empire State Building

(C) It may not be the tallest building in New York anymore (the Freedom Tower reclaimed the title for the World Trade Center in May 2012), but its status as most iconic will never change. Take in the panoramic views of the city from its observatories, or just enjoy it from afar—after dark it's illuminated by colored lights that correspond to different holidays and events.

Museum of Modern Art

(D) Airy and spacious, with soaring-ceiling galleries suffused with natural light and masterpieces that include Warhol's *Campbell's Soup Cans* and Van Gogh's *Starry Night,* this one-of-a-kind museum designed by Japanese architect Yoshio Taniguchi is as famous for its architecture as for its collections.

Brooklyn Bridge

(E) New York City's most famous bridge connects the island of Manhattan to the borough of Brooklyn, and serves thousands of pedestrians, vehicles, skaters, and bicyclists a day. Walking across is an essential New York experience.

Statue of Liberty
(F) Presented to the United States in 1886 as a gift from France, Lady Liberty is a near-universal symbol of freedom and democracy, standing 152 feet high atop an 89-foot pedestal on Liberty Island.

American Museum of Natural History
(G) The towering, spectacularly reassembled dinosaur skeletons that greet you when you enter this museum might stop you in your tracks, but there's much more to see here, including exhibits of ancient civilizations, the live Butterfly Conservatory (October–May), a hall of oceanic creatures overlooked by a 94-foot model of a blue whale, and space shows at the adjoining Rose Center for Earth and Space.

Central Park
The literal and spiritual center of Manhattan, Central Park has 843 acres of meandering paths, tranquil lakes, ponds, and open meadows. For equestrians, softball and soccer players, strollers, skaters, bird-watchers, boaters, picnickers, and outdoor performers, it's an oasis of fresh air and greenery amid the hustle of the city.

Ground Zero
The memorial at the World Trade Center site is a moving tribute to the lives lost on 9/11. After a decade of clean-up and construction, the memorial opened to the public on the 10th anniversary of the terrorist attacks; construction of a museum and work on other parts of the site continues.

The High Line
A botanical garden, a bridge to nowhere, a local hangout, and a work of art—using the city's architecture, greenery, and people as part of its composition—this once-abandoned railroad track rises above the west side of Chelsea neighborhood.

LIKE A LOCAL

New Yorkers love their city—and with good reason, as there's no place like it on earth. Living here can be challenging, from the high rents to battling crowds at Sunday brunch but the locals have plenty of tricks up their collective sleeves. At the risk of compromising our New York credibility (after all, we consider ourselves members of an exclusive club and guard our secrets accordingly), we've decided to share some insider info here. Just don't tell anyone we told you.

We Get Around

We hit the ground walking

Spend a day in a New Yorker's shoes and you'll understand why we have the reputation for being skinny: New Yorkers walk. Pounding the pavement is often be the fastest way to get around but remember—move quickly, we're in a hurry. If you need to check your smartphone, pull over and get out of the way.

We take the subway

If weather, distance, or time rules out walking, we take the subway; it's cheaper than a cab and often faster. The subway runs 24 hours a day, 7 days a week. There are maps posted in all stations, and locals are more than happy to show off their knowledge of the subway lines if you need directions. Even seasoned New Yorkers ask for or confirm directions, so don't be shy. If you're traveling with a smart phone, the app HopStop will help you figure out the best route. As for safety, the same advice applies here as to traveling in any major city: be alert, watch your bag, and don't travel on your own late at night.

All Hail the Taxi Cab

There is no shortage of yellow cabs in Manhattan; there's just a shortage of *available* cabs—especially when it's raining or you're in a hurry. You can tell whether a taxi is available by checking its rooftop light. If the center panel is lighted and the side panels are dark, the driver is looking for passengers (so stick out your arm!); taxis whose roof lights are lighted only at the edges—not the center—are off-duty.

Many visitors to the city expect to find locals summoning taxis with a loud whistle or a brash "Hey Taxi!" but in reality, we are much quieter about it, preferring to hail cabs with a raised arm or via a smart phone app. Several e-hail services are available in the city but Uber and Gett are the most popular with locals. Once you've signed up, a simple tap will search for a car and track it in real time as it comes to you; you pay with a prestored credit card. Uber has been building its business and reputation in NY since 2012 and is the best known on-demand car service, but their "surge price" levels for holidays and inclement weather have not endeared the service to locals in need of a ride on New Year's Eve or during a storm. Gett has two key differences: you can book a taxi in advance and you won't suffer surge pricing.

We work out

We work long hours, eat at our desks, and rush around but despite our busy schedules, we work out. Whether it's for vanity or sanity, we can be found early in the morning and late at night jogging around the reservoir in Central Park, and running or biking along the city's beautiful waterfront paths. Of course, this being New York, fitness is a competitive sport with long lines and waiting lists for the latest workout trends or "it" instructors. Fitness trends generating buzz (and bragging rights for locals) in 2014 were 24-hour gyms, spin classes in water, combination spin-yoga classes, dance-trampoline classes, Modo-Yoga, and high-intensity interval training (HIIT) classes. Consider packing a pair of (cute) sneakers for your next visit.

We're particular . . .

. . . about our coffee

There might be a chain coffee shop on every corner in New York City but you won't find many locals there. The so-called "city that never sleeps" is fueled with coffee, but not just any coffee. We're a bit particular, some might say snobby, about coffee, so—even if we're in a rush, which, of course, we are—we'll wait those few extra minutes for the best freshly roasted beans and pour-over brews. Join discerning locals at gourmet hot spots like Blue Bottle Coffee, Joe the Art of Coffee, Stumptown, La Colombe, and Third Rail Coffee. Most spots offer the added bonus of homemade pastries and treats, but don't expect to find a seat. Find your fuel by name, neighborhood, or location at ⊕ *NYCMugged.com*.

. . . about our food

New York offers dining experiences at every level, from budget to blowout, trendy to classic, with nearly all global cuisines represented; it's no wonder we have a reputation for eating out. That said, we do cook for ourselves on occasion (crazy rents to pay, after all), and when we do, we shop local. Local greenmarkets like Union Square Farmers Market offer a range of fresh fruit and vegetables as well as locally sourced meats, fish, and specialty foods. Join hungry locals to shop the stands on Monday, Wednesday, Friday, and Saturday from 8 am to 6 pm.

New Yorkers haven't lost their appetite for the various food-trucks parked around the city, offering everything from Korean tacos and vegan sandwiches, to gourmet donuts and Belgian waffles. Twitter feeds and blogs track their whereabouts (try ⊕ *NYCTruckFood.com*).

. . . and about our entertainment

You won't cross paths with many locals in the heart of packed Times Square but we're not so jaded as to ignore the wealth of Broadway and off-Broadway theatrical and musical offerings—we just don't like to pay full price for the experience. Instead, we look for discounted tickets at social buying sites like Groupon, Gilt City, and Living Social. Or we score deals at the discounted ticket booth TKTS, though we're more inclined to line up at the less-trafficked booth in Brooklyn than the one in Times Square. ■TIP➡ Use the free TKTS App for up-to-date ticket availability at each of the city's three booths. Otherwise we favor the off-off Broadway experience, staying in-the-know with sites like ⊕ *OffOffOnline.com*.

We like to take advantage of our city's amazing museums, too, although we tend to frequent during off hours, like early mornings on weekdays. We are members of our favorite museums (as much to skip lines as to support the arts), or we plan our visits around free or pay-as-you-wish nights. Another popular, and free, local art activity is skipping the major museums altogether and strolling from gallery to gallery in Chelsea.

SITTING IN A TV AUDIENCE

Tickets to tapings of TV shows are free, but can be hard to get on short notice. Most shows accept advance requests by email, phone, or online—but for the most popular shows, you might have to wait a few months. Same-day standby tickets are often available, but be prepared to wait in line for several hours, sometimes starting at 5 or 6 am, depending on how hot the show is, or the wattage of that day's celebrity guests. And we hate to tell you this, but standby tickets do not guarantee a seat in the audience. You can also follow your favorite shows on Twitter for updates on last-minute tickets.

The Shows

The Colbert Report. Stephen Colbert has a new gig as the host of The Late Show, starting in 2015, and the *The Colbert Report* will go off the air at the end of 2014. Until then, check the website or Twitter (@ColbertReport) for tickets. ⊠ *513 W. 54th St., between 10th and 11th Aves., Midtown West* ⊕ *www. colbertnation.com* Ⓜ *C, E to 50th St.*

The Daily Show with Jon Stewart. The amiable, and incisive Jon Stewart pokes fun at news headlines on this half-hour cable show. The program tapes from Monday through Thursday; you can request advance tickets by checking the calendar on the website. For standby tickets, show up before 2:30 pm on the day of the show. ■TIP→ Last-minute tickets are often announced on either The Daily Show Facebook, or on Twitter (@TheDailyShow). Audience members must be 18 or older. ⊠ *733 11th Ave., between 51st and 52nd Sts., Midtown West* ⊕ *www. thedailyshow.com/tickets.*

Good Morning America. Robin Roberts and George Stephanopoulos host this early-morning news and entertainment standby. *GMA* airs live, weekdays from 7 to 9 am, and ticket requests (required only if you want a studio tour after the show) should be requested online four to six months in advance. ■TIP→ Gather before 7 am on the corner of West 44th Street and Broadway to participate in outdoor segments. ⊠ *7 Times Sq., 44th St. and Broadway, Midtown West* ⊕ *abcnews.go.com/GMA/ mailform?id=12943471* Ⓜ *1, 2, 3, 7, N, Q, R, S to Times Sq.–42 St.*

The Late Show with David Letterman. Dave's famously offbeat humor and wacky Top Ten lists will be going off the air in 2015 but until then, check the website for how to get tickets. ⊠ *Ed Sullivan Theater, 1697 Broadway, between 53rd and 54th Sts., Midtown West* ☎ *212/975–5853* ⊕ *www. lateshowaudience.com* Ⓜ *1, C, E to 50th St.; B, D, E to 7th Ave.*

Late Night with Seth Meyers. *Saturday Night Live* alum Seth Meyers took the reins as host of *Late Night* on NBC in 2014 when former host Jimmy Fallon departed for *The Tonight Show.* Check the website for ticket details. ⊠ *30 Rockefeller Plaza, Midtown West* ⊕ *www.nbc.com/tickets-and-nbc-studio-tour#lnsm* Ⓜ *B, D, F, M to 47th–50th Rockefeller Center.*

Live! with Kelly and Michael. The sparks fly on this morning program, which books an eclectic roster of cohosts and guests. Tickets are available online about six weeks in advance, or by mail up to a year in advance. Standby tickets become available weekdays at 7 am at the **ABC Studios** (⊠ *7 Lincoln Sq., corner of 67th St. and Columbus Ave., Upper West Side*). Children under 10 are not permitted in the audience. ☎ *212/456–3054* ⊕ *www.dadt.com/live* Ⓜ *1 to 66th St.– Lincoln Center.*

Rachael Ray Show. This energetic, bubbly chef helms a daytime talk show that covers everything from cooking and fashion tips to celebrity interviews. The set looks like a cozy kitchen, and the show typically tapes on Tuesday, Wednesday, and Thursday at 11:30 am and 3:30 pm. Guests must be 16 or older to be in the audience. Advance tickets are only available on Rachael Ray's website. ■TIP→ Dress business-casual and avoid crazy prints per the suggested dress code if you want to be admitted. ⊠ *Chelsea Television Studios, 221 W. 26th St., between 7th and 8th Aves., Chelsea* ⊕ *www.rachaelrayshow. com* Ⓜ *1 to 28th St.*

Saturday Night Live. *SNL* continues to captivate audiences. Standby tickets—only one per person—are distributed at 7 am on the day of the show at the West 49th Street entrance to 30 Rockefeller Plaza. You may ask for a ticket for either the dress rehearsal (8 pm) or the live show (11:30 pm). Requests for advance tickets (two per applicant) must be submitted by email only in August to ✉ *snltickets@ nbcuni.com*; recipients are determined by lottery. You must be 16 or older to sit in the audience. ⊠ *NBC Studios, 30 Rockefeller Plaza, between 49th and 50th Sts., Midtown West* ☎ *212/664–3056* ⊕ *www. nbc.com/tickets* Ⓜ *B, D, F, M to 47th– 50th Sts./Rockefeller Center.*

Today. The *Today Show* doesn't have a studio audience but if you get yourself to the the corner of Rockefeller Center and 49th Street before dawn, with posterboard and markers (fun signs always get camera time), comfortable shoes (you'll be on your feet for hours), and a smiley, fun attitude you might get on camera. America's first morning news–talk show airs weekdays from 7 to 10 am in the

TIPS

■ Prepare to have your pockets and bags checked before you enter, and leave the camera at home, as snapping a shot during a show isn't allowed.

■ Wear layers: TV studios blast the air-conditioning.

■ Sitting in a TV audience can be more boring than watching the show at home. You'll have to wait intermittently while sets are changed and stars' makeup is refreshed; if your seats are in back, you may feel far from the action.

glass-enclosed, ground-level NBC studio. ⊠ *Rockefeller Plaza at W. 49th St., Midtown West* ⊕ *www.today.msnbc.msn. com* Ⓜ *B, D, F, M to 47th–50th Sts./ Rockefeller Center.*

The Tonight Show Starring Jimmy Fallon. In early 2014, musician, actor, and comedian Jimmy Fallon packed up his impressions and sketches, his roster of star friends, and his house band, the Roots, and moved from *Late Night* to *The Tonight Show,* into the big comedic shoes of Jay Leno and Johnny Carson before him. Thankfully for NYC audiences, Fallon did not have to move to Burbank for his new gig. The *Tonight* show is back in New York (where it resided until 1972). Visit the website to reserve free tickets. ⊠ *Studio 6B, Rockefeller Plaza, Midtown West* ☎ *212/664–3506* ⊕ *www. showclix.com/event/thetonightshowstar ringjimmyfallon.*

FREE AND ALMOST FREE

Sometimes it seems like everything in New York costs too much but, in fact, the city has tons of free (or almost free) attractions and activities; you just need to know where to look for them. Note that NYC is at its most free (mentally and financially) in summer when there are all sorts of outdoor events, but you can find a "wealth" of freebies year round.

Free Art

The $25 admission fee to the **Metropolitan Museum of Art** and the $22 fee to the **American Museum of Natural History** are actually *suggested* donations. Smaller donations may get some eye-rolling from the cashier, but it's a small price to pay for access to world-famous works. At the **Museum at FIT**, "the most fashionable museum in the city," the Fashion Institute of Technology's museum is home to a collection of some 50,000 garments and accessories from the 18th century to the present. It's free, off-the-beaten-museum-path, and fabulous. Another less trafficked—and free—gem, the **National Museum of the American Indian (Smithsonian Institution)** on the south side of Bowling Green in Lower Manhattan is in a beautiful Beaux Arts building. It's a small museum (by New York standards) but offers free music and dance performances as well as an extensive permanent collection of textiles, ceremonial objects, and decorative arts. Decidedly on the beaten path, and for good reason, **MoMA** is free on Friday between 4 and 8 pm, when the $25 entry fee is waived. Arrive as close to 4 as you can, and once you get your ticket (the line is long but fast), avoid the crowds by working your way down from the fifth floor. If you want to avoid the crowds altogether—and get ahead of the art game—take a gallery-crawl in and out of the hundreds of **galleries in Chelsea** for free access to up-and-coming and superstar artists alike. Unlike major museums, the galleries are rarely crowded (except for Thursday, when galleries often host openings with free wine and cheese!). You'll also find trendy a art scene in Williamsburg, Brooklyn. Most galleries are closed on Monday.

Free Entertainment

If you don't see enough movie stars on your wanderings around New York City you can catch stars on a big screen—under the stars—with a free summer flick. There are free screenings all across the five boroughs in summer, from Brooklyn Bridge Park to Bronx Terminal Market (⊕ *www.nycgovparks.org/events/free_summer_movies*). In Manhattan take your blanket and picnic basket to **Bryant Park**: a tradition since 1992, watching films alfresco surrounded by tall Midtown buildings is a summertime rite of passage for New Yorkers. Be prepared to stake out a good spot on the lawn early in the day. Movie schedules are posted at ⊕ *www.bryantpark.org*.

If you prefer live entertainment, catch tango dancers and jazz musicians outside Lincoln Center at the annual, free, monthlong Out of Doors festival, held in August. It includes more than 100 performances of spoken word, beatboxing, and bigwigs like Dave Brubeck and Arlo Guthrie. **Central Park Summerstage** is your free ticket to big-name performers like Afrobeat bandleader Seun Kuti and Columbia University's own Vampire Weekend. There's also a second series of concerts in Brooklyn.

Catch rising stars in music, drama, and dance at the **Juilliard School**'s free student concerts (check ⊕ *www.juilliard.edu* for a calendar of events). Free tickets are available at the Juilliard box office for theater performances; standby tickets are available an hour before the show.

One of the city's most beloved events and hottest free ticket is **Shakespeare in the Park,** usually features celebrities earning their olde English acting chops in outdoor performances in Central Park. Get in line early at the Public Theater for a shot at tickets, or head to the Delacorte Theater in Central Park. ⊕ *www.shakespeareinthepark.org.*

Like your theater a little less-scripted? Get gratis giggles at the **Upright Citizens Brigade** Theatre's improv comedy shows, where professional comedians, including UCB cofounder and *Saturday Night Live* alumna Amy Poehler, are sprinkled in with amateurs during the performances. Many of the shows are just $5; some are free. ⊕ *www.ucbtheatre.com.*

Another way to save your pennies for dinner is to catch a free reading at one of the city's bookstores—big (Barnes & Noble) and small (Housing Works Bookstore Café). Or you can get your fix of free words at KGB in the East Village, where authors have been reading since 1993. In Williamsburg, Pete's Candy Store has a reading series on alternate Thursday nights.

Free Rides

The Statue of Liberty never gets old, even for locals. That said, you won't find many lining up—or paying—for the pleasure of a glimpse of Lady Liberty. Join locals for a free ride on the **Staten Island Ferry** to see the Statue of Liberty, Ellis Island, and the southern tip of Manhattan from the water. A one-way trip takes 30 minutes and offers magnificent views—and inexpensive beer and snacks. Note that you have to disembark at St.

George Terminal in Staten Island before your return trip. Another cheap/sometimes-free ferry sure to (ahem) float your boat is the seven-minute ferry ride from Lower Manhattan to **Governor's Island,** a 172-acre island oasis in the heart of New York Harbor. You can visit the former military base turned sculpture park and public playground daily from late May to late September to bike, picnic, wander forts, take in spa treatments (as of 2015) and views of Lower Manhattan, and enjoy a variety of cultural offerings and festivals. Ferries are free on weekend mornings and $2 round trip (for adults) on all weekday and weekend-afternoon ferries. Give your sea legs a rest and take to the sky for an almost-free aerial ride on the **Roosevelt Island Tramway.** For the price of a subway ride ($2.25), you can glide over the East River on the only commuter cable in North America and score stunning city views while you're at it. The trip takes only a few minutes (board at the 59th Street and 2nd Avenue station) so you have plenty of time to explore Roosevelt Island and FDR Four Freedoms Park before you make the return trip.

MIDTOWN ARCHITECTURE: LOOK UP!

Midtown is the heart of the city during the workday. From every direction, people pour into the city to give it a jolt of energy. That vibrancy is intense, but is also an unmissable aspect of city life worth exploring for the average visitor. Midtown is home to many beautiful architectural sights, so don't be embarrassed to look at them.

The East Side: From the United Nations to Grand Central

Start near the river, at New York City's first glass-curtain skyscraper, the **UN Building** (⊠ *760 United Nations Plaza*), completed in 1949 and designed by Le Corbusier. (Technically, it's not on New York land, but we still count it.) The iconic structure is a monument to diplomacy, but being the city's first skyscraper isn't all glory: the air-conditioning is famously persnickety in summer. Continuing west, you'll pass the murals of the **Daily News Building** (⊠ *220 E. 42nd St.*) on the south side of the street. The lobby is home to a giant globe (from the era when the *News* had international correspondents) and murals are in the WPA-style, as the Art Deco building was finished in 1929. Also a can't-miss: the **Chrysler Building** (⊠ *405 Lexington Ave.*), which out–Art Decos any other structure in New York. (Dig the wheels with wings in place of gargoyles on the exterior.) Continue walking and you'll see **Grand Central Terminal** (⊠ *1 E. 42nd St.*), the largest train station in the world. This Beaux Arts structure was saved from the wrecking ball by concerned citizens in the '70s, a fate that similarly styled Penn Station didn't escape. Step inside for a look at the constellations painted on the soaring ceiling, for a nibble at the Grand Central Oyster Bar, or a cocktail at the swanky Campbell Apartment.

Midtown: Bryant Park and the New York Public Library

By the time you hit 5th Avenue, you'll be staring at the lions that guard the **New York Public Library** (⊠ *455 5th Ave.*). Built in 1911, the structure is a hub of learning and hosts many lecture series throughout the year. It's abutted by **Bryant Park,** which offers free Wi-Fi, ice skating in the winter, and films in the summer. The library, too, was brought back from the dead during New York's darkest days.

The West Side: The Heart of Times Square

Keep walking west and you'll hit the razzle and dazzle of **Times Square**. It's better than it's ever been. No, not from Guiliani's cleanup—those seedy days are long since passed, and Disney predominates—but thanks to a series of pedestrian-friendly improvements, including the closure of some lanes to traffic and the addition of lawn chairs, making it easier to navigate. Be sure to note the futuristic-looking **4 Times Square**, where Vogue magazine dictates the world of style from on high, and the kid-friendly confines of **Madame Tussaud's** (⊠ *234 W. 42nd St.*). Finish off by seeing the lights of Broadway from the many theaters on this stretch between 8th and 9th avenues.

1

Where to Start:	United Nations, especially for those who are architecturally inclined
Length:	1½ miles (two hours)
Where to Stop:	Grand Central, Bryant Park
Best Time to Go:	Early afternoons; weekends
Worst Time to Go:	Weekday evenings, when the after-work crush is at its peak
Highlights:	Grand Central, Chrysler Building, New York Public Library

NYC'S WATERFRONT PARKS

If Central Park makes you think, "Been there, done that," head to one of the city's several waterfront parks. Many New Yorkers are just discovering some of these green getaways, too.

Battery Park City

Built on landfill jutting out into the Hudson River, Battery Park City (BPC) is a high-rise residential neighborhood split in two by the World Financial Center and its marina. The Hudson River Park promenade borders BPC along the West Side Highway. In South Battery Park City, you'll pass by the Museum of Jewish Heritage, at 36 Battery Place. Nearby are several reasonably priced outdoor restaurants with stunning views of the Statue of Liberty. There is some interesting public art scattered throughout BPC, too. If you have kids, don't miss the excellent Teardop Park, with its huge slide.

Getting Here

By subway: South Battery Park: 1, R to Rector Place; 4, 5 to Wall Street. North Battery Park: 1, 2, 3, A, C to Chambers Street; E to World Trade Center. By bus: M9, M20, M22.

Brooklyn Bridge Park

A former industrial eyesore rusting along a narrow stretch of Brooklyn waterfront from Vinegar Hill to Brooklyn Heights, this newly developed 1.3-mile-long park is almost finished. It's replete with grassy lawns, rocky outcrops, bike paths, playgrounds, a pop-up pool in summer, soccer fields, basketball courts, volleyball courts, and a carousel. You'll also find picnic areas, an ice-cream factory nearby, food and film festivals in summer, water-taxi service to Governors Island, and thousands of visitors and locals taking advantage of it all. Perhaps the best feature of this new hipster destination is one

that's been here all along—the picture-postcard views of the Brooklyn Bridge and the city skyline, now framed by a thriving greenway and best appreciated from the rough-hewn granite-block seating under the Manhattan Bridge.

Getting Here

By subway: A, C to High Street; F to York Street. Instead of taking the subway, take a water taxi (⊕ *www.nywatertaxi.com*) to Fulton Ferry Landing, the East River Ferry (⊕ *www.nywaterway.com*) to Fulton Ferry Landing, or by walking across the Brooklyn Bridge.

The East River Park

This recently landscaped waterfront park, stretching from Montgomery Street to 12th Street along the East River, is one of the Lower East Side's best-kept secrets, with ball fields, bike paths, tennis courts, playgrounds, gardens, and picnic areas—along with impressive views of the Brooklyn skyline and the Williamsburg Bridge. You have to cross a footbridge over the FDR Drive to get to the park.

Getting Here

By subway: J, M, Z to Essex Street; F to 2nd Avenue.

Governors Island

A recent addition to the city's parks scene, this little island feels like a small town just 800 yards from the tip of Manhattan. Tourists love the unparalleled views of the harbor and Lower Manhattan, and locals love the out-of-the-city experience. The 172-acre park, built in part from landfill from subway excavations, was a base for the U.S. Army and Coast Guard for almost two centuries. Until 2003, it was off-limits to the public, which could be why the 19th-century homes here are so well preserved. The island is open to the public daily from

May to October, with programs, including art showings, concerts, and family programs. You can take a bike over on the ferry or rent one on the island. For more information, including updated ferry schedules and a calendar of activities, go to ⊕ *www.govisland.org.*

Getting Here

A $2 seven-minute ferry ride (free on weekend mornings) takes passengers to Governors Island from a dock at 10 South Street, next to the Staten Island Ferry. Get to the ferry by subway: 1 to South Ferry; 4, 5 to Bowling Green; or R, W to Whitehall Street. By bus: M1 (weekdays only), M6, M9, and M15.

The High Line

Once an elevated railroad track that serviced the long-ago factories along the lower west side, the High Line was converted into a park (really more of a promenade) that integrates landscaping with rail-inspired design and provides a fresh perspective on the city. Vegetation here includes 210 species of plants, trees, and shrubs intended to reflect the wild plants that flourished for decades after the tracks were abandoned in 1980. The park—30 feet above street level—is open between Gansevoort Street in the Meatpacking District to 34th Street. Sweeping views of the Hudson River and an extended sight line of the Meatpacking District are the highlights. For information on tours, public programs, and a calendar of events, go to ⊕ *www. thehighline.org* or call ☎ *212/500–6035.*

Getting Here

The High Line is accessible at Gansevoort and every two blocks between 14th and 30th streets with elevator access at 14th, 16th, 23rd, and 30th streets (no bikes allowed). It's two blocks west of the

subway station at 14th Street and 8th Avenue, served by the L, A, C, E. You can also take the C, E to 23rd Street and walk two blocks west. The 1, 2, 3 stops at 14th Street and 7th Avenue, three blocks away. By bus: M11 to Washington Street, M11 to 9th Avenue, M14 to 9th Avenue, M23 to 10th Avenue, M34 to 10th Avenue.

The Hudson River Park

This 5-mile greenway park hugs the Hudson River from 59th Street to Battery Park. Although the park has a unified design, it's divided into seven distinct sections that reflect the different Manhattan neighborhoods just across the West Side Highway. Along with refurbished piers with grass and trees, there are also attractions like the *Intrepid Sea, Air, and Space Museum* at Pier 86 across from 46th Street. A few blocks south, the Circle Line and World Yacht offer boat tours of the Hudson. At piers 96 and 40, the Downtown Boat House (⊕ *www.downtownboathouse.org*) offers free kayaking. There's a mammoth sports center, **Chelsea Piers,** between piers 59 and 61, and a playground, mini-golf course, and beach volleyball court at Pier 25. The park also sponsors free tours and classes, including free fishing. For a calendar of events and activities, go to ⊕ *www.hudsonriverpark.org.* North of Hudson River Park is one of Manhattan's more well-known parks, **Riverside Park** (⇨ *For more information see Chapter 12: Upper West Side*).

Getting Here

Hudson River Park is on the far west side of the city, adjacent to the West Side Highway. Crosstown buses at 14th, 23rd, and 42nd streets will get you close, but you'll still have to walk a bit. It's worth it.

NEW YORK CITY WITH KIDS

From space shuttles to vintage trains, climbing walls to climbing coasters, kite-flying festivals to hot dog–eating contests, not to mention zoos, parks, playgrounds, kid-centric shows, and more—the city that never sleeps has plenty of ways to tire out your kids.

Museums

There's a museum for every age, interest, and attention span in New York City. Some are aimed squarely at the younger set, but you shouldn't limit yourself or your kids to "children's" museums; most museums—especially the big players like MoMA, the Guggenheim, the Met, and the Whitney—offer programs to engage younger visitors (just ask at the admission desk). That said, sometimes toddlers want play places designed specifically for them, like the play center and interactive exhibits created for the under-five set at the **Children's Museum of Manhattan** and the arts and crafts rooms and ball pit at the **Children's Museum of Art.** The **American Museum of Natural History** is generally a top choice for kids of all ages and interests, visitors and locals alike. The giant dinosaurs and the huge blue whale alone are worth the trip, as is the live Butterfly Conservatory (October through May). You'll also find an IMAX theater, ancient-culture displays, and fabulous wildlife dioramas. The space shows at the Hayden Planetarium (tickets sold separately) are a big bang with kids. Nearby, the often overlooked (and under-trafficked) **DiMenna Children's History Museum**—in the recently renovated New-York Historical Society—invites kids (8 and up) to connect to the lives of real New York children from the past through hands-on activities that include video games, cross-stitching, and interactive maps. The **Lower East Side Tenement Museum** also offers a glimpse into the lives of early New Yorkers, in this case immigrant families. Guided tours (for ages 6 and up) visit restored tenement apartments where costumed "residents" bring history to life. You can also explore the history of public transit in NYC—from horse-power to subway—at the **New York Transit Museum.** In an old subway station in Brooklyn Heights, this museum has an old bus to pretend-drive, vintage subway cars, and retro ads and maps. The **Intrepid Sea, Air and Space Museum,** an aircraft carrier turned museum, houses the world's fastest jets, a Cold War–era submarine, the first space shuttle, an interactive Exploreum Hall, flight simulators, and more. When museums try to make learning fun, they usually fall flat with kids but the new kid museum on the block, the **Museum of Mathematics,** makes learning kaleidoscopic, and yes—fun—through interactive puzzles, games, displays, and hands-on tools like square-wheeled tricycles.

Parks and Playgrounds

If you're looking for space to let off steam in Manhattan, the 843-acre **Central Park** is a good start. You can take rowboats out on the lake, ride a carousel, explore the zoo, rent bikes, picnic in the meadows, or just wander and enjoy all the musicians, performers, and activity. Head to **DUMBO** (short for Down Under the Manhattan Bridge Overpass) for family-friendly **Brooklyn Bridge Park,** a picnic-perfect waterfront park with several inventive playgrounds, Jane's Carousel, Brooklyn Ice Cream Factory, a public swimming pool, and a variety of kid-centric music, arts, and kite-flying festivals. If it's too hot, too cold, or the kids just want too much of a good thing in one easy location, head to **Chelsea Piers,** between 18th and

23rd streets along Manhattan's Hudson River. With a climbing wall, batting cages, ice-skating rinks, basketball and volleyball courts, indoor soccer fields, bowling, sailing, golf, gymnastics, and an Explorer Center with a ball pit and slides, it's a five-block energy outlet for local and visiting kids of all ages.

Attractions

With all the screeching and honking, wild colors, and crazy behavior, New York City can feel like one big zoo, but if the kids want the real deal, there's a zoo in every borough of Manhattan. The **Bronx Zoo** is the city's—and country's—largest metropolitan wildlife park, and home to more than 4,000 animals, including endangered and threatened species. Plan to spend a whole day here so your kids don't have to choose between Congo Gorilla Forest and the Siberian cats at Tiger Mountain. Manhattan's **Central Park Zoo** is small but popular, and known to little kids as the setting for the animated *Madagascar* films. You'll find red pandas, snow leopards, a penguin house, performing sea lions, a polar bear pool, and a petting zoo. You can get face-to-face with even more interesting creatures in **Coney Island,** where the whole family can enjoy a walk along Coney Island's famous boardwalk to take in the beach, Luna Park's amusement rides, the landmark Cyclone wooden roller coaster (54-inch height requirement), minor league baseball games at the Cyclones' stadium—MCU Park, and Nathan's hot dogs (the infamous hot dog–eating contest takes place here every July 4). While the **New York Aquarium** is still only partially open due to continuing renovations (after 2012's Hurricane Sandy), the sea lion shows at its newly renovated Aquatheater are always a hit with kids, as is Mitik—the adorable orphaned baby walrus who was rescued off the coast of Alaska and adopted by the aquarium. If adorable creatures of the robotic variety are called for, hit **Sony Wonder Technology Lab.** The line to get into this futuristic fantasy world might be long (entry is free) but a talking robot keeps everyone entertained while you wait. Inside, kids can program their own robots; record their own digital music, movies, and games; and perform open-heart surgery using Haptic technology.

Shows

Once upon a time, it seemed like the only truly kid-friendly show on Broadway was *The Lion King*. These days, adults could complain that Broadway is selling itself to the youngest bidder, but who's complaining when the shows are so darn adult-friendly, too. *The Lion King* is still a firm favorite with kids, but it has solid competition with the likes of *Aladdin, Matilda, Cinderella, Newsies, Wicked*, the *Gazillion Bubble Show* (Off-Broadway), and *Blue Man Group* (Off-Broadway). Kids shows are popular so it's rare to find tickets at TKTS booths; book ahead if possible. Preteens and teens who are too cool for the Disney musical experience might appreciate **Monday Night Magic** at the Players Theatre in Greenwich Village. Founded in 1997, this longest running show off-Broadway features magicians from all over the world and a celebration of the art of magic with acts that involve illusion, mentalism, comedy, skill, and more. Kids ages 3–9 can partake of music, dance, comedy, storytelling, and dancing at Just Kidding at **Symphony Space,** a performing arts center on Broadway and 95th Street that inspires and entertains with established and emerging family-friendly artists. Interacting is encouraged.

NYC MUSEUMS, AN OVERVIEW

From the grand institutions along 5th Avenue's museum mile to an underground museum in a converted subway station in Brooklyn, to the dramatic new Whitney Museum in the Meatpacking District, New York City is home to an almost overwhelming collection of artistic riches, so it's a good idea to plan ahead. This overview includes museums listed elsewhere in the book; check the index for full listings.

Major Museums

It's hard to create a short list of top museums in New York City because, well, there are just so many top museums. That said, ambitious art lovers will likely focus on the Big Five. One of the most-visited museums in the world, the **Metropolitan Museum of Art** (known locally as "the Met," not to be confused with the Metropolitan Opera, also known as "the Met") is a must. It's collection consists of more than 2 million works of art representing 5,000 years of history. From its world famous dinosaur halls, its halls of fossils, gems, and human evolution, and its planetarium, the **American Museum of Natural History** is one of the most celebrated museums in the world. Both the **Museum of Modern Art (MoMA)** and the **Solomon R. Guggenheim Museum** are known as much for their incredible spaces—MoMA, a maze of glass walkways, was designed by Yoshio Taniguchi, and the nautilus-like Guggenheim was designed by Frank Lloyd Wright—as for their superlative collections of contemporary art and curated shows. The **Whitney Museum of American Art**, which is moving from its Upper East Side home to the Meatpacking District in spring 2015, is the city's hottest museum ticket, as much for its Highline and Hudson views as its expansive indoor and outdoor exhibition spaces.

Other Top Museums

There are many other important museums in the city. The **Frick Collection**, an elegant museum in the neoclassical mansion of industrialist Henry Clay Frick, is especially worthy of a visit. The **Morgan Library and Museum** is another mansion-museum founded on the vast and varied collections of a magnate—in this case J. P. Morgan. The **American Folk Art Museum** is dedicated to American folk art and the work of contemporary self-taught artists. The **New Museum** is the only museum dedicated solely to contemporary art in Manhattan. There are several museums to satisfy design-lovers including the **Museum of American Illustration and Museum of Comic and Cartoon Art at the Society of Illustrators**, the **Museum of Arts and Design**, the **Museum at FIT**, the **Skyscraper Museum**, and the **Cooper-Hewitt, National Design Museum, Smithsonian Institution**. Speaking of lovers, the provocative, adult-only **Museum of Sex** explores the history, evolution, and cultural significance of sex while the **Museum of American Finance** satisfies our obsession with all things money.

New York–Specific Museums

It's appropriate that the city's oldest museum, the **New-York Historical Society,** is dedicated to the city itself. Founded in 1805 this recently renovated neighbor of the American Museum of Natural History offers a unique and comprehensive overview of New York's history, as well as quirky and compelling exhibits. Other NY-centric museums to provide context and insight on the city's include the **Museum of the City of New York**, the **Lower East Side Tenement Museum**, the **Merchant's House Museum**, the **Fraunces Tavern Museum**, the **Ellis Island Immigration Museum**, the **New York City Police Museum**, the **New York City Fire Museum**, the **9/11 Memorial Museum** (at Ground Zero), and the **New York Transit Museum.**

Culturally Specific Museums

New York City is often referred to as a melting pot, which explains the profusion of culture-specific museums dedicated to sharing the broad and specific stories, struggles, and experiences of certain cultural and ethnic groups—often overlooked in mainstream museums. **El Museo del Barrio** focuses on Latina American and Caribbean art and features a popular collection of carved wooden folk-art figures from Puerto Rico. The **Hispanic Society of America Museum and Library** houses paintings by Goya, Velázquez, and El Greco, as well as an unsurpassed collection of Spanish, Portuguese, and Latin American artifacts. The **National Museum of the American Indian (Smithsonian Institution)**, explores the diversity of the Native American peoples through cultural artifacts, and regular music and dance performances. The **Jewish Museum**, the **Museum of Jewish Heritage**, and the **Museum at Eldridge Street** explore Jewish culture and art, and the Jewish experience in New York. The **Asia Society and Museum**, the **Museum of Chinese in America (MOCA)**, the **Japan Society**, and the **Rubin Museum of Art** are dedicated to the art and experiences of Asian communities. Other notable ethnic- or culture-specific museums include the **Leslie + Lohman Museum of Gay and Lesbian Art**, the **Ukranian Museum**, and the **Studio Museum in Harlem** (for artists of African descent locally, nationally, and internationally).

Museums Farther Afield

The **Brooklyn Museum** is the second-biggest museum in New York City and home to an impressive collection of European and American paintings and sculptures, an outstanding Egyptian collection, and a sculpture "memorial garden" of salvaged architectural elements from throughout New York City. A visit to Queens means innovative and experimental art at **MoMA PS1** and the small museum and garden of the **Noguchi Museum,** dedicated to the art of Isamu Noguchi, a prominent modern art Japanese-American sculptor. Other top museums in Queens include the **Museum of the Moving Image** and the **Queens Museum of Art**. The **Cloisters Museum and Gardens** (an outpost of the Met museum) in Fort Tyron Park in Upper Manhattan is a bit of a trek, relative to other city museums but we can pretty much guarantee you'll think it worth the trip.

Children's Museums

Some kids museums are fun just for the kids, like the **Children's Museum of the Arts,** the **Children's Museum of Manhattan,** and the **Brooklyn Children's Museum,** but many are fun for the entire family. Kids of all ages will appreciate the fleet of jets, the flight simulator, and other hands-on activities, the space shuttle Enterprise, and the Growler submarine at the **Intrepid Sea, Air and Space Museum.** Other crowd pleasers include **Madame Tussaud's New York,** the **Museum of Mathematics,** and the **New York Transit Museum.** The **DiMenna Children's History Museum** (at the New-York Historical Society) has interactive exhibits geared to help kids connect with children throughout New York's history.

NEW YORK CITY FESTIVALS

There's always *something* going on New York City but if you want to put a finger on the real pulse of New York, you should participate in a *big something* while you're here. Summer is an especially good time for festivals. Here are a few of our favorites:

Spring

Sakura Matsuri Cherry Blossom Festival. New Yorkers come out of hibernation in masses every spring to witness the extremely popular annual Sakura Matsuri Cherry Blossom Festival at the Brooklyn Botanic Garden. In addition to the blooming cherry trees, there are Taiko drumming performances, Japanese pop bands, Samurai swords, martial arts, tea ceremonies, and more. ⊕ *www.bbg. org* ⊙ *Mar.*

Tribeca Film Festival. Founded by Jane Rosenthal and Robert De Niro to contribute to the long-term recovery of Lower Manhattan after 9/11, the Tribeca Film Festival has become one of the most prominent film festivals in the world. There are upward of 250 films, more than 1,000 screenings, and even more buzz. ⊕ *www.tribecafilm.com* ⊙ *Mid- to late Apr.*

Summer

With festivals and events on city streets, at the beaches, and in almost every city park, New Yorkers take full advantage of the long summer days and nights. Free outdoor movie festivals are a huge draw in summer: choices include sci-fi movies with a view at Brooklyn Bridge Park (⊕ *www. brooklynbridgepark.org*); indie movies on city rooftops (⊕ *www.rooftopfilms.com*); and classics screened every Monday night in Midtown's Bryant Park (⊕ *www.bryant park.org*).

★ Fodor's Choice **Celebrate Brooklyn!.** Launched in 1979 to bring people back into Prospect Park after years of neglect, Celebrate Brooklyn! is one of the city's most popular, free, outdoor performing arts festivals, and *the* place to catch excellent live music in the great Brooklyn outdoors. The artists and ensembles reflect the borough's diversity, ranging from internationally acclaimed performers to up-and-coming musicians. The lineup also includes kids shows, movies with live music, ballet, and more. Performances are rain or shine and free (although, there is a suggested donation of $3), with the exception of ticketed benefit concerts which directly support the festival. Seats for free shows are first-come first-serve. Local restaurants provide the food. ■TIP→ Get there early and bring a blanket and an umbrella for shade. ⊠ *Prospect Park Bandshell, 9th St. and Prospect Park W entrance, Park Slope, Brooklyn* ⊕ *bricartsmedia.org/performing-arts/celebrate-brooklyn* ⊡ *Free* ⊙ *Jun.–Aug.* Ⓜ *F, G to 7th Ave.; 2, 3 to Grand Army Plaza.*

Midsummer Night Swing. If dancing in the street is your thing, join the Midsummer Night Swing festival, an outdoor music and dance party in Lincoln Center Plaza. Take lessons with pros or just take your chances on the floor! ⊕ *www.midsummer nightswing.org* ⊙ *Late June–early July.*

Museum Mile Festival. For one day every June, thousands of locals and visitors celebrate the Museum Mile Festival when 10 museums along 5th Avenue open their doors for free. ⊕ *www.museummile festival.org* ⊙ *Early June.*

Summer Streets. On three consecutive Saturdays every August, you can join hundreds of thousands of locals to let loose on nearly 7 miles of pedestrianized city streets for Summer Streets. From the Brooklyn Bridge to Central Park, along Park Avenue and connecting streets, New Yorkers hit the car-free streets to rock climb, zip line, dance, work out, experience art, or just ramble and the city's streets in a new way—all for free. ⊕ *www.nyc.gov/summerstreets* ⊗ *Aug.*

Other popular summer festivals and events include Coney Island's Mermaid Parade, the New York International Fringe Festival, SummerStage, and Shakespeare in the Park.

Fall

Brooklyn Book Festival. The Brooklyn Book Festival is a huge, (mostly) free public event with an array of established and emerging authors, readings, panels, discussions, parties, games, and signings, all held in clubs, parks, theaters, and libraries across Brooklyn. ⊕ *www.brooklynbookfestival.org* ⊗ *Sept.*

Feast of San Gennaro. Every year, thousands of locals and visitors flock to Little Italy for the 11-day Feast of San Gennaro. This festival is a mix of religion, delicious food, colorful parades, and live entertainment. Don't miss the cannoli-eating competition at the end of the week. ⊕ *www.sangennaro.org* ⊗ *Mid- to late Sept.*

New York City Marathon. Even if you're not joining the almost 50,000 runners taking a 26.2 mile run through New York's five boroughs on the first Sunday in November for the New York City Marathon, you'll want to experience the electric atmosphere and very best of New York with the 2 million spectators. ⊕ *www.tcsnycmarathon.org* ⊗ *1st Sun. in Nov.*

Other top fall events include the **Village Halloween Parade, Macy's Thanksgiving Day Parade,** and the **Rockefeller Center Tree Lighting Ceremony.**

Winter

Sure it can be icy-cold in New York in winter but locals know that the best way to stay warm is by running/skating from one event to another.

Holiday Train Show. The New York Botanical Garden's Holiday Train Show is one of the city's top seasonal attractions, especially for families. You'll find electric trains, more than 140 miniature replicas of city landmarks (made out of twigs and bark), and magical landscapes—and it's all housed in a conservatory so winter weather can't dampen the spirit. ⊕ *www.nybg.org* ⊗ *Mid-Nov.–mid-Jan.*

To ring in the Lunar New Year, the streets of Chinatown give way to food vendors hawking traditional eats, colorful costumes and decorations, and a major parade running from Little Italy through Chinatown and Lower Manhattan.

If you want to join in on a little local tomfoolery, join tens of thousands of Santafied locals who tear up the town for SantaCon (⊕ *www.nycsantacon.com*), or sign up for a No Pants Subway ride in January (⊕ *www.improveverywhere.com*).

SIGHTSEEING NEW YORK CITY

Sometimes a guided tour is a great idea, even if you usually prefer flying solo. They can be a great way to investigate out-of-the-way areas, or learn about interesting aspects of the city's history, inhabitants, or architecture. In addition to the listings below, these are some other highly recommended tours to keep in mind: Foraging with Steve Brill ☎ *914/835–2153* ⊕ *www.wildmanstevebrill.com.* A Slice of Brooklyn Pizza Tour ☎ *212/209–3370* ⊕ *www.asliceofbrooklyn.com.*

Boat Tours

Circle Line Sightseeing Cruise. In good weather a Circle Line Sightseeing Cruise around Manhattan Island is one of the best ways to get oriented in the city. Three-hour, $39 cruises run at least once daily; a shorter, two-hour "semi-Circle" option is $35. ✉ *Pier 83 at 42nd St., Midtown West* ☎ *212/563–3200* ⊕ *www.circleline42.com* ✉ *$39.*

Manhattan By Sail. If you're looking for a historical sailing experience, Manhattan By Sail has an 82-foot yacht dating from the 1920s. Themed sailings include a jazz cruise, lobster-and-beer-lovers sail, and a full-moon sail ($55; May to October). They also offer two-hour sunset sails in June, July, and August. ✉ *North Cove Marina at World Financial Center, Lower Manhattan* ☎ *212/619–0907* ⊕ *www.manhattanbysail.com* ✉ *$39.*

Bus Tours

Gray Line New York Sightseeing. Gray Line runs various "hop-on, hop-off" double-decker bus tours, including a downtown Manhattan loop, an upper Manhattan loop, a Brooklyn loop, and evening tours of the city. Prices vary. ✉ *777 8th Ave., between 46th and 47th Sts., Midtown West* ☎ *800/669–0051* ⊕ *www.graylinenewyork.com* ✉ *$49.*

Walking Tours

Big Onion Walking Tours. The wisecracking PhD candidates of Big Onion Walking Tours lead themed tours such as "Immigrant New York" and "Satan's Seat: New York During Prohibition," as well as multiethnic eating tours. Tours run daily; there's an additional $5 for tours that include stops to eat. ☎ *888/606–9255* ⊕ *www.bigonion.com* ✉ *$20.*

The Municipal Art Society of New York. MAS conducts walking tours that emphasize the architecture and history of particular neighborhoods. A daily walking tour of Grand Central explores the 100-year-old terminal's architecture, history, and hidden secrets. Tickets can be purchased in advance online or from the ticket booth in the main concourse. ✉ *111 W. 57th St.* ☎ *212/935–3960, 212/935–3960 for recorded info* ⊕ *www.mas.org* ✉ *$20.*

New York City Cultural Walking Tours. Alfred Pommer's walking tours cover such topics as buildings' gargoyles, Chelsea Historic District, and the Millionaire's Mile of 5th Avenue. Two-hour public tours run on some Sundays from March to December (no reservations needed); private tours can be scheduled at $60 per hour (minimum two hours). ☎ *212/979–2388* ⊕ *www.nycwalk.com* ✉ *$20.*

New York Food Tours. Options from these walking tours include "The Freakiest and Funniest Food" and a "Tastes of Chinatown" tour. Prices range from $52 for a 2½ hour East Village food and culture tour to $100 for a 3½ hour multicultural bar-hopping tour. ☎ *347/559–0111* ⊕ *www.foodtoursofny.com* ✉ *$52.*

THE STATUE OF LIBERTY AND ELLIS ISLAND: GATEWAY TO THE NEW WORLD

A quintessential part of a visit to New York, the trip to the Statue of Liberty and Ellis Island takes up the better part of a day. It involves a ferry ride, long lines, security checks, and ultimately, the rare opportunity to appreciate some of the most powerful symbols of America right up close. It's worth the effort. It's no overstatement to say that these two sights have played defining roles in American culture.

THE STATUE OF LIBERTY

Impressive from the shore, the Statue of Liberty is even more majestic up close. For millions of immigrants, the first glimpse of America was Lady Liberty, growing from a vaguely defined figure on the horizon into a towering, stately colossus. Visitors approaching Liberty Island on the ferry from Battery Park may experience a similar sense of wonder as they approach. Note that at press time most of Ellis Island is still closed due to damage from Hurricane Sandy. Check www.nps.gov/elis for updates.

What's Here

The 152-foot-tall **statue** of Liberty, officially named *La Liberté éclairant le monde* ("Liberty Enlightening the World") was a gift from the people of France to the United States. It was designed by French sculptor Frédéric Auguste Bartholdi, built in France, and shipped to America where it was assembled. The statue stands atop an 89-foot-tall **pedestal** designed by American architect Richard Morris Hunt. The lines of Emma Lazarus's sonnet "The New Colossus" ("Give me your tired, your poor, your huddled masses yearning to breathe free...") are inscribed on a plaque inside the pedestal.

Inside the pedestal is an informative and entertaining **museum**. Highlights include the torch's original glass flame (the current flame is 24-karat gold and lit at night by floodlights), full-scale copper replicas of Lady Liberty's face and one of her giant feet, Bartholdi's alternative designs for the statue, and a model of the interior framework designed by Gustave Eiffel)of Eiffel Tower fame).

The **observatory platform** at the top of the pedestal is a great place for a photo op; it's 16 stories high, and you'll have all of Lower Manhattan spread out in front of you. The observatory platform is accessible via elevator if you don't want to climb the stairs.

The **crown** is the statue's highest accessible point. It's reached by stairs (154 of them; about a 20 minute journey) from the observatory platform.

Liberty Island has a pleasant outdoor café.

Know Before You Go

Buy your tickets in advance. There are a limited number of same-day standby tickets available at ferry ticket offices, where you catch the ferry but we strongly advise planning early. Once you reach the island, there are no tickets available, and without a ticket there is absolutely no admittance into the pedestal or the museum.

You have three choices when buying your ticket to the Statue of Liberty:

A. You can just buy a ferry ticket. This will get you to Liberty Island and Ellis Island but it does not get you *into* the Statue of Liberty—either the pedestal or the crown. The ferry ticket does include a self-guided audio tour of Liberty Island (there's an adult version and a kids version). Pick up your audio guide when you exit the ferry at Liberty Island.

B. You can buy your ticket with pedestal access; there is no extra charge but you should do this in advance. Pedestal access includes access to the Liberty Island Museum.

C. For crown access, plan *far* in advance, as there are only 320 spots available each day and they sell out months in advance. There is a small extra fee.

Liberty Highlights

- The surreal chance to stand next to, and be dwarfed by, the original glass torch and the copper cast of Lady Liberty's foot.

- The vistas of New York from the observatory platform.

Statue Basics

☎ 212/363–3200;
877/523–9849 ticket
reservations

🌐 www.nps.gov/stli

🎫 Free; ferry $18
round-trip (includes Ellis
Island); crown tickets $3

🕐 Daily 9:30–5:00; extended
hours in summer.

Liberty helicopters

ALTERNATIVE VIEWS

■ The free Staten Island Ferry offers a great view of New York Harbor and of the Statue of Liberty from a distance (see Chapter 2).

■ Webcams placed around the statue's torch allow you to see what Lady Liberty sees—wide views of the New York City skyline, the Hudson River, and ships in the harbor—from your computer or phone.

■ Liberty Helicopters has sightseeing tours that fly over the crown and torch (see Chapter 1).

FAST FACT: To move the Statue of Liberty from its initial home on a Paris rooftop to its final home in the New York Harbor, the statue was broken down into 350 individual pieces and packed in 214 crates. It took four months to reassemble it.

FAST FACT: The face of Lady Liberty is actually a likeness of sculptor Frederic-Auguste Bartholdi's mother—quite a tribute.

Foundation of the pedestal to torch: 305'6"

Heel to top head: 111'6"

FAST FACT: Lady Liberty has formidable proportions. Her face is more than 8 feet tall, she has a 35-foot waistline, and she weighs 225 tons (450,000 pounds). Her crown has 7 rays, to represent the 7 continents; each is 9-feet long and weighs about 150 pounds.

ELLIS ISLAND

Chances are you'll be with a crowd of international tourists as you disembark at Ellis Island. Close your eyes and imagine the jostling crowd 100 times larger. Now imagine that your journey has lasted weeks at sea and that your day pack contains all your worldly possessions. You're hungry, tired, jobless, and homeless. This scenario just begins to set the stage for the story of the millions of immigrants who passed through Ellis Island. Between 1892 and 1924, approximately 12 million men, women, and children first set foot on U.S. soil at the Ellis Island federal immigration facility. By the time the facility closed in 1954, it had processed the ancestors of more than 40% of Americans living today. *At press time limited parts of Ellis Island have reopened after Hurricane Sandy. Visit www. nps.gov/elis/planyourvisit for updated information.

WHAT'S HERE

The island's main building, now a national monument, reopened in 1990 as the Ellis Island Immigration Museum, with more than 30 galleries of artifacts, photographs, and taped oral histories. The centerpiece of the museum is the **Registry Room** (also known as the Great Hall). It feels dignified and cavernous today, but photographs show that it took on many configurations over the years, always packed with humanity. While you're here, look out the Registry Room's tall, arched windows and try to imagine what passed through immigrants' minds as they viewed Lower Manhattan's skyline to one side and the Statue of Liberty to the other.

Along with the Registry Room, the museum includes the ground-level **Peopling of America Center**, which explores immigration to the United States before and after Ellis Island was a portal for immigrants. Graphics and poignant audio stories give firsthand accounts of the immigrants' journeys—from making the trip and arriving in the United States to their struggle and survival here. There is also the **American Family Immigration Center**, where you can search Ellis Island's records for your own ancestors, and the **American Flag of Faces**, an interactive display filled with images of immigrants submitted online (submit yours at *FlagofFaces.org*). Outside, the **American Immigrant Wall of Honor** has inscribed upon it the names of more than 600,000 immigrant Americans.

MAKING THE MOST OF YOUR VISIT

Because there's so much to take in, it's a good idea to make use of the museum's interpretive tools. Check at the visitor desk for free film tickets, ranger tour times, and special programs.

Consider starting your visit with a viewing of the free film *Island of Hope, Island of Tears*. A park ranger starts off with a short introduction, then the 25-minute film takes you through an immigrant's journey from the troubled conditions of European life (especially true for ethnic and religious minorities), to their nervous arrival at Ellis Island, and their introduction into American cities. The film is a primer into all the exhibits and will deeply enhance your experience.

The audio tour, which is included in the ticket price, is also worthwhile: it takes you through the exhibits, providing thorough, engaging commentary interspersed with recordings of immigrants recalling their experiences.

ELLIS ISLAND HIGHLIGHTS

■ Surveying the Great Hall.

■ The moving film *Island of Hope, Island of Tears*.

■ Exploring the Peopling of America Center to gain a deeper understanding of the history of immigration in America.

■ Reading the names on the American Immigrant Wall of Honor.

■ Researching your own family's history.

Ellis Island Basics

☎ 212/363–3200 Ellis Island; 212/561–4500 Wall of Honor information

⊕ www.nps.gov/stli

🚢 Free; ferry $18 round-trip (includes Liberty Island)

🕐 Daily 9:30–5:00; extended in summer.

IMMIGRANT HISTORY TIMELINE

Starting in the 1880s, troubled conditions throughout Europe persuaded both the poor and the persecuted to leave their family and homes to embark on what were often gruesome journeys to come to the golden shores of America.

1880s 5.7 million immigrants arrive in U.S.

1892 Federal immigration station opens on Ellis Island in January.

1901–1910 8.8 million immigrants arrive in U.S.; 6 million processed at Ellis Island.

1907 Highest number of immigrants (860,000) arrives in one year, including a record 11,747 on April 17.

1910 75% of the residents of New York, Chicago, Detroit, Cleveland, and Boston are now immigrants or children of immigrants.

1920s Federal laws set immigration quotas based on national origin.

1954 Ellis Island immigration station is closed.

New arrivals line up to have their eyes inspected.

FAST FACT: Some immigrants who passed through Ellis Island later became household names. A few include Charles Atlas (1903, Italy); Irving Berlin (1893, Russia); Frank Capra (1903, Italy); Bob Hope (1908, England); Knute Rockne (1893, Norway); and Baron Von Trapp and his family (1938, Germany).

FAST FACT: In 1897, a fire destroyed the original pine immigration structure on Ellis Island, including all immigration records dating back to 1855.

FAST FACT: The first test that immigrants had to pass was known as the "six-second medical exam." As they entered the Great Hall, they were watched by doctors; if anyone seemed disabed, their clothing was marked with chalk and they were sent for a full exam.

Four immigrants and their belongings, on a dock, look out over the water; view from behind.

PLANNING

ADMISSION

There is no admission fee for either the Statue of Liberty or Ellis Island, but the ferry ride (which goes round-trip from Battery Park to Liberty Island to Ellis Island) costs $18. Ferries leave from Battery Park (see Ch. 2) every 30 to 40 minutes, depending on the time of year. There are often long lines, so arrive early, especially if you have a reserved-time ticket. (Oversize bags and backpacks aren't permitted onboard.) Reserve tickets online—you'll still have to wait in line, both to pick up the tickets (or print your tickets at home) and to board the ferry, but you'll be able to pick up a Monument Pass for access to the pedestal, the museum, and the statue's interior. There is no fee for the Monument Pass, but you cannot enter the Statue of Liberty without it.

WHERE TO CATCH THE FERRY

Broadway and Battery Pl., Lower Manhattan Ⓜ Subway: 4, 5 to Bowling Green.

PLANNING TIPS

Buy tickets in advance. This is the only way to assure that you'll have tickets to actually enter the Statue of Liberty museum and observatory platform.

Be prepared for intense security. At the ferry security check, you will need to remove your coat; at the statue, you will need to remove your coat as well as your belt, watch, and any metal accessories. At this writing, no strollers, large umbrellas, or backpacks are allowed in the statue.

Check ferry schedules in advance. Before you go, check www.statuecruises.com.

Keep in mind that even though the last entry time for the monument is at 4:30 PM, **the last ferry to the Statue of Liberty and Ellis Island is at 3:30 PM.** You need to arrive by at least 3 PM (to allow for security checks and lines) if you want to make the last ferry of the day.

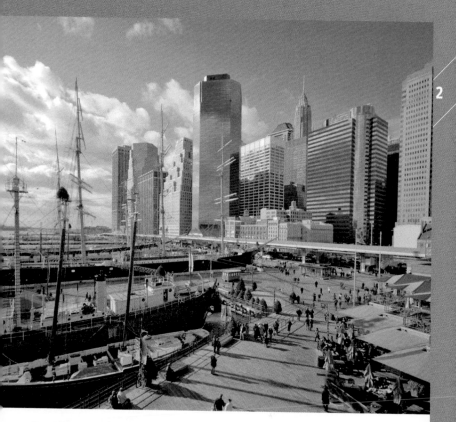

LOWER MANHATTAN

with the Financial District,
New York Harbor, and TriBeCa

GETTING ORIENTED

Lower Manhattan

0   1/8 mi
0   200 meters

TRIBECA

CHINATOWN

La Colombe Torrefaction

All Good Things

Hudson River Park

Independence Plaza

Zucker's Bagels

Federal Plaza

Foley Square

Woolworth Building

City Hall

Brooklyn Bridge Walkway

Brooklyn Bridge

St. Paul's Chapel

World Trade Center Site/ Ground Zero

South Street Seaport Historic District

Pier 17

Brookfield Place

Federal Reserve Bank of New York

North Cove Yacht Harbor

Battery Park City

Museum of American Finance

New York Stock Exchange (NYSE)

Wall St.

New York City Police Museum

South Cove

Museum of Jewish Heritage— A Living Memorial to the Holocaust

Skyscraper Museum

Bowling Green

Stone Street District

Fraunces Tavern Museum

Robert F. Wagner Jr. Park

National Museum of the American Indian (Smithsonian Institution)

FINANCIAL DISTRICT

Castle Clinton National Monument

Battery Park

Staten Island Ferry

Governors Island Ferry

Ellis Island

Statue of Liberty

Brooklyn-Battery Tunnel

Hudson River

East River

NEW YORK HARBOR

MAKING THE MOST OF YOUR TIME

Visit the Financial District during the weekend and you might feel like a lone explorer in a canyon of buildings; even on weeknights the decibel level of the neighborhood reduces significantly after about 6. Weekdays, however, the sidewalks bustle so much that you can expect to be jostled if you stand still too long. End your visit by watching the sunset over the Hudson River.

The sights of the New York Harbor are some of the most quintessential of New York, but be prepared for long lines for Ellis Island and the Statue of Liberty, especially on weekends. TriBeCa is one of the quieter neighborhoods in Manhattan, being mostly residential. There are pleasant shops, restaurants, and local bars, but the neighborhood tends not to be a tourist attraction unless the film festival is going on.

COFFEE AND QUICK BITES

All Good Things. Rub elbows with locals shopping for bread, cheese, and treats at this upscale food hall. Grab a quick bite for any meal of the day or gather ingredients for a picnic in Hudson River Park. ⊠ *102 Franklin St., TriBeCa* ☎ *212/966–3663* ⊕ *www.allgoodthingsny.com* Ⓜ *A, C, E to Canal St.; 1 to Franklin St.*

La Colombe Torrefaction. In this loftlike space just below Canal Street, expect excellent espresso drinks and impressive latte art. ⊠ *319 Church St., at Lispenard St., TriBeCa* ☎ *212/343–1515* ⊕ *www.lacolombe.com* Ⓜ *A, C, E to Canal St.*

Zucker's Bagels. This is one of the few places left in the city that still serves hand-rolled, kettle-boiled New York bagels. Coffee is from La Colombe and the morning egg sandwiches on a freshly sliced bagel are a neighborhood favorite. ⊠ *146 Chambers St., Financial District* ☎ *212/608–5844* ⊕ *www.zuckersbagels.com* Ⓜ *1, 2, 3 to Chambers St.*

TOP EXPERIENCES

Visiting the National 9/11 Memorial.

Riding the Staten Island Ferry.

Touring Ellis Island and the Statue of Liberty.

Snapping a photo in front of Wall Street's bull.

Strolling through Hudson River Park.

BEST FOR KIDS

Castle Clinton and Battery Park

South Street Seaport Museum

GETTING HERE

Many subway lines connect to the Financial District. The Fulton Street station is serviced by eight different subway lines (A, C, J, Z, 2, 3, 4, 5) and puts you within walking distance of City Hall, South Street Seaport, and the World Trade Center site (⇨ *Ground Zero feature in this chapter*). To get to the Brooklyn Bridge, take the 4, 5, or 6 to Brooklyn Bridge–City Hall.

For sights around New York Harbor, take the R to Whitehall, or the 4 or 5 to Bowling Green. (Note that you can also reach the Harbor area via the 1 train to South Ferry; it also stops in the heart of TriBeCa [Franklin Street].)

Sightseeing
★★★★★
Nightlife
★★
Dining
★★★★
Lodging
★★
Shopping
★★

Lower Manhattan, or in the parlance of New Yorkers emphatically giving directions to tourists, "all the way down-town," has long been where the action—and transaction—is. Originally the Dutch trading post called New Amsterdam (1626–47), this neighborhood is home to historic, cobbled streets next to soaring skyscrapers. This mix of old and new, the bustle of Wall Street, and a concentration of city land-marks all lure visitors to the tip of Manhattan.

FINANCIAL DISTRICT AND SOUTH STREET SEAPORT

Updated by
Jessica Colley

Little from Manhattan's colonial era is left in lower Manhattan (apart from a precious few structures built in the 1700s) but you can still feel a sense of history in the South Street Seaport's 19th-century brick facades and pedestrianized Stone Street lined with picnic tables. There's life to be found within the skyscraper-lined canyons of Wall Street and lower Broadway, as locals move into the neighborhood and fill the barstools in candlelit watering holes. Bounded by the East and Hudson rivers to the east and west, respectively, and by Chambers Street and Battery Park to the north and south, the Financial District is best appreciated by getting lost in its streets.

You'll want to see what's here, but above all you'll want to see what's not, most notably in that empty gulf among skyscrapers: the World Trade Center site where two 1-acre pools represent the footprints of the fallen Twin Towers.

TOP ATTRACTIONS

FAMILY   **Battery Park.** Jutting out at the southernmost point of Manhattan, tree-filled Battery Park is a respite from the narrow, winding, and (on weekdays) jam-packed streets of the Financial District. Even if you don't plan to stay for long, carve out a few minutes of sightseeing time to sit on a bench and take in the view, which includes the Statue of Liberty and Ellis Island. On clear days you can see all the way to Port Elizabeth's cranes, which seem to mimic Lady Liberty's stance; to Governors Island, a former Coast Guard installation now managed by the National Park Service; a hilly Staten Island in the distance; and the old railway terminal in Liberty State Park, on the mainland in Jersey City, New Jersey. Looking away from the water and toward Lower Manhattan's skyscrapers, there's a feeling that you're at the beginning of the city, and a sense of all the possibility it possesses just a few blocks in.

BROOKLYN BRIDGE FACTS

- Overall length: 6,016 feet

- Span of twin Gothic-arch towers: 1,595½ feet

- Distance from top of towers to East River: 272 feet

- Distance from roadway to the water: 133 feet

- Number of times the line "If you believe that, I've got a bridge to sell you" is used referring to the Brooklyn Bridge: infinite

The park's main structure is **Castle Clinton National Monument,** the ticket office site and takeoff point for ferries to the Statue of Liberty and Ellis Island. This monument was once 200 feet off the southern tip of the island located in what was called the Southwest Battery, and was erected during the War of 1812 to defend the city. (The East Battery sits across the harbor on Governors Island.) As dirt and debris from construction were dumped into the harbor, the island expanded, eventually engulfing the landmark. Later, from 1855 to 1890, it served as America's first official immigration center (Ellis Island opened in 1892).

Inside Battery Park are several monuments and statues, including *The Sphere,* which for three decades stood on the plaza at the World Trade Center as a symbol of peace. Damaged but still intact after the collapse of the towers, it serves as a memorial to those who lost their lives.

The southern link in a chain of parks connecting Battery Park north to Chambers Street, Robert F. Wagner Jr. Park has a flat, tidy lawn and wide benches from which to view the harbor or the stream of runners and in-line skaters on the promenade. A brick structure at the southeast section of Battery Park has public bathrooms and a restaurant with additional views from its flat roof. ⊠ *Battery Park* ☎ *212/417–2000* ⊕ *www.nycgovparks.org/parks/batterypark* Ⓜ *4, 5 to Bowling Green.*

Fodor's Choice ★ **Brooklyn Bridge.** "A drive-through cathedral" is how the journalist James Wolcott described the Brooklyn Bridge, one of New York's noblest and most recognized landmarks, perhaps outdoing Walt Whitman's comment that it was "[t]he best, most effective medicine my soul has yet partaken." The bridge stretches over the East River, connecting Manhattan and Brooklyn. A walk across its promenade—a boardwalk elevated above the roadway, shared by pedestrians, in-line skaters, and cyclists—takes about 40 minutes and delivers exhilarating views. If you start from downtown Manhattan, you'll end up in the heart of Brooklyn Heights (you can also take the subway to the Brooklyn side and walk back towards Manhattan). It's worth noting that on weekends when the weather is nice, the path can get pretty congested; it's most magical, and quietest, early in the morning or during sunset when the city lights come to life. ⊠ *E River Dr., Lower Manhattan* Ⓜ *4, 5, 6 to Brooklyn Bridge/ City Hall; J, Z to Chambers St.; A, C to High St.–Brooklyn Bridge.*

Ground Zero. *See highlighted feature in this chapter.*

New York Stock Exchange (NYSE). Unfortunately you can't tour it, but it's certainly worth ogling. At the intersection of Wall and Broad streets, the exchange is impossible to miss. The neoclassical building, designed by architect George B. Post, opened on April 22, 1903. It has six Corinthian columns supporting a pediment with a sculpture titled *Integrity Protecting the Works of Man,* featuring a tribute to the then-sources of American prosperity: Agriculture and Mining to the left of Integrity; Science, Industry, and Invention to the right. The Exchange was one of the world's first air-conditioned buildings. ⊠ *11 Wall St., Financial District* ☎ *212/656-3000* ⊕ *www.nyse.com* Ⓜ *1, 4, 5, N, R to Rector; 2, 3 to Wall St.; J, Z to Broad St.*

South Street Seaport Historic District. Had this charming cobblestone corner of the city not been declared a historic district in 1977, the city's largest concentration of early-19th-century commercial buildings would have been destroyed. Today, the area is largely filled with tourists, and if you've been to Boston's Quincy Market or Baltimore's Harborplace, you may feel a flash of déjà vu—the same company leased, restored, and adapted the existing buildings, with the result being the blend of a quasi-authentic historic district with a slightly homogenous shopping mall.

At the intersection of Fulton and Water streets, the gateway to the seaport, is the ***Titanic* Memorial,** a small white lighthouse that commemorates the sinking of the RMS *Titanic* in 1912. Beyond the lighthouse, Fulton Street turns into a busy pedestrian mall. On the south side of Fulton is the seaport's architectural centerpiece, **Schermerhorn Row,** a redbrick terrace of Georgian- and Federal-style warehouses and countinghouses built from 1811 to 1812. Some upper floors house gallery space, and the ground floors are occupied by shops, bars, and restaurants. Cross South Street, once known as the Street of Ships, under an elevated stretch of FDR Drive to **Pier 16,** where historic ships are docked, including the *Pioneer,* a 102-foot schooner built in 1885; the *Peking,* the second-largest sailing bark in existence; the iron-hulled *Wavertree*; and the lightship *Ambrose.* The Pier 16 ticket booth provides information and sells tickets to the museum, ships, tours, and exhibits. Pier 16 is the departure point for various seasonal cruises.

To the north is **Pier 17,** a former multilevel dockside shopping mall that is currently undergoing redevelopment and is expected to open in 2016 with a new rooftop space, restaurants, outdoor bars, and an amphitheater. Pier 17 used to be the home of the Fulton Fish Market, which first opened in South Manhattan in 1807; starting in 1939 it was housed in the New Market Building, just north of the Seaport, but that closed in 2005 when operations were moved to a new 400,000-square-foot facility in Hunt's Point in the Bronx. ⊠ *South*

Street Seaport, South Street Seaport ☎ *212/732–8257 for events and shopping info* ⊕ *www.southstreetseaport.com* Ⓜ *2, 3, 4, 5, A, C, J, Z to Fulton St./Broadway-Nassau.*

Stone Street Historic District. Nestled amid skyscrapers, the low-rise, two-block oasis of bars and restaurants along historic Stone Street feels more like a village than the center of the financial universe. In the summer, tables spill out into the cobblestone street and the mood is convivial—especially on Thursday and Friday nights. This was Manhattan's first paved street and today the cluster of buildings along here, with South William and Pearl streets, and Coenties Alley, make up the Stone Street Historic District. ⊠ *Financial District.*

WORTH NOTING

Bowling Green. Perhaps most recognized as the home of Arturo Di Modica's 7,000-pound, bronze *Charging Bull* statue (1989), Bowling Green, at the foot of Broadway, became New York's first public park in 1733. Legend has it that before that, this was the sight where Peter Minuit purchased the island of Manhattan from the Native Americans, in 1626, supposedly for what amounted to 24 U.S. dollars. On July 9, 1776, a few hours after citizens learned about the signing of the Declaration of Independence, rioters toppled a statue of British King George III that had occupied the spot for 11 years; much of the statue's lead was melted down into bullets. In 1783, when the occupying British forces fled the city, they defiantly hoisted a Union Jack on a greased, uncleated flagpole so it couldn't be lowered; patriot John Van Arsdale drove his own cleats into the pole to replace the flag with the Stars and Stripes. The copper-top subway entrance here is the original one, built in 1904–05. ⊠ *Broadway at Whitehall St., Financial District* Ⓜ *4, 5 to Bowling Green.*

City Hall. What once marked the northernmost point of Manhattan today houses the office of the mayor and serves as a gathering place for demonstrators voicing concerns and the news crews that cover their stories. This is the oldest City Hall in the country, a striking (but surprisingly small) building dating back to 1803. If the history of local politics and architecture is your thing, free tours are available (sign up in advance online). Tours begin outside. Indoors, highlights include the Victorian-style **City Council Chamber,** the Rotunda where President Lincoln lay in state in 1865 under a soaring dome supported by 10 Corinthian columns, and the **Governor's Room,** an elegantly preserved space with intricate portraits of historic figures and a writing table that George Washington used in 1789 when New York was the U.S. capital. If nothing else, take a moment to snap a photo of the columned exterior and see the small but lovely City Hall Park, bound by Broadway to the west and Chambers Street to the north. This park is an underrated place to stop and take a breath away from the typical congestion of Lower Manhattan. ⊠ *City Hall Park, Financial District* ☎ *212/788–2656 for tour reservations* ⊕ *www.nyc.gov/html/artcom/html/tours/city_hall. shtml* ⊡ *Free* ☉ *Tours available some weekdays; reserve online or by phone* Ⓜ *2, 3 to Park Place; R to City Hall; 4, 5, 6 to Brooklyn Bridge/ City Hall; J, Z, A, C to Chambers St.*

Continued on page 58

A GLIMPSE OF THE FUTURE WORLD TRADE CENTER

An illuminated antenna reaches to 1,776 feet to commemorate America's founding.

Tower 1
Designed by David Childs. At a height of 1,776 feet (and 104 stories) it is the tallest building in the United States.

Tower 2
Designed by Norman Foster. Ground was broken in 2010.

Tower 3
Designed by Richard Rogers. Ground was broken in 2010; when complete it will stand 80 feet with 5 levels of retail shops.

7 World Trade Center
Designed by David Childs. Opened in 2006. Across the street from Ground Zero.

Performing Arts Center
Funding still to be worked out. To be designed by Frank Gehry.

9/11 Museum
Street-level pavilion by Snøhetta; designed by Aedas.

Transportation Hub
Designed by Santiago Calatrava.

Tower 4
Designed by Fumihiko Maki. To be 72 stories tall when it's complete.

National September 11 Memorial
Entitled *Reflecting Absence*. Designed by Michael Arad and Peter Walker. Opened on 9/11/11.

GROUND ZERO
THE WORLD TRADE CENTER SITE

A decade after September 11, 2001, the 9/11 Memorial opened, giving Ground Zero's thousands of annual visitors a solemn place to reflect and think about that brutal day. After delays, its accompanying underground museum opened in 2014, on the same bedrock once used by the Twin Towers' foundation. It is a fitting place to display artifacts from 9/11 and its aftermath. As you plan your visit, set aside time to visit other key parts of the story, such as St. Paul's Chapel and the "Ten House" firehouse on Liberty Street.

(above) President Obama, Michelle Obama, former President George W. Bush, and Laura Bush at the National 9/11 Memorial. (below) Names on the 9/11 Memorial; (opposite) Rendition of the future WTC site.

THE TOWERS

The World Trade Towers, each 110 stories tall, were an impressive feat of engineering. Construction began in 1968, and the Twin Towers officially opened in 1973. Avoiding the typical construction used at the time, the architects gave each building an exterior skeleton made up of 244 slim steel columns and an inner "core" tube that supported the weight of the tower.

Approximately 50,000 people worked in the north tower (1 World Trade Center) and south tower (2 World Trade Center), and another 40,000 people visited the 16-acre complex every day. Beneath the towers was a multi-level mall with nearly 100 stores and restaurants.

The Twin Towers prior to 9/11

EVENTS OF THE DAY On September 11, 2001, terrorist hijackers steered two jets into the World Trade Center's Twin Towers, demolishing them and five outlying buildings.

■ The first hijacked jet, American Airlines Flight 11, crashed into the north tower, 1 World Trade Center, at 8:46 AM, cutting through floors 93 to 99. The tower collapsed at 10:28 AM. Cantor Fitzgerald, a brokerage firm headquartered between the 101st and 105th floors, lost 658 of its 1,050 employees. At the Windows on the World restaurant (floors 106 and 107), 100 patrons and 72 staff members died.

■ The second hijacked jet, United Airlines Flight 175, hit the south tower, 2 World Trade Center, at 9:03 AM, crashing through the 77th to 85th floors. The plane banked as it hit, so portions of the building remained undamaged on impact floors. Consequently, one stairwell initially remained passable from at least the 91st floor down. The tower collapsed at 9:58 AM.

■ The attack killed 2,753 people. (Deaths are still being counted; casualties after the fact included Jerry J. Borg who died in late 2010 from pulmonary sarcoidosis, a lung disease caused by inhaling toxins from the dust cloud that formed when the towers collapsed.) The fenced-in 16-acre work site that emerged from the rubble, almost immediately dubbed Ground Zero, came to symbolize the personal, political, and historical impact of September 11.

(above) Towers burning after attack.

THE DAMAGE

Why *did* the towers fall? A three-year federal study revealed several reasons. The two airplanes used in the attack, both Boeing 767s, hit their respective towers at roughly 500 mph. They both damaged the exterior columns, destroying core supports for at least three of the north tower's floors and up to six of the south tower's floors. Ensuing fires, fed by tens of thousands of gallons of jet fuel, further weakened the buildings. The collapse of the most heavily damaged floors then triggered a domino effect, causing the towers to crumple at an estimated speed of about 125 mph.

Many other area buildings suffered collateral damage. The World Financial Center office complex, to the west of Ground Zero, has as its centerpiece the 10-story glass-domed Winter Garden. After having nearly all its glass blown out in the attacks, the atrium reopened in September 2002 after repairs that included the installation of 2,000 windows and 1.2 million pounds of stone.

The 47-story 7 World Trade Center, to the north of Ground Zero, was struck by large chunks of falling debris from the north and south towers. The building remained standing at first, but subsequent fires caused it to collapse later that afternoon. A new 52-story 7 World Trade Center opened in May 2006 with a much smaller footprint than its predecessor.

St. Paul's Chapel, across the street from Ground Zero, sustained no major dam-

age; staff there credit a huge sycamore that toppled over during the attack. Its gigantic root system, now above ground, helped to shield the building and the headstones in its attached cemetery from falling debris.

Although the New York Stock Exchange's building wasn't physically harmed during the attacks, the market remained closed for six days (including 9/11). When trading resumed on September 17, the Dow Jones industrial average dropped 684.81 points, or 7.13 percent. The American Stock Exchange (Amex), however, sustained some damage on 9/11, and for two weeks Amex stocks and exchange-traded funds were traded on the NYSE floor.

(above) A New York City fire fighter looks up at what remains of the World Trade Center after its collapse; a 9/11 memorial wreath; the "Tribute in Light" memorial on the fifth anniversary of 9/11.

A vision of the future Manhattan skyline

It may have taken longer than most observers could have imagined, but a new World Trade Center is now a reality, at least partially. Following the master plan laid down by the architect Daniel Libeskind, the footprints of the original towers have been made into pools, their rushing waterfalls part of a powerful memorial. When all the work is finished—and there's still more to do—the World Trade Center will include office buildings, a transit hub, and a performing arts center.

NATIONAL SEPTEMBER 11 MEMORIAL

The architect Michael Arad, working in partnership with the landscape architect Peter Walker, won the international contest to design the memorial. It is entitled "Reflecting Absence," and it takes up about half of the 16-acre complex. It opened on the tenth anniversary of 9/11.

No buildings are in the space where the Twin Towers once stood. In their place are recessed waterfalls cascading thirty feet down into two subterranean reflecting pools that limn the Twin Towers' original footprints (each roughly an acre in size). The water then tumbles down into smaller square holes at the center of each pool. The effect manages to be both moving and solemn but not sentimental. In the words of Paul Goldberger, the *New Yorker's* architecture critic, "Arad figured out how to express the idea that what were once the largest solids in Manhattan are now a void, and he made the shape of this void into something monumental."

Future downtown skyline at dusk

Surrounding each waterfall on the plaza level is a low bronze wall with the names of the 2,887 victims of the 9/11 attacks (including those at the Pentagon and on flights 11, 77, 93, and 175), and the six people who died in the first World Trade Center bombing, in 1993. The names are sorted by affiliation, so that names lie etched near those of people they worked with or otherwise knew. Kiosks on the edge of the site help with finding out which panel holds a particular name or group (the information can also be found online, at *www.911memorial.org*, and through a smartphone app). Surrounding the waterfalls is a stark plaza punctuated with hundreds of swamp white-oak saplings, which some day will be 70 feet tall. Joining them is the so-called "survivor tree," a Callery pear tree that was plucked from the rubble, nursed back to health elsewhere, and replanted on the site as a symbol of resilience.

One World Trade Center towering over Lower Manhattan.

Fumihiko Maki, Larry Silverstein, and Norman Foster

Standing at an angle to the memorial's pools is the small center that will serve as the entrance to the memorial's accompanying museum, an ambitious project that has experienced some construction delays. From here, visitors will walk down a ramp to the bedrock the towers were built on, 71 feet below. One exhibit will be the "last column," the last piece of steel to be removed from the site, which was covered with slogans and memorials from rescue crews and others.

ONE WORLD TRADE CENTER

Known for a time as the Freedom Tower, this 104-story skyscraper has a roof that's 1,368 feet tall—identical to that of the taller of the Twin Towers. An illuminated antenna further increases the building's height to 1,776 feet to commemorate America's founding (and making it the country's tallest building). Designed by David Childs of Skidmore, Owings & Merrill, the new 1 WTC is expected to be finished in 2014. The three other office buildings on the site (all at various stages of construction) are each by a different prominent architect: Fumihiko Maki, Richard Rogers, and Norman Foster.

TRANSPORTATION HUB

Intended to connect New Jersey's PATH train with 13 of New York's subway lines, this transportation hub was designed by the Spanish architect Santiago Calatrava. Inspired by the image of a child releasing a dove, the massive glass-roofed building is likely to be awe-inspiring once it's finished, but soaring costs and a complicated design mean that the tentative completion date of 2014 may be delayed.

For more information on the new structures, visit www.lowermanhattan.info and www.911memorial.org.

A GROUND ZERO WALK

Names on the 9/11 Memorial Wall.

The firefighters' memorial.

This tour starts near the WTC Tribute Center, which runs its own well-regarded walking tours that include the memorial and other sites important to the history of 9/11. If you're just doing this walking tour, you can do it in any order.

1 One place to start your walk is at the corner of Liberty and Greenwich streets, just a short distance from where the World Trade Center's South Tower once stood. This is Ten House, a firehouse named for the number of its engine and ladder

companies. On 9/11, the station was nearly destroyed, and six of its members lost their lives after responding to the disaster. The station's restored exterior is now covered with a 56-foot bronze bas-relief "dedicated to those who fell and to those who carry on." The Tribute WTC Visitor Center, a project of the September 11th Families' Association, is next-door. Its exhibits give a heartbreaking picture of the many lives lost on that day.

2 Head around the corner to the National 9/11 Memorial, which incorporates the footprints of the Twin Towers into two pools of water. Make sure to visit the 9/11 Museum. Its 110,000 square feet, nearly all of them underground, take up the seven stories of space that were once occupied by the stores and parking garage under the original Twin Towers.

3 After you've finished paying your respects, head south to exit the memorial (the current exit, as of early 2013, leaves you near the corner of Albany and West streets), making a quick stop at the nearby 9/11 Memorial Visitor Center, at 90 West Street. From here, take the next left (onto Albany Street) and walk over to Trinity Place (which turns into Church Street), turn left (north) and continue until you reach the churchyard behind St. Paul's,

the Episcopal chapel that became a dormitory, mess hall, and medical center in the months after 9/11. Even George Washington's pew was called back into service for the exhausted rescue workers. Across the street, at 20 Vesey Street, is the 9/11 Memorial Preview Site, which has models of what the entire World Trade Center will look like once it's completed. It also has a good selection of books and other items about 9/11 and its aftermath.

Inspired by the giant sycamore that fell under the rubble and helped protect old headstones in St. Paul's graveyard, the *Trinity Root* sculpture, a 9/11 memorial pictured here, can be seen at Trinity Church

The Tribute WTC Visitor Center

VISITING THE MEMORIAL

There is airport-like security at the memorial, and no large bags are allowed, there's no bag storage, and there are no bathrooms. Entry is via free, timed tickets, available online; book ahead. Standby tickets are sometimes available at the site itself. Allow at least an hour to visit the memorial and museum, more at a busy times of the year.

VISITOR CENTERS

An information booth on Vesey Street, near the temporary PATH station, has maps of the area. The 9/11 Memorial Visitor Center (90 West St., 212/225–1009, www.911memorial. org) is open daily, 10–8:30, early Mar.–early Oct. and around Thanksgiving and Christmas; it's open 10–7 the rest of the year. The 9/11 Memorial Preview Site (20 Vesey St., 212/267–2047, free) is open daily, 10–7:30 early Mar.–early Oct. and around Thanksgiving and Christmas, and 9–7 other times. The **Tribute WTC Center** (120 Liberty St., 866/737–1184, www. tributewtc.org, $17) is open 10–6, Mon.–Sat., 10–5 on Sun.

TOURS

The Tribute WTC Center leads hour-long walking tours that include the National September 11 Memorial and nearby sites. The $22 cost ($5 if you've already paid to see the exhibits; keep your receipt) includes admission to the Tribute WTC Center exhibits ($12 for just the tour). You don't need to book in advance. Booking a tour with the Tribute WTC Visitor Center saves you having to get your own timed ticket for the 9/11 memorial.

GETTING THERE

Subway: **1**, **N**, **R** to Rector St.; **2**,**3**,**4**,**5**,**A**,**C**,**J**,**Z** to Fulton St./ Broadway-Nassau; **E** to World Trade Center/Church St.

PATH: Any line to World Trade Center.

Federal Reserve Bank of New York. With its imposing mix of sandstone, limestone, and ironwork, the Federal Reserve looks the way a bank ought to: strong and impregnable. The gold ingots in the subterranean vaults here are worth roughly $350 billion—reputedly a third of the world's gold reserves. Forty-five-minute-long tours (conducted six times a day and requiring reservations made at least five days in advance) include a visit to the gold vault, the trading desk, and "FedWorks," a multimedia exhibit center where you can track hypothetical trades. Visitors must show an officially issued photo ID, such as a driver's license or passport, and pass through scanning equipment to enter the building. The Fed advises arriving 20 minutes before your tour to accommodate security screening. Photography is not permitted. ⊠ *33 Liberty St., between William and Nassau Sts., Financial District* ☎ *212/720–6130* ⊕ *www.newyorkfed.org* 🖃 *Free* ☉ *Tour by advance reservation, weekdays 11:15–4* Ⓜ *A, C to Broadway-Nassau; J, Z, 2, 3, 4, 5 to Fulton St.*

Fraunces Tavern Museum. This former tavern, where General George Washington celebrated the end of the Revolutionary War in 1783, is now a museum covering two floors above a restaurant and bar. Here, in his pre-presidential days, Washington bid an emotional farewell to his officers upon the British evacuation of New York. Today this historic landmark has two fully furnished period rooms—including the Long Room, site of Washington's address—and other modest displays of 18th- and 19th-century American history. You'll find more tourists and Wall Street types than revolutionaries in the tavern and restaurant on the ground floor these days, but a cozy colonial atmosphere and a decent hearty meal is also on offer. ⊠ *54 Pearl St., at Broad St., Financial District* ☎ *212/425–1778* ⊕ *www.frauncestavernmuseum.org* 🖃 *$7* ☉ *Daily noon–5* Ⓜ *R to Whitehall St.; 4, 5 to Bowling Green; 1 to South Ferry; J, Z to Broad St.*

Museum of American Finance. Pre-9/11, a visit to the New York Stock Exchange was the ultimate high; the energy of the floor and the proximity to so much power couldn't be beat. Post-9/11 security prohibits tours of the Exchange but you can still get a feel—albeit a less exhilarating feel—for what makes the financial world go 'round (and down) by visiting this museum. Located in the grandiose former banking hall of the Bank of New York, this Smithsonian affiliate is home to artifacts of the financial market's history; interactive exhibits on the financial markets, banking, entrepreneurship, and Alexander Hamilton; and well-executed temporary exhibits. ⊠ *48 Wall St., at William St., Financial District* ☎ *212/908–4110* ⊕ *www.moaf.org* 🖃 *$8* ☉ *Tues.–Sat. 10–4* Ⓜ *2, 3 to Wall St.*

Museum of Jewish Heritage—A Living Memorial to the Holocaust. In a granite 85-foot hexagon at the southern end of Battery Park City, this museum pays tribute to the 6 million Jews who perished in the Holocaust. Architects Kevin Roche and John Dinkeloo built the museum in the shape of a Star of David, with three floors of exhibits demonstrating the dynamism of 20th-century Jewish culture. Visitors enter through a gallery that provides a context for the early-20th-century artifacts on the first floor: an elaborate screen hand-painted for the fall harvest festival of Sukkoth, wedding invitations, and tools used by Jewish tradesmen. Original documentary films play throughout the museum. The second floor details the rise of Nazism and anti-Semitism, and the ravages of

CLOSE UP

The Gangs of Five Points

In the mid-19th century the Five Points area was perhaps the city's most notorious and dangerous neighborhood. The confluence of five streets—Mulberry, Anthony (now Worth), Cross (now Park), Orange (now Baxter), and Little Water (no longer in existence)—had been built over a drainage pond that had been filled in the 1820s. When the buildings began to sink into the mosquito-filled muck, middle-class residents abandoned their homes. Buildings were chopped into tiny apartments that were rented to the poorest of the poor, who at this point were newly emancipated slaves and Irish immigrants fleeing

famine. Newspaper accounts at the time tell of daily robberies and other violent crimes. And with corrupt political leaders like William Marcy "Boss" Tweed more concerned with lining their pockets than patrolling the streets, keeping order was left to the club-wielding hooligans portrayed in *Gangs of New York*. The neighborhood, finally razed in the 1880s to make way for Columbus Park, has left a lasting legacy: In the music halls where different ethnic groups grudgingly came together, the Irish jig and the African-American shuffle combined to form a new type of fancy footwork called tap dancing.

the Holocaust. A gallery covers the doomed voyage of the SS *St. Louis*, a ship of German Jewish refugees that crossed the Atlantic twice in 1939 in search of a safe haven. Signs of hope are also on display, including a trumpet that Louis Bannet (the "Dutch Louis Armstrong") played for three years in the Auschwitz-Birkenau inmate orchestra. The third floor covers postwar Jewish life. Recent temporary exhibits explore the history of American Jews who tried to rescue European Jews leading up to and during the Holocaust, as well as the rich Jewish history of Oswiecim, the town the Germans called Auschwitz. The museum's east wing has a theater, a memorial garden, a library, more galleries, and a café. A free audio guide, with narration by Meryl Streep and Itzhak Perlman, is available at the admissions desk. ⊠ *36 Battery Pl., Battery Park City, Financial District* ☎ *646/437–4202* ⊕ *www.mjhnyc.org* 💲 *$12, free Wed. 4–8* ☉ *Thurs. and Sun.–Tues. 10–5:45, Wed. 10–8, Fri. and eve of Jewish holidays 10–3* Ⓜ *4, 5 to Bowling Green.*

National Museum of the American Indian (Smithsonian Institution). Massive granite columns rise to a pediment topped by a double row of statues at the impressive beaux arts Alexander Hamilton U.S. Custom House building (1907), which houses the New York branch of this Smithsonian museum (the other branch is in Washington DC). Inside, the egg-shape stairwell and rotunda embellished with shipping-theme murals (completed in the 1930s) are also worth a pause. The permanent exhibit, *Infinity of Nations*, is an encyclopedic survey of Native cultures from throughout the Americas, including 700 objects from ancient times to present day. The venue also presents changing exhibits, videos and films, dance, music, and storytelling programs. ⊠ *1 Bowling Green, between State and Whitehall Sts., Financial District* ☎ *212/514–3700* ⊕ *www.nmai.si.edu* 💲 *Free* ☉ *Mon.–Wed. and Fri.–Sun. 10–5, Thurs. 10–8* Ⓜ *4, 5 to Bowling Green.*

FAMILY   **New York City Police Museum.** Why are police called cops? Why does a police badge have eight points? When was fingerprinting first used to solve a crime? The answers to these questions and much more can be found at this museum dedicated to New York's Finest. The force's history from colonial times to the present is covered through the permanent *9/11 Remembered* installation—which includes a video featuring interviews with first responders to the attack—as well as rotating exhibits. The Hall of Heroes honors police officers who have fallen in the line of duty. The Junior Officers Discovery Zone, an interactive children's exhibit, includes a model of a mobile crime lab, a police car, fingerprint labs, and other tools used for investigations. Special events include a vintage police-car show the first weekend in June. At press time, the museum remains closed due to damage caused by Hurricane Sandy; a small, temporary exhibit is located at 45 Wall Street. Call or check online for re-opening date. ⊠ *100 Old Slip, near South St., Financial District* ☎ *212/480–3100* ⊕ *www.nycpolicemuseum.org* ⊠ *$8* ☉ *Mon.–Sat. 10–5, Sun. noon–5* Ⓜ *2, 3 to Wall St.*

Skyscraper Museum. Why get a crick in your neck—or worse, risk looking like a tourist—while appreciating New York City's famous skyline, when you can visit the Skyscraper Museum instead? At this small museum that shares a building with the Ritz Carlton in Battery Park City, you can appreciate highly detailed hand-carved miniature wood models of midtown and downtown Manhattan; explore the past, present, and future of the skyscraper—from New York City's Empire State Building to Dubai's Burj Khalifa (taller than the Empire State Building and Chicago's Sears Tower combined); and examine both the history of the Twin Towers at the World Trade Center and the ongoing rebuilding of Ground Zero. Expect models of current or future buildings, videos, drawings, floor plans, talks, and exhibits that reveal the influence of history, real estate, and individuals on shaping city skylines. ⊠ *39 Battery Pl., across from Museum of Jewish Heritage, Financial District* ☎ *212/968–1961* ⊕ *www.skyscraper.org* ⊠ *$5* ☉ *Wed.–Sun. noon–6* Ⓜ *4, 5 to Bowling Green.*

St. Paul's Chapel. For more than a year after the World Trade Center attacks, the chapel's fence served as a shrine for visitors seeking solace. People from around the world left tokens of grief and support, or signed one of the large drop cloths that hung from the fence. After serving as a 24-hour refuge where rescue and recovery workers could eat, pray, rest, and receive counseling, the chapel, which amazingly suffered no damage, reopened to the public in fall 2002. The powerful ongoing exhibit, titled Unwavering Spirit: Hope & Healing at Ground Zero, honors the efforts of rescue workers in the months after September 11 with photos, drawings, banners, and other items sent to them as memorials. Open since 1766, St. Paul's is the oldest public building in continuous use in Manhattan. ⊠ *209 Broadway, at Fulton St., Financial District* ☎ *212/602–0800* ⊕ *www.trinitywallstreet.org/about/ st-pauls* ☉ *Mon.–Sat. 10–6, Sun. 7 am–9 pm* Ⓜ *2, 3, 4, 5, A, C, J, Z to Broadway-Nassau; 4, 5 to Broadway-Nassau; E to Chambers; 6 to Brooklyn Bridge/City Hall.*

On a typical weekday, five ferries make roughly 110 trips back and forth between Staten Island and Manhattan, transporting about 60,000 passengers.

NEW YORK HARBOR

The southern tip of Manhattan has often served as a microcosm for a city that offers as many first shots as it does second chances, so it's appropriate that the key point of departure for the Statue of Liberty and Ellis Island is here. This experience should never be dismissed as too touristy. Like nothing else, the excursion will remind you that New York is a city of immigrants and survivors.

TOP ATTRACTIONS

Fodor's Choice
★

Ellis Island. *See highlighted feature at the end of Chapter 1.*

FAMILY
Fodor's Choice
★

Governors Island. Governors Island is open to the public from May to October: get there via a short, free ferry ride. It's essentially a big, charming park that looks like a small New England town—it's popular with locals for biking and running trails, festivals, art shows, concerts, and family programs. Wouter Van Twiller, a representative for Holland, supposedly purchased the island for his private use, in 1637, from Native Americans for two ax heads, a string of beads, and a handful of nails. It was confiscated by the Dutch a year later, and for the next decade its ownership switched back and forth between the Dutch and British until the Brits gained firm control of it in the 1670s. The island was officially named in 1784 for His Majesty's Governors, and was used by the American military until the 1960s, when the Coast Guard took it over. After their facilities were abandoned in 1995, the island was purchased by the public in 2002 and started welcoming visitors in 2003. The ferry to the island departs from the

Battery Maritime Building. ✉ *Ferry: Battery Maritime Building, 10 South St., Financial District* ⊕ *www.govisland.com* ✆ *Free* ⊙ *June–Oct., Fri. 10–5, weekends 10–7* Ⓜ *1 to South Ferry; 4, 5 to Bowling Green; R to Whitehall Street.*

Fodor's Choice
★

Staten Island Ferry. Every day, some 60,000 people ride the free ferry to Staten Island, one of the city's outer boroughs, and you should be one of them. Without paying a cent, you get phenomenal views of the Lower Manhattan skyline, the Statue of Liberty, and Ellis Island during the 25-minute boat ride across New York Harbor. You'll also pass tugboats, freighters, and cruise ships—a reminder that this is very much still a working harbor. The boat embarks every 15 to 30 minutes from the Whitehall Terminal at Whitehall and South streets, near the east end of Battery Park. You must disembark once you reach the opposite terminal, but you can just get back in line to board again if you don't plan to stay. ✉ *Battery Park, Financial District* ☎ *212/639–9675* ⊕ *www.siferry.com* ✆ *Free* Ⓜ *1 to South Ferry; R to Whitehall St.; 4, 5 to Bowling Green.*

Fodor's Choice
★

Statue of Liberty. *See highlighted feature at the end of Chapter 1.*

TRIBECA

Tucked on the west side, south of Canal Street, residential TriBeCa (the triangle below Canal Street) has a quieter vibe than most other Manhattan neighborhoods. Walk the photogenic streets, especially the stretch of Federal row houses on Harrison Street, and you'll understand why so many celebrities own apartments here. The two-block-long Staple Street, with its connecting overhead walkway, is a favorite of urban cinematographers. Although TriBeCa's money is often hidden behind grand cast-iron facades, you can get a taste of it at posh neighborhood restaurants and cocktail bars, or at the star-studded TriBeCa Film Festival in spring.

WORTH NOTING

FAMILY
Fodor's Choice
★

Hudson River Park. The quiet places of New York City are treasured by locals, and one of the best options is Hudson River Park, a 5-mile path from Battery Place to 59th Street. This riverside stretch has been renovated into a landscaped park, incorporating the piers that jut out into the Hudson, with walking and cycling paths, a seasonal mini golf course, dog runs, and skate parks. The TriBeCa portion consists of piers 25 and 26 and offers picnic spaces, playgrounds, and a sand volleyball court. The area adjacent to the West Village (piers 45 and 46) and near Chelsea (piers 63 and 64) are equally attractive, with lots of green spaces. ✉ *TriBeCa* ☎ *212/627–2020* ⊕ *www.hudsonriverpark. org* Ⓜ *1 to Franklin St.*

3

SOHO, NOLITA, LITTLE ITALY, AND CHINATOWN

GETTING ORIENTED

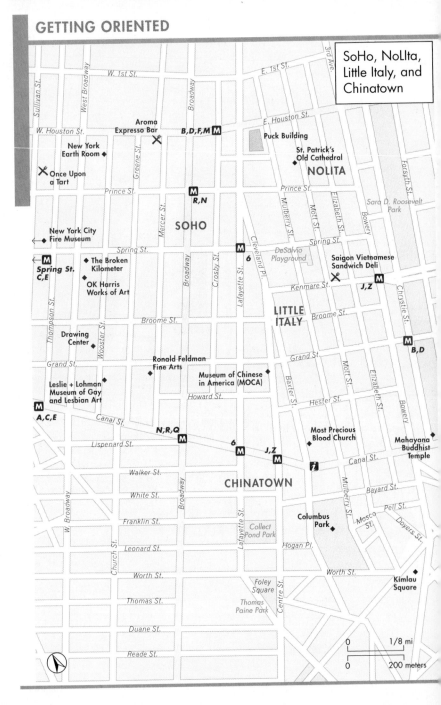

SoHo, NoLIta, Little Italy, and Chinatown

Sullivan St.
West Broadway
W. 1st St.
Broadway
E. 1st St.
3rd Ave.

W. Houston St.
Aroma Expresso Bar
B,D,F,M
E. Houston St.
Puck Building

New York Earth Room
Greene St.
St. Patrick's Old Cathedral
NOLITA
Forsyth St.

Once Upon a Tart
Prince St.
Mercer St.
R,N
Prince St.
Mulberry St.
Mott St.
Elizabeth St.
Bowery
Sara D. Roosevelt Park

New York City Fire Museum
SOHO
Spring St.
Spring St.

Spring St.
C,E
The Broken Kilometer
Broadway
Crosby St.
Lafayette St.
Cleveland Pl.
6
DeSalvio Playground
Saigon Vietnamese Sandwich Deli
J,Z
Chrystie St.

OK Harris Works of Art
Kenmare St.

Thompson St.
Broome St.
LITTLE ITALY
Broome St.

Drawing Center
Wooster St.
B,D

Grand St.
Ronald Feldman Fine Arts
Grand St.
Mott St.
Elizabeth St.
Bowery

Leslie + Lohman Museum of Gay and Lesbian Art
Museum of Chinese in America (MOCA)
Baxter St.

Howard St.
Hester St.

A,C,E
Canal St.
Most Precious Blood Church
Mahayana Buddhist Temple

Lispenard St.
N,R,Q
6
J,Z
Canal St.

Walker St.
CHINATOWN
Bayard St.

W. Broadway
White St.
Broadway
Columbus Park
Mosco St.
Pell St.
Doyers St.

Franklin St.
Lafayette St.
Collect Pond Park

Church St.
Leonard St.
Hogan Pl.

Worth St.
Worth St.
Kimlau Square

Foley Square
Centre St.

Thomas St.
Thomas Paine Park

Duane St.

Reade St.

0   1/8 mi
0   200 meters

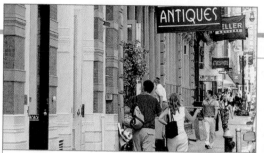

MAKING THE MOST OF YOUR TIME

If you're coming to shop in SoHo and NoLIta, there's no need to rush out the door, because most shops don't open until 10 or 11 am; many stay open until early evening. If art is your thing, avoid Sunday, because most galleries are closed. SoHo, with national chains lining its section of Broadway, is almost always a madhouse (unless it's raining), but weekdays are somewhat less frenetic. NoLIta, with less traffic, fewer chains, and more boutiques, is calmer and less crowded.

Little Italy is a small area nowadays, having lost ground to a growing Chinatown. Note that food-wise, most of the checkered-tablecloth spots in Little Italy itself are touristy, with mediocre food.

If you're visiting New York in mid-September, you'll time it right for the San Gennaro festival—a huge street fair in honor of the patron saint of Naples—and you, along with thousands of others, can easily spend some time exploring the many food and souvenir booths and playing games of chance. Given that few Italian-Americans live in the area anymore, it's not exactly like visiting old Napoli, but it is a fun way to spend an hour or two.

Chinatown bustles with local shoppers pretty much any time of day, but there are more tourists on the weekends, when it gets so busy there isn't much room on the sidewalk.

TOP EXPERIENCES

Browsing boutiques and people-watching in SoHo and NoLIta

Ogling the out-of-the-ordinary produce and seafood in Chinatown

Gallery hopping in SoHo

Eating dim sum in Chinatown

Sipping a cocktail in NoLIta

GETTING HERE AND AROUND

SoHo (South of Houston) is bounded by Houston Street, Canal Street, 6th Avenue, and Lafayette Street. To the east, NoLIta (North of Little Italy) is contained within Houston, the Bowery, Kenmare, and Lafayette. Plenty of subways service the area: take the 6, C, or E to Spring St.; the N or R to Prince St.; or the B, D, F, or M to Broadway–Lafayette St. For Chinatown, farther south, take the J, N, Q, R, Z, or 6 to Canal St. or the B or D to Grand St.

COFFEE AND QUICK BITES

Aroma Espresso Bar. Large windows are perfect for people-watching and the sandwiches, soups, pastries, and coffee beverages are top quality. ✉ *145 Greene St., at Houston St., SoHo* ☎ *212/533–1094* ⊕ *www.aroma. us* Ⓜ *N, R to Prince St.*

Once Upon a Tart. A great name, and sandwiches, soups, and sweets to back it up. ✉ *135 Sullivan St., between Houston and Prince Sts., SoHo* ☎ *212/387–8869* ⊕ *www.onceuponatart.com* Ⓜ *C, E to Spring St.*

Saigon Vietnamese Sandwich Deli. Predating the recent banh mi craze by perhaps a decade, this storefront serves delicious sandwiches. ✉ *369 Broome St., between Mott and Elizabeth Sts., SoHo* ☎ *212/219–8341* ⊕ *www. vietnamese-sandwich.com* Ⓜ *J to Bowery; 6 to Spring St.*

Sightseeing
★★★
Nightlife
★★★
Dining
★★★★
Lodging
★★★
Shopping
★★★★★

SoHo, NoLIta, Little Italy, and Chinatown all tend to be jam-packed with humanity, all the more perfect for people-watching as you shop, nibble, and wander. Parts of SoHo and NoLIta are destinations for super-trendy shopping as well as popular chains and department stores: the boutiques are often overpriced but it's undeniably glamorous. Little Italy and Chinatown are more about local shopping.

SOHO

Updated by
Jessica Colley

SoHo was the epicenter of New York's art scene in the late 1970s, and has since evolved into a shopping destination of mostly chain retailers. (Where are the galleries? They've scattered, with Chelsea taking the lion's share of the more established names, and the East Village, Lower East Side, and several Brooklyn neighborhoods incubating many up-and-comers.) Compared with other neighborhoods, SoHo takes more work to find a local vibe, but a bit of bohemia still exists. It can be found on the cobblestone side streets where there are still a few galleries, as well as sidewalks jammed with tables full of handmade beaded jewelry, tooled leather belts, and hats and purses. There are also unique clothing boutiques, gourmet food shops, Italian neighborhood staples, and even a few divey bars thrown into the mix.

WORTH NOTING

Drawing Center. At this nonprofit organization the focus is only on drawings—contemporary and historical. Works shown in the three galleries often push the envelope on what's considered drawing; many projects are commissioned especially by the center. ⊠ *35 Wooster St., between Broome and Grand Sts., SoHo* ☎ *212/219–2166* ⊕ *www. drawingcenter.org* ⊠ *$5* ⊙ *Wed. and Fri.–Sun. noon–6, Thurs. noon–8* Ⓜ *N, Q, R, J, Z, 6, A, C, E to Canal St.*

Leslie + Lohman Museum of Gay and Lesbian Art. Founded in the late 1980s, this museum has roots in the collection of its founders, Charles Leslie and Fritz Lohman. The well-curated exhibits are usually photographic, with much of it sexually charged or at least homoerotic. ⊠ *26 Wooster St., between Grand and Canal Sts., SoHo* ☎ *212/431–2609* ⊕ *www. leslielohman.org* ⊗ *Tues.–Sun. noon–6* Ⓜ *A, C, E to Canal St.*

> ## SOHO WAS HELL
>
> SoHo once had the less trendy moniker "Hell's Hundred Acres," so named because the crowded slums were repeatedly beset by frequent fires, but it boomed after the Civil War, when the neighborhood came to be known simply as the Eighth Ward and filled up with manufacturing and dry-goods stores.

New York City Fire Museum. In the former headquarters of Engine 30—a handsome Beaux Arts building dating from 1904—retired firefighters volunteer their time in the morning and early afternoon to answer visitors' questions. The collection of firefighting tools from the 18th century to the present includes hand-pulled and horse-drawn engines, speaking trumpets, pumps, and uniforms. A memorial exhibit with photos, paintings, children's artwork, and found objects relating to the September 11 attacks is also on view—a poignant reminder and tribute to the 343 firefighters who died on 9/11. The museum is two subway stops (via the E train) north of the Ground Zero site. ⊠ *278 Spring St., between Hudson and Varick Sts., SoHo* ☎ *212/691–1303* ⊕ *www.nycfiremuseum.org* 🖃 *$8* ⊗ *Daily 10–5* Ⓜ *C, E to Spring St.*

New York Earth Room. Noted "earthworks" artist Walter De Maria's 1977 avant-garde installation consists of 140 tons of gently sculpted soil (22 inches deep). It fills 3,600 square feet of a second-floor gallery maintained by the Dia Art Foundation since 1980. As the *New York Times* put it in 1999, "a loamy smell definitely permeates the space." You can't touch or walk on the dirt, nor can you take its photo. If you like this installation, check out De Maria's equally odd and impressive work called *The Broken Kilometer*, an 18.75-ton installation that consists of five columns of a total of 1,000 meter-long brass rods, which cover the wood floors of an open loft space. It's a few blocks away at 393 West Broadway, and has the same hours as the Earth Room. ⊠ *141 Wooster St., 2nd fl., between W. Houston and Prince Sts., SoHo* ☎ *212/989–5566* ⊕ *www.earthroom.org* 🖃 *Free* ⊗ *Wed.–Sun. noon–6 (closed 3–3:30 and mid-June–mid-Sept.)* Ⓜ *R to Prince St.; B, D, F, M to Broadway-Lafayette.*

OK Harris Works of Art. Since 1969, this contemporary fine-arts gallery has showed a wide range of painting, photography, and sculptures. The gallery is closed from mid-July through Labor Day. Its building was built in the 1860s for drying and storing tobacco. ⊠ *383 W. Broadway, between Spring and Broome Sts., SoHo* ☎ *212/431–3600* ⊕ *www. okharris.com* ⊗ *Mid-Sept.–June, Tues.–Sat. 10–6; early to mid-July, Tues.–Fri. noon–5* Ⓜ *C, E to Spring St.*

SoHo and NoLIta Architecture

There are plenty of beautiful people in SoHo and NoLIta, but tilt your eyes up, beyond the turn-of-the-20th-century lampposts adorned with cast-iron curlicues, and you'll also find some of New York's most impressive architecture. SoHo has one of the world's greatest concentrations of cast-iron buildings, created in response to fires that wiped out much of Lower Manhattan in the mid-18th century. Look down and you'll see Belgian brick cobblestones lining some of the streets. Along Broadway and the neighboring streets of SoHo, you'll see lights in the sidewalk: starting in the 1850s, these vault lights were set into sidewalks to permit daylight to reach basements.

The **King of Greene Street**, at 72–76 Greene, between Grand and Canal, is a five-story Renaissance-style 1873 building with a magnificent projecting porch of Corinthian columns and pilasters. These days it's unmistakably painted in high-gloss ivory. Over at 28–30 Greene Street is the **Queen of Greene Street**, a graceful 1873 cast-iron beauty that exemplifies the Second Empire style with its dormers, columns, window arches, projecting central bays, and roof.

The **Haughwout Building**, at 488–492 Broadway, north of Broome, is best known for what's no longer inside—the world's first commercial passenger elevator, invented by Elisha Graves Otis. The building's exterior is worth a look, though: nicknamed the Parthenon of Cast Iron, the five-story, Venetian palazzo–style structure was built in 1857 to house department-store merchant E. V. Haughwout's china, silver, and glassware store.

Each window is framed by Corinthian columns and rounded arches.

Built in 1904, the **Little Singer Building**, at 561 Broadway, is a masterpiece of cast-iron styling, its delicate facade covered with curlicues of wrought iron. The L-shape building's second facade is around the corner on Prince Street.

Charlton Street, not technically in SoHo but across 6th Avenue in the West Village, is Manhattan's longest stretch of Federal-style redbrick row houses from the 1820s and '30s. The high stoops, paneled front doors, leaded-glass windows, and narrow dormer windows are all intact. King and Vandam streets also have historic houses. Much of this was the site of a mansion called Richmond Hill, and, in the late 18th century the surrounding area was a beautiful wild meadow from where you could see the nearby "hamlet" of Greenwich Village.

Over in Little Italy/NoLIta, the magnificent old **Police Headquarters** building at 240 Centre Street, between Broome and Grand, might be familiar from Martin Scorsese's *Gangs of New York*. The 1909 Edwardian baroque structure with its striking copper dome was the headquarters of the New York City Police Department until 1973. Designed to "impress both the officer and the prisoner with the majesty of the law," it was converted into luxury condos in 1988 and is known today as the Police Building Apartments.

The 1885 Romanesque Revival **Puck Building**, at 295 Lafayette Street, on the southeast corner of Houston, is a former magazine headquarters and now a busy event space—look for the statue of Puck just over the door.

The stark, simple interior of OK Harris Works of Art illustrates the typical gallery space in SoHo.

Ronald Feldman Fine Arts. Founded in 1971 and in SoHo since the 1980s, this gallery represents more than 30 international contemporary artists; exhibits contemporary painting, sculpture, installations, drawings, and prints; and hosts performances. It has a large selection of Andy Warhol prints, paintings, and drawings. ⊠ *31 Mercer St., between Grand and Canal Sts., SoHo* ☎ *212/226–3232* ⊕ *www.feldmangallery.com* ⊗ *Winter, Tues.–Sat. 10–6; summer, Mon.–Thurs. 10–6, Fri. 10–3* Ⓜ *N, Q, R, J, A, C, E, 6 to Canal St.*

NOLITA

NoLIta is a lot less frantic and crowded than either SoHo or Chinatown, and the upscale boutiques, indie shops, quirky cafés, small eateries, and other gentrifying influences here evoke, in some ways, the spirit of old SoHo.

WORTH NOTING

St. Patrick's Old Cathedral. If you've watched *The Godfather,* you've peeked inside New York's first Roman Catholic cathedral— the interior shots of the infamous baptism scene were filmed here. Dedicated in 1815, this church lost its designation as the seat of New York's bishop when the current St. Patrick's opened uptown, in 1879. The unadorned exterior of the cathedral gives no hint of the splendors within, which include an 1868 Henry Erben pipe organ. The interior dates from the 1860s, after a large fire gutted most of the original design. The enormous marble altar surrounded by hand-carved niches (reredos) houses an extraordinary collection of sacred statuary

Some of the storefronts and signage in Chinatown are bilingual—but some are just in Chinese.

and other Gothic exuberance. There's a maze of mortuary vaults underneath the cathedral (older residents of Little Italy recall playing hide-and-seek in the vaults). Sunday Mass in English is at 9:15 and 12:45. ✉ *263 Mulberry St., corner of Mott and Prince Sts., NoLIta* ☎ *212/226–8075* ⊕ *www.oldcathedral.org* ⊗ *Daily 8–5 (hrs vary)* Ⓜ *R to Prince St.; 6 to Bleecker St.*

LITTLE ITALY

Just east of Broadway, you'll find the remains of what once was a thriving, lively community of Italian Americans: the tangle of streets that make up Little Italy. The few nostalgic blocks surrounding Mulberry Street between NoLIta and bustling Canal Street are still a cheerful salute to all things Italian, with red-green-and-white street decorations on permanent display and specialty grocers and cannelloni makers dishing up delights. It is all a bit touristy these days, and you should look elsewhere if you're looking for a great Italian restaurant meal. Still, Little Italy is fun to walk around, and several of the food stores on Grand Street are worth a stop if you're after an edible souvenir.

Every September, Mulberry Street becomes the giant Feast of San Gennaro, a crowded 11-day festival that sizzles with the smell of sausages and onions (don't miss John Fasullo's braciole, an iconic sandwich filled with filet of pork roasted over a coal pit and topped with peppers and onions). This is by far the city's most extensive annual street fair.

If you're looking for a bigger and more bustling Little Italy, head up to Arthur Avenue in the Bronx (⇨ *Chapter 15*) and you'll find several good restaurants and a cornucopia of authentic Italian goods, all of them marketed to New Yorkers and tourists alike.

WORTH NOTING

Most Precious Blood Church. The National Shrine of San Gennaro, a replica of the grotto at Lourdes, is the high point of Most Precious Blood Church's richly painted interior. The church becomes a focal point during the annual San Gennaro festival. Sunday Mass is in English at 9 and noon. ⊠ *113 Baxter St., between Canal and Hester Sts., Little Italy* ☎ *212/226–6427* Ⓜ *N, Q, R, 6 to Canal St.; J, Z to Canal St.*

> ### KIDS IN SOHO AND LITTLE ITALY
>
> This is primarily a grown-up section of town, unless you're raising dedicated shoppers, but there are a few things for the kids to do here. Check out the Scholastic bookstore (⊠ 557 Broadway) or blow off steam at Little Italy's DeSalvio Playground at the corner of Spring and Mulberry streets—it's nothing fancy, but the kids may enjoy clambering on the red, white, and green equipment.

CHINATOWN

Chinatown is a living, breathing, anything-but-quiet ethnic enclave: a quarter of the city's nearly 700,000 Chinese residents live here. The neighborhood started as a seven-block area, but now covers some 40-plus blocks above and below Canal Street (encroaching on what was once a thriving Little Italy), with 200-plus restaurants serving every imaginable regional Chinese cuisine crammed into about 2 square miles. Head to **Mott Street,** south of Canal, Chinatown's main thoroughfare, where the first Chinese immigrants (mostly men) settled in tenements in the late 1880s. Today, the street is dense with restaurants, hair salons and barbershops, massage parlors, bakeries, tea parlors, and souvenir shops, as well as Buddhist temples, herbalists, and acupuncturists. The few blocks above Canal overflow with food shops selling vegetables and fish (some still alive and squirming). Walk carefully, as the sidewalks can be slick from the ice underneath the eels, blue crabs, snapper, and shrimp that seem to look back at you as you pass by. If you plan it right, you can create a movable feast, starting with soup dumplings, a specialty from Shanghai, and continuing with Peking duck, a yellow custard cake, and a jasmine bubble tea, each at a different place. A city tourist-information kiosk on a traffic island where Canal, Baxter, and Walker streets meet can help you with tours, and also has a map that's very useful for unraveling the tangled streets in the area.

WORTH NOTING

Columbus Park. People-watching is the thing in this park. If you swing by in the morning, you'll see men and women practicing tai chi; the afternoons bring intense games of mah-jongg. In the mid-19th century the park was known as Five Points—the point where Mulberry Street, Anthony (now Worth) Street, Cross (now Park) Street, Orange (now Baxter) Street, and Little Water Street (no longer in existence) intersected—and was notoriously ruled by dangerous Irish gangs. In the 1880s a neighborhood-improvement campaign brought about the park's creation. ✉ *Chinatown* ⊕ *www.nycgovparks.org/parks/M015* Ⓜ *6, J, N, Q, Z to Canal St.*

Kimlau Square. Ten streets converge at this labyrinthine intersection crisscrossed at odd angles by pedestrian walkways. Standing on an island in this busy area is the **Kimlau Arch,** named for Ralph Kimlau, a bomber pilot who died in World War II; the arch is dedicated to all Chinese-Americans who "lost their Lives in Defense of Freedom and Democracy." A statue on the square's eastern edge pays tribute to a Qing Dynasty official named Lin Ze Xu, the Fujianese minister who sparked the Opium War by banning the drug. ✉ *Chatham Square, Bowery and E. Broadway, Chinatown* ⊕ *www.nycgovparks.org/parks/kimlausquare* Ⓜ *4, 5, 6 to Brooklyn Bridge/City Hall; J, Z to Chambers St.*

Mahayana Buddhist Temple. This pleasant and bright Buddhist temple is at a very busy corner, at the foot of the Manhattan Bridge Arch on the Bowery. There's an excellent gift shop on the second floor. Before its reincarnation as a place of worship in 1997, this was the Rosemary, a theater showing a mix of kung fu and porn movies. ✉ *133 Canal St., at the Bowery, Chinatown* ☏ *212/925–8787* ⊕ *en.mahayana.us* ✉ *Donations accepted* ◷ *Daily 8–6* Ⓜ *B, D to Grand St.*

The Museum of Chinese in America (MOCA). Founded in 1980, this museum is dedicated to preserving and presenting the history of the Chinese people and their descendants in the United States. Its current building, which opened in 2009 near the boundary between Chinatown and Little Italy (technically, many would say it's in Little Italy), was designed by Maya Lin, architect of the Vietnam Veterans Memorial in Washington, DC. MOCA's permanent exhibit on Chinese-American history, titled With a Single Step: Stories in the Making of America, includes artworks, personal and domestic artifacts, historical documentation, and films. Chinese laundry tools, a traditional general store, and antique business signs are some of the unique objects on display. Rotating shows, some of which examine the sometimes turbulent relations between Asian Americans and the rest of the country, are on display in the second gallery. MOCA sponsors workshops, walking tours, lectures, and family events. ✉ *215 Centre St., between Grand and Howard Sts., Chinatown* ☏ *212/619–4785* ⊕ *www.mocanyc.org* ✉ *$10* ◷ *Tues., Wed., and Fri.– Sun. 11–6, Thurs. 11–9* Ⓜ *6, J, M, N, Q, R, Z to Canal St.*

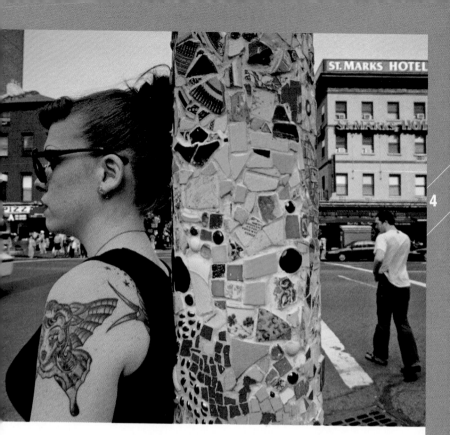

4

THE EAST VILLAGE
AND THE LOWER
EAST SIDE

GETTING ORIENTED

The East Village and the Lower East Side

MAKING THE MOST OF YOUR TIME

Houston Street runs east–west and neatly divides the East Village (north of Houston) and the Lower East Side (south of Houston). The eastern boundary of the East Village and Lower East Side is the East River; the western boundary is 4th Avenue and the Bowery. So many communities converge in these neighborhoods that each block seems like a new neighborhood unto itself.

The East Village lets loose on weekend nights, when nightlife seekers converge on the area, filling up the bars and spilling out onto the sidewalks. Weekday evenings are less frenetic, with more of a local vibe—although the term "local" around here always means a large number of students from New York University. Daytime is great for shopping in the local boutiques, and brunch on weekends around here generally can mean lines for hot spots like Prune and Back Forty, which fill with patrons lingering over coffee.

The Lower East Side does not tend to be an early-riser destination any day of the week. Although there's plenty to see during the day, nightfall offers a different vision: blocks that were previously empty rows of pulled-down gratings transform into clusters of throbbing bars. On the trendy streets around Rivington and Stanton, stores, bars, and cafés buzz all week.

GETTING HERE AND AROUND

For the East Village, take the N/R subway line to 8th Street, the 6 to Astor Place, or the L to 3rd Avenue. To reach Alphabet City, take the L to 1st Avenue or the F to 2nd Avenue. For the Lower East Side, head southeast from the 2nd Avenue stop on the F, or take the F/M/J/Z to the Delancey Street–Essex Street stop.

TOP EXPERIENCES

People-watching on St. Marks Place or at Tompkins Square Park

Shopping at boutiques and vintage clothing stores

Visiting the Lower East Side Tenement Museum

COFFEE AND QUICK BITES

Il Laboratorio del Gelato. Seasonal flavors make this gelato la crème de la crème. ⊠ *188 Ludlow St., at E. Houston St., Lower East Side* ☎ *212/343-9922* ⊕ *www.laboratoriodelgelato. com* Ⓜ *F to 2nd Ave.*

Katz's Delicatessen. Given Katz's location and its equally lost-in-time vibe, this old-school deli goes as well with a visit to the Tenement Museum as a Cel-Ray soda goes with pastrami (ask for a sample while you wait). Just don't lose your ticket. ⊠ *205 E. Houston St., at Ludlow St., Lower East Side* ☎ *212/254-2246* ⊕ *www.katzsdelicatessen. com* Ⓜ *F to 2nd Ave.*

Veniero's Pastry. This Italian bakery has been churning out cookies, coffee, and elaborate cakes and tarts since 1894—and the late hours it keeps only sweeten the deal. ⊠ *342 E. 11th St., between 1st and 2nd Aves., East Village* ☎ *212/674-7070* ⊕ *www.venierospastry.com* Ⓜ *6 to Astor Place; L to 1st Ave.*

4

Sightseeing
★★
Nightlife
★★★★★
Dining
★★★★★
Lodging
★★
Shopping
★★★★

American punk was born in the East Village, at the now-defunct CBGB, and the punk-rock and indie scene is kept alive at the many small music venues here and on the Lower East Side, as well as in Brooklyn. Both neighborhoods are tamer than they once were—as the arrival of Whole Foods and several glass-and-chrome condos attests—but there's definitely still a gritty edge. Spend some time wandering these bohemian side streets, and you'll be struck by the funky pastiche of ethnicities whose imprints are visible in the neighborhood's restaurants, shops, and, of course, people.

EAST VILLAGE

Updated by
Jessica Colley

The concept of "*La Bohème* meets hipsters in vintage clothing," better known as the musical *Rent*, pegged the East Village as a community of artists, activists, and other social dissenters—and this is still the essential vibe here, although the neighborhood has become more upscale in recent years. These days, for example, St. Marks Place evokes less of the gritty, counterculture scene it once had in favor of a pastiche of students, well-earning postgrads, and Japanese expats.

East of 1st Avenue is Alphabet City, once the city's seedy drug haunt but now an ever more gentrified neighborhood. There is still a young, artistic vibe in and around Tompkins Square Park.

TOP ATTRACTIONS

Alphabet City. The north-south avenues east of 1st Avenue, from Houston Street to 14th Street, are all labeled with letters, not numbers, which gives this area its nickname. Avenues A, B, and C are full of restaurants, cafés, stores, and bars that run from the low-rent and scruffy to the rarefied and genteel—the streets are more mixed than in other neighborhoods downtown. Parts of Avenues A and B run along Tompkins

Keep Your Eyes Peeled

The East Village's reputation for quirkiness is evidenced not only by its residents and sites but also in the many incongruous structures that somehow coexist so easily that they can go almost unnoticed. Keep your eyes open as you explore the streets. You never know what might turn up: the Hells Angels' Headquarters tucked into a residential block of 3rd Street between 1st and 2nd avenues, surrounded by a bevy of show-stopping bikes. The architectural "joke" on New York City atop the Red Square building on Houston Street at Norfolk, where a statue of Lenin points to the sky and a clock has lost its notion of time. The shingled Cape Cod–style house perched on the apartment building at the northwest corner of Houston and 1st Avenue, one of the city's many unique rooftop retreats. It's best viewed from the east. Two privately owned, nearly hidden but airy "marble" cemeteries (New York Marble Cemetery and the New York City Marble Cemetery) established in the 1830s on 2nd Avenue between 2nd and 3rd streets hold the remains of thousands in underground, marble-lined vaults thought to prevent the spread of disease in a time marked by cholera epidemics. The gardens are surrounded by 12-foot walls made of Tuckahoe marble, and are entered through wrought-iron gates. Although rarely open to the public they can be visited by appointment.

Square park. A close-knit Puerto Rican community makes its home around Avenue C, also called Loisaida Avenue (a Spanglish creation meaning "Lower East Side"). Although it's still filled with many Latino shops and bodegas, it's also now home to some trendy restaurants and bars. Avenue D remains rough around the edges—in part because of the uninterrupted row of projects that are on its east side. The East River Park, farther east, provides some nice views of Williamsburg and other parts of Brooklyn. To reach the park, cross Avenue D and take one of the pedestrian bridges that crosses the FDR Drive at East 10th or East 5th Streets, or cross the road at East Houston Street. ⊠ *East Village* Ⓜ 6 *to Astor Pl.; L to 1st Ave.; F to 2nd Ave.*

St. Marks Place. The longtime hub of the edgy East Village, St. Marks Place is the name given to idiosyncratic East 8th Street between 3rd Avenue and Avenue A. During the 1950s, beatniks Allen Ginsberg and Jack Kerouac lived and wrote in the area; the 1960s brought Bill Graham's Fillmore East (nearby, at 105 2nd Ave.), and Andy Warhol's Dom and the Electric Circus nightclub (both at 19–25 St. Marks Place), where the Velvet Underground performed. The studded, pink-haired, and shaved-head punk scene followed, and there's a good chance you'll still see some pierced rockers and teenage Goths on the block. Trash & Vaudeville, the punk store at No. 4, is the real deal—it's been open since 1971. Farther down, at No. 33, is where the punk store Manic Panic first foisted its lurid hair dyes and make-up on the world. And at No. 57 stood the short-lived Club 57, a church basement that attracted such 80s stalwarts as Keith Haring, Ann Magnuson, Klaus Nomi, Kenny Scharf, and Fab Five Freddy.

These days, there's not much cutting edge left. Some of the grungy facades lead to luxury condos, and the area has become a Little Japan, with several ramen and dumpling shops, some sake bars, and lots of young Japanese students. The blocks between 2nd and 3rd avenues can feel like a shopping arcade, crammed with body-piercing and tattoo salons, and shops selling cheap jewelry, sunglasses, incense, and out-there sloganed T-shirts. The cafés and bars along here and over to Avenue A attract customers late into the night. ⊠ *8th St., between 3rd Ave. and Ave. A, East Village* Ⓜ *6 to Astor Pl.*

FAMILY **Tompkins Square Park.** This leafy park fills up with locals year-round, partaking in picnics and drum circles, and making use of the playground and the dog run. Free Wi-Fi (strongest on the north side of the park) joins the shade, benches, and an elegant 1891 water fountain (donated by a teetotaling benefactor) as some of the best amenities here. There are movie screenings and music gatherings throughout the summer, a year-round farmers market on Sunday, and an annual Halloween dog costume event. But it wasn't always so rosy in the park: in 1988 police followed then-mayor David Dinkins's orders to clear the many homeless who had set up makeshift homes here, and homeless rights and anti-gentrification activists fought back with sticks and bottles. The park was reclaimed and reopened in 1992 with a midnight curfew, still in effect today. ⊠ *Bordered by Aves. A and B, and E. 7th and E. 10th Sts., East Village* ⊕ *www.nycgovparks.org/parks/tompkinssquarepark* Ⓜ *6 to Astor Pl.; L to 1st Ave.*

WORTH NOTING

Astor Place Subway Station. At the beginning of the 20th century almost all of the city's Interborough Rapid Transit (IRT) subway entrances resembled the one here—an ornate cast-iron replica of a Beaux Arts kiosk marking the subway entrance for the uptown No. 6 train. This traffic-island entrance, which was—and still is—the stop to get to the venerable Cooper Union college, is now on the National Register of Historic Places. Inside, plaques of beaver emblems line the tiled station walls, a reference to the fur trade that contributed to John Jacob Astor's fortune. Milton Glaser, the Cooper Union graduate who originated the "I [heart] NY" logo, designed the station's murals. ⊠ *Traffic island at E. 8th St. and 4th Ave., East Village* Ⓜ *6 to Astor Pl.*

The Hole. Run by Kathy Grayson, the former director of the highly influential Deitch Projects, this contemporary-arts gallery generally hosts two simultaneous shows a month. Its artists lean more toward the up-and-coming rather than the establishment. The on-site Hole Shop carries lots of quirky zines, posters, books, and art objects. ⊠ *312 Bowery, between Bleecker and Houston Sts., East Village* ☎ *212/466–1100* ⊕ *www.theholenyc.com* ☽ *Tues.–Sat. noon–7* Ⓜ *6 to Bleecker St.; B, D, F, M to Broadway-Lafayette.*

Merchant's House Museum. Built in 1832, this redbrick house, combining Federal and Greek Revival styles, provides a glimpse into the domestic life of the period 30 years before the Civil War. Retired merchant Seabury Tredwell and his descendants lived here from 1835 until 1933. The home became a museum in 1936, with the original furnishings and architectural features preserved; family memorabilia are also on display. The fourth-floor servants' bedroom, where the Tredwell family's Irish servants slept and did some of their work, offers a rare and intimate look at the lives of Irish domestics in the mid-1800s. A guided tour is offered at 2 pm. ⊠ *29 E. 4th St., between Bowery and Lafayette St., East Village* ☎ *212/777–1089* ⊕ *www.merchantshouse.org* 🕮 *$10* ☽ *Thurs.–Mon. noon–5, guided tours Thurs.–Mon. at 2* Ⓜ *6 to Astor Pl. or Bleecker St.; B, D, F, M to Broadway–Lafayette St.; R to 8th St.*

Museum of Reclaimed Urban Space. Opened in late 2012, this self-described "living archive of urban activism" covers the vexatious postwar period in New York, during which the city's public housing was often woefully mismanaged and hundreds of apartments lay abandoned and crumbling. Zines, photographs, and videos fill the small exhibit space inside a tenement's storefront and its basement. Squatters, community gardens, the Tompkins Square riots, and the renaissance of bicycling in the city are all given their due, as is Occupy Wall Street. Tours of community gardens, activist landmarks, and other squats, both legal and otherwise, are also run by the museum. ⊠ *C-Squat, 155 Avenue C, between 9th and 10th Sts., East Village* ☎ *973/818–8495* ⊕ *www.morusnyc.org* 🕮 *$5 suggested donation; tours $20* ☽ *Thurs.–Sun. and Tues. 11–7.*

St. Mark's Church in-the-Bowery. This charming 1799 fieldstone country church, which is Episcopalian, stands on what was once Governor Peter Stuyvesant's *bouwerie,* or farm. It's Manhattan's second oldest church, and both Stuyvesant and Commodore Perry are buried in vaults here. Check out the gorgeous modern stained-glass windows on the balcony, which replaced the more traditional windows (like those on the ground level) after a fire in the late '70s. Over the years St. Mark's has hosted many avant-garde arts events, including readings by poet Carl Sandburg and dance performances by Martha Graham and Merce Cunningham. The tradition has continued with Danspace, the Poetry Project, and the Incubator Arts Project, which give performances throughout the year. Services are held Sunday at 11. ⊠ *131 E. 10th St., at 2nd Ave., East Village* ☎ *212/674–6377* ⊕ *www.stmarksbowery.org* Ⓜ *6 to Astor Pl.; L to 3rd Ave.*

Stuyvesant Street. This diagonal slicing through the block bounded by 2nd and 3rd avenues and East 9th and 10th streets is unique in Manhattan: it's the oldest street laid out precisely along an east–west axis. Among the handsome 19th-century redbrick row houses are the Federal-style **Stuyvesant Fish House** at No. 21, built as a wedding gift for a great-great-granddaughter of the Dutch governor Peter Stuyvesant, and **Renwick Triangle,** an attractive group of Anglo-Italianate brick and brownstone residences, that face Stuyvesant and East 10th streets. Ⓜ *6 to Astor Pl.*

Ukrainian Museum. From the late nineteenth century through the end of World War II, tens of thousands of Ukrainians made their way to New York City—and particularly to "Little Ukraine," as much of the East Village was known. This museum, which opened in 2005, examines Ukrainian Americans' dual heritage, with a permanent collection made up of folk art, fine art, and documentary materials about the immigrants' lives. Ceramics, jewelry, hundreds of brilliantly colored Easter eggs, and an extensive collection of Ukrainian costumes and textiles are the highlights. If you're feeling like a little Ukrainian food to continue the experience, the nearby Veselka diner awaits. ✉ *222 E. 6th St., between 2nd and 3rd Aves., East Village* ☎ *212/228–0110* ⊕ *www.ukrainianmuseum.org* ✉ *$8* ⊘ *Wed.–Sun. 11:30–5* Ⓜ *6 to Astor Pl.*

LOWER EAST SIDE

Often referred to simply as LES, the Lower East Side was the historic "Gateway to America," after waves of Irish, German, Jewish, Hispanic, and Chinese immigrants pulled up stakes and moved to New York in search of a better life. Today, a cool arts and nightlife scene, several distinctively modern high-rises, and the ultracontemporary New Museum exist alongside buildings and cultural centers staunchly rooted in the past.

On Saturday night, the scene can be as raucous as in a college town, especially on Rivington and Orchard streets, but Ludlow Street, one block east of Orchard, has become the main drag for twentysomethings with attitude, its boutiques wedged in between bars and low-key restaurants.

The best time to experience the neighborhood's past is by day. The excellent Lower East Side Tenement Museum movingly captures the immigrant legacy of tough times and survival instincts. You might not find many pickles being sold from barrels anymore, but this remains a good place to nosh on typical Jewish food from Katz's Delicatessen or Russ & Daughters.

TOP ATTRACTIONS

Gallery Onetwentyeight. Inside this narrow space, artist Kazuko Miyamoto directs crisp and provocative group shows. The art space celebrated its 25th anniversary in 2012. ✉ *128 Rivington St., between Essex and Norfolk Sts., Lower East Side* ☎ *212/674–0244* ⊕ *www.galleryonetwentyeight.org* Ⓜ *F to Delancey St.; J, M, Z to Essex St.*

FAMILY

Fodor'sChoice

★

Lower East Side Tenement Museum. Step back in time and into the partially restored 1863 tenement building at 97 Orchard Street, where you can squeeze through the preserved apartments of immigrants, learn about the struggles of past generations, and gain historical perspective on the still contentious topic of immigration. This is America's first urban living-history museum dedicated to the life of immigrants. The museum itself is only accessible by guided tour, each offered at various times each day and limited to 15 people, so it's a good idea to buy tickets in advance. The building tour called "Hard Times" visits the homes of Natalie Gumpertz, a German-Jewish dressmaker (dating from 1878), and Adolph and Rosaria Baldizzi, Catholic immigrants from Sicily (1935). "Sweatshop Workers" visits the Levines' garment shop/apartment and the home of the Rogarshevsky family from Eastern

Europe (1918). "Irish Outsiders" explores the life of the Moores, an Irish American family living in the building in 1869, and shows a re-created tenement backyard. "Shop Life," which opened in 2012, looks at the various businesses run on the street level here, including a German-style bar, a kosher butcher, an auctioneer, and, in the 1970s, a discount underwear store. A two-hour extended experience tour with a chance for in-depth discussion is offered every day. Walking tours of the neighborhood are also held daily. Note that most tours don't allow kids under 5. ✉ *103 Orchard St., corner of Orchard and Delancey Sts., Lower East Side* ☎ *212/982–8420* ⊕ *www.tenement.org* ☞ *$25 for a building tour* ☾ *Fri.–Wed. 10–6:30, Thurs. 10–8:30* Ⓜ *B, D to Grand St.; F to Delancey St.; J, M, Z to Essex St.*

WORTH NOTING

Essex Street Market. Started in 1940 as an attempt by Mayor Fiorello LaGuardia to establish a place for street pushcarts and vendors (and thereby get them off the streets), the Essex Street Market was defined early on by the Jewish and Italian immigrants of the Lower East Side. After being run cooperatively by the merchants for years, the market was taken over by a private developer in 1992. Then in 1995, the New York City Economic Development Corporation assumed control and began a $1.5 million renovation and consolidation of the space. These days the market is reinvigorated and filled with small grocery stores, coffee shops, sellers of meat, fish, and gourmet cheeses, and even a barber and a botanica. Standouts include Saxelby Cheesemongers and local favorite Shopsins, an eccentric and strangely appealing restaurant that moved in here in 2007 after decades in the West Village. ✉ *120 Essex St., between Rivington and Delancey Sts., Lower East Side* ☎ *212/312–3603* ⊕ *www.essexstreetmarket.com* ☾ *Mon.–Sat. 8–7, Sun. 10–6; vendors' hrs vary* Ⓜ *F, V to Delancey St.; J, M, Z to Essex St.*

Museum at Eldridge Street. The exterior of this Orthodox synagogue, the first to be built by the many Eastern European Jews who settled in the Lower East Side in the late 19th century, is a striking mix of Romanesque, Gothic, and Moorish motifs. Inside is an exceptional hand-carved ark of mahogany and walnut, a sculptured wooden balcony, jewel-tone stained-glass windows, vibrantly painted and stenciled walls, and an enormous brass chandelier. The synagogue can be viewed as part of an hourlong tour, which begins at the small museum downstairs where interactive "touch tables" teach all ages about Eldridge Street and the Lower East Side. The crowning piece of the synagogue's decades-long restoration is a stained-glass window by artist Kiki Smith and architect Deborah Gans. Installed in 2010 to replace 1940s glass brick, the window weighs 6,000 pounds and has more than 1,200 pieces of glass. ✉ *12 Eldridge St., between Canal and Division Sts., Lower East Side* ☎ *212/219–0302* ⊕ *www.eldridgestreet.org* ☞ *$10* ☾ *Sun.–Thurs. 10–5, Fri. 10–3; tours on the hr* Ⓜ *F to E. Broadway; B, D to Grand St.; N, R to Canal St.*

New Museum. This seven-story, 60,000-square-foot structure—a glimmering metal mesh-clad assemblage of off-centered squares—caused some neighborhood uproar when it was built in 2007, with some residents slow to accept the nontraditional building. Not surprisingly, given the museum's name and the building, shows are all about contemporary art: previous exhibitions have included the popular Carsten Höller: Experience, with a slide connecting the fourth and second floors, and a sensory deprivation tank, among other things. Studio 231, the museum's adjacent, ground-floor space at 231 Bowery, gives emerging artists the opportunity to create work outside the confines of the main museum building in a studiolike space. If you're visiting on the weekend, check out the seventh-floor "sky room" and its panoramic view of Lower Manhattan. From 10 to noon on the first Saturday of every month, the museum runs free family-oriented programs and events. And Thursday's free night always brings a fun-loving, hipster-heavy crowd out of the woodwork. ⊠ *235 Bowery, at Prince St., Lower East Side* ☎ *212/219–1222* ⊕ *www.newmuseum.org* ▧ *$16 (free Thurs. 7–9)* ☉ *Wed. and Fri.–Sun. 11–6, Thurs. 11–9* Ⓜ *6 to Spring St.; F, M to 2nd Ave.*

Sperone Westwater. Founded in 1975 in SoHo, and after spending nearly a decade in Chelsea, Sperone Westwater now finds itself a major part of the art-ification of the Lower East Side. In 2010, the gallery moved into this nine-story building, which it commissioned for itself, a vote of confidence in both its Bowery surroundings and the continued importance of its artists, which have included Bruce Nauman, William Wegman, Gerhard Richter, and a host of blue-chip minimalists. The narrow building, designed by Norman Foster, rivals the New Museum (a few doors down) for crisp poise: in 2011 New York's Municipal Art Society deemed it the best new building of the year. Its Big Red Box, essentially a huge room-like freight elevator, is a major contributor to the building's good looks. ⊠ *257 Bowery, between E. Houston and Stanton Sts., Lower East Side* ☎ *212/999–7337* ⊕ *www.speronewestwater.com* Ⓜ *6 to Spring St.; F to 2nd Ave.*

5

GREENWICH VILLAGE AND THE WEST VILLAGE

Greenwich Village and the West Village

MEATPACKING DISTRICT

High Line Park

Little W. 12th St.

Gansevoort St.

Horatio St.

Jane St.

W. 12th St.

Bethune St.

Greenwich St.

Abingdon Square

Grounded

A,C,E,L

1,2,3 W. 14th St.

W. 13th St.

W. 12th St.

W. 11th St.

Patchin Place

Waverly Pl.

Ga Stre

Sheridan Square

Joe

W. 10th St.

Christopher Park

Bank St.

Perry St.

Charles St.

Hudson St.

Washington St.

West St.

Hudson River Park

Hudson River

WEST VILLAGE

Commerce St.

Christopher St.

Grove St.

Bedford St.

Bleecker St.

Cornel

Leroy St.

75 1/2 Bedford St.

Carmine St.

Barrow

Morton St.

Leroy St.

St. Luke's Place

Children's Museum of the Arts

Downing

West St.

0   1/8 mi

0   200 meters

TOP EXPERIENCES	MAKING THE MOST OF YOUR TIME
People-watching in Washington Square Park	Greenwich Village proper—around New York University and Washington Square Park—is busy any time of day with locals (especially students) and visitors. A trip to Washington Square Park is a must for people-watching and relaxing on a bench. There are lots of restaurants and shops in the neighborhood, though they do tend to be touristy.
Strolling and window-shopping along the pretty streets of the West Village	
Relaxing in one of the many cafés	The West Village—basically from 7th Avenue to the Hudson River—is more residential, and tends to be pretty quiet, with carefully tended, tree-lined streets that are pleasant for. Upscale boutiques line Bleecker Street and Greenwich Avenue (note that, confusingly, there is also a Greenwich Street in this neighborhood).
Walking along Hudson River Park by the water	
Eating your way along Bleecker Street	The windy streets of the West Village often seem mazelike, even to locals, because most of the streets here are named rather than numbered and they're not organized on a grid system. Assume that you're going to get a little bit lost—that's part of the fun—but don't hesitate to ask for directions.

COFFEE AND QUICK BITES

Coffee options abound in this part of town; these are some of our favorites.

Caffe Reggio. Dating back to the 1920s, this is one of the oldest coffeehouses in the city. The enormous espresso machine may have introduced cappuccino to New York. ⊠ *119 MacDougal St., between 3rd and Carmine Sts., Greenwich Village* ☎ *212/475-9557* ⊕ *www.cafe reggio.com* Ⓜ *A, B, C, D, E, F, M to West 4th St.*

Grounded. At this welcoming café, the lattes are joined by equally strong (and free) Wi-Fi. Pastries and people-watching are a cut above. ⊠ *28 Jane St., between 8th and Greenwich Aves., West Village* ☎ *212/647-0943* ⊕ *www.groundedcoffee. com* Ⓜ *1, 2, 3 to 14th St.*

Joe (West Village). The coffee is exquisitely sourced and prepared at this small corner café, the first of what is now a small chain. ⊠ *141 Waverly Pl., at Gay St., Greenwich Village* ☎ *212/924-6750* ⊕ *www.joe newyork.com* Ⓜ *A, B, C, D, E, F, M to West 4th St.*

GETTING HERE AND AROUND

The West 4th Street subway stop—serviced by the A, B, C, D, E, F, and M—puts you in the center of Greenwich Village. Farther west, the 1 train has stops at West Houston Street and at Christopher Street–Sheridan Square. The A, C, E, and L trains stop at 14th Street, which is the northern boundary of the West Village.

BEST FOR KIDS

Hudson River Park

Washington Square Park

Taking time out for pizza or dessert

Sightseeing
★★★
Nightlife
★★★★
Dining
★★★★★
Lodging
★★★
Shopping
★★★★

Long the home of writers, artists, bohemians, and bon vivants, the Village—subdivided here into Greenwich Village proper, surrounding Washington Square Park; and the West Village, between 7th Avenue and the Hudson River— is a magical section of the city. Greenwich Village, in prime New York University territory, has lots of young people, while the West Village is primarily residential, with lots of well-to-do couples and families and a substantial community of older gay men and some lesbians. Both areas also have many restaurants, cafés, and boutiques with a warm and charming neighborhood vibe.

GREENWICH VILLAGE

Updated by
Jessica Colley

Fertile doesn't even begin to describe Greenwich Village's yield of creative genius. In the late 1940s and early 1950s, abstract expressionist painters Franz Kline, Jackson Pollock, Mark Rothko, and Willem de Kooning congregated here, as did Beat writers Jack Kerouac, Allen Ginsberg, and Lawrence Ferlinghetti. The 1960s brought folk musicians and poets, notably Bob Dylan and Joan Baez. Its bohemian days may be long gone, but there is still a romantic allure lingering along tree-lined streets and at the back of the cafés, behind the frenetic clamor of NYU students and the professional veneer of multimillion-dollar town houses.

One of the neighborhood's top sites is Washington Square Park, where you can find just about every sort of person imaginable lounging on a summer day, from skateboarders and students to local moms and nannies to people who look like they've lived in the park for years, playing chess and checkers at the stone tables. The grand Washington Memorial Arch looks north to two blocks of lovingly preserved Greek Revival and Federal-style town houses known as the Row.

TOP ATTRACTIONS

Bleecker Street. Walking the stretch of Bleecker Street between 5th and 7th avenues provides a smattering of just about everything synonymous with Greenwich Village these days: NYU buildings, used-record stores, Italian cafés and food shops, pizza and takeout joints, some nightclubs, and funky boutiques. Grab an espresso and sample some of the city's best pizza. Notable along the Greenwich Village length of the street is Our Lady of Pompeii Church, at Bleecker and Carmine, where Mother Cabrini, a naturalized Italian immigrant who became the first American citizen to be a saint, often prayed. Foodies love the blocks between 6th and 7th avenues for the specialty purveyors like Murray's Cheese (No. 254). West of 7th Avenue, where Bleecker crosses the border into the West Village, things get more upscale, with fashion and home-furnishings boutiques featuring antiques, eyeglasses, shoes, and designer clothing. ⊠ *Greenwich Village* Ⓜ *A, B, C, D, E, F, M to West 4th St.*

FAMILY

Fodor's Choice

★

Washington Square Park. NYU students, street musicians, skateboarders, jugglers, chess players, and those just watching the grand opera of it all generate a maelstrom of activity in this physical and spiritual heart of Greenwich Village. The 9¾-acre park had inauspicious beginnings as a cemetery, principally for yellow-fever victims—an estimated 10,000–22,000 bodies lie below (a headstone was actually unearthed in 2009). At one time, plans to renovate the park called for the removal of the bodies; however, local resistance prevented this from happening. In the early 1800s the park was a parade ground and the site of public executions; bodies dangled from a conspicuous Hanging Elm that still stands at the northwest corner of the square. Today that gruesome past is all but forgotten, as playgrounds attract parents with tots in tow, dogs go leash-free inside the popular dog runs, and everyone else seems drawn toward the large central fountain.

The triumphal European-style **Washington Memorial Arch** stands at the square's north end, marking the start of 5th Avenue. The original wood-and-papier-mâché arch, originally situated a half block north, was erected in 1889 to commemorate the 100th anniversary of George Washington's presidential inauguration. The arch was reproduced in Tuckahoe marble in 1892, and the statues—*Washington as General Accompanied by Fame and Valor* on the left, and *Washington as Statesman Accompanied by Wisdom and Justice* on the right—were added in 1916 and 1918, respectively. ⊠ *5th Ave. between Waverly Pl. and 4th St., Greenwich Village* Ⓜ *A, B, C, D, E, F, M to W. 4th St.*

WORTH NOTING

Gay Street. A curved, one-block lane lined with small row houses, Gay Street was probably named after an early landowner and definitely had nothing to do with gay rights. In the 1930s this tiny thoroughfare and nearby Christopher Street became famous nationwide after Ruth McKenney began to publish somewhat zany autobiographical stories based on what happened when she and her sister moved to No. 14 Gay Street from Ohio. The stories, first published in the *New Yorker,* birthed many adaptations, including the 1953 Broadway musical *Wonderful Town* (revived in 2004) and the 1942 and 1955 movies

CLOSE UP

Halloween in the Village

All things weird and wonderful, all creatures great and small, all things witty and fantastical, New York City has them all—and on All Hallows' Eve they strut through the streets in New York's Halloween parade. White-sheeted ghouls feel dull compared with fishnets and leather, sequins and feathers posing and prancing along 6th Avenue in this vibrant display of vanity and insanity.

In 1973 mask-maker and puppeteer Ralph Lee paraded his puppets from house to house visiting friends and family along the winding streets of his Greenwich Village neighborhood. His merry march quickly outgrew its original, intimate route and now, decades later, it parades up 6th Avenue, from Spring Street to 21st Street, attracting 90,000 creatively costumed exhibitionists, artists, dancers, and musicians, hundreds of enormous puppets, scores of bands, and more than 2 million spectators. Anyone with a costume can join in, no advance registration

required, although the enthusiastic interaction between participants and spectators makes it just as much fun simply to watch. It's a safe "street event" for families and singles alike, and a joyful night unlike any other.

The parade lines up on 6th Avenue between Canal and Spring streets from 6:30 to 8:30 pm. The walk actually starts at 7, but it takes about two hours to leave the staging area. It's best to arrive from the south to avoid the crush of strollers and participants. Get there a few hours early if possible. Costumes are usually handmade, clever, and outrageous, and revelers are happy to strike a pose. The streets are crowded along the route, with the most congestion below 14th Street. Of course, the best way to truly experience the parade is to march, but if you're not feeling the face paint, it's possible to volunteer to help carry the puppets. For information visit ⊕ *www.halloween-nyc.com.*

—Jacinta O'Halloran

My Sister Eileen. ⊠ *Between Christopher St. and Waverly Pl., Greenwich Village* Ⓜ *1 to Christopher St./Sheridan Sq.; A, B, C, D, E, F, M to W. 4th St.*

Patchin Place. This little cul-de-sac off West 10th Street between Greenwich and 6th avenues has 10 diminutive 1848 row houses. Around the corner on 6th Avenue is a similar dead-end street, **Milligan Place,** with five small houses completed in 1852. The houses in both quiet enclaves were originally built for waiters who worked at 5th Avenue's high-society Brevoort Hotel, long since demolished. Later Patchin Place residents included writers Theodore Dreiser, e. e. cummings, Jane Bowles, and Djuna Barnes. Milligan Place became popular among playwrights, including Eugene O'Neill. Ⓜ *A, B, C, D, E, F, M to W. 4th St.*

The Row. Built from 1833 through 1837, this series of Greek Revival and Federal row houses along Washington Square North, between University Place and MacDougal Street, once belonged to merchants and bankers, then to writers and artists such as John Dos Passos and Edward Hopper. Many are now owned by New York University and used for housing and offices. Although the houses' facades remain

Out and On Display: George Segal's sculptures of two gay couples in Christopher Park illustrate gay pride in Greenwich Village.

beautifully preserved, the interiors have been drastically altered over the years. ✉ *1–13 and 19–26 Washington Sq. N, between University Pl. and MacDougal St., Greenwich Village* Ⓜ *A, B, C, D, E, F, M to W. 4th St.*

Washington Mews. A rarity in Manhattan, this pretty, brick-covered street—really a glorified alley—is lined on one side with the former stables of the houses on the Row on Washington Square North. Although the street is private and owned by New York University, which uses many of the stables for offices, it's open to pedestrian traffic from 7 am to 11 pm. ✉ *Between 8th St. and Washington Sq. N, between 5th Ave. and University Pl., Greenwich Village* Ⓜ *A, B, C, D, E, F, M to W. 4th St.*

WEST VILLAGE

High-rises and office towers have little business among the labyrinth of small curving streets, peculiar alleys, and historic town houses here, although a new boom in distinctive apartment living by designer architects has emerged around the western edges near the Hudson River. It's easy to see why the tree-lined streets of the West Village, which are primarily residential, are in such demand—think charming cafés, carefully disheveled celebrities out and about, and well-dressed children playing in parks.

It's easy to feel like a local while shopping here. Unlike 5th Avenue or SoHo, the pace is slower, the streets are relatively quiet, and the scale is small. This is the place to come for unusual finds as well as

Bleecker Street's Little Italy

Little Italy can be besieged by slow-moving crowds, touristy shops, and restaurant hosts hollering invitations to dine inside. Bleecker Street between 6th and 7th avenues, on the other hand, with its crowded cafés, bakeries, pizza parlors, and old-world merchants, offers a more pleasurable, equally vital alternative to the traditional tourist trap.

For an authentic Italian bakery experience, stop by **Pasticceria Rocco** (No. 243) for wonderful cannoli, cream puffs, and cookies packed up, or order an espresso and linger over the treats.

Step into the past at the old-style (and now high-end) butcher shops, such as **Ottomanelli & Sons** (No. 285) and **Faicco's Pork Store** (No. 260), where locals have bought their sausage and custom-cut pork since 1900.

The sweet (or stinky) smell of success is nowhere more evident than at **Murray's Cheese** (No. 254), at Cornelia Street. The original shop, opened in 1940 by Murray Greenberg (not Italian), was not much larger than the display case that stocked the stuff. Now it's a fromage-fiend's emporium, with everything from imported crackers and bamboo cutting boards to a full-service sandwich counter. Samples of cheese, salami, gelato, and other goodies are frequently offered.

There are also a few popular pizzerias along this strip; **Kesté Pizza & Vino** (No. 271) serves Neapolitan pies that some would argue give even Da Michele in Naples a run for its money. It is also the official location in the United States for the Associazione Pizzaiuoli Napoletani, whose mission is to promote pizzas made in the Neapolitan tradition, using Neapolitan products.

global-brand goods. The West Village section of Bleecker Street is a particularly good place to indulge all sorts of shopping appetites; high-fashion foragers prowl the stretch between West 10th Street and 8th Avenue. Hudson Street and Greenwich Avenue are also prime boutique-browsing territory.

Christopher Street has long been the symbolic heart of New York's gay and lesbian community, though places like Chelsea, Hell's Kitchen, and parts of Brooklyn attract more gay and lesbians these days. On Christopher, among cafés, lifestyle boutiques, and clothing shops, is one of the city's most acclaimed off-Broadway theaters, the Lucille Lortel, where major playwrights like David Mamet, Eugene Ionesco, and Edward Albee have their own markers in the sidewalk. Nearby, at 51–53 Christopher Street, is the site of the Stonewall Inn and the historic Stonewall riots, one of the signal events in the gay rights movement. Across the street is a green triangle named Christopher Park, where there are commemorative statues of two gay and lesbian couples.

TOP ATTRACTIONS

Hudson River Park. *See the listing in the TriBeCa section of Chapter 2: Lower Manhattan.*

WORTH NOTING

75½ Bedford Street. Rising real-estate rates inspired the construction of New York City's narrowest house—just 9½ feet wide and 32 feet deep—in 1873. Built on a lot that was originally a carriage entrance of the Isaacs-Hendricks House next door, this sliver of a building was home to actor John Barrymore and poet Edna St. Vincent Millay. ⊠ *75½ Bedford St., between Commerce and Morton Sts., West Village* Ⓜ *A, B, C, D, E, F, M to W. 4th St.*

FAMILY   **Children's Museum of the Arts.** The CMA seeks to give children ages 1 to 15 room to get really creative through a variety of mediums. Along with the requisite children's museum offerings like pencils, chalk, and paint, you'll find a clay bar; a media lab with mounted cameras and a recording studio; a small slide and colorful ball pond that kids can play in; an airy exhibition space with rotating exhibits (and workshops inspired by exhibits); a permanent collection of children's art from more than 50 countries; and classes in ceramics, origami, animation, filmmaking, and more. Check the website for a busy calendar of events. ⊠ *103 Charlton St., between Hudson and Greenwich Sts., West Village* ☎ *212/274–0986* ⊕ *www.cmany.org* ✉ *$11* ⊙ *Mon. and Wed. noon–5, Thurs. and Fri. noon–6, weekends 10–5; closed Tues.* Ⓜ *C, E to Spring St.*

Christopher Park. You might have to share a bench in this tiny park with George Segal's life-size sculptures of a lesbian couple. The painted bronzes, cast in 1980 and titled *Gay Liberation,* also include a gay male couple, captured in mid-chat nearby. ⊠ *Bordered by W. 4th, Grove, and Christopher Sts., West Village* Ⓜ *1 to Christopher St.– Sheridan Sq.*

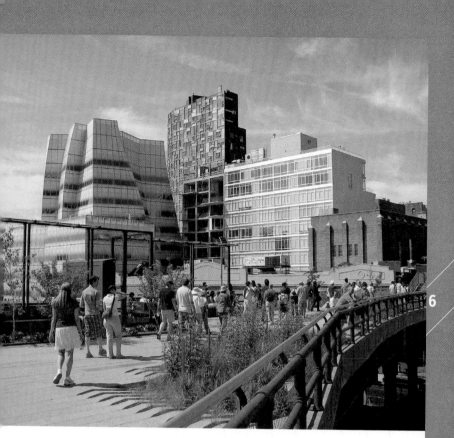

6

CHELSEA AND THE MEATPACKING DISTRICT

GETTING ORIENTED

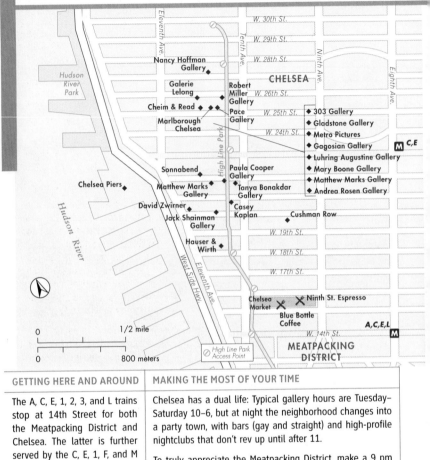

GETTING HERE AND AROUND

The A, C, E, 1, 2, 3, and L trains stop at 14th Street for both the Meatpacking District and Chelsea. The latter is further served by the C, E, 1, F, and M lines at 23rd Street and by the 1 train at 28th Street. 14th Street and 23rd Street are both also served by the PATH trains.

MAKING THE MOST OF YOUR TIME

Chelsea has a dual life: Typical gallery hours are Tuesday–Saturday 10–6, but at night the neighborhood changes into a party town, with bars (gay and straight) and high-profile nightclubs that don't rev up until after 11.

To truly appreciate the Meatpacking District, make a 9 pm or later dinner reservation at a hot restaurant, then hit the bars to see where the glitterati are this week.

If shopping is your pleasure, weekdays are great; come after noon, though, or you'll find most spots shuttered.

Chelsea and the Meatpacking District

W. 30th St.
W. 29th St.
W. 28th St.
W. 27th St.
Museum at FIT
W. 26th St.
W. 25th St.
W. 24th St.
W. 23rd St.
W. 22nd St.
W. 21st St.
W. 20th St.
W. 19th St.
W. 18th St.
W. 17th St.
Rubin Museum of Art
W. 16th St.
W. 15th St.
✕ **Donut Pub**
W. 14th St.
W. 13th St.

Sixth Ave.
Seventh Ave.
Fifth Ave.
Madison Ave.

Madison Square Park

Broadway

Union Square Park

M F,M
M
M F,M
M L
N,Q,R,4,5,6,L

TOP EXPERIENCES

Gallery hopping in Chelsea

Walking along the High Line

Checking out the Meatpacking District's nightlife

Eating your way through Chelsea Market

Shopping the ultrachic boutiques in the Meatpacking District

BEST FOR KIDS

Chelsea Piers

The High Line

Hudson River Park

COFFEE AND QUICK BITES

Blue Bottle Coffee. If you're serious about your coffee and equally serious about fresh-baked pastries, eco-friendly practices, and good old-fashioned service, you need to stop in at this trendy multi-level coffee shop in Chelsea. Seriously. ✉ *450 W. 15th St., Chelsea* ⊕ *www.bluebottlecoffee.com.*

Donut Pub. Care for an apple fritter, a red-velvet doughnut, or an old-fashioned cruller with your coffee? A 5 am sugar fix after a night clubbing in the Meatpacking District? Pull up a stool: it's open 24/7. ✉ *203 W. 14th St., at 7th Ave., Chelsea* ☎ *212/929–0126.*

Ninth Street Espresso. The Chelsea Market outpost of Ninth Street Espresso is popular all day, though the lines in the morning are longest. The lattes here are liquid gold. ✉ *Chelsea Market, 9th Ave. between 15th and 16th Sts., Chelsea* ☎ *212/228–2930.*

Sightseeing
★★★
Nightlife
★★★★★
Dining
★★★★★
Lodging
★★★
Shopping
★★★★

Chelsea long ago usurped SoHo as the epicenter of New York contemporary art galleries, but the opening of the High Line above 10th Avenue created a new artery of life in this part of the city. More foot traffic means more gentrification and more restaurants. Not surprisingly, this also means more real-estate development and rising rents, which means less of the smaller galleries that transformed Chelsea from a dead area to an art hub in the first place.

MEATPACKING DISTRICT

Updated by Jacinta O'Halloran

Concentrated in a few blocks of what is essentially the West Village, between the Hudson River and 9th Avenue, from Little West 12th Street to about West 17th Street, the Meatpacking District used to be the center of the wholesale meat industry for New York City. Other than beloved meat purveyor Pat LaFrieda, though, there are few meat markets left in this now rather quaint, cobblestoned area—but it's definitely a metaphorical meat market at night, when the city's trendiest frequent the equally trendy restaurants and bars here. The area is also home to some of the city's trendiest retailers, with boutiques of fashion designers like Alexander McQueen and Stella McCartney.

CHELSEA

Most of Chelsea's art galleries are found from about 20th to 27th streets, primarily between 10th and 11th avenues. The range of contemporary art on display includes almost every imaginable medium and style; if it's going on in the art world, it'll be in one of the 300 or so galleries here. While some of the small and midsize galleries have been squeezed uptown due to high rents, the big players in the art world are getting bigger. Giant standouts include the new five-story David Zwirner Gallery on 20th Street; Hauser & Wirth's cavernous industrial space on 18th Street; the Robert Miller Gallery on 26th Street, a titan in the New York art world representing the likes of Patti Smith and Alice Neel, among others; and the galleries of Gagosian, Matthew Marks, and Pace (which has expanded to four galleries in this neighborhood).

TOP ATTRACTIONS

FAMILY **Chelsea Market.** This former Nabisco plant—where the first Oreos were baked in 1912—now houses more than two dozen gourmet food, wine, and flower shops, as well as an Anthropologie store, and one of NYC's last independent book stores (Posman Books). Renowned specialty purveyors including L'Arte del Gelato, Fat Witch Bakery, Amy's Bread, Jacques Torres Chocolate, and Ninth Street Espresso flank the interior walkway that stretches from 9th to 10th avenues. Be sure to wander into the 15th St. Arcade where you'll find a bunch of great new kiosks offering everything from fresh minidoughnuts to authentic Mexican street food. The market's funky industrial design—a tangle of glass and metal for an awning, a factory pipe converted into an indoor waterfall—complements the eclectic assortment of shops. There is some seating inside but if the weather's nice, take your goodies to the High Line. ⊠ *75 9th Ave., between 15th and 16th Sts., Chelsea* ☏ *212/652–2117* ⊕ *www.chelseamarket.com* ⊙ *Mon.–Sat. 7–9, Sun. 8–8* Ⓜ *A, C, E, L to 14th St.*

David Zwirner. In 2013, Zwirner further solidified his commitment to contemporary art, and his place in the ranks of the most successful galleries in the art world, with this purpose-built, five-story exhibition and project space, created to compliment the programming of the gallery's three existing 19th Street locations a block away. Zwirner's galleries show works in all mediums by artists like Dan Flavin, Donald Judd, Palermo, Richard Serra, Gordon Matta-Clark, Doug Wheeler, and Yayoi Kusama. ⊠ *537 W. 20th St., between 10th and 11th Aves., Chelsea* ☏ *212/517–8677* ⊕ *www.davidzwirner.com* ⊙ *Tues.–Sat. 10–6* Ⓜ *C, E to 23rd St.*

Gagosian Gallery. This enterprising modern gallery has two large Chelsea branches (the other is at 522 West 21st Street, between 10th and 11th avenues) and a third on the Upper East Side, as well as nine more outposts in cities around the world. Perhaps the most powerful dealer in the business, the Gagosian Gallery shows works by heavy hitters such as Pablo Picasso, Jean-Michel Basquiat, sculptor Richard Serra, and the late pop-art icon Roy Lichtenstein. ⊠ *555 W. 24th St., at 11th Ave., Chelsea* ☏ *212/741–1111* ⊕ *www.gagosian.com* ⊙ *Tues.–Sat. 10–6* Ⓜ *C, E to 23rd St.*

Gladstone Gallery. The international roster of artists at this gallery's two Chelsea locations includes sculptor Anish Kapoor, photographer Sharon Lockhart, and multimedia artists Matthew Barney and Cecilia Edefalk. The other location is 530 West 21st Street, between 10th and 11th avenues. ⊠ *515 W. 24th St., between 10th and 11th Aves., Chelsea* ☏ *212/206–9300* ⊕ *www.gladstonegallery.com* ⊙ *Tues.–Sat. 10–6* Ⓜ *C, E to 23rd St.*

DID YOU KNOW?

Once teeming with more than 200 slaughterhouses, the Meatpacking District has done an abrupt 180 degrees in the last two decades to become the epicenter of all things hot.

Hauser & Wirth. On the site of the former Roxy nightclub and roller rink on 18th Street, this Hauser & Wirth gallery is the opposite of its narrow townhouse location on the Upper East Side. The space is huge (23,000 square feet) and cavernous, and begs for sprawling exhibits and large-scale works. Emerging and established contemporary artists in the powerful Hauser & Wirth fold that show here include Dieter Roth, Paul McCarthy, Eva Hesse, and Jason Rhoades. ⊠ *511 W. 18th St., between 10th and 11th Aves., Chelsea* ☎ *212/790–3900* ⊕ *www. hauserwirth.com* ⏱ *Tues.–Sat. 10–6* Ⓜ *C, E to 23rd St.*

Fodor'sChoice
★

The High Line. Once a railroad track carrying freight trains, this elevated space has been transformed into a green retreat in the spirit of Paris's Promenade Plantée and is one of the most visited parks in the city. A long "walking park" with benches, public art installations, and views of the Hudson River and the Manhattan skyline, the High Line runs north–south, crisscrossing 9th, 10th, and 11th avenues in West Chelsea along the way. Reclining chaise longues and strategically situated benches are perfect for a picnic lunch (Chelsea Market is a convenient place to pick up fixings). The first section of the High Line, between Gansevoort and West 20th streets, opened in 2009 and was immediately the talk of the town. The second section of the park, up to West 30th Street, opened in 2011, doubling the length of the walkway. The final section of the park, currently under construction, runs between West 30th and West 34th streets, wrapping around the Hudson Yards Redevelopment Project. Plans include a performance space, a kids' playspace, picnic areas, and panoramic views of the cityscape and Hudson River. Construction will be completed in three phases over the next several years, with the first phase opening in fall 2014. ⊠ *10th Ave. from Gansevoort St. to 30th St., Chelsea* ☎ *212/206–9922* ⊕ *www.thehighline. org* ⏱ *Daily 7–7* Ⓜ *L to 8th Ave.; 1 to 14th St., 23rd St., or 28th St.; 2 and 3 to 14th St.; A, C, E to 14th St.*

Hudson River Park. *See the listing in the TriBeCa section of Chapter 2.*

Marlborough Chelsea. With galleries in London, Monaco, and Madrid, the Marlborough empire also operates two of the largest and most influential galleries in New York City. The recently renovated Chelsea location (the other is on 57th Street) shows the latest work of modern artists, with a focus on sculptural forms, such as the boldly colorful paintings of Andrew Kuo. Red Grooms, Richard Estes, and Fernando Botero are just a few of the 20th-century luminaries represented. ⊠ *545 W. 25th St., between 10th and 11th Aves., Chelsea* ☎ *212/463–8634* ⊕ *www.marlboroughgallery.com* ⏱ *Tues.–Sat. 10–6* Ⓜ *C, E to 23rd St.*

Matthew Marks Gallery. A hot venue for both the New York and international art crowd, openings at any of the four Matthew Marks galleries are always an interesting scene—there are three other locations along 22nd Street between 10th and 11th avenues. Swiss artist Ugo Rondinone made his U.S. debut here, as did Andreas Gursky. Luigi Ghirri, Darren Almond, Robert Adams, Nan Goldin, Ellsworth Kelly, and a cast of illustrious others also show here. ⊠ *523 W. 24th St., between 10th and 11th Aves., Chelsea* ☎ *212/243–0200* ⊕ *www.matthewmarks. com* ⏱ *Tues.–Sat. 10–6* Ⓜ *C, E to 23rd St.*

You never know what you might see in Chelsea's galleries: works by well-known artists like Alexander Calder, or pieces by up-and-coming artists.

Museum at FIT. What this small, three-gallery museum housed in the Fashion Institute of Technology lacks in size, staging, and effects it more than makes up for in substance and style (and free admission). You won't find interactive mannequins, elaborate displays, or over-crowded galleries at the self-declared "most fashionable museum in New York City," but you will find carefully curated exhibits, an impressive permanent collection that includes more than 50,000 garments and accessories from the 18th century to the present, and dedicated followers and students sketching and leaning in to wow over seams and sequins. The Fashion and Textile History Gallery, on the main floor, provides ongoing historical context with a rotating selection of historically and artistically significant objects from the museum's permanent collection (the exhibits change every six months), but the real draw here are the special exhibitions in the lower level gallery; recent examples include *Elegance in an Age of Crisis: Fashions of the 1930s*; *Beyond Rebellion: Fashioning the Biker Jacket*; and *Exposed: A History of Lingerie*. Gallery FIT, also located on the main floor, is dedicated to student and faculty exhibitions. ✉ *227 W. 27th St., at 7th Ave., Chelsea* ☎ *212/217–4558* ⊕ *www.fitnyc.edu/museum* ✉ *Free* ☾ *Tues.–Fri. noon–8, Sat. 10–5* Ⓜ *1 to 28th St.*

Pace Gallery. The impressive roster of artists represented by the Pace Gallery includes a variety of upper-echelon artists, sculptors, and photographers, including Elizabeth Murray, Chuck Close, Sol LeWitt, and Robert Rauschenberg. ■**TIP→ This gallery has street cred: hip hop artist Jay-Z filmed his performance art piece *Picasso Baby* at this location in 2013.** Pace has four spaces in Chelsea, along West 25th Street,

Chelsea Galleries 101

CLOSE UP

Good art, bad art, edgy art, downright disturbing art—it's all here waiting to please and provoke in the contemporary art capital of the world. For the uninitiated, the concentration of nearly 300 galleries within a seven-block radius can be overwhelming, and the sometimes cool receptions on entering and deafening silence, intimidating. Art galleries are not exactly famous for their customer-service skills, but they're free, and you don't need a degree in art appreciation to stare at a canvas or an installation.

There's no required code of conduct, although most galleries are library-quiet and cell phones are seriously frowned on. Don't worry, you won't be pressured to buy anything; staff will probably be doing their best to ignore you.

Galleries are generally open Tuesday through Saturday from 10 to 6. Gallery hop on a Saturday afternoon—the highest-traffic day—if you want company. You can usually find a binder with the artist's resume, examples of previous work, and exhibit details (usually including prices) at the front desk. If not, ask. Also ask whether there's information you can take with you.

You can't see everything in one afternoon, so if you have specific interests, plan ahead. Find gallery information and current exhibit details by checking the listings in the *New Yorker* or the weekend section of the *New York Times*. Learn more about the galleries and the genres and artists they represent at ⊕ www.artincontext.org.

—Jacinta O'Halloran

as well as a Midtown location (on East 57th Street). ⊠ *534 W. 25th St., between 10th and 11th Aves., Chelsea* ☎ *212/929–7000* ⊕ *www. thepacegallery.com* ⊙ *Tues.–Sat. 10–6* Ⓜ *C, E to 23rd St.* ⊠ *510 West 25th St., between 10th and 11th Aves., Chelsea* ☎ *212/255–4044* ⊙ *Tues.–Sat. 10–6*

Paula Cooper Gallery. SoHo pioneer Paula Cooper moved to Chelsea in 1996, and enlisted architect Richard Gluckman to transform a warehouse into a dramatic space with tall ceilings and handsome skylights. There are now two galleries (the other is at 521 West 21st Street) that showcase the minimalist sculptures of Carl Andre, among other works. ⊠ *534 W. 21st St., between 10th and 11th Aves., Chelsea* ☎ *212/255–1105* ⊕ *www. paulacoopergallery.com* ⊙ *Tues.–Sat. 10–6* Ⓜ *C, E to 23rd St.*

WORTH NOTING

303 Gallery. International cutting-edge artists shown here include up-and-coming New York artist Jacob Kassay, photographer Doug Aitken, and installation artists Karen Kilimnik and Jane and Louise Wilson. In 2013, the gallery moved from its home on West 21st Street to a spot under the High Line at 24th Street, with plans to move back to 21st Street to anchor a new high-rise in 2015. 303 may retain both locations in 2015 so be sure to call and confirm before you visit. ⊠ *507 W. 24th St., between 10th and 11th Aves., Chelsea* ☎ *212/255–1121* ⊕ *www.303gallery.com* ⊙ *Tues.–Sat. 10–6; closed Aug.* Ⓜ *C, E to 23rd St.*

Andrea Rosen Gallery. Artists on the cutting edge, such as Felix Gonzalez-Torres, video-artists Ryan Trecartin and Lizzie Fitch, sculptor Andrea Zittel, and painter and installation artist Matthew Ritchie, are on view here. In late 2012, Rosen opened a second space, Gallery 2, just down the street (at 544 West 24th Street) from the gallery headquarters, with more experimental shows that place less emphasis on commercial appeal or success. ⊠ *525 W. 24th St., between 10th and 11th Aves., Chelsea* ☎ *212/627–6000, 212/627–6100 for Gallery 2* ⊕ *www. andrearosengallery.com* ⊗ *Tues.–Sat. 10–6* Ⓜ *C, E to 23rd St.*

Casey Kaplan. Founded in 1995, the Casey Kaplan gallery represents contemporary artists from Europe and the Americas. Sophisticated and ambitious exhibitions have included works by such artists as Nathan Carter, Henning Bohl, Giorgio Griffa, Matthew Brannon, Johannes Wohnseifer, and Julia Schmidt. ⊠ *525 W. 21st St., between 10th and 11th Aves., Chelsea* ☎ *212/645–7335* ⊕ *www.caseykaplangallery.com* ⊗ *Tues.–Sat. 10–6* Ⓜ *C, E to 23rd St.*

Cheim & Read. This prestigious gallery represents artists such as Louise Bourgeois, William Eggleston, Joan Mitchell, Jenny Holzer, Donald Baechler, and Jack Pierson. ⊠ *547 W. 25th St., between 10th and 11th Aves., Chelsea* ☎ *212/242–7727* ⊕ *www.cheimread.com* ⊗ *Tues.–Sat. 10–6* Ⓜ *C, E to 23rd St.*

FAMILY **Chelsea Piers.** This sports-and-entertainment complex along the Hudson River between 17th and 23rd streets, a phenomenal example of adaptive reuse, is the size of four 80-story buildings if they were laid out flat. There's pretty much every kind of sports activity going on inside and out, from golf (check out the multitier, all-weather, outdoor driving range) to ice-skating, rock climbing, soccer, bowling, gymnastics, and basketball. Plus there's a spa, elite sport-specific training, film studios, and a brewery with a restaurant. Chelsea Piers is also the jumping-off point for some of the city's varied water tours and dinner cruises. ⊠ *Piers 59–62 on Hudson River from 17th to 23rd Sts. (entrance at 23rd St.), Chelsea* ☎ *212/336–6666* ⊕ *www.chelseapiers. com* Ⓜ *C, E to 23rd St.*

Cushman Row. Built in 1840 for merchant and developer Don Alonzo Cushman, this string of red brick beauties between 9th and 10th avenues represents some of the country's most perfect examples of Greek Revival row houses. Original details include small wreath-encircled attic windows, deeply recessed doorways with brownstone frames, and striking iron balustrades and fences. Note the pineapples, a traditional symbol of welcome, on top of the black iron newels in front of No. 416. ⊠ *406–418 W. 20th St., between 9th and 10th Aves., Chelsea* Ⓜ *C, E to 23rd St.*

Galerie Lelong. This large gallery presents challenging installations and art, as well as many Latin American artists. Look for work by Yoko Ono, Alfredo Jaar, Andy Goldsworthy, Cildo Meireles, Ana Mendieta, Hélio Oiticica, Nalini Malani, and Petah Coyne. ⊠ *528 W. 26th St., between 10th and 11th Aves., Chelsea* ☎ *212/315–0470* ⊕ *www. galerielelong.com* ⊗ *Tues.–Sat. 10–6* Ⓜ *C, E to 23rd St.*

Jack Shainman Gallery. Emerging and established artists such as Tallur L. N., a young sculptor from India, and Kerry James Marshall, who deals with African-American issues, are shown here. You might find portrait paintings by Barkley L. Hendricks and photography from South African photojournalist Zwelethu Mthethwa. ⊠ *513 W. 20th St., between 10th and 11th Aves., Chelsea* ☎ *212/645–1701* ⊕ *www.jackshainman.com* ☉ *Tues.–Sat. 10–6* Ⓜ *C, E to 23rd St.*

Luhring Augustine Gallery. Owners Lawrence Luhring and Roland Augustine have been working with established and emerging artists from Europe, Japan, and America, since 1985. In 2012, Luhring Augustine opened a Brooklyn outpost (at 25 Knickerbocker Avenue in Bushwick) for large-scale installations and long-term projects. ⊠ *531 W. 24th St., between 10th and 11th Aves., Chelsea* ☎ *212/206–9100* ⊕ *www.luhringaugustine.com* ☉ *Tues.–Sat. 10–6* Ⓜ *C, E to 23rd St.*

Mary Boone Gallery. Based in SoHo in the late seventies, when it was a hot showcase for younger artists, the Mary Boone Gallery relocated to Midtown (745 Fifth Avenue, near 58th Street) in 1996 and then opened this additional branch in a former garage in Chelsea in 2000. The space here allows for large-scale works and dramatic installations. Boone continues to show established artists such as Barbara Kruger and Eric Fischl, as well as newcomers such as Pierre Bismuth, Jacob Hashimoto, and Hilary Harkness. ⊠ *541 W. 24th St., between 10th and 11th Aves., Chelsea* ☎ *212/752–2929* ⊕ *www.maryboonegallery.com* ☉ *Tues.–Sat. 10–6* Ⓜ *C, E to 23rd St.*

Metro Pictures. The hottest talents in contemporary art shown here include Cindy Sherman, Olaf Breuning, Louise Lawlor, Trevor Paglen, T. J. Wilcox, and B. Wurtz. ⊠ *519 W. 24th St., between 10th and 11th Aves., Chelsea* ☎ *212/206–7100* ⊕ *www.metropicturesgallery.com* ☉ *Tues.–Sat. 10–6* Ⓜ *C, E to 23rd St.*

Nancy Hoffman Gallery. Contemporary painting, sculpture, drawing, photography, and video works by an impressive array of international artists are on display in this light-filled space that has high ceilings and a sculpture garden. Artists range from Viola Frey, known for her heroic-scale ceramic male and female figures, to other well-established artists such as Don Eddy and Joseph Raffael, to a strong group of young artists embarking with their first solo shows. Artists from this gallery were featured in the first virtual "art exhibition" in space—on astronauts' computer screens. ⊠ *520 W. 27th St., between 10th and 11th Aves., Chelsea* ☎ *212/966–6676* ⊕ *www.nancyhoffmangallery.com* ☉ *Sept.–July, Tues.–Sat. 10–6; Aug., weekdays 10–5* Ⓜ *C, E to 23rd St.*

Robert Miller Gallery. The Robert Miller Gallery—founded in 1977 by Robert Miller, a titan of the New York art world—represents some of the biggest names in modern painting and photography, including Diane Arbus, Patti Smith, and the estates of Lee Krasner and Alice Neel. ⊠ *524 W. 26th St., between 10th and 11th Aves., Chelsea* ☎ *212/366–4774* ⊕ *www.robertmillergallery.com* ☼ *Sept.–June, Tues.–Sat 10–6; July, weekdays 10–6; Aug., by appointment only* Ⓜ *C, E to 23rd St.*

Rubin Museum of Art. This sleek and serene museum spread over six floors is the largest in the Western Hemisphere dedicated to the art of the Himalayas and the pieces shown here include paintings on cloth, metal sculptures, and textiles dating from the 2nd century onward. Many of the works from areas such as Tibet, Nepal, southwest China, and India are related to Buddhism, Hinduism, Bon, and other eastern religions. You'll find a pleasant café and gift shop on the ground floor. ⊠ *150 W. 17th St., near 7th Ave., Chelsea* ☎ *212/620–5000* ⊕ *www. rmanyc.org* ⊠ *$15* ☼ *Mon. and Thurs. 11–5, Wed. 11–9, Fri. 11–10, weekends 11–6* Ⓜ *1 to 18th St.*

Sonnabend. This pioneer of the SoHo art scene continues to show important contemporary artists in its Chelsea space, including Jeff Koons, Rona Pondick, Elger Esser, and Clifford Ross. ⊠ *536 W. 22nd St., between 10th and 11th Aves., Chelsea* ☎ *212/627–1018* ⊕ *www. sonnabendgallery.com* ☼ *Tues.–Sat. 10–6* Ⓜ *C, E to 23rd St.*

Tanya Bonakdar Gallery. Contemporary artists such as Uta Barth, whose blurry photos challenge ideas about perception, and Ernesto Neto, a Brazilian artist who has made stunning room-size installations of large nylon sacks filled with spices, are shown here. ⊠ *521 W. 21st St., between 10th and 11th Aves., Chelsea* ☎ *212/414–4144* ⊕ *www. tanyabonakdargallery.com* ☼ *Tues.–Sat. 10–6* Ⓜ *C, E to 23rd St.*

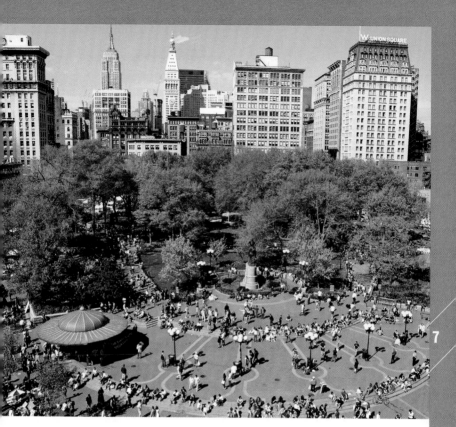

7

UNION SQUARE, THE FLATIRON DISTRICT, AND GRAMERCY PARK

GETTING ORIENTED

Union Square,
the Flatiron District,
and Gramercy Park

B,D,F
M,N,Q,R
Herald
Square

E. 34th St.

E. 33rd St.

6

W. 32nd St.

E. 32nd St.

E. 31st St.

E. 30th St.

E. 29th St.

N,R

W. 28th St.

E. 28th St.

Little
India

Museum
of Sex

W. 27th St.

E. 27th St.

Museum
of Mathematics

E. 26th St.

W. 26th St.

Appellate Division
Courthouse

E. 25th St.

W. 25th St.

Madison
Square Park

W. 24th St.

E. 24th St.

Eataly

Metropolitan Life
Insurance Company Tower

F,M

W. 23rd St.

N,R

E. 23rd St.

Flatiron Building

6

W. 22nd St.

E. 22nd St.

**FLATIRON
DISTRICT**

E. 21st St.

Gramercy
Park

W. 20th St.

E. 20th St.

W. 19th St.

E. 19th St.

City
Bakery

GRAMERCY PARK

W. 18th St.

71 Irving Place

Irving
Place

E. 18th St.

W. 17th St.

E. 17th St.

W. 16th St.

Union Square Park
& Greenmarket

Stuyvesant
Square

W. 15th St.

L,F,M

L,N,Q,R
4,5,6

L

W. 14th St.

E. 14th St.

W. 13th St.

E. 13th St.

W. 12th St.

E. 12th St.

0   1/8 mile

E. 11th St.

0   200 meters

E. 10th St.

MAKING THE MOST OF YOUR TIME

Union Square seems like it's busy at just about every time of day and night, with commuters and people hanging out on the steps to eat lunch or just hang out, but market days—Monday, Wednesday, Friday, and Saturday—are even busier. Early weekday mornings are quietest, before the market is set up, though without all the people, the area loses its allure.

This is definitely an area for strolling, shopping, and eating, so plan your visit around a meal—or several.

If you're planning to eat at the Shake Shack in Madison Square Park, come at noon if you can; the lines here can get pretty long.

COFFEE AND QUICK BITES

71 Irving Place. Steps from Union Square, this cozy little café roast their own beans—always a good sign—and serves up good people-watching along with sandwiches, muffins, and snacks. ✉ *71 Irving Pl., Gramercy Park* ☎ *212/995–5252* ⊕ *www.irvingfarm.com/locations/gramercy-cafe.*

City Bakery. Pretzel croissants, chocolate-chip cookies, and superthick hot chocolate are just some of the signature snacks here. ✉ *3 W. 18th St., Flatiron District* ☎ *212/366–1414.*

Eataly. Ignore the overpriced produce market by the front entrance of Mario Batali's Italian food emporium and make a beeline for La Piazza for sandwiches made with meticulously sourced ingredients (you can eat them at the standup tables nearby); a full-service pizza and pasta restaurant; a raw bar and fish eatery; and a spot for quaffing wines by the glass and beers on tap. There's also a corridor that's a gourmand's dream, with Italian chocolates, coffees, gelati, and pastries. ✉ *200 5th Ave., at 23rd St., Flatiron District* ☎ *212/229–2560* ⊕ *www.eataly.com.*

TOP EXPERIENCES

Strolling in Union Square Park and checking out the produce and other goodies at the greenmarket

Browsing the miles of books in the Strand bookstore

Picnicking in Madison Square Park

GETTING HERE AND AROUND

Union Square/14th Street is a major subway hub, with the L, N, Q, R, 4, 5, and 6 lines all converging here. For Madison Square Park, take the local R train to 23rd Street. The 6 also stops at 23rd and 28th streets.

7

Sightseeing
★★★★
Nightlife
★
Dining
★★★
Lodging
★★★
Shopping
★★★★

Union Square is a hub of seemingly never-ending activity and people-watching that anchors the quieter neighborhoods of Gramercy and the Flatiron District. When that certain brand of New Yorker says they don't like to travel above 14th Street, they're usually thinking about Union Square as the cut-off.

UNION SQUARE

Updated
by Jacinta
O'Halloran

The energy of Union Square reaches its peak during its greenmarket days (Monday, Wednesday, Friday, and Saturday), when more than 140 regional farmers and food purveyors set up shop on the square's north and west sides to peddle everything from produce to meat and fresh fish to baked goods. The market is a great place to rub elbows with—and get elbowed by—local shoppers and chefs and a great source for tasty souvenirs (locally produced honeys, jams, pickles, and cheeses) as well as lunch. Find a bench in the park to savor your goodies and take in the scene. Sometimes political rallies happen here, too.

Even on a nonmarket day, Union Square regularly has vendors of all kinds, selling everything from art to jewelry to T-shirts. New York University students, nannies with their charges, visitors, and locals alike all gather in this open space that can at times feel more like an outdoor version of Grand Central Terminal than a park. Just south of Union Square, on Broadway at 12th Street, is the Strand, the giant bookstore that attracts book lovers like a magnet.

It was in this square, on September 5, 1882, that Labor Day was born, when more than 10,000 New York City unionized workers took an unpaid day off to march from City Hall to Union Square.

TOP ATTRACTIONS

Union Square Park and Greenmarket. A park, farmers' market, meeting place, and site of rallies and demonstrations, this pocket of green space sits in the center of a bustling residential and commercial neighborhood. The name Union originally signified that two

main roads—Broadway and 4th Avenue—crossed here, but it took on a different meaning in the late 19th and early 20th centuries, when the square became a rallying spot for labor protests; many unions, as well as fringe political parties, moved their headquarters nearby.

Union Square is at its best on Monday, Wednesday, Friday, and Saturday (8–6), when the largest of the city's greenmarkets brings farmers and food purveyors from the tri-state area. Browse the stands of fruit and vegetables, flowers, plants, fresh-baked pies and breads, cheeses, cider, New York State wines, fish, and meat. Between Thanksgiving and Christmas, there is a popular gift market where artisans sell gift items and food in candy-cane-stripe booths at the square's southwest end.

New York University dormitories, theaters, and cavernous commercial spaces occupy the handsomely restored 19th-century commercial buildings that surround the park, along with chain coffee shops and restaurants. The run of diverse architectural styles on the building at 33 Union Square West, the Decker Building, is as imaginative as its former contents: this was once home to Andy Warhol's studio. The building at 17th Street and Union Square East, now housing the New York Film Academy and the Union Square Theater, was the final home of Tammany Hall, an organization famous in its day as a corrupt and powerful political machine. Statues in the park include those of George Washington, Abraham Lincoln, Mahatma Gandhi (often wreathed in flowers), and the Marquis de Lafayette sculpted by Frederic Auguste Bartholdi, creator of the Statue of Liberty. Plaques in the sidewalk on the southeast and southwest sides chronicle the park's history from the 1600s to 1800s. After years of legal battles, the once-crumbling pavilion at the northern end of the park reopened as a restaurant in summer 2014. Expect crowds. ⊠ *E. 14th to E. 17th Sts., between Broadway and Park Ave. S, Union Square* Ⓜ *L, N, Q, R, 4, 5, 6 to Union Sq./14th St.*

FLATIRON DISTRICT

The Flatiron District—anchored by Madison Square Park on the north and Union Square to the south—is one of the city's busiest neighborhoods, particularly along 5th Avenue and Park Avenue South. Once known as Ladies' Mile because of the fashionable row of department stores where women routinely shopped, the area is still a favorite for lady-spotting because of the number of modeling agencies and photography studios here. Lovely Madison Square Park, a pleasant green space hemmed in by the neighborhood's notable architecture—from the triangular Flatiron to the dazzling, gold-pyramid-topped New York Life Building and the Metropolitan Life Tower with its elegant clock

The wedge-shape Flatiron Building got its nickname because of its resemblance to the shape of a clothes iron; its original name is the Fuller Building.

face—is the best place to savor the view. Sit and admire the scene with a burger and shake from the park's always-busy Shake Shack or takeout from the mother of all Italian markets, Eataly, across the street from the west side of the park.

TOP ATTRACTIONS

Flatiron Building. When completed in 1902, the Fuller Building, as it was originally known, caused a sensation. Architect Daniel Burnham made ingenious use of the triangular wedge of land at 23rd Street, 5th Avenue, and Broadway, employing a revolutionary steel frame that allowed for the building's 22-story, 286-foot height. Covered with a limestone and white terra-cotta facade in the Italian Renaissance style, the building's shape resembled a clothing iron, hence its nickname. When it became apparent that the building generated strong winds, gawkers would loiter at 23rd Street hoping to catch sight of ladies' billowing skirts. Local traffic cops had to shoo away the male peepers—one purported origin of the phrase "23 skidoo." There is a small display of historic building and area photos in the lobby, but otherwise you will have to settle for appreciating this building from the outside, at least for now; the building may be converted to a luxury hotel when current occupant leases expire in 2018. ✉ *175 5th Ave., bordered by Broadway, E. 22nd and E. 23rd Sts., Flatiron District* Ⓜ *N, R to 23rd St.*

Madison Square Park. The benches of this elegant tree-filled park afford great views of some of the city's oldest and most charming skyscrapers (the Flatiron Building, the Metropolitan Life Insurance Tower, the gold-crowned New York Life Insurance Building, and the Empire State Building) and serve as a perfect vantage point for people-, pigeon-,

Lounging on the grass in Madison Square Park.

and dog-watching. Add free Wi-Fi, the Shake Shack, temporary art exhibits, and summer and fall concerts, and you'll realize that a bench here is definitely the place to be. New York City's first baseball games were played in this 7-acre park in 1845 (though New Jerseyans are quick to point out that the game was actually invented across the Hudson in Hoboken). On the north end of the park, an imposing 1881 statue by Augustus Saint-Gaudens memorializes Civil War naval hero Admiral David Farragut. An 1876 statue of Secretary of State William Henry Seward (the Seward of the term from "Seward's Folly," coined when the United States purchased Alaska from the Russian Empire in 1867) sits in the park's southwest corner, though it's rumored that the sculptor placed a reproduction of the statesman's head on a statue of Abraham Lincoln's body. ⊠ *E. 23rd to E. 26th Sts., between 5th and Madison Aves., Flatiron District* ☎ *212/538–1884* ⊕ *www.madisonsquarepark.org* Ⓜ *N, R to 23rd St.*

WORTH NOTING

Appellate Division Courthouse. Sculpted by Frederick Ruckstuhl, figures representing Wisdom and Force flank the main portal of this imposing Beaux Arts courthouse, built in 1899. Melding the structure's purpose with artistic symbolism, statues of great lawmakers line the roof balustrade, including Moses, Justinian, and Confucius. In total, sculptures by 16 artists adorn the ornate building, a showcase of themes relating to the law. This is one of the most important appellate courts in the country: it hears more than 3,000 appeals and 6,000 motions a year, and also admits approximately 3,000 new attorneys to the bar each year. Inside the courtroom is a stunning stained-glass dome set into a gilt ceiling. The main hall and the courtroom are open to visitors from 9 to 5, weekdays. All sessions, which are generally held Tuesday to Thursday at 2, are open to the public. (Visitors can call the main number ahead of time to be sure court is in session.) ✉ 27 Madison Ave. (entrance on 25th St.), Flatiron District ☎ 212/340–0400 ⊕ www. courts.state.ny.us/courts/ad1 ⊙ Weekdays 9–5 Ⓜ N, R, 6 to 23rd St.

Metropolitan Life Insurance Company Tower. When it was added to the original building on this site, in 1909, the 700-foot tower resembling the campanile of St. Mark's in Venice made this 1893 building the world's tallest; it was surpassed in height a few years later (by the Woolworth Building). It was stripped of much of its classical details during renovations in the early 1960s but remains a prominent feature of the Midtown skyline today. The clock's four faces are each three stories high, and their minute hands weigh half a ton each. In late 2014, Marriott International and Ian Schrager will open a 355 luxury-room hotel—The New York Edition Hotel—in the long-vacant clock tower portion of the building. ✉ 1 Madison Ave., between 23rd and 24th Sts., Flatiron District Ⓜ N, R, 6 to 23rd St.

FAMILY **Museum of Mathematics.** There's no exact formula to get kids excited about math, but the sleek, new two-floor Museum of Mathematics (MoMath)—the only cultural institution devoted to math in all of North America—comes close to finding the perfect ratio of fun-to-math. Kids can ride square-wheeled trikes, create human fractal trees, build virtual 3-D geometric shapes (which can be printed out on a 3-D printer), use lasers to explore cross-sections of objects, solve dozens of puzzles, and just generally bend their minds while they unknowingly multiply brain cells (sshh!). ■TIP→ **Kids will need closed-toed shoes for the Square-Wheeled Trikes.** Exhibits are best suited to kids ages 6 and up, but preschoolers will still enjoy many of the interactive exhibits, like the Math Square—a light-up floor programmed with math games, simulations, and patterns. The museum closes at 2:30 pm the first Wednesday of every month. ✉ 11 E. 26th St., between 5th and Madison, Flatiron District ☎ 212/542–0566 ⊕ www.momath.org 🎟 $15 ⊙ Daily 10–5 Ⓜ N, R to 28th St.

Museum of Sex. Ponder the profound history and cultural significance of sex at this 14,000-square-foot museum while staring at vintage pornographic photos, S&M paraphernalia, anti-masturbation devices from the 1800s, explicit film clips, vintage condom tins, and a collection of artwork. Recent exhibits have included a rare Milton Greene photo essay of Linda Lovelace and probed such topics as desire on the Internet and the sex lives of animals. The subject matter is given serious curatorial treatment, though the gift shop is full of fun sexual kitsch. Only patrons over 18 are admitted. After visiting the museum's exhibitions, sate your appetite with a kinky cocktail or gourmet coffee and pastry in the museum's new bar and restaurant, Play. ✉ 233 5th Ave., entrance on 27th St., Flatiron ☎ 212/689–6337 ⊕ www. museumofsex.com 🎟 $17.50 ⊙ Sun.–Thurs. 10–8, Fri. and Sat. 10–9 Ⓜ N, R to 28th St.

GRAMERCY PARK

The haste and hullabaloo of the city calms considerably in the residential neighborhood of Gramercy Park. Dignified Gramercy Park, named for its 1831 gated garden ringed by historic buildings and private clubs, is an early example of the city's best creative urban planning. Just north of the park is Ian Schrager's reincarnation of the Gramercy Park Hotel on Lexington Avenue. And south of the park, running north–south from 14th Street, is Irving Place, a short street honoring Washington Irving, that feels calm, green, and exclusive, and has a combination of old and new eateries, stores, and architecture. Pete's Tavern (⇨ *Nightlife*), on Irving Place since 1864, maintains its claim as the oldest original bar in the city. Two famous writers, O. Henry (*Gift of the Magi*) and Ludwig Bemelmans (*Madeline*), were "inspired" here, probably from the amazing eggnog or Pete's House Ale.

TOP ATTRACTIONS

Gramercy Park. You may not be able to enter this private park (the only truly private park in Manhattan—only those residing around it have keys), but a look through the bars in the wrought-iron fence that encloses it is worth your time, as is a stroll around its perimeter. The beautifully planted 2-acre park, designed by developer Samuel B. Ruggles, dates from 1831, and is flanked by grand examples of early-19th-century architecture and permeated with the character of its many celebrated occupants.

When Ruggles bought the property, it was known as Krom Moerasje ("little crooked swamp"), named by the Dutch settlers. He drained the swamp and set aside 42 lots for a park to be accessible exclusively to those who bought the surrounding lots in his planned London-style residential square. The park is still owned by residents of buildings in the surrounding square, although neighbors from the area can now buy visiting privileges. ■ TIP➜ Guests of the Gramercy Park Hotel can enjoy coveted access to this private park. In 1966 the New York City Landmarks Preservation Commission designated Gramercy Park a historic district. Notable buildings: No. 15 was once home to Samuel Tilden, governor of New York. It was designed by Calvert Vaux in Gothic Revival brownstone with black granite trim and included a secret passageway to 19th Street so Tilden could escape his political enemies. It is now home to the 100-year-old National Arts Club. Next door at No. 16 Gramercy Park South lived the actor Edwin Booth, perhaps most famous for being the brother of Lincoln's assassin. In 1888 he turned his Gothic-trim home into the Players Club, a clubhouse for actors and theatrical types who were not welcome in regular society. A bronze statue of Edwin Booth as Hamlet has pride of place inside the park. ✉ *Lexington Ave. and E. 21st St., Gramercy Park* Ⓜ *L, N, Q, R, 4, 5, 6 to Union Sq./14th St.*

MIDTOWN EAST

with Murray Hill

GETTING ORIENTED

Midtown East

N,Q,R

N,Q,R,4,5,6

E. 59th St.

E. 58th St.

E. 57th St.

E. 56th St.

Trump Tower

Pace Gallery

Little Collins

Sony Wonder Technology Lab

E. 55th St.

E. 54th St.

Third Ave.

Second Ave.

Seagram Building

E,M

E,M

E,M

6

E. 51st St.

St. Patrick's Cathedral

MIDTOWN EAST

E. 50th St.

Beekman Place

First Ave.

E. 49th St.

E. 48th St.

Japan Society

Fifth Ave.

Madison Ave.

Park Ave.

Lexington Ave.

E. 47th St.

E. 46th St.

United Nations Headquarters

Helmsley Building

E. 45th St.

E. 44th St.

FDR Dr.

Grand Central Terminal

Grand Central Market

E. 43rd St.

Chrysler Building

E. 42nd St.

Tudor City

7

4,5,6,7,S

Daily News Building

Bryant Park

E. 41st St.

Queens-Midtown Tunnel

East River

E. 40th St.

E. 39th St.

MURRAY HILL

E. 38th St.

Lucid Cafe

Morgan Library and Museum

E. 37th St.

E. 36th St.

B. Altman Building/ New York Public Library— Science, Industry, and Business Library (SIBL)

E. 35th St.

E. 34th St.

Empire State Building

E. 33rd St.

0   1/4 mi

Koreatown

E. 32nd St.

Curry Hill

0   1/4 km

MAKING THE MOST OF YOUR TIME

The east side of Midtown is somewhat more laid back than the west side, but there's still lots to keep you busy. Wherever you're headed, try to make sure you at least pass through Grand Central, which celebrated its 100th birthday in 2013—it'll be a madhouse on weekday mornings or right after work, and extremely quiet on the weekends, so you might want to visit on a weekday afternoon.

If you're planning to visit the Empire State Building, try to do so either early or late in the day—morning is the least crowded time, and late at night the city lights are dazzling. Allow at least two hours for your visit if you plan to visit the observation deck.

It's also worth making time for a quick trip out of the United States to visit the "international zone" of the United Nations; take a tour or just wander the grounds and promenade.

TOP EXPERIENCES

Standing in the center of Grand Central Terminal's main concourse and taking in the fiber-optic map of the constellations overhead

Strolling down 5th Avenue, where some of the world's top luxury brands have flagship stores, especially around the holidays when store windows are dressed to impress

Viewing the rare manuscripts at the Morgan Library

Enjoying panoramic views of the city—at dusk—from the top of the Empire State Building

Ogling at the neo-Gothic architecture, stained glass, and sculptures at iconic St. Patrick's Cathedral. Soaking up the cathedral's peace and serenity (even amid renovations)

Dining with locals in Koreatown and Curry Hill

GETTING HERE

To get to the east side of Midtown, take the 4, 5, 6, or the 7 to Grand Central. The S, or Shuttle, travels back and forth between Grand Central and Times Square.

You can reach the Empire State Building via the B, D, F, M, N, Q, or R train to 34th Street or the 6 to 33rd Street. The 6 also stops at 23rd and 28th streets.

COFFEE AND QUICK BITES

Grand Central Market. The concourse on the lower level of Grand Central Terminal is a cornucopia of gourmet snack options, including Eli Zabar's, Ciao Bella Gelato, Li-Lac Chocolates, and even an outpost of Junior's, the famed Brooklyn restaurant known for their classic cheesecake. ⊠ *Grand Central Terminal, main entrance at E. 42nd St., at Park Ave., Midtown East.*

Little Collins. This Australian import pays as much attention to what it puts on your plate as to what it pours in your coffee mug. ⊠ *667 Lexington Ave., near 56th St., Midtown East* ☎ *212/308–1969* ⊕ *www.little collinsnyc.com.*

Lucid Cafe. A cozy (okay, tiny) coffee spot in Murray Hill with excellent coffee, espresso, hot chocolates, and tasty pastries. ⊠ *311 Lexington Ave., at 38th St., Midtown East* ☎ *212/867–3490.*

8

Sightseeing
★★★★★

Nightlife
★★

Dining
★★★★

Lodging
★★★★★

Shopping
★★★★★

Fifth Avenue is Manhattan's dividing line, marking the divergence of east side and west side, but the avenue itself seems to connote so much of what the city's East Side is all about. This is where some of the city's most iconic buildings are found, including the Empire State Building, which is technically in the Murray Hill neighborhood.

MIDTOWN EAST

Updated
by Jacinta
O'Halloran

In terms of architecture, Midtown East has some of the city's most notable gems, including the stately Chrysler Building, considered an art deco triumph, and the bustling Beaux Arts masterpiece Grand Central Terminal. At night the streets around here are relatively quiet, but the restaurants are filled with expense-account diners celebrating successes. Some of the most formal dining rooms and most expensive meals in town can be found here. The lower section of 5th Avenue is also a shopper's paradise, home to megabrand flagships such as Louis Vuitton, Yves Saint Laurent, and Chanel, and some of the world's most famous jewelry stores, including Tiffany, Van Cleef & Arpels, and Harry Winston. Upscale department stores like Bloomingdales and Saks Fifth Avenue are also around here.

TOP ATTRACTIONS

Chrysler Building. A monument to modern times and the mighty automotive industry, the former Chrysler headquarters wins many a New Yorker's vote for the city's most iconic and beloved skyscraper (the world's tallest for 40 days until the Empire State Building stole the honor). Architect William Van Alen, who designed this 1930 Art Deco masterpiece, incorporated car details into its form: American eagle gargoyles made of chromium nickel sprout from the 61st floor, resembling car-hood ornaments used on 1920s Chryslers; winged urns festooning the 31st floor reference the car's radiator caps. Most breathtaking is the pinnacle, with tiered crescents and spiked windows that radiate out like a magnificent steel sunburst. View it at sunset to catch the light gleaming off the tip.

Even better, observe it at night, when its peak illuminates the sky. The inside is sadly off-limits apart from the amazing time-capsule lobby replete with chrome "grillwork," intricately patterned wood elevator doors, marble walls and floors, and an enormous ceiling mural saluting transportation and the human endeavor. ⊠ *405 Lexington Ave., at 42nd St., Midtown East* Ⓜ *4, 5, 6, 7, S to 42nd St./Grand Central.*

Fodor's Choice ★ **Grand Central Terminal.** Grand Central is not only the world's largest (76 acres) and the nation's busiest (nearly 700,000 commuters and subway riders use it daily) railway station, but also one of the world's most magnificent, majestic public spaces. Past the glimmering chandeliers of the waiting room is the jaw-dropping **main concourse:** 200 feet long, 120 feet wide, and 120 feet (roughly 12 stories) high, modeled after an ancient Roman public bath. In spite of it being completely cavernous, Grand Central manages to evoke a certain sense of warmth rarely found in buildings its size. Overhead, a twinkling fiber-optic map of the constellations covers the robin's egg–blue ceiling. To admire it all with some sense of peace, avoid visiting at rush hour.

To escape the crowds, head up one of the sweeping staircases at either end, where three upscale restaurants occupy the balcony space. Any would make an enjoyable perch from which to survey the concourse, but for a real taste of the station's early years, head beyond the western staircase to the **Campbell Apartment,** a clubby cocktail lounge in the restored private offices and salon of 1920s tycoon John W. Campbell. Located around and below the main concourse are fantastic shops and eateries (this is, of course, home to the eponymous Grand Central Oyster Bar), making this one of the best—if somewhat labyrinthine— "malls" in the city.

To best admire Grand Central's exquisite Beaux Arts architecture, start from its ornate south face on East 42nd Street, modeled after a Roman triumphal arch. Crowning the facade's Corinthian columns and 75-foot-high arched windows, a graceful clock keeps time for hurried commuters. In the central window stands an 1869 bronze statue of Cornelius Vanderbilt, who built the station to house his railroad empire. Also noteworthy is the 1½-ton, cast-iron bald eagle displaying its 13-foot wingspan atop a ball near the corner of 42nd Street and Vanderbilt Avenue.

Grand Central still functions primarily as a railroad station, and might resemble its artless cross-town counterpart, Penn Station, were it not for Jacqueline Kennedy Onassis's 1975 public information campaign to save it as a landmark. Underground, more than 60 ingeniously integrated railroad tracks carry trains upstate and to Connecticut via Metro-North Commuter Rail. The subway connects here as well. The **Municipal Art Society** (☎ *212/935–3960* ⊕ *www.mas.org/tours*) leads an official daily walking tour to explore the 100-year-old terminal's architecture, history, and hidden secrets. Tours begin in the main concourse at 12:30 and last 75 minutes. Tickets ($20) can be purchased in advance online (⊕ *www.docentour.com/gct*) or from the ticket booth in the main concourse. ⊠ *Main entrance, E. 42nd St. at Park Ave., Midtown East* ☎ *212/935–3960* ⊕ *www.grandcentralterminal.com* Ⓜ *4, 5, 6, 7, S to 42nd St./Grand Central.*

8

Irish pride takes to the streets and sweeps up 5th Avenue in the annual St. Patrick's Day Parade.

St. Patrick's Cathedral. This Gothic edifice—the largest Catholic cathedral in the United States, seating approximately 2,400 people—is among Manhattan's most striking churches, with its double spires topping out at 330 feet. St. Pat's, as locals call it, holds a special place in the hearts of many New Yorkers and offers a calm and quiet refuge in the heart of buzzy midtown . . . despite the throngs of tourists (the cathedral receives more than 5.5 million visitors annually) and ongoing renovations.

The church dates back to 1858–79 and has begun to show its age. Hence, the cocoon of scaffolding, inside and out, as it undergoes an extensive $177 million rehabilitation project. The cathedral is open during renovations, and is slowly revealing its shiny new-old self: the stone faces of the spires that tower above 5th Avenue have been cleaned and caulked and the copper crosses that crown them polished. Interior scaffolding is constantly on the move as work progresses but if you're lucky, you can catch a glimpse of the organ loft and the famous rose window (considered stained-glass artist Charles Connick's greatest work). You can still check out the statues in the alcoves around the nave, including a modern depiction of the first American-born saint, Mother Elizabeth Ann Seton. ■TIP→ Make sure to check out the ornately carved bronze double doors, each weighing 9,200 pounds and featuring sculptures of saints.

The church's Pietà sculpture is three times larger than the Pietà in St. Peter's Rome. Construction does not interfere with daily masses or the free guided tours held at 10 am most days (call ahead to confirm). ⊠ *5th Ave., between 50th and 51st Sts., Midtown East* ☎ *212/753–2261 for rectory* ⊕ *www.saintpatrickscathedral.org* ☉ *Daily 6:30 am–8:45 pm* Ⓜ *E, M to 5th Ave./53rd St.*

FAMILY **Sony Wonder Technology Lab.** Have kids in tow? The free Sony Wonder Technology Lab in the Sony Building lets them program robots, remix songs, perform virtual heart surgery, and see their dance moves performed by favorite Sony-animated characters in real time through motion capture. An evolutionary timeline explores how technology keeps getting faster, sharper, smaller, and more portable (fascinating, even if your new smartphone is aging in your pocket.) The lab also shows classic and contemporary films for both young and adult audiences in its HD theater on Thursdays and Saturdays. Admission is free but reservations are strongly recommended; they can be made a minimum of 7 days and up to 3 months from the time of visit. ■TIP→ A limited number of same-day tickets are available on a first-come basis. ✉ *550 Madison Ave., at 56th St., Midtown East* ☎ *212/833-8100* ⊕ *www.sonywondertechlab.com* ⊗ *Tues.–Sat. 9:30–5:30* Ⓜ *N, Q, R to 5th Ave./59th St.*

United Nations Headquarters. Officially an "international zone" and not part of the United States, the U.N. Headquarters is a working symbol of global cooperation. Built between 1947 and 1961, the headquarters sits on a lushly landscaped, 18-acre tract on the East River, fronted by flags of member nations. The main reason to visit is the 45-minute guided tour (given in 20 languages; reservations can be made through the website), which includes the **General Assembly** and major council chambers, though some rooms may be closed on any given day. ■TIP→ Arrive 30 minutes before the start of your tour for security screening. Bring proper ID. The newly renovated Conference Building, which includes the original chambers of the Security Council, the Trusteeship Council, and the Economic and Social Council, as well as gifts from U.N. Member States like the mosaic representation of Norman Rockwell's "The Golden Rule" are all back on public display. The tour also includes displays on war, peacekeeping, nuclear nonproliferation, human rights, and refugees, and passes corridors overflowing with imaginatively diverse artwork. Free tickets to assemblies are sometimes available on a first-come, first-served basis before sessions begin; pick them up in the General Assembly lobby. If you just want to wander around, the grounds include a beautiful riverside promenade, a rose garden with 1,400 specimens, and sculptures donated by member nations. The complex's buildings (the slim, 505-foot-tall green-glass **Secretariat Building**; the much smaller, domed **General Assembly Building** (reopening after renovation in fall 2014); and the **Dag Hammarskjöld Library**) evoke the influential French modernist Le Corbusier (who was on the team of architects that designed the complex), and the surrounding park and plaza remain visionary. During renovations, the visitors' gate is temporarily located on 47th Street and 1st Avenue. Call before you visit to confirm. The public concourse has a coffee shop, gift shops, a bookstore, and a post office where you can mail letters with U.N. stamps. ✉ *Visitor entrance, 1st Ave. at 46th St., Midtown East* ☎ *212/963-8687* ⊕ *visit.un.org* 🎟 *Tour $16 (plus $2 service charge for online ticketing)* ⊗ *Tours weekdays 9:45–4:15. Tours in English leave every 30 mins; for other languages, check schedule online* Ⓜ *4, 5, 6, 7, S to 42nd St./Grand Central* ☞ *Children under 5 not admitted.*

8

WORTH NOTING

Daily News Building. The landmark lobby of this art deco tower contains an illuminated 12-foot globe that revolves beneath a black glass dome. Around it, spreading across the floor like a giant compass and literally positioning New York at the center of the world, bronze lines indicate mileage to various international destinations. Movie fans may recognize the building from its role as the offices of the fictional newspaper the Daily Planet in the original *Superman* movie. The Daily News hasn't called this building home since the mid-1990s. Only the lobby is open to the public. ⊠ *220 E. 42nd St., between 2nd and 3rd Aves., Midtown East* ☎ *212/210–2100* Ⓜ *4, 5, 6, 7, S to 42nd St./Grand Central.*

Helmsley Building. This Warren & Wetmore–designed 1929 landmark was intended to match neighboring Grand Central in bearing, and it succeeded, with a gold-and-copper roof topped with an enormous lantern (originally housing a 6,000-watt light) and distinctive dual archways for traffic on Park Avenue. The building's history gets quirky, however: When the millionaire real estate investor Harry Helmsley purchased the building in 1977, he changed its name from the New York Central Building to the New York General Building in order to save money by replacing only two letters in the facade (only later did he rename it after himself). During a renovation the following year, however, he actually gilded the building, applying gold paint even to limestone and bronze—it was removed by a succeeding owner. In 2010, after a $100 million renovation, the Helmsley Building (technically 230 Park or "the building formerly known as the Helmsley Building and informally still known as the Helmsley Building") became the first prewar office tower to receive LEED Gold certification for energy efficiency. Despite being blocked from view from the south by the MetLife Building (originally the Pan Am Building), the Helmsley Building remains a defining—and now "green," as opposed to gold—feature of one of the world's most lavish avenues. ⊠ *230 Park Ave., between 45th and 46th Sts., Midtown East* Ⓜ *4, 5, 6, 7, S to 42nd St./Grand Central.*

Japan Society. The stylish, serene lobby of the Japan Society has interior bamboo gardens linked by a second-floor waterfall. Works by well-known Japanese artists are exhibited in the second-floor gallery. Past shows have included the first American retrospective of Sakai Hôitsu, a samurai aristocrat turned Buddhist monk who dedicated his life to art and poetry; a display of artwork created by children from Tohoku after Japan's 2011 earthquake; and *Points of Departure: Treasures of Japan from the Brooklyn Museum*—more than 2,000 years of Japan's art-making history drawn from Brooklyn's renowned collection of Japanese art. In July, the museum hosts an annual film festival, Japan Cuts, showcasing contemporary Japanese cinema. ⊠ *333 E. 47th St., between 1st and 2nd Aves., Midtown East* ☎ *212/832–1155* ⊕ *www. japansociety.org* ☑ *$12 (gallery)* ☉ *Gallery Tues.–Thurs. 11–6, Fri. 11–9, weekends 11–5; building hrs vary* Ⓜ *6 to 51st St./Lexington Ave.; E, M to Lexington–3rd Aves./53rd St.*

The restoration and cleaning of Grand Central in the late 1990s uncovered the elaborate astronomical design on the ceiling of the main concourse.

Pace Gallery (Midtown). This leading contemporary art gallery—now with several outposts in Chelsea as well as two in London and a gallery in Beijing—focuses on such modern and contemporary artists as Julian Schnabel, Mark Rothko, James Turrell, and New York School painter Ad Reinhardt. ✉ *32 E. 57th St., between Park and Madison Aves., 2nd fl., Midtown East* ☎ *212/421–3292* ⊕ *www.thepacegallery.com* ⊙ *Tues.–Sat. 10–6* Ⓜ *N, R to 5th Ave.*

Seagram Building. Ludwig Mies van der Rohe, a pioneer of modern architecture, built this boxlike bronze-and-glass tower in 1958. The austere facade belies its wit: I-beams, used to hold buildings up, here are merely attached to the surface, representing the *idea* of support. The Seagram Building's innovative ground-level plaza, extending out to the sidewalk, has since become a common element in urban skyscraper design. With its two giant fountains and welcoming steps, it's also a popular lunch spot with midtown workers. Visit late in the afternoon to avoid crowds. ✉ *375 Park Ave., between 52nd and 53rd Sts., Midtown East* Ⓜ *6 to 51st St./Lexington Ave.; E, M to Lexington–3rd Aves./53rd St.*

Trump Tower. The tallest all-glass building in Manhattan when it was completed in 1983, this skyscraper's ostentatious atrium flaunts that decade's unbridled luxury, with expensive boutiques and gaudy brass everywhere. You'll half expect the pleasant-sounding waterfall streaming down to the lower-level food court to flow with champagne. These days, the building is best known for its appearances on TV reality show, "Celebrity Apprentice," where Donald Trump hires and fires celebrities. ✉ *725 5th Ave., at 56th St., Midtown East* ☎ *212/832–2000* ⊕ *www.trump.com* Ⓜ *N, R to 5th Ave./59th St.*

8

Tudor City. Before Donald Trump, there was Fred F. French. In 1925 the prominent real-estate developer became one of the first to buy up a large number of buildings—more than 100, in fact, most of them tenements—and join their properties into a single new development. He designed a collection of nine apartment buildings and two parks in the "garden city" mode, which placed a building's green space not in an enclosed courtyard but in the foreground. French also elevated the entire development 70 feet (40 stone steps) above the river and built a 39-by-50-foot "Tudor City" sign atop one of the 22-story buildings. The development's residential towers opened between 1927 and 1930, borrowing a marketable air of sophistication from Tudor-style stone-work, stained-glass windows, and lobby design flourishes. Tudor City has featured in numerous films, and its gardens remain a popular lunch spot among office workers. ⊠ *Between E. 40th and E. 43rd Sts., and 1st and 2nd Aves., Midtown East* Ⓜ *4, 5, 6, 7, S to 42nd St./Grand Central.*

MURRAY HILL

Murray Hill stretches roughly from about 30th to 40th streets between 5th and 3rd avenues and is a mix of high-rises, restaurants, and bars filled mostly with a postcollege crowd. The small but solid enclave of Little India (also known as Curry Hill), primarily around Lexington and 28th Street, is a good area to sample authentic cuisine and shop for traditional cloth-ing and other goods in a handful of boutiques. Farther north a few side streets are tree-lined and townhouse-filled with some high-profile haunts, including the Morgan Library and Museum with its vast book stacks and rare manuscripts. But perhaps the biggest reason to visit this neighborhood is to see New York's biggest icon, the Empire State Building.

TOP ATTRACTIONS

FAMILY

Fodor's Choice

★

Empire State Building. With a pencil-slim silhouette, recognizable virtu-ally worldwide, the Empire State Building is an art deco monument to progress, a symbol for New York City, and a star in some great roman-tic scenes, on- and off-screen. Its cinematic résumé—the building has appeared in more than 250 movies—means that it remains a fixture of popular imagination, and many visitors come to relive favorite movie scenes. You might just find yourself at the top of the building with *Elf* look-alikes or even the building's own *King Kong* impersonator.

Built in 1931 at the peak of the skyscraper craze, this 103-story lime-stone giant opened after a mere 13 months of construction. The frame-work rose at an astonishing rate of 4½ stories per week, making the Empire State Building the fastest-rising skyscraper ever built.

There are three lines to get to the top of the Empire State Build-ing; a line for tickets, a line for security, and a line for the eleva-tors. ■TIP→ **Save time by purchasing your tickets in advance (⊕ *www. esbnyc.com*). You can't skip the security line, but you can skip to the front of both the ticket line and the line for elevators by purchasing an Express ticket ($50). If you don't want to pony up for express service, do yourself a favor and skip that last elevator line at the 80th floor by taking the stairs.**

CLOSE UP

The Lights of the Empire State Building

At night the Empire State Building (ESB) lights up the Manhattan skyline with a colorful view as awe-inspiring from a distance as the view from the top. The colors at the top of the building are changed regularly to reflect seasons, events, and holidays, so New Yorkers and visitors from around the world always have a reason to look at this icon in a new light.

The building's first light show was in November 1932, when a simple searchlight was used to spread the news that New York–born Franklin Delano Roosevelt had been elected president of the United States. Douglas Leigh, sign designer and mastermind of Times Square's kinetic billboard ads, tried to brighten up prospects at the "Empty State Building" after the Depression by negotiating with the Coca-Cola Company to occupy the top floors. He proposed that Coca-Cola could change the lights of the building to serve as a weather forecast and then publish a small guide on its bottles to decipher the colors. Coca-Cola loved this idea, but the deal fell through because of the bombing at Pearl Harbor, when the U.S. government needed office space in the building.

In 1956 the revolving "freedom lights" were installed to welcome people to America; then in 1964 the top 30 floors of the building were illuminated to mark the New York World's Fair. Douglas Leigh revisited the lights of the ESB in 1976, when he was made chairman of City Decor to welcome the Democratic Convention. He introduced the idea of color lighting, and so the building's tower was ablaze in red, white, and blue to welcome the convention and to mark the celebration of the American Bicentennial. The color lights were a huge success, and they remained red, white, and blue for the rest of the year.

Leigh's next suggestion of tying the lights to different holidays, a variation on his weather theme for Coca-Cola, is the basic scheme still used today. In 1977 the lighting system was updated to comply with energy conservation programs and to allow for a wider range of colors. Leigh further improved this new system in 1984 by designing an automated color-changing system so vertical fluorescents in the mast could be changed.

In November 2012, the Empire State Building debuted its new LED light system, synchronizing its undulating lights to Alicia Keys' "Girl on Fire" and Jay Z's "Empire State of Mind." For the building's first major exterior lighting renovation in many years, Philips Color Kinetic created a system that can produce both intensely saturated full-color light and dimmable cool white light, allowing for an astonishing and flexible range of dramatic or subtle lighting effects.

For a full lighting schedule, visit ⊕ *www.esbnyc.com.*

—Jacinta O'Halloran

If this is your first visit, keep yourself entertained during your ascent by renting a headset with an audio tour by Tony, a fictional but "authentic" native New Yorker, available in eight languages.

The 86th-floor observatory (1,050 feet high) has both a glass-enclosed area (heated in winter and cooled in summer) and an outdoor deck spanning the building's circumference. Don't be shy about going outside into the wind (even in winter) or you'll miss half the experience. Also, don't be deterred by crowds; there's an unspoken etiquette when it comes to sharing the views and backdrop, and there's plenty of city to go around. Bring quarters for the high-powered binoculars—on clear days you can see up to 80 miles—or bring binoculars so you can get a look at some of the city's rooftop gardens. If it rains, the deck will be less crowded and you can view the city between the clouds or watch the rain travel sideways around the building from the shelter of the enclosed walkway.

The views of the city from the 86th-floor deck are spectacular, but the views from 16 stories up on the 102nd-floor observatory are even more so—yet fewer visitors make it this far. Instead of rushing back to elevator lines, ask yourself when you'll be back again and then head up to the enclosed 102nd floor. The ticket for both the 86th-floor and 102nd-floor decks costs $44, but you will be rewarded with peaceful, bird's-eye views of the entire city. There are fewer visitors angling for photo ops.

■TIP➔ Even if you skip the view from up top, be sure to step into the lobby and take in the ceiling, beautifully restored in 2009. The gilded gears and sweeping Art Deco lines are a romantic tribute to the machine age and part of the original vision for the building. ✉ *350 5th Ave., at 34th St., Murray Hill* ☎ *212/736–3100, 877/692–8439* ⊕ *www.esbnyc. com* ✇ *$27, $44 for 86th-fl. and 102nd-fl. decks* ☉ *Daily 8 am–2 am; last elevator up leaves at 1:15 am*

NY SKYRIDE. Although some parents blanch when they discover how much it costs and how it lurches, the second-floor NY SKYRIDE, New York's only aerial virtual tour simulator, is a favorite of the 7- and 8-year-old set, and it's cheaper than an actual aerial tour of New York. Narrated by actor Kevin Bacon, the ride takes the viewer on a 30 minute virtual tour of New York, soaring by the Brooklyn Bridge, the Statue of Liberty, Central Park, Times Square, Yankee Stadium, and other top attractions along the way. There's also a brief but poignant trip back in time to visit the World Trade Center's Twin Towers. It's a fun way to get a sense of the city's highlights, though teenagers may find the technology a little dated. ■TIP➔ When you purchase a SKYRIDE–Empire State Building combo ticket (at significant discount online), you'll visit the SKYRIDE first and then join the line for the observation deck at the elevators, skipping up to half the wait. ✉ *Empire State Building, entrance on 33rd St.* ☎ *212/279–9777, 888/759–7433* ⊕ *www.skyride.com* ✇ *$42 ($29 online), $59 ($49 online) combo SKYRIDE and observatory* ☉ *Daily 8 am–10 pm* Ⓜ *B, D, F, N, Q, R, M to 34th St./Herald Sq.; 6 to 33rd St.*

The view from Midtown over the East River and into Queens

Morgan Library and Museum. The treasures inside this museum, gathered by John Pierpont Morgan (1837–1913), one of New York's wealthiest financiers, are exceptional: medieval and Renaissance illuminated manuscripts, old master drawings and prints, rare books, and autographed literary and musical manuscripts. Crowning achievements produced on paper, from the Middle Ages to the 20th century, are on view here: letters penned by John Keats and Thomas Jefferson; a summary of the theory of relativity in Einstein's own elegant handwriting; three Gutenberg Bibles; drawings by Dürer, da Vinci, Rubens, and Rembrandt; the only known manuscript fragment of Milton's *Paradise Lost*; Thoreau's journals; and original manuscripts and letters by Charlotte Brontë, Jane Austen, Thomas Pynchon, and others.

Outside on East 36th Street, the sphinx in the right-hand sculptured panel of the original library's facade is rumored to wear the face of architect Charles McKim. ✉ *225 Madison Ave., at 36th St., Murray Hill* ☎ *212/685–0008* ⊕ *www.themorgan.org* ✎ *$18; free Fri. 7–9* ☺ *Tues.–Thurs. 10:30–5, Fri. 10:30–9, Sat. 10–6, Sun. 11–6* Ⓜ *B, D, F, N, Q, R, V to 34th St./Herald Sq.; 6 to 33rd St.*

WORTH NOTING

FAMILY **B. Altman Building/New York Public Library–Science, Industry, and Business Library (SIBL).** In 1906 department-store magnate Benjamin Altman gambled that his fashionable patrons would follow him uptown from his popular store in the area now known as the Ladies' Mile Historic District. His new store, one of the first of the grand department stores on 5th Avenue, was designed to blend with the mansions nearby. Note in particular the beautiful entrance on 5th Avenue. In 1996 the New York

Public Library (NYPL) set up a high-tech library here. A 33-foot-high atrium unites the building's two floors, the lending library off the lobby and the research collections below. Downstairs a wall of electronic ticker tapes and TVs tuned to business-news stations beams information and instructions to patrons. As part of the controversial Central Library Plan, the NYPL plans to sell this library and its Mid-Manhattan circu-lating library to fund renovations of the iconic Main Building on 42nd Street and Fifth Avenue. The sale has been delayed but is still probable so visit while you can! A free one-hour tour is offered Thursday at 2; meet at the reception desk. ⊠ *188 Madison Ave., between 34th and 35th Sts., Murray Hill* ☎ *917/275–6975* ⊕ *www.nypl.org* ☽ *Mon., Fri., and Sat. 11–6, Tues.–Thurs. 10–8* Ⓜ *6 to 33rd St.*

Curry Hill. Affectionately nicknamed in reference to the neighborhood (Murray Hill), Curry Hill is an aromatic three-block cluster of Indian restaurants, and one of the city's most exciting dining destinations. There are nearly 25 Indian restaurants peppered (or is it spiced?) around Lexington Avenue between 26th and 28th streets, and while the neigh-borhood is popular with in-the-know New Yorkers, it is decidedly off-the-beaten-tourist-track. You'll find culinary offerings from a variety of regional cuisines and for every appetite, be it a filling biryani or a quickie *chaat* (savory snack): highlights include a *saag paneer* (spin-ach dish with cheese) or a bowl of curry at one of the neighborhood's founding restaurants, Curry in a Hurry (28th and Lex); vegetarian food with Kosher certification at Bhojan (between 27th and 28th on Lex); *kati* rolls (meat or veggie filling wrapped in flatbread) and other urban Indian street snacks at Desi Galli (between 27th and 28th on Lex), and Indo-Chinese offerings at Chinese Mirch (28th and Lex). Don't leave the neighborhood without sampling a *dosa*—a fermented crêpe often filled with spiced potato and served with dipping sauces—and shop-ping the spice markets. ■TIP→ Too full to walk? Curry Hill is a great place to score a cab as Indian cab drivers regularly stop here for food. ⊠ *Lexington Ave. between 26th and 28th Sts., Murray Hill.*

Koreatown. Despite sitting in the shade of the Empire State Building, and within steps of Herald Square, Koreatown (aka K-Town) isn't a tourist destination. In fact, it feels decidedly off-the-beaten track. Tech-nically, Koreatown runs 31st through 36th streets and between Fifth and Sixth avenues, though the main drag is 32nd Street between Fifth and Broadway. Known as Korea Way, this strip is home to 24/7 Korean barbecue joints, karaoke bars, and spas, all piled on top of each other. Fill up on *kimchi* (spicy pickled cabbage), *kimbap* (seaweed rice), and red bean doughnuts (delicious), then try some authentic Asian karaoke ⊠ *Bordered by 31st and 36th Sts., 5th and 6th Aves., Murray Hill* Ⓜ *B, D, F, N, Q, R, M to 34th St./Herald Sq.; 6 to 33rd St.*

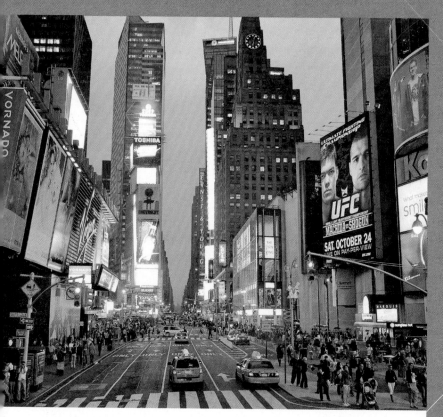

MIDTOWN WEST

with Times Square and Rockefeller Center

GETTING ORIENTED

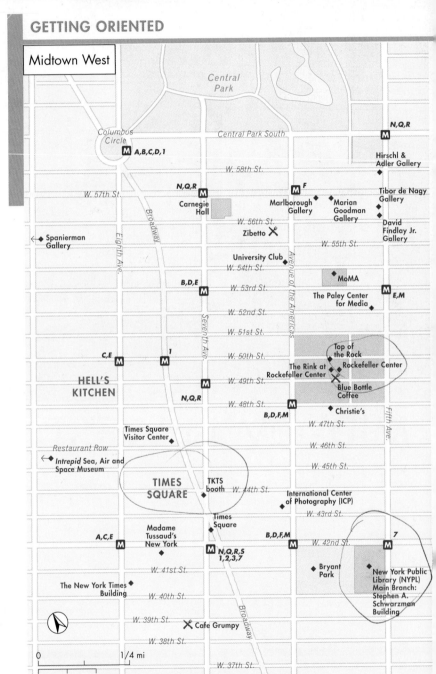

Midtown West

Central Park

Columbus Circle
M A,B,C,D,1

Central Park South

Hirschl & Adler Gallery

W. 58th St.

M N,Q,R

M N,Q,R
W. 57th St.

Carnegie Hall

M F

Marlborough Gallery

Marian Goodman Gallery

Tibor de Nagy Gallery

W. 56th St.

Zibetto ✕

David Findlay Jr. Gallery

← ◆ Spanierman Gallery

W. 55th St.

University Club
W. 54th St.

M B,D,E
W. 53rd St.

MoMA

M E,M

W. 52nd St.

The Paley Center for Media

W. 51st St.

M C,E   **M** 1
W. 50th St.

Top of the Rock

Rockefeller Center

The Rink at Rockefeller Center

HELL'S KITCHEN

W. 49th St.

Blue Bottle Coffee

M N,Q,R

W. 48th St.

M

Christie's

B,D,F,M

W. 47th St.

Times Square Visitor Center ◆

W. 46th St.

Restaurant Row

W. 45th St.

←◆ Intrepid Sea, Air and Space Museum

TIMES SQUARE

TKTS booth   W. 44th St.

International Center of Photography (ICP)

W. 43rd St.

Times Square

Madame Tussaud's New York

B,D,F,M

7

M A,C,E

M N,Q,R,S
1,2,3,7

M
W. 42nd St.

W. 41st St.

Bryant Park

New York Public Library (NYPL) Main Branch: Stephen A. Schwarzman Building

The New York Times Building ◆

W. 40th St.

W. 39th St.

✕ Cafe Grumpy

0   1/4 mi

W. 38th St.

0   1/4 km

W. 37th St.

MAKING THE MOST OF YOUR TIME

Most people think of Times Square when they think of Midtown but there's a lot more going on here. The Museum of Modern Art (MoMA) is one of the neighborhood's top attractions, and definitely worth a visit, as is Bryant Park—a cool oasis for Midtown's workers and locals. If you have enough time, hop in a cab and head over to 12th Avenue to visit the space shuttle Enterprise at the *Intrepid* Sea, Air & Space Museum.

Times Square is almost always a frenetic mass of people, staring up at the lights and the giant televisions. If you're in a hurry to get somewhere, try to avoid walking—or cabbing—through here. If you're staying in Midtown, you can take advantage of the prime location and rise early to be first in line at landmarks, museums, or the TKTS booth for discount day-of theater tickets (⇨ *Chapter 20: Performing Arts*).

TOP EXPERIENCES

Summer film screenings at dusk in Bryant Park

Skating at Rockefeller Center

Checking out the views from the Top of the Rock; opinions vary on whether the better views are from here or from the Empire State Building. Either way, if you go at night, the city spreads out below in a mesmerizing blanket of lights.

Soaking in the art and serenity of MoMA's sculpture garden

GETTING HERE

You can get to Midtown via (almost) all the subways; many make numerous stops throughout the area. For Midtown West, the 1, 2, 3, 7, A, C, E, N, Q, and R serve Times Square–42nd Street. The S, or Shuttle, travels back and forth between Times Square and Grand Central. The B, D, F, and M trains serve Rockefeller Center.

COFFEE AND QUICK BITES

Blue Bottle Coffee. Known for their meticulous methods—drip coffee poured by hand, freshly roasted organic beans (prepared in a Brooklyn roastery), and delicious treats and pastries (also rushed fresh from Brooklyn)—the Rock Center outpost of this cult California coffee fave is the perfect refueling spot amid the chaos of Midtown. ⊠ *1 Rockefeller Plaza, Concourse level, Midtown West* ⊕ *www.bluebottlecoffee.com/ cafes/rockefeller-center.*

✕ **Cafe Grumpy.** Stop by this Garment District outlet of the New York minichain and turn any sign of grumpiness into a smile with coffee roasted at the Greenpoint, Brooklyn, location. $ *Average main: $7* ⊠ *200 W. 39th St., Midtown West* ☎ *646/499-8749* ⊕ *www.cafegrumpy.com* ☉ *Closed weekends dinner* Ⓜ *1, 2, 3, 7, N, Q, R, S to Times Sq.*

Zibetto Espresso Bar. You won't find any seats but you will find arguably the best espresso drinks in New York, served in ceramic cups (with a glass of water). ⊠ *1385 6th Ave., at 56th St., Midtown West* ⊕ *www. zibettoespressobar.com.*

9

Sightseeing
★★★★★

Nightlife
★★★

Dining
★★★★★

Lodging
★★★★★

Shopping
★★★★★

Big is the buzz in Times Square where giant TV screens, towering skyscrapers, and Broadway theaters play starring roles alongside megastores like Hershey's and Toys "R" Us. Love it or hate it, Times Square is the flashy and flashing heart of Midtown. A visit to New York demands a photo op in Times Square. Just don't forget that there's also a lot more to see and experience on this side of Midtown.

Updated
by Jacinta
O'Halloran

Luckily, you needn't go far from Times Square to get away from the crowds. Head over to 9th Avenue—also known as Hell's Kitchen (though the food here is heavenly)—and the calmer side streets, home to a mixed bag of locals, many who work in the theater industry. There are lots of eclectic restaurants, pretheater dining options, and cute boutiques for shopping. Head over to the Avenue of the Americas (6th Avenue) and you'll find Bryant Park's zen, green space, stretched out like a yoga mat at the backdoor of the New York Public Library (another refuge from Midtown madness).

You can score good seats to some of the hottest Broadway and Off Broadway shows for half the going rate at the TKTS booth in Duffy Square at 47th Street and Broadway (⇨ *Chapter 20, Performing Arts*). Although people think of Broadway as the heart of the theater scene, few theaters actually line the thoroughfare. For some of the grandes dames, head west on 45th Street. There are several Broadway beauties here, including the **Booth**, the **Schoenfeld**, the **Jacobs**, the **Music Box**, and the **Imperial**. On the southern side of 45th Street there's the pedestrians-only **Shubert Alley**, distinguished by colorful posters advertising the latest hit plays and musicals, and the **Shubert Theatre**, one of Broadway's most lustrous gems. Head west along 44th Street to see the **Helen Hayes**, the **Broadhurst**, the **Majestic**, and the **St. James**.

You might be surprised to learn that Chelsea is not the only gallery hub in the city; 57th Street between 5th and 6th Avenues is home to some of the city's most prestigious galleries. There's also the International Center of Photography just minutes from Times Square at 43rd Street.

TOP ATTRACTIONS

FAMILY **Bryant Park.** This lovely green space nestled among landmarks and skyscrapers is one of Manhattan's most popular parks. Tall London plane trees line the perimeter of the sunny central lawn, overlooking stone terraces, formal flower beds, gravel pathways, and a smattering of kiosks selling everything from sandwiches to egg creams (in season). The garden tables scattered about fill with lunching office workers and folks enjoying the park's free Wi-Fi (signs show you how to log on). In summer you can check out free live jazz and "Broadway in Bryant Park" musical theater performances, as well as author readings. Most popular of all is the Summer Film Festival: locals leave work early to snag a spot on the lawn for the outdoor screenings each Monday at dusk. At the east side of the park, near a squatting bronze cast of Gertrude Stein, is the stylish Bryant Park Grill, which has a rooftop garden, and the adjacent open-air Bryant Park Café, open seasonally. The 5th Avenue terrace is home to a different food truck at lunchtime every day during the week. On the south side of the park is an old-fashioned **carousel** (🎠 $2) where kids can ride fanciful rabbits and frogs instead of horses, and attend storytellings and magic shows. Big kids can play with the park's selection of lawn and tabletop games, which includes everything from Quoits and Scrabble to Chinese Checkers and Scandinavian Kubb. Come November the park rolls out the artificial frozen **"pond"** (🕙 *Nov.–Mar., Sun–Thurs. 8 am–10 pm, Fri. and Sat. 8 am–midnight* 🎿 *Skate rental $15*) for ice skating. Surrounding the ice rink are the Christmas market–like stalls of the **Holiday Shops,** selling handcrafted goods and local foods. ✉ *6th Ave. between 40th and 42nd Sts., Midtown West* ☎ *212/768–4242* ⊕ *www.bryantpark.org* 🕙 *Vendor hrs vary by month. See website for exact times.* Ⓜ *B, D, F, M to 42nd St.–Bryant Park; 7 to 5th Ave.*

FAMILY *Intrepid* **Sea, Air & Space Museum.** The centerpiece of the *Intrepid* Sea, Air & Space Museum complex is the 900-foot *Intrepid* aircraft carrier, Manhattan's only floating museum. The carrier's most trying moment of service, the day it was attacked in World War II by kamikaze pilots, is recounted in a multimedia presentation. The museum faced its own trying period when forced to close for several months due to extensive flooding after 2012's Superstorm Sandy. Fortunately, the *Intrepid*'s unparalleled collection of aircraft was not damaged in the storm. The museum reopened in late December 2012 with a reinforced home for the space shuttle *Enterprise,* NASA's first prototype orbiter which joined the Intrepid in July 2012. *Enterprise* is temporarily housed in a climate-controlled bubble tent on the flight deck of the *Intrepid,* but visitors can check out plans for what will eventually be its permanent home, on the interactive wall outside the Space Shuttle Pavilion. While *Enterprise* never flew in space, it is presented in a dramatic darkened display with blue lighting to evoke the atmosphere of flight. Images and displays share the shuttle's history and that of NASA's 30-year space shuttle program.

Docked alongside the *Intrepid,* and also part of the museum, is the *Growler,* a strategic-missile submarine. The interactive Exploreum contains 18 hands-on exhibits. You can experience a flight simulator, transmit messages in Morse code, and see what it was like to live aboard the massive carrier. Ticket booths and gift shops have been relocated to the museum's plaza while the visitor Welcome Center is being rebuilt. ■TIP➔ There are frequent ticket discounts if you purchase through the museum website. ✉ *Pier 86, W. 46th St. and 12th Ave., Midtown West* ☎ *212/245–0072, 877/957–7447* ⊕ *www. intrepidmuseum.org* ✑ *$22; $29 combo Space Shuttle and general admission* ☉ *Apr.–Oct., weekdays 10–5, weekends 10–6; Nov.–Mar., daily 10–5; last admission 1 hr before closing* Ⓜ *A, C, E to 42nd St.– Port Authority; M42 bus to pier.*

Radio City Music Hall. *See the listing in Chapter 20: Performing Arts.*

Rockefeller Center. If Times Square is New York's crossroads, Rockefeller Center is its communal gathering place, where the entire world converges to snap pictures, skate on the ice rink, peek in on a taping of the *Today* show, shop, eat, and take in the monumental art deco structures and public sculptures from the past century. Totaling more than 75 shops and 45 eateries (including Thomas Keller's Bouchon Bakery), the complex runs from 47th to 52nd streets between 5th and 7th avenues. Special events and huge pieces of art dominate the central plazas in spring and summer. In December an enormous twinkling tree towers above the ice-skating rink, causing huge crowds of visitors from across the country and the globe to shuffle through with necks craned and cameras flashing. The first official tree-lighting ceremony was held in 1933.

The world's most famous ice-skating rink *(⇨ see the Rink at Rockefeller Center)* occupies Rockefeller Center's sunken lower plaza October through April and converts to a café in summer. The gold-leaf statue of the fire-stealing Greek hero **Prometheus**—Rockefeller Center's most famous sculpture—hovers above, forming the backdrop to zillions of photos. Carved into the wall behind it, a quotation from Aeschylus reads "Prometheus, teacher in every art, brought the fire that hath proved to mortals a means to mighty ends." ■TIP➔ The lower plaza also provides access to the marble-lined corridors underneath Rockefeller Center, which house restaurants, a post office, and clean public restrooms—a rarity in Midtown.

Rising up on the Lower Plaza's west side is the 70-story (850-foot-tall) art deco **GE Building**, a testament to modern urban development. Here Rockefeller commissioned and then destroyed a mural by Diego Rivera upon learning that it featured Vladimir Lenin. He replaced it with the monumental *American Progress* by José María Sert, still on view in the lobby, flanked by additional murals by Sert and English artist Frank Brangwyn. While in the lobby, pick up a free "Rockefeller Center Visitor's Guide" at the **information desk.** Up on the 65th floor sits the now-shuttered city icon and Landmark Rainbow Room, a glittering big-band ballroom from 1934 through 2009. Higher up, Top of the Rock *(⇨ Top of the Rock)* offers what many consider the finest panoramic views of the city. ✉ *30 Rockefeller Plaza* ⊕ *www. rockefellercenter.com.*

The iconic marquee at Radio City Music Hall

FAMILY **The Rink at Rockefeller Center.** Set in the shadow of the giant Rockefeller Center Christmas Tree, the city's most iconic ice-skating rink is a quintessential experience for visitors and a long-standing tradition for many locals. Skaters swoop or stumble across the ice while crowds gather at street level to watch the spins and spills. General admission skating is on a first-come, first-serve basis so it is best to come early, and on weekdays, to avoid crowds. First Skate tickets (reserved online) allow 7 am access to the rink, followed by a complimentary hot chocolate/coffee and pastry. VIP Skate packages ($50–$105) allow guests to skate past the long lines to complimentary skate rental, 90 minutes of ice time, and hot chocolate and cookies. Other packages include Sky Skate ($40), which includes admission to the rink, skate rental, and admission to the Top of the Rock Observation Deck, and Engagement on Ice packages ($350–$1,000), which provide exclusive ice time, a romantic backdrop, and a variety of romantic add-ons to seal the deal. The rink is a café in summer. ⊠ *30 Rockefeller Center* ⊕ *www.therinkatrockcenter.com* ⊠ *$27, $12 skate rental* ⊙ *Daily 8:30 am–midnight.*

Times Square. Hands down, this is the most frenetic part of New York City, a cacophony of flashing lights and shoulder-to-shoulder crowds that many New Yorkers studiously avoid. Originally named after the *New York Times* (whose headquarters have relocated nearby), the area has seen many changes since the first subway line, which included a 42nd street station, opened in 1904. You won't find speakeasies and unsavory clubs around here nowadays: it's more of a vibrant, family friendly destination, with a pedestrianized stretch of Broadway and stadium seating behind discount theater ticket–seller TKTS, all under the glare of brand names like MTV and M&Ms. If you like sensory overload, the chaotic mix of huge underwear billboards, flashing digital displays, on-location television broadcasts, naked cowboys, and Elmo clones will give you your fix. The focus of the entertainment may have shifted over the years, but showtime is still the heart of New York's theater scene and there are forty Broadway theaters nearby. ✉ *Broadway between 42nd and 44th Sts., Midtown West* ☎ *212/768–1560* ⊕ *www.timessquarenyc.org* Ⓜ *1, 2, 3, 7, N, Q, R, S to Times Square–42 St.*

Times Square Visitor Center. After its $1.8 million renovation, this visitor center is the place to take shelter when the crowds start to overwhelm you. Unlike its gaudy, flashy neighbors, the center is housed in an elegant, theater-like space with brass doors, marble accents, framed art, chandeliers, and wood paneling. The space is theater-like for a reason; Times Square Visitor Center was once the high-end Embassy Theater, opened in 1925 by Loews. As well as a rare glimpse of the Times Square of old (really old), you'll find a past New Year's Eve ball and a New Year's Eve "Wishing Wall," where you can write on confetti that will become one of the actual pieces to flutter down at midnight on January 1. You can also watch a video on Times Square's unsavory past in a mock-peep booth. Stop by for multilingual kiosks, Metro-Cards, a peek in the gift shop, sightseeing and theater tickets, and free (clean!) restrooms. The center partners with Manhattan Walking Tours to offer a 90-minute walking tour of the area—the Broadway Walking tour (☉ *Daily at 9:30, 11:30, 2* ⊕ *www.walkinbroadway.com*). ✉ *1560 Broadway (entrance on 7th Ave.), between 46th and 47th Sts., Midtown West* ☎ *212/768–1560* ⊕ *www.timessquarenyc.org* ✉ *Walking tours, $25* ☉ *Daily 8–8. Tours leave daily at 9:45, 11, 12:30, 1:45, 3, and 4:45* Ⓜ *1, 2, 3, 7, N, Q, R, S to 42nd St./Times Sq.*

Fodor's Choice ★ **Top of the Rock.** Rockefeller Center's multifloor observation deck, the Top of the Rock, on the 69th–70th floors of the building, provides views that rival those from the Empire State Building—some would say they're even better because the views include the Empire State Building. Arriving just before sunset affords a view of the city that morphs before your eyes into a dazzling wash of colors, with a bird's-eye view of the tops of the Empire State Building, the Citicorp Building, and the Chrysler Building, and sweeping views northward to Central Park and south to the Statue of Liberty. Reserved-time ticketing eliminates long lines. Indoor exhibits include films of Rockefeller Center's history and a model of the building. Especially interesting is a Plexiglas screen on the floor with footage showing Rock Center construction workers dangling on beams high above the streets; the brave can even "walk" across a beam to get a sense of what it might have been like to erect this skyscraper. A Sun & Stars ticket ($40) allows you to visit twice and see the city as it rises and sets in the same day. ✉ *30 Rockefeller Plaza (entrance on 50th St. between 5th and 6th Aves.), Midtown West* ☎ *212/698–2000, 212/698–2000* ⊕ *www.topoftherocknyc.com* ✉ *$27* ☉ *Daily 8–midnight (last elevator at 11 pm)* Ⓜ *B, D, F, M to 47th–50th Sts./Rockefeller Center.*

Ice-skating under the sculpture of Prometheus, at Rockefeller Center, is a winter ritual for many local and visiting families.

WORTH NOTING

Christie's. One of the first items to be sold at the New York outpost of this infamous auction house, when it opened in 2000, was the "Happy Birthday" dress worn by Marilyn Monroe when she sang to President Kennedy (it sold for more than $1.2 million, in case you were wondering). Yes, the auction house has come a long way since James Christie launched his business in England by selling two chamber pots, among other household goods, in 1766. The lobby's specially commissioned abstract Sol Lewitt mural alone makes it worth visiting the 310,000-square-foot space, but you can also participate in Christie's auctions via live online video. ⊠ *20 Rockefeller Plaza, 49th St. between 5th and 6th Aves., Midtown West* ☎ *212/636–2000* ⊕ *www.christies. com* ☉ *Weekdays 9:30–5, weekend hrs vary; hrs vary for specific exhibits* Ⓜ *B, D, F, M to 47th–50th Sts./Rockefeller Center.*

David Findlay Jr. Gallery. This well-established gallery exhibits work by contemporary and 20th-century American artists from Whistler to Herman Cherry, Byron Brown, and David Aronson, and specializes in the New York School. ⊠ *724 5th Ave., 8th fl., Midtown West* ☎ *212/486–7660* ⊕ *www.davidfindlayjr.com* ☉ *Mon.–Sat. 10–5:30* Ⓜ *N, R to 5th Ave.*

Hirschl & Adler Gallery. Although this gallery has a selection of European works, it's best known for American paintings, prints, and decorative arts. The celebrated 19th- and 20th-century artists whose works are featured include Stuart Davis, Childe Hassam, Camille Pissarro, and John Singleton Copley. ⊠ *730 5th Ave., at 57th St., 4th fl., Midtown West* ☎ *212/535–8810* ⊕ *www.hirschlandadler.com* ☉ *Tues.–Fri. 9:30–5:15, Sat. 9:30–4:45* Ⓜ *N, R to 5th Ave. St./Hunter College.*

International Center of Photography. Founded in 1974 by photojournalist Cornell Capa (photographer Robert Capa's brother), this top-notch photography museum and school has a collection of over 150,000 original prints spanning the history of photography from daguerreotypes to large-scale pigment prints. Changing exhibits display work by famous and should-be-famous photographers, while themed group shows focus on topics such as ecology, health, religion, science, war, and candid street shots. The gift shop has amazing imagery on postcards, posters, and prints, and outstanding photography books. ⊠ *1133 Ave. of the Americas, at 43rd St., Midtown West* ☎ *212/857–0000* ⊕ *www.icp. org* ⊠ *$14* ☉ *Tues.–Thurs. and weekends 10–6, Fri. 10–8* Ⓜ *B, D, F, M to 42nd St.*

Madame Tussaud's New York. Sit in the Oval Office with President Obama, sing along with Lady Gaga, pose with your favorite heartthrob—be it Justin Bieber or Justin Timberlake, or enjoy a royal chat with the Duke and Duchess of Cambridge, William and Kate. Much of the fun here comes from the photo opportunities—you're encouraged to pose with and touch the nearly 200 realistic replicas of the famous, the infamous, and the downright super. The new Marvel 4D Experience includes wax likenesses of heroes like The Hulk, Captain America, Ironman, and Thor, as well as a short animated movie shown on a 360-degree screen that surrounds the viewer. Other interactive options at the museum include a karaoke café, a celebrity walk down the red carpet, and a haunted town populated with both wax figures and real people. ■TIP→ Closing hours can vary during peak seasons so call ahead to verify. ⊠ *234 W. 42nd St., between 7th and 8th Aves., Midtown West* ☎ *866/841–3505* ⊕ *www.madame-tussauds.com* ⊠ *$36 (discounts available online)* ☉ *Sun.–Thurs. 10–8, Fri. and Sat. 10–10* Ⓜ *1, 2, 3, 7, A, C, E, N, Q, R, S to 42nd St.*

Marian Goodman Gallery. Perhaps the most respected contemporary art dealer in town, the Marian Goodman Gallery has been introducing top European artists to American audiences for over thirty years. The stable of excellent contemporary artists here includes Gerhard Richter, Jeff Wall, William Kentridge, Thomas Schutte, and Steve McQueen. ⊠ *24 W. 57th St., between 5th and 6th Aves., Midtown West* ☎ *212/977–7160* ⊕ *www.mariangoodman.com* ☉ *Mon.–Sat. 10–6* Ⓜ *F to 57th St.*

Marlborough Gallery (Midtown). The Marlborough gallery has an international reputation, representing modern artists such as Magdalena Abakanowicz, Zao Wou-Ki, Red Grooms, and photorealist Richard Estes. Look for sculptures by Tom Otterness—his whimsical bronzes are found in several subway stations. There is also a branch in Chelsea. ⊠ *40 W. 57th St., between 5th and 6th Aves., Midtown West* ☎ *212/541–4900* ⊕ *www.marlboroughgallery.com* ☉ *Mon.–Sat. 10–5:30* Ⓜ *F to 57th St.*

New York Public Library (NYPL) Main Branch: Stephen A. Schwarzman Building. In 2011 the "Library with the Lions" celebrated its centennial as a masterpiece of Beaux Arts design and one of the great research institutions in the world, with more than 6 million books, 12 million manuscripts, and 3 million pictures. The party ended in 2012 when the board

Art in Rockefeller Center

The mosaics, murals, and sculptures that grace Rockefeller Center—many of them Art Deco masterpieces—were all part of John D. Rockefeller Jr.'s plans. In 1932, as the steel girders on the first of the buildings were heading heavenward, Rockefeller put together a team of advisers to find artists who could make the project "as beautiful as possible." More than 50 artists were commissioned for 200 individual works.

Some artists scoffed at the idea of decorating an office building: Picasso declined to meet with Rockefeller, and Matisse replied that busy businessmen wouldn't be in the "quiet and reflective state of mind" needed to appreciate his art. Those who agreed to contribute, including muralists Diego Rivera and José María Sert, were relatively unknown, though a group of American artists protested Rockefeller's decision to hire "alien" artists.

As Rockefeller Center neared completion in 1932, Rockefeller still needed a mural for the lobby of the main building and he wanted the subject of the 63-by-17-foot mural to be grandiose: "human intelligence in control of the forces of nature." He hired Rivera.

With its depiction of massive machinery moving mankind forward, Rivera's *Man at the Crossroads* seemed exactly what Rockefeller wanted—until it was realized that a portrait of Soviet Premier Vladimir Lenin surrounded by red-kerchiefed workers occupied a space in the center. Rockefeller, who was building what was essentially a monument to capitalism, was less than thrilled. When Rivera was accused of propagandizing, he famously replied, "All art is propaganda."

Rivera refused to remove the offending portrait and, in early 1934, as Rivera was working, representatives for Rockefeller informed him that his services were no longer required. Within a half hour, tar paper had been hung over the mural. Despite negotiations to move it to the Museum of Modern Art, Rockefeller was determined to get rid of the mural once and for all. Not content to have it painted over, he ordered ax-wielding workers to chip away the entire wall.

Rockefeller ordered the mural replaced by a less offensive one by Sert. Rivera did have the last word: he re-created the mural in the Palacio de Bellas Artes in Mexico City, adding a portrait of Rockefeller among the champagne-swilling swells ignoring the plight of the workers.

The largest of the original artworks that remained is Lee Lawrie's two-ton sculpture, *Atlas.* Its building also stirred controversy, as it was said to resemble Italy's fascist dictator, Benito Mussolini. The sculpture, depicting a muscle-bound man holding up the world, drew protests in 1936. Some even derided Paul Manship's golden *Prometheus,* which soars over the ice-skating rink, when it was unveiled the same year. Both are now considered to be among the best public artworks of the 20th century.

Lawrie's sculpture *Wisdom,* perched over the main entrance of 20 Rockefeller Plaza, is another gem. Also look for Isamu Noguchi's stainless-steel plaque *News* over the entrance of the Bank of America Building at 50 Rockefeller Plaza and Attilio Piccirilli's 2-ton glass-block panel called *Youth Leading Industry* over the entrance of the International Building.

9

THE MUSEUM OF MODERN ART (MOMA)

⊠ *11 W. 53rd St., between 5th and 6th Aves., Midtown West* ☎ *212/708-9400* ⊕ *www.moma.org* ⌨ *$25* ⊙ *Sat.–Thurs. 10:30–5:30, Fri. 10:30–8* Ⓜ *E, M to 5th Ave./53rd St.; B, D, F, M to 47th–50th Sts./Rockefeller Center.*

TIPS

■ MoMa's new Audio+ app is free and allows visitors to listen to commentaries for selected artworks, and to access, share, and save additional content. Audio+-enabled iPods can be rented at the museum or downloaded the app from MoMA's website. Wi-Fi is free, too.

■ MoMA also has three movie theaters; passes to the day's screenings are included with admission.

■ Tickets to MoMA include free admission to its affiliated PS1 in Queens. Save your ticket and you can go in for free any time within 30 days of your original purchase.

■ Grab a quick bite at one of MoMA's two cafés—Cafe 2 and Terrace 5, or dine leisurely at the upscale Modern. In summer there is gelato in the Sculpture Garden.

Art enthusiasts and novices alike are often awestruck by the masterpieces here, including Picasso's *Les Demoiselles d'Avignon* and van Gogh's *The Starry Night.* In 2004, the museum's $425 million facelift by Yoshio Taniguchi increased exhibition space by nearly 50%, including space to accommodate large-scale installations. The museum continues to collect: most recently it obtained a collection of Occupy Wall Street screenprints. In 2013, the museum inspired heady debate as to what constitutes art when it acquired a selection of video games and consoles and created a new category in MoMA's collection. One of the top research facilities in modern and contemporary art is housed inside the museum's eight-story Education and Research building. Note the gallery housing Monet's *Water Lilies* triptych is closed for renovations as of spring 2014.

Highlights

In addition to the art, one of the main draws of MoMA is the building itself. A maze of glass walkways permits art viewing from many angles.

The 110-foot atrium entrance (accessed from the museum's lobby on either 53rd or 54th Street) leads to the movie theaters and the main-floor restaurant, Modern, with Alsatian-inspired cuisine.

A favorite resting spot is the Abby Aldrich Rockefeller Sculpture Garden. Designed by Philip Johnson, it features Barnett Newman's *Broken Obelisk* (1962–69). The glass wall lets visitors look into the surrounding galleries from the garden, where there's also a reflecting pool and trees.

Contemporary art (1970 to the present) from the museum's seven curatorial departments shares the second floor of the six-story building, and the skylighted top floor showcases an impressive lineup of changing exhibits.

of this National Historic Landmark approved a controversial $300 million plan to convert the 5th Avenue flagship into the world's largest combined research and circulating library—a plan that will create two floors of storage space under adjacent **Bryant Park**, create additional public space and computer terminals, and eventually fold two other Manhattan branches under its roof. The plan met with much debate, discussion, and a few lawsuits so the board and its design team are reevaluating options and revisiting the design. When and if construction commences on the project, the library will close for two years, so enjoy the beautiful architecture and

peaceful escape from Midtown's bustle while you can—check the website for details. The marble staircase at the library's grand 5th Avenue entrance is an excellent perch for people-watching, before or after you explore the opulent interior.

The library's bronze front doors open into **Astor Hall,** which leads to several special exhibit galleries and, to the left, a stunning periodicals room with wall paintings of New York publishing houses. Ascend the sweeping double staircase to a second-floor balconied corridor overlooking the hall, with panels highlighting the library's development. Make sure to continue up to the magisterial **Rose Main Reading Room**—297 feet long (almost two full north–south city blocks), 78 feet wide, and just over 51 feet high; walk through to best appreciate the rows of oak tables and the extraordinary ceiling. Several additional third-floor galleries show rotating exhibits on print and photography (past exhibits have included old New York restaurant menus and a 1455 Gutenberg Bible). Free one-hour tours leave Monday–Saturday at 11 and 2, and Sunday at 2 from Astor Hall. Women's bathrooms are on the ground floor and third floor, and there's a men's bathroom on the third floor. ⊠ *5th Ave., between 40th and 42nd Sts., Midtown West* ☎ *212/930–0800 for exhibit information* ⊕ *www.nypl.org* ☉ *Mon. and Thurs.–Sat. 10–6, Sun. 1–5, Tues. and Wed. 10–8; exhibitions until 6* Ⓜ *B, D, F, M to 42nd St.; 7 to 5th Ave.*

The New York Times Building. This 52-story building with its distinctive, ladderlike ceramic rods is a testament to clean-lined modernism. The architect, Renzo Piano, extended the ceramic rods beyond the top of the building so that it would give the impression of dissolving into the sky. One of the skyscraper's best features—and the one that's open to the public—is the building's lobby atrium, which includes an open-air moss garden with 50-foot paper birch trees and a wooden footbridge, a 560-screen media art installation titled *Moveable Type* streaming a mix of the newspaper's near-real time and archival content, and a flagship store by minimalist home goods designer MUJI. You never know which famous journalists you'll spy on the coffee line in Dean & DeLuca. Unfortunately, tours are not offered. ✉ *620 8th Ave., between 40th and 41st Sts., Midtown West* 🕾 *212/984–8128* ⊕ *www. newyorktimesbuilding.com* Ⓜ *A, C, E to 42nd St.; 1, 2, 3, 7, N, Q, R, S to 42nd St./Times Sq.*

The Paley Center for Media. With three galleries of photographs and artifacts that document the history of broadcasting, a computerized catalog of more than 150,000 television and radio programs, and public seminars, lectures, and programs, the Paley Center for Media examines the past and constantly-evolving present state of media. The past is the main draw here. If you want to see a performance of "Turkey Lurkey Time" from the 1969 Tony Awards, for example, type the name of the song, show, or performer into a computer terminal, then proceed to one of the semiprivate screening areas to watch your selection. People nearby might be watching classic comedies from the '50s, miniseries from the '70s, or news broadcasts from the '90s. Possibly the most entertaining part of these TV shows from yesteryear is the fact that the original commercials are still embedded in many of the programs; if ads are your thing you can also skip the programming altogether and watch compilations of classic commercials. ✉ *25 W. 52nd St., between 5th and 6th Aves., Midtown West* 🕾 *212/621–6800* ⊕ *www.paleycenter.org* 🖾 *$10* ☉ *Wed., Fri., and weekends noon–6, Thurs. noon–8* Ⓜ *E, M to 5th Ave./53rd St.; B, D, F, V to 47th–50th Sts./Rockefeller Center.*

Spanierman Gallery. This venerable gallery deals in 19th- and early-20th-century American painting and sculpture. Their inventory list and scholarship is amazing, and they frequently sell to museums looking to broaden their own collections. Just down the block at 53 East 58th St., Spanierman Modern (⊕ *www.spaniermanmodern.com*) represents contemporary artists such as Judith Godwin and Frank Bowling. ✉ *625 W. 55th St., between 11th and 12th Aves., Midtown West* 🕾 *212/832–0208* ⊕ *www.spanierman.com* ☉ *Weekdays 9:30–5:30* Ⓜ *N, Q, R to 57th St.*

Tibor de Nagy Gallery. Founded in 1950, this gallery shows works by 20th-century artists such as Biala, Nell Blaine, Jane Freilicher, and Shirley Jaffe. Instrumental in bringing many of America's finest abstract expressionist artists to public attention in the mid-20th century, the gallery now shows abstract and realistic work. ✉ *724 5th Ave., 12th fl., between 56th and 57th Sts., Midtown West* 🕾 *212/262–5050* ⊕ *www. tibordenagy.com* ☉ *Tues.–Sat. 10–5:30* Ⓜ *N, R to 5th Ave.*

THE UPPER EAST SIDE

10

GETTING ORIENTED

Upper East Side

El Museo del Barrio
Museum of the City of New York
The Jewish Museum
Cooper-Hewitt National Design Museum
Solomon R. Guggenheim Museum
Neue Galerie New York
Museum Mile
Metropolitan Museum of Art
Peter Findlay Gallery
Acquavella Galleries
Mitchell-Innes & Nash
Lady M Cake Boutique
Leo Castelli
The Carlyle Hotel/ Bemelman's Bar
Joe
Jane Kahan
Whitney Museum of American Art (moving to Meatpacking District in 2015)
Frick Collection
Asia Society and Museum
Museum of American Illustration

Two Little Red Hens
Gracie Mansion
Carl Schurz Park
Roosevelt Island
Sotheby's
Mount Vernon Hotel Museum and Garden

UPPER EAST SIDE

CENTRAL PARK

Fifth Ave
Madison Ave
Park Ave
Lexington Ave
Third Ave
Second Ave
First Ave
York Ave
East End Ave

FDR Dr.
East River
East River
Queensboro Bridge
Roosevelt Island Tram

E. 97th St.
E. 96th St.
E. 95th St.
E. 94th St.
E. 93rd St.
E. 92nd St.
E. 91st St.
E. 90th St.
E. 89th St.
E. 88th St.
E. 87th St.
E. 86th St.
E. 85th St.
E. 84th St.
E. 83rd St.
E. 82nd St.
E. 81st St.
E. 80th St.
E. 79th St.
E. 78th St.
E. 77th St.
E. 76th St.
E. 75th St.
E. 74th St.
E. 73rd St.
E. 72nd St.
E. 71st St.
E. 70th St.
E. 69th St.
E. 68th St.
E. 67th St.
E. 66th St.
E. 65th St.
E. 64th St.
E. 63rd St.
E. 62nd St.
E. 61st St.
E. 60th St.
E. 59th St.
E. 58th St.

M 6
M 4,5,6
M 6
M 6
M F
M N,Q,R
M N,Q,R,4,5,6

0   1/4 mile
0   400 meters

MAKING THE MOST OF YOUR TIME

The Upper East Side lends itself to a surprising variety of simple but distinct itineraries: exploring the landmarks on Museum Mile; languorous gallery grazing; window shopping on Madison Avenue; or bar hopping for just-out-of-college kids on 2nd Avenue. If it's the museums you're after, make sure to plan at least a few hours per museum—with some snack/coffee breaks. There's a lot to see, so we'd advise not more than one museum a day.

The Upper East Side's town houses, boutiques, consignment stores, and hidden gardens are easy to miss unless you take some time to wander. If all that walking wears you out, you can always hit one of the nail salons and indulge in a neighborhood stereotype of the pampered Upper East Sider. A well-deserved post–Museum Mile foot rub and mani/pedi are surprisingly reasonably priced.

GETTING HERE

Take the Lexington Avenue 4 or 5 express trains to 59th or 86th streets. The 6 local train also stops at 59th, 68th, 77th, 86th, and 96th streets. If you're coming from Midtown, the F train will let you out at Lexington Avenue at 63rd Street, where you can transfer to the 4, 5, or 6 after a short walk (and without paying subway fare again). From the Upper West Side, take one of the crosstown buses, the M66, M72, M79, M86, or M96. You can also take the N or R train to 59th Street and Lexington Avenue.

TOP EXPERIENCES

Exploring any of the world-class museums up here—permanent exhibits or temporary shows may guide your interest; make sure to plan a relaxing, restorative lunch, too.

Window-shopping on Madison Avenue

Strolling in Central Park (⇨ see Chapter 11)

Appreciating the views from the cable car on the ride to the recently opened Four Freedoms Park on Roosevelt Island

COFFEE AND QUICK BITES

Joe (Upper East Side). One of the city's best coffee chains, Joe provides the kind of quality caffeine and sweets you'll need to make it up and down museum mile (and maybe even around the park). ⊠ *1045 Lexington Ave., at 1st Ave., Upper East Side* ☏ *212/988–2500.*

Lady M Cake Boutique. You don't know it yet but you're here for the signature Mille Crêpes cake. Twenty crêpes stacked together with a delicious cream filling. Don't fight it! ⊠ *41 E. 78th St., at Madison Ave., Upper East Side* ☏ *212/452–2222.*

Two Little Red Hens. With first-rate joe and delicious cupcakes, cheesecake, and cookies to match, it's no wonder this busy little bakery is a legend with locals. ⊠ *1652 2nd Ave., at 86th St., Upper East Side* ☏ *212/452–0476.*

10

To many New Yorkers the Upper East Side connotes old money and high society—alongside Central Park, between 5th and Lexington avenues, up to East 96th Street, the trappings of wealth are everywhere apparent: posh buildings, Madison Avenue's flagship boutiques, and doormen in braided livery. It's also a key destination for visitors because some of the most fantastic museums in the country are here.

Updated
by Jacinta
O'Halloran

Although a glance up and down the manicured grass meridian of Park Avenue may conjure scenes from *Bonfire of the Vanities* or *Gossip Girl*, there's more than palatial apartments, elite private schools, and highfalutin clubs up here—starting with fantastic museums. The **Metropolitan Museum of Art**, the **Solomon R. Guggenheim Museum**, the **Whitney Museum** (until spring 2015 when it moves downtown), and many others lie on and around "Museum Mile," as do a number of art galleries. For a local taste of the luxe life, hit up Madison Avenue for its lavish boutiques; strolling this platinum-card corridor between East 60th and East 82nd street is like stepping into the pages of a glossy magazine. Many fashion houses have their flagships here and showcase their lush threads in exquisite settings. Compared with the megastores of Midtown, Madison Avenue feels quieter; it's significantly less crowded and more conducive to leisurely shopping (window or otherwise). Beyond clothing, the boutiques here carry baubles to satisfy anyone's champagne wishes, whether it's a box of truffles at **La Maison du Chocolat** or an intriguing read at **Crawford Doyle Booksellers.**

Venture east of Lexington Avenue and you encounter a less wealthy—and more diverse—Upper East Side, one inhabited by couples seeking some of the last (relatively) affordable places to raise a family south of 100th Street, and recent college grads getting a foothold in the city (on weekend nights 2nd Avenue resembles a miles-long fraternity and sorority reunion). One neighborhood particularly worth exploring is northeast-lying Yorkville, especially between 78th and 86th streets east of 2nd Avenue. Once a remote hamlet with a large German population, its several remaining ethnic food shops, 19th-century row houses, and—one of the city's best-kept secrets—**Carl Schurz Park,** make for a good half-day's exploration, as does touring the most striking residence there, **Gracie Mansion.**

If art galleries are your thing, there are some elegant places to visit on the Upper East Side. In keeping with the tony surroundings, the emphasis here is on works by established masters rather than up-and-coming (or even still-living) artists. Their locations are eminent as well: large townhouses and upper stories in and around Madison and 5th avenues. Note that galleries often have limited hours, so make sure to check in advance.

TOP ATTRACTIONS

Asia Society and Museum. The Asian art collection of Mr. and Mrs. John D. Rockefeller III forms the core of this museum's holdings, which include South Asian stone and bronze sculptures; art from India, Nepal, Pakistan, and Afghanistan; bronze vessels, ceramics, sculpture, and paintings from China; Korean ceramics; and paintings, wooden sculptures, and ceramics from Japan. Founded in 1956, the society has a regular program of lectures, films, and performances, in addition to changing exhibitions of traditional and contemporary art. Trees grow in the glass-enclosed, skylit Garden Court Café, which serves an eclectic Asian menu for lunch and dinner. ■TIP➔ Admission is free on Friday from 6 to 9 (September to July). ✉ *725 Park Ave., at 70th St., Upper East Side* ☎ *212/288–6400* ⊕ *www.asiasociety.org* ✉ *$12* ⊗ *Tues.–Sun. 11–6 (Fri. until 9 from Labor Day to July 1)* Ⓜ *6 to 68th St./Hunter College.*

Cooper-Hewitt, National Design Museum, Smithsonian Institution. The Cooper-Hewitt is closed while undergoing renovations that will increase the museum's exhibition space by 60% while also enhancing visitor interactivity and accessibility. The new and improved Cooper-Hewitt is scheduled to reopen in fall 2014. In the meantime the museum is staging exhibitions around the city; check the website for more information. ✉ *2 E. 91st St., at 5th Ave., Upper East Side* ☎ *212/849–1549* ⊕ *www. cooperhewitt.org* Ⓜ *4, 5, 6 to 86th St.*

El Museo del Barrio. *El barrio* is Spanish for "the neighborhood" and the nickname for East Harlem, a largely Spanish-speaking Puerto Rican and Dominican community. El Museo del Barrio, on the edge of this neighborhood, focuses on Latin American and Caribbean art, with some ten percent of its collection concentrated on works by self-taught artists from New York, Puerto Rico, the Caribbean, and Latin America. The more than 6,500-object permanent collection includes over 400 pre-Columbian artifacts, sculpture, photography, film and video, and traditional art from all over Latin America. The collection of 360 *santos,* carved wooden folk-art figures from Puerto Rico, is popular. El Museo hosts performances, lectures, films, and cultural events, including a monthong Dia de los Muertos celebration. ✉ *1230 5th Ave., between 104th and 105th Sts., Upper East Side* ☎ *212/831–7272* ⊕ *www.elmuseo.org* ✉ *$9 suggested donation* ⊗ *Wed.–Sat. 11–6* Ⓜ *6 to 103rd St.*

10

Fodor's Choice
★

Frick Collection. Henry Clay Frick made his fortune amid the soot and smoke of Pittsburgh, where he was a coke (a coal fuel derivative) and steel baron, but this lovely museum, once Frick's private New York residence, is decidedly removed from soot. With an exceptional collection of works from the Renaissance through the late 19th century that includes Édouard Manet's *The Bullfight* (1864), a Chinard portrait bust (1809), three Vermeers, three Rembrandts, works by El Greco, Goya, van Dyck, Hogarth, Degas, and Turner, as well as sculpture, decorative arts, and 18th century French furniture, everything here is a highlight. The Portico Gallery, an enclosed portico along the building's 5th Avenue garden, houses the museum's growing collection of sculpture. An audio guide, available in several languages, is included with admission, as are the year-round temporary exhibits. The tranquil indoor garden court is a magical spot for a rest. Children under 10 are not admitted, and those ages 10–16 with adult only. ⊠ *1 E. 70th St., at 5th Ave., Upper East Side* ☎ *212/288–0700* ⊕ *www.frick.org* ☜ *$20* ⊙ *Tues.–Sat. 10–6, Sun. 11–5* Ⓜ *6 to 68th St./Hunter College.*

Gracie Mansion. The official mayor's residence, Gracie Mansion was built in 1799 by shipping merchant Archibald Gracie, and enlarged in 1966. Tours of the impressive interior—which must be scheduled in advance (by phone or email) and take place at limited hours—guide you through the building's history and its colorful rooms furnished over centuries and packed with American objets d'art. Nine mayors have lived here since it became the official residence in 1942, though Michael Bloomberg broke with tradition and chose to stay in his own 79th Street townhouse during his three terms as mayor. In January 2014, the newly prepped, polished, and spruced up mansion became home to newly elected Mayor Bill de Blasio and his family. Mayor de Blasio is the first mayor to live in Gracie Mansion since Mayor Rudolph W. Giuliani. De Blasio's predecessor, Mayor Michael Bloomberg, poured millions into renovations at Gracie Mansion without spending a single night there. ⊠ *Carl Schurz Park, East End Ave. at 88th St., Upper East Side* ☎ *212/570–4778* ✉ *gracietours@cityhall.nyc.gov* ☜ *$7* ⊙ *45-min guided tours Wed. 10–2* Ⓜ *4, 5, 6 to 86th St.*

The Jewish Museum. In a Gothic-style 1908 mansion, the Jewish Museum draws on a large collection of art and ceremonial objects to explore Jewish identity and culture spanning more than 4,000 years. The two-floor permanent exhibition *Culture and Continuity: The Jewish Journey* displays nearly 800 objects complemented by interactive media. The wide-ranging collection includes a 3rd-century Roman burial plaque, 20th-century sculpture by Elie Nadelman, and contemporary art from artists such as Marc Chagall and Man Ray. ■**TIP➔ Admission to the museum is free on Saturday and pay-what-you-wish on Thursday 5–8.** ⊠ *1109 5th Ave., at 92nd St., Upper East Side* ☎ *212/423–3200* ⊕ *www.jewishmuseum.org* ☜ *$15* ⊙ *Fri. 11–4, Sat.–Tues. 11–5:45, Thurs. 11–8; closed Fri. mid-Mar.–Oct.* Ⓜ *6 to 96th St.*

Fodor's Choice
★

Metropolitan Museum of Art. *See highlighted listing in this chapter.*

SOLOMON R. GUGGENHEIM MUSEUM

✉ *1071 5th Ave., between 88th and 89th Sts., Upper East Side* ☎ *212/423–3840* ⊕ *www.guggenheim.org* 💲 *$22* ⏱ *Sun.–Wed. 10–5:45, Fri. 10–5:45, Sat. 10–7:45* Ⓜ *4, 5, 6 to 86th St.*

TIPS

■ The museum's free app (download to your own device or borrow one from the desk next to Admissions) provides an enhanced visit before, during, and after your time in the museum. Features include detailed floor maps, multimedia guides to exhibits, interviews with artists, and access to the permanent collection.

■ The museum often runs special programs—including lectures, conversations, and film screenings—in conjunction with major exhibitions. Check the museum's website for details of upcoming events.

■ Take it from the top: Escape the crowded lobby and keep your legs fresh for the rest of the museum by taking the elevator to the top and working your way down the spiral.

■ The museum is pay-what-you-wish Saturday from 5:45 to 7:45. Lines can be long, so arrive early. The last tickets are handed out at 7:15.

■ Eat before you visit; restaurants on Lexington Avenue offer more varied fare than the museum's small Café 3 espresso and snack bar on the third floor.

Frank Lloyd Wright's landmark nautilus-like museum building is renowned as much for its famous architecture as for its superlative collection of art and its well-curated shows. Opened in 1959, shortly after Wright's death, the Guggenheim is acclaimed as one of the greatest buildings of the 20th century. Inside, under a 96-foot-high glass dome, a ramp spirals down past the artworks of the current exhibits (the ramp is just over a quarter mile long, if you're wondering). The museum has strong holdings of Wassily Kandinsky, Paul Klee, Marc Chagall, Pablo Picasso, and Robert Mapplethorpe.

Highlights

Wright's design was criticized by some who believed that the distinctive building detracted from the art within, but the interior nautilus design allows artworks to be viewed from several different angles and distances. Be sure to notice not only what's in front of you but also what's across the spiral from you.

Even if you aren't planning to eat, stop at the museum's modern American restaurant, the Wright, for its stunning design created by Andre Kikoski.

On permanent display, the museum's Thannhauser Collection is made up primarily of works by French Impressionists and Postimpressionists Van Gogh, Toulouse-Lautrec, Cézanne, Renoir, and Manet. Perhaps more than any other 20th-century painter, Wassily Kandinsky, one of the first "pure" abstract artists, has been closely linked to the museum's history: beginning with the acquisition of his masterpiece *Composition 8* (1923) in 1930, the collection has grown to encompass more than 150 works.

10

WHITNEY MUSEUM OF AMERICAN ART

✉ *945 Madison Ave., at
75th St., Upper East Side*
☎ *212/570–3600 8639*
🌐 *www.whitney.org* 🎫 *$20*
🕐 *Wed., Thurs., and weekends
11–6, Fri. 1–9* Ⓜ *6 to 77th St.*

TIPS

■ After 6 on Friday the price of admission is pay-what-you-wish. On some Fridays the Whitney Live series presents new artists and reinterpretations of American classics. Be forewarned that this combination may result in long lines.

■ The Untitled restaurant in the basement (by Danny Meyer of the Union Square Café), serves updated diner classics; it's open for breakfast and lunch Tuesday through Saturday, and for dinner Thursday through Saturday.

With its bold collection of 20th- and 21st-century contemporary American art, the Whitney presents an eclectic mix drawn from more than 19,000 works in its permanent collection. The museum was originally a gallery in the studio of sculptor and collector Gertrude Vanderbilt Whitney, whose talent and taste were accompanied by the money of two wealthy families. In 1930, after the Met turned down Whitney's offer to donate her collection of 20th-century American art, she established an independent museum in Greenwich Village. The museum moved uptown in 1966, into the minimalist granite building designed by Marcel Breuer and Hamilton Smith. In spring 2015, the Whitney will head downtown again to a new space designed by architect Renzo Piano, situated between the High Line and the Hudson River. The new museum will feature more than 50,000 square feet of state-of-the-art gallery space, as well as 13,000 square feet of outdoor space for installations, performances, and events, and a multiuse theater. Exhibits will continue at the uptown location until late 2014. After the opening of the Whitney's new building, the Metropolitan Museum of Art will present exhibitions and special programs at the Whitney's old location for at least eight years.

Highlights

Start on the fifth floor, where the galleries house rotating exhibitions of postwar and contemporary works from the permanent collection by artists such as Jackson Pollock, Jim Dine, Jasper Johns, Mark Rothko, Chuck Close, Cindy Sherman, and Roy Lichtenstein.

The lower floors feature exhibitions of contemporary artists such as Kara Walker and Gordon Matta-Clark as well as retrospective exhibitions that focus on movements and themes in American art.

Museum of the City of New York. In a Colonial Revival building designed for the museum in the 1930s, the city's history and many quirks are revealed through engaging exhibits here. The museum is currently in the last phase of a three-part, $90 million renovation that will upgrade and modernize the entire facility. Renovations are expected to be complete in mid-to-late 2015. In the meantime, the museum remains open, and rotating exhibits on subjects such as architecture, fashion, history, and politics are still on display. Recent exhibits *City as Canvas: New York City Graffiti* and *Gilded New York* provided contrasting visual accounts of the city—exploring street art in New York City during the 1970s and 80s and the culture of the elite class at the end of the 19th century. Don't miss *Timescapes*, a 25-minute media projection that innovatively illustrates New York's physical expansion and population changes, or *Activist New York*, an ongoing exploration of the city's history of social activism. The museum hosts New York–centric lectures, films, and walking tours. ■**TIP**➔ When you're finished touring the museum, cross the street and stroll through the Vanderbilt Gates to enter the Conservatory Garden, one of Central Park's hidden gems. ✉ *1220 5th Ave., at 103rd St., Upper East Side* ☎ *212/534-1672* ⊕ *www.mcny.org* ✉ *$10 suggested donation* ⊙ *Daily 10–6* Ⓜ *6 to 103rd St.*

Neue Galerie New York. Early-20th-century German and Austrian art and design are the focus here, with works by Gustav Klimt, Wassily Kandinsky, Paul Klee, Egon Schiele, Josef Hoffman, and other designers from the Wiener Werkstätte taking center stage. The Neue Galerie was founded by the late art dealer Serge Sabarsky and cosmetics heir and art collector Ronald S. Lauder. It's situated in a 1914 wood- and marble-floored mansion designed by Carrère and Hastings, which was once home to Mrs. Cornelius Vanderbilt III. An audio guide is included with admission. Note that children under 12 are not admitted, and teens 12–16 must be accompanied by an adult. **Café Sabarsky**, in an elegant, high-ceiling space below the Neue Galerie, is a destination in its own right, for their Viennese coffee, cakes, strudels, and Sacher tortes (⊙ *Mon. and Wed. 9–6, Thurs.–Sun. 9–9*). If you seek something more than a sugar fix, the savory menu includes trout crepes and Hungarian goulash. Café Fledermaus, on the lower level of the museum, offers the same menu as Café Sabarsky. ■**TIP**➔ Admission is free 6–8 on the first Friday of every month. ✉ *1048 5th Ave., at 86th St., Upper East Side* ☎ *212/628-6200* ⊕ *www.neuegalerie.org* ✉ *$20* ⊙ *Thurs.–Mon. 11–6* Ⓜ *4, 5, 6 to 86th St.* ☞ *Children under 12 not admitted.*

WORTH NOTING

Acquavella Galleries. The 19th- and 20th-century museum-quality art shown inside this five-story marble-floored French neo-classical mansion tends to be by the big names, from Impressionists through Pop artists, including Picasso, Lucian Freud, James Rosenquist, and Wayne Thiebaud. ✉ *18 E. 79th St., between 5th and Madison Aves., Upper East Side* ☎ *212/734-6300* ⊕ *www.acquavellagalleries.com* ⊙ *Mon.– Sat. 10–5* Ⓜ *6 to 77th St.*

10

Continued on page 165

Mesmerizing carvings in the ancient Egyptian Temple of Dendur.

THE METROPOLITAN MUSEUM OF ART

If the city held no other museum than the colossal Metropolitan Museum of Art, you could still occupy yourself for days roaming its labyrinthine corridors. Because the Metropolitan Museum has more than 2 million works of art representing 5,000 years of history, you're going to have to make tough choices. Looking at everything here could take a week.

Before you begin exploring the museum, check the museum's floor plan, available at all entrances, for location of the major wings and collections. Google Maps will help you find your way through the museum. The service tracks your location with a blue dot and guides you through exhibits, across floors, and to bathrooms and exits. It can even help you avoid the gift shop if you're visiting with kids!

The posted adult admission, though only a suggestion, is one that's strongly encouraged. Whatever you choose to pay, admission includes all special exhibits and same-day entrance to the Cloisters (see Chapter 12). The Met's audio guide costs an additional $7, and if you intend to stay more than an hour or so, it's worth it. The generally perceptive commentary covers museum highlights and directors' picks, with separate commentary tracks directed at kids.

If you want to avoid the crowds, visit weekday mornings. Also good are Friday and Saturday evenings, when live classical music plays from the Great Hall balcony. If the Great Hall (the main entrance) is mobbed, avoid the chaos by heading to the street-level entrance to the left of the main stairs, near 81st Street. Ticket lines and coat checks are much less ferocious here.

What to see? Check out the museum highlights on the following pages.

⊠ 5th Ave. at 82nd St., Upper East Side

Ⓜ Subway: 4, 5, 6 to 86th St.

☎ 212/535–7710

⊕ www.metmuseum.org

⊠ $25 suggested donation

🕐 Sun.–Thurs. 10–5:30, Fri. and Sat. 10–9

MUSEUM HIGHLIGHTS

Egyptian Art

A major star is the **Temple of Dendur** (circa 15 BC), in a huge atrium to itself and with a moatlike pool of water to represent its original location near the Nile. The temple was commissioned by the Roman emperor Augustus to honor the goddess Isis and the sons of a Nubian chieftain. Look for the scratched-in graffiti from 19th-century Western explorers on the inside. Egypt gave the temple as a gift to the U.S. in 1965; it would have been submerged after the construction of the Aswan High Dam.

The Egyptian collection as a whole covers 4,000 years of history, with papyrus pages from the Egyptian Book of the Dead, stone sarcophagi inscribed with hieroglyphics, and tombs. The galleries should be walked through counterclockwise from the Ancient Kingdom (2650–2150 BC), to the period under Roman rule (30 BC–400 AD). In the latter, keep an eye out for the enormous, bulbous **Sarcophagus of Horkhebil**, sculpted from basalt.

Greek and Roman Art

Today's tabloids have nothing on ancient Greece and Rome. They had it all—sex, cults, drugs, unrelenting violence, and, of course, stunning art. The recently redone Greek and Roman galleries encompass 6,000 works of art that reveal aspects of everyday life in these influential cultures.

The urnlike terracotta kraters were used by the Greeks for mixing wine and water at parties and other events. Given that, it's not surprising that most depict slightly racy scenes. Some of the most impressive can be found in the gallery covering 5th century BC.

On the mezzanine of the Roman galleries, the Etruscan bronze chariot from 650 BC depicts scenes from the life of Achilles. Notice how the simplistic Etruscan style in combination with the Greek influence evolved into the naturalistic Roman statues below.

The frescoes from a bedroom in the Villa of P. Fannius Synistor preserved by the explosion of Mt. Vesuvius in 79 AD give us a glimpse into the stylistic achievement of perspective in Roman painting.

Temple of Dendur

ART TO TAKE HOME

You don't have to pay admission to get to the mammoth gift shop on the first floor. One of the better souvenirs here is also one of the more reasonable: the Met's own **illustrated guide** to 869 of the best items in its collection ($19.95).

Engelhard Court

An artifact from ancient Greece.

SECOND FLOOR

MEZZANINES

Petrie Court Café

Modern Art

Elevator to Roof Garden

The American Wing

The Cafeteria (on ground floor)

European Sculpture and Decorative Arts

Arms and Armor

Arts of Africa, Oceania & Americas

Equestrian Court

Shop

Temple of Dendur

Greek and Roman Art

Access Route

Great Hall

Egyptian Art

FIRST FLOOR

Modern Art

The American Wing

European Painting

19th-Century European Painting and Sculpture

Asian Galleries

Access Route

Eastern Art

Balcony Café

Astor Court

5th Avenue

The American Wing of the Metropolitan Museum of Art.

American Wing

After years of extensive renovations, the Met's revital-ized **New American Wing Galleries for Paintings, Sculpture, and Decorative Arts** reopened in 2012 with 30,000 square feet of skylit space to showcase one of the best and largest collections of American art in the country.

There's much to see, from Colonial furniture to the works of the great masters, including John Singleton Copley, Gilbert Stuart, Thomas Cole, Frederic Edwin Church, Winslow Homer, and Thomas Eakins, among others. The highlight of the new installation is Emanuel Gottlieb Leutze's magnificent 1851 painting, *Washington Crossing the Delaware*. Hung in an immense gilded frame (recreated from an 1864 photograph of the painting), Leutze's iconic work is displayed just as it was at a fundraiser for Union soldiers in 1864—flanked by Frederic Church's *Heart of the Andes* and Albert Bierstadt's *Rocky Mountains*.

Also not to be missed are John Singer Sargent's *Madame X*, a once-scandalous portrait of a Parisian socialite; the recreation of the entrance hall of the 18th Century Van Rensselaer Manor House in Albany, New York; and the collection of portrait miniatures—detailed watercolors to be carried or gifted as tokens of love.

TIME TO EAT? INSIDE THE MUSEUM

The **Petrie Court Café**, at the back of the 1st-floor European Sculpture Court, has waiter service. Prices range from $12 for a sandwich to $21 for organic chicken salad. Afternoon tea is served from 2:30 PM to 4:30 PM during the week. Dinner is served on weekends.

The **Great Hall Balcony Bar** is located on the second floor belcony overlooking the Great Hall. On Fridays and Saturdays, 4 PM TO 8:30 PM waiters serve appetizers and cocktails accompanied by live classical music.

The **cafeteria** on the ground floor has stations for pasta, main courses, antipasti, and sandwiches.

Looking for one of the best views in town? The **Roof Garden** (open May–Oct.) exhibits contemporary sculpture, but most people take the elevator here to have a drink or snack while checking out Central Park and the skyline.

Tiffany

Arms and Armor

The **Equestrian Court**, where the knights are mounted on armored models of horses, is one of the most dramatic rooms in the museum. For a bird's-eye view, check it out again from the balconies in the Musical Instruments collection on the second floor.

European Sculpture and Decorative Arts

Among the many sculptures in the sun-filled Petrie Court, *Ugolino and His Sons* still stands out for the despairing poses of its subjects. Ugolino, a nobleman whose family's tragic story is told in Dante's *Inferno*, was punished for treason by being left to starve to death with his grandsons and sons in a locked tower. (It's not clear if putting such a sculpture so near the Petrie Court's café is some curator's idea of a joke or not.) By the way, the redbrick and granite wall on the court's north side is the museum's original entrance.

The newly renovated Wrightsman Galleries for French Decorative Arts on the first floor displays the opulence that caused Louis the XVI to lose his head. The blindingly golden Boiserie from the Hotel de Cabris, a remnant of French 18th century Neo-classical interiors, represents the finest collection of French decorative arts in the country.

Anna Wintour Costume Center

In May 2014, after a two-year renovation, the Met's Costume Institute reopened with a newly designed 4,200-square-foot main gallery, an updated costume conservation laboratory, expanded study and storage facilities, and a new name—the Anna Wintour Costume Center. Named for the legendary *Vogue* editor-in-chief and Met Trustee (responsible for the annual Met Gala), and housing one of the most comprehensive costume collections in the world, the new Costume Center (northeast end of the museum on the ground floor) is sure to be a huge draw for fashion lovers.

European Paintings

On the second floor, the 13th- to 18th-century paintings are grouped at the top of the Great Hall's stairs.

Recently, the Met spent about $45 million to buy Duccio di Buoninsegna's *Madonna and Child,* painted circa 1300. The last remaining Duccio in private hands, this painting, the size of a piece of typewriter paper, is unimpressive at first glance. The work, though rigid, represents a revolution in Byzantine art. The humanity reflected in the baby Jesus grabbing his mother's veil changed European painting.

TIME TO EAT?
OUTSIDE THE MUSEUM

Because museum admission is good all day, you can always leave for lunch and come back later. A block from the museum, **Caffe Grazie** (26 E. 84th St., between Madison and Fifth Aves., 212/717–4407) offers casual Italian dining in a lovely townhouse. Options include omelets, pizzas, sandwiches, and salads, but they're best known for the Italian Bento-Box with its tastings of savory and sweets.

At the fairly inexpensive sit-down eatery **Le Pain Quotidien** (1131 Madison Ave., at 84th St., 212/327–4900), the hungry dine at long communal tables on high-quality sandwiches (around $9), salads, and pastries.

10

Equestrian Court (1930)

Rembrandt's masterful *Aristotle with a Bust of Homer* (1653) shows a philosopher contemplating worldly gains versus values through its play of light and use of symbols. Around Aristotle is a gold medal of Alexander the Great, one of the philosopher's students.

In the room dedicated to **Monet** you can get to all his greatest hits—poplar trees, haystacks, water lilies, and the Rouen Cathedral. The muted tones of Pissaro are followed by a room full of bright and garish colors announcing works by Gauguin, Matisse, and Van Gogh.

Vincent van Gogh,
Wheatfield with Cypresses

Islamic Galleries

In late 2011, after an eight-year renovation, the Met reopened its Islamic galleries, a suite of 15 galleries housing one of the world's premier collections of Islamic art. Now known as the "Art of the Arab Lands, Turkey, Iran, Central Asia, and Later South Asia," the collection comprises more than 12,000 works of art and traces the course of Islamic Civilization over a span of 13 centuries. Highlights include an 11-foot-high 14th century mihrab, or prayer niche, decorated with glazed ceramic tiles; the recently restored Emperor's Carpet—a 16th century Persian carpet that was presented to the Hapsburg Emperor Leopold I by Peter the Great of Russia; the Damascus Room—a Syrian Ottoman reception room decorated with poetic verses; and glass, ceramics, and metalwork from Egypt, Syria, Iraq, and Iran.

Asian Galleries

The serene **Astor Court**, which has its own skylight and pond of real-life koi (goldfish), is a model of a scholar's court garden in Soochow, China.

The Han dynasty (206 BC–220 AD) introduced the practice of sending the dead on to the afterlife with small objects to help them there. Keep an eye out for these **small clay figures**, which include farm animals (enclosed in barnyards) and dancing entertainers.

On display in a glass case in the center of an early-Chinese gallery is a complete set of 14 **bronze altar vessels**. Dating 1100 BC—800 AD, these green and slightly crusty pieces were used for worshipping ancestors. The Met displays some of its finest **Asian stoneware and porcelain** along the balcony overlooking the Great Hall.

The teak dome and minature balconies from a **Jain meeting hall** in western India were carved in the 16th century. Just about the entire surface is covered with musicians, animals, gods, and servants.

WHAT'S NEW

Under construction for two years, the front steps of the Met—one of Manhattan's most iconic meeting places—reopens in late 2014 as a European-style plaza with additional public seating, a modernized fountain, landscaping, and improved museum access. Food and ticket kiosks may be added in early 2015.

Standing eight-armed
Avalokiteshvara

FAMILY **Carl Schurz Park.** Facing the East River, this park, named for a German immigrant who was a prominent newspaper editor in the 19th century, is so tranquil you'd never guess you're directly above FDR Drive. Walk along the promenade, where you can take in views of the river and the Roosevelt Island Lighthouse across the way. To the north are Randall's and Wards islands and the RFK Bridge (aka the Triborough Bridge)—as well as the more immediate sight of locals pushing strollers, riding bikes, or walking their dogs. If you enter the park at its 86th Street entrance or if you're exiting there, you'll find yourself approaching the grounds of a Federal-style wood-frame house that belies the grandeur of its name—Gracie Mansion.

■ **TIP→** Exit the park at 86th Street and cross East End Avenue for a stroll through Henderson Place, a miniature historic district of 24 connected Queen Anne–style houses in a dead end. The small redbrick houses, built in 1881 "for persons of moderate means," have turrets marking the corner of each block and symmetrical roof gables, pediments, parapets, chimneys, and dormer windows. ⊠ *East End Ave. to the East River, and 84th to 90th Sts., Upper East Side* ☎ *212/459–4455* ⊕ *www.carlschurzparknyc.org* Ⓜ *4, 5, 6 to 86th St.*

Jane Kahan. This welcoming gallery represents some lofty works. In addition to tapestries by modern masters like Pablo Picasso, Joan Miró, and Alexander Calder—one of this gallery's specialties—you'll see works by late-19th- and early-20th-century modern artists such as Fernand Léger and Marc Chagall. ⊠ *922 Madison Ave., 2nd fl., between 73rd and 74th Sts., Upper East Side* ☎ *212/744–1490* ⊕ *www.janekahan.com* ☉ *Labor Day–Memorial Day, Tues.–Sat. 10–6; summer, weekdays 11–5* Ⓜ *6 to 77th St.*

Leo Castelli. Castelli was one of the most influential dealers of the 20th century. He helped foster the careers of many important artists, including one of his first discoveries, Jasper Johns. The gallery shows works by Roy Lichtenstein, Andy Warhol, Ed Ruscha, Jackson Pollock, Robert Morris, and other heavies. ⊠ *18 E. 77th St., between 5th and Madison Aves., Upper East Side* ☎ *212/249–4470* ⊕ *www.castelligallery.com* ☉ *Tues.–Sat. 10–6* Ⓜ *6 to 77th St.*

Mitchell-Innes & Nash. This sleek spot represents the estates of Roy Lichtenstein and Jack Tworkov as well as other Impressionist, modern, and contemporary masters. ⊠ *1018 Madison Ave., between 78th and 79th Sts., Upper East Side* ☎ *212/744–7400* ⊕ *www.miandn.com* ☉ *Weekdays 10–5* Ⓜ *6 to 77th St.*

FAMILY **Mount Vernon Hotel Museum and Garden.** Built in 1799, this former carriage house became a day hotel (a sort of country club) in 1826. Now restored and owned by the Colonial Dames of America, it provides a glimpse of the days when the city ended at 14th Street and this area was a country escape for New Yorkers. A 45-minute tour passes through the eight rooms that display furniture and artifacts of the Federal and Empire periods. Many rooms have real artifacts such as clothes, hats, and fans that children can handle. There is a lovely adjoining garden, designed in an 18th-century style. ⊠ *421 E. 61st St., between York and 1st Aves., Upper East Side* ☎ *212/838–6878* ⊕ *www.mvhm.org* 🖅 *$8* ☉ *Tues.–Sun. 11–4* Ⓜ *4, 5, 6, N, Q, R to 59th St./Lexington Ave.*

10

Museum of American Illustration and Museum of Comic and Cartoon Art at the Society of Illustrators. Founded in 1901, the museum of the Society of Illustrators presents its annual "Oscars," a juried, international competition, from January to March. The best in children's book illustrations is featured October through November. In between are eclectic exhibitions on science fiction, fashion, political, and historical illustrations. In 2012, the Society of Illustrators incorporated the holdings of the Museum of Comic and Cartoon Art (MoCCA) into its collections. MoCCA's collection is housed in its own gallery on the second floor and continues its workshops, programs, and comic festival (MoCCA Fest). ⊠ *128 E. 63rd St., between Lexington and Park Aves., Upper East Side* ☎ *212/838–2560* ⊕ *www.societyillustrators.org* ⊿ *Free* ☉ *Tues. 10–8, Wed.–Fri. 10–5, Sat. noon–4* Ⓜ *F to 63rd St.; 4, 5, 6, N, R to 59th St./Lexington Ave.*

Peter Findlay Gallery. Covering 19th- and 20th-century works by European artists, this gallery shows work by Mary Cassatt, Paul Klee, and Alberto Giacometti. ⊠ *16 E. 79th St., 2nd fl., Upper East Side* ☎ *212/644–4433* ⊕ *www.findlay.com* ☉ *Weekdays 1:30–5* Ⓜ *6 to 77th St.*

FAMILY **Roosevelt Island.** The 2-mile-long East River slice of land that parallels Manhattan from East 48th to East 85th streets is now a quasi-suburb of more than 12,000 people, and the vestiges of its infamous asylums, hospitals, and prisons make this an offbeat trip for the historically curious. At the south tip are the eerie ruins of a **Smallpox Hospital,** built in 1854 in a Gothic Revival style by the prominent architect James Renwick Jr. (Among many other works, Renwick also designed St. Patrick's Cathedral and the Smithsonian Institution Building.) Neighboring the hospital ruins is the recently opened **Four Freedoms Park,** a memorial to Franklin Delano Roosevelt designed by famed architect Louis I. Kahn. After decades of delays, the 4-acre park—once just a landfill with wasted dramatic city views—opened in late 2012, to much fanfare. The monument to President Roosevelt is essentially a large, open granite box with a giant bust of FDR, and a wall inscribed with the words of the wartime Four Freedoms speech which the park honors. Visitors can stroll the stone walkways and the symmetrical tree-lined pebble paths that run along the manicured lawn and enjoy unique views of the United Nations and East River. ∎TIP→ Free guided walking tours of FDR Four Freedoms Park are available Saturday at 11, on a first-come basis. Visitors can also request a private tour in advance for $20 per person (minimum 6 people). On a small park at the island's north tip is a lighthouse built in 1872 by island convicts. You can get to the island by subway, but why would you when you can take the five-minute ride on the **Roosevelt Island Tramway,** the only commuter cable car in North America, which lifts you 250 feet in the air, with impressive views of Queens and Manhattan. A visitor center (open May to September), made from an old trolley kiosk, stands to your left as you exit the tram. Red buses service the island for 25¢ a ride. ⊠ *Tramway entrance at 2nd Ave. and either 59th St. or 60th St., Upper East Side* ☎ *212/688–4836 for visitor center* ⊕ *www.fdrfourfreedomspark. org* ⊿ *$2.50 (MetroCard)* ☉ *Park Wed.–Mon. 9–5, tram Sun.–Thurs. 6 am–2 am, Fri. and Sat. 6 am–3:30 am (leaves approximately every 15 mins)* Ⓜ *F to Roosevelt Island.*

11

Central Park

WORD OF MOUTH

"Central Park was fabulous! I love that this busy, bustling city has such a huge expanse of peaceful parkland."

— cathies

OUR BACKYARD

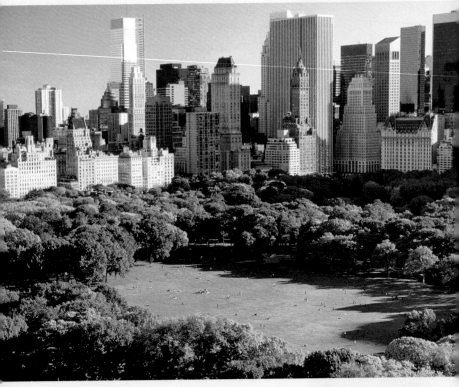

HOW A SWAMP BECAME AN OASIS

1855 Using the power of eminent domain, New York City acquires 843 acres of undeveloped swamp for the then-obscene sum of $5 million, displacing 1,600 people living there.

1857 The landscape architect Frederick Law Olmsted becomes superintendent of a park that does not yet exist. He spends days clearing dirt and evicting squatters and evenings working with architect Calvert Vaux on what will become the Greensward plan. The plan is the winning entry in the city's competition to develop a design for the park.

While the Panic of 1857 creates widespread unemployment, thousands of workers begin moving five million cubic yards of dirt and planting more than five million trees and plants. Beleaguered by bureaucrats, Olmsted and Vaux unsuccessfully submit resignations several times.

1873 The Greensward plan is completed. It has been the basic blueprint for Central Park ever since.

More than thirty-eight million people visit Central Park each year; on an average summer weekend day, a quarter of a million children and adults flood these precincts, frolicking in the 21 playgrounds and 26 ballfields, and collapsing on more than 9,000 benches, which would span seven miles if you lined them up. There are more than 55 monuments and sculptures in the park, and countless ways to have fun.

30 THINGS WE LOVE TO DO IN CENTRAL PARK

1 Take a rowboat out on the lake

2 Clap for the sea lions at the zoo

3 Jog around the Reservoir

4 Ice-skate at Trump Wollman Rink

5 Watch rollerbladers show off

6 Go bird-watching at the Ramble

7 Doze in Sheep Meadow

8 Rent a bike at the Boathouse

9 Sit on the hill behind the Met Museum

10 See a free concert or play

11 Catch a softball game

12 Bask in fall foliage

13 Remember John Lennon at Strawberry Fields

14 Take a Central Park Conservancy Tour

15 Rent a gondola and a gondolier

16 Cross the park on the bridle path

17 Stand under the 72nd Street Wisteria Pergola

18 Hear the Delacorte Clock's musical chimes

19 Crunch the snow before anyone else

20 Pilot a model boat at Conservatory Water

21 Stroll through Shakespeare Garden

22 Fish at Harlem Meer

23 Sunbathe on Hernshead

24 Smell the Conservatory Garden tulips

25 Shoot photos from Bow Bridge

26 Ride the Carousel

27 People-watch at Bethesda Fountain

28 Picnic on the Great Lawn

29 Pet the bronze Balto statue

30 Climb to the top of Belvedere Castle

(top left) Monarch butterfly pollinates at Conservatory Garden (top center) Bethesda Fountain (top right) Chrysanthemums near Sheep Meadow (center) The skyline with some of the park's 26,000 trees (bottom) Park skaters in the 1860s.

On the map: 111th St., Central Park N., Duke Ellington Circle, Frederick Douglass Circle, Harlem Meer, Great Hill, North Meadow, East Meadow, Central Park W., Fifth Ave., 96th St. Transverse, Jacqueline Kennedy Onassis Reservoir, West Drive, East Drive, 86th St. Transverse, Great Lawn, Fifth Ave., 79th St. Transverse, The Ramble, The Lake, West Drive, 72nd St. Drive, East Drive, Fifth Ave., Sheep Meadow, Central Park W., 66th St. Transverse, Center Dr., The Pond, Central Park S., Columbus Circle, 6th Ave., Grand Army Plaza

PARK BASICS

Several entrances lead into the park. You can enter from the east, west, south, and north by paved pedestrian walkways, just off Fifth Avenue, Central Park North (110th St.), Central Park West, and Central Park South (59th St.).

Four roads, or transverses, cut through the park from east to west—66th, 79th, 86th, and 96th streets. The East and West drives are both along the north–south axis; Center Drive enters the south edge of the park at Sixth Avenue and connects with East Drive around 66th Street.

There are five Visitor Centers—the Dairy (just south of the 66th St. transverse), Belvedere Castle (just north of the 79th Street transverse), the Chess & Checkers House (mid-park at 64th St.), and the Charles A. Dana Discovery Center (at the top of the park at Central Park North) and the North Meadow Recreation Center (mid-park, near 96th St.)—that have directions, park maps, event calendars, and volunteers who can guide you.

TOURS

The **Central Park Conservancy** gives several different free walking tours of the park based on the season. Most tours are 60 to 90 minutes and explore the park's history, ecology, and design. Custom tours are also available. If you'd rather go it alone, the Conservancy also offers an audio guide you can follow on your cell phone. Each description is read by a different celebrity or NYC VIP. Self-guided tours of the Ramble and North Woods are available as PDFs for download. For more information, see *centralparknyc.org*.

WHERE AM I?

Along the main loop and some paths, lampposts are marked with location codes. Posts bear a letter—always "E" (for east) or "W" (for west)—and four numbers. The first two numbers tell you the nearest cross street. The second two tell you how far you are from either 5th Ave. or Central Park West (depending on whether it's an "E" or "W" post). Download the free Central Park app (www.centralparknyc.org/digital); with its interactive GPS-enabled map, event calendar, and site info and you'll never get lost in the park again.

PERFORMERS AND THE PARK: SOULMATES

It was inevitable that Central Park, conceived to give so much and ask little in return, would attract artists and art lovers who feel the same way.

Be they superstars like Paul Simon, Diana Ross, or Elton John or one of the amateur musicians, animal handlers, or jugglers who delight passersby, they all share the urge to entertain and give back to the city, the park, and its visitors.

Information on scheduled events is provided, but if you can't catch one, don't fret: you'll be rewarded by the serendipitous, particularly on summer and autumn days. Just keep your ears peeled for the music, applause, and laughter. The Central Park Conservancy, in cooperation with other arts patrons, organizes a series of free events, including the Harlem Meer Performance Festival and the Great Lawn performances by the New York Philharmonic. SummerStage has yielded a cornucopia of international performers.

Perhaps the brass ring of park performances is Shakespeare in the Park, which celebrated its 50th year in 2012. Every summer's performances of works by the Bard (and others) wow as many as 90,000 New Yorkers and visitors. Free tickets (two per person) are given out starting at noon for the performance that evening, but you need to line up by midmorning or earlier, depending on the show. Tickets are also distributed via online lottery on the show day at www.*shakespeareinthepark.org*. Either way, the trouble is worth it, as casts are often studded with stars like Meryl Streep, Oliver Platt, Natalie Portman, Morgan Freeman, Denzel Washington, and Kevin Kline.

GOINGS ON

Central Park Conservancy Film Festival: Five nights at end of summer; Rumsey Playfield, near E. 72nd St. entrance.

Global Citizen: VIPs of rock and roll join 60,000 fans to raise their voices for change in this one-day annual concert in late Sept.

Harlem Meer Performance Festival: Late June–early Sept., Sun.; at Dana Discovery Center, near Lenox Ave. entrance.

Jazz & Colors: Live jazz and fall foliage at this one-day concert in November.

New York Philharmonic: Two performances in the summer; Great Lawn.

Shakespeare in the Park: June–early Aug., Tues.–Sun. evenings.

Storytelling: June–Sept., Sat. 11 AM; Hans Christian Andersen Statue at 72nd St. and 5th Ave.

SummerStage: Late May or June–early Sept.; Rumsey Playfield.

Swedish Cottage Marionette Theatre: Since 1947, puppeteers have entertained in this 1876 Swedish schoolhouse.

(center) N.Y. Philharmonic associate conductor Xian Zhang (right) Shakespeare's *Much Ado About Nothing*

FROM 59TH TO 72ND ST.

The busy southern section of Central Park is where most visitors get their first impression; it's also where most of the park's child-friendly attractions are centered. Artists line the entrances off Central Park South, and horse carriages await passengers. But no matter how many people gather here, you can always find a spot to picnic, ponder, or just take in the beauty, especially on a sunny day.

At the southeast corner of the park, you will come upon one of its prettiest areas, the **Pond**. Swans and ducks cruise on its calm waters, and if you follow the shore line to Gapstow Bridge and look southward, you'll see much of New York City's skyline: to the left (east) are the peak-roofed Sherry-Netherland Hotel, the black-and-white GM Building, the Chippendale-style top of the Sony Building, and the black-glass Trump Tower. In front of you is the château-style Plaza Hotel.

Opening in late October, **Trump Wollman Skating Rink** sits inside the park against a backdrop of Central Park South skyscrapers. You can rent skates, buy snacks, and have a perfect city-type outing. There's a

lively feeling here with lots of great music playing and a terrace so you can watch if you're not into skating.

The **Friedsam Memorial Carousel**, also known as the Central Park Carousel, was built in 1908. It has 58 nearly life-size hand-carved horses and remains a favorite among young and old. Its original Wurlitzer organ plays calliope waltzes, polkas, and standards. Even if you don't need visitor infomation, the **Dairy** is worth a stop for its Swiss-chalet exterior.

If you saw the film *Madagascar*, you may recognize the **Central Park Zoo**. Here, the polar bears play at the Polar Circle, monkeys frolic in the open-air Temperate Territory, and the Rain Forest showcases flora and fauna that you wouldn't expect to see in Manhattan. An unusual exhibit is the ant colony—even New York City's zoo has a sense of humor. Stick around to see the sea lion feedings (call for times) and to watch the animal statues dance to a variety of nursery rhymes at the **Delacorte Musical Clock** just outside, on the hour and half-hour from 8 AM to 5 PM.

Wedged between the zoo and the clock is **The Arsenal**, the second-oldest building in the park. Inside are rotating

exhibits that often cover park history and landscape art.

North of the clock is **Tisch Children's Zoo**, where kids can pet and feed sheep, goats, rabbits, cows, and pigs. Enter through the trunk of a make-believe tree and arrive at The Enchanted Forest, filled with huge "acorns,"

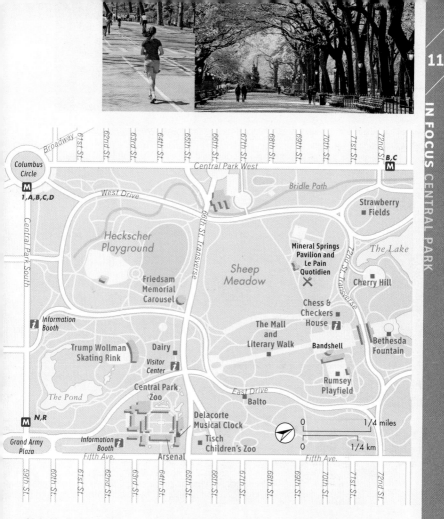

a climbable "spider web," and hoppable "lily pads."

Perhaps more pettable than any of the zoo's occupants is a decidedly more inert creature, perched on a rockpile at East Drive and 67th Street: **Balto**. Shiny in places from constant touching, this bronze statue commemorates a real-life sled dog who led a team of huskies that carried medicine for 674 mi across perilous ice to Nome, Alaska, during a 1925 diphtheria epidemic.

The Mall, at the intersection of Central Drive and East Drive, is arguably the most elegant area of Central Park. In the beginning of the 20th century, it was the place to see and be seen. Today, these formal walkways are still a wonderful place to stroll, meander, or sit and take in the "parade" under a canopy of the largest col-

lection of American elms in North America. The mall's southern end, known as **Literary Walk**, is lined with statues of authors and artists such as Robert Burns and William Shakespeare.

(from left to right) Riding on the outside track (recommended) of the Carousel; Getting in a workout on a park drive loop; The Mall, where Dustin Hoffman's character famously teaches his son to ride a bike in *Kramer vs. Kramer*.

The large expanse to the west of the Mall is known as the **Sheep Meadow**, the only "beach" that some native New Yorkers have ever known. Join in on a Frisbee or football game, admire the tenacity of kite flyers, or indulge simultaneously in the three simplest meadow pleasures of them all—picnicking, sunbathing, and languorously reading a book or magazine.

There's a reason why the ornate **Bethesda Fountain**, off the 72nd Street transverse, shows up in so many movies set in New York City: the view from the staircase above is one of the most romantic in the city. The statue in the center of the fountain, **The Angel of the Waters**, designed by Emma Stebbins, is surrounded by four figures symbolizing Temperance, Purity,

Health, and Peace. There's a good amount of New York–style street entertainment here, too, with break dancers, acrobats, and singers all vying for your spare change. It's also a great place to meet, sit, and admire the beautiful lake with its swans. For a glimpse of the West Side skyline, walk slightly west to **Cherry Hill**. Originally a watering area for horses, this circular plaza

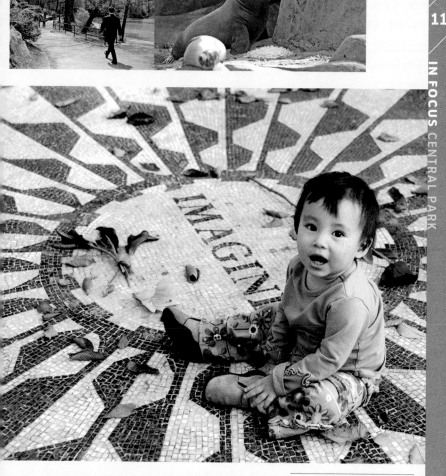

has a small wrought-iron-and-gilt fountain. It's particularly beautiful in the spring when the cherry trees are in full pink-and-white bloom. Farther west are the Oak Bridge and the lovely Ladies Pavilion, emblematic of the park's past.

Across from the Dakota apartment building on Central Park West is **Strawberry Fields**, named for the Beatles' 1967 classic, "Strawberry Fields Forever." Sometimes called the "international garden of peace," this spot draws fans who come to reflect among its shrubs, trees, and flower beds, and lay flowers on the black-and-white "Imagine" mosaic. On December 8, hundreds of Beatles fans mark the anniversary of Lennon's death by gathering here.

(top from left to right) Horse-drawn carriages; Artist painting the oft-rendered Gapstow bridge, which spans the northeast end of the Pond; Cutting through the park is a classic midday timesaver and post-work respite; Seals at the Central Park Zoo (center left); Nighttime at Wollman Rink serves up twinkling skyscrapers and skaters of all abilities (center right); The late John Lennon and his widow, Yoko Ono, often visited the site of what would become Strawberry Fields.

FROM 72ND ST. TO THE RESERVOIR

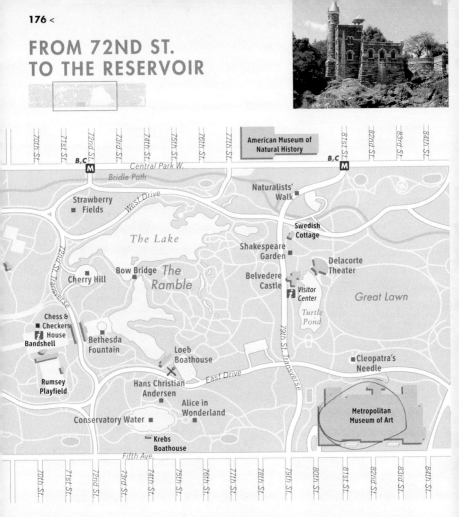

Playgrounds, lawns, jogging and biking paths, and striking buildings populate the midsection of the park. You can soak up the sun, have a picnic, or even play in a pick-up basketball or baseball game by the Great Lawn; get your cultural fix at the Metropolitan Museum of Art; or train for the next New York City Marathon along the Reservoir.

A block from Fifth Avenue, just north of the 72nd Street entrance, is a peaceful section of the park where you'll find the **Conservatory Water**, named for a conservatory that was never built. Generations of New Yorkers have grown up racing radio-controlled model sailboats here. It's a tradition that happens each Saturday at 10 AM from April through Oct. During those months smaller boats are available for rent

daily. At the north end is the **Alice in Wonderland** statue; on the west side of the pond, a bronze statue of **Hans Christian Andersen**, the Ugly Duckling at his feet, is the site of Saturday storytelling hours during summer.

At the neo-Victorian **Loeb Boathouse** on the park's 18-acre Lake, you can rent a rowboat, kayak, bike, or ride in an authentic Venetian gondola. The attached café is a worthy pit stop.

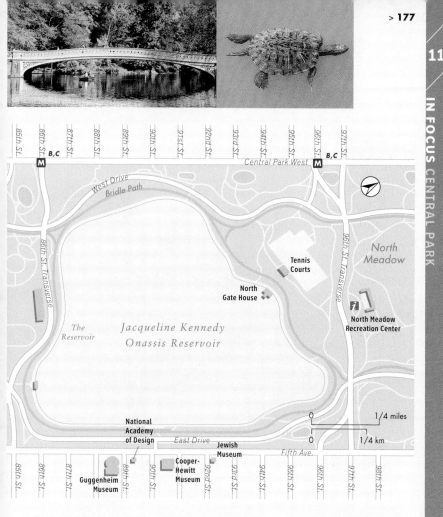

Designed to resemble upstate New York's Adirondack Mountain region, the **Ramble** covers 38 acres and is laced with twisting, climbing paths. This is prime bird-watching territory, since it's a rest stop along a major migratory route and a shelter for many of the more than 230 species of birds that have been sighted in the park; bring your binoculars. Because the Ramble is so dense and isolated,

however, don't wander here alone, or after dark. Head south through the Ramble and you'll come to the beautiful cast-iron **Bow Bridge**, spanning part of the Lake between the Ramble and Bethesda Fountain. From the center of the bridge, you can get a sweeping view of the park as well as of the apartment buildings on both the East Side and the West Side.

North of the Ramble atop Vista Rock, **Belvedere Castle** is the second-highest natural point in the park. If you can't get tickets for Delacorte Theater, you can climb to one of the castle's

(from left to right) Belvedere means "beautiful view" in Italian, a clue to why we climb to the top of Belvedere Castle; Birders, photographers, and couples of all ages are drawn to Bow Bridge; Red-eared slider turtles frolic in Turtle Pond, at the base of Belvedere Castle.

three terraces and look down on the stage. You'll also get a fantastic view of the Great Lawn—it's particularly beautiful during the fall foliage months—and of the park's myriad bird visitors. Since 1919 the castle has served as a U.S. Weather Bureau station, and meteorological instruments are set on top of the tower. If you enter the Castle from the lower level, you can visit the Henry Luce Nature Observa-

tory, which has nature exhibits, children's workshops, and educational programs.

Somewhat hidden behind Belvedere Castle, **Shakespeare Garden** is an informal jumble of flowers, trees, and pathways, inspired by the flora mentioned in Shakespeare's plays and poetry. Bronze plaques throughout the garden bear the bard's lines mentioning the plants.

The Great Lawn hums with action on weekends, on warm days, and on most summer evenings, when its baseball fields and picnic grounds fill with city folks and visitors alike. Its 13 acres have endured millions of footsteps, thousands of ball games, hundreds of downpours, dozens of concerts, fireworks displays, and even a papal mass. On a beautiful day, everyone seems to be here.

Chancing upon the 70-ft-tall **Cleopatra's Needle** always feels a bit seren-dipitous and delightfully jarring, even to the most cynical New Yorkers. This weathered hieroglyphic-covered obelisk began life in Heliopolis, Egypt, around 1500 BC, but has only a little to do with Cleopatra—it's just New York's nickname for the work. It was eventually carted off to Alexandria by the Romans in 12 BC, and

it landed here on January 22, 1881, when the khedive of Egypt made it a gift to the city.

At the southwest corner of the Great Lawn is the fan-shaped **Delacorte Theater**, home to the summer Shake-speare in the Park festival.

If you want to take in sev-eral sites in a single brisk jaunt, consider walking the **Naturalists' Walk.** On this path you can wind your way

toward the Swedish Cot-tage, the Shakespeare Gar-den, and Belvedere Castle on a landscaped nature

(top, from left to right) A female Canada goose and goslings on Turtle Pond; Cyclists make good use of the bike paths; Bikers as well as joggers boost their egos by outpacing the hansom car-riages; Racing boats at Conserva-tory Water (center) In the 1930s, a flock of sheep was evicted from what would later be known as the Sheep Meadow.

walk with spectacular rock outcrops, a stream that attracts bird life, a woodland area with various native trees, stepping-stone trails, and, thankfully, benches.

North of the Great Lawn and the 86th Street transverse is a popular gathering place for New Yorkers and visitors alike, the **Jacqueline Kennedy Onassis Reservoir**. Rain or shine, you'll see runners of all ages and paces heading counterclockwise around the 1.58-mi dirt path that encircles the water. The path in turn is surrounded by hundreds of trees that burst into color in the spring and fall. The 106-acre reservoir, finished in 1862, was a source of fresh water for Manhattanites. It holds more than a billion gallons, but it's no longer used for drinking water; the city's main reservoirs are upstate. From the top of the stairs at 90th Street just off 5th Avenue you have a 360-degree panorama of the city's exciting skyscrapers and often-brilliant sunsets. On the south side, there are benches so you can rest and recharge.

More locals than tourists know about the wilder-looking, less-crowded northern part of Central Park, and there are hidden gems lurking here that enable even the most tightly wound among us to decompress, at least for a short while.

Walking along Fifth Avenue to 105th Street, you'll see a magnificent wrought-iron gate—once part of the 5th Avenue mansion of Cornelius Vanderbilt II—that marks the entrance to the **Conservatory Garden**. As you walk through it, you enter a different world, a quiet place that's positively idyllic for reading and slowing down. The Italian-style **Central Garden** is a beauty, with an expansive lawn, a strikingly simple fountain, and a wisteria-draped pergola that just oozes romance.

The French-inspired **North Garden** is a colorful place with plants placed into elaborate patterns. Springtime is magical—thousands of tulips come to life in a circle around the garden's striking Untermyer Fountain and its three bronze dancers; in the fall, chrysanthemums take their place. The English-style **South Garden** conjures up images from the classic children's book *The Secret Garden*. The garden is

a beautiful hodgepodge of trees, bushes, and flowers that bloom year-round. A free tour is conducted on Saturday at 11 AM, from April through October.

At **Harlem Meer**, the third-largest body of water in Central Park, you can borrow fishing poles (identification required) from mid-April through October and try your hand at catching (and releasing) the largemouth bass, catfish, golden shiners, and bluegills that are stocked in the water's 11 acres. You can also learn about the upper park's geography, ecology, and

history at the Victorian-style **Charles A. Dana Discovery Center**.

Although only a shell of this stone building remains, **Blockhouse #1** serves as a historical marker: the structure was built in 1814 as a cliffside fortification against the British. The area is deserted and dense with trees, so go as a group here, and avoid it at night.

(left) A pensive raccoon in the park's northern reaches; (center) A jogger makes her counterclockwise progress along the reservoir; (right) Inside the Central Park Conservancy Garden.

CONTACT INFORMATION

Central Park Conservancy
☎ 212/310–6600
🌐 www.centralparknyc.org

Central Park SummerStage
☎ 212/360–2777
🌐 www.summerstage.org

Central Park Wildlife Center (Central Park Zoo)
☎ 212/439–6500
🌐 www.centralparkzoo.org

Central Park Visitor Centers
☎ 212/794–6564 (Dairy)
🌐 www.nycgovparks.org

Charles A. Dana Discovery Center
☎ 212/860–1370

Loeb Boathouse, Boathouse Restaurant
☎ 212/517–2233
🌐 www.thecentral parkboathouse.com

Shakespeare in the Park
☎ 212/539–8500 (Public Theater)
🌐 www.shakespeareinthe park.org

Swedish Cottage Marionette Theatre
☎ 212/988–9093
🌐 www.cityparks foundation.org

Trump Wollman Rink
☎ 212/439–6900
🌐 www.wollmanskating rink.com

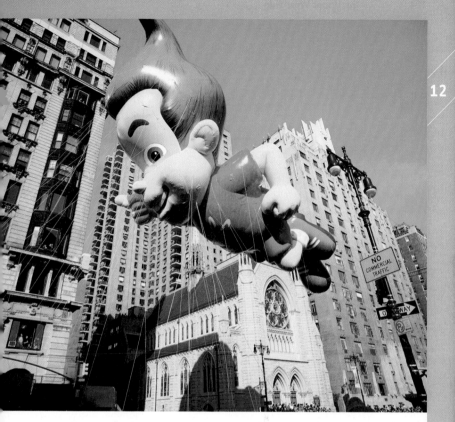

THE UPPER WEST SIDE

with the Cloisters

GETTING ORIENTED

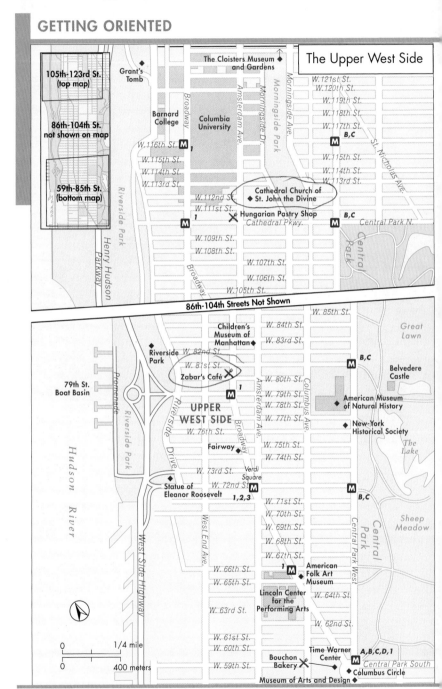

105th-123rd St. (top map)

86th-104th St. not shown on map

59th-85th St. (bottom map)

The Upper West Side

Grant's Tomb

The Cloisters Museum and Gardens

W.121st St.
W.120th St.
W.119th St.
W.118th St.
W.117th St.
B,C

Broadway

Barnard College

Columbia University

Amsterdam Ave.

Morningside Dr.

Morningside Park

St. Nicholas Ave.

W.116th St. **M** 1
W.115th St.
W.114th St.
W.113rd St.

W.115th St.
W.114th St.
W.113th St.

Riverside Park

Henry Hudson Parkway

W.112nd St.
W.111th St.

Cathedral Church of
◆ St. John the Divine

Broadway

M 1   ✗ Hungarian Pastry Shop
Cathedral Pkwy.   **B,C**   Central Park N.

W.109th St.
W.108th St.

Central Park

W.107th St.
W.106th St.
W.105th St.

86th-104th Streets Not Shown

W. 85th St.

Great Lawn

Children's Museum of Manhattan ◆

W. 84th St.
W. 83rd St.

M **B,C**

◆ Riverside Park   W. 82nd St.
W. 81st St.

Belvedere Castle

Zabar's Café ✗

Amsterdam Ave.

Columbus Ave.

79th St. Boat Basin

Promenade

Riverside Park

Riverside Drive

M 1

W. 80th St.
W. 79th St.
W. 78th St.
W. 77th St.

American Museum
◆ of Natural History

UPPER WEST SIDE

W. 76th St.

Broadway

◆ New-York
Historical Society

Hudson River

Fairway ◆

W. 75th St.
W. 74th St.

The Lake

W. 73rd St.   Verdi Square

Statue of ◆
Eleanor Roosevelt

West End Ave.

W. 72nd St
M
1,2,3

W. 71st St.
W. 70th St.
W. 69th St.
W. 68th St.
W. 67th St.

M **B,C**

Central Park West

Central Park

Sheep Meadow

West Side Highway

American
◆ Folk Art
Museum

M

W. 66th St.
W. 65th St.

Lincoln Center for the Performing Arts

W. 64th St.

W. 63rd St.

W. 62nd St.

W. 61st St.
W. 60th St.
W. 59th St.

Bouchon ✗
Bakery

Time Warner ◆
Center   **M**   **A,B,C,D,1**
Central Park South
◆ Columbus Circle

Museum of Arts and Design ◆

0   1/4 mile
0   400 meters

MAKING THE MOST OF YOUR TIME

Broadway is one of the most walkable and interesting thoroughfares on the Upper West Side because of its broad sidewalks and aggressive mix of retail stores, restaurants, and apartment buildings. If you head north from the Lincoln Center area (around 65th Street) to about 81st Street (about 1 mile), you'll get a feel for the neighborhood's local color, particularly above 72nd Street. Up here you'll encounter residents of every conceivable age and ethnicity either shambling or sprinting, street vendors hawking used and newish books, and such beloved landmarks as the 72nd Street subway station, the Beacon Theater, the produce mecca Fairway (the cause of perhaps the most perpetually congested block), and Zabar's (a food spot that launches a memorable assault on all five of your senses—and your wallet). The Upper West Side's other two main avenues—Columbus and Amsterdam—are more residential but also have myriad restaurants and shops.

If you're intrigued by having the city's only Ivy League school close at hand, hop the 1 train to 116th Street and emerge on the east side of the street, which puts you smack in front of Columbia University and its Graduate School of Journalism. Pass through the gates and up the walk for a look at a cluster of buildings so elegant you'll understand why it's an iconic NYC setting.

GETTING HERE

The A, B, C, D, and 1 subway lines will take you to Columbus Circle. From there, the B and C lines run along Central Park, stopping at 72nd, 81st, 86th, 96th, 103rd, and 110th streets. The 1 train runs up Broadway, making local stops at 66th, 72nd, 79th, 86th, 96th, 103rd, 110th, 116th, and 125th streets. The 2 and 3 trains, the express trains that also go along Broadway, stop at 72nd and 96th.

TOP EXPERIENCES

12

Walking along Broadway—for the shopping, people-watching, and snacking

Grazing at Zabar's

Strolling through Riverside Park past the boat basin

Strolling in Central Park (⇨ *See Chapter 11*)

Standing below the gigantic blue whale at the American Museum of Natural History

Basking in the views, gardens, and medieval masterpieces at the Cloisters Museum and Gardens

COFFEE AND QUICK BITES

Bouchon Bakery. In busy Columbus Circle's Time Warner shopping center, this busy little bakery serves excellent sandwiches, quiches, pastries, and coffee. ⊠ *Time Warner Center, 10 Columbus Circle, 3rd fl., Upper West Side* ☎ *212/823–9366.*

Hungarian Pastry Shop. Linger over a Danish and bottomless coffee with the Columbia kids and professors at this old-world (cash only) café and bakery. ⊠ *1030 Amsterdam Ave., at 111th St., Upper West Side* ☎ *212/866–4230.*

Zabar's Cafe. Fast-track the Zabar's experience with a gourmet coffee and sandwich, pickled lox, or slice of cheesecake. ⊠ *2245 Broadway, at 80th St., Upper West Side* ☎ *212/787–2000.*

Sightseeing	The Upper West Side is one of the city's quieter, more
★★★	residential neighborhoods, with wide sidewalks and a
Nightlife	
★★	(relatively) slower pace. There's more of a residential feel
Dining	here than in many other parts of Manhattan. You'll see
★★	
Lodging	lots of families with strollers and young children up here.
★	
Shopping	The Cloisters, in Inwood, has the Metropolitan Museum's
★★★★	medieval collection.

THE UPPER WEST SIDE

Updated
by Jacinta
O'Halloran

The tree-lined side streets of the Upper West Side are lovely, with high stoops leading up to stately brownstones. Central Park, of course, is one of the main attractions here, no matter the season or time of day, though locals know that Riverside Park, along the Hudson River, can be even more appealing, with smaller crowds.

The Upper West Side also has its share of cultural institutions, from the 16-acre **Lincoln Center** complex, to the impressive and quirky collection at the **New-York Historical Society,** to Columbus Circle's **Museum of Arts and Design** and the much-loved **American Museum of Natural History.**

Most people think the area north of 106th Street and south of 125th Street on the West Side is just an extension of the Upper West Side. But technically it's called Morningside Heights, and it's largely dominated by Columbia University, along with a cluster of academic, religious, and medical institutions, including Barnard College and the **Cathedral Church of St. John the Divine.**

TOP ATTRACTIONS

Fodor'sChoice   **American Museum of Natural History.** *See highlighted feature in this chapter.*

★   **Cathedral Church of St. John the Divine.** The largest Gothic-style cathedral in the world, even with its towers and transepts still unfinished, this divine behemoth comfortably asserts its bulk in the country's most vertical city. The seat of the Episcopal diocese in New York, it acts as a sanctuary for all, giving special services that include a celebration of New York's gay and lesbian community as well as the annual Blessing of the Bikes, when cyclists

12

of all faiths bring their wheels for a holy-water benediction. The cathedral hosts **musical performances** (⊕ *www.stjohndivine.org*) and has held funerals and memorial services for such artists as Duke Ellington, Jim Henson, George Balanchine, James Baldwin, and Alvin Ailey. Built in two long spurts starting in 1892, the cathedral remains only two-thirds complete. What began as a Romanesque-Byzantine structure under the original architects George Heins and Christopher Grant Lafarge shifted (upon Heins's death in 1911) to French Gothic under the direction of Gothic Revival purist Ralph Adams Cram. You can spot the juxtaposition of the two medieval styles by comparing the finished Gothic arches, which are pointed, with the still-uncovered arches, which are rounded in the Byzantine style.

To get the full effect of the cathedral's size, approach from Broadway on 112th Street. Above the 3-ton central bronze doors is the intricately carved **Portal of Paradise,** which depicts St. John witnessing the Transfiguration of Jesus, and 32 biblical characters. Then step inside to the cavernous nave. More than 600 feet long, it holds some 5,000 worshippers, and the 162-foot-tall dome crossing could comfortably contain the Statue of Liberty (minus its pedestal). The **Great Rose Window,** made from more than 10,000 pieces of colored glass, is the largest stained-glass window in the United States.

At the end of the nave, surrounding the altar, are seven chapels expressing the cathedral's interfaith tradition and international mission—with menorahs, Shinto vases, and dedications to various ethnic groups. The **Saint Saviour Chapel** contains a three-panel bronze altar in white-gold leaf with religious scenes by artist Keith Haring (his last work before he died in 1990).

Outside, in the cathedral's south grounds, is the eye-catching **Peace Fountain.** It depicts the struggle of good and evil with the archangel Michael decapitating Satan. Encircling it are whimsical animals cast in bronze from pieces sculpted by children.

On the first Sunday of October the Cathedral Church of St. John the Divine is truly a zoo. In honor of St. Francis of Assisi, the patron saint of animals, the church holds its usual Sunday service with a twist: in past years upward of 3,500 New Yorkers have shown up to have their pets blessed. A procession is led by such guest animals as elephants, camels, llamas, and golden eagles. Seats are first-come, first-served for this popular event, so come at least an hour ahead of time. Sunday services are at 8, 9, 11, and 4. "Highlight Tours" and "Vertical Tours" are offered throughout the week: check the website to reserve. ⊠ *1047 Amsterdam Ave., at 112th St., Upper West Side* ☎ *212/316–7540, 866/811–4111 for tour reservations* ⊕ *www.stjohndivine.org* 🎟 *Tours $6–$15* ☉ *Daily 7:30–6; visitor center daily 9–5; tours Mon. at 11 and 2, Tues.–Sat. at 11 and 1, Sun. at 2* Ⓜ *1 to 110th St./Cathedral Pkwy.*

FAMILY **Central Park.** *See Chapter 11.*

Fodor's Choice
★

Lincoln Center for the Performing Arts. *See the listing in Chapter 20, Performing Arts.*

Fodor's Choice
★

New-York Historical Society. Manhattan's oldest museum, founded in 1804, was brought up-to-date and out of the shadow of its more

Continued on page 196

INSECTS AND MYRIAPODS

INSECTS and MYRIAPODS

SEGMENTED WOR

AMERICAN MUSEUM OF NATURAL HISTORY

Theodore Roosevelt Memorial Hall

The largest natural history museum in the world is also one of the most impressive sights in New York. Four city blocks make up its 45 exhibition halls, which hold more than 30 million artifacts and wonders from the land, the sea, and outer space. With all those wonders, you won't be able to see everything on a single visit, but you can easily hit the highlights in half a day.

Before you begin, plan a route before setting out. Be sure to pick up a map when you pay your admission. The museum's four floors (and lower level) are mazelike.

Visitors can use the free AMNH Explorer app to navigate the museum. It tracks your location, has turn-by-turn directions, profiles of iconic museum objects, and tours, and guides you to bathrooms and exits. There are free companion apps to support special exhibits; check the website. The museum has devices you can borrow if you don't have an app-friendly phone.

Enter the museum at the below-street-level entrance connected to the 81st Street subway station for the shortest lines (look for the subway entrance to the left of the museum's steps). The entrance on Central Park West, where the vast steps lead up into the impressive, barrel-ceilinged

Theodore Roosevelt Rotunda, is central and a good starting place for exploring.

The Rose Center for Earth and Space is attached to the museum. Enter from West 81st Street, where a path slopes down to the entrance, after which elevators and stairs descend to the ticket line on the lower level.

What to see? Check out the museum highlights on the following pages.

✉ Central Park West at W. 79th St., Upper West Side

Ⓜ Subway: B, C to 81st St.

☎ 212/769–5100

🌐 www.amnh.org

💵 $22 suggested donation, includes admission to Rose Center for Earth and Space

🕐 Daily 10–5:45.

Left, Spectrum of Life Wall

MUSEUM HIGHLIGHTS

Left, Woolly Mammoth
Above, Tyrannosaurus rex

Dinosaurs and Mammals

An amazing assembly of dinosaur and mammal fossils covers the entire fourth floor. The organization can be hard to grasp at first, so head to the **Wallace Orientation Center,** where a short film explains how each of the Fossil Halls lead into each other. You'll want to spend at least an hour here—the highlights include a *T. rex,* an *Apatosaurus* (formerly called a Brontosaurus), and the *Buettneria,* which resembles a modern-day crocodile.

The specimens are not in chronological order; they're put together based on their shared characteristics. Key branching-off points—a watertight egg, a grasping hand—are highlighted in the center of rooms and surrounded by related fossil groups. Check out the touch screens here; they make a complex topic more comprehensible.

Reptiles and Amphibians

Head for the Reptiles and Amphibians Hall on the third floor to check out the Komodo Dragon lizards and a 23-foot-long python skeleton. The weirdest display is the enlarged model of the Suriname toad *Pipa pipa,* whose young hatch from the female's back. The Primates Hall carries brief but interesting comparisons between apes, monkeys, and humans. Also on the third floor is the upper gallery of the famed Akeley Hall of African Mammals.

SPECIAL SHOWS AND NEW EXHIBITS

Special exhibits, the IMAX theater, and the Space Show cost extra. The timed tickets are available in advance at the museum's Web site and are sold same day at the door. Between October and May, don't miss the warm, plant-filled Butterfly Conservatory, where blue morphos, monarchs, and other butterflies flit and feed. Ten minutes is probably enough time to enjoy it.

THIRD FLOOR

Wallach
Orientation
Center

Café on 4

Vertebrate
Origins

Milstein Hall
of Advanced
Mammals

Saurischian
Dinosaurs

Astor Turret

Primitive
Mammals

Akeley Hall
of African
Mammals

Ornithischian
Dinosaurs

FOURTH FLOOR

Hayden Planetarium
Space Theater

Reptiles and
Amphibians Hall

Rose Center for
Earth and Space

Ross Hall of
Meteorites

FIRST FLOOR

Guggenheim
Hall of Minerals

Columbus Ave.
Entrance

Entrance
(open seasonally)

ker Hall
Human
rigins

Morgan Memorial
Hall of Gems

Café on 1

Akeley
Hall of
African
Mammals

Rose Center for
Earth and Space

Big
Bang

xit
nly

Entrance

Lefrak
IMAX
Theater

Entrance

Milstein
Hall of
Ocean Life

Heilbrunn
Cosmic
Pathway

Information,
Group Tickets,
and Will Call

Heilbrunn Cosmic
Pathway

Main Entrance

Hall of
Biodiversity

81st St. Entrance

Gottesman Hall
of Planet Earth

Rose Center for
Earth and Space

SECOND FLOOR

Entrance

Theodore Roosevelt
Memorial Hall

Theodore Roosevelt Memorial

After a $40 million renovation, the two-story Theodore Roosevelt Memorial re-opened in late 2012. It includes the restored Central Park West entrance, the Theodore Roosevelt Rotunda, and the Theodore Roosevelt Memorial Hall. Highlights are a new bronze statue of a seated Roosevelt, celebratory murals honoring the Conservation President, touch-screen timelines, and film footage. The Hall of North American Mammals was also restored as part of the memorial to Roosevelt; the hall originally opened in 1942 and many of its displays feature scenes from National Parks that were signed into being by the president.

Akeley Hall of African Mammals

Opened in 1936, this hall on the third floor, its 28 dramatically lighted dioramas is one of the most beloved parts of the museum.

The hall was the life's work of the explorer Carl Akeley, who came up with the idea for the hall, raised the funds for the expeditions, gathered specimens, and sketched landscape studies for what would become the stunning backgrounds. (The backgrounds themselves were painted by James Perry Wilson, whose works can be found throughout the museum.)

Akeley died a decade before the hall opened on an expedition in what's now Rwanda. His gravesite is near the landscape portrayed in the gorilla diorama, completed after his death as a memorial to him and his work.

Hall of Human Origins

The Spitzer Hall of Human Origins on the first floor is a comprehensive exhibit that allows visitors to draw their own conclusions about human evolution by presenting both the scientific methods and the material evidence that goes into evolutionary theory.

The exhibit then traces the evolution of our species over six million years of fossil record and spells out our ancestors' physical and intellectual advancements. Highlights include casts of our famous hairy relative "Lucy," who walked the plains of Africa over 1.8 million years ago.

Hall of Biodiversity

The small **Hall of Biodiversity** on the first floor includes a shady replica of a Central African Republic rain forest. Nearby, the **Spectrum of Life Wall** showcases 1,500 specimens and models, helping show just how weird life can get. The wall opens into the gaping Milstein Hall of Ocean Life, designed to give it an underwater glow and to show off the 94-foot model of a **blue whale** that's suspended from the ceiling.

Blue Whale

ROSE CENTER FOR EARTH AND SPACE

The vast expanses of space and time involved in the creation of the universe can be hard to grasp even with the guiding hand of a museum, so you may want to visit the center when you're at your sharpest. The stunning glass building's centerpiece is the aluminum-clad Hayden Sphere, 87 feet in diameter. Enclosed within are the planetarium, called the Space Theater, and an audiovisual Big Bang presentation consisting of four minutes of narration by Maya Angelou, indistinct washes of color, and frightening bursts of sound. The rock-filled **Hall of Planet Earth** is particularly timely given the earthquakes and other natural disasters of recent years: one section uses a working earthquake monitor to help explain just what causes such seismic violence.

The Space Theater

At the Space Theater, the stage is the dome above you and the actors, heavenly projections. One of the world's largest virtual reality simulators, the theater uses surround sound and slight vibrations in the seats, to immerse you in scenes of planets, star clusters, and galaxies. *Dark Universe* puts Hollywood effects to shame as it explores the cosmos and just how little we know about it.

Tip: The Museum's Cosmic Discoveries app allows you to take the universe, and all its galaxies and planets, with you when you leave. The app offers images, findings, and bulletins all culled from the museum's archives and curated by the museum's astrophysicists. ⊕ *www.amnh.org/apps*

TIME TO EAT?

Inside the museum:
The main food court on the lower level serves sandwiches, pizza, hamburgers and global street food. The animal- and planet-shaped cookies are draws for kids; adults should check out the barbecue station.

The small **Café on 4**, in a turret next to the fossil halls, offers garden views and sells premade sandwiches and salads, soup, yogurt, and desserts.

The über-white **Café on 1**, tucked away beside the Hall of Human Origins, sells warm sandwiches, soup, salads, beer and wine at New York prices.

TIME TO PLAY

Nights at the museum aren't just for kids! Bust out your moonwalk and enjoy a few *cosmic*politans at the Rose Center's monthly One Step Beyond series, featuring live bands, DJs, VJs, cocktails, and dynamic visuals. Get tickets at amnh.org/plan-your-visit/one-step-beyond

TIME TO WATCH

Each October, the AMNH hosts the Margaret Mead Film & Video Festival, the longest-running premiere showcase for international documentaries in the United States. Tickets are made available one month prior to the festival, and online at www.amnh.org/mead

AMNH TALKS TO FODOR'S

Rose Center for Earth and Space

Interview with Ellen V. Futter, President of the American Museum of Natural History, conducted by Michelle Delio.

If You Only Have an Hour: The American Museum of Natural History has the world's finest collection of dinosaur fossils, so a visit to the fourth-floor's Fossil Halls, where more than 600 specimens are on display, is a must. An extraordinarily high percentage of the specimens on view—85%—are real fossilized bones as opposed to casts. At most museums those percentages are reversed, so here visitors have the chance to see the real thing including T. rex, velociraptor, and triceratops.

What to Hit Next? The museum also is renowned for its habitat dioramas, which are considered among the finest examples in the world. Visits to the Akeley Hall of African Mammals, the Hall of North American Mammals, and the Sanford Hall of North American Birds provide an overview of the diorama arts—pioneered and advanced at the museum—while allowing visitors to come face-to-face with some glorious and beautiful animals depicted in their natural habitats—habitats which in many cases no longer exist in such pristine conditions.

If You're Looking to Be Starstruck: Even if you don't have time to take in a space show in the Hayden Planetarium, the Rose Center for Earth and Space has lots of fascinating exhibits describing the vast range of sizes in the cosmos; the 13-billion-year-history of the universe; the nature of galaxies, stars, and planets; and the dynamic features of our own unique planet Earth—all enclosed in a facility with spectacular award-winning architecture.

Hidden gems

The museum consists of 45 exhibition halls in 25 interconnected buildings so there are gems around every corner. Some lesser-known treasures include:

Star of India: The 563-carat Star of India, the largest and most famous star sapphire in the world, is displayed in the Morgan Memorial Hall of Gems.

ID PLEASE!

Once a year (usually in May or June—check website for details), the museum invites visitors to share rocks, teeth, shells, insects, feathers, and other curiosities with their scientists and anthropologists. Previous Identification Days have yielded rocks from the Jurassic Period, a fossilized walrus skull, and a 5,000-year-old stone spear point from Morocco. Lines can be long, but it's *so* interesting.

Black Smokers: These sulfide chimneys—collected during groundbreaking museum expeditions to the Pacific Ocean—are the only such specimens exhibited anywhere. Black smokers form around hot springs on the deep ocean floor and support a microbial community that does not live off sunlight but instead on the chemical energy of the Earth. Some of these microbes are considered the most ancient forms of life on Earth and may offer clues to the development of life here and the possibility of life elsewhere. See them in the Gottesman Hall of Planet Earth.

Spectrum of Life: The Hall of Biodiversity aims to showcase the glorious diversity of life on Earth resulting from 3.5 billion years of evolution. The impressive "Spectrum of Life" display is a 100-foot-long installation of more than 1,500 specimens and models—microorganisms and mammals, bacteria and beetles, fungi and fish. Use the computer workstations to learn more about the species depicted in each area.

Dodo: One of the museum's rarest treasures is the skeleton of a dodo bird, displayed along with other endangered or extinct species in the "Endangered Case" in the Hall of Biodiversity.

Small Dioramas: Tucked along the sides of the Hall of North American Mammals are two easy-to-miss corridors displaying a number of exquisitely rendered dioramas. In these jewel-box-like displays, some a mere 3 feet deep, you will see the smaller animals such as wolves galloping through a snowy night, a Canada lynx stalking a snowshoe hare, and a spotted skunk standing on its hands, preparing to spray a cacomistle, to name just a few of the evocative scenes.

Dinosaur Eggs: In 1993 museum scientists working in the Gobi Desert of Mongolia were the first to unearth fossilized embryos in dinosaur eggs, as well as the fossil of an adult oviraptor in a brooding posture over its nest. This discovery provided invaluable information about dinosaur gestation and revolutionized thinking about dinosaur behavior. Look for the display in the museum's Fossil Halls on the fourth floor.

Ross Terrace: In warmer months the Ross Terrace, with its fountains and cosmic theme, offers a wonderful outdoor spot for resting and reflecting, while providing a spectacular view of the Rose Center for Earth and Space.

Star of India

A diorama featuring a Komodo Dragon, the largest and most powerful lizard in the world.

MOST INTERESTING OBJECT?

What's most interesting about the American Museum of Natural History is not any single object on exhibit, but the sheer range and scope of what you can experience here. Think of it is a field guide to the natural world, the universe, and the cultures of humanity—all under one roof. The experience of visiting the museum is ultimately about awakening a sense of discovery, wonder, awe, and stewardship of this Earth we call home.

celebrated museum-neighbor (yes, that place with the dinosaurs) with a three-year $70 million renovation, completed in 2011. In the process, an under-the-radar museum and one of the city's finest research libraries stepped into the spotlight, delivering a contemporary glass facade, sleek technology and interactivity, a new children's museum, restaurant, and inventive exhibitions that showcase the museum's eclectic collections and voice. While the museum's permanent collection of more than 6 million pieces of art, literature, and memorabilia sheds light on America's history, art, and architecture, it's the special exhibits like the recent *The Black Fives* (a history of the African American basketball teams that existed in New York City and elsewhere from the early 1900s through 1950) and *Keith Haring All-Over* (featuring everyday items transformed by famed New York artist Keith Haring) that showcase this museum's fresh—and often surprising—insight on all things New York.

The **DiMenna Children's History Museum** on the lower level invites children to become "history detectives" and explore New York's past through interactive displays and the stories of iconic New York children through the centuries. ■TIP→ Unlike most other children's museums, this museum is geared to mature elementary school kids and middle schoolers, not toddlers. Caffé Storico, the light-filled restaurant on the first floor (with a separate entrance), serves upscale Italian food at lunch and dinner, and is open for brunch on the weekends. ⊠ *170 Central Park W, Upper West Side* ☎ *212/873-3400* ⊕ *www.nyhistory.org* 🖃 *$18* ⊙ *Tues.–Thurs. and Sat. 10–6, Fri. 10–8, Sun. 11–5* Ⓜ *B, C to 81st St.*

WORTH NOTING

American Folk Art Museum. After a near-death, or rather, near-*debt* experience in late 2011, the American Folk Art Museum left its home of 10 years on 53rd Street, adjacent to the MoMA, and returned to its humble rental near Lincoln Center. Here, minus the distractions of an artsy facade and celebrity neighbor, the focus returns to its incredible collection of contemporary self-taught artists of the 20th and 21st centuries, including the single largest collection of reclusive Chicago artist Henry Darger, known for his painstakingly detailed collage paintings of fantasy worlds. Recent exhibitions have included *Folk Couture: Fashion and Folk Art*, which featured the work of 13 established and emerging designers who created an original ensemble based on a selection of paintings, sculptures, photographs, quilts, and furniture chosen from the museum's collection. The gift shop has an impressive collection of handcrafted items. ⊠ *2 Lincoln Sq., Columbus Ave. at 66th St., Upper West Side* ☎ *212/595-9533* ⊕ *www.folkartmuseum.org* 🖃 *Free* ⊙ *Tues.–Sat. noon–7:30, Sun. noon–6* Ⓜ *1 to 66th St./Lincoln Center; A, B, C, D to 59th St./Columbus Circle.*

FAMILY   **Children's Museum of Manhattan.** In this five-story exploratorium, children ages 1–7 are invited to paint their own masterpieces, float boats down a "stream" (weather permitting), rescue animals with Dora and Diego (in an exhibition created in collaboration with Nickelodeon), and walk through giant interactive organs to explore the connections between food, sleep, and play. Special exhibits focus on the works of prominent artists, like the recent *Red Grooms' New York City*, and promote physical fitness, like *You Make the Call: Learn to be an NFL Official*. Seasonal programs include a Grinch Holiday workshop. Art workshops, science programs, and storytelling sessions are held daily. ■TIP→ Admission is free 5–8 pm on the first Friday of every month. ✉ *212 W. 83rd St., between Broadway and Amsterdam Ave., Upper West Side* ☎ *212/721–1223* ⊕ *www.cmom.org* ☛ *$11* ⊙ *Tues.–Fri. and Sun. 10–5, Sat. 10–7* Ⓜ *1 to 79th St. or 86th St.*

Columbus Circle. This busy traffic circle at Central Park's southwest corner anchors the Upper West Side and makes a good starting place for exploring the neighborhood if you're coming from south of 59th Street. The central 700-ton granite monument (capped by a marble statue of Christopher Columbus) serves as a popular meeting place. To some people, Columbus Circle is synonymous with the **Time Warner Center** (⊕ *www.shopsatcolumbuscircle.com*) and its several floors of shops and restaurants—including takeout-friendly Bouchon Bakery and Whole Foods, both perfect places to pick up picnic fixings to take to Central Park. ✉ *Broadway between 57th and 59th Sts.* Ⓜ *A, B, C, D, 1 to 59 St./Columbus Circle.*

Grant's Tomb (*General Grant National Memorial*). Walk through upper Riverside Park and you're sure to notice this towering granite mausoleum (1897), the final resting place of Civil War general and two-term president Ulysses S. Grant and his wife, Julia Dent Grant. As the old joke goes, who's buried here? Nobody—they're *entombed* in a crypt beneath a domed rotunda, surrounded by photographs and Grant memorabilia. Once a more popular sight than the Statue of Liberty, this pillared Classical Revival edifice feels more like a relic of yesteryear, but it remains a moving tribute. The words engraved on the tomb, "Let Us Have Peace," recall Grant's speech to the Republican convention upon his presidential nomination. Surrounding the memorial are the so-called "rolling benches," which bring to mind the works of architect Antonio Gaudí's Park Güell, in Barcelona. Made in the 1970s as a public art project, they are now as beloved as they are incongruous with the grand memorial they surround. Free public talks are available in the visitor center (across the street from the tomb), from Thurs through Monday at 11:15, 1:15, and 3:15. ✉ *Riverside Dr. at 122nd St., Upper West Side* ☎ *212/666–1640* ⊕ *www.nps.gov/gegr* ☛ *Free* ⊙ *Thurs.–Mon. 9–5* Ⓜ *1 to 116th St. St.*

Museum of Arts and Design. In a funky-looking white building right across the street from the Time Warner Center, the Museum of Arts and Design celebrates joyful quirkiness and personal, sometimes even obsessive, artistic visions. The art is human-scale here, much of it neatly housed in display cases rather than on the walls, with a strong focus on contemporary jewelry, glass, ceramic, fiber, wood, and mixed-media works. Recent exhibits included *Out of Hand: Materializing the Postdigital*, which examined the use of computer-assisted production in creative fields, and *Body & Soul: New International Ceramics,* which explored the use of ceramics to convey emotion. ■TIP→ Thursday evening admission is pay-what-you-wish. ✉ *2 Columbus Circle, 59th St. at 8th Ave., Upper West Side* ☎ *212/299–7777* ⊕ *www.madmuseum.org* ☛ *$16* ⊙ *Tues., Wed., and weekends 10–6, Thurs. and Fri. 10–9* Ⓜ *A, B, C, D, 1 to Columbus Circle/59th St.; N, Q, R to 57th St./7th Ave.; F to 57th St./6th Ave.*

FAMILY **Riverside Park.** Surrounded by concrete and skyscrapers, you might not realize that there is an expansive green space running along the water just blocks away. Riverside Park—which, along with the Riverside Park South extension, runs along the Hudson from 58th to 156th streets—dishes out a dose of tranquility. The original sections of Riverside Park, designed by Frederick Law Olmsted and Calvert Vaux of Central Park fame and laid out between 1873 and 1888, are outshone by Olmsted's "other" park—Central Park—but with its waterfront bike and walking paths and lighter crowds, this green space holds its own.

There are several access points to the park, including one at 72nd Street and Riverside Drive (look for the **statue of Eleanor Roosevelt**) where you'll reach the waterfront path after heading through an underpass beneath the West Side Highway. You can then head north along the Hudson River, past the **79th Street Boat Basin,** where you can watch a flotilla of houseboats bobbing in the water. Above it, a ramp leads to the Rotunda, home in summer to the **Boat Basin Café,** an open-air café that's open for lunch and dinner in the warmer months (from about March through October). The **91st Street Garden,** planted by community gardeners, explodes with flowers in most seasons and is a level up from the water: leave the waterside path near 92nd Street by taking another underpass and then heading up the path on the right. To the south, cresting a hill along Riverside Drive at West 89th Street, stands the **Civil War Soldiers' and Sailors' Monument** (1902), an imposing 96-foot-high circle of white-marble columns designed by Paul M. Duboy, who also designed the Ansonia Hotel—a once-famous residential hotel (now an apartment building) on Broadway and West 74th Street. ⊠ *58th to 156th St., between Riverside Dr. and the Hudson R., Upper West Side* ⊕ *www. nycgovparks.org/parks/riversidepark* Ⓜ *1, 2, 3 to 72nd St.*

INWOOD

The Cloisters Museum and Gardens. Perched on a wooded hill in Fort Tryon Park, near Manhattan's northwestern tip, the Cloisters Museum and Gardens, which shelter the medieval collection of the Metropolitan Museum of Art, is a scenic destination in its own right. Colonnaded walks connect authentic French and Spanish monastic cloisters, a French Romanesque chapel, a 12th-century chapter house, and a Romanesque apse. One room is devoted to the 15th- and 16th-century Unicorn Tapestries from around 1500—a must-see masterpiece of medieval mythology. The tomb effigies are another highlight. Two of the three enclosed gardens shelter more than 250 species of plants similar to those grown during the Middle Ages, including flowers, herbs, and medicinals; the third is an ornamental garden planted with both modern and medieval plants, providing color and fragrance from early spring until late fall. Concerts of medieval music are held here regularly (concert tickets include same-day admission to the museum). The outdoor Trie Café is open 10 to 4:15 daily except Monday, April through October, and serves sandwiches, coffee, and snacks. ■TIP→ **Fee includes same-day admission to the Metropolitan Museum of Art's main building at 82nd Street.** ⊠ *99 Margaret Corbin Dr., Ft. Tryon Park, Upper West Side* ☎ *212/923–3700* ⊕ *www.metmuseum. org* ⊠ *$25 suggested donation* ⊙ *Mar.–Oct., daily 10–5:15; Nov.–Feb., daily 10–4:45* Ⓜ *A to 190th St.*

HARLEM

GETTING ORIENTED

Harlem

0   1/4 mile

0   400 meters

Highbridge Park

Morris-Jumel Mansion

C

B,D

Hispanic Society of America Museum and Library

W. 155th St.

Sugar Hill

W. 153rd St.

W. 152nd St.

W. 151st St.

W. 150th St.

W. 149th St.

The Chipped Cup

W. 148th St.

3

W. 147th St.

THE BRONX

W. 146th St.

3

A,B,C,D

W. 145th St.

145 St. Bridge

Convent Avenue Baptist Church

W. 144th St.

Harlem River

W. 143rd St.

Hamilton Terrace

W. 142nd St.

W. 141st St.

Hamilton Grange

W. 140th St.

Strivers' Row

W. 139th St.

City College

W. 138th St.

Abyssinian Baptist Church

W. 137th St.

W. 136th St.

2,3

E. 135th St.

B,C

W. 135th St.

W. 134th St.

W. 133rd St.

W. 132nd St.

E. 131st St.

W. 130th St.

E. 129th St.

W. 129th St.

W. 128th St.

W. 127th St.

Apollo Theater

W. 127th St.

125th St-Metro North

W. 126th St.

A,B,C,D

African Sq.

2,3

Dr. Martin Luther King Jr. Blvd. (125th St.)

Studio Museum in Harlem

Greater Refuge Temple

W. 124th St.

HARLEM

W. 123rd St.

W. 123rd St.

Marcus Garvey Park

W. 122nd St.

W. 121st St.

W. 121st St.

W. 120th St.

E. 119th St.

Barnard College

E. 118th St.

Columbia University

Canaan Baptist Church of Christ

E. 117th St.

Levain Bakery

2,3

Malcolm Shabazz Harlem Market

E. 116th St.

W. 116th St.

B,C

E. 115th St.

First Corinthian Baptist Church

W. 114th St.

Memorial Baptist Church

Masjid Malcolm Shabazz

W. 113th St.

W. 112th St.

Cathedral Church of St. John the Divine

W. 111th St.

Cathedral Pkwy.

B,C

Central Park North

2,3

E. 110th St.

W. 109th St.

CENTRAL PARK

Harlem Meer

13

MAKING THE MOST OF YOUR TIME

Harlem's simplest pleasures are free. Take time to walk the areas around Strivers' Row, Hamilton Heights, Sugar Hill, and 116th Street to see some impressive—and often fanciful—architecture. Hear the sweet sounds of a choir practice as you stroll by any of Harlem's churches (which number in the hundreds). See well-curated exhibits showcasing the work of contemporary artists of African descent at the Studio Museum in Harlem (open Thursday–Sunday), or visit the Morris-Jumel Mansion for a trip back in time to colonial New York.

GETTING HERE AND AROUND

The 2 and 3 subway lines stop on Lenox Avenue; the 1 goes along Broadway, to the west; and the A, B, C, and D trains travel along St. Nicholas and 8th avenues. And yes, as the song goes, the A train is still usually "the quickest way to Harlem."

The city's north–south avenues take on different names in Harlem: 6th Avenue is called both Malcolm X Boulevard *and* Lenox Avenue; 7th Avenue is Adam Clayton Powell Jr. Boulevard (it's named for the influential minister and congressman); and 8th Avenue is Frederick Douglass Boulevard. West 125th Street, the major east–west street and Harlem's commercial center, is also known as Dr. Martin Luther King Jr. Boulevard.

SAFETY

Harlem is more residential than many parts of the city and home to many families, so it gets quiet at night. Like everywhere else in New York, use common sense and steer clear of deserted side streets after dark.

TOP EXPERIENCES

Join Harlem's hippest for cocktails and music (live or DJ-spun) at Red Rooster/Ginny's Supper Club.

Attend a gospel service.

Visit the Studio Museum in Harlem.

Have fried chicken and waffles for breakfast, lunch, or dinner at a number of soul-food spots.

COFFEE AND QUICK BITES

The Chipped Cup. Below busy Broadway, this coffeehouse offers fair-trade organic coffee, espresso drinks, tea, fresh pastries, and free Wi-Fi in a parlorlike atmosphere with a vibrant, neighborhood vibe. ✉ *3610 Broadway, between 148th and 149th Sts., Hamilton Heights* ⊕ *Located below street level* ☎ *212/368–8881* ⊕ *www.chippedcupcoffee.com* ⊗ *Weekdays 7 am–8 pm, weekends 8–8* Ⓜ *1 to 145th St.*

Levain Bakery. From coffee and cakes to breads and scones, this bakery has something for every sweet tooth. It's the cookies, however, that make them famous. Choose from varieties such as Chocolate Chip Walnut and Dark Chocolate Chocolate Chip; they're big enough to share, but after one bite you may not want to. ✉ *2167 Frederick Douglass Blvd., between 116th and 117th Sts.* ☎ *646/455–0952* ⊕ *www.levainbakery.com* ⊗ *Mon.–Sat. 8–7, Sun. 9–7.*

Sightseeing
★★

Nightlife
★★★★

Dining
★★★

Lodging
★★

Shopping
★★

Harlem is known throughout the world as a center of African-American culture, music, and life. The neighborhood invites visitors to see historic jewels such as the Apollo Theater, architecturally splendid churches, cultural magnets like the Studio Museum in Harlem and the Schomburg Center for Research in Black Culture, as well as an ongoing list of new and renovated sites and buildings.

Updated by
Anuja Madar

In Harlem, things are changing quickly. Luckily, its original charm and personalities are still around if you know where to look. While some iconic establishments have closed, newer spots aim to take their place by both paying homage to the area's roots and appealing to the young families and professionals who are buying up new high-rise condos and restoring old brownstone and limestone buildings.

Harlem's 125th Street is at the heart of the neighborhood. Bill Clinton's New York office is at 55 West 125th Street, and the legendary Apollo Theater stands at No. 253. Growth has brought outposts of Starbucks, Old Navy, and H&M (with Whole Foods set to open in 2015), which make it hard to distinguish 125th Street from the city's other heavily commercialized areas. But there are still a few things that set it apart: an energy created by sidewalk vendors hawking bootleg DVDs, incense, and African shea butter; impromptu drum circles; and some of the best people-watching in Manhattan.

To get a taste of today's Harlem, spend time visiting its past and present. On 116th Street, particularly between St. Nicholas and Lenox avenues (Malcolm X Boulevard), you'll find some of the area's most interesting religious buildings. Admire the ornate theatrical facade of the giant **First Corinthian Baptist Church,** or fill your soul with the mellifluous gospel music of the **Canaan Baptist Church of Christ's** choir during a Sunday service. Take a hint from the parishioners and follow up with smothered chicken and waffles at **Sylvia's,** at 328 Malcolm X Boulevard.

After lunch, walk by the green-domed **Masjid Malcolm Shabazz**—a mosque attended primarily by West Africans and African Americans.

Finish at **Malcolm Shabazz Harlem Market** where you can bargain for African and African-inspired jewelry, masks, crafts, and caftans at good prices.

Nowhere is the "new Harlem" more visible than along Lenox Avenue and Frederick Douglass Boulevard, between 110th and 126th streets. Here you'll find restaurants, bars, and a few boutiques. Grab a bar stool at Red Rooster, where celebrity chef Marcus Samuelsson has created a restaurant-bar-lounge that draws tourists from across the globe and NYC residents from below 14th Street. While you might not be able to score a table, a visit here is more for the scene and creative cocktails than the food. Just west on 125th Street, check out contemporary African-American-oriented artworks at the **Studio Museum in Harlem.** If you're here on Thursday or Friday, exhibits are open until 9, and on Sunday admission is free.

TOP ATTRACTIONS

Abyssinian Baptist Church. This 1923 Gothic-style church holds one of Harlem's richest legacies, dating to 1808 when a group of parishioners defected from the segregated First Baptist Church of New York City and established the first African-American Baptist church in New York State. Among its legendary pastors was Adam Clayton Powell Jr., a powerful orator and civil rights leader and the first black U.S. congressman. Today sermons by Rev. Dr. Calvin O. Butts III are fiery, and the several choirs are excellent. Dress your best, remember to not take pictures or videos, get there early—at least two hours ahead of time—and be prepared to wait in line outside (rain or shine). ⊠ *132 Odell Clark Pl. (W. 138th St.), between Adam Clayton Powell Jr. Blvd. and Lenox Ave. ⊹ Tourist entrance is on the southeast corner of 138th and Adam Clayton Powell, Jr. Blvd. ☏ 212/862–7474 ⊕ www.abyssinian. org ☉ Visitor services Wed. at 7 pm and Sun. at 11 am; no visitor services on major holidays. Ⓜ 2, 3 to 135th St.*

Apollo Theater. *See the listing in Chapter 20 Performing Arts.*

Canaan Baptist Church of Christ. The heavenly gospel music during Rev. Dr. Thomas D. Johnson Jr.'s Sunday-morning services makes up for this church's unassuming, concrete-box-like exterior. Pastor emeritus Wyatt Tee Walker worked with Dr. Martin Luther King Jr., who delivered his famous "A Knock at Midnight" sermon here. Visitors may enter once parishioners are seated. To attend, arrive at least an hour before services. ⊠ *132 W. 116th St., between Malcolm X and Adam Clayton Powell Jr. Blvds. ☏ 212/866–0301 ⊕ www.cbccnyc.org ☉ Services Sun. at 8 and 10 am Ⓜ 2, 3 to 116th St.*

Hamilton Heights. To taste this neighborhood's Harlem Renaissance days, walk down tree-lined Convent Avenue, detouring onto adjacent **Hamilton Terrace,** and see a time capsule of elegant stone row houses in mint condition. One of the neighborhood's most beautiful blocks, it's popular with film and TV crews. Continue down Convent Avenue and see the looming Gothic spires (1905) of City College. The stately Oxford-inspired buildings here are New York to the core: they are clad with the schist rock unearthed when the city was building what is now the 1

D.I.Y. Harlem Gospel Tours

For the past decade, the popularity of Sunday gospel tours has surged. While some in the community see it as an opportunity to broaden horizons and encourage diversity, others find tours disruptive and complain that tourists take seats away from regular parishioners (churches regularly fill to capacity). If you plan on attending a service, here are some tips:

Most churches have Sunday services at 11, but you may need to arrive as much as two hours early (depending on the church) to get in. Dress nicely—no shorts, sneakers, or jeans—be as quiet as possible, do not leave in the middle of the service and do not take photos or videos or use your cell phone. Most important, remember that parishioners do not consider the service, or themselves, to be tourist attractions or entertainment.

A bus tour is generally an inauthentic (and more expensive) way to experience Harlem. Explore the neighborhood and churches on your own, or join a small tour like those offered by **Harlem Heritage Tours** (☎ 212/280–7888 ⊕ www.harlemheritage.com).

Their tours ($39) get high marks from past clients and are run by guides who were born and raised in Harlem; groups are no larger than 25 people.

The following are some of the uptown churches with Sunday services:

Abyssinian Baptist Church is one of the few churches that does not allow tour groups. Service for visitors is at 11. Arrive at least two hours ahead of time for this service. **Canaan Baptist Church of Christ** has services at 8 and 10. **Convent Avenue Baptist Church** (⊠ 420 W. 145th St., between Convent and St. Nicholas Aves., Harlem ☎ 212/234–6767 ⊕ www. conventchurch.org) has services at 8, 11, and 5. **First Corinthian Baptist Church** has services at 8 and 10:45.

Greater Refuge Temple (⊠ 2081 Adam Clayton Powell Jr. Blvd., at 124th St., Harlem ☎ 212/866–1700 ⊕ www.greaterrefugetemple.org) has services at 11, 4, and 7:30. **Memorial Baptist Church** (⊠ 141 W. 115th St., between Adam Clayton Powell Jr. and Malcolm X Blvds., Harlem ☎ 212/663–8830 ⊕ www.mbcvisionharlem.org) has service at 11.

subway line. Otherwise, walk down 141st Street and visit the ⇨ *Hamilton Grange National Memorial*, founding father Alexander Hamilton's Federal-style mansion. When you're ready to move on, head southeast, which will bring you to Strivers' Row. ⊠ *Convent Ave., between 138th and 150th Sts.* Ⓜ *A, B, C, D to 145th St.*

Morris-Jumel Mansion. During the Revolutionary War, General Washington used this wooden, pillared 8,500-square-foot house (1765) as his headquarters, and when he visited as president in 1790, he brought along John Quincy Adams, Jefferson, and Hamilton. Inside are rooms furnished with period decorations—upstairs, keep an eye out for the hand-painted wallpaper (original to the house) and a "commode chair," stuck in a corner of the dressing room. Outside, behind the house, is a Colonial-era marker that says it's 11 miles to New York: a reminder of what a small sliver of Manhattan the city was at that time. East of the house is the block-long Sylvan Terrace, a row of crisp two-story

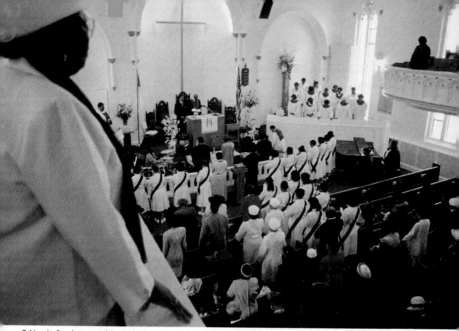

Taking in Sunday gospel in Harlem

clapboard houses built in 1882. ⊠ *65 Jumel Terr., north of 160th St., between St. Nicholas and Edgecombe Aves.* ☎ *212/923–8008* ⊕ *www. morrisjumel.org* ✉ *$5, guided tours $6* ⊙ *Wed.–Sun. 10–4, guided tours Sat. at noon* Ⓜ *C to 163rd St.*

Strivers' Row. This block of gorgeous 1890s Georgian and neo-Italian homes earned its nickname in the 1920s from less affluent Harlemites who felt its residents were "striving" to become well-to-do. Some of the few remaining private service alleys, used when deliveries arrived via horse and cart, lie behind these houses and are visible through iron gates. Note the gatepost between Nos. 251 and 253 on West 138th Street that says, "Private Road. Walk Your Horses." The houses were built by the contractor David H. King Jr., whose works also include the base for the Statue of Liberty and the oldest parts of the Cathedral Church of St. John the Divine. When the houses failed to sell to whites, the properties on these blocks were sold to African-American doctors, lawyers, and other professionals; the composers and musicians W. C. Handy and Eubie Blake were also among the residents. If you have the time, detour a block north to see the palazzo-style group of houses designed by Stanford White, on the north side of West 139th Street. ⊠ *W. 138th and W. 139th Sts., between Adam Clayton Powell Jr. and Frederick Douglass Blvds.* Ⓜ *B, C to 135th St.*

Studio Museum in Harlem. Contemporary art by African-American, Caribbean, and African artists is the focus of this small museum with a light-filled sculpture garden. Recent exhibits included *Gordon Parks: A Harlem Family 1967*, documenting the life of the Fontenelle family, who Parks photographed for *Life* magazine, and the science fiction-inspired

Harlem's Jazz Age

It was in Harlem that Billie Holiday got her first singing job, Duke Ellington made his first recording, and Louis Armstrong was propelled to stardom. Jazz was king during the Harlem Renaissance in the 1920s and '30s, and though Chicago and New Orleans may duke it out for the "birthplace of jazz" title, New York was where jazz musicians came to be heard.

In the 1920s socialites made the trek uptown to Harlem's Cotton Club and Connie's Inn (131st Street and 7th Avenue) to hear "black" music. Both clubs were white-owned and barred blacks from entering, except as performers. (The rules changed years later.) Connie's introduced New Yorkers to Louis Armstrong. The Cotton Club—Harlem's most popular

nightspot by far—booked such big names as Fletcher Henderson, Coleman Hawkins, Duke Ellington, Cab Calloway, and Ethel Waters. After shows ended at the paying clubs, musicians would head to after-hours establishments with black patrons, such as Small's Paradise, Minton's Playhouse (which reopened in 2013), and Basement Brownies, where they'd hammer out new riffs into the wee hours.

While you can't go back in time to Harlem's jazz heyday, and most of the old places are long closed, you can still find good live music at the recently reopened **Minton's** (⊠ 206 W. 118th St.) and **Ginny's Supper Club** (⊠ 310 Lennox Ave., in the Red Rooster's basement).

Robert Pruitt: Women. Three artists in residence present their works each year. The gift shop is small but packs a lot of punch; don't miss its fantastic collection of coffee table books. ⊠ *144 W. 125th St., between Lenox Ave. and Adam Clayton Powell Jr. Blvd.* ☎ *212/864–4500* ⊕ *www.studiomuseum.org* ✉ *$7 suggested donation, free on Sun.* ☉ *Thurs. and Fri. noon–9, Sat. 10–6, Sun. noon–6* Ⓜ *2, 3 to 125th St.*

WORTH NOTING

First Corinthian Baptist Church. One of the most ornate structures in Harlem, this church kicked off its life in 1913 as the Regent Theatre, one of the country's early movie palaces that replaced the nickelodeons. Its elaborately columned and arched facade loosely resembles the Doges' Palace in Venice. The Regent was sold to the church in 1964. To attend services, arrive at least an hour ahead of time. ⊠ *1912 Adam Clayton Powell Jr. Blvd., at 7th Ave.* ☎ *212/864–5976* ⊕ *www.fcbcsermons. com* ☉ *Services Fri. at 6:30 pm and Sun. at 8 and 10:45 am* Ⓜ *2, 3 to 116th St.*

Hamilton Grange National Memorial. Founding father Alexander Hamilton and his wife raised eight kids in this Federal-style country home, which he called his "sweet project." Located on Hamilton's 32 acres, the Grange, named after his father's childhood home in Scotland, has moved three times since it was built in 1802. It now stands in St. Nicholas Park and offers a lesson in Hamilton's life, from his illegitimate birth in the West Indies and his appointment as the nation's first Secretary of

Treasury to his authoring of *The Federalist Papers* and his death following a duel with Vice President Aaron Burr. The house's ground floor, formerly servants' quarters, hosts an interactive exhibit that includes a short film on Hamilton's life. Upstairs a parlor, study, dining room, and two guest rooms are open for viewing. ⊠ *414 W. 141st St., between St. Nicholas and Convent Aves.* ☎ *646/548–2310* ⊕ *www.nps.gov/hagr/ index.htm* 🎫 *Free* ⊙ *Wed.–Sun. 9–5* Ⓜ *1 to 137th St.; A, B, C, D to 145th St.* ☞ *Self-guided tours of the furnished rooms are 12–1 and 3–4 only. Thirty-minute ranger-led tours are at 10, 11, 1, 2, and 4.*

The Hispanic Society of America Museum and Library. This is the best collection of Hispanic and Spanish art outside the Prado in Madrid, with paintings, sculptures, textiles, manuscripts, music, and decorative arts from ancient Iberia through the 20th century. There are notable pieces by Goya, El Greco, Murillo, Velázquez and Zurbarán. An entire room is filled with a collection of antique iron knockers. ⊠ *Audubon Terrace, 613 W. 155th St., Broadway between 155th and 156th Sts. (entrance up steps to left)* ☎ *212/926–2234* ⊕ *www.hispanicsociety.org* 🎫 *Free* ⊙ *Tues.–Sat. 10–4:30, Sun. 1–4* Ⓜ *1 to 157th St.*

Masjid Malcolm Shabazz (*Mosque*). Talk about religious conversions. In the mid-'60s, the Lenox Casino was transformed into this house of worship and cultural center, and given bright yellow arches and a huge green onion dome that loudly proclaims its presence in a neighborhood of churches. Once functioning as Temple No. 7 under the Nation of Islam with a message of pro-black racism, the mosque was bombed after the assassination of Malcolm X, who had preached here. It was rebuilt and renamed in honor of the name Malcolm took at the end of his life, El-Hajj Malik Shabazz; its philosophy now is one of inclusion. Next door is Graceline Court, a 16-story luxury condominium building that cantilevers somewhat awkwardly over the mosque. Farther east on 116th Street is the outdoor **Malcolm Shabazz Harlem Market**, where you can find African and African-inspired jewelry, art, clothing and fabrics. ⊠ *102 W. 116th St., at Lenox Ave.* ☎ *212/662–2200* Ⓜ *2, 3 to 116th St.*

Sugar Hill. Standing on the bluff of Sugar Hill overlooking Jackie Robinson Park, outside the slightly run-down **409 Edgecombe Avenue** you'd never guess that here resided such influential African-Americans as NAACP founder W. E. B. DuBois and Supreme Court Justice Thurgood Marshall, or that farther north at **555 Edgecombe,** known as the "Triple Nickel," writers Langston Hughes and Zora Neale Hurston and jazz musicians Duke Ellington, Count Basie, and others lived and played. And it's also here that for nearly 20 years musician Marjorie Eliot has been hosting jazz concerts in her apartment, 3F, at 3:30 every Sunday. Farther down, at 345 Edgecombe, you can't miss the **Benzinger House** with its flared mansard roof. Amidst all this history, the modern-looking Sugar Hill Children's Museum of Art & Storytelling, at 155th Street and St. Nicholas Avenue, is set to open in 2014. Its design has earned it the nickname Sugar Cube Building. ⊠ *Bounded by 145th and 155th Sts., and Edgecombe and St. Nicholas Aves.* Ⓜ *A, B, C, D to 145th St.*

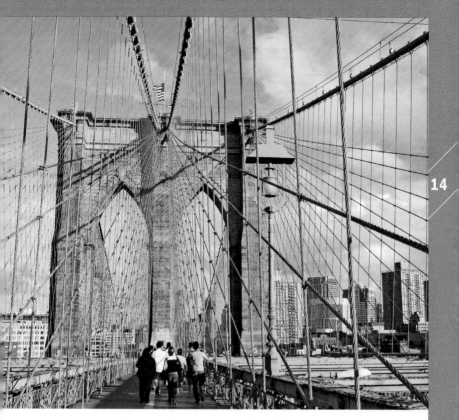

BROOKLYN

GETTING ORIENTED

Brooklyn

Manhattan Bridge

278

Williamsburg
see map

Brooklyn Heights
and DUMBO
see map

DUMBO

WILLIAMSBURG

Flushing Ave.

Myrtle Ave.

De Kalb Ave.

BROOKLYN
HEIGHTS

FORT
GREENE

BEDFORD
STUYVESANT

*Governors
Island*

COBBLE
HILL BOERUM
HILL

◆ Brooklyn
Academy
of Music

Atlantic Ave.

CARROLL
GARDENS

Union St.

Carroll Gardens
Cobble Hill,
Boerum Hill,
and Fort Greene
see map

RED
HOOK

9th St.

PROSPECT
HEIGHTS

CROWN
HEIGHTS

*Upper New
York Bay*

27

PARK
SLOPE

◆ Brooklyn
Museum

◆ Brooklyn
Botanic Garden

Eastern Pkwy.

Empire Blvd.

Utica Ave.

*Prospect
Park*

New York Ave.

Park Slope and
Prospect Heights
see map

27

*Greenwood
Cemetery*

*Holy Cross
Cemetery*

SUNSET
PARK

38th St.

DITMAS
PARK

Foster Ave.

278

KENSINGTON

14th Ave.

McDonald Ave.

Ocean Pkwy.

Coney Island Ave.

Ocean Ave.

Flatbush Ave.

FLATBUSH

BAY
RIDGE

278

Fort Hamilton Pkwy.

Avenue J

4th Ave.

76th St.

BOROUGH
PARK

MIDWOOD

Belt Parkway

FORT
HAMILTON

86th St.

14th Ave.

Coney Island

STILLWELL AVE.

M D,F,N,Q

Mermaid Ave.

W. 8th St.

*Lower New
York Bay*

BATH
BEACH

Coney Island
Circus Sideshow

Coney
Island
Museum

W. 8TH ST.

M F,Q

W. 8th St.

W. 5th St.

Nathan's Famous ✕

◆ ◆

Surf Ave.

New York
Aquarium

*Asser Levy
Park*

The Bowery

The Cyclone
and Luna Park

Surf Ave.

Belt Parkway

W. 19th St.

W. 16th St.

W. 15th St.

Stillwell Ave.

Jones Walk

W. 12th St.

W. 10th St.

Deno's
Wonder Wheel
Amusement Park

◆ Brighton Beach
Boardwalk

Boardwalk

0   1/4 mile

0   400 meters

Atlantic Ocean

**Coney
Island**
see inset

SHEEPSHEAD
BAY

Shore Parkway

SEA
GATE

CONEY
ISLAND

BRIGHTON
BEACH

MANHATTAN
BEACH

*Manhattan
Beach Park*

0   1 mi

0   1 km

Surf Ave.

14

TOP EXPERIENCES

Late-night music or bar-hopping in Williamsburg

Screaming at the top of the Cyclone roller coaster

Smelling the roses, and everything else, at the Brooklyn Botanic Garden

Catching a show at BAM or Barclay's Center

Pizza at Grimaldi's or ice cream from the Brooklyn Ice Cream Factory after a walk across the Brooklyn Bridge

GETTING HERE

To get to Williamsburg, take the L train from any 14th Street station in Manhattan to Bedford Avenue, the first stop in Brooklyn.

You can reach Brooklyn Heights via the 2 or 3 train to Clark Street, the R to Court Street, or the 4 or 5 to Borough Hall.

To get to DUMBO, take the F train to York Street, the A or C to High Street, or walk from Brooklyn Heights.

The F train to 7th Avenue will take you to the center of Park Slope. From there, walk uphill to reach Prospect Park or walk north on 7th Avenue to get to the shops. The hipper boutiques and eateries are two long blocks west, on 5th Avenue, best accessed on the R train to Union Street.

To reach the Brooklyn Museum, Brooklyn Botanic Garden, and Prospect Park take the 2 or 3 train to Eastern Parkway–Brooklyn Museum.

Coney Island is the last stop on the D, F, N, and Q trains; the Q or B will take you to Brighton Beach. Allow a good part of the day for these, since it takes about an hour to reach the ocean from Manhattan.

COFFEE AND QUICK BITES

Almondine Bakery. The best French bakery this side of Montmartre is on Water Street. Chocolate raspberry croissants, mille-feuille, macarons, and pear tarts are baked on site, as well as baguettes, quiche, and sandwiches—perfect snacks to take to the park. ⊠ *85 Water St., DUMBO* ☏ *718/797–5056* ⊕ *www.almondinebakery.com* Ⓜ *F to York St.*

Brooklyn Farmacy. Step back in time in this fully restored 1920s-era soda fountain to enjoy all kinds of ice-cream treats, as well as savory snacks. ⊠ *513 Henry St., Carroll Gardens* ☏ *718/522–6260* ⊕ *brooklynfarmacy.blogspot.com* Ⓜ *F to Carroll St.*

Bakeri. This comforting, compact Williamsburg café serves seasonal, sweet and savory pastries, plus cakes, muffins, scones, and cookies. Take a coffee to-go or sit among the artfully dressed clientele. ⊠ *150 Wythe Ave., Williamsburg* ☏ *718/388–8037* ⊕ *www.bakeribrooklyn.com* Ⓜ *L to Bedford Ave.*

One Girl Cookies. Top-notch snacks include a variety of whoopie pies, cakes, and cookies in flavors like chocolate-cinnamon-ganache and Thai-ginger-oatmeal, served with Stumptown Coffee. ⊠ *33 Main St., DUMBO* ☏ *347/338–1268* ⊕ *www.onegirlcookies.com/dumbo* Ⓜ *F to York St.; A, C to High St.*

Sightseeing
★★★
Nightlife
★★★★
Dining
★★★★ ★
Lodging
★ ★
Shopping
★★★

Brooklyn is changing rapidly, and it has been for a while. Hardly Manhattan's wimpy sidekick, this is the largest and most populous of all the boroughs, with more than 2.5 million residents and a ton of cool places to eat, drink, shop, and explore, including the glamorous Barclay's Center arena, home to the Brooklyn Nets NBA basketball team, as well as a new waterfront park extending from the Manhattan Bridge to Atlantic Avenue and beyond.

Updated
by Michael
Hornburg

Brooklyn was a city itself until the end of the 19th century, with its own widely circulated newspaper (the *Brooklyn Eagle*), its own expansive park (Prospect Park), and its own baseball team that would eventually be called the Brooklyn Dodgers. And in 1883, it got its own bridge: the Brooklyn Bridge, which drew the attention of the entire country.

Today, Brooklyn's young family-friendly vibe encompasses lovely brownstone-filled neighborhoods like **Brooklyn Heights, Cobble Hill, Carroll Gardens, Boerum Hill, Fort Greene, Park Slope,** and **Prospect Heights.** And of course, Brooklyn is also home to hipsters—if you're looking for the their epicenter, head to **Williamsburg,** where young artists started infiltrating the residential neighborhood back in the late 1990s. The area quickly became known for its galleries, and then for the funky bars, restaurants, and music venues.

With the exception of art exhibits at the Brooklyn Museum, the lush grounds of the Brooklyn Botanic Garden, and cutting-edge performances at the Brooklyn Academy of Music, this isn't really a destination for "sights." Instead, the neighborhoods' real draws are their residential vibe, proudly local restaurants, and down-home shops and bars.

Brooklyn is Book Country

Brooklyn has been a mecca for writers and literature since the days of *Uncle Tom's Cabin,* written by a preacher's daughter in Brooklyn Heights. Since then writers have flocked here for the cheap rent and quiet streets. Henry Miller, Norman Mailer, Truman Capote, Arthur Miller (with Marilyn Monroe), Paul and Jane Bowles, Carson McCullers, James Purdy, and Walt Whitman created more than one masterpiece.

Today, amid the gentrification, Brooklyn continues to lure famous and near-famous writers and musicians from all over the world. Local residents include power-writer couples Paul Auster and Siri Hustvedt, Jonathan Safran Foer and Nicole Krauss, Jhumpa Lahiri, and Martin Amis, just to name a few.

Perhaps reflecting the plethora of writers in the neighborhood, the borough has a relatively high density of both used and new bookstores, and also several small presses, including Melville House, a press with a storefront bookstore.

And with all these writers so close by, it only makes sense that Brooklyn has a fabulous book festival, to boot. The Brooklyn Book Festival happens every year at Borough Hall, on the third weekend in September. Authors gather for readings and signings, and independent publishers display their wares.

14

BROOKLYN HEIGHTS

Brooklyn's toniest neighborhood offers residents something that wealthy Manhattanites will never have: a stunning view of the Manhattan skyline from the Brooklyn Heights Promenade. First developed in the mid-1800s as the business center of the then-independent city of Brooklyn, Brooklyn Heights showcases historic cobblestone streets of pristine brownstones.

There is a lot of history in Brooklyn Heights itself. In the early to mid-20th century the Heights was a bohemian haven, home to a virtual "who's who" of writers like Arthur Miller, Truman Capote, Henry Miller, Alfred Kazin, Carson McCullers, Paul Bowles, Marianne Moore, Norman Mailer, and W. E. B. Du Bois.

The majestic **Brooklyn Bridge** has one foot in Brooklyn Heights, near DUMBO, and a walk across it either to or from Lower Manhattan is one of the quintessential New York experiences.

Much of Brooklyn Heights's early architecture has been preserved, thanks to its designation as New York's first historic district in the 1960s. Some 600 buildings built in the 19th century represent a wide range of American architecture styles. Many of the best line **Columbia Heights,** a residential street that runs parallel to the promenade, but any of its adjoining streets are also worth strolling. On **Willow Street** be sure to note No. 22, Henry Ward Beecher's prim Greek Revival brownstone, and Nos. 155–159. These three brick Federal row houses are said to have been stops on the Underground Railroad. The skylight in the pavement by the gate to No. 157 provided the light for an underground tunnel leading to an 1880 carriage house. Plymouth Church, where Beecher preached, saw the likes of Abraham Lincoln, Charles Dickens, and Ralph Waldo Emerson in its congregation.

TOP ATTRACTIONS

Fodor's Choice ★ **Brooklyn Bridge.** (⇨ *Chapter 2*) Ⓜ *4, 5, 6 to Brooklyn Bridge–City Hall; J, Z to Chambers St.; A, C to High St.*

FAMILY Fodor's Choice ★ **Brooklyn Heights Promenade.** Stretching from Orange Street to Remsen Street, the Brooklyn Heights esplanade provides enthralling views of Manhattan, especially in the evening when the lights of the city sparkle across the East River. Find a bench and take in the skyline, the Statue of Liberty, and the Brooklyn Bridge—an impressive 1883 steel suspension bridge designed by John Augustus Roebling. Frank Gehry's majestic 8 Spruce Street, Manhattan's tallest residential tower, is visible, as well as the new World Trade Center tower. Below the promenade is the Brooklyn–Queens Expressway and Brooklyn Bridge Park. Ⓜ *2, 3 to Clark St.; A, C to High St.; R to Court St.*

FAMILY **New York Transit Museum.** Step down into a 1930s subway station, where you'll find more than 60,000 square feet devoted to the history of public transportation. Visitors can wander around the collection of vintage trains and turnstiles and sit behind the wheel of city buses. The old subway advertisements and signs are amusing. The gift store is a great place for NYC-theme souvenirs (there's also a shop at Grand Central). ✉ *Boerum Pl. at Schermerhorn St., Brooklyn Heights* ☎ *718/694–1600* ⊕ *www.mta.info/museum* 🎫 *$7* ⊘ *Tues.–Fri. 10–4, weekends 11–5* Ⓜ *2, 3, 4, 5 to Borough Hall; A, C, G to Hoyt-Schemerhorn; A, C, F, N, R to Jay St.; N, R to Court St.*

WORTH NOTING

Brooklyn Borough Hall. Built in 1848 as Brooklyn's City Hall, this Greek Revival landmark is one of Brooklyn's handsomest buildings. Adorned with Tuckahoe marble, it features a hammered square rotunda and a two-story Beaux Arts courtroom. Today the building serves as the office of Brooklyn's borough president and the home of the **Brooklyn Tourism & Visitors Center** (☎ *718/802–3846* ⊕ *www.visitbrooklyn.org*), which has historical exhibits, a gift shop, and helpful information. It's open weekdays 10–6. Each Tuesday and Saturday, as well as Thursday from April to December, a greenmarket sets up on the flagstone plaza in front. ✉ *209 Joralemon St., between Court and Adams Sts., Brooklyn Heights* ☎ *718/802–3700* ⊕ *www.brooklyn-usa.org* 🎫 *Free* Ⓜ *2, 3, 4, 5 to Borough Hall; M, R to Court St; A, C, F to Jay St.*

Brooklyn Historical Society. Housed in an 1881 Queen Anne–style National Landmark building (one of the gems of the neighborhood), the Brooklyn Historical Society displays memorabilia, artifacts, art, and interactive exhibitions. Upstairs, an impressive library—which contains an original copy of the Emancipation Proclamation—is invaluable to researchers. New renovations include two art galleries, a 200-seat event space, and a gift shop. The building's ornately carved front door has also been restored. ✉ *128 Pierrepont St., at Clinton St., Brooklyn Heights* ☎ *718/222–4111* ⊕ *www.brooklynhistory.org* 🎫 *$6* ⊘ *Wed.–Sun. noon–5* Ⓜ *2, 3, 4, 5 to Borough Hall; A, C, F to Jay St.; R to Court St.*

Hanging out in Brooklyn Bridge Park, with a view of the iconic bridge rising in the background

DOWNTOWN BROOKLYN

There's not much reason for the typical tourist to head to Downtown Brooklyn but it's a convenient location near the Brooklyn Bridge and Brooklyn Heights, and walking distance to neighborhoods like Cobble Hill, Boerum Hill, and DUMBO. Subway stops in the area include Borough Hall on the 2, 3, 4, and 5 trains; Court St. or Jay St.–Metro Tech on the N and R trains.

DUMBO

Once home to bustling factories and dry-goods warehouses, DUMBO (Down Under the Manhattan Bridge Overpass) is now among the most chic and expensive neighborhoods in the city. Tucked downhill from Brooklyn Heights, beside the East River and below thrumming subway lines running along the Brooklyn and Manhattan Bridges, the scene is the epitome of old-meets-new. Warehouses that lured artists in the 1970s now house tech startups and indie book publishers. Luxury condos, high-end shops, and artisan coffeehouses line cobblestone streets, lending tony energy to what was once known as Fulton Landing. Inventor and engineer Robert Fulton introduced steamboat ferry service from Brooklyn to Manhattan in 1814 and once again there is ferry service along the East River to Williamsburg, Greenpoint, and Long Island City, as well as to Manhattan.

An integral part of DUMBO is Brooklyn Bridge Park, and the stroller set and nine-to-five lunch crowds flock to its benches and green spaces, as do brides galore posing for wedding pictures with the perfect background.

Gallery-hopping is also a good reason to head to DUMBO—most are open afternoons, Wednesday or Thursday through Sunday.

TOP ATTRACTIONS

FAMILY **Brooklyn Bridge Park.** On the waterfront between the Brooklyn Bridge and the Manhattan Bridge, this vast park is a great place for a riverside picnic or to just enjoy the view. There are several sections of the park, including Pier 1, Pier 6, the Main Street Lot (with DUMBO's free Wi-Fi network), and the newly renovated Empire–Fulton Ferry. The large playground at Pier 1 has a replica of a boat for make-believe voyages across the East River. In the Empire–Fulton Ferry part of the park is one of the park's new highlights, the fabulously restored **Jane's Carousel**, originally built in 1922 and now housed in a plexiglass pavilion designed by renowned French architect Jean Nouvel. The carousel runs all year (☉ *Mid-May–Oct., Wed.–Mon. 11–7; Oct.–mid-May, Thurs.–Sun. 11–6*) and rides are $2, or you can buy 12 tickets for $20.

From April to October the park is home to a wide range of arts performances, and on Thursday nights in July and August, Movies with a View projects classic New York films on an outdoor screen with no cover charge. ⊠ *New Dock St. at Water St., DUMBO* ☎ *718/222–9939* ⊕ *www.brooklynbridgepark.org* 🎟 *Free* ☉ *Daily 6 am–1 am* Ⓜ *A, C to High St.; F to York St.*

NEED A BREAK? **Brooklyn Ice Cream Factory.** The original of two locations occupies a fireboat house on the Fulton Ferry Pier, offering views of the Brooklyn Bridge and Manhattan skyline. Ice cream, made on-site in small batches, come with classic sundae toppings like hot fudge and whipped cream. ⊠ *1 Water St., DUMBO* ⊕ *www.brooklynicecreamfactory.com* Ⓜ *A, C to High St.; F to York St.*

WORTH NOTING

Smack Mellon. Inside a 12,000-square-foot restored boiler building with a 35-foot ceiling, Smack Mellon exhibits work by up-and-coming artists, and nurtures them with studio space and other support. ⊠ *92 Plymouth St., at Washington St., DUMBO* ☎ *718/834–8761* ⊕ *www.smackmellon.org* ☉ *Wed.–Sun. 12–6* Ⓜ *F to York; A, C to High Street.*

SHOPPING

Jacques Torres Chocolate. You'll feel like Charlie getting a peek at the Oompa Loompas as you peer into the small chocolate factory while munching on an unusually flavored chocolate bonbon or sipping a cup of thick, rich hot chocolate. (For the latter, try the "wicked" flavor, spiked with chipotle peppers and cinnamon.) During summer months, the adjacent ice-cream shop serves scoops, sundaes, and ice-cream sandwiches, with flavors from salted caramel to black current sorbet. ⊠ *66 Water St., DUMBO* ☎ *718/875–1269* ⊕ *www.mrchocolate.com* Ⓜ *F to York St.; A, C to High St.*

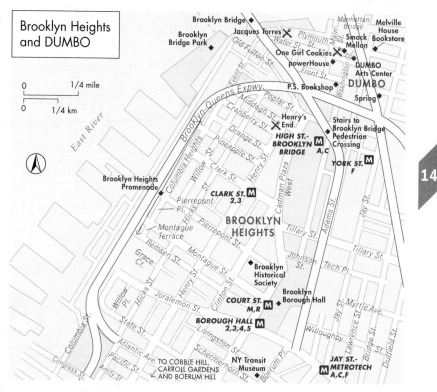

Brooklyn Heights and DUMBO

0   1/4 mile

0   1/4 km

East River

Brooklyn Bridge ◆

Jacques Torres ✕

Manhattan Bridge

Melville House Bookstore

Brooklyn Bridge Park ◆

Old Fulton St.

Water St.

Plymouth St.

Main St.

Smack Mellon

One Girl Cookies ✕

powerHouse ◆

Front St.

DUMBO Arts Center

Washington St.

P.S. Bookshop ◆

DUMBO

Brooklyn-Queens Expwy.

Poplar St.

Spring ◆

Front St.

Middagh St.

Cranberry St.

Henry's End ✕

Stairs to Brooklyn Bridge Pedestrian Crossing

Orange St.

HIGH ST.-BROOKLYN BRIDGE Ⓜ A,C

Pineapple St.

Columbia Heights

Willow St.

Clark St.

Henry St.

YORK ST. Ⓜ F

Brooklyn Heights Promenade

Cadman Plaza West

CLARK ST. Ⓜ 2,3

Pierrepont Pl.

Hicks St.

Pierrepont St.

BROOKLYN HEIGHTS

Jay St.

Adams St.

Montague Terrace

Remsen St.

Montague St.

Tillary St.

Tillary St.

Grace Ct.

Clinton St.

Johnson St.

Tech Pl.

Willow Pl.

Hicks St.

Henry St.

Joralemon St.

◆ Brooklyn Historical Society

Brooklyn ◆ Borough Hall

Myrtle Ave.

COURT ST. Ⓜ M,R

State St.

BOROUGH HALL Ⓜ 2,3,4,5

Livingston St.

Jay St.

Lawrence St.

Bridge St.

Duffield St.

Columbia St.

Atlantic Ave.

Schermerhorn St.

NY Transit Museum ◆

Willoughby St.

Congress St.

Pacific St.

Amity St.

TO COBBLE HILL, CARROLL GARDENS AND BOERUM HILL

Boerum Pl.

JAY ST.-METROTECH Ⓜ A,C,F

14

Melville House Bookstore. Get a taste of the local literary scene inside this independent publisher's shop that hosts art exhibits and evening events, and stocks books from Brooklyn presses like Ugly Duckling and Akashic. ✉ *145 Plymouth St., DUMBO* ☎ *718/722–9204* ⊕ *www.mhpbooks.com* ⊗ *Weekdays 12–6* Ⓜ *F to York St.; A, C to High St.*

The powerHouse Arena. This stunning 5,000-square-foot space with soaring 24-foot ceilings, glass frontage, and amphitheater-style seating does multiple duty as gallery, boutique, bookstore, and performance space. It's a must-stop for culture hawks and bookworms. ✉ *37 Main St., DUMBO* ☎ *718/666–3049* ⊕ *www.powerhousearena.com* Ⓜ *F to York St.; A, C to High St.*

P.S. Bookshop. The largest used bookstore in Brooklyn is in the center of DUMBO. They have signed first editions, and a large selection of art and photography books. ✉ *72 Front St., DUMBO* ☎ *718/222–3340* ⊕ *www.psbnyc.com.*

CARROLL GARDENS

Traditionally Italian Carroll Gardens began drawing Manhattan families in the 1990s, but still retains some of its old-school roots. Wedged between Gowanus and Red Hook, the scene is pleasantly less polished than northern neighbor Cobble Hill. Unpretentious delis and sweet-smelling Italian bakeries sit beside posh restaurants and a hipster version of a yacht club. Court and Smith streets host most of the foot traffic, while the neighborhood's prettiest Italianate brownstone homes and namesake front gardens occupy 1st Place through 4th Place.

SHOPPING

Brooklyn Collective. A rotating cast of local artists and designers populate this lovely little shop on Columbia Street with everything from fine art and jewelry to designer socks and dresses, as well as one-of-a-kind furniture and hand-printed pillowcases. Everything is handmade in Brooklyn. ⊠ *212 Columbia St., Carroll Gardens* ☎ *718/596–6231* ⊕ *www.brooklyncollective.com* Ⓜ *F, G to Carroll St.*

Store 518. Led by dancer-turned-designer Nadia Tarr, this Carroll Gardens shop sells a distinctive array of ladylike jewelry, playful home goods, and vintage toys. Items are stored in drawers and chests throughout the whimsical store, perfect for an afternoon browse. It's only open Thursday through Sunday. ⊠ *518 Court St., Carroll Gardens* ☎ *646/256–5041* ⊕ *www.store518.com* Ⓜ *F, G to Carroll St.*

COBBLE HILL

Adjacent to Boerum Hill and north of Carroll Gardens, Cobble Hill stands out for its 19th-century architecture and leafy, compact parks. Dutch residents called the area Cobleshill in reference to a Revolutionary War–era land mound, which was flattened by British soldiers to prevent strategic use by George Washington's troops. These days, most of the 22-block neighborhood is landmarked as Brooklyn's second-oldest district, a mix of brick townhouses, brownstones, and Victorian schoolhouses, where only the Gothic revival churches exceed a 50-foot height limit. Historically working-class, the neighborhood has adopted all the trappings of haute Brooklyn, especially along busy Court Street: an independent bookstore, artisanal coffee shops, and a boutique devoted to vintage eyewear. But a quiet grace pervades the streets. Swing by the circular Cobble Hill Park, ringed by trees and edged by cozy Verandah Place, a narrow block that once held servants quarters.

SHOPPING

Rapisarda. Funky and whimsical, this tiny Cobble Hill boutique has heaps of fun gift items—from cute bags and swimsuits to quirky footwear, all presented in a stylish colorful fashion by the Brazilian-born owner. ⊠ *117 Court St., near Amity St., Cobble Hill* ☎ *718/797–6863* ⊕ *www.rapisarda.com.*

Carroll Gardens, Cobble Hill, Boerum Hill, and Fort Greene

14

Refinery. This Smith Street storefront has been around since before the Brooklyn boom, touting super-cool gifts. Choose between the many stylish bags—Refinery's forte—as well as quirky jewelry and other fun paraphernalia. ✉ *248 Smith St., at Douglass St., Cobble Hill* ☎ *718/643–7861* ⊕ *www.brooklynrefinery.com* ⊗ *Closed Mon.* Ⓜ *F to Bergen St.*

BOERUM HILL

Understated elegance defines Boerum Hill, where redbrick townhouses and brownstones line quiet, leafy thoroughfares from 4th Avenue to Smith Street and Schemerhorn to Warren. The neighborhood saw an influx of immigrants in the late 1800s, with completion of the Brooklyn Bridge and emergence of trolley cars, but fell into disrepair after World War II. Now fully gentrified, the setting is laden with beautiful cafés that are worth a visit. Despite its air of sophistication, Boerum Hill presents moments of levity, namely artist Susan Gardner's sparkly mosaic-covered brownstone at 108 Wyckoff Street.

WILLIAMSBURG

These days, it's impossible to walk through North Brooklyn without encountering something new. Fabulous boutiques, vintage shops, and forward-thinking restaurants crop up constantly, lending an energy that verges on overwhelming. The neighborhood has certainly glossed itself up in recent years, evidenced by pricey cocktail bars, high-rise waterfront condos, and moneyed hipsters sauntering down Bedford Avenue. But Williamsburg's past is also endlessly intriguing: for much of the 20th century this industrial area on the East River was home to a mix of working-class Americans. Rising Manhattan rents in the 1990s sent an influx of East Village artists and musicians onto the L train, and since then the area has rapidly, albeit creatively, gentrified. And while some side streets may appear graffitied and creepy, rest assured that there's likely to be a DIY concert-gallery space in one of those seemingly abandoned factories.

Williamsburg's 70-plus galleries are distributed randomly, with no single main drag. Plan your trip ahead of time using the online **Brooklyn Art Guide** at ⊕ *www.wagmag.org.* (You can also pick up a copy at neighborhood galleries and some cafés.) Hours vary widely, but most are open weekends (call ahead). Although serendipitous poking is the best way to sample the art, two longtime galleries—Sideshow and Pierogi—are must-sees.

TOP ATTRACTIONS

Pierogi Gallery. Nope, it's not a restaurant, it's an art gallery. Check out the famous "Flat Files," an online collection of the portfolios of more than 900 young contemporary artists. **The Boiler,** an affiliated space nearby (⊠ *191 N. 14th St.* ☎ *718/599–2144*), has more limited hours. ⊠ *177 N. 9th St., between Bedford and Driggs Aves., Williamsburg* ☎ *718/599–2144* ⊕ *www.pierogi2000.com* ☿ *Pierogi Tues.–Sun. 11–6, The Boiler Thurs.–Sun. 12–6* Ⓜ *L to Bedford Ave.*

Sideshow Gallery. The focus is on local Williamsburg artists at this pioneering gallery, but there are traveling exhibits as well, and sometimes readings and concerts. ⊠ *319 Bedford Ave., Williamsburg* ☎ *718/486–8180* ⊕ *www.sideshowgallery.com* Ⓜ *L to Bedford; J, M to Marcy.*

Fodor's Choice
★

Smorgasburg. The ultimate eating extravaganza, Smorgasburg does for local and regional culinary startups what the Brooklyn Flea does for independent designers and craftspeople. April through mid-November, rain or shine, 25 to 50 food vendors sell prepared and packaged treats like gourmet s'mores, savory jams, and Asian-influenced hot dogs. Bring your appetite to East River State Park (90 Kent Avenue at North 7th Street) on Sunday; on Saturday, Smorgasburg is part of the Fort Greene Flea Market (176 Lafayette, in Fort Greene). Smorgasburg moves inside for the winter, from December to March, at 80 North 5th Street (at Wythe Avenue) in Williamsburg. ⊕ *www.smorgasburg.com* ☿ *Apr.–mid-Nov., weekends 11–6; Dec.–Mar., weekends 10–6* Ⓜ *Williamsburg locations: L to Bedford Ave. Fort Greene location: C to Lafayette St.; G to Clinton/Washington.*

SHOPPING

For Shopping, there are boutiques along Bedford Avenue, but you'll also find stores along Grand Street, and on many side streets, especially North 6th.

A&G Merch. Contemporary, stylish, and affordable home accessories with an urban bent, from large to small, are what you'll find at this Brooklyn shop. ☒ *111 N. 6th St., Williamsburg* ☎ *718/388–1779* ⊕ *www.aandgmerch.com* ☉ *Weekends 11–7* Ⓜ *L to Bedford Ave.*

Beacon's Closet. Local fashionistas and out-of-towners alike flock to Beacon's Closet for its huge selection of used and vintage clothing and accessories where real deals can be scored if you devote some time to browsing. Word on the street is that Beacon's is moving to Greenpoint in the near future, so check before you plan a visit. ☒ *88 N. 11th St., Williamsburg* ☎ *718/486–0816* ⊕ *www.beaconscloset. com* Ⓜ *L to Bedford Ave.*

Catbird. One of the standout boutiques on Bedford, Catbird is a doll-house-size shop with shelves filled with handmade jewelry, home accessories, and whimsical hats. ☒ *219 Bedford Ave., near N. 5th St., Williamsburg* ☎ *718/599–3457* ⊕ *www.catbirdnyc.com* Ⓜ *L to Bedford Ave.*

In God We Trust. Having mastered the distinctly Brooklyn, manicured yet rumpled combination, this clothing and accessories boutique draws a steady stream of cool kids to Bedford Avenue. Look for quietly elegant dresses from Brooklyn designer Samantha Pleet, and delicate utilitarian jewelry made locally by IGWT. Other locations are in Greenpoint (⊠ *70 Greenpoint Ave.*) and lower Manhattan (⊠ *265 Lafayette St.*). ⊠ *129 Bedford Ave., Williamsburg* ☎ *718/384–0700* ⊕ *www.ingodwetrustnyc. com/stores/bedford* Ⓜ *L to Bedford Ave.*

Junk. You can be the judge about whether this place lives up (or down) to its name. It's a basement collection of vintage Americana from books and LPs to furniture, art, photos, radios, buttons, glassware, and clothing. The stock evolves continuously and is loaded with everything you're not looking for and more. A great place to pick up a New York souvenir that doesn't say "I [heart] NY" on it. ⊠ *197 N. 9th St., Williamsburg* ☎ *718/640–6299* ⊕ *www.motherofjunk2.blogspot.com* Ⓜ *L to Bedford Ave.*

Pema New York. Nestled in the north end of Williamsburg, this Tibetan-inspired boutique carries affordable women's casual wear and eclectic jewelry, including pieces by local designer Alexis Bittar. The in-house collection of accessories by Migmar Tsering includes hemp wear and wool hats hand knit in the Himalayas. ⊠ *225 Bedford Ave., near N. 5th St., Williamsburg* ☎ *718/388–8814* ⊕ *www.pemany.com* Ⓜ *L to Bedford Ave.*

Realform Girdle Building. The Realform Girdle Building is the closest thing Williamsburg has to a mall. It houses a small café, several hip yet inexpensive boutiques selling vintage clothing and lingerie, and an art bookstore. ⊠ *218 Bedford Ave., Williamsburg* Ⓜ *L to Bedford Ave.*

Rough Trade Records. This newly opened London-based store sells LPs/CDs and books, and doubles as a small 250-seat concert venue and art gallery. Look for in-store events when artists are releasing new records. ⊠ *64 N. 9th St., Williamsburg* ☎ *718/388–4111* Ⓜ *L to Bedford Ave.*

GREENPOINT

Greenpoint is still a predominantly Polish neighborhood, but the overflow of hipsters from Williamsburg, just to the south, are starting to move in. It's very residential, with some local restaurants and bars around Nassau and Manhattan avenues.

BUSHWICK

Bushwick is still a pretty industrial neighborhood, with relatively small pockets of hipsterdom. There's some great street art but the area can also feel a bit sketchy. Roberta's, the renowned pizza restaurant, is tucked away amid factories.

FORT GREENE

Thriving Fort Greene is one of the latest hot Brooklyn neighborhoods, full of young professionals and families drawn here by leafy streets and great food and drink venues. The bars here are just cool enough to rival

Williamsburg's, but with a slightly older and less image-conscious crowd. It can be a trek to get to from Manhattan, but the rewards are many, including some of the best restaurants in Brooklyn, lovely brownstones, and beautiful Fort Greene Park. As with many other areas of Brooklyn, Fort Greene has long been a home to famous writers and musicians like Notorious B.I.G. and Cecil Taylor, and fittingly it's also the locale of one of the city's top performing-arts powerhouses, the Brooklyn Academy of Music, known as BAM (⇨ *Chapter 20: Performing Arts*).

SHOPPING

Fodor'sChoice
★

Brooklyn Flea. Quirky, inclusive, and full of unclaimed treasures—that's Brooklyn in a nutshell, and it also describes the Brooklyn Flea. The Flea is a hybrid of traditional flea market, garage sale, and crafts fair, a tumble of the expensive, the cheap, and the strange. Some vendors hawk high-end items like antique doors refashioned into tables, rescued fixtures from prewar houses, or mid-century lamps like those in *Mad Men*. The most "Brooklyn-y" component is the local artisans, and buying their one-of-a-kind handmade wares gives shoppers the altruistic feeling of supporting arts and crafts, whether it's a silk-screen T-shirt of a giant squid, tongue-in-cheek charm bracelets with little daggers, or hand-stitched stuffed elephants. Finally, there is plenty of bric-a-brac to sift through: great stuff that may not be practical (mink stoles, *Star Wars* collectibles), but that makes for fun browsing.

When you've exhausted the shopping side of things, the Flea has fantastic food options. You'll find minicupcakes from Kumquat Cupcakery, juicy sandwiches from Porchetta, gooey grilled cheese from Milk Truck, and family-farmed coffee from Crop to Cup.

The Flea takes place in two locations every weekend from mid-March to late November: on Saturday, in the parking lot of Bishop Laughlin Memorial High School, at 176 Lafayette Avenue, between Clermont and Vanderbilt Avenue, in Fort Greene. On Sunday, it's in East River State Park, at 90 Kent Avenue, Williamsburg. In winter, from December to March, the Flea moves inside, to a Williamsburg warehouse at 80 North 5th Street (at Wythe Avenue) in Williamsburg. ⊕ *www. brooklynflea.com* ⊗ *Mid-Mar.–late Nov., weekends 10–5; Nov.–Mar., weekends 11–6* Ⓜ *Fort Greene: C to Lafayette Ave. Williamsburg: L to Bedford Ave.*

PARK SLOPE

Full of young families, well-dressed dog walkers, and impeccably curated shops, the neighborhood that literally slopes down from Prospect Park can feel like a veritable Norman Rockwell painting. Add to all that a slew of laptop-friendly coffeehouses and turn-of-the-20th-century brownstones—remnants of the days when Park Slope had the nation's highest per-capita income—and it's no surprise that academics and writers have flocked here. Park Slope's busiest drags, 5th and 7th avenues, present plenty of shopping and noshing opportunities. Head to the elegant, 585-acre Prospect Park for long strolls or bicycle rides past lazy meadows, shady forests, and lakes designed by Olmsted and

Vaux of Central Park fame (look out for free summertime concerts). Adjacent is Brooklyn Botanic Garden, which features a variety of public classes and the springtime Cherry Blossom Festival. Also perched on the park is the Brooklyn Museum, lauded for collections of American, Egyptian, and feminist art.

TOP ATTRACTIONS

FAMILY   **Brooklyn Botanic Garden.** The 52 acres of this beloved Brooklyn retreat, one of the finest botanic gardens in the country, are a must-see, especially in spring and summer. A major attraction is the beguiling Japanese Hill-and-Pond Garden—complete with a blazing red *torii* gate and Shinto shrine. Nearby, the Japanese cherry arbor turns into a breathtaking cloud of pink every spring; the Sakura Matsuri, a two-day cherry blossom festival, is a hugely popular event.

Wander through the Cranford Rose Garden (5,000 plants, 1,200 varieties); the Fragrance Garden, designed especially for the blind; and the Shakespeare Garden, featuring more than 80 plants immortalized by the Bard. At the Steinhardt Conservatory, desert, tropical, temperate, and aquatic vegetation thrives. Don't miss the extraordinary C. V. Starr Bonsai Museum for close to 100 miniature Japanese specimens, some more than a century old. Near the conservatory are a café and a gift shop, with bulbs, plants, and gardening books as well as jewelry.

Entrances to the garden are on Eastern Parkway, next to the subway station; on Washington Avenue, behind the Brooklyn Museum; and on Flatbush Avenue at Empire Boulevard. Free garden tours meet at the front gate every weekend at 1 pm. ⊠ *900 Washington Ave., between Crown and Carroll Sts., Park Slope* ☎ *718/623–7200* ⊕ *www.bbg. org* ⊠ *$10 (free all day Tues., Sat. before noon, and weekdays mid-Nov.–mid-Feb.), combo ticket with Brooklyn Museum $20* ☉ *Mar.–Oct.: grounds Tues.–Fri. 8–6, weekends 10–6; conservatory Tues.–Sun. 10–5:30. Nov.–Feb.: grounds Tues.–Fri. 8–4:30, weekends 10–4:30; conservatory daily 10–4. Closed Mon.* Ⓜ *2, 3 to Eastern Pkwy.; B, Q to Prospect Park.*

Fodor's Choice   **Brooklyn Museum.** Although it may be overshadowed by the big name
★   museums in Manhattan, the Brooklyn Museum, with more than 1 million pieces in its permanent collection—from Rodin sculptures to Andean textiles and Assyrian wall reliefs—and a roster of consistently popular shows and neighborhood events, is a worthwhile and relatively peaceful museum-going experience.

Along with changing exhibitions, highlights include one of the best collections of Egyptian art in the world and impressive collections of African, pre-Columbian, and Native American art. It's also worth seeking out the museum's works by Georgia O'Keeffe, Winslow Homer, John Singer Sargent, George Bellows, Thomas Eakins, and Milton Avery—all stunners. The Elizabeth A. Sackler Center for Feminist Art hosts traveling exhibits in addition to serving as the permanent home to Judy Chicago's installation *The Dinner Party* (1974–79). On the first Saturday of each month (except September) the museum throws a popular free evening of art, music, dancing, film screenings, and readings, from 5 to 11 pm; there are several cash bars. ⊠ *200 Eastern Pkwy., at Washington*

Park Slope and
Prospect Heights

Ave., Park Slope ☏ 718/638–5000 ⊕ www.brooklynmuseum.org
✉ $12 suggested donation (free 1st Sat. of month 5–11), combo ticket
with Brooklyn Botanic Garden $20 ☉ Wed., Fri., and weekends 11–6,
Thurs. 11–10; 1st Sat. of month 11–11 Ⓜ 2, 3 to Eastern Pkwy./Brook-
lyn Museum.

FAMILY **Prospect Park.** Brooklyn residents are fiercely passionate about Prospect
Park, and with good reason. Gently curved paths beg for long walks
and bike rides, while free summer concerts, winter sledding hills, a new
ice-skating rink as of winter 2013, and vivid autumn leaves make the
park a year-round destination. Designed by Frederick Law Olmsted and
Calvert Vaux, the park was completed in the late 1880s. Olmsted once
said that he was prouder of it than of any of his other works—including Manhattan's Central Park.

A good way to experience the park is to walk along its 3.5-mile circular
drive and make detours off it as you wish. The drive is closed to cars at
all times except weekday rush hours. Families with children should head
straight for the eastern side, where most kids' attractions are clustered.

The park's north entrance is at **Grand Army Plaza**, where the Soldiers'
and Sailors' Memorial Arch honors Civil War veterans. (Look familiar?
It's patterned after the Arc de Triomphe in Paris.) Three heroic sculptural groupings adorn the arch: atop, a dynamic four-horse chariot; to

either side, the victorious Union Army and Navy of the Civil War. The inner arch has bas-reliefs of presidents Abraham Lincoln and Ulysses S. Grant, sculpted by Thomas Eakins and William O'Donovan, respectively. To the northwest of the arch, Neptune and a passel of debauched Tritons leer over the edges of the **Bailey Fountain**. On Saturdays year-round a greenmarket at the plaza sells produce, flowers and plants, cheese, and baked goods. ⊠ *450 Flatbush Ave., Park Slope* ☎ *718/965–8951* ⊕ *www.prospectpark.org*

Prospect Park Audubon Center and Visitor Center at the Boathouse. Styled after Sansovino's 16th-century Library at St. Mark's in Venice, the Prospect Park Audubon Center and Visitor Center at the Boathouse, built in 1904, sits opposite the Lullwater Bridge, creating an idyllic spot for watching pedal boats and wildlife, or just taking a break at the café. Interactive exhibits, park tours, and educational programs for kids make this a fun place to learn about nature. On a nice day, take a ride on the electric boat to tour the Lullwater and Prospect Lake. Sign up for a bird-watching tour to see some of the 200 species here. ⊠ *Prospect Park, just inside the Lincoln Rd./Ocean Ave. entrance, Park Slope* ☎ *718/287–3400* ⊕ *www.prospectpark.org/audubon* ⊠ *Audubon Center free, electric-boat tours $10* ⊙ *Audubon Center: Apr.–June, Thurs.–Sun. noon–5; July–Aug., Thurs.–Sun. noon–6; Sept., weekends noon–5; Oct.–Mar., weekends noon–4; closed Jan and Feb. except school holidays; call for program and tour times. Electric-boat tours: May–Aug., Thurs.–Sun. noon–4:30; Sept.–mid-Oct., weekends 12:30–4, every 30 mins.*

Prospect Park Band Shell. The band shell is the home of the annual Celebrate Brooklyn Festival, which from early June through mid-August sponsors free films and concerts that have included Afro-Caribbean jazz, flamenco dance troupes from Spain, David Byrne and other big name musicians, and the Brooklyn Philharmonic. Films are shown on a 50-foot-wide outdoor screen, one of the world's largest. ⊠ *Prospect Park, Park Slope* ☎ *718/855–7882 for Celebrate Brooklyn Festival* ⊕ *www.bricartsmedia.org.*

Prospect Park Carousel. Climb aboard a giraffe or sit inside a dragon-pulled chariot at the immaculately restored Prospect Park Carousel, handcrafted in 1912 by master carver Charles Carmel. ⊠ *Prospect Park, Park Slope* ☎ *718/282–7789* ⊠ *$2 per ride* ⊙ *Apr.–June, Sept., and Oct., Thurs.–Sun. noon–5; July–Labor Day, Thurs.–Sun. noon–6.*

Prospect Park Zoo. Of the 400 inhabitants and 125 species at the small, friendly, Prospect Park Zoo, kids seem especially fond of the sea lions and the red pandas. An outdoor discovery trail has a simulated prairie-dog burrow, a duck pond, and kangaroos and wallabies in habitat. Be aware that there are no cafés, only vending machines. ⊠ *450 Flatbush Ave., Prospect Park, Park Slope* ☎ *718/399–7339* ⊕ *www.prospectparkzoo.com* ⊠ *$8* ⊙ *Apr.–Oct., weekdays 10–5, weekends 10–5:30; Nov.–Mar., daily 10–4:30. Last entry 30 mins before closing* Ⓜ *2, 3 to Eastern Pkwy.; B, Q to Prospect Park.*

A view of the pond at the Brooklyn Botanic Garden, seen through the blossoming cherry trees

WORTH NOTING

FAMILY **Brooklyn Children's Museum.** A mile east of Grand Army Plaza is the oldest children's museum in the world, now housed in a sparkling Rafael Viñoly–designed "green" building. Kids will have a blast, trekking through natural habitats found in the city, running a bakery, creating African-patterned fabric, and even becoming DJs, mixing the rhythms of the outdoors to make music. ⊠ *145 Brooklyn Ave., at St. Marks Ave., Park Slope* ☎ *718/735–4400* ⊕ *www.brooklynkids.org* ✉ *$9* ⊙ *Tues.–Sun. 10–5* Ⓜ *C to Kingston–Throop Aves.; 3 to Kingston Ave., A, C to Nostrand Ave.*

NEED A BREAK?
Gorilla Coffee. Brooklyn's gourmet coffee boom started here in 2002 when the borough's caffeine connoisseurs got introduced to Gorilla's organic, Fair Trade–certified beans from Central and South America, Africa, and Indonesia. Pair your perfectly pulled espresso with a buttery, flaky pastry from Manhattan's Balthazar. ⊠ *97 5th Ave., Park Slope* ☎ *718/230–3244* ⊕ *www.gorillacoffee.com* Ⓜ *2, 3, 4, 5, B, D, N, Q, R to Atlantic Ave.–Barclays Center*

SHOPPING

Seventh Avenue is Park Slope's main shopping street, with long-established restaurants, bookstores, shops, cafés, bakeries, churches, and real-estate agents (a favorite neighborhood pastime is window-shopping for new apartments). More fun, however, are the newer restaurants and cute boutiques along 5th Avenue.

Bird. Well-traveled owner Jen Mankins embodies Brooklyn's refined eclecticism, a vibe that's on full display inside her boutiques. An extremely well-curated selection of designers—think Band of Outsiders, Vena Cava, and 3.1 Phillip Lim—makes Bird one of the best of the many excellent women's clothing stores dotting the area. There are two other Brooklyn locations (in Cobble Hill, at 220 Smith Street [☎718/797–3774], and the Ole Sondresen–designed store in Williamsburg, at 203 Grand Street [☎718/388–1655]). ⊠ *316 5th Ave., between 2nd and 3rd Sts., Park Slope* ☎718/768–4940 ⊕ *www.shopbird.com.*

FAMILY **Brooklyn Superhero Supply Co.** Where else can young superheroes purchase capes, grappling hooks, secret identity kits, and more from staff who never drop the game of pretend? Proceeds benefit the free drop-in tutoring center (run by nonprofit organization 826NYC) in a "secret lair" behind a swinging bookcase. ⊠ *372 5th Ave., at 7th St., Park Slope* ☎718/499–9884 ⊕ *www.superherosupplies.com.*

PROSPECT HEIGHTS

An influx of creative young professionals and impressive eats has lifted Prospect Heights out from the shadow of nearby Park Slope. Swing by on a Saturday to hit the borough's flagship farmer's market, Grand Army Plaza Greenmarket, where cooking demos and fresh produce entice the food-loving hoards. For years Vanderbilt Avenue was the main thoroughfare for food and drink but today it's spreading north to Washington Avenue.

CONEY ISLAND

Coney Island is practically synonymous with the sounds, smells, and sights of a New York City summer: hot dogs and ice cream, suntan lotion, roller coasters, excited crowds, and weathered old men fishing.

Named Konijn Eiland (Rabbit Island) by the Dutch for its wild rabbit population, the Coney Island peninsula has a boardwalk, a 2½-mile-long beach, amusement parks, and the **New York Aquarium,** still partially closed after sustaining damage from Hurricane Sandy. Nathan's Famous (⊠ *1310 Surf Ave.*) is the quintessential hot dog spot.

Among the other entertainments out here are the freakish attractions at **Coney Island Circus Sideshow** and the heart-stopping plunge of the granddaddy of all roller coasters—the **Cyclone.** The minor-league baseball team, the Cyclones, plays at MCU Park, where music concerts are held in summer. The area's banner day is during the raucous Mermaid Parade, held in June. A fireworks display lights up the sky Friday night from late June through Labor Day.

TOP ATTRACTIONS

FAMILY **The Cyclone and Luna Park.** The highlight of Coney Island's amusement park will always be the Cyclone. One of the oldest roller coasters still operating, the world-famous, wood-and-steel colossus first roared around the tracks in 1927 and is still making riders scream. Luna Park is the amusement grounds that grew up in place of Astroland; it's fun

Strolling on the boardwalk at Coney Island

if you keep your expectations in check—the rides are mostly for kids. ✉ *834 Surf Ave., at W. 10th St., Coney Island* ☎ *718/265–2100* ⊕ *www. lunaparknyc.com* 🎟 *Cyclone: $9* ⏱ *Luna Park & Cyclone: Apr.–May, weekends, noon–8; June–Aug., daily noon–midnight. Schedule varies, so check website* Ⓜ *B, F, N, Q to Coney Island–Stillwell Ave.*

FAMILY **New York Aquarium.** New York City's only aquarium is also the nation's oldest but the New York Aquarium was hit hard by Hurricane Sandy in 2012 and is still recovering. As of early 2014 many exhibits were still closed but the park is still open year-round, with the Aquatheater open and animal feedings still take place (check the schedules). There are exciting plans for rebuilding and expansion. Admission prices have been adjusted during the process. ✉ *502 Surf Ave., at W. 8th St., Coney Island* ☎ *718/265–3474* ⊕ *www.nyaquarium.com* 🎟 *$9.95* ⏱ *Sept.–May, 10–4:30; June–Sept., 10–6* Ⓜ *F, Q to W. 8th St.; N, D to Coney Island–Stillwell Ave.*

WORTH NOTING

Coney Island Circus Sideshow. Step right up for lively circus-sideshow entertainment, complete with a fire-eater, sword swallower, snake charmer, and contortionist. ✉ *1208 Surf Ave., at W. 12th St., Coney Island* ☎ *718/372–5159* ⊕ *www.coneyisland.com/sideshow.shtml* 🎟 *$10* ⏱ *Sideshows: Apr.–Sept., hrs vary* Ⓜ *D, F, N, Q to Coney Island–Stillwell Ave.*

FAMILY **Deno's Wonder Wheel Amusement Park.** You'll get a wide perspective from atop the 150-foot-tall Wonder Wheel at Deno's Amusement Park. The Wonder Wheel was built in 1920 and although it appears tame, the swinging cars will quicken your heart rate. There are plenty of rides to amuse the kids at this park, which sits just beside the famed Cyclone. ⊠ *3059 Denos Vourderis Pl., at W. 12th St., Coney Island* ☎ *718/372–2592* ⊕ *www.wonderwheel.com* 🕮 *$7 per ride, 4 rides for $25* ⊙ *Memorial Day–Labor Day, daily 11 am–midnight; Apr., May, Sept., and Oct., weekends noon–9* Ⓜ *D, F, N, Q to Coney Island– Stillwell Ave.*

BRIGHTON BEACH

A pleasant stroll just down the boardwalk from Coney Island is Brighton Beach, named after Britain's beach resort. In the early 1900s Brighton Beach was a resort in its own right, with seaside hotels that catered to rich Manhattan families visiting for the summer. Since the 1970s and '80s Brighton Beach has been known for its 100,000 Soviet émigrés. To get to the heart of "Little Odessa" from Coney Island, walk about a mile east along the boardwalk to Brighton 1st Place, then head up to Brighton Beach Avenue. To get here from Manhattan directly, take the B or Q train to the Brighton Beach stop; the trip takes about an hour from Midtown Manhattan.

TOP ATTRACTIONS

Brighton Beach boardwalk. The Brighton Beach section of the boardwalk, especially between Brighton 3rd and 6th streets, bustles with restaurants serving traditional Russian dishes. The beach tends to be slightly less crowded in summer than at Coney Island, filled with local sunbathers and Manhattanites who've come out for the day. Brighton Beach is about a mile from Coney Island. ⊠ *Between Ocean Pkwy. and Coney Island Ave., Brighton Beach* Ⓜ *B or Q to Coney Island.*

SHOPPING

Brighton Beach Avenue. The shops, bakeries, markets, and restaurants along Brighton Beach Avenue, the neighborhood's main artery, cater primarily to the neighborhood's Russian community but shopping along here is a primary reason to visit. This is the place to find knishes with every filling imaginable, borscht, *blini* (small crêpes or pancakes), fruit and veggies, Russian liquor and chocolates, and cups of dark-roast coffee, plus caviar at prices that can put Manhattan purveyors to shame. ⊠ *Brighton Beach Ave. from Brighton 1st to Brighton 6th Sts., Brighton Beach* Ⓜ *Q to Brighton Beach.*

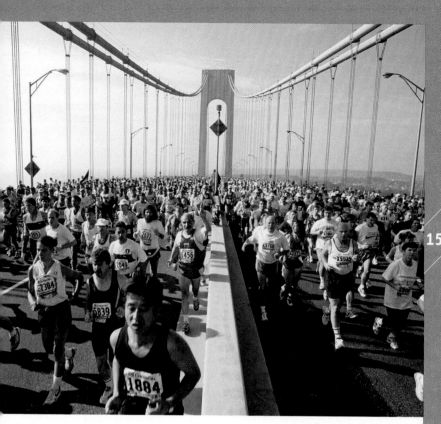

QUEENS, THE BRONX, AND STATEN ISLAND

GETTING ORIENTED

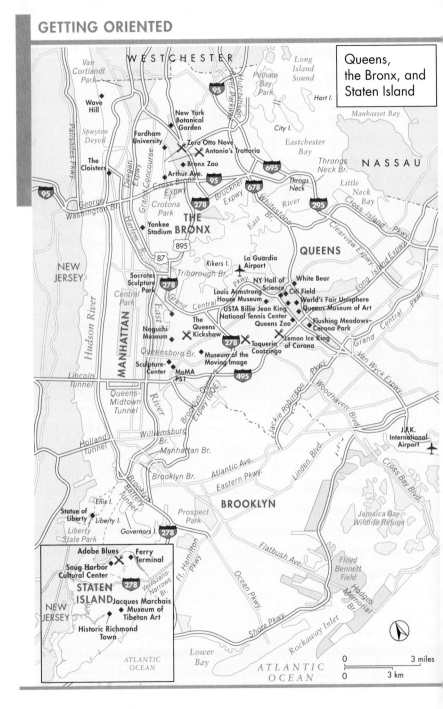

Queens,
the Bronx, and
Staten Island

TOP EXPERIENCES

Ethnic eats in Queens

Catching a game at Yankee Stadium or Citi Field

Taking a free ride on the Staten Island Ferry

MAKING THE MOST OF YOUR TIME

Queens is rich with superb museums. An afternoon in Long Island City and Astoria will enable you to take in the PS1 Contemporary Art Center, the Museum of the Moving Image, and the Noguchi Museum. After that, jump on the 7 train and have dinner in Jackson Heights or Flushing at one of the borough's excellent restaurants.

It is easy to spend a full day at either of the Bronx's treasures: the New York Botanical Garden or the Bronx Zoo. To visit both, start early and plan on a late lunch or early dinner in the Arthur Avenue area. The garden and the zoo are less crowded on weekdays during the school year.

Many tourists' only sight of Staten Island is during a round-trip ride on the ferry, but the borough also holds unexpected offerings in its small museums and historic villages. Set aside the better part of a day for Historic Richmond Town, and add on a couple of hours for the Museum of Tibetan Art.

GETTING HERE

Queens is served by many subway lines. To get to Astoria, take the N or Q train. For Long Island City, take the E, M, G or 7 train. To get to Jackson Heights, take the 7 train to the 74th Street–Broadway stop. You can also take the E, F, R, or M train to Jackson Heights–Roosevelt Avenue.

The Bronx is serviced by the 1, 2, 4, 5, 6, B, and D trains. The attractions in the Bronx are spread out across the borough, so you'll need to take different lines to get where you want to go, and it's not necessarily convenient to make connections across town. The B, D, and 4 trains all go to Yankee Stadium, and the B and D continue uptown to the vicinity of Arthur Avenue. The 2 and 5 trains take you to the Bronx Zoo and to Arthur Avenue.

From the scenic (and free) Staten Island Ferry you can catch a local bus to attractions. Tell the driver where you're going, and ask about the return schedule.

COFFEE AND QUICK BITES

The Queens Kickshaw. Head here for specialty coffee, a variety of grilled cheese sandwiches, and craft ales. ✉ 40–17 Broadway, at 41st St., Astoria Ⓜ M, R to Steinway St. ☎ 718/777–0913 ⊕ www.thequeenskickshaw.com.

Taqueria Coatzingo. Grab an al pastor taco and take a seat at this cheap, authentic Mexican taqueria. You'll probably want seconds. ✉ 7605 Roosevelt Ave., Elmhurst, Jackson Heights ☎ 718/424–1977 Ⓜ 7 to 74th St.–Broadway; E, F, M, R to Jackson Hts.–Roosevelt Ave. ☞ Cash only.

White Bear. This is the perfect place to begin your culinary adventure through New York's other Chinatown. Order the #6: a dozen wontons with hot sauce for $4.50. ✉ 135–02 Roosevelt Ave., Flushing Ⓜ 7 to Flushing–Main St. ☎ 718/961–2322.

Zero Otto Nove. For serious Neapolitan pizza, pasta, and fine wines, head straight to Zero Otto Nove. ✉ 2357 Arthur Ave, at E. 186th St., Bronx ☎ 718/220–1027 ⊕ www.089bx.roberto089.com ⊗ Closed Mon. Ⓜ N, R to 23rd St.

Sightseeing
★★★
Nightlife
★★★
Dining
★★★★
Lodging
★
Shopping
★★★★

Many tourists miss out on Queens, the Bronx, and Staten Island—the three boroughs of New York City other than the biggies, Manhattan and Brooklyn—and that's a shame. There are some noteworthy restaurants, museums, and attractions, and the subway's handful of express trains means that they're closer than you might think.

QUEENS

Updated by
Josh Rogol

Just for the museums and restaurants alone, a short 15-minute trip on the 7 train from Grand Central or Times Square to **Long Island City** and **Astoria** is truly worth it. In Long Island City, major must-sees are **MoMA PS1** and the **Noguchi Museum.** No trip to Astoria—nicknamed "Little Athens"—would be complete without sampling Greek cuisine and stopping at the **Museum of the Moving Image.**

Jackson Heights is home to the city's largest Indian population. It's a wonderful place to spend an afternoon browsing its shops and dining in one of the many authentic ethnic restaurants.

Top reasons to trek out to **Flushing** and **Corona** include seeing a ballgame at the New York Mets' stadium, **Citi Field,** spending time at the expansive **Flushing Meadows–Corona Park**—especially if traveling with kids, and devouring a wide array of Asian fare in downtown Flushing's Chinatown.

ASTORIA

Astoria, nicknamed "Little Athens," was the center of Greek immigrant life in New York City for more than 60 years. An increase in Greek affluence has meant that many have left the borough, but they still return for authentic restaurants, grocery stores, and churches. Here you can buy kalamata olives and salty sheep's-milk feta from storeowners who can tell you where to go for the best spinach pie. Today substantial numbers of Arab, Asian, Eastern European, Irish,

TIPS FOR QUEENS ADDRESSES

Addresses in Queens can seem confusing at first. Not only are there 30th Street and 30th Avenue, but there are also 30th Place and 30th Road, all next to one another. Then there are those hyphenated building numbers. But the system is actually logical. Sequentially numbered avenues run east-to-west, and sequentially numbered streets run north-to-south. If there are any smaller roads between avenues, they have the same number as the nearest avenue, and are called roads or drives. Similarly, smaller side roads between streets are called places or lanes. Thus, 30th Place is one block east of 30th Street. Most buildings have two pairs of numbers, separated by a hyphen. The first pair indicates the nearest cross street, and the second gives the location on the block. So 47–10 30th Place is 10 houses away from the corner of 47th Avenue and 30th Place. Logical, right? If this all still seems confusing to you, there's good news: locals are used to giving directions to visitors.

15

and Latino immigrants also live in Astoria. The heart of what remains of the Greek community is on Broadway, between 31st and Steinway streets. Thirtieth Avenue is another busy thoroughfare, with almost every kind of food store imaginable. Astoria is also home to the nation's only museum devoted to the art, technology, and history of film, TV, and digital media. The **Museum of the Moving Image** has countless hands-on exhibits that allow visitors to edit, direct, and step into favorite movies and television shows.

TOP ATTRACTIONS

Fodor'sChoice **Museum of the Moving Image.** Like switching to a widescreen television,
★ the Museum of the Moving Image is twice as nice as it was before the 2011 expansion and renovation. The Thomas Lesser design includes a three-story addition and a panoramic entrance to this museum full of Hollywood and television memorabilia. Exhibitions range from "Behind the Screen" which demonstrates how movies are produced and shot to watching the live editing of Mets baseball games as they happen on SNY. Classic family films are shown as matinees on Saturdays and Sundays, while the museum also has a section devoted to video artists for visitors looking for some culture. Film buffs will love the film retrospectives, lectures, and other special programs. ✉ 36–01 35th Ave., at 37th St., Astoria ☎ 718/777–6888 ⊕ www.movingimage. us ☑ $12 (free after 4 on Fri.) ☉ Wed. and Thurs. 10:30–5, Fri. 10:30–8, weekends 11:30–7 Ⓜ R, M to Steinway St.; N, Q to 36th Ave.

LONG ISLAND CITY

Long Island City (LIC for short) is the outer-borough art capital, with **MoMA PS1**, which presents experimental and formally innovative work; the **Noguchi Museum**, showcasing the work of Japanese-American sculptor Isamu Noguchi in a large, peaceful garden and galleries; and **Socrates Sculpture Park**.

Filmmaking in Astoria

Hollywood may be the king of movie-making now, but in the early days of sound, Queens was where it was at. In the 1920s such stars as Gloria Swanson, Rudolph Valentino, and Claudette Colbert all acted in one of the more than 100 films made at Astoria Studios. Opened in 1920 by the film company that would become Paramount, "the Big House" was the largest and most important filmmaking studio in the country.

Though Astoria's ideal location provided easy access to Broadway and vaudeville stars, Hollywood's weather soon lured most studios away. Astoria was able to hold its own for a while longer, creating such films as the Marx Brothers classics *The Cocoanuts* and *Animal Crackers*. But in 1942 the studio was sold to the U.S. Army. It became the Signal Corps Photographic Center, producing training films and documentaries, including Frank Capra's classic seven-film series *Why We Fight*. The army retained the studio until 1970.

In 1980 the city leased the studio to real-estate developer George S. Kaufman, in partnership with Alan King and Johnny Carson. Kaufman-Astoria Studios, with seven stages, is a thriving operation once again, used for television series (*Sesame Street; Law & Order; Nurse Jackie*) as well as movies (*The Wiz; Eat, Pray, Love;* and *The Bourne Legacy*). In 2013 the studio expanded by an entire city block after completing construction on what is now New York City's only outdoor backlot, Although it is not open to the public, movie buffs can hope to spot stars at the Studio Café and learn more about the craft next door at the fantastic Museum of the Moving Image.

TOP ATTRACTIONS

Fodor's Choice ★ **MoMA PS1.** A pioneer in the "alternative-space" movement, PS1 rose from the ruins of an abandoned school in 1976 as a sort of community arts center for the future. MoMA PS1 focuses on the work of currently active experimental and innovative artists. Long-term installations include work by Sol LeWitt and Pipilotti Rist. Every available corner of the enormous 100-room building is used; discover art not only in galleries but also on the rooftop, in the boiler room, and even in some bathrooms. Also inside the museum is **M. Wells Dinette**, a cafe designed to resemble a school classroom, with daily specials lining the chalkboard and lunch served at your "desk." On summer Saturdays, MoMA PS1 presents "Warm Up", an outdoor dance party series attracting a hip art-school crowd that's held in the courtyard from noon–9. Similarly, their "Sunday Sessions" are held in the Dome and feature various artistic installations, scholarly lectures, and special performances. ⊠ *22–25 Jackson Ave., at 46th Ave., Long Island City* ☎ *718/784–2084* ⊕ *www. momaps1.org* ⊠ *$10 (free with MoMA entrance ticket, within 14 days of visit); Warm Up admission $18* ⊗ *Thurs.–Mon. noon–6* Ⓜ *7 to Court Sq.; E, M to Court Square–23 St.; G to 21st St.*

The Noguchi Museum. In 1985 the Japanese-American sculptor Isamu Noguchi (1904–88) transformed this former photo-engraving plant into a place to display his modernist and earlier works. A peaceful central

Astoria and
Long Island City

garden is surrounded by gallery buildings, and there are more than 250
pieces done in stone, metal, clay, and other materials, on display. Temporary exhibits have featured his collaborations with others, such as
industrial designer Isamu Kenmochi. The museum is about a mile from
subway stops; check the website for complete directions. On Sunday a
shuttle bus leaves from the northeast corner of Park Avenue and 70th
Street in Manhattan (in front of the Asia Society) hourly, beginning at
12:30 with return trips ending at 5; the round trip costs $10. ✉ 9–01
33rd Rd., at Vernon Blvd., Long Island City ☎ 718/204–7088 ⊕ www.
noguchi.org ☞ $10 (1st Fri. of month, pay what you wish) ◷ Wed.–Fri.
10–5, weekends 11–6 Ⓜ N or Q to Broadway.

WORTH NOTING

SculptureCenter. Founded by artists in 1928 to exhibit innovative contemporary work, SculptureCenter now occupies a former trolley repair
shop renovated by artist Maya Lin and architect David Hotson, not
far from MoMA PS1. Their indoor and outdoor exhibition spaces
sometimes close between shows; call ahead before visiting. ✉ 44–19
Purves St., at Jackson Ave., Long Island City ☎ 718/361–1750 ⊕ www.
sculpture-center.org ☞ $5 suggested donation ◷ Thurs.–Mon. 11–6
Ⓜ 7 or G to Court Sq.; E, M to Court Sq.–23rd Street; N or Q to
Queensboro Plaza.

FAMILY   **Socrates Sculpture Park.** In 1986 local artist Mark di Suvero and other residents rallied to transform what had been an abandoned landfill and illegal dump site into this 4.5-acre waterfront park devoted to public art. Today a superb view of the East River and Manhattan frames changing exhibitions of contemporary sculptures and multimedia installations. Free public programs include art workshops and an annual outdoor international film series (July and August, Wednesday evenings). Socrates is open 365 days a year, but the best time to visit is during warmer months. Check online for a list of current and upcoming exhibitions. ✉ *32–01 Vernon Blvd., at Broadway, Long Island City* ☎ *718/956–1819* ⊕ *www. socratessculpturepark.org* ⎙ *Free* ⊘ *10–sunset* Ⓜ *N, Q to Broadway.*

JACKSON HEIGHTS

Even in the diverse borough of Queens, Jackson Heights stands out for being a true polycultural neighborhood. In just a few blocks surrounding the three-way intersection of Roosevelt Avenue, 74th Street, and Broadway, you can find shops and restaurants catering to the area's strong Indian, Bangladeshi, Colombian, Mexican, and Ecuadorian communities. Built as a planned "garden community" in the late 1910s, the area boasts many prewar apartments with elaborate block-long interior gardens as well as English-style homes. Celebs who grew up in the area include Lucy Liu and Gene Simmons. It's also the birthplace of the board game Scrabble.

FLUSHING AND CORONA

Before it became a part of New York City, Queens consisted of many small independent townships. So it makes sense that the historic town of Flushing is today a microcosm of a larger city, including a bustling downtown area, fantastic restaurants, and bucolic suburbanlike streets nearby.

Flushing may seem like a strange name for a town, but it's an English adaptation of the original (and hard-to-pronounce) Dutch name Vlissingen. The Dutch named it for a favorite port city in the Netherlands.

Next door, quiet Corona could easily be overlooked, but that would be a mistake. Here you'll find two huge legacies: the music of Satchmo and the cooling simplicity of an Italian ice.

TOP ATTRACTIONS

Fodor'sChoice   **Citi Field.** Opened in 2009, the Mets' newest stadium was designed to
★   hark back to Ebbets Field (where the Dodgers played in Brooklyn until 1957) with a brick exterior and plenty of bells and whistles, from a batting cage and Wiffle-ball field to the original giant apple taken from the team's old residence, Shea Stadium. Even those who aren't Mets fans but simply love baseball should come to see the Jackie Robinson Rotunda, a soaring multistory entrance and history exhibit dedicated to the Dodgers player who shattered baseball's color barrier. While here, don't miss tasting your way through the more-than-fabulous food court behind center field, where you'll find Shake Shack burgers, Blue Smoke ribs, a selection of close to 40 beers at the Big Apple Brews stand, and even lobster rolls and tacos. Though it seats fewer people than Shea by about 15,000,

tickets are not hard to come by, especially later in the season. Still feeling nostalgic for the old Shea? Stop by the Mets Hall of Fame & Museum or pay your respects at the plaque in the parking lot. ⊠ *123–01 Roosevelt Ave., 126th St. and Roosevelt Ave., Flushing/ Corona* ☏ *718/507–8499* ⊕ *newyork.mets.mlb.com* Ⓜ *7 to Mets–Willets Point.*

FAMILY **Flushing Meadows–Corona Park.** Standing in the lush grass of this park, you'd never imagine that it was once a swamp and dumping ground. But the gleaming Unisphere (an enormous 140-foot-high steel globe) might tip you off that this 897-acre park was also the site of two World's Fairs. Take advantage of the park's barbecue pits and sports fields, but also don't forget that there's an art museum, a petting zoo, golf and minigolf, and even a model-plane field. There's way too much to see here to pack into a day, so aim to hit a few primary spots, noting that while several are clustered together on the northwest side of the park, visitors should be prepared for long peaceful walks in between. The flat grounds are ideal for family biking; rent bikes near the park entrance or Meadow Lake from March to October. ■ TIP→ Although the park is great in daytime, avoid visiting once it gets dark; there has been some crime in this area. ⊠ *Between 111th St./Grand Central Pkwy. and Van Wyck Expwy. at 44th Ave., Flushing/ Corona* ⊕ *www.nycgovparks.org/ parks/fmcp* Ⓜ *7 to 111th St. or Mets – Willets Point.*

The jungle habitat at the Bronx Zoo will make you forget the surrounding urban jungle.

New York Hall of Science. At the northwestern edge of Flushing Meadows–Corona Park, the New York Hall of Science has more than 400 hands-on exhibits that make science a playground for inquisitive minds of all ages. Climb aboard a replica of John Glenn's space capsule, throw a fastball and investigate its speed, or explore Charles and Ray Eames's classic Mathematica exhibition. ⊠ *47–01 111th St., Flushing/Corona* ☎ *718/699–0005* ⊕ *www.nysci.org* ✉ *$11 (free Fri. 2–5 and Sun. 10–11 Sept.–June)* ☉ *Sept.–March, Tues.–Fri. 9:30–5, weekends 10–6; April–Aug., weekdays 9:30–5, weekends 10–6* Ⓜ *7 to 111th St.; walk 3 blocks south.*

Fodor's Choice ★ **Queens Museum of Art.** Between the zoo and the Unisphere in Flushing Meadows–Corona Park, you'll find the Queens Museum of Art. Don't miss the astonishing Panorama, a nearly 900,000-building model of N.Y.C. made for the 1964 World's Fair. Many unsuspecting park visitors looking for a bathroom instead find themselves spending hours checking out the intricate structures that replicate every block in the city. There are also rotating exhibitions of contemporary art and a permanent collection of Louis Comfort Tiffany stained glass. The museum recently doubled in size after a major expansion project, which resulted in more exhibitions and education departments, a café, a bookstore, and places for children's activities. ⊠ *Flushing Meadows–Corona Park, New York City Building, Flushing/Corona* ☎ *718/592–9700* ⊕ *www.queensmuseum.org* ✉ *$8 suggested donation* ☉ *Wed.–Sun. 12–6; call for extended hrs in July and Aug.* Ⓜ *7 to 111th St. or Mets–Willets Point.*

FAMILY **Queens Zoo.** Behind the Hall of Science in Flushing Meadows–Corona Park lies the intimate Queens Zoo, whose small scale is especially well suited to easily tired young visitors. In only 11 acres you'll find

North American animals such as bears, mountain lions, bald eagles, and pudu—the world's smallest deer. Buckminster Fuller's geodesic dome from the 1964 World's Fair is now the aviary. Across the street is a petting zoo. ✉ *53–51 111th St., at 53rd Ave., Flushing/Corona* ☎ *718/271–1500* ⊕ *www.queenszoo.com* 🎟 *$8* ⊙ *Apr.–Oct., weekdays 10–5, weekends and holidays 10–5:30; Nov.–March, daily 10–4:30; last ticket sold 30 mins before closing* Ⓜ *7 to 111th St., walk south to park; Q58 to Corona Ave., walk east to 111th St.*

USTA Billie Jean King National Tennis Center. Each August, 700,000 fans come here for the U.S. Open, which claims the title of highest-attended annual sporting event in the world. The rest of the year, the 39 courts (19 outdoor and 12 indoor, all DecoTurf, plus 4 clay bubbled courts and 4 stadium courts) are open to the public for $22–$66 hourly. Make reservations up to two days in advance. ✉ *Flushing Meadows–Corona Park, Flushing/Corona* ☎ *718/760–6200* ⊕ *www.ntc.usta.com* ⊙ *Daily 6 am–midnight; closed major holidays and 1 month around U.S. Open* Ⓜ *7 to Mets–Willets Point.*

WORTH NOTING

Louis Armstrong House Museum. For the last 28 years of his life the famed jazz musician lived in this modest three-story house in Corona with his wife Lucille. Take a guided 40-minute tour and note the difference between the rooms vividly decorated by Lucille in charming midcentury style and Louis's dark den, cluttered with phonographs and reel-to-reel tape recorders. Although photographs and family mementos throughout the house impart knowledge about Satchmo's life, it's in his den that you'll really understand his spirit. ✉ *34–56 107th St., at 37th Ave., Corona* ☎ *718/478–8274* ⊕ *www.louisarmstronghouse.org* 🎟 *$10 (includes guided house tour)* ⊙ *Tues.–Fri. 10–5, weekends 12–5; tours hourly (last tour at 4)* Ⓜ *7 to 103rd St.–Corona Plaza.*

NEED A BREAK?

Lemon Ice King of Corona. If you're looking for an authentic Queens experience, there are few as true as eating an Italian ice from the Lemon Ice King of Corona on a hot summer day. There are no seats and the service can often be gruff at this neighborhood institution of more than 60 years, but none of that will matter after your first taste. And yes, there are plenty of flavors other than lemon. ✉ *52–02 108th St., at 52nd Ave., Flushing/Corona* ☎ *718/699–5133* ⊕ *www.thelemonicekingofcorona.com.*

THE BRONX

The Bronx is the city's most maligned and misunderstood borough. Its reputation as a gritty, down-and-out place is a little outdated, and there's lots of beauty to be found, if you know where to look. There is more parkland in the Bronx than in any other borough, as well as one of the world's finest botanical collections, the largest metropolitan zoo in the country, and, of course, Yankee Stadium. (The Bronx does cover a large area, though, so the attractions are spread out.) Whether you're relaxing at a ballgame, indulging in fresh mozzarella and cannolis on Arthur Avenue or scoping out exotic species at the zoo, there's plenty of fun to be had here.

TOP ATTRACTIONS

FAMILY
Fodor'sChoice
★

The Bronx Zoo. When it opened its gates in 1899, the Bronx Zoo had only 843 animals. But today, with 250 acres and more than 4,000 animals (of more than 650 species), it's the largest metropolitan zoo in the United States. Get up close and personal with exotic creatures in outdoor settings that re-create natural habitats; you're often separated from them by no more than a moat or wall of glass. Don't miss the **Congo Gorilla Forest,** a 6.5-acre re-creation of a lush African rain forest with two troops of lowland gorillas, as well as white-bearded DeBrazza's monkeys, okapis, and red river hogs. At **Tiger Mountain** an open viewing shelter lets you get incredibly close to Siberian tigers, who frolic in a pool, lounge outside (even in cold weather), and enjoy daily "enrichment sessions" with keepers. As the big cats are often napping at midday, aim to visit in the morning or evening. In the new $62 million exhibit **Madagascar!,** the formality of the old Lion House has been replaced with a verdant re-creation of one of the most threatened natural habitats in the world. Here you'll see adorable lemurs and far-from-adorable hissing cockroaches.

Go on a minisafari via the **Wild Asia Monorail,** open May–October, weather permitting. As you wend your way through the forest, see Asian elephants, Indo-Chinese tigers, Indian rhinoceroses, gaur (the world's largest cattle), Mongolian wild horses, and several deer and antelope species. ■TIP➔ Try to visit the most popular exhibits, such as Congo Gorilla Forest, early to avoid lines later in the day. In winter the outdoor exhibitions have fewer animals on view, but there are also fewer crowds, and plenty of indoor exhibits to savor. Also note that there is an extra charge for some exhibits. If you want to see everything, you'll save money by purchasing the Total Experience ticket. ⊠ *2300 Southern Blvd., near E. 187 St.* ☎ *718/367–1010* ⊕ *www.bronxzoo.com* ✉ *General admission: $16.95 (extra charge for some exhibits). Total Experience: $20.95–$33.95. Free Wed. (suggested donation $16). Parking: $15 cars, $18 buses* ☉ *Apr.–Oct., weekdays 10–5, weekends and holidays 10–5:30; Nov.–Mar., daily 10–4:30. Last ticket sold 30 mins before closing* Ⓜ *2, 5 to E. Tremont/West Farms, then walk 2 blocks up Boston Rd. to zoo's Asia entrance; 2, 5 to Pelham Pkwy or BxM11 express bus to Bronx River entrance; Metro-North Harlem line to Fordham, then take the Bx9 bus to 183rd St. and Southern Blvd.*

Fodor'sChoice
★

The New York Botanical Garden. Considered one of the leading botany centers of the world, this 250-acre garden is one of the best reasons to make a trip to the Bronx. Built around the dramatic gorge of the Bronx River, the Garden offers lush indoor and outdoor gardens, and acres of natural forest, as well as classes, concerts, and special exhibits. Be astounded by the captivating fragrance of the Peggy Rockefeller Rose Garden's 4,000 plants of more than 600 varieties; see intricate orchids that look like the stuff of science fiction; relax in the quiet of the forest or the calm of the Conservatory; or take a jaunt through the Everett Children's Adventure Garden: a 12-acre, indoor-outdoor museum with a boulder maze, giant animal topiaries, and a plant discovery center.

The Garden's roses bloom in June and September, but there's plenty to see year-round. The Victorian-style **Enid A. Haupt Conservatory** houses re-creations of misty tropical rain forests and arid African and North American deserts as well as exhibitions, such as the annual Holiday Train Show and the Orchid Show. The **All-Garden Pass** (🎟 *$20*) gives you access to the Conservatory, Rock Garden, Native Plant Garden, Tram Tour, Everett Children's Adventure Garden, and exhibits in the library.

The most direct way to the Garden is via **Metro-North Railroad** (⊕ *www.mta.info/mnr*) from Grand Central Terminal (Harlem local line, Botanical Garden stop). Round-trip tickets are $12.50 to $16.50, depending on time of day. A cheaper alternative is to take the B, D or 4 train to Bedford Park Boulevard, then walk east. ⊠ *2900 Southern Blvd.* ☎ *718/817–8700* ⊕ *www.nybg.org* 🎟 *Grounds only $13 (free Sat. 9–10 and all day Wed.), All-Garden Pass $20 ($25 during special events); parking $12 weekdays, $15 weekends and during special events* ⊙ *Tues.–Sun. 10–6 (mid-Jan.–Feb. 10–5); select holiday Mon. 10–6 (check website!)* Ⓜ *B, D, 4 to Bedford Park Blvd., then walk 8 blocks downhill to the garden or take the Bx26 bus; Metro-North (Harlem local line) to Botanical Garden.*

Fodor'sChoice   **Yankee Stadium.** Fans are still nostalgic about the original, legendary
★   Yankee Stadium, which saw its last season in 2008. The new $1.5 bil-
lion Yankee Stadium, however (right across the street from the House
that Ruth Built) got off to a good start, with the Yankees winning the
World Series in its inaugural year. Tickets can be pricey, but the experience is like watching baseball in a modern-day coliseum. It's incredibly
opulent and over-the-top: traditional white frieze adorns the stadium's
top; inside, limestone-and-marble hallways are lined with photos of past
Yankee greats; lower-level seats have cushions, cup holders, and a boffo
meatery, NYY Steak. Like the team, the amenities don't come cheap.
But the spirit of the original still remains. History buffs and hardcore
fans should visit Monument Park (closes 45 minutes prior to first pitch),
with plaques of past Yankee legends, by center field—it survived from
its original left field location at the old stadium. Aside from the subway, you can also get here by taking Metro-North to the Yankees—E.
153rd Street Station. ⊠ *1 E. 161st St., at River Ave.* ☏ *718/293–6000*
⊕ *newyork.yankees.mlb.com* Ⓜ *B, D, or 4 to 161st St.–Yankee Stadium;
Metro-North to Yankees–E. 153rd St.*

WORTH NOTING

Arthur Avenue (Belmont). Manhattan's Little Italy is sadly overrun with
mediocre restaurants aimed at tourists, but Belmont, the Little Italy of
the Bronx, is a real, thriving Italian-American community. Unless you
have family in the area, the main reason to come here is for the food:
eating it, buying it, looking at it fondly through windows. A secondary, but just as important, reason is chatting with shopkeepers so you
can steal their recipes.

Nearly a century after pushcarts on Arthur Avenue catered to Italian-
American workers constructing the zoo and Botanical Garden, the area
teems with meat markets, bakeries, and cheese makers. There are long
debates about which store or restaurant is the "best," but thanks to
generations of Italian grandmothers, vendors here wouldn't dare offer
anything less than superfresh, handmade foods.

Although the area is no longer solely Italian—many Latinos and Alba-
nians share this neighborhood now—Italians dominate the food scene.
The covered **Arthur Avenue Retail Market** is a terrific starting point.
It houses more than a dozen vendors. Regulars mostly shop on Saturday afternoon; you'll find many stores shuttered on Sunday and
after 6 pm. ⊠ *Arthur Ave. between Crescent Ave./E. 184th St. and E.
188th Sts., and 187th St. from Lorillard Pl. to Hughes Ave.* ⊕ *www.
arthuravenuebronx.com* Ⓜ *B, D, 4 to Fordham Rd., then Bx12 east; 2,
5 to Pelham Pkwy., then Bx12 west; Metro-North Railroad from Grand
Central Terminal (Harlem local line, Fordham stop) then 15-min walk.*

**OFF THE
BEATEN
PATH**

Wave Hill. Drawn by stunning views of the Hudson River and New
Jersey's dramatic cliffs, 19th-century Manhattan millionaires built
summer homes in the Bronx suburb of Riverdale. One of the most
magnificent, Wave Hill, is now a 28-acre public garden and cultural
center that attracts green thumbs from all over the world. Along with
exquisite gardens, grand beech and oak trees adorn wide lawns, an elegant pergola overlooks the majestic river view, and benches on curving

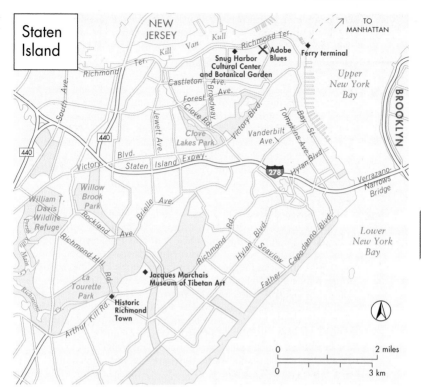

pathways provide quiet respite. Wave Hill House (1843) and Glyndor House (1927) are now home to art exhibitions, Sunday concerts, and gardening workshops. Even England's Queen Mother stayed here during a visit. It's worth the schlep. ⊠ *Independence Ave. at W. 249th St.* ☎ *718/549–3200* ⊕ *www.wavehill.org* ✈ *$8 (free Sat. 9–noon and some Tues.; check website)* ⊗ *Mid-Mar.–Oct., Tues.–Sun. 9–5:30; Nov.– mid-Mar., Tues.–Sun. 9–4:30; closed Mon. except holidays. Free garden tours Sun. at 2* Ⓜ *1 to W. 242nd St. (free hourly shuttle service 9:10 and 3:10); 1 to 231st St., then Bx7 or Bx10 bus to 252nd St. and Riverdale Ave.; A to W. 207th St., then Bx7 or Bx20 bus to W. 252nd St.; Metro-North Railroad to Riverdale (free hourly shuttle service 9:45 and 3:45).*

STATEN ISLAND

Legally part of New York City since 1898, Staten Island is in many ways a world apart. The "Forgotten Borough," as some locals refer to it, is geographically more separate, less populous, politically more conservative, and ethnically more homogeneous than the rest of the city.

Hurricane Sandy hit New York City in October 2012 and Staten Island was among the hardest hit areas. Many residential properties and small neighborhood businesses were severely damaged, but all of the cultural and destination points remained fairly unharmed. Rebuilding is ongoing, but gradual and it's expected that restoration efforts will continue over the next few years.

Despite this setback, Staten Island is full of surprises. Along with suburban sprawl, there are wonderful small museums, including a premier collection of Tibetan art, walkable woodlands, and a historic village replicating New York's rural past. And for a view of the skyline and the Statue of Liberty, nothing beats the 25-minute free ferry trip to Staten Island. To explore the borough, take the Staten Island Ferry from the southern tip of Manhattan. After you disembark, grab an S40 bus to the **Snug Harbor Cultural Center** (about 10 minutes) or take the S74 and combine visits to the **Tibetan Museum** and **Historic Richmond Town.**

TOP ATTRACTIONS

FAMILY
Fodor's Choice
★

Historic Richmond Town. Think of Virginia's Colonial Williamsburg (the polar opposite of Brooklyn's scene-y Williamsburg), and you'll understand the appeal of Richmond Town. This 100-acre village, constructed from 1695 to the 19th century, was the site of Staten Island's original county seat. Fifteen of the site's 27 historic buildings are open to the public. Highlights include the Gothic Revival **Courthouse,** the one-room **General Store,** and the **Voorlezer's House,** one of the oldest buildings on the site. It served as a residence, a place of worship, and an elementary school. Also on site is the **Staten Island Historical Society Museum,** built in 1848 as the second county clerk's and surrogate's office, which now houses Staten Island artifacts plus changing exhibits about the island. Audio tours are free with admission.

You may see staff in period dress demonstrate Early American crafts and trades such as tinsmithing or basket making, though the general era meant to be re-created is 1820–1860. December brings a monthlong Christmas celebration. Take the S74–Richmond Road bus (30 minutes) or a car service (about $15) from the ferry terminal. ⊠ *441 Clarke Ave., Richmondtown* ☎ *718/351–1611* ⊕ *www.historicrichmondtown.org* ⊠ *$8 (free on Fri.)* ⊙ *Wed.–Sun. 1–5; guided tours Wed.–Fri. at 2:30, weekends at 2 and 3:30* Ⓜ *S74 bus to St. Patrick's Pl.*

Jacques Marchais Museum of Tibetan Art. At the top of a hill sits this replica of a Tibetan monastery containing one of the largest collections of Tibetan and Himalayan sculpture, paintings, and artifacts outside Tibet. Meditate with visiting Buddhist monks, or just enjoy the peaceful views from the terraced garden. ⊠ *338 Lighthouse Ave., Lighthouse Hill* ☎ *718/987–3500* ⊕ *www.tibetanmuseum.org* ⊠ *$6* ⊙ *Apr.–Dec., Wed.–Sun. 1–5; Feb.–Mar., Fri.–Sun. 1–5; Jan. by appointment only* Ⓜ *S74 bus to Lighthouse Ave. (30–45 mins from the Staten Island Ferry Terminal) and walk uphill 15 mins.*

WORTH NOTING

Snug Harbor Cultural Center and Botanical Garden. Once part of a sprawling farm, this 83-acre community is now a popular spot to see maritime art, frolic in the **Children's Museum** (⊕ *www.statenislandkids.org*), or take a stroll through lush gardens.

LIFE RING BUOY
WITH LINE

Made up of 28 mostly restored historic buildings, Snug Harbor's center is a row of mid-19th-century Greek Revival temples. Main Hall—the oldest building on the property—is home to the **Eleanor Proske Visitors Center** (🖻 *$5, including Newhouse Center*), which has exhibits on art and Snug Harbor's history. The adjacent **Newhouse Center for Contemporary Art** (🖀 *718/425–3524* 🖻 *$5, including visitor center*) shows multidisciplinary videos, mixed media, and performances. Next door at the **Noble Maritime Collection** (🖀 *718/447–6490* ⊕ *www.noblemaritime.org,* 🖻 *Suggested donation*) an old seamen's dormitory is now a museum of ocean-inspired artwork.

From the Staten Island Ferry terminal, take the S40 bus 2 miles (about seven minutes) to the Snug Harbor Road stop. Or grab a car service at the ferry terminal. (The ride should cost you $5–$8.) ⊠ *1000 Richmond Terr., between Snug Harbor Rd. and Tyson Ave., Randall Manor* 🖀 *718/448–2500* ⊕ *www.snug-harbor.org* 🖻 *Grounds and gardens free; New York Chinese Scholar's Garden $5; art galleries $5; garden and gallery combo ticket $8; children's museum $6* ⊙ *Grounds daily dawn–dusk except major holidays. Botanical Gardens Tues.–Sun. 10–5. Visitor center and galleries Wed.–Sun. noon–5. Noble Maritime Thurs.–Sun. 1–5 or by appt. Children's Museum school days noon–5, weekends and holidays 10–5.*

WHERE TO EAT

Updated by
David Farley

Ready to take a bite out of New York? Hope you've come hungry. In a city where creativity is expressed in many ways, the food scene takes center stage, with literally thousands of ways to get an authentic taste of what Gotham is all about. Whether they're lining up at street stands, gobbling down legendary deli and diner grub, or chasing a coveted reservation at the latest celebrity-chef venue, New Yorkers are a demanding yet appreciative audience.

Every neighborhood offers temptations high, low, and in between, meaning there's truly something for every taste, whim, and budget. No matter how you approach dining out here, you can't go wrong. Planning a day of shopping among the glittering boutique flagships along 5th and Madison? Stop into one of the Upper East Side's storied restaurants for a repast among the "ladies who lunch." Clubbing in the Meatpacking District? Tuck into a meal at eateries as trendy as their patrons. Craving authentic ethnic? From food trucks to hidden joints, there are almost more choices than there are appetites. Recent years have also seen entire food categories, from ramen to meatballs to mac 'n' cheese, riffed-upon and fetishized.

Amid newfound economic realities, there's been a revived appreciation for value, meaning you can tap into wallet-friendly choices at every end of the spectrum. At many restaurants you'll also notice an almost religious reverence for seasonal, locally sourced cuisine. And don't forget—New York is still home to more celebrity chefs than any other city. Your chances of running into your favorite cookbook author, Food Network celeb, or paparazzi-friendly chef are higher, adding even more star wattage to a restaurant scene with an already through-the-roof glamour quotient. Ready, set, eat. Rest assured, this city will do its part to satisfy your appetite.

HARLEM
BBQ and soul food reign supreme

UPPER EAST SIDE
pricey neighborhood joints

UPPER WEST SIDE
casual & family-friendly

MIDTOWN WEST
mostly overpriced; some great steakhouses

MIDTOWN EAST
expense-account dining

QUEENS
Excellent ethnic fare

CHELSEA
reliable, casual spots

MURRAY HILL
a.k.a Curry Hill, great Indian restaurants

FLATIRON DISTRICT
stylish, upscale eateries

GRAMERCY

UNION SQUARE
foodie haven

MEATPACKING DISTRICT
flashy hotspots

GREENWICH VILLAGE
shabby-chic restaurants and hip gastropubs

EAST VILLAGE
cheap eats, great ethnic food

NOLITA
hipster hangouts

LOWER EAST SIDE
edgy, DIY resto-bars

SOHO
pricey bistros and glamorous lounges

LITTLE ITALY
red-sauce factories

TRIBECA
swanky lounges, sophisticated dining

CHINATOWN
dim-sum palaces, noodle shops, Asian bakeries

LOWER MANHATTAN
upscale haunts

BROOKLYN
Cool local restaurants in hip neighborhoods

NEW JERSEY

Hudson River

East River

Roosevelt Island

W. 86th St.
E. 86th St.
West Ave.
Amsterdam Ave.
Columbus Ave.
Central Park West
5th Ave.
West End Ave.
Riverside Dr.
Madison Ave.
Park Ave.
Lexington Ave.
1st Ave.
E. 65th St.
Henry Hudson Pkwy.
Broadway
E. 59th St.
E. 57th St.
Queensboro Bridge
W. 57th St.
50th St.
Queens-Midtown Tunnel
Lincoln Tunnel
W. 42nd St.
E. 42nd St.
11th Ave.
10th Ave.
9th Ave.
8th Ave.
7th Ave.
Ave. of the Americas
5th Ave.
Broadway
Madison Ave.
Park Ave.
3rd Ave.
2nd Ave.
1st Ave.
W. 34th St.
E. 23rd St.
W. 14th St.
E. 14th St.
Avenue B
Avenue C
West Side Hwy.
W. Houston St.
E. Houston St.
Williamsburg Bridge
Delancey St.
Holland Tunnel
Canal St.
West St.
W. Broadway
Chambers St.
Manhattan Bridge
Brooklyn Bridge
EDR Dr.

BEST BETS FOR NEW YORK CITY DINING

With thousands of restaurants to choose from, how will you decide where to eat? Fodor's writers and editors have selected their favorite restaurants by price, cuisine, and experience in the Best Bets lists below.

M. Wells Dinette, p. 338

Marea, p. 316

Northern Spy Food Co., p. 279

Osteria Morini, p. 272

Roberta's, p. 337

Fodor'sChoice★

Aldea, $$$, p. 300

Alder, $$, p. 273

Babbo, $$$, p. 286

Back Forty West, $$, p. 269

Bar Boulud, $$$, p. 322

The Breslin Bar and Dining Room, $$$, p. 300

Burger Joint, $, p. 312

Café Sabarsky, $$, p. 319

Candle 79, $$, p. 320

Carbone, $$$$, p. 287

The City Bakery, $, p. 300

Clinton St. Baking Co., $$, p. 282

Co., $$, p. 296

Daniel, $$$$, p. 320

Danji, $, p. 313

Edi & the Wolf, $$, p. 275

Eleven Madison Park, $$$$, p. 301

Empellon Taqueria, $$$, p. 292

Emporio, $$, p. 266

The Fat Radish, $$, p. 283

Fatty Crab, $$, p. 292

Freemans $$, p. 283

Gotham Bar & Grill, $$$$, p. 304

I Sodi, $$$, p. 293

Katz's Delicatessen, $, p. 283

Le Bernardin, $$$$, p. 315

M. Wells Dinette, $$, p. 338

Marea, $$, p. 316

Mission Chinese Food, $, p. 284

Momofuku Ko, $$$$, p. 278

Momofuku Noodle Bar, $, p. 279

NoMad, $$$, p. 302

North End Grill, $$$, p. 262

Northern Spy Food Co., $$, p. 279

Osteria Morini, $$, p. 272

Per Se, $$$$, p. 325

Peter Luger, $$$$, p. 336

Plataforma Churrascaria Rodizio, $$$, p. 317

Pok Pok Ny, $ p. 329

Reynards, $$, p. 336

Roberta's, $$, p. 337

Saxon & Parole, $$, p. 281

Shake Shack, $, p. 303

Tía Pol, $, p. 297

Torrisi Italian Specialties, $$$$, p. 268

Best by Price

$

Bubby's, p. 261

Burger Joint, p. 312

Cascabel Taqueria, p. 320

City Bakery, p. 300

Gray's Papaya, p. 324

Katz's Delicatessen, p. 283

Legend, p. 296

Mexicana Mama, p. 293

Mile End, p. 278

Mission Chinese Food, p. 284

Momofuku Noodle Bar, p. 279

Pok Pok Ny, p. 329

Shake Shack, p. 303

Somtum Der, p. 281

Tía Pol, $, p. 297

$$

Arturo's, p. 286

Café Sabarsky, p. 319

Candle 79, p. 320

Emporio, p. 266

Fatty Crab, p. 292

$$$

ABC Kitchen, p. 299

Babbo, p. 286

Balthazar, p. 269

Bar Boulud, p. 322

Craft, p. 301

Minetta Tavern, p. 289

NoMad, p. 302

The Standard Grill, p. 299

$$$$

Eleven Madison Park, p. 301

Jean Georges, p. 324

Le Bernardin, p. 315

The Modern and Bar Room, p. 316

Per Se, p. 325

Best by Cuisine

AMERICAN

ABC Kitchen, p. 299

Back Forty West, p. 269

Cookshop, p. 296

Gramercy Tavern, p. 303

Hundred Acres, p. 270

Northern Spy Food Co., p. 279

Per Se, p. 325

CHINESE

Grand Sichuan, p. 276
Great New York Noodletown, p. 263
Joe's Shanghai, p. 264
Legend, p. 296
Mission Chinese Food, p. 284
Shun Lee Palace, p. 309
Tasty Hand-Pulled Noodles, p. 265
Xi'an Famous Foods, p. 265

FRENCH

Bar Boulud, p. 322
Daniel, p. 320
Jean Georges, p. 324
Lafayette Grand Café & Bakery, p. 277
Le Bernardin, p. 315
The Modern and Bar Room, p. 316

GREEK

Kefi, p. 324
Pylos, p. 280
Snack, p. 272

INDIAN

Tamarind, p. 263

ITALIAN

Babbo, p. 286
Emporio, p. 266
Lupa, p. 288
Marea, p. 316
Osteria Morini, p. 272
Scarpetta, p. 298
Torrisi Italian Specialties, p. 268

JAPANESE

Ippudo, p. 277
Kuruma Zushi, p. 307
Sushi of Gari, p. 321
Sushi Nakazawa, p. 295
Sushi Yasuda, p. 309

MEDITERRANEAN

Aldea, p. 300
August, p. 290
Il Buco, p. 276
NoMad, p. 302
Picholine, p. 326

MEXICAN

Cascabel Taqueria, p. 320
Empellon Taqueria, p. 292
Maya, p. 321
Mexicana Mama, p. 293
Toloache, p. 318

NEW AMERICAN

Craft, p. 301
Eleven Madison Park, p. 301
Hundred Acres, p. 270
The Red Cat, p. 297

PIZZA

Arturo's, p. 286
Co., p. 296
Esca, p. 313
Grimaldi's, p. 331
Keste Pizza & Vino, p. 288
Lombardi's, p. 267

SEAFOOD

Grand Central Oyster Bar & Restaurant, p. 307
The John Dory, p. 302
Marea, p. 316
Mary's Fish Camp, p. 293
Pearl Oyster Bar, p. 294

SPANISH

Boqueria, p. 300
Casa Mono, p. 303
Tía Pol, p. 297

STEAKHOUSE

BLT Prime, p. 303
BLT Steak, p. 306
Peter Luger's, p. 336
Porter House, p. 326
Sparks Steakhouse, p. 309

Best by Experience

BRUNCH

Balthazar, p. 269
Bubby's, p. 261
Cookshop, p. 296
Hundred Acres, p. 270
Sarabeth's Kitchen, p. 326

CELEB-SPOTTING

ABC Kitchen, p. 299
Balthazar, p. 269
The Breslin Bar and Dining Room, p. 300
Café Boulud, p. 319

DBGB Kitchen & Bar, p. 275
Four Seasons, p. 307
Minetta Tavern, p. 289
Nobu, p. 262
The Standard Grill, p. 299

CHILD-FRIENDLY

Bubby's, p. 261
Carmine's, p. 312
City Bakery, p. 300
Joe's Shanghai, p. 264
Lombardi's, p. 267
Odeon, p. 262

GREAT VIEW

Asiate, p. 322
Marea, p. 316
Michael Jordan's The Steakhouse NYC, p. 308
Per Se, p. 325
Porter House, p. 326

LATE-NIGHT DINING

Balthazar, p. 269
The Breslin Bar and Dining Room, p. 300
DBGB Kitchen & Bar, p. 275
Emporio, p. 266
Fatty Crab, p. 292
Minetta Tavern, p. 289
Osteria Morini, p. 272
The Standard Grill, p. 299

16

EAT LIKE A LOCAL

A handful of foods are associated with New York City: apples (obviously), pizza, pastrami, hot dogs, bagels—the list of earthly delights is long and delicious. These are, generally speaking, what the locals tend to talk about.

FOOD TRUCKS

The food-truck movement is officially on. It seems there's a special truck for everything from ethnic eats to fresh-baked sweets. The southern end of Washington Square, for example, near NYU, is a prime location, with trucks lined up serving the cuisines of Holland, Colombia, Cambodia, and Mexico, but you can find food trucks parked all over town, some with legendary followings and Twitter feeds to help you find them. Thompson Hotels, which has several properties in New York, even has a Food Truck Concierge.

PIZZA

There are few things more Big Apple than a slice of pizza, its bottom crust crispy from the coal oven. There are take-out joints for slices, and sit-down restaurants that only serve whole pies; some are thin-crust, some are thick, some even have fried dough. And everyone has a favorite. There's no question that pizza will always be synonymous with New York, but pizza crust is something that's being elevated to a real art form these days.

SOUL FOOD IN HARLEM

Sylvia Woods, the "Queen of Soul Food" and proprietor of the eponymous Harlem restaurant, may have ascended to that great soul food restaurant in the sky, but the cuisine lives on in this historic African American neighborhood—in fact, more now than ever, since celeb-chef Marcus Samuelsson moved into the area, opening the Red Rooster, a global eatery that gives a big nod to soul food.

CHINESE FOOD

There's Chinese food and then there's New York's downtown Chinatown Chinese food, which some visitors might find head-scratchingly unfamiliar. That's because Chinatown boasts a diverse population from China's many regions, which means menus are going to look deliciously foreign to the uninitiated. Go ahead, point and order something you've never heard of. Restaurants serving dim sum, which are basically different kinds of small fried or steamed dumplings, are popular for breakfast on the weekends.

BURGERS

Hamburgers will forever be a part of the Big Apple dining landscape. But it so happens that it's never been a better time to be a burger eater, and nearly every restaurant—American or not—has some kind of burger on its menu. If you're a discriminating burger lover, look for the name Pat LaFrieda, a meat purveyor par excellence. Just don't expect to save any money; it's not unusual to see a $20 hamburger on a menu.

GASTROPUBS

The gastropub phenomenon, imported from London, began with the Spotted

Pig in the West Village, and within a few years, every neighborhood had one. And why not? Blending a casual pub atmosphere with way-better-than-average pub grub is a fun and tasty combination that's hard to beat.

BANH MI SANDWICHES

The banh mi sandwich has grabbed the attention of Big Apple eaters and it has not let go in recent years. This French-influenced Vietnamese sandwich consists of pork, pâté, carrots, cilantro, and jalapeño peppers stuffed into a baguette. This is a delicacy worth seeking out, so check the menus at our top Asian restaurant picks.

LOCAVORE

The focus on local food and beverages has definitely taken hold at NYC restaurants. Menus flaunt the nearby provenance of their meat and produce, whether it's from upstate New York or from the restaurant's rooftop garden. Wine lists frequently feature excellent Long Island wines, as well as bourbon and other spirits brewed as close as the Brooklyn Navy Yards or in the Hudson Valley.

16

PLANNING

CHILDREN

Though it's unusual to see children in the dining rooms of Manhattan's most elite restaurants, dining with youngsters in New York does not have to mean culinary exile. Many of the restaurants reviewed in this chapter are excellent choices for families, and are marked as such.

RESERVATIONS

It's always a good idea to plan ahead. Some renowned restaurants like Per Se, Daniel, Brooklyn Fare, and Momofuku Ko are booked weeks or even months in advance. If that's the case, you can get lucky at the last minute if you're flexible—and friendly. Most restaurants keep a few tables open for walk-ins and VIPs. Show up for dinner early (5:30) or late (after 10), and politely inquire about any last-minute vacancies or cancellations.

Occasionally, an eatery may take your credit-card number and ask you to call the day before your scheduled meal to reconfirm: don't forget or you could lose out, or possibly be charged for your oversight.

WHAT TO WEAR

New Yorkers like to dress up, and so should you. Whatever your style, dial it up a notch. Have some fun while you're at it. Pull out the clothes you've been saving for a special occasion and get glamorous. Unfair as it is, the way you look can influence how you're treated—and where you're seated. Generally speaking, jeans and a button-down shirt will suffice at most table-service restaurants in the $ to $$ range. In reviews, we note dress only when a jacket or jacket and tie are required. If you have doubts, call the restaurant and ask.

TIPPING AND TAXES

In most restaurants, tip the waiter 15%–20%. (To figure out a 20% tip quickly, just move the decimal point one place to the left on your total and double that amount.) Bills for parties of six or more sometimes include the tip. Tip at least $1 per drink at the bar, and $1 for each coat checked. Never tip the maître d' unless you're out to impress your guests or expect to pay another visit soon.

SMOKING

Smoking is prohibited in all enclosed public spaces in New York City, including restaurants and bars.

HOURS

New Yorkers seem ready to eat at any hour. Many restaurants stay open between lunch and dinner, some offer late-night seating, and still others serve around the clock. Restaurants that serve breakfast often do so until noon or later. Restaurants in the East Village, the Lower East Side, SoHo, TriBeCa, and Greenwich Village are likely to remain open late, whereas Midtown spots and those in the Theater and Financial districts and uptown generally close earlier. Unless otherwise noted, the restaurants listed in this guide are open daily for lunch and dinner.

PRICES

Be sure to ask the price of the daily specials recited by the waiter. The charge for specials at some restaurants is noticeably out of line with the other prices on the menu. Beware of the $10 bottle of water; ask for tap water instead. And always review your bill.

If you eat early or late, you may be able to take advantage of a prix-fixe deal not offered at peak hours. Most upscale restaurants offer great lunch deals.

Credit cards are widely accepted, but many restaurants (particularly smaller ones downtown) accept only cash. If you plan to use a credit card, it's a good idea to confirm that it is acceptable when making reservations or before sitting down to eat.

Prices in the reviews are the average cost of a main course at dinner or, if dinner is not served, at lunch.

CHECK BEFORE YOU GO

The nature of the restaurant industry means that places open and close in a New York minute. It's always a good idea to phone ahead and make sure your restaurant is still turning tables.

16

RESTAURANT REVIEWS

Listed alphabetically within neighborhoods. Use the coordinate (⊕ 1:B2) at the end of each listing to locate a property on the corresponding map at the end of the chapter.

LOWER MANHATTAN

FINANCIAL DISTRICT

The southern tip of the island, once skyscraper-laden and nightlife-starved, has been getting buzzier in the last few years. Exciting new bars and restaurants have opened (the old dependable steakhouses and bistros are still here).

$
ITALIAN
FAMILY

✕ **Adrienne's Pizza Bar.** It's hip to be square at this downtown pizzeria. Father-and-son team Harry and Peter Poulakakos's square (also known as Grandma) pies are worth the trek, and make a convenient stop en route to the Statue of Liberty. They also do a mean traditional round pizza, and first timers should opt for the signature Old Fashioned: thin crispy crust loaded with tangy tomato sauce, fresh mozzarella, and Parmesan cheese. Salads and pasta are also on the menu. Service has never been Adrienne's forte, so be flattered if you get someone to crack a smile. ⑤ *Average main: $17* ⊠ *54 Stone St., near Hanover Sq., Financial District* ☎ *212/248–3838* ⊕ *www. adriennespizzabar.com* ⊕ *1:E4.*

$$$$
STEAKHOUSE

✕ **Delmonico's.** The oldest continually operating restaurant in New York City (it opened in 1837), austere Delmonico's is steeped in cultural, political, and culinary history. Lobster Newburg and Baked Alaska were invented here—and are still served. Inside the stately mahogany-panel dining room, tuck into the classic Delmonico's steak, a 20-ounce boneless ribeye smothered with frizzled onions, and don't forget to order creamed spinach on the side. The cheesy spaetzle with pancetta is also sinfully sublime. The dining room gets busy early with an after-work Wall Street crowd, making reservations essential. $ *Average main: $37* ✉ *56 Beaver St., at William St., Financial District* ☎ *212/509–1144* ⊕ *www.delmoniconsy.com* ⌲ *Reservations essential* ⊘ *Closed Sun. No lunch Sat.* Ⓜ *2, 3 to Wall St.; R to Whitehall St./South Ferry; 4, 5 to Bowling Green* ✛ *1:D4.*

$ CAFÉ ✕ **Financier Patisserie.** On the cobblestone pedestrian street that has become the Financial District's restaurant row, this charming patisserie serves excellent pastries and delicious savory foods, like mushroom bisque, salads, and hot or cold sandwiches (we have cravings for the panini pressed with prosciutto, fig jam, mascarpone, and arugula). After lunch, relax with a cappuccino and a *financier* (almond tea cake), or an elegant pastry. In warm weather, perch at an outdoor table and watch Manhattanites buzz by. There are locations all over town. $ *Average main: $7* ✉ *62 Stone St., between Mill La. and Hanover Sq., Financial District* ☎ *212/344–5600* ⊕ *www.financierpastries.com* ⌲ *Reservations not accepted* ⊘ *Closed Sun.* Ⓜ *2, 3 to Wall St.; 4, 5 to Bowling Green* ✛ *1:E4.*

$$$ STEAKHOUSE ✕ **Harry's Café and Steak.** Its noise-dampening acoustics and maze of underground nooks combine to make Harry's Steak—the fine-dining half of the restaurant (Harry's Café is more casual, but the menu is the same)—one of the city's most intimate steakhouses. Settle in to one of the leather booths and start with a classic shrimp cocktail or the tomato trio, starring thick beefsteak slices topped with bacon and blue cheese, mozzarella and basil, and shaved onion with ranch dressing. The star attraction—prime aged porterhouse for two—is nicely encrusted with sea salt and a good match for buttery mashed potatoes infused with sweet roasted shallots and thick steak sauce spooned from Mason jars. Weekend brunch is popular, too. $ *Average main: $35* ✉ *1 Hanover Sq., between Stone and Pearl Sts., Financial District* ☎ *212/785–9200* ⊕ *www.harrysnyc.com* ⌲ *Reservations essential* ⊘ *Closed Sun.* Ⓜ *4, 5 to Bowling Green; 2, 3 to Wall St.* ✛ *1:E4.*

$ AMERICAN ✕ **Ulysses'.** Nestled alongside skyscrapers and the towering New York Stock Exchange, Stone Street is a two-block restaurant oasis that feels more like a village than the center of the financial universe. After the market closes, Wall Streeters head to Ulysses', a popular pub with 17 beers on tap and more than 50 bottled beers. Hungry? There are also decent pub-grub options, like scallop lollipops, fried oysters, nachos, and wings. $ *Average main: $9* ✉ *95 Pearl St., near Hanover Sq., Financial District* ☎ *212/482–0400* ⊕ *www.ulyssesnyc.com* ✛ *1:E4.*

TRIBECA

TriBeCa and its restaurants are a playground for the rich and famous. Fortunately, glamorous dining rooms in converted warehouses have been joined in the last few years by more casual spots.

$$$ AUSTRIAN FAMILY ✕ **Blaue Gans.** Chef Kurt Gutenbruner, one of the most lauded Austrian chefs in New York, runs this sprawling brasserie like an all-day clubhouse. Pop in for a late morning or early afternoon snack—the coffee comes topped with schlag, the donuts filled with apricot jam. Or swing by in the evening for central European standards like sausage,

schnitzel, potato dumplings, and beef goulash. And you can wash it all down with a hoppy Austrian brew. ⑤ *Average main: $25* ✉ *139 Duane St., near W. Broadway, TriBeCa* ☎ *212/571–8880* ⊕ *www. kg-ny.com* Ⓜ *1, 2, 3, A, C to Chambers St.* ✛ *1:C1.*

$ ✕ **Bubby's.** Neighborhood crowds clamoring for coffee and freshly
AMERICAN   squeezed juice line up for brunch at this TriBeCa mainstay, but Bub-
FAMILY   by's is good for lunch and dinner, too, if you're in the mood for comfort food like mac 'n' cheese or fried chicken. The dining room is homey and comfortable, with big windows; in summer, patrons sit at tables outside with their dogs. Brunch options include just about everything, including homemade granola, sour-cream pancakes with bananas and strawberries, and huevos rancheros with guacamole and grits. ⑤ *Average main: $17* ✉ *120 Hudson St., at N. Moore St., TriBeCa* ☎ *212/219–0666* ⊕ *www.bubbys.com* Ⓜ *1 to Franklin St.* ✛ *1:C1.*

$$$ ✕ **The Harrison.** It's been more than a decade since Jimmy Bradley opened
AMERICAN   the Harrison, following his success with the Red Cat in Chelsea, but it's still a quintessential neighborhood eatery. The warm, woody room serves as a relaxed backdrop for the seasonal American food, like English-cut lamb loin with baby carrots and fennel, and malt-vinegar mayo. Desserts, including an ice cream–brownie sandwich with Sazerac caramel, are at once accessible and sophisticated. ⑤ *Average main: $27* ✉ *355 Greenwich St., at Harrison St., TriBeCa* ☎ *212/274–9310* ⊕ *www.theharrison.com* ⚄ *Reservations essential* ☾ *No lunch weekends* Ⓜ *1 to Franklin St.* ✛ *1:B1.*

$ ✕ **Kitchenette.** This small, comfy restaurant lives up to its name with
AMERICAN   tables so close together, you're likely to make new friends. Indeed,
FAMILY   the dining room pretty much feels like a breakfast nook, and the food tastes like your mom made it—provided she's a great cook. Think comfort food: fried chicken, barbecue brisket with mashed potatoes, and even a turkey dinner. There are no frills here, just solid cooking, friendly service, and a long line at peak times. At brunch don't miss the peach pancakes or the baked cinnamon-swirl French toast. ⑤ *Average main: $15* ✉ *156 Chambers St., near Greenwich St., TriBeCa* ☎ *212/267–6740* ⊕ *www.kitchenetterestaurant.com* Ⓜ *1, 2, 3, A, C to Chambers St.* ✛ *1:C2.*

$$$ ✕ **Locanda Verde.** Chef Andrew Carmellini, an acolyte of Daniel Boulud,
ITALIAN   has definitely made a name for himself in New York City with this Robert De Niro–backed restaurant, and then with the Dutch in SoHo. The space at Locanda Verde is warm and welcoming, with accents of brick and wood and large windows that open to the street, weather permitting, while the menu is full of inspired Italian comfort food that hits the mark. Standouts include small plates like blue crab crostino with jalapeños and the pumpkin agnolotti in brown sage butter that diners reminisce about. Several draft beers, along with more than a dozen wines by the glass, make an already hopping bar scene even more of a draw. ⑤ *Average main: $26* ✉ *377 Greenwich St., at N. Moore St., TriBeCa* ☎ *212/925–3797* ⊕ *www.locandaverdenyc.com* ⚄ *Reservations essential* Ⓜ *1 to Franklin St.* ✛ *1:B1.*

16

$$$ ✕ **Marc Forgione.** Chef Marc Forgione has restaurant success in his blood
AMERICAN (his father was one of the New York food scene megastars with his
1980s restaurant, An American Place) but he more than holds his own
at this neighborhood restaurant that continues to attract crowds for
the ambitious, creative New American cuisine. The menu changes fre-
quently but whatever you order will be bold, flavorful, and inventive
without a hint of preciousness. Meat dishes are excellent and well-
prepared but Forgione has a special way with seafood. His chili lobster
appetizer, a take on a dish you'll find all over Asia, comes with Texas
toast for mopping up the spicy, buttery sauce. Tartare (perhaps kingfish,
hamachi, or salmon, depending on the day) is accented with avocado in
a pool of sweet, soy-lashed sauce. ⑤ *Average main: $30* ⊠ *134 Reade
St., between Hudson and Greenwich Sts., TriBeCa* ☎ *212/941–9401*
⊕ *www.marcforgione.com* ⌂ *Reservations essential* ⊗ *No lunch* Ⓜ *1,
2, 3 to Chambers St.* ✛ *1:C1.*

$$$$ ✕ **Nobu.** At this large, bustling TriBeCa dining room (or its sister
JAPANESE location uptown), you might just spot a celeb or two. New York's
famed Japanese restaurant has gained a lot of competition in recent
years, but this is still the destination for the innovative Japanese cui-
sine Nobu Matsuhisa made famous (though he's rarely in attendance
these days). Dishes like fresh yellowtail sashimi with jalapeño, rock
shrimp tempura, or miso-marinated Chilean sea bass continue to
draw huge crowds. Put yourself in the hands of the chef by order-
ing the *omakase* (tasting menu), and specify how much you want to
spend, then let the kitchen do the rest. Can't get reservations? Try
your luck at the first-come, first-served **Nobu Next Door** (literally
next door), with a similar menu plus a sushi bar. ⑤ *Average main:
$37* ⊠ *105 Hudson St., at Franklin St., TriBeCa* ☎ *212/219–0500*
⊕ *www.myriadrestaurantgroup.com* ⌂ *Reservations essential* ⊗ *No
lunch Sun.* Ⓜ *1 to Franklin St.* ✛ *1:B1.*

$$$ ✕ **North End Grill.** The Financial District movers and shakers who fre-
SEAFOOD quent this handsome, seafood-heavy restaurant are in good hands.
Fodor's Choice Floyd Cardoz, who made a name for himself at the now-shuttered
★ elevated Indian eatery, Tabla, mans the stoves, churning out inspired
fare like memorable grilled octopus, pumpkin soup bobbing with crab,
and succulent whole fish (for two). Carnivores can dig into a juicy
Berkshire pork chop, lamb loin topped with a minty chickpea puree,
or the whopping 16-ounce ribeye. Save some stomach space for a
sweet ending: the sticky toffee pudding with vanilla bourbon ice cream
is sublime. At lunch, don't pass up the amazing bacon-shrimp burger
on a soft pretzel roll. ⑤ *Average main: $26* ⊠ *104 North End Ave., at
Murray St., TriBeCa* ☎ *646/747–1600* ⊕ *www.northendgrillnyc.com*
Ⓜ *1, 2, 3 to Chambers St.; E to World Trade Center* ✛ *1:B2.*

$$$ ✕ **Odeon.** New Yorkers change hangouts faster than they can press
FRENCH speed-dial, but this spot has managed to maintain its quality and flair
FAMILY for more than 30 years. It still feels like *the* spot in TriBeCa to get a
late-night bite. The neo–Art Deco room is still packed nightly with
revelers, and the pleasant service and well-chosen wine list are always
in style. The bistro-menu highlights include *frisée aux lardons* (bacon-
enhanced frisee salad) with poached farm egg, grilled NY strip steak,

and slow-cooked cod with baby leeks and fennel confit. ⑤ *Average main: $28* ✉ *145 West Broadway, between Duane and Thomas Sts., TriBeCa* ☎ *212/233–0507* ⊕ *www.theodeonrestaurant.com* Ⓜ *1, 2, 3, A, C to Chambers St.* ✛ *1:C1; 2:D6.*

$$$ ✕ **Tamarind.** Many consider Tamarind to be Manhattan's best Indian
INDIAN restaurant and the elegant atmosphere makes it a different experience from what you'll find in many other NYC Indian restaurants. Forsaking the usual brass, beads, sitar, and darkness, you'll find an airy modern dining room. Welcoming hosts, owner Avtar Walia and his nephew, general manager Gary, practically reinvent charm. The busy kitchen offers multiregional dishes, some familiar (tandoori chicken, a searing lamb vindaloo), some unique (succulent venison chops in a vigorously spiced cranberry sauce, she-crab soup with saffron, nutmeg, and ginger juice). The more intriguing a dish sounds, the better it turns out to be. ⑤ *Average main: $25* ✉ *99 Hudson St., at Franklin St., TriBeCa, New York, New York* ☎ *212/674–7400* ⊕ *www.tamarindrestaurantsnyc.com* Ⓜ *1 to Franklin St.; A,C, E to Canal St.* ✛ *2:C6.*

SOHO, NOLITA, LITTLE ITALY, AND CHINATOWN

16

CHINATOWN

Chinatown beckons adventurous diners with restaurants representing numerous regional cuisines of China, including Cantonese-, Szechuan-, Hunan-, Fujian-, Shanghai-, and Hong Kong–style cooking. Malaysian and Vietnamese restaurants also have taken root here, and the neighborhood continues to grow rapidly, encroaching into what was Little Italy.

$ ✕ **456 Shanghai Cuisine.** Come to this Chintown eatery for above-
CHINESE average Chinese fare, such as General Tsao's chicken, pork buns, and cold sesame noodles, but do yourself a favor and ask for an order of soup dumplings (*xiao long bao*) as soon as you sit down. You won't regret it. The dumplings, doughy and thin on the outside, encase morsels of crab swimming in a bold porky broth, and are truly a wonder of the culinary world—456 does them as good as (or better than) anyone in the city. ⑤ *Average main: $14* ✉ *69 Mott St., between Canal and Bayard Sts., Chinatown* ☎ *212/964–0003* Ⓜ *J, N, Q, J to Canal St.* ✛ *2:F5.*

$ ✕ **Great New York Noodletown.** Although the soups and noodles are
CHINESE unbeatable at this no-frills restaurant, what you should really order
FAMILY are the window decorations—the hanging lacquered ducks and roasted pork, which are listed on a simple board hung on the wall and superb served with pungent garlic-and-ginger sauce on the side. Seasonal specialties like duck with flowering chives and salt-baked soft-shell crabs are excellent. So is the *congee*, or rice porridge, available with any number of garnishes. Solo diners may end up at a communal table. Noodletown is open late—till 4 am on Friday and Saturday. ⑤ *Average main: $10* ✉ *28 Bowery, at Bayard St., Chinatown* ☎ *212/349–0923* ▭ *No credit cards* Ⓜ *6, J, M, Z to Canal St.; B, D to Grand St.* ✛ *2:G5.*

Head to Chinatown for some authentic taste experiences.

$ ✕ **Jing Fong.** On weekend mornings people pack this vast dim sum pal-
CHINESE ace so be prepared to wait. Once your number is called you'll take
FAMILY the escalator up to the carnivalesque third-floor dining room, where
servers push carts crammed with tasty goodness. Expect to be plied
with delights like steamed dumplings, crispy spring rolls, barbecue pork
buns, and shrimp balls. For adventurous eaters, there's chicken feet,
tripe, and snails. Arrive early for the best selection, and save room
for mango pudding. $⑤ Average main: $16 ✉ 20 Elizabeth St., 2nd fl.,
between Bayard and Canal Sts., Chinatown ☎ 212/964–5256 ⊕ www.
jingfongny.com Ⓜ 6, J, M, N, Q, R, Z to Canal St. ✛ 2:F5.$

$ ✕ **Joe's Shanghai.** Joe opened his first Shanghai restaurant in Queens
CHINESE in 1995 but, buoyed by the accolades accorded his steamed soup
FAMILY dumplings—filled with a rich, fragrant broth and ground pork or
pork-crabmeat mixture—several Manhattan outposts soon followed.
The trick is to take a bite of the dumpling and slurp out the soup,
then eat the rest. There's almost always a wait, but the line moves
fast. The soup dumplings are a must but you can fill out your order
from the extensive menu. There's another Joe's Shanghai in Midtown
West, at 24 W. 56th Street, between 5th and 6th avenues (where
credit cards are accepted). $⑤ Average main: $16 ✉ 9 Pell St., between
the Bowery and Mott St., Chinatown ☎ 212/233–8888 ⊕ www.
joeshanghairestaurants.com ▭ No credit cards Ⓜ 6, J, M, N, Q, R, Z
to Canal St. ✛ 2:F5.$

$ ✕ **New Malaysia.** This Malaysian restaurant is a real find. Literally.
MALAYSIAN You could stroll right by it and never know it existed. That's because
it's in a passageway between Bowery and Elizabeth Street. It's worth
the trouble, though, as the menu is loaded with Malaysian favorites

like roti flatbread with curry and delicious red-bean and coconut-milk drinks. The atmosphere is casual and table service is relaxed, which means you might need to flag down your server. ⑤ *Average main: $14* ✉ *48 Bowery, near Canal St., Chinatown* ☎ *212/964–0284* Ⓜ *B, D to Grand St.* ✛ *2:G5.*

$$
CHINESE
✕ **Peking Duck House.** This Chinatown institution is the place to go in New York for authentic Peking duck. Although the restaurant offers a full Chinese menu, everyone—and we mean everyone—orders the duck. Begin, as most tables do, with an order of Shanghai soup dumplings, then move on to the bird. It's carved tableside with plenty of fanfare—crisp burnished skin separated from moist flesh. Roll up the duck, with hoisin and scallions, in tender steamed pancakes. The menu at the Midtown East location (236 E. 53rd Street) is a bit pricier. ⑤ *Average main: $19* ✉ *28 Mott St., at Mosco St., Chinatown* ☎ *212/227–1810* ⊕ *www.pekingduckhousenyc.com* Ⓜ *6, J, M, N, Q, R, Z to Canal St.* ✛ *2:F5.*

$
CHINESE
✕ **Tasty Hand-Pulled Noodles.** The name says it all. And it doesn't lie. The open kitchen at this salt-of-the-earth Chinatown restaurant (located on the charming, curved Doyers Street), means you can watch the noodle-slinger in action while awaiting your bowl of, um, tasty hand-pulled noodles. Just choose your ingredients—beef, pork, oxtail, eel, chicken, lamb, or shrimp, among others—and prepare to eat the most delicious bowl of $5 noodles since that last trip to Shanghai. The restaurant is small so be prepared to possibly share a table with a fellow diner. ⑤ *Average main: $5* ✉ *1 Doyers St., at Bowery, Chinatown* ☎ *212/791–1817* ⊕ *www.tastyhandpullednoodles.com* ▭ *No credit cards* Ⓜ *6, J, M, N, Q, R, W, Z to Canal St.* ✛ *2:F6.*

$
CHINESE
✕ **Vanessa's Dumpling House.** One of the best deals in Chinatown can be found at Vanessa's Dumpling House: sizzling pork-and-chive dumplings are four for a buck. There are also vegetarian options. The restaurant is very casual: order at the counter and then grab a seat at a table, if you can find one. Vanessa's is especially popular with Lower East Side revelers looking to pad their stomach before more debauchery. ⑤ *Average main: $8* ✉ *118 Eldridge St., near Broome St., Chinatown* ☎ *212/625–8008* ⊕ *www.vanessasdumplinghouse.com* ⌖ *Reservations not accepted* ▭ *No credit cards* Ⓜ *B, D to Grand St.* ✛ *2:G4.*

$
VIETNAMESE
✕ **Xe Lua.** A good Vietnamese restaurant in Manhattan is hard to find, which is why you should seek out Xe Lua, in Chinatown just below Little Italy. Quick service and the marathon-length menu should satisfy any palate but the real standouts are the clay pot dishes: cooked and served in—you guessed it—a clay pot, the pork, chicken, veggies, or whatever you order become slightly caramelized, giving a subtle sweetness to the dish. The *pho* (the soupy national dish of Vietnam) is also a good bet, as the broth seems to have a bolder taste here than at other places. ⑤ *Average main: $11* ✉ *86 Mulberry St., between Canal and Bayard Sts., Chinatown* ☎ *212/577–8887* ⊕ *www.xeluarestaurantnyc. com* Ⓜ *6, J, M, N, Q, R, W, Z to Canal St.* ✛ *2:F5.*

$
CHINESE
✕ **Xi'an Famous Foods.** Serving the very unrepresented cuisine of far western China, Xi'an Famous Foods serves Chinese food like you might not have tasted before. The restaurant first made a name for

16

itself at its original location, in the dingy basement food court of a mall in Flushing, Queens, but this spot—shinier, brighter, and cleaner—offers the same exciting fare. First-timers should try the spicy cumin lamb burger, which is mouth-wateringly delicious. Some of the dishes challenge the bounds of adventurousness in eating (lamb offal soup, anyone?) but don't let that scare you off. It's cheap enough to experiment, so tuck into that bowl of oxtail noodle soup and enjoy. $ *Average main: $10* ⊠ *67 Bayard St., Chinatown* ☎ *212/608–4170* Ⓜ *B, D to Grand St.* ✛ *2:F5.*

LITTLE ITALY

These days Little Italy is a tourist trap of pasta factories that just aren't very good. Don't despair, though: there is seriously good Italian food in just about every other neighborhood in the city—including nearby NoLIta.

NOLITA

In NoLIta, SoHo's trendy next-door neighborhood, the spirit of old, pre-chain-store SoHo prevails. Diminutive eateries, squeezed between up-and-coming designer boutiques, flank the narrow streets of this atmospheric neighborhood.

$
FRENCH

✗ **Café Gitane.** Specializing in simple salads, sandwiches, and a selection of hot mains, this French-Moroccan café draws models and model-gazers to its rather cramped NoLIta location (which is cash only). The clientele and the waitstaff seem to have wandered in fresh off the runway. The scene is quietest in the morning, when there are flaky croissants and big bowls of café au lait. There's a larger branch on the far edge of the West Village. $ *Average main: $15* ⊠ *242 Mott St., near Prince St., NoLIta* ☎ *212/334–9552* ⊕ *www.cafegitanenyc.com* ⌲ *Reservations not accepted* ▭ *No credit cards* Ⓜ *6 to Spring St.; N, R to Prince St.* ✛ *2:F3.*

$
ECLECTIC
FAMILY

✗ **Café Habana.** The Mexican-style grilled corn, liberally sprinkled with chili powder, lime, and cotija cheese is undoubtedly worth getting your hands dirty at this crowded hip luncheonette. Follow up with a classic Cuban sandwich (roast pork, ham, Swiss cheese, pickles, and chipotle mayo), fish tacos, or one of the innovative salads. Be prepared for a wait at lunchtime or on weekend afternoons. The cocktails are good, too. There's a take-out shop with a few seats down the street at 229 Elizabeth. $ *Average main: $12* ⊠ *17 Prince St., at Elizabeth St., NoLIta* ☎ *212/625–2001* ⊕ *www.cafehabana.com* ⌲ *Reservations not accepted* Ⓜ *B, D, F, M to Broadway–Lafayette* ✛ *2:F3.*

$$
ITALIAN
Fodor's Choice
★

✗ **Emporio.** The brick-lined front room of this homey Roman eatery in NoLIta is a gathering spot for happy hour at the bar, where you'll find an appetizing selection of free small bites like frittata, white-bean salad, and ham-and-spinach *tramezzini* (finger sandwiches). The centerpiece of the large, skylighted back room is a wood-fired oven that turns out crisp, thin-crusted pizzas topped with quality ingredients like prosciutto and buffalo mozzarella. Service is solicitous but not speedy, so you can linger over a bottle of wine from the copious selection. House-made pastas like garganelli with pork sausage and house-made ragù, and entrées like whole roasted fish with grilled lemon, are also excellent.

$ *Average main: $22* ✉ *231 Mott St., between Prince and Spring Sts., NoLIta* ☎ *212/966–1234* ⊕ *www.emporiony.com* Ⓜ *B, D, F, M, A, C, E to W. 4th St.; 6 to Bleecker St.* ✛ *2:F3.*

$$
MEXICAN

✕ **La Esquina.** Anchoring a downtown corner under a bright neon sign, La Esquina looks like nothing more than a fast-food taqueria, with cheap tacos sold to-go until 2 in the morning. Just around the corner, though, is a modestly priced café serving those same tacos along with more ambitious fare like *chiles rellenos* (stuffed peppers) and *carne asada* (grilled meat). The real hipster draw, however, is hidden from sight: the basement brasserie, like a Mexican speakeasy, is accessible by reservation only, through an unmarked door just inside the ground-floor taqueria. Once inside, you'll discover a buzzy subterranean scene with pretty people drinking potent margaritas, dining on upscale Mexican fare. Prices downstairs are high, but portions are large. $ *Average main: $20* ✉ *106 Kenmare, between Cleveland Pl. and Lafayette St., NoLIta* ☎ *646/613–7100* ⊕ *www.esquinanyc.com* Ⓜ *6 to Spring St.* ✛ *2:E4.*

$
PIZZA
FAMILY

✕ **Lombardi's Pizza.** Brick walls, red-and-white checkered tablecloths and the aroma of thin-crust pies emerging from the coal oven set the mood for dining on some of the best pizza in Manhattan. Lombardi's has served pizza since 1905 (though not in the same location), and business doesn't seem to have died down a bit. The mozzarella is always fresh, resulting in an almost greaseless slice, and the toppings, such as meatballs, pancetta, or imported anchovies, are also top quality. The clam pizza, with freshly shucked clams, garlic oil, Pecorino Romano cheese, and parsley, is well known among aficionados. $ *Average main: $16* ✉ *32 Spring St., at Mott St., NoLIta* ☎ *212/941–7994* ⊕ *www. firstpizza.com* ⌕ *Reservations not accepted* ▭ *No credit cards* Ⓜ *6 to Spring St.; B, D, F, M to Broadway–Lafayette* ✛ *2:F4.*

$$$
ITALIAN

✕ **Peasant.** The crowd at this rustic restaurant is stylishly urban. Inspired by the proverbial "peasant" cuisine where meals were prepared in the kitchen hearth, chef-owner Frank DeCarlo cooks all of his wonderful food in a bank of wood- or charcoal-burning ovens, from which the heady aroma of garlic perfumes the room. Don't fill up on the crusty bread and fresh ricotta or you'll miss out on flavorful Italian fare like sizzling sardines that arrive in terra-cotta pots, or spit-roasted leg of lamb with bitter *trevisano* lettuce and polenta. $ *Average main: $25* ✉ *194 Elizabeth St., between Spring and Prince Sts., NoLIta* ☎ *212/965–9511* ⊕ *www.peasantnyc.com* ⌕ *Reservations essential* ⊘ *Closed Mon. No lunch* Ⓜ *6 to Spring St.; R to Prince St.* ✛ *2:F3.*

$$$
ECLECTIC

✕ **Public.** To start with, the space here is complex and sophisticated, with soaring ceilings and whitewashed brick walls, skylights, fireplaces, three dining areas, and a vast bar. You've come for the food, though, and you won't be disappointed. The menu flaunts its nonconformity, and dishes like Australian barramundi fish, served with vanilla-celeriac puree and braised garlic greens, demonstrates a light yet adventurous touch. Brunch at Public is a local favorite, with exotic dishes like coconut pancakes topped with fresh ricotta, mango, and lime syrup, and a juicy venison burger. Standout desserts include a chocolate mousse with tahini ice cream and sesame candy. $ *Average main: $25* ✉ *210*

16

Elizabeth St., between Prince and Spring Sts., NoLIta ☎ *212/343–7011* ⊕ *www.public-nyc.com* ⊗ *No lunch weekdays* Ⓜ *6 to Spring St.; N, R to Prince St.; J, M to Bowery* ✛ *2:F3.*

$$ ✕ **Rubirosa.** Named for a jet-setting Dominican playboy, this Rubirosa
ITALIAN is only Latin and lascivious in name. Owner Angelo "A. J." Pappalardo has created an exciting Italian-American eatery that locals have shown an insatiable appetite for (so be prepared to wait). The kitchen isn't trying to reinvent anything here, they simply serve high-quality classic Italian dishes: from pasta with red sauce or a fork-tender veal chop Milanese to the thin-crust pizza—the recipe for the latter comes from Mr. Pappalardo's parents who have run the popular Staten Island pizza joint, Joe & Pat's, since anyone can remember. You don't have to be a jet-setter or a playboy to love this place. Just come hungry. ⑤ *Average main: $18* ⊠ *235 Mulberry St., between Prince and Spring Sts., NoLIta* ☎ *212/965–0500* ⊕ *rubirosanyc.com* Ⓜ *6 to Spring St.* ✛ *2:F3.*

$ ✕ **The Smile.** Subterranean and almost hidden, The Smile will turn your
AMERICAN frown upside down if you like hipsters, celebrities, and, most especially, hipster celebrities. Lounge among the fashionably conscious clientele (who are trying oh-so-hard to not look that way) and munch on breakfast-y items (breakfast is served until 4:30 pm) like chunky granola, or go for one of the giant sandwiches or spaghetti with heirloom tomato sauce. Dinner options, like a whole trout, brisket, hangar steak, or roasted chicken, are more ambitious. Just be sure you wear shoes that scream "this season." ⑤ *Average main: $15* ⊠ *26 Bond St., between Lafayette St. and Bowery, NoLIta* ☎ *646/329–5836* ⊕ *www.thesmilenyc.com* Ⓜ *B, D, F, M to Broadway–Lafayette; 6 to Astor Pl.* ✛ *2:E2.*

$$$$ ✕ **Torrisi Italian Specialties.** Italian-American cuisine is in-style, and this
ITALIAN hot spot is bringing locals back to Mulberry, a street otherwise flanked
FAMILY by mediocre, touristy Italian restaurants. Run by chefs Mario Carbone
Fodor's Choice and Rich Torrisi (both of whom have logged time in the kitchens of some
★ of the city's most lauded Italian eateries), this 25-seat restaurant isn't easy to get in to so reserve ahead. The $100 seven-course prix fixe is available at lunch (Friday–Sunday only) and dinner. The menu changes regularly and it's hard to know what you're going to get until you sit down–from Jamaican jerk oxtail to a crunchy pork chop or spaghetti with clams. For a simpler meal, head next door to Torrisi spinoff Parm, which serves great Italian-accented sandwiches. ⑤ *Average main: $75* ⊠ *250 Mulberry St., near Prince St., NoLIta* ☎ *212/965–0955* ⊕ *www.torrisinyc.com* ⇧ *Reservations essential* ⊗ *No lunch Mon.–Thurs.* Ⓜ *N, R to Prince St.* ✛ *2:F3.*

$$$ ✕ **Uncle Boons.** If you're looking for quality Thai fare in Manhattan, a
THAI good choice is Uncle Boon's in NoLIta. The chefs are a husband and wife team who originally met in the kitchen at Michelin-starred Per Se. You'd have to look underneath the layers to find evidence of über-haute cuisine here—but that just means that the simple, tasty Thai fare here is very good. Skip the green papaya salad—usually a must at Thai places but somehow bland here—and go right for the hearty fare, such as the *khao soi,* an ultra-tender chicken leg doused in a deliciously tangy yellow curry, or anything that's grilled. ⑤ *Average main: $22* ⊠ *7 Spring St., near Elizabeth St., NoLIta* ☎ *646/370–6650* ⊕ *www.uncleboons. com* ⊗ *Closed Mon.* Ⓜ *B, D to Grand St.* ✛ *2:F3.*

SOHO

Sure, eating in SoHo may not feel very low key, with mostly pricey eateries full of fashionistas and the "see and be seen" crowd. But the restaurants here are too hot to dampen any hungry spirits, and worth the fight for a table.

$$$ ╳ **Aquagrill.** A SoHo standard for fresh seafood, this lively neighbor-
SEAFOOD hood eatery also makes its own pastries and baked goods—includ-ing the bread for its brunchtime challah French toast with cinnamon apples and pecan butter. Fans rave about the lunchtime $24.50 prix-fixe Shucker Special—a half-dozen oysters with homemade soup or chowder and a salad. Dinner specialties include roasted Dungeness crab cake napoleon with sundried-tomato oil, and falafel-crusted salmon. Des-serts are excellent, too, especially the chocolate tasting plate with its molten chocolate cake, milk chocolate ice cream, and white chocolate mousse. Service is warm and welcoming. ⑤ *Average main: $28* ✉ *210 Spring St., at 6th Ave., SoHo* ☎ *212/274–0505* ⊕ *www.aquagrill.com* ⌂ *Reservations essential* Ⓜ *C, E to Spring St.* ✛ *2:D4.*

$$ ╳ **Back Forty West.** The SoHo spinoff of the popular East Village restaurant,
AMERICAN Back Forty, where chef Peter Hoffman was doing sustainable farm-to-table
Fodor'sChoice fare long before it became a near-obligatory restaurant trend in the Big
★ Apple, outdoes the original. Neighborhood denizens and shoppers flock here for well-executed comfort food. The menu changes with the season but expect dishes like coconut-milk-spiked scallop ceviche, pumpkin hummus, a very good grass-fed burger, and grilled trout from the Catskills, served alongside quality cocktails and a short but excellent list of beer and wine. Add in rustic, homey decor and you'll feel like you're hundreds of miles form that shopping mecca known as SoHo. ⑤ *Average main: $17* ✉ *70 Prince St., at Crosby St., SoHo* ☎ *212/219–8570* ⊕ *www.backfortynyc. com* ☺ *No dinner Sun.* Ⓜ *B, D, F, M, to Broadway-Lafayette St.* ✛ *2:E3.*

$$$ ╳ **Balthazar.** Even with long waits and excruciating noise levels, most
FRENCH out-of-towners agree that it's worth making reservations to experience restaurateur Keith McNally's flagship, a painstakingly accurate repro-duction of a Parisian brasserie with an insider New York feel. Like the decor, entrées re-create French classics: Gruyère-topped onion soup, steak frites, and icy tiers of crab, oysters, and other pristine shellfish. Brunch is still one of the toughest tables in town. The best strategy to experience this perennial fave is to go at off-hours, or on weekdays for breakfast, to miss the crush. ⑤ *Average main: $28* ✉ *80 Spring St., between Broadway and Crosby St., SoHo* ☎ *212/965–1414* ⊕ *www. balthazarny.com* ⌂ *Reservations essential* Ⓜ *6 to Spring St.; N, R to Prince St.; B, D, F, M to Broadway–Lafayette* ✛ *2:E4.*

$ ╳ **Balthazar Bakery.** Follow the beguiling scent of fresh-baked bread
CAFÉ to Balthazar Bakery, next door to Keith McNally's always-packed Balthazar restaurant. Choices include fresh-baked baguettes and other varieties of French breads, as well as gourmet sandwiches, soups, and memorable pastries to take out (there is no seating). Try the berry noi-sette tart or coconut cake, or keep it simple with an eggy canelé or a but-tery lemon or chocolate madeleine. ⑤ *Average main: $23* ✉ *80 Spring St., near Crosby St., SoHo* ☎ *212/965–1785* ⊕ *www.balthazarbakery. com* ⌂ *Reservations not accepted* ☺ *No dinner* ✛ *2:E4.*

16

$$
MODERN
AMERICAN

✕**Blue Ribbon.** After 20-plus years, Blue Ribbon still has a reputation not just for top-notch seafood and eclectic menu items, but also as a serious late-night foodie hangout. Join the genial hubbub for midnight noshing, namely the beef marrow with oxtail marmalade and the renowned raw-bar platters. Trustafarians, literary types, chefs, designers—a good-looking gang—generally fill this dark box of a room until 4 am. The menu appears standard at first blush, but it's not. Try the duck club sandwich or the matzo ball soup; the latter is a heady brew filled with the sacrilegious combo of seafood and traditional Jewish dumplings. $ *Average main: $32* ⊠ *97 Sullivan St., between Prince and Spring Sts., SoHo* ☎ *212/274–0404* ⊕ *www.blueribbonrestaurants.com* ⌲ *Reservations not accepted* ⊘ *No lunch* Ⓜ *C, E to Spring St.; R to Prince St.* ✛ *2:D3.*

$$$
JAPANESE

✕**Blue Ribbon Sushi.** Sushi, like pizza, attracts plenty of opinionated fanatics, and Blue Ribbon Sushi gets consistent raves for their über-fresh sushi and sashimi. Stick to the excellent raw fish and specials here if you're a purist, or branch out and try one of the experimental rolls: the Blue Ribbon—lobster, *shiso* (Japanese basil), and black caviar—is popular. The dark, intimate nooks, minimalist design, and servers with downtown attitude attract a stylish crowd that doesn't mind waiting for a table or for chilled sake. As expected from the quality and the location, it's not cheap. $ *Average main: $24* ⊠ *119 Sullivan St., between Prince and Spring Sts., SoHo* ☎ *212/343–0404* ⊕ *www.blueribbonrestaurants.com* ⌲ *Reservations not accepted* Ⓜ *C, E to Spring St.; R to Prince St.* ✛ *2:D3.*

$$$
AMERICAN

✕**The Dutch.** Perpetually packed with the "see and be seen" crowd, chef Andrew Carmellini's homage to American cuisine is really an encapsulation of recent food and dining trends: there's an excellent burger (and at $19 it should be), a Kentucky-size bourbon collection behind the bar, greenmarket-driven comfort food dishes like fried chicken, and bacon paired with things you would have not likely seen a couple decades ago (in this case, scallops with bacon jam). And it all works well at this SoHo restaurant. So much so, you might consider returning for weekend brunch when the housemade bologna sandwich or cornmeal flapjacks make appearances on the menu. $ *Average main: $27* ⊠ *131 Sullivan St., at Prince St., SoHo* ☎ *212/677–6200* ⊕ *www.thedutchnyc. com* ⌲ *Reservations essential* Ⓜ *C, E to Spring St.* ✛ *2:D3.*

$$$
MODERN
AMERICAN

✕**Hundred Acres.** Set on a quiet block of Greenwich Village, the rustic, farmhouse-slash-greenhouse that is Hundred Acres is a lovely place to while away a long lunch or quiet dinner. The market-driven creative comfort food keeps the neighborhood patrons and out-of-towners-in-the-know coming back again and again. Mains run the gamut from fish to meat: think a luscious pork shank with polenta and rhubarb chutney; shrimp and grits; or a classic burger made from pasture-raised beef, topped with Vermont cheddar and served with fries and Vidalia onion mayonnaise. Weekend brunch is a standout affair, with a list of variations on the bloody-mary theme and treats like a country pâté sandwich and goat cheese–sage bread pudding. $ *Average main: $26* ⊠ *38 MacDougal St., between Houston and Prince Sts., SoHo* ☎ *212/475–7500* ⊕ *www.hundredacresnyc.com* Ⓜ *1 to Houston; C, E to Spring St.; N, R to Prince St.* ✛ *2:D3.*

$$ ✗**Lucky Strike.** Whether you're lucky enough to nab a table at this
BISTRO sceney SoHo bistro at 1 pm or 1 am, Lucky Strike always seems like
the place to be. Bedecked in classic bistro trappings—copper hammered stools, mirrors with menu items scrawled on them—the restaurant would look just as perfect in the Bastille neighborhood of Paris
as it does in this swanky part of the Big Apple. The kitchen offerings
are a straightforward affair: croque-monsieur, grilled salmon, and
salade Niçoise are old standbys, with a turkey burger thrown in to
accommodate the *Americain* palate. ⑤ *Average main: $17* ✉ *59 Grand
St., between W. Broadway and Wooster St., SoHo* ☎ *212/941–0772*
⊕ *www.luckystrikeny.com* Ⓜ *1 to Canal St.* ✛ *2:D4.*

$$$ ✗**Lure Fishbar.** Decorated like the clubby interior of a sleek luxury liner,
SEAFOOD Lure offers oceanic fare prepared in multiple culinary styles. From the
sushi bar, you can feast on options like the Lure House Roll—a shrimp
tempura roll crowned with spicy tuna and Japanese tartar sauce—or
you can opt for creative dishes from the kitchen, like steamed branzino with oyster mushrooms, scallions, and ponzu sauce, or Manila
clams over pancetta-studded linguine. For an all-American treat, you
can't go wrong with a classic lobster roll on brioche. The dark subterranean bar is a good spot for cocktails and a snack. Brunch is served
on weekends. ⑤ *Average main: $29* ✉ *142 Mercer St., at Prince St.,
SoHo* ☎ *212/431–7676* ⊕ *www.lurefishbar.com* ◷ *No lunch weekends*
Ⓜ *6 to Bleecker St.; B, D, F, M to Broadway–Lafayette St.; N, R to
Prince St.* ✛ *2:E3.*

$ ✗**MarieBelle.** Practically invisible from the front of the chocolate
CAFÉ emporium, the back entry to the Cacao Bar opens into a sweet, high-
FAMILY ceiling, 12-table hot-chocolate shop. Most people order the Aztec,
European-style (that's 60% Colombian chocolate mixed with hot
water—no cocoa powder here!). The first sip is startlingly rich but
not too dense. American-style, made with milk, is sweeter. And not
to worry if you're visiting in spring or summer: you can opt for Aztec
iced chocolate—the warm-weather version of her decadent cacao
elixir—or the house-made chocolate gelato. For more substantial
snacking, choose a salad or sandwich from the dainty lunch menu.
⑤ *Average main: $12* ✉ *484 Broome St., between West Broadway
and Wooster St., SoHo* ☎ *212/925–6999* ⊕ *www.mariebelle.com*
⌲ *Reservations not accepted* ◷ *No dinner* Ⓜ *6 to Spring St.; A, C, E
to Canal St.* ✛ *2:D4.*

$$$ ✗**The Mercer Kitchen.** Part of Alsatian superchef Jean-Georges Vongeri-
ASIAN FUSION chten's culinary empire, the celebrity-laden front room of this SoHo
spot in the Mercer Hotel is as much about scene as it is cuisine. Which
isn't a bad thing. Dishes here look toward Asia (as is the proclivity
of Mr. Vongerichten), using simple ingredients and pairings to create
deliciousness for the taste buds. Think scallops with lentils and pancetta or crispy squid with black-olive tartar sauce. It's all good enough
to make you feign disinterest over the A-list celeb who just walked in.
⑤ *Average main: $28* ✉ *Mercer Hotel, 99 Prince St., at Mercer St.,
SoHo* ☎ *212/966–5454* ⊕ *www.jean-georges.com* Ⓜ *6 to Spring St.;
N, R to Prince St.* ✛ *2:E3.*

16

$$ ✗ **Osteria Morini.** Less formal than chef Michael White's other renowned
ITALIAN Italian restaurants (like Marea in Midtown West), the atmosphere at
Fodor'sChoice Osteria Morini is lively and upbeat, with communal tables at the
★ center and a rock-and-roll soundtrack. The food still steals the show,
though. Start with a selection of cheeses and cured meats, then move
on to hearty pastas—a lusty ragù Bolognese or garganelli with pro-
sciutto and truffle butter, for example—and main courses like oven-
baked polenta accompanied by either sausage or mushrooms. Waits
can be long, so try to come early or late, or grab one of the few bar
seats for an inventive cocktail or a glass of Italian wine. Brunch is
served on the weekends. $ *Average main: $25* ✉ *218 Lafayette St.,
between Spring and Broome Sts., SoHo* ☎ *212/965–8777* ⊕ *www.
osteriamorini.com* ⌕ *Reservations essential* ☾ *No lunch weekends*
Ⓜ *6 to Spring St.* ✛ *2:E4.*

$$$ ✗ **Raoul's.** One of the first trendy spots in SoHo, this arty French res-
FRENCH taurant has yet to lose its touch, either in the kitchen or with the atmo-
sphere. Expect a chic bar scene—especially late at night—filled with
polished PYTs, amazing photos on every piece of available wall space,
and a lovely back room that you reach through the kitchen. The winding stairs to the upstairs dining room are narrow and a bit treacherous
if you're wearing your highest heels. Food-wise, it's bistro-inspired, with
oysters and salads to start, and pastas, fish, and meat options for mains.
$ *Average main: $29* ✉ *180 Prince St., between Sullivan and Thompson
Sts., SoHo* ☎ *212/966–3518* ⊕ *www.raouls.com* ☾ *No lunch* Ⓜ *C, E to
Spring St.* ✛ *2:D3.*

$$ ✗ **Snack.** This SoHo cubbyhole may look like just another drop-in café,
GREEK but the food served inside will transport you to Greece. Typical mezes
like tzakiki, taramosalata, hummus, and skordalia are several notches
better than what you'd get elsewhere, but the menu options range
beyond snacks: pop in at lunch for a braised-lamb sandwich or spin-
ach pie, or linger in the evenings over votive-lighted tables and pastitsio
or stuffed peppers. The light-filled West Village location, Snack Tav-
erna, is somewhat roomier and also serves breakfast daily and brunch
on weekends. $ *Average main: $19* ✉ *105 Thompson St, near Prince
St., SoHo* ☎ *212/925–1040* ⊕ *www.snacksoho.com* ⌕ *Reservations not
accepted* Ⓜ *C, E to Spring St.* ✛ *2:D3.*

$$ ✗ **Spring Street Natural.** When this SoHo spot first fired up its burners in
AMERICAN 1973, restaurants emphasizing organic, whole, and natural ingredients
were mostly limited to San Francisco and college towns. The dining
landscape may have caught up, but Spring Street Natural is still going
strong, powered by a loyal clientele who come here for healthy food
that actually tastes good. Start with the creamy organic hummus (and
warm pita bread) before moving on to pan-roasted free-range chicken
(accompanied by sweet potato–poblano pepper gratin) or the panc-
etta-laced pumpkin ravioli. If you're too full for dessert, order a glass
of organic wine, sit back and stare out the floor-to-ceiling windows,
gawking at the occasional celebrity and the SoHo shoppers. $ *Average
main: $18* ✉ *62 Spring St., at Lafayette St., SoHo* ☎ *212/966–0290*
⊕ *www.springstreetnatural.com* Ⓜ *6 to Spring St.* ✛ *2:E4.*

CLOSE UP

Restaurant Chains Worth a Taste

When you're on the go or don't have time for a leisurely meal, there are several very good chain restaurants and sandwich bars that have popped up around New York City. The ones listed below are usually reasonably priced and are the best in their category.

Dos Toros. Fresh and inexpensive tacos, burritos, and salads are the calling card at this local minichain with several locations in Manhattan and one in Brooklyn. The brothers who run the joint moved to NYC from San Francisco and were disappointed with the taqueria options here so they took matters into their own hands. Order at the counter and grab a seat. ⊕ www.dostoros.com.

Le Pain Quotidien. Part bakery, part café, this Belgian chain with locations throughout the city serves fresh salads and sandwiches at lunch and is great for breakfast. You can grab a snack to go or stay and eat breakfast, lunch, or dinner with waiter service. There are more than 20 locations throughout Manhattan, including in Central Park. ⊕ www.lepainquotidien.com.

Pret A Manger. This sandwich shop started in London in 1986 and opened their first American outpost in 2000. These days you can find them in various locations around NYC—there are several in Midtown, catering to the bustling lunch crowds. The sandwiches are excellent, and the salads are good too. ⊕ www.pret.com.

Shake Shack. This homegrown chain has expanded across the United States and beyond but it got it start in Madison Square Park. There are multiple locations in Manhattan and Brooklyn to enjoy burgers, hot dogs, and shakes. ⊕ www.shakeshack.com.

'Wichcraft. Tom Colicchio may be best known these days as head judge of Bravo's *Top Chef*, but his fine dining restaurants Craft and Craftbar are also well known around Manhattan and beyond. At 'wichcraft, the sandwich shop he started with several partners back in 2003, the creations have a deliciously distinctive chef's touch. ⊕ www.wichcraftnyc.com.

16

EAST VILLAGE AND LOWER EAST SIDE

EAST VILLAGE

This neighborhood, once a grungy ghetto for punk rockers and drug addicts, has gotten itself into shape, with great restaurants on every block—from amazing, inexpensive Asian spots to Michelin-starred destinations. St. Marks Place is the center of New York's downtown Little Tokyo, and East 6th Street is its Indian row.

$$

AMERICAN

Fodor'sChoice

★

✕ **Alder.** Chef Wylie Dufresne, who still runs the show at acclaimed avant-garde eatery, wd~50, has followed in the footsteps of many of his peers and opened a casual dining spot. Alder has a modern gastropub vibe but, as Dufresne has shown in the past, looks can be deceiving, and there is more than meets the eye—and the mouth—here. The rye pasta with toasted caraway and pastrami is an ingenious re-imagining of the classic New York deli sandwich. The crackers in the New England clam chowder are made from pureed oysters and they pack quite a flavorful punch when they hit the palate. Pair anything with one of the carefully selected craft beers or innovative cocktails. Sunday brunch is also fun: try the bacon, egg, and cheese gyoza or the pastrami hash, with one of the unique bloody marys. $ *Average main: $18* ✉ *157 2nd Ave., near 10th St., East Village* ☎ *212/539–1900* ⊕ *www.aldernyc.com* ⌂ *Reservations essential* ☾ *No brunch Sat.* Ⓜ *L to Third Ave.* ✛ *3:G5.*

$$ ✗ **APT-13.** On buddingly hip Avenue C in the East Village (where few nonlocals seem to wander), Apt-13 is worth the trek, though a bit pricey for the neighborhood. Chef John Keller sends out fancy but comforting American fare like beer-steamed clams, and BBQ pork (crispy pig-trotter croquettes), and miso-marinated black cod fish sticks, while Leo DeGroff, son of famed mixologist, Dale, is in charge of one of the most exciting cocktail programs in the city. Sip on a crisp Jackie Rose (made with applejack, pomegranate liqueur, house-made grenadine, and lemon juice) or a cava-and-passion-fruit-blended Flamenco and chat with the friendly "villagers." $ *Average main: $24* ✉ *115 Ave. C, near 7th St., East Village* ☎ *917/475–1213* ⊕ *www.apt-13.com* ☾ *Closed Mon.* Ⓜ *L to 1st Ave.* ✛ *3:H5.*

$ ✗ **Artichoke Pizza.** Grab a gargantuan slice at this popular take-out joint, or order whole pies in the small adjacent no-frills dining room. In the wee hours, lines often snake for the artichoke-spinach slice, which tastes like cheesy dip on crackers. Those in the know opt for the less greasy Margherita slice. Make sure you're hungry and be prepared to stand in line a while. Or try the more formal Artichoke outpost underneath the High Line at 114 10th Ave. $ *Average main: $5* ✉ *328 E. 14th St., between 1st and 2nd Aves., East Village* ☎ *212/228–2004* ⊕ *www.artichokepizza.com* ⌂ *Reservations not accepted* Ⓜ *L to 1st Ave.* ✛ *3:H4.*

PIZZA
FAMILY

$$ ✗ **Back Forty.** Pioneering chef Peter Hoffman, a longtime leader in promoting local, sustainable food, attracts a devoted crowd to this casual neighborhood restaurant, where the homey decor features a pastoral mural behind the bar. The simply prepared dinner selections include a perfect grilled trout, moist pan-roasted chicken, and a wide array of seasonal sides, perhaps including roasted Brussels sprouts with maple-cider vinegar. Wash it all down with a house cocktail like the excellent, bourbon-based Back Forty. Brunch is served on weekends and there are frequent seasonal special events like crab boil dinners in summer. Weather permitting, snag a table in the leafy garden out back. The new Back Forty West, on Prince Street, between Lafayette and Crosby, is garnering equally stellar reviews. $ *Average main: $19* ✉ *190 Ave. B, at 12th St., East Village* ☎ *212/388–1990* ⊕ *www.backfortynyc.com* ☾ *No lunch weekdays* Ⓜ *L to 1st Ave.* ✛ *3:H4.*

AMERICAN

$$ ✗ **Café Mogador.** An East Village dining institution if there ever was one, Café Mogador is a frequent stop for locals and, for some, a hip place to be seen. Since 1983, the restaurant has been serving above-average Morrocan cuisine in a date-friendly candlelight atmosphere. Finish off that creamy hummus before the chicken tagine arrives, nurse that glass of Italian wine, and ponder the fact that most of the people around you were 3-feet tall when this family-run restaurant first fired up its couscous-cooking burners. $ *Average main: $15* ✉ *101 St. Marks Pl., near 2nd Ave., East Village* ☎ *212/677–2226* ⊕ *www.cafemogador.com* Ⓜ *F to 2nd Ave.; L to 1st Ave.* ✛ *2:G1.*

MOROCCAN

$ ✕ **Crif Dogs.** Gluttony reigns at Crif Dogs, where you can indulge in
FAST FOOD creative—and delicious—hot dog creations. Try the Chihuahua, bacon-
FAMILY wrapped and layered with avocado and sour cream, or the Tsunami,
bacon-wrapped with pineapple and teriyaki. There are vegetarian dogs,
too, for those who are into that kind of thing. The tater tots will ban-
ish all memories of the high school cafeteria. And that phone booth in
the corner? Use that to enter secret, chic cocktail bar, PDT. ⑤ *Average
main: $5* ⊠ *113 St. Marks Pl., at Ave. A, East Village* ☎ *212/614–2728*
⊕ *www.crifdogs.com* ✛ *3:H5.*

$$ ✕ **DBGB Kitchen & Bar.** The downtown arm of Daniel Boulud's New York
FRENCH City restaurant fleet, DBGB forgoes the white tablecloths, formal service,
and steep prices found at the famed chef's fancier digs, and instead pays
homage to the grittier, younger feel of its East Village location. (The name
is a wink to the legendary rock club CBGB.) Lined with shelves of pots,
plates, and pans (not to mention copperware donated by renowned chefs
from around the world), the dining room gives way to a partially open
kitchen where you can catch the chefs preparing Boulud's take on French-
and German-inspired pub fare. The menu features 14 different varieties of
sausages, decadent burgers (the aptly named "piggy" burger, a juicy beef
patty topped with a generous portion of pulled pork, jalapeño mayon-
naise, and mustard-vinegar slaw on a cheddar bun), and classic entrées like
steak frites and lemon-and-rosemary roasted chicken. ⑤ *Average main: $26*
⊠ *299 Bowery, between Houston and 1st Sts., East Village* ☎ *212/933–
5300* ⊕ *www.dbgb.com* ⚓ *Reservations essential* Ⓜ *F to 2nd Ave.* ✛ *2:F2.*

$$ ✕ **Edi & the Wolf.** For those who have always wanted to spend an evening
AUSTRIAN in a countryside Austrian pub—and who hasn't?—but don't have the
Fodor'sChoice means to hop on a plane to Vienna, there's Edi & the Wolf, an outstand-
★ ing restaurant deep in the section of the East Village called Alphabet
City. The rustic interior (usually crammed with stylish thirtysomethings)
is the perfect venue to sample dishes like honey-and-beer-accented ribs,
pork belly–laced poached eggs, and, of course, Wiener schnitzel, which
is refreshingly free of grease and super tender. The well-edited beer selection focuses on central Europe. Try the dark Czech brew, Krusovice
(pronounced Kroo-sho-veetzay) ⑤ *Average main: $22* ⊠ *102 Ave. C, at
7th St., East Village* ☎ *212/598–1040* ⊕ *www.ediandthewolf.com* Ⓜ *F
to 2nd Ave.; L to 1st Ave.* ✛ *2:H1.*

$$ ✕ **Five Points.** Describing a menu in terms of "seasonal" and "market-
AMERICAN driven" might be old news but chef Marc Meyer really makes the most
of the greenmarket, and showcases it in a cozy, convivial dining room.
Expect plump chilled oysters, exemplary Caesar salad, and splendid
house-made pasta, followed by the likes of pan-seared day-boat halibut
with cucumber gazpacho and chopped tomato salsa, and grilled lamb
chops with rosemary potatoes, mint-yogurt sauce, and black-olive-
stuffed tomato. Weekend brunch is one of the best in the city, and prices
are quite friendly. Weekday lunch is served, too, usually without the
wait that hungry stomachs have come to expect at other times. ⑤ *Aver-
age main: $24* ⊠ *31 Great Jones St., between Lafayette St. and Bow-
ery, East Village* ☎ *212/253–5700* ⊕ *www.fivepointsrestaurant.com*
⚓ *Reservations essential* Ⓜ *6 to Bleecker St.; B, D, F, M to Broadway–
Lafayette St.* ✛ *2:F2; 3:G6.*

16

$$ ✕**Gemma.** There's something almost formulaic about this restaurant
ITALIAN on the ground floor of the hip Bowery Hotel: from the rustic, wood-
bedecked interior to the stone-wall interior facade to the "see and be
seen" crowd who frequent the place and the menu of above-average
Italian staples (from pizza to pastas). But the food here is good, the ser-
vice is attentive, and nabbing an outside table may make you feel cooler
than you are for a couple of hours, so what difference does it make?
Answer: no difference, until it's time to pay the bill. Weekend brunch
is also a good bet. $ *Average main: $19 ⊠ 335 Bowery, at 3rd St., East
Village* ☎ *212/505–9100* ⊕ *www.theboweryhotel.com* 🙅 *Reservations
not accepted* Ⓜ *F to 2nd Ave.* ✛ *2:F2.*

$$ ✕**Gnocco.** Owners Pierluigi Palazzo and Gianluca Giavonetti named
ITALIAN their restaurant not after gnocchi but after a regional Italian specialty—
deep-fried dough bites typically served with Northern Italian sliced
meats like capicola, salami, and aged prosciutto. The *gnocchi* are certainly good, but the menu has so many other options you'll be forgiven
if you skip them in favor of the salads, house-made pasta specials,
pizza topped with mozzarella, truffles, and mushrooms, and hearty
entrées like pork tenderloin in a balsamic emulsion with flakes of Grana
Padano cheese—preferably all enjoyed in the roomy, canopied garden
out back. $ *Average main: $20 ⊠ 337 E. 10th St., between Aves. A and
B, East Village* ☎ *212/677–1913* ⊕ *www.gnocco.com* Ⓜ *L to 1st Ave.;
6 to Astor Pl.* ✛ *2:H1.*

$ ✕**Grand Sichuan.** Yes, it's a local Chinese chainlet, and no, you don't
CHINESE come here for the ambience, but the food—like fiery Sichuan *dan
dan* noodles, king pao chicken, double-cooked pork, or crab soup
dumplings—is good and inexpensive. Check the website for other locations around town. $ *Average main: $17 ⊠ 19–23 St. Marks Pl., near
3rd Ave., East Village* ☎ *212/529–4800* ⊕ *www.thegrandsichuan.com*
Ⓜ *6 to Astor Pl.* ✛ *2:F1.*

$$ ✕**Hecho en Dumbo.** "Made in Dumbo"—referring to the restaurant's
MEXICAN former location in the Brooklyn neighborhood, DUMBO—specializes
in *antojitos,* or "little cravings." The result is something equivalent to
Mexican comfort food for the hip thirtysomethings who frequent this
restaurant on the ever-happening Bowery. Variations on the theme of
tacos may dominate the menu, but Hecho shines with house dishes like
roasted kid and wine-braised oxtail served over Oaxacan mole sauce.
Pair your meal with one of their delicious margaritas (no bottled mix
used here), sangria, or perhaps a michelada—beer and tomato juice
on ice with lime and a salted rim. $ *Average main: $17 ⊠ 354 Bow-
ery, between Great Jones and 4th Sts., East Village* ☎ *212/937–4245*
⊕ *www.hechoendumbo.com* Ⓜ *6 to Astor Pl.* ✛ *2:F2.*

$$$ ✕**Il Buco.** The unabashed clutter of vintage kitchen gadgets and table-
ITALIAN ware harks back to Il Buco's past as an antiques store and the effect
is a romantic country-house feel with excellent food. This is a favorite for a cozy, intimate meal. The menu focuses on meat and produce
from local farms, with several excellent pasta choices, and a variety of
Mediterranean tapas-like appetizers. Call ahead to book the intimate
wine cellar for dinner. The Il Buco Alimentari & Vineria, around the
corner at 53 Great Jones St., is a more casual setting, with a small

market up front selling gourmet cheese and house-cured meats, and a wine bar in the back. ⑤ *Average main: $28* ⊠ *47 Bond St., between Bowery and Lafayette St., NoHo* ☎ *212/533–1932* ⊕ *www.ilbuco. com* ☾ *No lunch Sun.* Ⓜ *6 to Bleecker St.; B, D, F, M to Broadway– Lafayette St.* ⊹ *2:F2.*

$
JAPANESE
⤫ **Ippudo.** Crowds wait hours for the ramen noodles at Ippudo, the first American branch of the Japanese chain, and if you ask, loyal patrons will say it's all about the rich, pork-based broth—there is a vegetarian version available but it lacks the depth of flavor. Those really in the know, though, make sure to order the sleeper hit appetizers like the peppery chicken wings or the pork buns. It's not a hole in the wall ramen spot, so although a meal here is relatively inexpensive, it's not dirt cheap. There's a new Ippudo outpost in Midtown at 321 W. 51st St. ⑤ *Average main: $16* ⊠ *65 4th Ave., between 9th and 10th Sts., East Village* ☎ *212/388–0088* ⊕ *www.ippudony.com* ⩜ *Reservations not accepted* Ⓜ *4, 5, 6, L to Union Square* ⊹ *3:G5.*

$$$$
JAPANESE
⤫ **Jewel Bako.** Tiny Jewel Bako is arguably the best sushi restaurant in the East Village, gleaming in a minefield of cheap, often inferior sushi houses. The futuristic bamboo tunnel of a dining room is gorgeous, but try to nab a place at the sushi bar and put yourself in the hands of sushi master Yoshi Kousaka. The five-course *omakase*, or chef's menu, starts at $115. (A less expensive sushi or sashimi omakase is $65.) You'll be served only what's freshest and best. ⑤ *Average main: $50* ⊠ *239 E. 5th St., between 2nd and 3rd Aves., East Village* ☎ *212/979–1012* ⩜ *Reservations essential* ☾ *Closed Sun. No lunch* Ⓜ *6 to Astor Pl.* ⊹ *3:G6.*

$$
FRENCH
⤫ **Lafayette Grand Cafe & Bakery.** Food media darling, chef Andrew Carmellini (of Locanda Verde and the Dutch) goes Gallic here. After nearly a decade of Italian dominance on the Big Apple restaurant scene, French is back in vogue again and Lafayette is a return to Carmellini's roots, as he got his start cooking in the kitchens of the great Daniel Boulud. There's no culinary trickery happening here, just straightforward and very satisfying bistro fare. Creamy duck confit-spiked pumpkin risotto, a silky beef tartare, and steak frites are all excellent. And so is the people-watching at this "see and be seen" spot. ⑤ *Average main: $24* ⊠ *380 Lafayette St., at 4th St., East Village* ☎ *212/533–3000* ⊕ *www.lafayetteny.com* Ⓜ *6 to Bleecker St.; B, D, F, M to Broadway-Lafayette* ⊹ *3:F6.*

$
MIDDLE EASTERN
FAMILY
⤫ **Mamoun's Falafel.** Mamoun's is an institution. Bustling day and night, this hole-in-the-wall is the place to go for speedy, hot, super-cheap, and delicious Middle Eastern food. Tahini-topped pitas are packed with fresh, green-on-the-inside falafel balls. Be warned: the hot sauce is incendiary. The small space has a few tables, but this is food you can easily eat on the go. Best of all, it's open every night until at least 4 am. The original Mamoun's is still on MacDougal Street, near Washington Square Park in Greenwich Village. ⑤ *Average main: $7* ⊠ *22 St. Marks Pl., between 2nd and 3rd Aves., East Village* ☎ *212/387–7747* ⊕ *mamouns.com* ⩜ *Reservations not accepted* ▭ *No credit cards* Ⓜ *6 to Astor Place* ⊹ *3:G5.*

16

$
DELI
✕ **Mile End.** Named for a neighborhood in Montréal where the city's famed bagel bakeries exist, Mile End became the darling of the city's fooderati when it opened in January 2010 in Brooklyn. By the time this NoHo location began rolling out its light, chewy, and slightly sweet Montréal bagels in May 2012, the place was already an institution. The bagels are authentic but the real reason to come here is for the impressive deli fare, including pastrami, roast beef, and smoked meat sandwiches. The poutine—french fries with cheese curds and gravy—is a delicious mess. Dinner is served at the original Brooklyn location in Boerum Hill, at 97A Hoyt Street. ⑤ *Average main: $10* ⊠ *53 Bond St., near Bowery, East Village* ☎ *212/529–2990* ⊕ *www.mileenddeli.com* ☾ *Closed Mon. No dinner Sun.* Ⓜ *6 to Bleecker St.* ✛ *2:F2.*

$
JAPANESE
✕ **Minca.** It may have received less fanfare than some other East Village noodle bars, but the ramen at this tiny, cramped spot is among the best in the city; the fact that visiting Japanese students eat here is a good sign. Try to get a seat at the bar, where you can watch the chefs prepare your food. Start with homemade *gyoza* dumplings, then dive your spoon and chopsticks into one of the many types of ramen. The *shoyu* (soy sauce) Minca ramen is unfailingly good, but anything with pork is a good bet. ⑤ *Average main: $13* ⊠ *536 E. 5th St., between Aves. A and B, East Village* ☎ *212/505–8001* ⊕ *www.newyorkramen.com* ☜ *Reservations not accepted* ▭ *No credit cards* Ⓜ *F to 2nd Ave.* ✛ *2:H2.*

$$$$
ASIAN
Fodor'sChoice
★
✕ **Momofuku Ko.** A seasonal tasting menu full of clever combinations and esoteric ingredients explains the deafening buzz for James Beard Award–winning chef David Chang's most formal dining option. Ko's small, intimate space is sparsely furnished with a counter of blonde wood and only a dozen stools. Diners get to see Ko's chefs in action as they prepare all manner of inventive dishes, including a signature preparation of frozen foie gras torchon grated over lychee fruits and white-wine gelée. Reservations can be made only online, no more than 7 days ahead for dinner and 14 days ahead for lunch, and are extremely difficult to get. Log on at 10 am (credit-card number needed just to get in the system) when new reservations are available, and keep hitting reload. ⑤ *Average main: $60* ⊠ *163 1st Ave., at 10th St., East Village* ⊕ *www.momofuku.com* ☜ *Reservations essential* ☾ *No lunch Mon.– Thurs.* Ⓜ *L to 1st Ave.; 6 to Astor Pl.* ✛ *3:H5.*

$
CAFÉ
FAMILY
✕ **Momofuku Milk Bar.** This combination bakery, ice cream parlor, and sandwich shop offers quick-serve access to chef David Chang's cultish pork buns, along with some truly psychedelic treats by pastry whiz Christina Tosi. Swing by for a kimchee croissant and a glass of "cereal" milk, or for treats like the curiously flavored soft-serve ice cream (cereal-milk, lemon verbena), "candy bar pie" (a sweet bomb of caramel, peanut-butter nougat, and pretzels atop a chocolate-cookie crust), one of the addictive cookies (try the "compost" cookies, with pretzels, chocolate chips, and/or whatever inspires the bakers that day), or any of the intriguing savories (the "volcano" is a cheese and potato pastry that is impossible to eat daintily). ⑤ *Average main: $6* ⊠ *251 E. 13th St., East Village* ☎ *347/577-9504* ⊕ *www.milkbarstore.com* ☜ *Reservations not accepted* ✛ *3:G4.*

$ ╳ **Momofuku Noodle Bar.** Chef-owner David Chang has created a shrine
ASIAN to ramen with this stylish 70-seat restaurant. His riff on the Japa-
Fodor's Choice nese classic features haute ingredients like Berkshire pork, free-range
★ chicken, and organic produce—though there are plenty of other innovative options on the menu. His modern take on pork buns with cucumber
and scallions is phenomenal—worth the trip alone. You'll probably
have to wait if you go at regular meal times, but seats at the long counter
open up fairly quickly, and the lively atmosphere is part of the fun. The
excellent fried-chicken meal, featuring triple-fried Korean-style chicken
and southern-style, with a variety of accoutrements feeds four-to-eight
people and is available by special reservations only on the website.
$ *Average main: $16* ⊠ *171 1st Ave., between 10th and 11 Sts., East
Village* ☏ *212/777–7773* ⊕ *www.momofuku.com* ≋ *Reservations not
accepted* Ⓜ *L to 1st Ave.* ✛ *3:H5.*

$$ ╳ **Momofuku Ssäm Bar.** New York foodies have been salivating over chef
ASIAN David Chang's Asian-influenced fare since he opened his first restau-
rant, Momofuku, a Japanese noodle shop, in 2004, and Ssäm Bar,
with a more extensive menu, is equally worth the raves. The restaurant
is packed nightly with downtown diners cut from the same cloth as
the pierced and tattooed waitstaff and cooks, and the no-reservation
policy (except for large parties or special dinners) means you'll likely
have to wait for a chance to try Chang's truly inventive flavor com-
binations. The menu is constantly changing but the not-to-be-missed
riff on the classic Chinese steamed pork bun is almost always avail-
able. Have a nightcap at Chang's inventive cocktail bar, Booker &
Dax, right around the corner. $ *Average main: $24* ⊠ *207 2nd Ave.,
at 13th St., East Village* ☏ *212/254–3500* ⊕ *www.momofuku.com/
ssam* Ⓜ *L to 1st Ave.* ✛ *3:G4.*

$ ╳ **Motorino Pizza.** The Manhattan branch of the Williamsburg origi-
PIZZA nal has brought its impossibly high standards—and long lines—to a
new borough. The authentic Neapolitan pies are made with glutinous,
dough-friendly double-zero flour and San Marzano tomatoes, and the
crusts are lightly charred. You can't go wrong with any of the signature
traditional pizzas, like marinara; margherita with fresh tomatoes, moz-
zarella, and basil; or a pie with spicy sopressata, sausage and garlic; but
the seasonal selections are also tempting. Check out the brunch pizza
(with egg and pancetta) on the weekends. Antipasti like octopus and fin-
gerling potato salad with celery-chili oil, and cockle-clam crostini round
out the menu. Weekdays, the lunchtime prix fixe means pizza and salad
is a bargain at $12 per person. $ *Average main: $15* ⊠ *349 E. 12th St.,
at 1st Ave., East Village* ☏ *212/777–2644* ⊕ *www.motorinopizza.com*
≋ *Reservations not accepted* Ⓜ *L to 1st Ave.* ✛ *3:H4.*

$$ ╳ **Northern Spy Food Co.** A gem in the East Village, named for an apple
AMERICAN variety, Northern Spy is run by two San Francisco transplants who have
Fodor's Choice a West Coast perspective on the farm-to-table movement. Start your
★ meal with the freekeh risotto, a traditional dish made with a quirky
little-known grain, or a giant mound of shredded kale tossed with cheddar, pecorino, and toasted almonds. Main courses are winners, too—
choose tender meatballs in marinara sauce, roast chicken for two, or
baked polenta, eggs, and mushrooms topped with crème fraîche. There

16

is also an interesting, reasonably priced list of wines and beers, and a selection of housemade desserts like chocolate cake with sea salt and caramel. $ *Average main: $22* ✉ *511 E. 12th St., between 1st Ave. and Ave. A, East Village* ☎ *212/228–5100* ⊕ *www.northernspyfoodco.com* ♿ *Reservations not accepted* Ⓜ *L to 1st Ave.* ✛ *3:H4.*

$ ✕ **Pinche Taqueria.** Offshoots of a popular Tijuana taco shop established
MEXICAN   in 1973 and still going strong, these slim taquerias (the word "pinche"
FAMILY   can be translated as "tiny") do fish tacos the west coast way, with lightly battered fish, crunchy cabbage, and a dollop of cilantro *crema*. The tacos *al pastor*—filled with succulent pork slow-roasted on a rotating spit—are of a similarly superior caliber, stuffed into warm, house-made corn tortillas and generously anointed with fresh guacamole. There's another location just around the corner at 227 Mott Street (near Prince) and at 103 West 14th Street; all these spots get busy at prime meal times. $ *Average main: $6* ✉ *333 Lafayette St., near Bleecker St., East Village* ☎ *212/343–9977* ⊕ *www.pinchetaqueria.us* ♿ *Reservations not accepted* Ⓜ *B, D, F, M to Lafayette St.* ✛ *2:E2.*

$ ✕ **Porchetta.** Super-succulent Italian roast pork—dusted in fennel pol-
ITALIAN   len and covered in crisp cracklin' skin—is the star attraction here. It is, in fact, just about the only thing this tiny spot offers. Order your pork in a sandwich or as a platter with stewed greens and roasted potatoes. There's not much room inside for dining on-site, but the benches out front are ideal when the weather cooperates. $ *Average main: $11* ✉ *110 E. 7th St., near 1st Ave., East Village* ☎ *212/777–2151* ⊕ *www.porchettanyc.com* ♿ *Reservations not accepted* Ⓜ *6 to Astor Pl.* ✛ *3:H5.*

$$ ✕ **Prune.** There's just something very right-on about the food at Prune,
AMERICAN   a cozy treasure of a restaurant serving eclectic, well-executed American food from cult chef Gabrielle Hamilton. The choices change with the season, but you might find braised rabbit legs in vinegar sauce, whole grilled fish with fennel oil and chunky sea salt, or roasted marrow bones with parsley salad and toast points. If they're on the menu, try the pillowy, fired sweetbreads. There's usually a wait, and the quarters are very cramped, so don't expect to feel comfortable lingering at your rickety wooden table. Desserts, like ricotta ice cream with salted-caramel croutons, are irresistible, and on weekends lines form early for the restaurant's deservedly popular brunch. $ *Average main: $22* ✉ *54 E. 1st St., between 1st and 2nd Aves., East Village* ☎ *212/677–6221* ⊕ *www.prunerestaurant.com* ♿ *Reservations essential* Ⓜ *F to 2nd Ave.* ✛ *2:G2.*

$$ ✕ **Pylos.** The perfect setting for a relaxed dinner or an intimate spe-
GREEK   cial occasion, this tastefully refined, light-filled East Village restaurant emphasizes rustic Greek cooking from all over Greece. There are delicious versions of hearty comfort food dishes like pastitsio and moussaka on the menu but the lighter dishes—especially fish—let the flavors shine through. There is an extensive selection of interesting hot and cold mezes—start with the traditional trio of *tzatkziki* (garlicky yogurt dip), *taramosalata* (lemony fish roe dip), and *melitzanosalta* (an eggplant-based dip) and explore from there. Accompany your meal with some vino from the all-Greek wine list; the light white

Atlantis wine from the island of Santorini is particularly enjoyable—and affordable. ⓢ *Average main: $25* ⊠ *128 E. 7th St., near Ave. A, East Village* ☎ *212/473-0220* ⊕ *www.pylosrestaurant.com* Ⓜ *F to 2nd Ave.; L to 1st Ave.* ✛ *3:H5.*

$$ ✕ **Saxon & Parole.** One of the hottest spots on this burgeoning stretch of
MODERN the Bowery, this eatery may be named for two 19th century racehorses
AMERICAN but the food—and the extremely good-looking crowd—is nothing that
Fodor's Choice you'd find in a barnyard. Settle into this cozy, sceney spot, order a cock-
★ tail, and peruse a menu loaded with the Zeitgeist dishes of New York dining: roasted bone marrow, Brussels sprouts, pork belly, chicken liver mousse, and, of course, an overpriced-but-excellent burger. The kitchen executes it all to complete deliciousness. The bar scene is lively, so plan to come early for a cocktail. ⓢ *Average main: $22* ⊠ *316 Bowery, at Bleecker St., East Village* ☎ *212/254-0350* ⊕ *saxonandparole.com* Ⓜ *B, D, F, M to Broadway–Lafayette St.* ✛ *2:F2.*

$ ✕ **Sembrado en Nueva York.** Chef Danny Mena, who runs the show at Hecho en Dumbo, has created a quaint taco joint that acts as a love letter to mezcal and Mexico City. The signature taco is *al pastor* (grilled pork spiked with chunks of refreshing pineapple) but the salt-cured steak and chorizo varieties are just as palate pleasing. Don't fill up before trying a *costra*: this Mexico City specialty is cheese caramelized on a grill that acts as a tortilla for the taco. It adds a new flavor and texture to the taco that will make you wonder why this hasn't caught on elsewhere. Wash it all down with a margarita laced with smokey mescal (there are over 25 to choose from). ⓢ *Average main: $7* ⊠ *432 E. 13th St., near 1st Ave., East Village* ☎ *212/729-4206* ⊕ *www.sembradonyc. com* Ⓜ *L to 1st Ave.* ✛ *3:H4.*

$ ✕ **Somtum Der.** There once was a time when New Yorkers had to ven-
THAI ture to Queens to get good Thai food but that's no longer the case. Not only have a handful of great Thai restaurants opened in Manhattan in recent years, but many of them hail from Isaan, a region in northeast Thailand that emphasizes light, spicy fare. Somtum Der, originally based in Bangkok, is one of the best. Start with the namesake somtum, a palate-singeing green-papaya salad before moving on to the *larb moo*, a mound of minced pork mixed with veggies and chilies. Also worth trying is the fried chicken that will make you believe the southern United States no longer has a monopoly on crispy bird. The restaurant is small and can get quite noisy. ⓢ *Average main: $15* ⊠ *85 Ave. A, East Village* ☎ *212/260-8570* ⊕ *www.somtumder.com* Ⓜ *F to 2nd Ave.* ✛ *3:H6.*

$ ✕ **Veniero's Pasticceria.** Since 1894, this bustling bakery-café has sold
CAFÉ every kind of Italian *dolce* (sweet), from cherry-topped cookies to
FAMILY creamy cannoli and flaky *sfogliatelle* (shell-shaped, filled pastry). Cheesecake lovers will rejoice in Veniero's version, which is slathered with ricotta instead of cream cheese. In all, the hungry visitor with a serious sweet tooth can choose from more than 150 different types of desserts. A wine license means you can top off an evening with a bottle of red. Veniero's is worth a look, even if you're not hungry. ⓢ *Average main: $5* ⊠ *342 E. 11th St., near 1st Ave., East Village* ☎ *212/674-7070* ⊕ *www.venierospastry.com* ⌲ *Reservations not accepted* Ⓜ *6 to Astor Pl.; L to 1st Ave.* ✛ *3:H5.*

16

$ ✕ **Veselka.** The name means "rainbow" in Ukrainian, and you can order
EASTERN   potato pierogis 24 hours a day at this East Village stalwart, which
EUROPEAN   opened in 1954. The authentic Ukrainian-cuisine-slash-diner-food is
FAMILY   the perfect stick-to-your-ribs end to a night on the town—or to begin
a new day, as the restaurant serves a full array of breakfast staples. It's
a neighborhood experience, with tables of families sharing space with
the hipsters. The spacious, sunny interior is great for people-watching;
don't take the servers' studied indifference personally. $ *Average main:*
$11 ⊠ *144 2nd Ave., at 9th St., East Village* ☎ *212/228–9682* ⊕ *www.*
veselka.com ⌂ *Reservations not accepted* ✛ *3:H5.*
Westville East. *Branch location at 173 Avenue A, near 11th Street. See*
West Village for full review.

$ ✕ **Zum Schneider.** Located in Alphabet City—the wilds of the East Vil-
GERMAN   lage—this garrulous Teutonic spot will teach you the ABCs of beer
drinking and hearty eating. Grab a table outside when the weather's
nice, among the young hipsters who frequent the spot, and get ready for
some kraut-laden fun. After quaffing a huge liter stein of the sudsy stuff,
you may want to eat and the menu, naturally, is a veritable sausage-
palooza. In addition to the usual meaty fare, such as Wiener schnitzel
and goulash, there are, well, more sausages. The crispy potato pancakes
are a good bet, too. $ *Average main: $16* ⊠ *107 Ave. C, at 7th St., East*
Village ☎ *212/598–1098* ⊕ *www.zumschneider.com* Ⓜ *L to 1st Ave.; F*
to 2nd Ave. ✛ *2:H1.*

LOWER EAST SIDE

The Lower East Side, home to generations of immigrant newcomers, has
become quite the culinary hub over the last 15 years, with everything
from molecular gastronomy to hipster Chinese cuisine. You can't walk
a block without hitting a place that will make your stomach growl.

$$ ✕ **Clinton St. Baking Co.** There once was a time when this Lower East
AMERICAN   Side restaurant was *the* place to come for brunch. Specifically, it was
Fodor'sChoice   *the* place to eat blueberry pancakes, which many regulars professed
★   were the best in the city, if not the state, or the whole country. But all
that changed when owners Neil Kleinberg and DeDe Lahman opened
their beloved eatery for lunch and dinner. Oh, it's still a great place
for brunch but now you can eat those pancakes (along with a good
Black Angus burger or a crab cake sandwich) any time of day you
like. February is pancake month, when, in addition to the blueberry
pancakes, every weekday brings a special incarnation of the pancake.
$ *Average main: $18* ⊠ *4 Clinton St., near Houston St., Lower East*
Side ☎ *646/602–6263* ⊕ *www.clintonstreetbaking.com* ☾ *No dinner*
Sun. Ⓜ *F to 2nd Ave.* ✛ *2:H2.*

$ ✕ **Congee Village.** Don't be put off by the name—this boisterous China-
CHINESE   town icon serves much more than the eponymous rice porridge. Indeed,
the menu is enormous, covering an encyclopedic range of unusual
Cantonese classics. The bamboo-cloaked dining room is great with
a group of people, but being wedged in at a communal table with a
boisterous family is part of the experience. If you're feeling adventur-
ous, try the duck tongues in XO sauce or salt-and-pepper frog, or
stick to familiar classics. Either way, the congee is a great way to start.

$ *Average main: $15* ⊠ *100 Allen St., near Delancey St., Lower East Side* ☎ *212/941–1818* ⊕ *www.congeevillagerestaurants.com* Ⓜ *F to Delancey St.* ✛ *2:G3.*

$ ⨉ **Doughnut Plant.** If the cupcake craze is getting you down, head to the Doughnut Plant, where the all-American junk food staple is elevated to high art. Fresh seasonal ingredients go into these decadent treats, with real fruit and imported chocolate mixed into the batter. Traditionalists will croon over the vanilla bean doughnut but there are plenty of exotic flavors to tempt tastebuds: the dense, fudgy blackout is covered in crumb topping; carrot cake doughnuts have a cream cheese filling. The Lower East Side location is open every day from 6:30 am to 8 pm. There's a second location in Chelsea, next to the Chelsea Hotel; doughnuts are also available around the city at Dean & Deluca and Zabar's. $ *Average main: $5* ⊠ *379 Grand St., near Essex St., Lower East Side* ☎ *212/505–3700* ⊕ *www.doughnutplant.com* ⚐ *Reservations not accepted* ▭ *No credit cards* Ⓜ *F to Delancey St.* ✛ *2:G4.*

CAFÉ
FAMILY

$$ ⨉ **The Fat Radish.** The phrase "seasonal British" might have once seemed puzzling but with seasonal ingredients very much in vogue and British cuisine making a name for itself, this handsome, hip, and sceney Lower East Side (almost Chinatown) restaurant is worth a visit. The menu is eclectic but full of excellent choices. Think green curried monkfish, a cheeseburger served with duck fat fries, pork sausage and mussel stew, and, as the name vaguely suggests, plenty of farm-to-table fresh veggie dishes. Match that with quality craft British brews and potent cocktails and you'll be championing English cuisine in no time. $ *Average main: $21* ⊠ *17 Orchard St., near Canal St., Lower East Side* ☎ *212/300–4053* ⊕ *thefatradishnyc.com* Ⓜ *F to E. Broadway* ✛ *2:G5.*

BRITISH
Fodor'sChoice
★

16

$$ ⨉ **Freemans.** It's hard to believe now but there was once a time when New York restaurant interiors looked like they were trying hard not to look cool, when there was no taxidermy or ironic tchotchkes littered around the room, when the menu wasn't filled with old school (albeit very good) lodge-ish dishes like hunters stew, potted pork, and grilled trout with an equally inspired cocktails menu. But we have Freemans to thank for that. Down a little-used alleyway on the Lower East Side, trendsetting Freemans is as hip and popular as when it opened in 2004. Just don't try too hard to look cool. $ *Average main: $18* ⊠ *End of Freeman Alley, near Rivington St., Lower East Side* ☎ *212/420–0012* ⊕ *www.freemansrestaurant.com* Ⓜ *F to 2nd Ave.* ✛ *2:F3.*

AMERICAN
Fodor'sChoice
★

$ ⨉ **Katz's Delicatessen.** Everything and nothing has changed at Katz's since it first opened in 1888, when the neighborhood was dominated by Jewish immigrants. The rows of Formica tables, the long self-service counter, and such signs as "Send a salami to your boy in the army" are all completely authentic. The lines still form on the weekends for giant, succulent hand-carved corned beef and pastrami sandwiches, soul-warming soups, juicy hot dogs, and crisp half-sour pickles. Weeknights are more laid back. You'll get a ticket when you walk in and then get it punched at the various stations where you pick up your food; don't lose your ticket or you'll have to pay the lost ticket fee. $ *Average main: $15* ⊠ *205 E. Houston St., at Ludlow St., Lower East Side* ☎ *212/254–2246* ⊕ *www.katzdeli.com* Ⓜ *F to 2nd Ave.* ✛ *2:G2.*

DELI
Fodor'sChoice
★

$$ ✕ **Loreley Restaurant & Biergarten.** Once upon a time, beer gardens dotted
GERMAN the New York City landscape in the way that Starbucks does now, but
after World War I and Prohibition, most of these outdoor drinking spots
vanished. And then in 2003 came Loreley (which eventually kicked off
a new beer garden craze in the city). But don't mistake this Lower East
Side hotspot for a place where geriatrics in lederhosen swing their plus-
size steins of beer to polka music. Instead, there's a better than good
chance that you'll find a gaggle of hipsters nursing German craft beers
while bobbing their heads to the new Radiohead album and munching
on plates of sausage, meatballs, or schnitzel. The space out back may
be more concrete than garden, but it's a pleasure on a mild evening.
ⓢ *Average main: $16* ✉ *7 Rivington St., near Bowery, Lower East Side*
☎ *212/253–7077* ⊕ *www.loreleynyc.com* Ⓜ *J to Bowery; B, D to Grand
St.; F to 2nd Ave.* ✛ *2:F3.*

$ ✕ **The Meatball Shop.** New York's first full-service meatball restaurant has
ITALIAN a pedigree chef, a professional waitstaff, a wine list, and a hip crowd. And
FAMILY the meatballs, oh, the meatballs. Choose beef, pork, chicken, or veggie,
or "special" ball options that range from chili cheese balls to Greek lamb
balls to Buffalo chicken balls, then decide if you want them served simple
as is, in sliders or a hero, as a salad, or as a platter; all with an appropriate
choice of sauce and cheese. The meatball concept quickly caught on and
there are now five locations: four in Manhattan and one in Williamsburg.
Mix 'n' match ice-cream sandwiches—choose your flavor and cookie—
are worth saving room for. ⓢ *Average main: $10* ✉ *84 Stanton St., near
Allen St., Lower East Side* ☎ *212/982–8895* ⊕ *www.themeatballshop.
com* ☝ *Reservations not accepted* Ⓜ *F, V to 2nd Ave.* ✛ *2:G3.*

$ ✕ **Mission Chinese Food.** When the news spread that chef Danny Bowien
CHINESE was bringing his popular San Franisco Chinese spot to the Lower East
Fodor'sChoice Side, you could almost hear a collective shout of blogosphere glee. And
★ it hasn't disappointed. The food here, cheaper than it really should be,
is billed as Szechuan but is really at the chef's whim. Nearly everything
on the menu is a hit, but first timers should definitely get the signa-
tures: *kung pao* pastrami and the succulent thrice-cooked bacon, both
of which should come with a side of Lipitor. The spicy chiken wings
are also worth ordering—and they're really spicy. ⓢ *Average main:
$15* ✉ *154 Orchard St., Lower East Side* ☎ *212/529–8800* ⊕ *www.
missionchinesefood.com* Ⓜ *F to 2nd Ave.* ✛ *2:G3.*

$$$ ✕ **Rayuela.** There's a young, sexy vibe at this vibrant Lower East Side
LATIN AMERICAN restaurant where diners come for creative Latin cuisine. The bilevel
eatery has a dining area, a ceviche bar, and—growing in the center of
the restaurant—an olive tree. Ceviches are excellent, and there are several to choose from, as well as a selection of tapas. The kitchen excels
with fish but the rice dishes are worthy of acclaim, too. For maximum
enjoyment, come early for a predinner drink at the bar: standout cocktails include the pisco made with sour lime juice and foamy egg white.
Latin-inspired brunch is served on weekends. ⓢ *Average main: $28*
✉ *165 Allen St., between Rivington and Stanton Sts., Lower East Side*
☎ *212/253–8840* ⊕ *www.rayuelanyc.com* ☾ *No lunch* Ⓜ *F to 2nd Ave.;
J, M, Z to Essex and Delancey Sts.* ✛ *2:G3.*

$$ ✕ **Schiller's Liquor Bar.** It may not be as hard to get in as it was back in
BISTRO 2003 when Keith McNally first opened this sceney hangout on the Lower
FAMILY East Side but it still has the allure, with excellent bistro fare, sexy cock-
tails, and the kind of atmosphere that is as comfortable for celebrities or
parents with a strollers. This is vintage Parisian à la McNally: verdigris
mirrored panels, forever-in-style subway tiles, a tin ceiling, and a check-
ered floor, while Cuban sandwiches and steak frites reveal a steady hand
in the kitchen. This is also the place for a late-night bite, since the kitchen
is open until midnight every night except Friday and Saturday, when
food is served until 3 am. Breakfast is served weekdays until 4 pm, with
brunch on the weekends. ⑤ *Average main: $20* ⊠ *131 Rivington St., at
Norfolk St., Lower East Side* ☎ *212/260–4555* ⊕ *www.schillersny.com*
Ⓜ *F to Delancey St.; J, M, Z to Essex St.* ✛ *2:G3.*

$ ✕ **Shopsin's.** Don't ask for substitutions or sauce on the side at New
ECLECTIC York's most eccentric eatery because Kenny Shopsin, owner and chef,
FAMILY really may toss you out or ban you for life; somehow the attitude is part
of the appeal here. Though the eclectic menu runs to literally hundreds
of items—from pumpkin pancakes to chilaquiles, and from chili cheese-
burgers to lamb-curry soups—even the strangest foods conjured up in
his tight diner kitchen taste pretty great. The mac 'n' cheese pancakes
have loyal followers (they're even better with hot sauce). The space in
the Essex market is tiny, so expect to wait. Parties of more than four
aren't accepted. ⑤ *Average main: $17* ⊠ *Essex Market, 120 Essex St.,
near Rivington St., Lower East Side* ⊕ *www.shopsins.com* ⌳ *Reserva-
tions not accepted* ▭ *No credit cards* ☉ *Closed Mon. and Tues. No
dinner* Ⓜ *J, M, Z to Essex St.* ✛ *2:G3.*

$$ ✕ **The Stanton Social.** This swanky Lower East Side favorite lures the
ECLECTIC crowds with an expansive and eclectic small-plates menu, accompa-
nied by a perfectly calibrated cocktail list. Come before 7 if you want
to be able to hear your fellow diners speak, but the people-watching
and shared dishes are good at any hour. Try the gooey, Gruyère-topped
onion soup dumplings, juicy Kobe beef sliders, and wasabi-crusted
salmon. Downstairs feels like a more traditional dining room, whereas
the second level features a buzzy bar. The late-night lounge area, decorated with cherry-blossom wallpaper and red leather upholstery, turns
more nightclubby the later it gets. Brunch—with options like spicy
lobster Benedict, and appropriate cocktails—might blow your mind.
Whatever time you come, save room for the fresh doughnuts. ⑤ *Average
main: $20* ⊠ *99 Stanton St., between Ludlow and Orchard Sts., Lower
East Side* ☎ *212/995–0099* ⊕ *www.thestantonsocial.com* ⌳ *Reservations essential* ☉ *No lunch* Ⓜ *F to 2nd Ave.* ✛ *2:G3.*

$ ✕ **Sugar Sweet Sunshine.** The brainchild of two former Magnolia Bak-
CAFÉ ery employees, Sugar Sweet's cupcakes are far superior; try the chocolate-
FAMILY almond Gooey Gooey, or the cream-cheese-frosting-topped pumpkin. The
real showstopper? Swoon-inducing banana pudding incorporating slices
of ripe fruit and crumbled Nilla wafers suspended in decadent vanilla pudding. Cupcakes are the perfect on-the-go treat but if you prefer to hang out,
there are cozy couches for lounging. ⑤ *Average main: $5* ⊠ *126 Rivington
St., between Essex and Norfolk Sts., Lower East Side* ☎ *212/995–1960*
⊕ *www.sugarsweetsunshine.com* ⌳ *Reservations not accepted* ✛ *2:G3.*

16

$$$
MODERN
AMERICAN

✕ **wd~50.** Chef Wylie Dufresne—the mad genius and early progenitor of molecular gastronomy cuisine in New York—mixes colors, flavors, and textures with a masterful hand, and the staff encourage diners to feel at ease trying the deconstructed interpretations of modern food. You might think you know what an everything bagel with lox and cream cheese or eggs Benedict might look like but you're in for a surprise. Expect the unexpected when it comes to taste combinations like corned duck with rye crisp and purple mustard or lamb shoulder with pistachio "polenta." This style of cooking isn't news anymore, but dinner here is still an eye-opening experience, although presentation and conceptualization sometimes outshine the flavors. Tasting menus (including a dessert-tasting one) allow you to really experience the chef's creativity. ⑤ *Average main: $34* ⊠ *50 Clinton St., between Rivington and Stanton Sts., Lower East Side* ☎ *212/477–2900* ⊕ *www.wd-50.com* ◐ *No lunch.* Ⓜ *F to Delancey St.; J, M, Z to Essex St.* ✛ *2:H3.*

GREENWICH VILLAGE AND THE WEST VILLAGE

GREENWICH VILLAGE

Greenwich Village's bohemian days may have faded, but the romantic allure of its tiny bistros, bars, and cafés remains. Around New York University, shabby-chic eateries and take-out joints cater to students, but there are a growing number of more sophisticated dining spots, too. Avoid the generally schlocky restaurants on Bleecker Street.

$$
PIZZA
FAMILY

✕ **Arturo's.** Few guidebooks list this classic New York pizzeria, but the jam-packed room and pleasantly smoky scent foreshadow a satisfying meal. There's a full menu of Italian classics, but don't be fooled: pizza is the main event. The thin-crust beauties are cooked in a coal oven, and emerge sizzling with simple toppings like pepperoni, sausage, and eggplant. Monday to Thursday you can call ahead to reserve a table; weekends, be prepared to wait and salivate. If you like the whimsical paintings that plaster the walls, ask the waiter the price: they're for sale. ⑤ *Average main: $18* ⊠ *106 W. Houston St., near Thompson St., Greenwich Village* ☎ *212/677–3820* ◐ *No lunch* Ⓜ *1 to Houston St.; B, D, F, M to Broadway–Lafayette St.* ✛ *2:D3.*

$$$
ITALIAN
Fodor's Choice
★

✕ **Babbo Ristorante.** It shouldn't take more than one bite of the ethereal homemade pasta or tender barbecued squab with roast beet farrotto for you to understand why it's so hard to get a reservation at Mario Batali's casually elegant restaurant. The menu strays widely from Italian standards and hits numerous high points, in particular with the "mint love letters": ravioli filled with pureed peas, ricotta, and fresh mint, finished with spicy lamb sausage ragout; and rabbit with Brussels sprouts, house-made pancetta, and carrot vinaigrette. This is the perfect spot for a raucous celebratory dinner with flowing wine and festive banter. But be forewarned: if anyone in your party is hard of hearing, or bothered by loud rock music, choose someplace more sedate. ⑤ *Average main: $30* ⊠ *110 Waverly Pl., between MacDougal St. and 6th Ave., Greenwich Village* ☎ *212/777–0303* ⊕ *www.babbonyc.com* ⌕ *Reservations essential* ◐ *No lunch Sun. and Mon.* Ⓜ *A, B, C, D, E, F, M to W. 4th St.* ✛ *2:C1.*

$ ✕**Bleecker Street Pizza.** Flavor reigns at this bustling corner pizzeria. It's
PIZZA the perfect place to stop for a stand-up slice at the counter: the thin-
FAMILY crusted Nonna Maria is topped with garlicky marinara, grated and
fresh mozzarella, and freshly grated Parmesan and is worth the trek to
the West Village. If you're not smitten with "Grandma Maria," there
are also Sicilian slices and whole white (that's no tomato sauce) pies
available. $ *Average main: $4* ✉ *69 7th Ave. S, at Bleecker St., West
Village* ☎ *212/924–4466* ⊕ *www.bleeckerstreetpizza.net* ⚬ *Reservations
not accepted* ✛ *:C2.*

$$$ ✕**Blue Hill.** This tasteful, sophisticated den of a restaurant—formerly a
MODERN speakeasy—on a quiet side street maintains an impeccable reputation
AMERICAN for excellence and consistency under the leadership of chef Dan Barber.
The Obamas even stopped by here for dinner, shutting down the street
for one of their "date nights." Part of the slow-food, sustainable agricul-
ture movement, Blue Hill mostly uses ingredients grown or raised within
200 miles, including the Four Season Farm at Stone Barns Center for
Food and Agriculture, Barber's second culinary project in nearby West-
chester County. The chefs produce precisely cooked and elegantly con-
structed food such as wild striped bass with potato-and-clam chowder
and house-cured *guanciale* (pork jowl), and a smoked-tomato soup with
American caviar. $ *Average main: $29* ✉ *75 Washington Pl., between
Washington Sq. W and 6th Ave., Greenwich Village* ☎ *212/539–1776*
⊕ *www.bluehillfarm.com* ⚬ *Reservations essential* ☽ *No lunch* Ⓜ *A, B,
C, D, E, F, M to W. 4th St.* ✛ *2:C1.*

$$$$ ✕**Carbone.** Mario Carbone and Rich Torrisi are on a roll. Since open-
ITALIAN ing the hit Torrisi Italian Specialties in early 2010 the two chefs can't
Fodor's Choice seem to do wrong. Case in point: Carbone. The achingly popular place
★ not only sticks to the Italian-American formula that has won Carbone
and Torrisi acclaim but takes it a step further: the white-table-clothed
Greenwich Village restaurant successfully emulates the Big Apple Ital-
ian restaurants of the 1950s with revived dishesl like veal Marsala,
ribeye Diana, and baked clams. It's not cheap, though, so bring a fat
wallet. $ *Average main: $45* ✉ *181 Thompson St., north of Houston
St., Greenwich Village* ☎ *212/254–3000* ⊕ *www.carbonenewyork.com*
⚬ *Reservations essential* ☽ *No lunch weekends* Ⓜ *A, C, E B, D, F, M
to W. 4th St.* ✛ *2:D2.*

$$$ ✕**Charlie Bird.** Perpetually packed since the day it opened in the spring of
ITALIAN 2013, Charlie Bird is the love child of sommelier Robert Bohr, who was
in charge of wine at vino-mad Cru, and chef Ryan Hardy, who made a
name for himself at Little Nell in Aspen and, more recently, sharpened
his skills as the private chef for food-loving Jay-Z and Beyonce. It's no
coincidence the restaurant has a hip-hop theme (expect old school and
'90s rap on the hi-fi). The Italian-leaning menu is divided into small
and large plates, vegetables, a "raw" section, and pasta. The uni-loaded
duck egg spaghetti marries surf-and-turf in a deeply satisfying way while
the scallops are subtly laced with lardo, giving them an umami boost.
$ *Average main: $30* ✉ *5 King St., at 6th Ave., Greenwich Village*
☎ *212/235–7133* ⊕ *www.charliebirdnyc.com* ⚬ *Reservations essential*
Ⓜ *A, C, E, M, B, D, F to W. 4th St.* ✛ *2:C3.*

16

$ ✕ **Kati Roll Company.** You can think of a kati roll as a South Asian taco:
INDIAN   griddled parathas stuffed with savory-spiced grilled meat, shrimp, paneer, chickpea mash, or spiced mashed potato. They're the only things sold at this tiny, popular lunch spot cheerfully festooned with Bollywood posters. This is an excellent and inexpensive lunch option but be warned that lines often form at weekday lunch, and there are only a few seats, so a good plan is to take your kati roll to a nearby park bench. There are also locations at 39th Street and 6th Avenue and 53rd Street and 3rd Avenue. ⑤ *Average main: $6* ✉ *99 MacDougal St., near Bleecker St., Greenwich Village* ☎ *212/730–4280* ⊕ *www.the katirollcompany.com* ⚏ *Reservations not accepted* ▬ *No credit cards* Ⓜ *A, C, B, D, E, F, M to W. 4th St.* ✛ *2:D2.*

$ ✕ **Keste Pizza & Vino.** At the back of the long, narrow Keste Pizza & Vino
PIZZA   restaurant is a beautiful, tiled, wood-fired oven that cooks what might be Manhattan's most authentic Neapolitan pies at 1,000 degrees. Blistered and chewy around the edges, the Margherita pie gives way to a softer center pooled with San Marzano tomato sauce and housemade mozzarella. There are numerous pizza options, including white pies and ones with gluten-free crusts. This is a definite contender for best pizza in New York. The dining room is casual and the location means it's almost always busy. ⑤ *Average main: $15* ✉ *271 Bleecker St., between 6th and 7th Aves., West Village* ☎ *212/243–1500* ⊕ *www.kestepizzeria.com* ⚏ *Reservations not accepted* Ⓜ *A, B, C, D, E, F, M to W. 4th St.* ✛ *2:C2.*

$$ ✕ **Lupa.** Even the most hard-to-please connoisseurs have a soft spot
ITALIAN   for Lupa, Mario Batali and Joseph Bastianich's "downscale" Roman trattoria. Rough-hewn wood, great Italian wines, and simple preparations with top-quality ingredients define the restaurant, along with the "gentle" prices. People come repeatedly for dishes such as ricotta gnocchi with sweet-sausage ragout, house-made salumi, and sardines with golden raisins and pine nuts. The restaurant is split into two rooms: a boisterous space up front, with plenty of natural light, where walk-ins are welcome; the back room is more intimate, for those with reservations, and feels something like you're dining in a culinary cocoon, in the best sense. ⑤ *Average main: $22* ✉ *170 Thompson St., between Bleecker and Houston Sts., Greenwich Village* ☎ *212/982–5089* ⊕ *www.luparestaurant.com* Ⓜ *A, B, C, D, E, F, M to W. 4th St.* ✛ *2:D3.*

$$ ✕ **Mermaid Oyster Bar.** If you're craving a great raw bar, lobster roll, or
SEAFOOD   soft-shell crab sandwich (in season), Mermaid Oyster Bar gives nearby classics Mary's Fish Camp and Pearl Oyster Bar a run for their money. Almost every dish is a winner here, but the lobster bisque laced with Manzanilla sherry and toasted pumpkin seeds, the blackened striped bass with roasted squash and Swiss chard, and the spicy seafood bucatini fra diavolo are all standouts. From the bar, try something from the list of pitch-perfect cocktails, like a Dark and Stormy, made with black rum and ginger beer, or a Pimm's cooler with refreshing pieces of fresh cucumber. There are two other locations in Manhattan: on the Upper West Side and in the East Village. ⑤ *Average main: $22* ✉ *79 MacDougal St., at Houston St., Greenwich Village* ☎ *212/260–0100* ⊕ *www.themermaidnyc.com* ☉ *No lunch* Ⓜ *1 to Houston St.; C, E to Spring St.* ✛ *2:D2.*

$$$ ✕ **Minetta Tavern.** By converting a moribund 80-year-old Italian restaurant
MODERN into a cozy hot spot, restaurateur Keith McNally has created yet another
AMERICAN hit. Try early and often to score reservations, so that you can sample
creations like buttery trout meunière, bone marrow on toast, expertly
aged steaks, and the celebrated Black Label burger, a gorgeous assembly
of meat topped with caramelized onions and—for the brave—an added
layer of cheese. The barroom, with its original details intact, is great for
people-watching. Landing a table in the back room, with its original
mural depicting West Village life and wall-to-wall photos of famous and
infamous customers from eras gone by, makes sweet-talking the reser-
vationist worth your while. $ *Average main: $27* ✉ *113 MacDougal
St., between Bleecker and 3rd Sts., Greenwich Village* ☎ *212/475–3850*
⊕ *www.minettatavernny.com* ⌕ *Reservations essential* ☾ *No lunch Mon.
and Tues.* Ⓜ *A, B, C, D, E, F, M to W. 4th St.* ✛ *2:D2.*

$ ✕ **Peanut Butter & Co. Sandwich Shop.** For a childhood classic kicked up a
AMERICAN notch, head to Peanut Butter & Co. Sandwich Shop. You can go with
FAMILY a standard PB&J, or explore any of the menu's 20 options, including
the Elvis (grilled with peanut butter, bananas, and honey), the Preg-
nant Lady (peanut butter and pickles), or the sandwich of the week,
with expertly paired ingredients such as cherry jam, cream cheese, and
Crunch Time peanut butter. Pair your sandwich with a milkshake—
there are traditional flavors as well as more innovative combos. And of
course there are peanut butter cookies for dessert, as well as sundaes.
$ *Average main: $8* ✉ *240 Sullivan St., near 3rd St., Greenwich Village*
☎ *212/677–3995* ⊕ *ilovepeanutbutter.com* ⌕ *Reservations not accepted*
Ⓜ *A, B, C, D, E, F, M to W. 4th St.* ✛ *2:D2.*

$ ✕ **Umami Burger.** *Umami,* known as the "sixth taste," is the sensation on
BURGER our palate when we eat something savory. It's also the name of restau-
rant minichain whose New York location serves one of the best burgers
in the city. The signature burger looks like a regular burger (except for
the "u" branded into the top of the bun), but looks are deceiving. Dig,
if you will, the umami-building process: carmelized onions are doused
with star anise, the sweet-accented ketchup is made in house, and the
patty is sprinkled with sea kelp powder and bonito flake, then sprayed
with an oyster extract. The Manly Burger goes a step further, adding
beer cheddar and bacon lardons. Starters include salads, fries, truffle
fries, sweet potato fries, and onion rings. $ *Average main: $12* ✉ *432
6th Ave., near 10th St., Greenwich Village* ☎ *212/677–8626* ⊕ *www.
umami.com* Ⓜ *A, C, E, B, D, F, M to W. 4th St.* ✛ *3:D5.*

WEST VILLAGE

The West Village has mastered the art of destination restaurants that
feel like neighborhood eateries. Places here are homey, yet remarkable
enough to attract diners from all over the city.

$$$ ✕ **Annisa.** *Annisa* may mean "the women" in Arabic, but the food at this
MODERN ASIAN sedate West Village restaurant is inspired by Asia. And it's top notch.
Chef Anita Lo, one of the most underrated chefs in New York, cooks
up miraculous dishes like foie-gras soup dumplings, barbequed squid
with basil and peanuts, and Japanese curry–spiked rabbit. But be sure
to save room for dessert: the pecan and salted butterscotch beignets
with bourbon ice cream are good enough to make you want to come

16

back a second or third time. ⑤ *Average main: $30* ✉ *13 Barrow St., between 4th St. and 7th Ave. S, West Village* ☎ *212/741–6699* ⊕ *www. annisarestaurant.com* Ⓜ *1 to Christopher St.* ✛ *2:C2.*

$$$ ✕ **August.** Rustic simplicity is the theme at this bustling West Village
EUROPEAN eatery, where many of the dishes come from the wood-burning oven in the dining room. Fish is always a good choice here, be it baked skate or pan-roasted cod, and meaty entrées like the pork chop or dry-aged sirloin are excellently cooked. Starters are more inventive; try the foie gras terrine with rhubarb compote. Wood-planed floors and an arched cork ceiling envelop the busy 40-seat dining room; you can also dine at the bar. For a quieter meal, ask for a table in the glass-enclosed 15-seat atrium in back. ⑤ *Average main: $34* ✉ *359 Bleecker St., at Charles St., West Village* ☎ *212/929–8727* ⊕ *www.augustny.com* ✍ *Reservations essential* Ⓜ *1 to Christopher St./Sheridan Sq.; A, B, C, D, E, F, M to W. 4th St.* ✛ *3:C5.*

$$ ✕ **Barbuto.** Chef Jonathan Waxman made a name for himself with
ITALIAN his French-inspired California cuisine. Barbuto specializes in rustic preparations with bright flavors, like house-made duck sausage with creamy polenta, red wine–braised short ribs, and pasta carbonara, though the menu changes daily, depending on what's available. The chef's acclaimed roasted chicken is usually on the menu in one form or another. The airy, sophisticated space continues to get busy so make a reservation. The restaurant is particularly pleasant in nice weather when the giant garage-door-like windows open onto the street and you can watch the neighborhood go by. ⑤ *Average main: $17* ✉ *775 Washington St., between Jane and 12th Sts., West Village* ☎ *212/924–9700* ⊕ *www.barbutonyc.com* Ⓜ *A, C, E, to 14th St.; L to 8th Ave.; 1 to Christopher St./Sheridan Sq.* ✛ *3:B5.*

$$$ ✕ **Blue Ribbon Bakery.** A neighborhood standard for good, if expen-
ECLECTIC sive, food, this outpost of the Blue Ribbon empire has an eclectic menu featuring substantial sandwiches on homemade bread (freshly baked in the oven downstairs), small plates, legendary bread pudding, and entrées that span the globe, from hummus to grilled catfish with sautéed collards and sweet potatoes. The cavelike basement dining room is dark and intimate; upstairs is more open and light-filled, with large windows looking out onto a pretty West Village corner. Brunch is notoriously crowded. ⑤ *Average main: $25* ✉ *35 Downing St., at Bedford St., Greenwich Village* ☎ *212/337–0404* ⊕ *www. blueribbonrestaurants.com* Ⓜ *1 to Houston St.; A, B, C, D, E, F, M to W. 4th St.* ✛ *2:C2.*

$$ ✕ **Chez Sardine.** If you filtered a Japanese *izakaya* (generally serving
JAPANESE small plates to go with drinks) through downtown Manhattan, you'd get something like sceney Chez Sardine. This diminutive eatery (hence the name), at the busy West Village intersection of W. 4th and W. 10th streets, is run by neighborhood restaurateur Gabe Stulman (of Fedora, Perla, Joseph Leonard, and Jeffrey's Grocery). Regulars go ga-ga for the foie-gras and smoked-cheddar grilled-cheese sandwich, a sumptuous blend of haute and low-brow tastes. Likewise, the smokey bacon miso soup and the pork and unagi roll, a divinely delicious marriage of surf-and-turf if there ever was one, are worth a visit in and of themselves.

Reservations are strongly recommended. $ *Average main: $20* ✉ *183 W. 10th St., at 4th St., West Village* ☎ *646/360–3705* ⊕ *www.chezsardine. com* ☾ *1 to Christopher St./Sheridan Sq.* ✛ *3:D5.*

$$$$
MODERN
AMERICAN
✕ **Commerce.** This former speakeasy harks back to days gone by with its Diego Rivera–style murals, vintage sconces, and restored subway tiles, but the crowd really comes for chef Harold Moore's seasonal cuisine. Appetizers range from a red cabbage, apple, and pecan salad to yuzu-marinated hamachi ceviche. Entrées are just as vibrant: bright, sweet peas offset pristine halibut, and the shareable roast chicken, presented tableside, is served with foie-gras bread stuffing. Brunch has a Middle Eastern influence, with scrambled eggs and hummus atop a pillowy pita, and a mean *shakshuka*—baked eggs nestled in a pepper, onion, and tomato sauce. Even the contents of the bread basket are a pleasure here. In an interesting twist, especially given the restaurant's name, only credit cards are accepted: no cash. $ *Average main: $36* ✉ *50 Commerce St., West Village* ☎ *212/524–2301* ⊕ *www.commercerestaurant. com* ☾ *No lunch* Ⓜ *1 to Christopher St./Sheridan Sq.; A, B, C, D, E, F, M to W. 4th St.* ✛ *2:B2.*

$$$
ITALIAN
✕ **dell'anima.** Lines still snake out the door of this neighborhood favorite so it's a good idea to make a reservation. Once you're in, check out the open kitchen, where the stylish crowd converges to watch chefs prepare authentic Italian dishes with a modern twist. Starters might include sweetbreads, bone marrow, or charred octopus with chorizo, while traditional first courses like pasta alla carbonara with speck (smoked and cured pork), egg, and pecorino are impeccable. The signature *pollo al diavolo* (spicy chicken) is seared with enough smoke and heat for all seasons. Anfora, their wine bar next door, is good for an after-dinner drink if you want to linger. $ *Average main: $26* ✉ *38 8th Ave., at Jane St., West Village* ☎ *212/366–6633* ⊕ *www.dellanima.com* ☾ *No lunch weekdays* Ⓜ *A, C, E to 14th St.; L to 8th Ave.* ✛ *3:C5.*

$$
SEAFOOD
✕ **Ditch Plains.** Named for a surf spot in Montauk, this laid-back neighborhood restaurant serves an eclectic bill of beachfront fare—from fish tacos, lobster rolls, and fish-and-chips to clam chowder and crab dip. There are options for landlubbers and vegetarians, too. It's not quite a beach shack, but the food and the setting, with an upbeat rock soundtrack, are designed for conviviality, and the wine-list prices are extremely friendly, with whole and half bottles sold just above cost. The bloody marys are recommended, too. Brunch is served every day from 11 am. $ *Average main: $16* ✉ *29 Bedford St., near Downing St., West Village* ☎ *212/633–0202* ⊕ *www.ditch-plains.com* ⬧ *Reservations not accepted* Ⓜ *1 to Houston St.* ✛ *2:C3.*

$$
KOREAN
✕ **Do Hwa.** If anyone in New York is responsible for making Korean food cool and user-friendly, it is the mother-daughter team behind this chic and perennially popular restaurant and its East Village sister, Dok Suni's. Jenny Kwak and her mother, Myung Ja, serve home cooking in the form of *kalbi jim* (braised short ribs), *bibimbop* (a spicy, mix-it-yourself vegetable-and-rice dish), and other favorites that may not be as pungent as they are uptown in Korea Town but are satisfying nevertheless—and the atmosphere is definitely more sophisticated. The bar, where movies are projected onto the side wall, gets pretty

16

happening, too. $ *Average main: $23* ✉ *55 Carmine St., between Bedford St. and 7th Ave., West Village* ☎ *212/414–1224* ⊕ *www. dohwanyc.com* ◷ *No lunch weekends* Ⓜ *1 to Houston St.; A, B, C, D, E, F, M to W. 4th St.* ✛ *2:C2.*

$$$
MEXICAN
Fodor'sChoice
★

✕**Empellón Taqueria.** Chef Alex Stupak worked for years as the wizard-like pastry chef at wd~50, New York's premier home to molecular gastronomy. So when he left to open—wait for it—a taqueria, many Manhattan diners either scratched their heads or wondered if they'd be served deconstructed tacos. Instead, they got simple yet well-executed fare using top-notch ingredients. There are straightforward options—fish tempura, lamb, steak—as well as surprising variations, like tacos with sweat breads and a chorizo gravy poured over it. There are, of course, also several variations on the margarita theme, too, including one using the Japanese citrus, yuzu. Empellon isn't really south-of-the-border in its authenticity but when it's this good, who cares? $ *Average main: $23* ✉ *230 W. 4th St., at 10th St., West Village* ☎ *212/367–0999* ⊕ *www.empellon.com* Ⓜ *1 to Christopher St./Sheridan Sq.* ✛ *2:B1.*

$$
MALAYSIAN
Fodor'sChoice
★

✕**Fatty Crab.** This rustic Malaysian cantina showcases the exciting cuisine of chef Zak Pelaccio, who spent years cooking at famous French restaurants before escaping to Southeast Asia for a year, where he fell in love with the flavors of the region. Start with the addictive pickled watermelon and crispy pork salad, an improbable combination that's both refreshing and decadent. The can't-miss signature dish is chili crab—cracked Dungeness crab in a pool of rich, spicy chili sauce, served with bread for dipping. It's messy for sure, but worth rolling up your sleeves. The small space fills up quickly and be warned that the tables are practically on top of each other, but it's lots of fun. $ *Average main: $18* ✉ *643 Hudson St., between Gansevoort and Horatio Sts., West Village* ☎ *212/352–3592* ⊕ *www.fattycrab.com* ⬧ *Reservations not accepted* Ⓜ *A, C, E to 14th St.; L to 8th Ave.* ✛ *3:C5.*

$$$
ECLECTIC

✕**Fedora.** Up until 2011, subterranean Fedora was an ancient, little-patronized restaurant with an even more ancient owner (for whom the restaurant was named). But charming Fedora—the old Italian owner—has left the building and restaurateur Gabe Stulman took over the spot, vowing to keep the place largely intact. At least the decor. Now "see and be seen" folk cram the long narrow space, munching on French Canadian–accented fare like garlic cream–topped duck breast and scallops paired with bone marrow, and sipping cocktails including the creatively named (and made) signature cocktails. Fedora (the restaurant) will never be the same and that's maybe a good thing. $ *Average main: $25* ✉ *239 W. 4th St., between Charles and 10th Sts., West Village* ☎ *646/449–9336* ⊕ *www.fedoranyc.com* Ⓜ *1 to Christopher St./Sheridan Sq.* ✛ *2:B1.*

$$
ITALIAN

✕**Frankies Spuntino.** The Frankies—that is, owners and chefs Frank Falcinelli and Frank Castronovo—have a winning formula at their West Village restaurant: serve hearty not-necessarily-by-the-book Italian-inflected fare using local, organic, and humanely raised ingredients in a laid-back atmosphere. Most menu items change seasonally but expect pasta dishes like pappardelle with mushrooms and chestnuts, black spaghetti with mussels, cockels, and pistachios, sweet potato gnocchi with oxtail ragù. The large menu also includes crostini, fresh salads, cured meats, and cheese plates. It's a casual, family friendly, neighborhood spot. $ *Average main: $18* ⊠ *570 Hudson St., at 11th St., West Village* ☎ *212/924–0818* ⊕ *www.frankiesspuntino.com* Ⓜ *C, E to 14th St.; L to 8th Ave.* ✣ *2:B1.*

$$$
ITALIAN
Fodor'sChoice
★

✕ **I Sodi.** In a city of what seems like a million Italian restaurants, this minimalist-designed Tuscan-focused eatery in the West Village is a real find. Spikey-haired owner, Rita Sodi, a Florentine who formerly worked in the fashion industry, ensures the traditional fare coming from the kitchen is satisfying. The menu changes weekly based on seasonal ingredients but expect a bevy of pasta dishes topped with good stuff like duck ragù and artichoke-laced lasagna, as well as not-very-Lipitor-friendly pancetta-wrapped pork and rabbit. Hoist a glass of grappa at the end of the meal and be happy you're in the right place. $ *Average main: $26* ⊠ *105 Christopher St., between Bleecker and Hudson Sts., West Village* ☎ *212/414–5774* ⊕ *www.isodinyc.com* Ⓜ *1 to Christopher St.– Sheridan Sq.* ✣ *2:B2.*

$$
MODERN
AMERICAN

✕ **The Little Owl.** This tiny neighborhood joint, with seating for 28 people, is exceptionally eager to please—and the attitude, along with the food, is a winning combination. The menu is congruently small, which actually makes it easier to decide what you want. And what you want are the pork-veal-beef-pecorino-cheese meatball "sliders," or miniburgers. The unusually juicy pork loin chop, served with Parmesan butter beans and wild dandelion greens, is gigantic, and hugely satisfying. Raspberry-filled beignets, served with a ramekin of warm Nutella, are otherworldly. It's quintessential West Village: quirky and wonderful. Fans of sitcom *Friends* might recognize the apartment building that houses the restaurant. $ *Average main: $24* ⊠ *90 Bedford St., at Grove St., West Village* ☎ *212/741–4695* ⊕ *www.thelittleowlnyc.com* ⌧ *Reservations essential* Ⓜ *1 to Christopher St./Sheridan Sq.; A, B, C, D, E, F, M to W. 4th St.* ✣ *3:D6.*

16

$$
SEAFOOD

✕ **Mary's Fish Camp.** Diners still line up down the street before the restaurant opens for dinner to get a table at this small but bustling seafood shack. The result of a split between Pearl Oyster Bar's partners, Mary's is a more intimate space, but the two have similar menus: excellent fried oysters, chowders, and, of course, the sweet lobster roll with crisp fries, all of which will have you licking your fingers. The killer hot fudge sundae is worth saving room for. The staff here are warm and friendly, too. This is the kind of place everyone wishes was in their neighborhood. $ *Average main: $21* ⊠ *64 Charles St., at 4th St., West Village* ☎ *646/486–2185* ⊕ *marysfishcamp.com* ⌧ *Reservations not accepted* ☾ *Closed Sun.* Ⓜ *1 to Christopher St./Sheridan Sq.* ✣ *2:B1.*

$
MEXICAN

✕ **Mexicana Mama.** This small, colorful, and popular space serves vividly flavored fare and the kitchen is serious enough to create four different salsas daily. The tomato-habanero salsa is simply unforgettable; cream tames the habaneros, but only slightly. Three chili-roasted pork tacos are also filled with piquant Chihuahua cheese and black beans, and served over Mexican rice and avocado cubes. Quesadillas are made with fresh corn tortillas, filled with that melted Chihuahua cheese and your choice of chicken, barbacoa beef, chicken mole, or a daily special vegetable filling. For dessert, look no further than the eggy flan in flavors like caramel or cinnamon. $ *Average main: $13* ✉ *525 Hudson St., near Charles St., West Village* ☎ *212/924–4119* ▭ *No credit cards* ⊘ *Closed Mon.* Ⓜ *1 to Christopher St./Sheridan Sq.; A, B, C, D, E, F, M to W. 4th St.* ⊹ *3:C6.*

$ ✕ **Moustache.** There's typically a crowd waiting outside for one of the
MIDDLE EASTERN copper-top tables at this casual Middle Eastern neighborhood restaurant. The focal point is the perfect pita that accompanies tasty salads like lemony chickpea and spinach, hearty lentil and bulgur, or falafel. Also delicious is *lahambajin,* spicy ground lamb on a crispy flat crust. For entrées, try the leg of lamb, the juicy baby lamb sandwich, or merguez sausage sandwiches. Service is slow but friendly. There are also locations in the East Village and in East Harlem. $ *Average main: $12* ✉ *90 Bedford St., between Barrow and Grove Sts., West Village* ☎ *212/229–2220* ⊕ *moustachepitza.com* ⌫ *Reservations not accepted* ▭ *No credit cards* Ⓜ *1 to Christopher St./Sheridan Sq.* ⊹ *2:B2.*

$$$ ✕ **Pearl Oyster Bar.** There have been many imitators and few real com-
SEAFOOD petitors to this West Village seafood institution. Since 1997, Rebecca Charles has been serving arguably the best lobster roll in New York City in a no-frills space down charming, restaurant-lined Cornelia Street—and expanded next door to accommodate the throngs. But that's not the only reason you should cast your net here. Pan-roasted sea scallops and plus-size crab cakes may compete with the legendary lobster roll for your taste buds' attention. Service is very efficient; you might even say rushed. $ *Average main: $25* ✉ *18 Cornelia St., between 4th and Bleecker Sts., West Village* ☎ *212/691–8211* ⊕ *www.pearloysterbar. com* ⊘ *Closed Sun.* Ⓜ *A, B, C, D, E, F, M to W. 4th St.* ⊹ *2:C2.*

$$$ ✕ **RedFarm.** Conceived and run by Ed Schoenfeld, an expert on Chinese
CHINESE cuisine, and Joe Ng, known as the dumpling king of New York, this bilevel West Village restaurant specializes in—you guessed it—Chinese-style dumplings. At least partly. The menu focuses mostly on dim sum—small plates and snacks (often in dumpling form)—as well as Chinese-American dishes like three-chili chicken and chicken in garlic sauce. The lobster dumplings and the crab and pork soup dumplings are culinary wonders and nearly obligatory for first timers. But come with a wallet the size of China itself because the dishes add up. There's also a location on Broadway and 76th St. $ *Average main: $30* ✉ *529 Hudson St., between 10th and Charles Sts., West Village* ☎ *212/792–9700* ⊕ *www.redfarmnyc.com* Ⓜ *1 to Christopher St.–Sheridan Sq.; C, E to 8th Ave.* ⊹ *2:B2.*

Snack Taverna. *Branch location at 63 Bedford Street, at Morton. See SoHo for full review.*

$$ ✕ **The Spotted Pig.** Part cozy English pub, part laid-back neighbor-
BRITISH hood hangout, part gastronome's lure, the Spotted Pig showcases the impeccable food of the now legendary London chef April Bloomfield (Mario Batali and his partners consulted). Dishes like arugula salad with tangy radishes and Parmesan, smoked haddock–and-corn chowder with homemade crackers, are studies in texture and flavor contrast. Shoestring potatoes accompany the Roquefort cheeseburger. Chase it with a glass of foam-dripping Old Speckled Hen. This neighborhood hangout still packs it in, so come early, or late. The Breslin is another

of Bloomfield's standout New York restaurants with an überclubby feel. $ *Average main: $23* ✉ *314 W. 11th St., at Greenwich St., West Village* ☎ *212/620–0393* ⊕ *www.thespottedpig.com* ⌲ *Reservations not accepted* Ⓜ *A, C, E to 14th St.; L to 8th Ave.* ✛ *2:A1.*

$$$$
JAPANESE

✕ **Sushi Nakazawa.** Daisuke dreams of sushi. Fans of the acclaimed 2011 documentary *Jiro Dreams of Sushi* may remember Daisuke Nakazawa, the apprentice to the great Tokyo-based sushi master Jiro Ono, who spent the near entirety of the film trying to perfect the egg custard. He finally succeeded—just as he has succeeded in wooing even the most finicky New York diners. It's all *omakase* (a tasting menu set by the chef) here, so sit back and enjoy two hours of being fed by one of the best sushi chefs in New York. Mr. Nakazawa practices an old Tokyo style of sushi making—putting all his highly fresh fish on a thumb-size bundle of rice. (Sorry, fans of sashimi.) Reserve at least a month in advance. $ *Average main: $150* ✉ *23 Commerce St., near Bedford St., West Village* ☎ *212/924–2212* ⊕ *www.sushinakazawa.com* ⌲ *Reservations essential* Ⓜ *1 to Christopher St./Sheridan Sq.* ✛ *3:D6.*

$
MIDDLE EASTERN

✕ **Taïm.** There's a real chef behind this tiny sliver of a restaurant—New York's only gourmet falafel stand. Taïm means "tasty" in Hebrew, and Tel Aviv transplant Einat Admony's fried chickpea balls are delicious, and available in several beguiling flavors (try them infused with spicy harissa sauce) along with a tantalizing display of à la carte salads (the carrots with Moroccan spices is a standout). There's also a location in NoLIta, on Spring Street between Mott and Mulberry, as well as a food truck that makes its way around the city (you can find it via Twitter). $ *Average main: $9* ✉ *222 Waverly Pl., near Perry St., West Village* ☎ *212/691–1287* ⊕ *www.taimfalafel.com* ⌲ *Reservations not accepted* ▭ *No credit cards* Ⓜ *1 to Christopher St.* ✛ *2:B1.*

$$$
AUSTRIAN

✕ **Wallsé.** The modern Austrian menu at Kurt Gutenbrunner's lovely, light-filled neighborhood restaurant has a strong emphasis on Austrian tradition and urban New York attitude. It's hard to argue with such dishes as Wiener schnitzel with potato-cucumber salad and lingonberries, or venison goulash with spaetzle and Brussels sprouts, and it's often lighter than you'd think Austrian food would be. Desserts do Vienna proud: apple-walnut strudel is served with apple sorbet. The atmosphere is casual but sophisticated—perfect for either a weeknight dinner or a special occasion. $ *Average main: $33* ✉ *344 W. 11th St., at Washington St., West Village* ☎ *212/352–2300* ⊕ *www.wallse.com* ⌲ *Reservations essential* ☾ *No lunch weekdays and Saturday* Ⓜ *1 to Christopher St./Sheridan Sq.; A, C, E to 14th St.; L to 8th Ave.* ✛ *3:B6.*

$
AMERICAN
FAMILY

✕ **Westville.** If New York's neighborhoods were small country towns, they'd all have restaurants just like Westville. These adorable spots—with branches in the East and West Village, Chelsea, and west SoHo—serve simple wholesome fare, at reasonable prices. Salads, grilled chicken, burgers, and chops are all good, but the seasonal sides, which change daily based on what's fresh at the market, are the real star attraction (the "Market Plate" with any three sides is a popular dinner option). Dessert is worth saving room for, too, especially the daily pie selections. Expect to wait on weekend nights. $ *Average main: $11* ✉ *210 W. 10th St., near Bleecker St., West Village* ☎ *212/741–7971* ⊕ *www.westvillenyc.com* Ⓜ *1 to Christopher St.* ✛ *3:C6.*

16

CHELSEA AND THE MEATPACKING DISTRICT

CHELSEA

Several big-name chefs have moved to the western part of this neighborhood in recent years, putting Chelsea on the dining map. For a tasty quick bite or a gift for your favorite foodie, stop by **Chelsea Market.**

$
PIZZA
Fodor'sChoice
★

× **Co.** Co., or "Company" as it's pronounced, took the New York pizza scene by red-sauce-scented storm when it opened in early 2009. Bread master Jim Lahey, who made a name for himself at the Sullivan Street Baking Company, crafts simple but memorable pies, the dough and crust of which play a starring role. The simple Margherita (tomato sauce, mozzarella, basil) is a good way to sample Co.'s fare, but diners are always tempted by unorthodox pizzas like the carmelized-onion-walnut-puree pie or the béchamel-and-Parmesan-topped version. If you can, take a few friends, so you can order several pies. This casual Chelsea pizzeria is anything but half baked. ⑤ *Average main: $16 ✉ 230 9th Ave., at 24th St., Chelsea* ☎ *212/243–1105* ⊕ *www.co-pane.com* ⊙ *No lunch Mon.* Ⓜ *C, E to 23rd St.* ✛ *3:B2.*

$$$
AMERICAN

× **Cookshop.** One of far-west Chelsea's first hot restaurants, Cookshop manages a casual elegance while focusing on seasonal, farm-fresh cuisine that continues to wow. Outdoor seating on 10th Avenue is quite peaceful in the evening; during the day you can survey a cross-section of gallery-hoppers and shoppers. Divine cocktails, made with fresh fruit juices, are veritable elixirs of well-being. Line up early for brunch; it's worth the wait for dishes like baked eggs over duck and Swiss chard, or the fluffiest pancakes in town. Dinner is also a triumph, with a variety of perfectly prepared dishes like whitefish with lemony asparagus and hen-of-the-woods mushrooms or a simply roasted chicken. ⑤ *Average main: $26 ✉ 156 10th Ave., at 20th St., Chelsea* ☎ *212/924–4440* ⊕ *www.cookshopny.com* Ⓜ *A, C, E to 23rd St.* ✛ *3:B3.*

$
ECLECTIC

× **Coppelia.** Named for a legendary ice cream shop in Havana, Coppelia is neither Cuban nor an ice-cream parlor. At least not strictly speaking. Chef Julian Medina has created a 24-hour pan-Latin diner that works on many levels—for a quick breakfast, a casual lunch, or a post-club late-night bite. The continent-sized menu emphasizes comfort food, with satisfying dishes like the pork belly spiked mac 'n' cheese, mountainous nachos, grilled cheese with jalapeño and bacon, and even kimchi-stuffed tacos. And if you had your *corazon* set on ice cream, there's plenty of it on the dessert menu. ⑤ *Average main: $15 ✉ 207 W. 14th St., between 7th and 8th Aves., Chelsea* ☎ *212/858–5001* ⊕ *www. ybandco.com* Ⓜ *1, 2, 3 to 14th St.* ✛ *3:C4.*

$
CHINESE

× **Legend.** Sure, there's nothing Chinese about the generic name; and the location, on a stretch of 7th Avenue in Chelsea, is flanked by forgettable eating options. But do your taste buds a favor and eat at this affordable Sichuan spot, whose quiet opening was followed by a lot of buzz among New York's fooderati. The long menu is not for the indecisive but nearly anything is a hit, including the double-cooked bacon, the massive and flaky whole roasted fish, and the ultra-spicy *ma po* tofu. Dishes here lean toward the fiery side so be prepared. ⑤ *Average main: $14 ✉ 88 7th*

Ave., *between 15th and 16th Sts.,*
Chelsea ☎ *212/929–1778* ⊕ *www.*
legendrestaurant88.com Ⓜ *1, 2, 3*
to 14th St. ✥ *3:D4.*

$$
MODERN
AMERICAN

✕ **The Red Cat.** Elegant yet unpretentious, a lovely neighborhood spot *and* a destination restaurant, the Red Cat and its American-meets-Mediterranean menu is a great place for a long chat with a friend, to celebrate an auspicious occasion, to have a business dinner, or just the

kind of place to go for an excellent meal. The menu changes frequently, based on what's in season, but expect an eclectic menu of well-executed pastas, burgers, saffron-laced seafood, and meaty numbers. Factor in the affordable wine list and you'll most definitely feel like one lucky cat. Ⓢ *Average main: $25* ✉ *227 10th Ave., between 23rd and 24th Sts., Chelsea* ☎ *212/242–1122* ⊕ *www.redcatrestaurants.com* ☾ *No lunch Mon. and Tues.* Ⓜ *C, E to 23rd St.* ✥ *3:A2.*

$
SPANISH
Fodor's Choice
★

✕ **Tia Pol.** It may be sardine-can small and dark, but that doesn't stop this popular tapas bar from being packed most nights. This is one of the best tapas spots in town, with a welcoming vibe, a dozen reasonably priced Spanish wines by the glass, and charm to spare. One of the most original tapas has become a signature here: bittersweet chocolate smeared on a baguette disc and topped with salty Spanish chorizo. *Patatas bravas* (rough-cut potatoes served with spicy aioli) are so addictive, you won't want to share them. The pork loin, piquillo pepper, and mild tetilla cheese sandwich is scrumptious, and so is the Galician octopus terrine. Tia Pol also makes for a great spot to stop and snack midway through a High Line jaunt. Ⓢ *Average main: $13* ✉ *205 10th Ave., between 22nd and 23rd Sts., Chelsea* ☎ *212/675–8805* ⊕ *www.tiapol.com* ⌕ *Reservations essential* ☾ *No lunch Mon.* Ⓜ *C, E to 23rd St.* ✥ *3:A2.*

$$
SOUTHERN

✕ **Tipsy Parson.** If New York's Chelsea neighborhood were magically transported to the American South, it might taste something like the Tipsy Parson, a hip southern-accented eatery with a menu of artery-hardening delights. Named for a boozy southern dessert, the TP and its menu are all about comfort in the belly and soul: fried pickles, home-made peanut butter with crackers, bourbon-laced chicken liver mousse, and seafood pot pie are designed to make you leave full and happy. The restaurant's close proximity to the High Line means you can walk it all off afterward. Ⓢ *Average main: $24* ✉ *156 9th Ave., between 19th and 20th Sts., Chelsea* ☎ *212/620–4545* ⊕ *www.tipsyparson.com* Ⓜ *C, E to 8th Ave.* ✥ *3:B3.*

$$
SWISS

✕ **Trestle on Tenth.** Cozy and warm with an inviting exposed brick interior, this Swiss brasserie is a true west Chelsea neighborhood spot. Locals and gallery hoppers quaff foamy beers or glasses of wine from the reasonable list while awaiting hearty Alpine-inspired dishes. Crispy duck necks, calf's liver with potato *rösti* and butter lettuce with bacon are fan favorites here. It's not art—for that hit up one of the many galleries in the neighborhood—but it will make you yearn for Alpine

16

landscapes. The location is convenient to the High Line. $ *Average main: $20* ✉ *242 10th Ave., at 24th St., Chelsea* ☏ *212/645–5659* ⊕ *www.trestleontenth.com* Ⓜ *C, E to 23rd St.* ✛ *3:A2.*

$$ ✕**Txikito.** After being wined and dined at this popular Chelsea Spanish
SPANISH restaurant, you'd never guess that chef Alexandra Raij is from the very un-Spanish-like Minneapolis. Her husband and business partner is, though, and the duo put on an impressive show. The theme is *cucina Vasca,* or Basque cuisine, one of the most exciting regions in Iberia for eating. Raij captures the moment by serving standouts like juicy lamb meatballs in a minty broth, crispy beef tongue, and an addictive crabmeat gratin. The wine list at Txikito (pronounced Chi-kee-toe) is loaded with great bottles of Rioja and tempranillo, many of which are from Basque winemakers. $ *Average main: $15* ✉ *240 9th Ave., at 25th St., Chelsea* ☏ *212/242–4730* ⊕ *www.txikitonyc.com* Ⓜ *C, E to 23rd St.* ✛ *3:B2.*

MEATPACKING DISTRICT

Europeans, models, actors, and the people who love them stroll the sidewalks like a catwalk, going from one hot restaurant to the next in this cobblestone-street-laden neighborhood, which has become almost too sceney for its own good. There's plenty of great eating here—you just might have to wait a while (or impersonate a celebrity) to get a table.

$$$$ ✕**Del Posto.** Much more formal than Babbo, Del Posto is Mario Batali's
ITALIAN grown-up venue (in partnership with Lidia and Joe Bastianich), and the dining room—with its sweeping staircase, formal decor, and live tinkling from a baby grand—has the feel of an opulent hotel lobby. This is one of the most consistently dazzling special-occasion spots in the city and the food is stellar. There are a variety of set menus to choose from ($126 for four courses, $179 for eight courses; there are à la carte options for parties of four and under): pitch-perfect risotto is made fresh to order for two people or more; meat dishes like roasted veal chops are standout, and pastas are ethereal—all with Old World tableside service. For a smaller taste of the experience, come for a cocktail and sample the bargain bar menu. $ *Average main: $60* ✉ *85 10th Ave., between 15th and 16th Sts., Meatpacking District* ☏ *212/497–8090* ⊕ *www.delposto. com* Ⓜ *A, C, E to 14th St.; L to 8th Ave.* ✛ *3:A4.*

$$$ ✕**Scarpetta.** Chef Scott Conant left L'Impero and Alto to open Scar-
ITALIAN petta, a critical darling since day one, adjacent to the glitz of the Meatpacking District. Walk past the bar into the polished dining room, where orange belts loop around mirrors and a retractable roof ushers in natural light. For a rousing start, try the braised octopus paired with chickpeas and a tangy paprika viniagrette before enjoying one of the house-made pastas, like the al dente tagliatelle laced with strands of tender lamb ragout or his signature spaghetti with tomato sauce. Save room for dessert: the Amadei chcocolate cake with burnt-caramel gelato brings "à la mode" to a whole new level. $ *Average main: $29* ✉ *355 W. 14th St., at 9th Ave., Meatpacking District* ☏ *212/691–0555* ⊕ *www.scarpettanyc.com* ☾ *No lunch* Ⓜ *A, C, E to 14th St.; L to 8th Ave.* ✛ *3:B4.*

$$ ✕ **Spice Market.** Set in a cavernous space amid embroidered curtains and
ASIAN   artifacts from Burma, India, and Malaysia, chef Jean-Georges Vongeri-
chten's playful take on Southeast Asian street food will keep you asking
the waiters for information: what exactly was in that? Sometimes the
playfulness works, sometimes it doesn't, but don't miss the steamed lob-
ster with garlic, ginger, and dried chili, or the squid salad with papaya
and cashews. This may not be the hottest new restaurant on the block
anymore but it's still a fun Meatpacking venue with food that doesn't
disappoint. ⑤ *Average main: $22* ✉ *403 W. 13th St., at 9th Ave., Meat-
packing District* ☎ *212/675–2322* ⊕ *www.spicemarketnewyork.com*
🍴 *Reservations essential* Ⓜ *A, C, E to 14th St.; L to 8th Ave.* ✛ *3:B4.*

$$$ ✕ **The Standard Grill.** Hotelier Andre Balasz created a scene for celebs,
AMERICAN fashion-industry insiders, and the common folk, too, who all cluster at
this buzzy restaurant inside the Standard Hotel. In warm weather the
spacious outdoor seating area is perfect for sampling creative cocktails;
there's an indoor bar, too, and two dining rooms—a casual one in front
and a larger room in back, with a floor whimsically made up of thousands of glittering pennies. The menu is comfort-luxe, with dishes like
roast chicken for two in a cast-iron skillet and delicious moist trout
with a currant-and-pine nut relish. For dessert, there's a nearly obscene
chocolate mousse that comes with silicone spatulas in lieu of spoons.
A late-night menu is offered until 4 am. ⑤ *Average main: $30* ✉ *848
Washington St., between Little W. 12th and 13th Sts., Meatpacking
District* ☎ *212/645–4100* ⊕ *www.thestandardgrill.com* Ⓜ *A, C, E to
14th St.; L to 8th Ave.* ✛ *3:B4.*

16

UNION SQUARE WITH THE FLATIRON
DISTRICT AND GRAMERCY

FLATIRON DISTRICT

The popular Union Square Farmer's Market has done wonders for
the dining landscape in the area. Chefs, wanting to be close to the
green bounty, have opened up restaurants nearby, particularly in the
Flatiron District.

$$$ ✕ **ABC Kitchen.** Much more than a shopping break, Jean Georges Vong-
AMERICAN erichten's popular restaurant, inside posh housewares emporium ABC
Carpet and Home, is more like a love letter to greenmarket cuisine.
Underneath the exposed concrete beams, a chic crowd devours fresh,
flavorful appetizers like the roasted carrot salad with avocado, crème
frâiche, and toasted pumpkin seeds or pretzel-dusted calamari. Win-
ning entrées include roast suckling pig with smoked bacon marmalade
and sea bass with chilies and herbs. The restaurant is committed to all
the right causes—environmentalism, sustainability, supporting local
farmers—all of which are announced in a near manifesto-length list
on the back of the menu; thankfully, ABC Kitchen pulls it off without
seeming patronizing or preachy. ⑤ *Average main: $28* ✉ *35 E. 18th St.,
between Broadway and Park Ave. S, Flatiron District* ☎ *212/475–5829*
⊕ *www.abckitchennyc.com* 🍴 *Reservations essential* Ⓜ *L, N, R, Q, 4,
5, 6 to 14th St./Union Square* ✛ *3:F3.*

$$$
MEDITERRANEAN
Fodor's Choice
★

✕**Aldea.** Bouley alumnus George Mendes's popular restaurant relies on his Portuguese heritage as inspiration and rises to new heights. Although there are no bad seats in this sleek bilevel space decorated with touches of wood, glass, and blue accents, watching Mendes work in his spotless tiled kitchen from one of the seats at the chef's counter in the back is undeniably exciting. *Petiscos* (small bites) like cubes of crisp pork belly with apple cider reveal sophisticated cooking techniques and flavors. A delicate matsutake mushroom broth floated with a slow-poached egg is edged with a subtle brace of pine while sea-salted cod is subtle with a deep flavor strata that will leave your palate satisfied long after the meal is over. ⑤ *Average main: $33* ✉ *31 W. 17th St., between 5th and 6th Aves., Flatiron District* ☎ *212/675–7223* ⊕ *www.aldearestaurant.com* ⌂ *Reservations essential* ⊘ *Closed Sun. No lunch Sat.* Ⓜ *L, N, R, Q, 4, 5, 6 to 14th St./Union Sq.; F, M to 14th St. and 6th Ave.* ✛ *3:E3.*

$$
SPANISH

✕**Boqueria.** Perenially packed, this convivial tapas spot has leather banquettes lining the main room but if you want to make friends, opt for the communal table running down the center of the dining room—if you can get a seat. There are a few seats at the bar, too. Fried quail eggs and chorizo on roasted bread are even better than they sound, and the mushroom and ham croquettes are a mainstay. Traditional churros come with a thick hot chocolate for dipping. The original spot in the Flatiron District was so popular it spawned an offshoot in SoHo, at 171 Spring Street. ⑤ *Average main: $19* ✉ *53 W. 19th St., between 5th and 6th Aves., Flatiron District* ☎ *212/255–4160* ⊕ *www.boquerianyc.com* ⌂ *Reservations not accepted* Ⓜ *6, F, R, M to 23rd St.* ✛ *3:E3.*

$$$
BRITISH
Fodor's Choice
★

✕**The Breslin Bar and Dining Room.** A sceney meatopia inside the ever-trendy Ace Hotel, the Breslin is not for the Lipitor crowd. English chef April Bloomfield, who also runs the John Dory right next door and the excellent Spotted Pig in the West Village, hardens arteries with peanuts fried in pork fat, whipped lardo on pizza bianca, blood sausage accompanied by a fried duck egg, and a delicious feta-topped lamb burger. The dimly lighted, wood-bedecked interior is like a culinary womb, inspiring thoughts of planting yourself there all day or night nursing pints of cask-conditioned ale or scotch-based cocktails. And you wouldn't be the first (or last) to have actually done it. ⑤ *Average main: $30* ✉ *20 W. 29th St., at Broadway, Flatiron District* ☎ *212/679–1939* Ⓜ *N, R to 28th St.* ✛ *3:E1.*

$
AMERICAN
FAMILY
Fodor's Choice
★

✕**The City Bakery.** This self-service bakery-restaurant has the urban aesthetic to match its name. Chef-owner Maury Rubin's baked goods—giant cookies; addictively flaky, salty-sweet pretzel croissants; elegant caramel tarts—are unfailingly rich and outstandingly delicious, but another major draw is the salad bar. It may seem overpriced, but the large selection of impeccably fresh food, including whole sides of baked salmon, roasted vegetables, soups, and several Asian-accented dishes, delivers bang for the buck. Much of the produce comes from the nearby farmers' market. In winter the bakery hosts a hot-chocolate festival; in summer it's lemonade time. ⑤ *Average main: $12* ✉ *3 W. 18th St., between 5th and 6th Aves., Flatiron*

District ☎ *212/366–1414* ⊕ *www.thecitybakery.com* ⌔ *Reservations not accepted* ☺ *No dinner* Ⓜ *L, N, Q, R, 4, 5, 6 to 14th St./Union Sq.; F, M to 14th St.* ✛ *3:E3.*

$$$$ ✕ **Craft.** A meal here is like a luscious choose-your-own-adventure
MODERN game since every delectable dish comes à la carte. Craft is *Top Chef*
AMERICAN head judge Tom Colicchio's flagship in a miniempire of excellent restaurants around the country, including the upscale Craftbar and Craftsteak brands, as well as grab-and-go sandwich bars called 'wich-craft. Just about everything here is exceptionally prepared with little fuss, from simple yet intriguing starters (like harissa-spiked octopus) and sides (including the justly famous variety of roasted mushrooms, including oysters, trumpets, chanterelles, and hen-of-the-woods) to desserts (warm chocolate tart with buttermilk ice cream, cinnamon custard, and cashews). The serene dining room of burnished dark wood and dangling radiant bulbs is more welcoming than it sounds. ⑤ *Average main: $40* ✉ *43 E. 19th St., between Broadway and Park Ave. S, Flatiron District* ☎ *212/780–0880* ⊕ *www.craftrestaurant.com* ⌔ *Reservations essential* ☺ *No lunch* Ⓜ *L, N, Q, R, 4, 5, 6 to 14th St./Union Sq.* ✛ *3:F3.*

$$ ✕ **Craftbar.** The casual sibling to Tom Colicchio's Craft is a bargain in
MODERN comparison, but still not cheap, though the food continues to garner
AMERICAN raves and the service is consistently excellent. The menu features asser-tive seasonal cooking similar to what you can find at the upscale flagship just around the corner. The small-plates category on the menu elevates tiny nibbles like sausage-stuffed fried sage leaves or addictive fluffy salt-cod croquettes to temptations that make you forget the main course entirely. The rest of the menu is eclectic enough to satisfy. ⑤ *Average main: $25* ✉ *900 Broadway, between 19th and 20th Sts., Flatiron District* ☎ *212/461–4300* ⊕ *www.craftbarnyc.com* ⌔ *Reservations essential* Ⓜ *L, N, Q, R, 4, 5, 6 to 14th St./Union Sq.* ✛ *3:F3.*

$$$ ✕ **Eataly.** The cavernous Eataly, from Mario Batali & Co., is a temple
ITALIAN of all things Italian. Ignore the overpriced produce market by the front entrance and make a beeline for La Piazza for sandwiches made with meticulously sourced ingredients (you can eat at the standup tables nearby). There's also a full-service pizza and pasta restaurant, a raw bar and fish eatery, and a wine bar for quaffing wines by the glass and beers on tap. Gourmet Italian chocolates, coffees, gelati, and pastries are all delicious to take away, too, though none of this is cheap. Upstairs, the covered, roof-top birrreria is open in all weather and serves hearty Austrian and German food as well as Italian specialties, and excellent beer, of course. ⑤ *Average main: $25* ✉ *200 5th Ave., at 23rd St., Flat-iron District* ☎ *646/398–5100* ⊕ *www.eatalyny.com* ⌔ *Reservations not accepted* ✛ *3:E2.*

$$$$ ✕ **Eleven Madison Park.** Luxury, precision, and creativity are the driving
MODERN forces at this internationally renowned restaurant overlooking Madison
AMERICAN Park. Swiss-born chef Daniel Humm oversees the kitchen, concocting
Fodor's Choice unexpected dishes that change often. It's a tasting-menu-only format,
★ and dishes are kept miminalist, giving Humm and company maximum latitude to work their magic on the plate. Not that they're resting on their laurels and accolades; the restaurant seems to reinvent itself when

16

you least expect it, its most recent incarnation a focus on elevated versions of classic New York fare. Think cognac-doused, truffle-sprinkled foie gras and Sichuan peppercorn–encrusted duck. Reservations should be made two months in advance. ⑤ *Average main: $225* ✉ *11 Madison Ave., at 24th St., Flatiron District* ☎ *212/889–0905* ⊕ *www. elevenmadisonpark.com* ⌲ *Reservations essential* ⊗ *No lunch Sun.– Wed.* Ⓜ *N, R, 6 to 23rd St.* ✛ *3:F2.*

$$
SEAFOOD

✗ **The John Dory.** Chef April Bloomfield and former rock band manager-turned-restaurateur Ken Friedman can do no wrong. Their third restaurant—after the gastropub-y Spotted Pig and the Breslin—turns its attention to the sea. Fish tanks with brightly colored reefs and floor-to-ceiling windows create an eye-pleasing venue for the seafood feast that awaits those who snagged tables at this restaurant off the lobby of the hip Ace Hotel. The menu is dominated by small plates—chorizo-stuffed squid, an excellent lobster roll—but focuses on the *crudo* (raw) dishes. The happy-hour special of a half-dozen oysters or clams and a choice of sparkling wine or a pint of ale for $18 is the perfect start to an evening. ⑤ *Average main: $20* ✉ *1196 Broadway, at 29th St., Flatiron District* ☎ *212/792–9000* ⊕ *www.thejohndory.com* ⌲ *Reservations not accepted* Ⓜ *N, R to 28th St.* ✛ *3:E1.*

$$$
MODERN
AMERICAN
Fodor'sChoice
★

✗ **NoMad.** Named for the hotel, which itself is named for the up-and-coming neighborhood, north of Madison Square Park, the NoMad is brought to you by Daniel Humm and Will Guidara, the masterminds behind much-lauded Eleven Madison Park. The atmosphere is a blend of lively and sophisticated—plush velvet chairs and drapes for the hip young crowd that frequents the place. The food is similarly vibrant yet simple: seared scallops are paired with pumpkin, juicy suckling pig goes very nicely with pear confit and mustard. The poached egg and quinoa dish unexpectedly transforms into a stew once the yokes are broken. The restaurant's pièce de résistance is the whole roasted chicken for two, which looks basic until the foie gras and black truffles are uncovered. Have a nightcap in the dimly lit and atmospheric Library Bar, which has floor-to-ceiling bookshelves and comfy chairs. ⑤ *Average main: $34* ✉ *1170 Broadway, at 28th St., Flatiron District* ☎ *347/472–5660* ⊕ *www.thenomadhotel.com* ⌲ *Reservations essential* Ⓜ *N, R to 28th St.* ✛ *3:E2.*

$$$
ITALIAN

✗ **SD26.** The charming father-daughter restaurant team of Tony and Marisa May closed uptown's San Domenico to open this more casual, yet still impressive, Italian spot. The cavernous main dining room, decorated with a constellation of pinpoint lights and ringed with more intimate tables and banquettes, speaks to a fresher, more modern approach than its predecessor. The food—pappardelle with wild boar ragu, smoked lobster with porcini mushrooms and orange segments—is a refreshing mix of classic and forward-thinking. Expect a personal greeting from either father or daughter before your meal comes to an end. ⑤ *Average main: $26* ✉ *19 E. 26th St., between 5th and Madison Aves., Flatiron District* ☎ *212/265–5959* ⊕ *www. sd26ny.com* ⌲ *Reservations essential* ⊗ *No lunch weekends* Ⓜ *R to 23rd St. and 5th Ave.* ✛ *3:F2.*

$ ✕ **Shake Shack.** Although there are other locations of Danny Meyer's
AMERICAN patties 'n shakes joint around town (including Brooklyn), this is where
Fodor's Choice it all began. Here in Madison Square Park there's no indoor seating—
★ just snaking outdoor lines. ■TIP➔ **Check the "Shack Cam" from their
Web site to gauge your wait.** Fresh Angus beef burgers are ground daily,
and a single will run you from $4.60 to $8.80, depending on what you
want on it. For a burger on the go, they're decidedly tasty. For a few
more bucks you can order a double, a stacks, or a vegetarian 'Shroom
Burger—a super-rich melty Muenster-and-cheddar-cheese-stuffed, fried
portobello, topped with lettuce, tomato, and Shack sauce. The menu
also offers beef and bird (chicken) hot dogs, french fries, a variety of
delicious frozen custard desserts, and—of course—shakes! ⑤ *Average
main: $6 ⊠ Madison Square Park near Madison Ave. and 23rd St.,
Flatiron District* ☎ *212/889–6600* ⊕ *www.shakeshack.com* Ⓜ *N, R, 6
to 23rd St.* ✛ *3:F2.*

GRAMERCY

This leafy, high-rent neighborhood, which has an old-world, old-
money feel, is home to a few gem restaurants, tucked away down
the long blocks of brownstones. Gramercy is a great place for a stroll
before dinner.

$$$$ ✕ **BLT Prime.** A masculine, vivacious space is the showcase for bold,
STEAKHOUSE appealing Franco-American cuisine. Menu specials are scrawled on a
blackboard. Everything is served à la carte, and prices are high, but
so is the quality of every dish. Although there are poultry, veal, and
lamb dishes on the menu—from lemon-rosemary chicken to a lamb
T-bone—steaks are the main event. The dry-aged USDA Prime steaks—
pulled from a 30-foot-wide dry-aging room—are broiled at 1,700
degrees, spread lightly with herb butter and offered with a choice of
sauce (the béarnaise is perfection). ⑤ *Average main: $40 ⊠ 111 E. 22nd
St., between Lexington and Park Aves., Gramercy* ☎ *212/995–8500*
⊕ *www.bltprime.com* ⌔ *Reservations essential* ◎ *No lunch* Ⓜ *6, R to
23rd St.* ✛ *3:F2.*

$$ ✕ **Casa Mono.** Andy Nusser put in his time cooking Italian under Mario
SPANISH Batali at Babbo before an obsession with Spain landed him his own
acclaimed Iberian niche. The perennially cramped and crowded Casa
Mono sends patrons to Bar Jamón, the annex wine-and-ham bar next
door, where you can pick at plates of *jamón serrano* while awaiting the
main feature. Our favorites seats are at the Casa Mono counter over-
looking the chef's open kitchen. Though most menu items are delectably
shareable, of particular note are all things seared *à la plancha,* including
blistered peppers and garlic-kissed mushrooms. Like his mentor, Nusser
has a weakness for the neglected cuts of meat so check your food fears
at the door. ⑤ *Average main: $20 ⊠ 52 Irving Pl., at 17th St., Gramercy*
☎ *212/253–2773* ⊕ *www.casamononyc.com* Ⓜ *4, 5, 6, L, N, Q, R to
Union Sq.* ✛ *3:G3.*

$$$$ ✕ **Gramercy Tavern.** Danny Meyer's intensely popular restaurant tops
AMERICAN many a New Yorker's list of favorite dining spots. In front, the first-
come, first-served tavern has a lighter menu—including a value-packed
three-course prix fixe—along with great craft beers and cocktails
scrawled on a board at the bar. The more formal dining room has

16

an American prix-fixe menu, where choices include seasonal dishes such as marinated sea scallops with pickled peppers and fresh grapes, and rack of lamb with sunchokes, hazelnuts, and exotic mushrooms. Meyer's restaurants—he owns several well-regarded eateries in the city—are renowned for their food and hospitality, and Gramercy Tavern sets the standard. ⑤ *Average main: $35* ⊠ *42 E. 20th St., between Broadway and Park Ave. S, Gramercy* ☎ *212/477–0777* ⊕ *www.gramercytavern.com* ⚑ *Reservations essential* ⊗ *No lunch weekends* Ⓜ *6, R to 23rd St.* ✛ *3:F3.*

$$$ ✕ **Maialino.** Named for its signature dish—suckling pig—the perpetu-
ROMAN ally packed restaurant in the Gramercy Park Hotel is what it might look like if Manhattan and Rome collided: fashionable people eating in an Eternal City ambience. And if you haven't been to the Italian capital in a while, there's plenty to reintroduce your taste buds to *la dolce vita*: excellent fried artichokes, spaghetti alla carbonara (made with *guanciale,* or pig cheek, just like in Rome), and sausage-studded pasta dish *lumaconi alla Norcia*. It's enough to make a toast to the good life—that is, if your dining companions can hear you over the chatter of the fashion models and bankers at surrounding tables. ⑤ *Average main: $26* ⊠ *2 Lexington Ave., at 21st St., Gramercy* ☎ *212/777–2410* ⊕ *www.maialinonyc.com* ⚑ *Reservations essential* Ⓜ *6 to 23rd St.* ✛ *3:G3.*

UNION SQUARE

Once the main spot in New York to go for protests, Union Square is now the stage for another type of communal experience: breaking bread. You'll find no shortage of appealing options at whatever price range (including picnic provisions from the wonderful greenmarket, open Monday, Wednesday, Friday, and Saturday).

$$$$ ✕ **Gotham Bar & Grill.** A culinary landmark, Gotham Bar & Grill is
AMERICAN every bit as thrilling as it was when it opened in 1984. Celebrated chef
Fodor'sChoice Alfred Portale, who made the blueprint for "architectural food"—that
★ is, towers of stacked ingredients—builds on a foundation of simple, clean flavors. People come for Portale's transcendent preparations: no rack of lamb is more tender, no seafood salad sweeter. The stellar 20,000-bottle cellar provides the perfect accompaniments—at a price. The three-course $34 greenmarket-driven prix-fixe lunch from noon to 2:30 weekdays is a steal, even if it's not as sophisticated as dinner. Take a stroll through the Union Square greenmarket before, or after, lunch to see the chef's inspirations. Desserts are also memorable. ⑤ *Average main: $41* ⊠ *12 E. 12th St., between 5th Ave. and University Pl., Union Square* ☎ *212/620–4020* ⊕ *www.gothambarandgrill.com* ⊗ *No lunch weekends* Ⓜ *L, N, Q, R, 4, 5, 6 to 14th St./Union Sq.* ✛ *3:E4.*

$ ✕ **Republic.** When Republic first opened, it was one of very few places
ASIAN to get an Asian-style noodle bowl with a stylish edge. Many have followed in its footsteps—and some are better—but for window shoppers, greenmarketers, and anyone else in the Union Square area, this is a fun stop for a meal. The look is a cross between a downtown art gallery and a Japanese school cafeteria, and the young waitstaff dressed in black T-shirts and jeans hold remote-control ordering devices to accelerate the already speedy service. Sit at the long, bluestone bar or at the picnic-style

Get an idea of what produce is in season at the Union Square greenmarket, then look for it on menus around town.

tables and order appetizers such as smoky grilled eggplant and luscious fried wontons. Spicy coconut chicken soup and Vietnamese-style barbecued pork are menu standouts. ⑤ *Average main: $14* ✉ *37 Union Sq. W, between 16th and 17th Sts., Union Square* ☎ *212/627–7172* ⊕ *www.thinknoodles.com* ⌕ *Reservations not accepted* Ⓜ *L, N, Q, R, 4, 5, 6 to 14th St./Union Sq.* ✛ *3:F4.*

$$$
MODERN
MEXICAN
✕ **Rosa Mexicano.** The idea that you can't find good south-of-the-border cuisine in the Big Apple is quickly fading, thanks in part to this Union Square restaurant (there are two other locations, at Lincoln Center and Midtown East). Although the spacious, colorfully lighted interior might tip you off that if authenticity is what you seek you should look elsewhere, if you're looking for high-quality, well-executed Mex-flavored fare, step right up, hombre. Start with an order of guac (made tableside) and dig in, moving on, perhaps, to the pork belly and scallop tacos, soul-comforting chicken tortilla pie, or the crispy pork shank. All of which taste better with a margarita. Happy hour (Sunday–Thursday only) at the bar is a great deal but it gets crowded. ⑤ *Average main: $28* ✉ *9 E. 18th St., between 5th Ave. and Union Sq., Flatiron* ☎ *212/533–3350* ⊕ *www.rosamexicano.com* Ⓜ *R, N, Q, 4, 5, 6, L to 14th St./Union Sq.* ✛ *3:F3.*

$$$
MODERN
AMERICAN
✕ **Tocqueville.** Hidden just steps from busy Union Square, Tocqueville is a refined dining oasis that's a secret even to many New York foodies. Enter through the austere reception area, past the heavy curtains and a six-seat bar, and you'll find the intimate dining area where chef-owner Marco Moreira's signature starter is the unctuous sea urchin angel-hair carbonara. Main courses are steeped in French tradition, but with international flavors like saffron-and-fennel-spiked grilled octopus,

and smoked duck breast paired with baby bok choy and Asian pear. The three-course $29 prix-fixe lunch is the ultimate deal. Jacket and tie are recommended. $ *Average main: $28* ⊠ *1 E. 15th St., between 5th Ave. and Union Sq. W, Union Square* ☏ *212/647–1515* ⊕ *www.tocquevillerestaurant.com* ⌂ *Reservations essential* ☽ *No lunch Sun.* Ⓜ *L, N, Q, R, 4, 5, 6 to 14th St./Union Sq.* ✛ *3:E4.*

$$$ ✗ **Union Square Cafe.** When he opened Union Square Cafe in 1985,
AMERICAN Danny Meyer changed the American restaurant landscape: his combination of upscale food and unpretentious but focused service sparked a revolution. This landmark spot still draws devotees with the crowd-pleasing menu, warm atmosphere, and, of course, the service. Wood paneling and white walls are hung with splashy modern paintings; in addition to the three dining areas, there's a long bar ideal for solo diners. The cuisine is American with a thick Italian accent—hearty pastas, seafood, and meat, as well as an excellent roast chicken—and the lunchtime burger is a perennial favorite. $ *Average main: $29* ⊠ *21 E. 16th St., between 5th Ave. and Union Sq. W, Union Square* ☏ *212/243–4020* ⊕ *www.unionsquarecafe.com* ⌂ *Reservations essential* Ⓜ *L, N, Q, R, 4, 5, 6 to 14th St./Union Sq.* ✛ *3:F4.*

MIDTOWN EAST WITH MURRAY HILL

MIDTOWN EAST

Midtown East's streets are relatively quiet at night and on weekends, but the restaurants are filled with expense-account diners celebrating their successes. Some of the most formal dining rooms and most expensive meals in town can be found here.

$$$$ ✗ **Aquavit and Aquavit Café.** Celebrity chef and co-owner Marcus Samu-
SCANDINAVIAN elsson may no longer be in the kitchen here, but you'd never know it from the impeccable cuisine and service at this fine-dining restaurant and upscale café, now in the hands of able executive chef Marcus Jenmark. The elegant atmosphere features warm woods and modern decor from a Scandinavian design team. Dishes can be ordered à la carte or you can opt for the $95 five-course dinner. Standout dishes include foie gras paired with liquorice, lamb and sweet potato, and, for dessert, smoked vanilla crème brûlée. Head to the sumptuous bar area to sample housemade aquavit. $ *Average main: $65* ⊠ *65 E. 55th St., between Madison and Park Aves., Midtown East* ☏ *212/307–7311* ⊕ *www.aquavit.org* ⌂ *Reservations essential* ☽ *Closed Sun., no lunch Sat.* Ⓜ *E, M to 5th Ave./53rd St.* ✛ *4:F2.*

$$$ ✗ **BLT Steak.** Chef Laurent Tourondel may no longer be involved with his
STEAKHOUSE namesake steak house, but this classy space, decked out in beige with resin-top black tables, still draws crowds. As soon as you're settled, puffy Gruyère popovers arrive still steaming. The no-muss, no-fuss menu is nonetheless large, and so are the portions of supple crab cakes with celery-infused mayonnaise and luscious, ruby tuna tartare with avocado ramped up with soy-lime dressing. A veal chop crusted with rosemary and Parmesan lends new depth to the meat. Sides and desserts, like a killer peanut butter–chocolate mousse with banana ice cream, are all superior. $ *Average main: $33* ⊠ *106 E. 57th St., between Lexington*

and Park Aves., Midtown East ☎ *212/752–7470* ⊕ *www.bltsteak. com* ⌲ *Reservations essential* ⊘ *No lunch weekends* Ⓜ *4, 5, 6, N, R to 59th St./Lexington Ave.* ✛ *4:F1.*

$$$$
AMERICAN
✕ **The Four Seasons.** The landmark Seagram Building houses one of America's most famous restaurants, truly an only-in-New-York experience. Owners Alex Von Bider and Julian Niccolini supervise the seating chart like hawks, placing power players in finance, entertainment, and New York society in prime positions for maximum visibility. The stark Grill Room, birthplace of the power lunch, has one of the best bars in New York (and the $28 two-course bar lunch is a steal). Illuminated trees and a gurgling Carrara marble pool characterize the more romantic Pool Room. The menu changes seasonally; there's a $75 prix-fixe pretheater dinner—a delicious indulgence. You can't go wrong with classic dishes like Dover sole, filet mignon, or crispy duck, but the restaurant moves with the times, so expect seasonal specials featuring luxe ingredients and preparations. Ⓢ *Average main: $60* ✉ *99 E. 52nd St., between Park and Lexington Aves., Midtown East* ☎ *212/754–9494* ⊕ *www.fourseasonsrestaurant. com* ⌲ *Reservations essential* 🎩 *Jacket required* ⊘ *Closed Sun. No lunch Sat.* Ⓜ *E, M to Lexington Ave./53rd St.; 6 to 51st St.* ✛ *4:F2.*

$$$
SEAFOOD
✕ **Grand Central Oyster Bar & Restaurant.** Nestled deep in the belly of Grand Central Station, the vast Oyster Bar has been a worthy seafood destination since 1913, and it's still a worthy destination, whether you're about to catch a train or craving seafood. Sit at the counter for the fried oyster po'boy or to slurp an assortment of bracingly fresh oysters before having a steaming bowl of clam chowder washed down with an ice-cold beer. This is also the place to experience the pleasure of fresh, unadorned seafood such as lobster with drawn butter or grilled herring in season—generally a better option than anything that sounds too complicated, like cream-smothered seafood pan roasts. Ⓢ *Average main: $30* ✉ *Grand Central Station dining concourse, E. 42nd St. at Vanderbilt Ave., Midtown East* ☎ *212/490–6650* ⊕ *www.oysterbarny. com* ⊘ *Closed Sun.* Ⓜ *4, 5, 6, 7, S to 42nd St./Grand Central* ✛ *4:F4.*

$$$$
JAPANESE
✕ **Kuruma Zushi.** Only a small sign in Japanese indicates the location of this extraordinary restaurant that serves only sushi and sashimi. Bypass the tables, sit at the sushi bar, and put yourself in the hands of Toshishiro Uezu, the chef-owner. Among the selections are hard-to-find fish that Uezu imports directly from Japan. The most attentive, pampering service staff in the city completes the wildly expensive experience. The showstopping chef's omakase, priced at whatever the market dictates and the type of fish being offered, could run as much as $250 but it's a multicourse feast you'll never forget. Ⓢ *Average main: $155* ✉ *7 E. 47th St., 2nd fl., Midtown East* ☎ *212/317–2802* ⊕ *www.kurumazushi. com* ⌲ *Reservations essential* ⊘ *Closed Sun.* Ⓜ *4, 5, 6, 7, S to 42nd St./ Grand Central* ✛ *4:E3.*

16

$$$$ ✕ **Le Cirque.** Impresario-owner Sirio Maccioni still presides over this
FRENCH dining room, filled nightly with a who's who of political, business, and
society circles—regulars who've table-hopped from Le Cirque's first
incarnation to its latest, in a glass-enclosed aerie on the ground floor of
the Bloomberg headquarters. The menu strikes a balance between the
creative and classic: Dover sole, fileted table-side, gives way to more
avant-garde preparations like foie gras ravioli. Desserts, too, have a
split personality, with the menu divided into the "classic" and "new."
The foot-tall napoleon that seems to arrive at every second table is an
old favorite, but newer creations like the praline tortellini with exotic
fruit also satisfy. Though jackets are still required in the dining room,
things are more relaxed in the casual wine lounge. ⑤ *Average main: $60*
✉ *151 E. 58th St., at Lexington Ave., Midtown East* ☎ *212/644–0202*
⊕ *www.lecirque.com* ⌫ *Reservations essential* ⊘ *Closed Sun. No lunch*
Sat. Ⓜ *4, 5, 6, N, R to Lexington Ave./59th St.* ✛ *4:F1.*

$$$ ✕ **Michael Jordan's The Steakhouse NYC.** Don't be dissuaded by the fact
STEAKHOUSE that this place is technically part of a chain: there's nowhere remotely
like it. The handsomely appointed space in Grand Central Terminal,
hung with gracious filigree chandeliers, overlooks one of the most
famous interiors in America. Start with the stack of soft, toasted bread
soldiers in a pool of hot Gorgonzola fondue. Pristine oysters make a
great prelude for a prime dry-aged ribeye or a 2½-pound lobster, grilled,
steamed, sautéed, or broiled. Sides, like creamy mac 'n' cheese and
a crispy rosemary hash-brown cake, are equally tempting. ⑤ *Average*
main: $30 ✉ *Grand Central Terminal west balcony, 23 Vanderbilt Ave.,*
between 43rd and 44th Sts., Midtown East ☎ *212/655–2300* ⊕ *www.*
michaeljordansnyc.com ⌫ *Reservations essential* ⊘ *No lunch Sun.* Ⓜ *4,*
5, 6, 7 to 42nd St./Grand Central ✛ *4:F4.*

$$ ✕ **Mint Restaurant & Lounge.** With a delightful dining room splashed with
INDIAN bright colors and flattering lighting, and executive chef and owner
Gary Sikka's brightly seasoned dishes, Mint has joined the ranks of
the best Indian restaurants in town. The large menu includes rarely
encountered specialties from Goa and Sikkim. Freshly grilled, moist
ground lamb kebabs deliver a slow burn to the palate. Chili heat punc-
tuates other spices in the lamb vindaloo, resulting in a well-rounded
array of savory flavors. Finish with carrot pudding with saffron and
coconut flakes. ⑤ *Average main: $20* ✉ *150 E. 50th St., Midtown*
East ☎ *516/307–8677* ⊕ *mintny.com* Ⓜ *6, E, M to 51st St./Lexington*
Ave. ✛ *4:G3.*

$$$ ✕ **The Palm Restaurant.** They may have added tablecloths, but it would
STEAKHOUSE take more than that to hide the brusque, no-nonsense nature of this
legendary steakhouse. The steak is always impeccable, and the Nova
Scotia lobsters are so big—3 pounds and up—that there may not be
room at the table for such classic side dishes as rich creamed spinach,
served family-style for two or more. The "half-and-half" side combi-
nation of cottage-fried potatoes and fried onions is particularly addic-
tive. There are other locations (the original, Palm 1, is on 2nd Avenue
at 58th Street, there's one in the mid 50s, one in TriBeca, and one at
JFK airport), but because of its perch near the Theater District and
Midtown businesses, this is the one with the most action. ⑤ *Average*

main: $30 ⊠ 837 2nd Ave., between 44th and 45th Sts., Midtown East
☎ *212/687–2953* ⊕ *www.thepalm.com* ⊘ *No lunch Sun.* Ⓜ *4, 5, 6, 7,*
S to Grand Central ✛ *4:G4; 1:B2.*

$$ ╳ **P. J. Clarke's.** This East Side institution has been dispensing burgers
AMERICAN and beer for more than a century. Despite renovations and several dif-
ferent owners over the years, the original P. J. Clarke's (there's also an
offshoot in Midtown West, on 63rd Street at Columbus) maintains the
beveled-glass and scuffed-wood look of an old-time saloon. Many of
the bartenders and patrons are as much a fixture as the decor. More
civilized at lunchtime, the bar area heaves with an after-work mob on
weekday evenings. Pull up a stool if you can for superlative bar food,
like clams casino and the signature burger smothered in creamy béar-
naise. Ⓢ *Average main: $18* ⊠ *915 3rd Ave., at 55th St., Midtown East*
☎ *212/317–1616* ⊕ *www.pjclarkes.com* Ⓜ *E to 53rd St.; 4, 5, 6 to 59th*
St.; N, Q, R to 59th St./Lexington Ave. ✛ *4:G2; 1:B3; 5:C5.*

$$$ ╳ **Shun Lee Palace.** If you want inexpensive Cantonese food without
CHINESE pretensions, head to Chinatown; but if you prefer to be pampered and
don't mind spending a lot of money, this is the place, which has been
elegantly serving classic Chinese fare for over four decades. Beijing pan-
fried dumplings make a good starter, and rack of lamb Szechuan-style,
grilled with scallions and garlic, is a popular entrée. The "Lion's Head,"
a slow-baked pork dish, is one of the most tender porky things you'll
eat. Beijing duck, served tableside with thin pancakes, is a signature
dish here—and for good reason. Ⓢ *Average main: $28* ⊠ *155 E. 55th*
St., between Lexington and 3rd Aves., Midtown East ☎ *212/371–8844*
⊕ *www.shunleepalace.net* ⌂ *Reservations essential* Ⓜ *N, R, 4, 5, 6 to*
59th St./Lexington Ave. ✛ *4:G2.*

$$$$ ╳ **Sparks Steakhouse.** Magnums of wines that cost more than most peo-
STEAKHOUSE ple earn in a week festoon the large dining rooms of this classic New
York steakhouse. Tasty fresh seafood is given more than fair play on
the menu, and the extra-thick lamb and veal chops are also noteworthy.
But Sparks is really about dry-aged steak. Classic sides of hash browns,
creamed spinach, sautéed mushrooms, and grilled onions are all you
need to complete the experience—plus maybe a martini. Ⓢ *Average*
main: $38 ⊠ *210 E. 46th St., between 2nd and 3rd Aves., Midtown*
East ☎ *212/687–4855* ⊕ *www.sparkssteakhouse.com* ⌂ *Reservations*
essential ⊘ *Closed Sun. No lunch Sat.* Ⓜ *4, 5, 6, 7, S to 42nd St./Grand*
Central ✛ *4:G4.*

$$$ ╳ **Sushi Yasuda.** Devotees mourned the return of namesake chef
JAPANESE Naomichi Yasuda to Japan, but things are in capable hands with his
handpicked successor, Misturu Tamura. Here, the sleek bamboo-lined
interior is as elegant as the food. Whether using fish flown in daily from
Japan or the creamiest sea urchin, the chef makes sushi so fresh and
delicate, it melts in your mouth. A number of special appetizers change
daily (crispy fried eel backbone is a surprising treat), and a fine selec-
tion of sake and beer complements the lovely food. Try to sit at the bar,
which was hand-crafted by Yasuda out of imported Japanese materials.
Ⓢ *Average main: $30* ⊠ *204 E. 43rd St., between 2nd and 3rd Aves.,*
Midtown East ☎ *212/972–1001* ⊕ *www.sushiyasuda.com* ⊘ *Closed*
Sun. No lunch Sat. Ⓜ *4, 5, 6, 7 to 42nd St./Grand Central* ✛ *4:G4.*

16

MURRAY HILL

This area has a residential feel with plenty of bistros perfect for a casual meal. Lexington Avenue's "Curry Hill" section between 27th and 29th streets is home to Indian spice shops, cafés, and restaurants.

$$
DELI

✕ **2nd Ave Deli.** It may no longer be on 2nd Avenue, but the most recent incarnation of this East Village institution—about a mile uptown, in midtown—is still delivering on its longtime traditional matzo-ball soup, overstuffed triple-decker sandwiches filled with house-cured pastrami, and other old-world specialties. Hot open sandwiches, like juicy beef brisket served with gravy and french fries, may be a heart attack on a plate, but hey, you only live once. Even better, you can now get your fill of kasha *varnishkes,* carrot tzimmes, and potato kugel until the wee hours of the night. There's also an outpost on the Upper East Side. ⑤ *Average main: $23* ✉ *162 E. 33rd St., between Lexington and 3rd Aves., Midtown East* ☎ *212/689–9000* ⊕ *www.2ndavedeli.com/* Ⓜ *6 to 33rd St./Lexington Ave.* ✛ *4:G6.*

$$$
BRASSERIE

✕ **Artisanal.** This spacious brasserie is a shrine to cheese, the passion of chef-owner Terrance Brennan. Though service can be spotty, gastronomes and business lunchers still flock here for the more than 150 cheeses—available for on-site sampling or retail sale—then stay to enjoy their selections with one of 160 wines by the glass. Hot *fromage*-imbued fare also is satisfying, with preparations like addictive gougère cheese puffs, onion soup gratiné, and several types of fondue. For curd-averse customers, steak frites or selections from the raw bar should satisfy. ⑤ *Average main: $27* ✉ *2 Park Ave., at 32nd St., Midtown East* ☎ *212/725–8585* ⊕ *www.artisanalbistro.com* ⚏ *Reservations essential* Ⓜ *6 to 33rd St.* ✛ *3:F1.*

$$
FRENCH
FAMILY

✕ **Les Halles.** This local hangout, owned by Philippe Lajaunie since 1990 and benefiting from the celebrity of former executive chef and writer/TV host Anthony Bourdain (although he has little to do with the restaurant these days), is boisterous and unpretentious—just like a true French brasserie. A good bet is steak frites—with fries regarded by some as the best in New York. Other prime choices include crispy duck-leg confit with frisée salad, blood sausage with caramelized apples, and steak tartare, prepared tableside. Another Les Halles is in Lower Manhattan at 15 John Street. ⑤ *Average main: $22* ✉ *411 Park Ave. S, between 28th and 29th Sts., Flatiron District* ☎ *212/679–4111* ⊕ *www.leshalles. net* Ⓜ *6 to 28th St.* ✛ *3:F1.*

MIDTOWN WEST

It's true that tourist traps abound on Broadway, but fortunately you needn't head far from Times Square to score a stellar meal. Just move away from the bright lights and unrelenting foot traffic that clogs the area. On calmer side streets and in adjoining Hell's Kitchen there are excellent dining options for budget travelers and expense-account diners alike. Some of the best steakhouses and Italian restaurants are here, and many eateries offer budget pretheater dinners and prix-fixe lunch menus to draw in new business.

$$$$ ✕ **'21' Club.** Tradition's the thing at this townhouse landmark, a for-
AMERICAN mer speakeasy that opened in 1929. Chef John Greeley tries to satisfy
everyone with standards like the famous '21' burger and Dover sole
with brown butter, and with more modern dishes, such as sautéed pork
belly with butternut squash puree, but the food is almost secondary to
the restaurant's storied past. Belongings donated by famous patrons—
for example, John McEnroe's tennis racket or Howard Hughes's
model plane—hang from the ceiling. Men, a jacket is required but
you can leave your tie at home. $ *Average main: $41* ✉ *21 W. 52nd
St., between 5th and 6th Aves., Midtown West* ☎ *212/582-7200*
⊕ *www.21club.com* 🏛 *Jacket required* ⊗ *Closed Sun. No lunch Sat.
and Mon.* Ⓜ *E, M to 53rd St./5th Ave.; B, D, F, M to 47th–50th Sts./
Rockefeller Center* ✛ *4:D2.*

$$$$ ✕ **Aureole.** An island of fine dining just a stone's throw from bustling
MODERN Times Square, Aureole is the second act of a New York classic from
AMERICAN Charlie Palmer and his executive chef, Marcus Gleadow-Ware. From
the street, a curved second-story corridor hosting the restaurant's storied wine collection beckons. A welcoming front barroom serves a more
casual, yet refined, menu with dishes like a cheddar-bacon burger with
pickled ramp mayonnaise. The dining room, with its abundance of
flowers, is the place to hobnob with expense-account diners and pretheater revelers. For dinner, starters like the pumpkin risotto with shrimp
is a treat, and the $118 "parallel tasting" offers the menu's greatest
hits. There is no à la carte option in the main dining room. $ *Average
main: $50* ✉ *135 W. 42nd St., between Broadway and 6th Ave., Mid-
town West* ☎ *212/319-1660* ⊕ *www.charliepalmer.com* ✍ *Reservations
essential* Ⓜ *B, D, F, M to 42nd St./Bryant Park; 1, 2, 3, 9, N, R, Q to
42nd St./Times Sq.* ✛ *4:D4.*

$$$ ✕ **Bar Americain.** Celeb chef Bobby Flay's largest Manhattan restaurant
SOUTHERN is the soaring Bar Americain. The 200-seat two-story space looks like
a dining room on a luxury liner. This is not food for the faint-of-heart:
Flay piles on the butter, cream, and endless varieties of bacon. South-
ern-inflected brasserie fare includes deviled eggs with smoked shrimp,
chicken with hatch-green-chili spoonbread and black-pepper vinegar
sauce, and duck confit flavored with a bourbon-based sauce and fig
chutney. Slightly naughtier are the éclairs piped with whiskey-infused
pastry cream and burnished with a burnt-sugar glaze. Brunch, featuring
dishes like biscuits and cream gravy with sausage and scrambled eggs,
is delicious. $ *Average main: $35* ✉ *152 W. 52nd St., between 6th and
7th Aves., Midtown West* ☎ *212/265-9700* ⊕ *www.baramericain.com*
✍ *Reservations essential* Ⓜ *B, D, E to 7th Ave.; 1, C, E to 50th St.; N,
R to 49th St.* ✛ *4:C2.*

$$ ✕ **Becco.** An ingenious concept makes Becco a prime Restaurant Row
ITALIAN choice for time-constrained theatergoers. There are two pricing sce-
narios: one includes an all-you-can-eat selection of antipasti and three
pastas served hot out of pans that waiters circulate around the dining
room; the other adds a generous entrée to the mix. The pasta selection
changes daily, but often includes gnocchi, fresh ravioli, and fettuc-
cine in a cream sauce. The entrées include braised veal shank, grilled
double-cut pork chop, and rack of lamb, among other selections.

16

⑤ *Average main: $23* ⊠ *355 W. 46th St., between 8th and 9th Aves., Midtown West* ☎ *212/397–7597* ⊕ *www.becco-nyc.com* Ⓜ *A, C, E to 42nd St.* ✛ *4:B3.*

$$$ ✕ **Benoit.** Who needs to go to Paris when the world's most famous
FRENCH French chef, Alain Ducasse, can come to you? Ducasse imported his famous Right Bank bistro to the Big Apple in 2008 and it's been a hit with Gallic-loving eaters ever since. The decor—cozy red velour banquettes and wall lamps illuminating each table—is plucked straight from the City of Light. So is the menu, which doesn't reinvent anything as much as it replicates. And that's okay, especially when the fennel-inflected *loup de mer* (sea bass) or the tender roasted veal loin are so well executed. It's not exactly cheap for simple bisto fare—then again, neither is a round-trip ticket to Paris. ⑤ *Average main: $27* ⊠ *60 W. 55th St., between 5th and 6th Aves., Midtown West* ☎ *646/943–7373* ⊕ *www.benoitny.com* Ⓜ *B, D, E to 7th Ave.; F to 57th St.* ✛ *4:D2.*

$$$ ✕ **Brasserie Ruhlmann.** In a plush 120-seat dining room with just enough
BRASSERIE Art Deco touches to harmonize with its Rockefeller Center setting, the sublime French bistro cookery is on display. The room has a refined air but the staff is so friendly that the place could never be stuffy. The raw bar, with its selection of pedigreed oysters, is a great way to begin, or opt for a blue crab salad over mâche with a honey-lime vinaigrette. If it's on the menu, order braised rabbit nestled in mustard cream on a bed of fresh pappardelle, sprinkled with pitted cherries. Desserts like Floating Island—delicately baked meringue floating on a pond of crème anglaise—are embellished with a flurry of spun sugar. ⑤ *Average main: $28* ⊠ *45 Rockefeller Plaza, 50th St. between 5th and 6th Aves., Midtown West* ☎ *212/974–2020* ⊕ *www.brasserieruhlmann.com* ⌂ *Reservations essential* ☉ *No dinner Sun.* Ⓜ *B, D, F, M to 47th–50th Sts./ Rockefeller Center* ✛ *4:D3.*

$ ✕ **Burger Joint.** What's a college burger bar, done up in particleboard
BURGER and rec-room decor straight out of a *Happy Days* episode, doing
Fodor's Choice hidden inside a five-star Midtown hotel? This tongue-in-cheek lunch
★ spot, hidden behind a heavy red velvet curtain in the Parker Meridien hotel, does such boisterous midweek business that lines often snake through the lobby (which means you're best off coming at noon or earlier). Stepping behind the curtain, you can find baseball cap–wearing, grease-spattered cooks dispensing paper-wrapped cheeseburgers and crisp, thin fries. Forget Kobe beef or foie gras—these burgers are straightforward, cheap, and delicious. ⑤ *Average main: $8* ⊠ *Parker Meridien,118 W. 57th St., between 6th and 7th Aves., Midtown West* ☎ *212/245–5000* ⊕ *www.parkermeridien.com* ▭ *No credit cards* Ⓜ *F, N, Q, R to 57th St.* ✛ *4:D1.*

$$ ✕ **Carmine's.** Savvy New Yorkers line up early for the affordable family-
ITALIAN style meals at this large, busy Midtown eatery. Family photos line
FAMILY the walls, and there's a convivial feeling amid all the Times Square hubbub. Don't be fooled: Carmine's may be huge, but it fills up with families carbo-loading for a day of sightseeing or a night of theater on Broadway. Hungry diners are rewarded with mountains of such popular, toothsome viands as fried calamari, linguine with white clam sauce, chicken parmigiana, and veal saltimbocca. ⑤ *Average*

main: $24 ✉ *200 W. 44th St., between Broadway and 8th Ave., Midtown West* ☎ *212/221–3800* ⊕ *www.carminesnyc.com* Ⓜ *A, C, E to 42nd St.–Port Authority; N, Q, R, S, 1, 2, 3, 7 to 42nd St./Times Sq.* ✛ *4:C4; 6:A5.*

$
KOREAN
Fodor'sChoice
★

✗ **Danji.** Diminutive and dark, Danji is no ordinary Korean restaurant. Helmed by talented chef Hooni Kim, this Hell's Kitchen spot is a standout among the rows of restaurants that attract theater-going tourists in the neighborhood. That's because Kim's take on Korean cuisine is inventive and inspired. The menu is split in two, and both sides contain a number of winning dishes. Start with the scallion-and-pepper pancake and the trio of kimchi from the "traditional" side, then set your taste buds singing with Korean chicken wings and unctuous pork belly sliders from the "modern" side of the menu. Then count your blessings that you're not eating a mediocre meal like the rest of the out-of-town visitors in the neighorhood. ⑤ *Average main: $17* ✉ *346 W. 52nd St., between 8th and 9th Aves., Midtown West* ☎ *212/586–2880* ⊕ *www. danjinyc.com* ⊘ *Closed Sun.* Ⓜ *C or E to 50th St.* ✛ *4:B2.*

$$$
FRENCH

✗ **db Bistro Moderne.** Daniel Boulud's "casual bistro" (it's neither, actually) consists of two elegantly appointed dining rooms. The menu features classic dishes like Nantucket Bay scallops or hanger steak exquisitely prepared. Ever the trendsetter, Boulud's $32 db hamburger stuffed with braised short ribs, foie gras, and black truffles, is the patty credited with kick-starting the whole gourmet burger trend. And, yes, it's worth every penny. Although it may not be the trendy destination it once was, it's still a treat and the service is friendly without being overbearing. ⑤ *Average main: $31* ✉ *55 W. 44th St., between 5th and 6th Aves., Midtown West* ☎ *212/391–2400* ⊕ *www.dbbistro.com* ⌂ *Reservations essential* Ⓜ *B, D, F, M to 42nd St./Bryant Park; 7 to 5th Ave./ Bryant Park* ✛ *4:D4.*

$$
AMERICAN
FAMILY

✗ **Ellen's Stardust Diner.** If you haven't had enough Broadway singing and dancing, you'll get a kick out of Ellen's, a retro, 1950s-style diner, complete with a singing waitstaff. The menu focuses on all-American classics like meat loaf and chicken potpie, and the waiters and waitresses serenading you on roller skates have the talent to prove this restaurant is right on Broadway. It's the kind of over-the-top family-style fun that you'd expect from the close-to-Times-Square location so don't expect a sophisticated—or quiet—dining experience. ⑤ *Average main: $20* ✉ *1650 Broadway, at 51st St., Midtown West* ☎ *212/956–5151* ⊕ *www. ellensstardustdiner.com* ✛ *4:C3.*

$$$
SEAFOOD

✗ **Esca.** The name is Italian for "bait," and this restaurant, courtesy of partners Mario Batali, Joe Bastianich, and longtime chef David Pasternack, lures diners in with delectable crudo—such as tilefish with orange and Sardinian oil or pink snapper with a sprinkle of crunchy red clay salt—and hooks them with such entrées as whole, salt-crusted branzino, sea bass for two, or bucatini with spicy baby octopus. The menu changes daily. Bastianich is in charge of the wine cellar, so you can expect an adventurous list of Italian bottles. ⑤ *Average main: $33* ✉ *402 W. 43rd St., at 9th Ave., Midtown West* ☎ *212/564–7272* ⊕ *www.esca-nyc.com* ⌂ *Reservations essential* ⊘ *No lunch Sun.* Ⓜ *A, C, E to 42nd St.* ✛ *4:A4.*

16

$ ✕ **Five Napkin Burger.** This perennially packed Hell's Kitchen burger place/
AMERICAN brasserie has been a magnet for burger lovers since day one. Bottles of
Maker's Mark line the sleek, alluringly lighted bar in the back, a collection
of antique butcher's scales hangs on a tile wall near the kitchen, and meat
hooks dangle from the ceiling between the light fixtures. Though there
are many menu distractions—deep-fried pickles, warm artichoke dip, to
name a few—the main attractions are the juicy burgers, like the original
10-ounce chuck with a tangle of onions, Gruyère cheese, and rosemary
aioli. There's a patty variety for everyone, including a ground lamb kofta
and an onion ring–topped ahi-tuna burger. For dessert, have an über-thick
black-and-white malted milkshake. ⑤ *Average main: $16* ☒ *630 9th Ave.,
at 45th St, Midtown West* ☎ *212/757-2277* ⊕ *www.5napkinburger.com*
Ⓜ *A, C, E to 42nd St./8th Ave.* ✛ *4:B4.*

$ ✕ **Gahm Mi Oak.** The deconstructed industrial design, inexpensive
KOREAN 24-hour menu, and late-night hours attract a young, stylish crowd—
there are even photos on the menu to help bleary-eyed revelers order.
Every item on the limited menu goes well with *soju*, a Korean spirit,
or beer. Korean-style fried mung-bean pancakes with scallions, onions,
carrots, and ground pork are addictive, and the kimchi is renowned.
Try the *sul long tang*, a milky ox-bone soup with thin slices of beef, rice,
and noodles that is reputed to be an effective hangover cure. ⑤ *Average
main: $14* ☒ *43 W. 32nd St., between 5th Ave. and Broadway, Midtown
West* ☎ *212/695-4113* ⊕ *www.gahmmioak.com* ⌲ *Reservations not
accepted* Ⓜ *B, D, F, N, Q, R, M to 34th St./Herald Sq.* ✛ *3:E1.*

$ ✕ **La Bonne Soupe.** Midtown office workers and in-the-know out-of-
FRENCH towners keep this French restaurant bustling for the ever-popular La
Bonne Soupe special—you get a bowl of their excellent soup with bread,
salad, a beverage (house wine, beer, soda, or coffee), and dessert for
$19.50. À la carte options include bistro classics like crêpes, omelets,
salads, quiches, sandwiches, and croque-madame or -monsieur. It's not
the hippest place in town but you'll leave feeling satisfied. There's often
a line at lunchtime but there are two floors of tables so you won't go
hungry for long. ⑤ *Average main: $16* ☒ *48 W. 55th St., between 5th
and 6th Aves., Midtown West* ☎ *212/586-7650* ⊕ *www.labonnesoupe.
com* Ⓜ *B, D, F, M to 47-50 Sts./Rockefeller Center* ✛ *4:E2.*

$$$$ ✕ **The Lambs Club.** Restaurateur Geoffrey Zakarian's opulent supper club
MODERN on the ground floor of the Chatwal Hotel has superb Art Deco detail-
AMERICAN ing, blood-red leather banquettes, and a roaring fireplace. Cocktails
are concocted by hipster mixologist Sasha Petraske, who eschews the
experimental in favor of classics like the sidecar and the martini, done
well. The food is typical Zakarian, meaning New American cuisine
with luxe touches in dishes like veal sweetbreads with peppered jus
and grilled treviso lettuce, or seared scallops with porcini mushrooms
and Indian-spiced sauce. The lunchtime menu is padded with appealing
choices, but the sleeper meal here is breakfast. Dishes like a house-made
biscuit with fried egg, bacon, and cheddar, or fluffy lemon-ricotta pancakes, may just fill you up for the rest of the day. ⑤ *Average main: $36*
☒ *132 W. 44th St., between 6th Ave. and Broadway, Midtown West*
☎ *212/997-5262* ⊕ *www.thelambsclub.com* Ⓜ *1, 2, 3 to 42nd St., B,
D, F, M to 47th–50th Sts./Rockefeller Center.* ✛ *4:D4.*

$$$$
FRENCH
Fodor's Choice
★

✕ **Le Bernardin.** Owner Maguy LeCoze presides over the teak-panel dining room at this trendsetting French seafood restaurant, and chef-partner Eric Ripert works magic with anything that swims—preferring at times not to cook it at all. Deceptively simple dishes such as poached lobster in rich coconut-ginger soup or crispy spiced black bass in a Peking duck bouillon are typical of his style. It's widely agreed that there's no beating Le Bernardin for thrilling cuisine, seafood or otherwise, coupled with some of the finest desserts in town and a wine list as deep as the Atlantic. It's prix fixe only, and there are nonfish options (pasta and meat) by request. ⑤ *Average main: $155* ⌧ *155 W. 51st St., between 6th and 7th Aves., Midtown West* ☎ *212/554–1515* ⊕ *www. le-bernardin.com* ⊡ *Jacket required* ⊘ *Closed Sun. No lunch Sat.* Ⓜ *1 to 50th St.; R to 49th St.; B, D, F, M to 47th–50th Sts./Rockefeller Center* ✛ *4:C2.*

$
BAKERY

✕ **Le Pain Quotidien.** This international Belgian chain brings its homeland ingredients with it, treating New Yorkers to crusty organic breads, jams, chocolate, and other specialty products. You can grab a snack to go or stay and eat breakfast, lunch, or dinner at communal or private tables with waiter service. Come for a steaming latte and croissant in the morning or a tartine (open-faced sandwich) at noon. There are more than 20 locations throughout Manhattan, including in Central Park. ⑤ *Average main: $13* ⌧ *1271 Ave. of the Americas, at 50th St., Midtown West* ☎ *646/462–4165* ⊕ *www.lepainquotidien.com* Ⓜ *B, D, F, V to 47–50th Sts./Rockefeller Center* ✛ *4:D3.*

$$
ITALIAN

✕ **Lugo Caffé.** The area around Madison Square Garden is a restaurant wasteland with the rare sparkling exception of Lugo Caffé, founded by an Italian menswear line. Locals rejoiced at the introduction of this spacious Italian "brasserie" offering comfort food with a *Dolce Vita* twist all day long. Stop by for an espresso and pastry in the morning. Later, a single menu presents lunch, aperitivo, and dinner options, which include grazing portions of salumi, cheeses, and vegetable dishes like eggplant caponata, Tuscan bean salad, and grilled zucchini with pine nuts. Fuller meals of Neapolitan-style pizzas, house-made pastas, and grilled meats and fish also are commendable. ⑤ *Average main: $24* ⌧ *1 Penn Plaza, 33rd St. and 8th Ave., Midtown West* ☎ *212/760–2700* ⊕ *www.lugocaffe.com* ⊘ *Only dinner weekends* Ⓜ *A, C, E to 34th St.; 1, 2, 3 to 34th St.* ✛ *4:C6.*

$$$
ASIAN

✕ **Má Pêche.** Starkly decorated and set in the basement of the Chambers Hotel, Má Pêche is just blocks from MoMA. And as the largest restaurant in David Chang's empire, you've got a better shot of nabbing a seat. The menus are a bit more refined (and expensive) than those at Momofuku Noodle Bar and Ssäm Bar, with elegantly composed plates that might include lamb shank accompanied by eggplant, raisins, and rice, or seared swordfish with black beans, braised celery, and crisped shallots. On the way out you can pick up sweets from the uptown offshoot of Momofuku Milk Bar, like the addictive, buttery Crack Pie or intriguingly flavored softserve. ⑤ *Average main: $26* ⌧ *15 West 56th St., between 5th and 6th Aves., Midtown West* ☎ *212/757–5878* ⊕ *www.momofuku.com/ma-peche* ⊘ *No lunch Sun.* ✛ *4:E1.*

16

$$
SEAFOOD
Fodor'sChoice
★

✕ **Marea.** Carefully sourced, meticulously prepared fish and seafood take center stage at this well-pedigreed restaurant. Large picture windows in the dining room offer expansive views of Central Park South, and silver-dipped shells on pedestals decorate the dining room. No expense is spared in importing the very best of the ocean's bounty, beginning with crudo—think scallops with orange, wild fennel, and arugula—that are becoming the restaurant's signature. You'd be remiss, though, if you skipped the pastas that made chef Michael White famous. They're served here in lusty iterations like rich fusilli with octopus and bone marrow and spaghetti with sea urchin. Whole fish like roasted turbot and salt-baked snapper are equally showstopping. Service is flawless. $ *Average main: $23* ✉ *240 Central Park S, between Broadway and 7th Ave., Midtown West* ☎ *212/582–5100* ⊕ *www.marea-nyc.com* ⌕ *Reservations essential* Ⓜ *A, B, C, D, 1 to Columbus Circle* ✛ *4:B1.*

$$
MEDITERRANEAN

✕ **Marseille.** With great food and a convenient location near several Broadway theaters, Marseille is perpetually packed. The Mediterranean creations are continually impressive, including the bouillabaisse, the signature dish of the region for which the restaurant is named—a mélange of mussels, shrimp, and white fish in a fragrant broth, topped with a garlicky crouton and served with rouille on the side. Also worth a bite is the charred octopus with fennel and tomatoes. Leave room for the spongy beignets with chocolate and raspberry dipping sauces. $ *Average main: $22* ✉ *630 9th Ave., at 44th St., Midtown West* ☎ *212/333–2323* ⊕ *www.marseillenyc.com* ⌕ *Reservations essential* Ⓜ *A, C, E to 42nd St./Port Authority Bus Terminal* ✛ *4:B4.*

$$$$
FRENCH

✕ **The Modern and Bar Room.** Both spots competing for the title of the country's best museum restaurant sit side by side on the ground floor of the New York MoMA. The Modern, run by restaurateur Danny Meyer, is two restaurants in one, and both offer the dazzling food of Alsatian chef Gabriel Kreuther. The formal dining room features a view of the museum's sculpture garden and an ambitious, pricey, prix-fixe menu with standouts like chorizo-crusted codfish with white coco-bean puree. The far more accessible and popular Bar Room lies just beyond a partition, and this is where you can find a dizzying collection of shareable plates, like the refreshing arctic char tartare and oysters with leeks and caviar. Two or three make a fine if extravagant afternoon snack—double that number and you have a full meal. $ *Average main: $45* ✉ *9 W. 53rd St., between 5th and 6th Aves., Midtown West* ☎ *212/333–1220* ⊕ *www.themodernnyc.com* ☾ *Closed Sun.* Ⓜ *E, M to 5th Ave./53rd St.* ✛ *4:D2.*

$$$
SEAFOOD

✕ **Oceana.** Entering Oceana is like walking into the dressy stateroom of a modern luxury ocean liner. Floor-to-ceiling windows look out both north and west, and the arrestingly designed raw bar backed with Mediterranean-hue ceramics offers stunningly fresh choices—you would expect gorgeous oysters at a restaurant called Oceana, and you get them. Chef Ben Pollinger has all the skill and confidence necessary to serve some of the most vivid and delicious seafood in town. A "contemporary appetizer" section features items like marinated cucumber with cucumber, apple, and toasted spices. Grilled whole fish like halibut, swordfish, and crispy wild striped bass are served with a perfect rotating roster of sauces like classic romesco and grilled pineapple salsa. Thai-style red snapper comes with tender silk squash, crisp jicama, and a kaffir-saffron broth. $ *Average main: $33* ⊠ *120 W. 49th St., at 6th Ave., Midtown West* ☎ *212/759–5941* ⊕ *www.oceanarestaurant. com* ⌕ *Reservations essential* ⊙ *Only dinner weekends* Ⓜ *E, M to 53rd St./5th Ave.* ✛ *4:D3.*

$$$
BRAZILIAN
Fodor'sChoice
★

✕ **Plataforma Churrascaria Rodizio.** This sprawling, boisterous shrine to meat, with its all-you-can-eat prix-fixe menu, is best experienced with a group of ravenous friends. A *caipirinha*, featuring cachaça sugarcane liquor, sugar, and lime, will kick things off nicely. Follow up with a trip to the fabulous salad bar, piled with vegetables, meats, and cheeses—but remember, there's about to be a parade of all manner of grilled meats and poultry, from pork ribs to chicken hearts, delivered to the table on long skewers. Everyone at the table gets a coaster-sized disc that's red on one side and green on the other: turn the green side up when you're ready for more; pace yourself so you can try all the different delicacies. It's definitely a fun evening, but make sure to come hungry. $ *Average main: $33* ⊠ *316 W. 49th St., between 8th and 9th Aves., Midtown West* ☎ *212/245–0505* ⊕ *www.plataformaonline.com* ⌕ *Reservations essential* Ⓜ *C, E to 50th St.* ✛ *4:B3.*

16

$$
ECLECTIC

✕ **Plaza Food Hall by Todd English.** At the Plaza Food Hall in the basement of the Plaza Hotel, celeb chef Todd English oversees a series of minirestaurants, each with its own counter with seating ideal for a quick snack or a full-fledged meal. Entry is a little confusing; though the place is made up of individual food concepts, you'll be seated by a hostess at any available counter. One you're settled, get up and survey your choices, then sit down and place one order from your waiter. There's a glistening raw bar, a burger joint, and a wood-burning pizza station where you can sample some of English's iconic pies, such as fig and prosciutto. It's one of the most varied and affordable daytime food options in an area of town that can still feel like a lunchtime wasteland. $ *Average main: $18* ⊠ *1 W. 59th St., at 5th Ave., Midtown East* ☎ *212/986–9260* ⊕ *www.theplazafoodhall.com* Ⓜ *N, Q, R to 5th Ave./59th St.* ✛ *4:E1.*

$$$
STEAKHOUSE

✕ **Quality Meats.** The handsome design at Quality Meats is inspired by classic New York City butcher shops in its use of warm wood, stainless steel, and white marble. Sit at the bar to peruse the extensive menu of wines and single-malt scotches, or sip a classic martini. Then retire to the dining room for memorable fare like the massive chunky crab cake, seared scallops, and sophisticated riffs on steakhouse classics like beef Wellington. The grilled bacon, peanut butter, and apple starter is a must for any first-timer. $ *Average main: $37* ⊠ *57 W. 58th St., near 6th Ave., Midtown East* ☎ *212/371–7777* ⊕ *www.qualitymeatsnyc.com* ⌕ *Reservations essential* ⊙ *No lunch weekends.* ✛ *4:D1.*

$$$
AUSTRIAN

✕ **Seäsonal Restaurant and Weinbar.** Partners and executive chefs Wolfgang Ban and Eduard Frauneder have brought something *neu* to Midtown: a swanky Austrian-German restaurant and Weinbar. With its sculptural ceiling lighting, elliptical bar, and contemporary Austrian and German art, Seäsonal feels more "downtown" than you'd expect from such central Midtown digs. The cuisine is sophisticated and contemporary, yet still steeped in regional traditions. Appetizers like the foie-gras terrine and the cheese ravioli with smoked chanterelle mushrooms delight with their contrasting lightness and intensity of flavor. Mains, such as the pumpkin seed–crusted black sea bass with butternut squash and black truffles, and the classic Wiener schnitzel, will definitely please your palate. Seäsonal's Weinbar features a distinctive selection of wines from emerging Austrian and German winemakers. ⑤ *Average main: $27* ⊠ *132 W. 58th St., between 6th and 7th Aves., Midtown West* ☎ *212/957–5550* ⊕ *www.seasonalnyc.com* Ⓜ *F to 57th St./6th Ave.* ✛ *4:D1.*

$$
ITALIAN

✕ **Sosa Borella.** This is one of the Theater District's top spots for reliable food at a reasonable cost. The bilevel, casual Argentinian-Italian eatery is an inviting and friendly space where diners choose from a wide range of options. The lunch menu features staples like warm sandwiches and entrée-size salads, whereas the dinner menu is slightly gussied up with meat, fish, and pasta dishes (the rich agnolotti with lamb Bolognese sauce, topped with a wedge of grilled pecorino cheese, is a must-try). The freshly baked bread served at the beginning of the meal with pesto dipping sauce is a nice touch as you wait for your meal. The service can be slow at times, so leave yourself plenty of time before the show. ⑤ *Average main: $25* ⊠ *832 8th Ave., between 50th and 51st Sts., Midtown West* ☎ *212/262–8282* ⊕ *www.sosaborella.com* Ⓜ *C, E, 1 to 50th St.* ✛ *4:B3.*

$$
MEXICAN

✕ **Toloache.** Make a quick detour off heavily trafficked Broadway into this pleasantly bustling Mexican cantina for one of the best dining options around Times Square. The bilevel eatery has a festive, celebratory vibe, with several seating options: bar, balcony, main dining room, and ceviche bar. Foodies flock here for three types of guacamole (traditional, fruited, and spicy), a trio of well-executed ceviches, and dishes like the Mexico City–style tacos with Negra Modelo–braised brisket, and quesadillas studded with black truffle and *huitlacoche* (a corn fungus). There's an extensive tequila selection—upward of 100 brands. Adventurous palates will be drawn to tacos featuring chili-studded dried grasshoppers, lobes of seared foie gras, and caramelized veal sweetbreads. There's another location in Greenwich Village. ⑤ *Average main: $19* ⊠ *251 W. 50th St., near 8th Ave., Midtown West* ☎ *212/581–1818* ⊕ *www.toloachenyc.com* Ⓜ *1, C, E to 50th St.; N, R to 49th St.* ✛ *4:B3.*

$$$$
STEAKHOUSE

✕ **Uncle Jack's Steakhouse.** Surpassing even its celebrated flagship restaurant in Bayside, Queens, Uncle Jack's soars directly into the pantheon of the best steakhouses in Manhattan. As in most great steakhouses, you can feel the testosterone throbbing all through the place. The space is vast and gorgeously appointed, and service is swift and focused. USDA Prime steaks are dry-aged for 21 days. Australian lobster tails are so enormous, they have to be served carved, yet the flesh is meltingly tender. Humongous pork chops, dripping with juice, are accompanied by chipotle sauerkraut. It's hard to go wrong at Jack's—just make sure you come with an empty stomach. ⑤ *Average main: $67* ⊠ *440 9th Ave., between 34th and 35th Sts., Midtown West* ☎ *212/244–0005* ⊕ *www. unclejacks.com* ⌕ *Reservations essential* ☾ *No lunch weekends* Ⓜ *A, C, E to 34th St./Penn Station.* ✛ *4:B6.*

UPPER EAST SIDE

Long viewed as an enclave of the privileged, the Upper East Side has plenty of elegant, pricey eateries that serve the society "ladies who lunch" and bankers looking forward to a steak and single-malt scotch at the end of the day. However, visitors to Museum Mile and 5th Avenue shopping areas need not be put off. Whether you're looking to celebrate a special occasion or just want to grab a quick bite, you'll find something here for almost any budget.

$$$$ ✕**Alloro.** Italian chef Salvatore Corea and his wife, Gina, a native New **ITALIAN** Yorker, are living their dream of opening an old-fashioned family-run restaurant on the Upper East Side. It's not Corea's first New York restaurant endeavor—he's opened three other successful venues in the city, but Alloro is his first venture with his wife, and judging by the friendly vibe and the delicious dishes coming out of the *cucina*, it's working swimmingly well. Chef Corea's creative take on traditional, regional Italian cuisines leads the way for delicious dishes, like creamy Parmesan risotto with Lambrusco-wine caramel. Both the sliced ribeye over corn puree and the filet of sole in pumpkin-Amaretto crust are fantastic. Gluten-free pasta selections are also available. ⑤ *Average main: $38* ✉ *307 E. 77th St., near 2nd Ave., Upper East Side* ☎ *212/535–2866* ⊕ *www.alloronyc.com* ◷ *Closed Sun.* Ⓜ *6 to 77th St.* ✛ *5:H2.*

$$$$ ✕**Café Boulud.** Manhattan's who's who in business, politics, and the art **FRENCH** world come to hobnob at Daniel Boulud's café-in-name-only, where the food and service are top-notch. The menu, overseen by Boulud protégé Gavin Kaysen, is divided into four parts: under La Tradition you can find classic French dishes such as roasted duck breast Montmorency with cherry chutney, green Swiss chard, and baby turnips; Le Potager tempts with lemon ricotta ravioli; La Saison follows the rhythms of the season; and Le Voyage reinterprets cuisines of the world. Start with a drink at the chic Bar Pleiades. ⑤ *Average main: $40* ✉ *Surrey Hotel, 20 E. 76th St., between 5th and Madison Aves., Upper East Side* ☎ *212/772–2600* ⊕ *www.danielboulud.com* ◿ *Reservations essential* Ⓜ *6 to 77th St.* ✛ *5:F3.*

$$ ✕**Café d'Alsace.** Unusually comfortable burgundy banquettes, huge **BRASSERIE** antiqued mirrors, and low lighting that makes everyone look fabulous characterize this Alsatian gem. Start with a house cocktail—say, L'Alsacien, in which the aperitif Belle de Brillet meets cognac, pear, and fresh lemon in a happy union. Standouts include the *tarte flambé*, a *fromage-blanc*-topped flat bread scattered with tawny caramelized onions and hunks of bacon. The *choucroute garnie* entrée comes in a cast-iron kettle that keeps it piping hot. Sausages, smoked pork breast, and pork belly are so carefully braised that everything comes out in perfect harmony. Can't decide what to wash it all down with? Let the in-house beer sommelier help you out. ⑤ *Average main: $22* ✉ *1695 2nd Ave., at 88th St., Upper East Side* ☎ *212/722–5133* ⊕ *www.cafedalsace. com* Ⓜ *4, 5, 6 to 86th St.* ✛ *6:G6.*

$$ ✕**Café Sabarsky.** In the Neue Galerie, this stately coffeehouse is meant **AUSTRIAN** to duplicate the Vienese café experience. And it does a good job, with **Fodor's**Choice Art Deco furnishings, a selection of daily newspapers, and cases filled ★ with cakes, strudels, and Sacher tortes. Museumgoers and locals love

16

to linger here over coffee. There is also a menu of heartier fare—created by Michelin-starred chef Kurt Gutenbrunner—of goulash, sandwiches, smoked pork-stuffed potato dumplings, and variations on the theme of sausage. ⑤ *Average main: $18* ⊠ *Neue Galerie, 1048 5th Ave., near 86th St., Upper East Side* ☎ *212/240–9557* ⊕ *www. cafesabarsky.com* ⚌ *Reservations not accepted* Ⓜ *4, 5, 6 to 86th St.* ✛ *6:E6.*

$$ × **Candle 79.** The Upper East Side may seem like an unlikely place for
VEGETARIAN
Fodor'sChoice
★

gourmet vegan fare, but the people behind Candle 79 have found a formula that would work in any neighborhood. The elegant, bilevel space, done in warm, autumnal tones, is far from the health-food stereotype. Appetizers like rice balls with tempeh bacon may sound like hippie throwbacks, but they taste more like well-executed trattoria fare. Signature dishes include the seitan piccata, which replaces the usual protein with a vegetarian substitute and is so well made that you would never miss the meat. Salads, soups, desserts, and entrées are all fresh and made with local, organic, seasonal produce. There's also an impressive list of organic wines and sakes. ⑤ *Average main: $22* ⊠ *154 E. 79th St., at Lexington Ave., Upper East Side* ☎ *212/537–7179* ⊕ *www.candle79. com* Ⓜ *6 to 77th St./Lexington Ave.* ✛ *5:G2.*

$ × **Cascabel Taqueria.** At Cascabel, the wrestling-theme decor is a whimsi-
MEXICAN
cal backdrop for reasonably priced Mexican food. Tacos are inventive without veering too far from the comfort-food norm. The Camaron scatters plump roasted shrimp among fresh oregano, garlic oil, and black beans. The beef tongue is slow-braised, then topped with spring onion and serrano chilies. There's also fresh, creamy guacamole with house-fried chips, pert tortilla soup with queso fresco cheese and chicken, and dinner-only platters like adobe-marinated Berkshire pork butt. At lunchtime, sandwiches—like shredded chicken with mango and smashed avocado—hit the spot with a cold Mexican beer. Inside seating is limited, but in temperate weather the outdoor tables expand your possibilities. ⑤ *Average main: $13* ⊠ *1538 2nd Ave., between 80th and 81st Sts., Upper East Side* ☎ *212/717–8226* ⊕ *www.nyctacos.com* Ⓜ *6 to 77th St.* ✛ *5:H2.*

$$$ × **Central Park Boathouse Restaurant.** There are plenty of pushcarts offer-
AMERICAN
ing hot dogs and sodas, but if you're looking to soak up Central Park's magical ambience in an elegant setting, head for the Central Park Boathouse, which overlooks the gondola lake. There you can relax on the outdoor deck with a glass of wine and a cheese plate, or go for a more formal meal inside the restaurant. In warmer months the restaurant can get crowded: go for a late lunch or an early-evening cocktail. Note that dinner is not served in the winter months. ⑤ *Average main: $30* ⊠ *E. 72nd St., at Park Dr. N, Upper East Side* ☎ *212/517–2233* ⊕ *www. thecentralparkboathouse.com* ⚌ *Reservations not accepted* ⊗ *No dinner Dec.–Mar.* ✛ *5:E3.*

$$$$ × **Daniel.** Celebrity-chef Daniel Boulud has created one of the most ele-
FRENCH
Fodor'sChoice
★

gant dining experiences in Manhattan. The prix fixe–only menu (there are à la carte selections in the elegant lounge and bar) is predominantly French, with such modern classics as turbot on Himalayan salt with an ale-and-gingerbread sauce, and a duo of dry-aged Angus black beef featuring meltingly tender red wine–braised short ribs and seared rib-eye with black trumpet mushrooms and Gorgonzola cream. Equally impressive are the serious artwork, professional service, extensive wine list, and masterful cocktails. Don't forget the decadent desserts and overflowing cheese trolley. A three-course vegetarian menu is also available. $ *Average main: $125* ⊠ *60 E. 65th St., between Madison and Park Aves., Upper East Side* ☎ *212/288–0033* ⊕ *www.danielnyc. com* ⚏ *Reservations essential* ⌂ *Jacket required* ⊘ *Closed Sun. No lunch* Ⓜ *6 to 68th/Hunter College* ✛ *5:F5.*

$$$
EASTERN
EUROPEAN
✕ **Hospoda.** The word may mean "pub" in Czech, but this chic Upper East Side, Central Europe–inspired spot is far from the dingy Prague drinking holes of years past. On the ground floor of the Bohemian National Hall, a Czech cultural center, the interior is dominated by artsy, backlit wall engravings, while in the kitchen Chef Oldrich Seha-jdak, who has been at the forefront in revolutionizing Czech cuisine at Prague's acclaimed restaurant La Degustation, has created a menu of updated European and Czech fare. Pork belly paired with scallops and duck with butternut squash are a couple of the standout dishes here. The Pilsner Urquell, shipped in air-conditioned containers from the brewery in Plzen, is especially delicious here. Remember to say "*Na zdravi,*" cheers in Czech, before your first sip. $ *Average main: $25* ⊠ *321 E. 73rd St., between 1st and 2nd Aves., Upper East Side* ☎ *212/861–1038* ⊕ *www.hospodanyc.com* ⊘ *No lunch* Ⓜ *6 to 68th St.* ✛ *5:H3.*

$$
MEXICAN
✕ **Maya.** The upscale-hacienda appearance of this justifiably popular restaurant showcases some of the best Mexican food in the city, cour-tesy of pioneering Mexican chef Richard Sandoval. Begin with a fresh mango mojito, then tuck into delicious roasted corn soup with huitla-coche dumplings, stuffed poblano peppers, and a smoky filet mignon taco with jalapeño escabeche. Next indulge in the tender roasted pork carnitas or the spicy chipotle shirmp. The bottomless margarita brunch on the weekends can get loud but the local Upper East Siders still enjoy it. $ *Average main: $24* ⊠ *1191 1st Ave., between 64th and 65th Sts., Upper East Side* ☎ *212/585–1818* ⊕ *www.modernmexican. com* Ⓜ *6 to 68th St./Hunter College* ✛ *5:H5.*

$$
JAPANESE
✕ **Sushi of Gari.** Options at this popular sushi restaurant range from the ordinary (California roll) to such exotic choices as tuna with creamy tofu sauce, miso-marinated cod, or Japanese yellowtail with jalapeño. Japanese noodles (udon or soba) and meat dishes such as teriyaki and negimaki (scallions rolled in thinly sliced beef) are well prepared. Some of the inventive non-sushi items on the menu are worth a try, especially the fried cream cheese dumplings. Reservations are recom-mended. There are other locations, too, including one across the park at 370 Columbus Avenue. $ *Average main: $24* ⊠ *402 E. 78th St., at 1st Ave., Upper East Side* ☎ *212/517–5340* ⊕ *www.sushiofgari.com* ⊘ *No lunch* Ⓜ *6 to 77th St.* ✛ *5:H2.*

16

UPPER WEST SIDE

The area around Lincoln Center is a fine-dining hub; as you head north you'll find a mix of casual and sophisticated neighborhood spots.

$$$$
ASIAN

✕ **Asiate.** The unparalleled view is reason enough to visit Asiate's pristine dining room, perched on the 35th floor of the Time Warner Center in the Mandarin Oriental Hotel. Artfully positioned tables and minimalist decor help direct eyes to the windows, which peer over Central Park. At night crystalline lights reflect in the glass, creating a magical effect. The kitchen turns out contemporary dishes with an Asian influence that pair unlikely ingredients: think foie-gras and hazelnut brittle, or branzino and truffles. Professional, attentive service helps foster an atmosphere of dreamlike luxury. The restaurant has prix-fixe menus only, and an illustrious wine collection housing 2,000 bottles. ⑤ *Average main: $100* ✉ *Mandarin Oriental Hotel, 80 Columbus Circle, 35th fl., at 60th St., Upper West Side* ☎ *212/805–8881* ⊕ *www.mandarinoriental.com* Ⓜ *A, B, C, D, 1 to 59th St./Columbus Circle* ✛ *5:C6.*

$$$
FRENCH
Fodor's Choice
★

✕ **Bar Boulud.** Acclaimed French chef Daniel Boulud, known for upscale New York City eateries Daniel and Café Boulud, shows diners his more casual side with this lively contemporary bistro and wine bar. The long, narrow space accommodates 100 people and has a 14-seat round table for special wine-theme tastings. The menu emphasizes charcuterie, including terrines and pâtés designed by Parisian charcutier Gilles Verot, who relocated just to work with Boulud, as well as traditional French bistro dishes like steak frites and *poulet rôti à l'ail* (roast chicken with garlic mashed potatoes). The 500-bottle wine list is heavy on wines from Burgundy and the Rhône Valley. Wallet watchers won't feel left out: a pretheater three-course menu starts at $45, and weekend brunch has four courses plus coffee for $32. ⑤ *Average main: $26* ✉ *1900 Broadway, between 63rd and 64th Sts., Upper West Side* ☎ *212/595–0303* ⊕ *www.barboulud.com* Ⓜ *1 to 66th St./Lincoln Center; 1, A, C, B, D to 59th St.* ✛ *5:B5.*

$$
AMERICAN

✕ **Barney Greengrass.** At this Upper West Side landmark, brusque waiters send out stellar smoked salmon, sturgeon, and whitefish to a happy crowd packed to the gills at small Formica tables. Split a fish platter with bagels, cream cheese, and other fixings, or get your velvety nova scrambled with eggs and buttery caramelized onions. If you're still hungry, go for a plate of cheese blintzes or the to-die-for chopped liver. Be warned that the weekend brunch wait can exceed an hour so you're better off coming during the week. ⑤ *Average main: $18* ✉ *541 Amsterdam Ave., between 86th and 87th Sts., Upper West Side* ☎ *212/724–4707* ⊕ *www.barneygreengrass.com* ⌦ *Reservations not accepted* ▭ *No credit cards* ۞ *Closed Mon.* Ⓜ *1, B, C to 86th St.* ✛ *6:B6.*

$
CAFÉ

✕ **Bouchon Bakery.** Never mind that you're in the middle of a shopping mall under a Samsung sign—soups and sandwiches don't get much more luxurious than this. Acclaimed chef Thomas Keller's low-key lunch spot (one floor down from his extravagant flagship, Per Se) draws long lines for good reason. Share a mason jar of salmon rillettes—an unctuous spread of cooked and smoked salmon folded around crème fraîche and butter—then move on to one of the fork-and-knife open-faced tartines, like the tuna niçoise. When a sandwich has this much pedigree, $13.50 is actually a bargain. Grab dessert to go, a fresh maca-roon or éclair, from the nearby bakery window. ⑤ *Average main: $14* ⊠ *Time Warner Center, 10 Columbus Circle, 3rd fl., Upper West Side* ☎ *212/823–9366* ⊕ *www.bouchonbakery.com* Ⓜ *1, A, B, C, D to 59th St./Columbus Circle* ⊹ *5:C6.*

$$
FRENCH
✕ **Café Luxembourg.** The old soul of the Lincoln Center neighborhood seems to inhabit the tiled and mirrored walls of this lively, cramped restaurant, where West End Avenue regulars—including lots of on-air talent from nearby ABC News—are greeted with kisses, and musicians and audience members pack the room after a concert. The bar's always hopping, and the menu (served until 11 pm Sunday through Tuesday and until midnight from Wednesday through Saturday) includes dishes like steak tartare and lobster roll alongside dishes with a more con-temporary spin like pan-seared trout with haricots verts, hazelnuts, and tomato-caper compote. ⑤ *Average main: $20* ⊠ *200 W. 70th St., between Amsterdam and West End Aves., Upper West Side* ☎ *212/873–7411* ⊕ *www.cafeluxembourg.com* ⌂ *Reservations essential* Ⓜ *1, 2, 3, B, C to 72nd St.* ⊹ *5:A4.*

$$
ITALIAN
FAMILY
✕ **Carmine's.** Set on a nondescript block of Broadway, this branch of the Italian family-style mainstay is a favorite for families celebrating special occasions, pre-prom groups of teens, and plain old folks who come for the tried-and-true menu items like fried calamari, linguine with white clam sauce, chicken parmigiana, and veal saltimbocca, all served in mountain-ous portions. Family photos line the walls, there's a groaning antipasti table filled with savory meats, cheese, and salads, and there's a convivial feeling amid the organized chaos. ⑤ *Average main: $24* ⊠ *2450 Broad-way, between 90th and 91st Sts., Upper West Side* ☎ *212/362–2200* ⊕ *www.carminesnyc.com* Ⓜ *1, 2, 3, to 96th St./Broadway* ⊹ *6:A6.*

$$$$
AMERICAN
✕ **Dovetail.** Inside Dovetail, chef-owner John Fraser's subdued townhouse and restaurant, cream-color walls and maple panels create a warm, sooth-ing atmosphere. The menu, which changes daily based on seasonal and available ingredients, features refined but hearty dishes. Seek solace from winter temperatures with the earthy gnocchi topped with matsutake mushrooms, poppy seeds, and lemon. Tender lamb is heightened by potatoes, artichokes, and olives. The savory feast continues with pastry chef Michal Shelkowitz's Earl Grey pumpkin cake with lemon curd and cinnamon-toast ice cream. ⑤ *Average main: $40* ⊠ *103 W. 77th St., at Columbus Ave., Upper West Side* ☎ *212/362–3800* ⊕ *www.dovetailnyc. com* ☾ *No lunch* Ⓜ *1 to 79th St.; B, C to 81st St.* ⊹ *5:B2.*

$$
CAFÉ
✕ **Fairway Café.** Fairway Supermarket is a neighborhood institution, living up to its reputation for great prices on gourmet products—and shopping-cart jockeying down the narrow aisles. Upstairs, though, is the respite of Fairway Café, a large, brick-walled room with windows overlooking Broadway. Up front you can grab a pastry and coffee to go, but there's a full menu of fairly priced entrées as well. The place is run by Mitchell London, who's known for his juicy, well-marbled steaks—try the ribeye and you may never go back to Brooklyn's Peter Luger steakhouse again. ⑤ *Average main: $22* ⊠ *2127 Broadway, between 74th and 75th Sts., Upper West Side* ☎ *212/994–9555* ⊕ *www. fairwaymarket.com* Ⓜ *1, 2 3 to 72nd St.* ⊹ *5:A3.*

16

$$ ✗**Fishtag.** Upper West Siders aren't going to be throwing chef Michael
MEDITERRANEAN Psilakis and his Greek-heavy Mediterranean fare back into the water
any time soon. At Anthos, a big-box Midtown eatery that shuttered a
few years ago, Psilakis was lauded for his prowess on the grill. He brings
the same skills to Fishtag with dishes like grilled striped bass and grilled
swordfish. Fanatics of Anthos' insanely good lamb burger can breath
easy, as it's on the menu here. The wine list is long and categorized
with subtitles like "Funky & Earthy" and "Explosive & Bold" and
brew imbibers will declare Fishtag a good catch when they see 20 craft
beers on the menu. $ *Average main: $20* ⊠ *222 W. 79th St., between
Broadway and Amsterdam Ave., Upper West Side* ☎ *212/362–7470*
⊕ *www.michaelpsilakis.com* Ⓜ *1 to 79th St.* ✛ *5:A2.*

$ ✗**Gray's Papaya.** It's a stand-up, takeout dive. And, yes, limos do some-
AMERICAN times stop here for these legendary hot dogs. These traditional, juicy
all-beef dogs are delicious, and quite the economical meal. The recession
special is two hot dogs and a drink for $5. There are cheap breakfast
offerings, too, like the quintessential egg and cheese on a roll. Although
there used to be several locations of Gray's Papaya, this is the only
one left. $ *Average main: $4* ⊠ *2090 Broadway, at 72nd St., Upper
West Side, New York, New York* ☎ *212/799–0243* ⌳ *Reservations not
accepted* ▭ *No credit cards* Ⓜ *1, 2, 3 to 72nd St.* ✛ *5:B4.*

$$ ✗**Isabella's.** Set in the shadow of the Museum of Natural History, Isa-
AMERICAN bella's has been a brunch-and-beyond stalwart for decades. Brunch
FAMILY is especially busy, even though the restaurant is large; lunch is less
crowded, and a great time to try neighborhood-institution salads like
the seafood-loaded Cobb or grilled artichoke hearts with Parmesan
and lemon-thyme vinaigrette. Another winner: the crab cake sandwich layered with lush avocado. Try for a table outside when the
weather's nice; it's a great perspective on the neighborhood. $ *Aver-
age main: $20* ⊠ *359 Columbus Ave., at 77th St., Upper West Side*
☎ *212/724–2100* ⊕ *www.isabellas.com* Ⓜ *B, C to 81st St./Museum of
Natural History* ✛ *5:B3.*

$$$$ ✗**Jean Georges.** This culinary temple in the Trump International Hotel
FRENCH and Towers focuses wholly on *chef celebre* Jean-Georges Vongerichten's spectacular creations. The chef may now have restaurants sprinkled around the globe but this is the spot in his culinary empire you
want to be at. Some dishes approach the limits of the taste universe,
like foie-gras brûlée with spiced fig jam and ice-wine reduction. Others
are models of simplicity, like slow-cooked cod with warm vegetable
vinaigrette. Exceedingly personalized service and a well-selected wine
list contribute to an unforgettable meal. It's prix fixe only. For Jean
Georges on a budget, try the prix-fixe lunch in the front room, Nouga-
tine. $ *Average main: $120* ⊠ *1 Central Park W, at 59th St., Upper
West Side* ☎ *212/299–3900* ⊕ *www.jean-georges.com* ⌳ *Reservations
essential* ⋔ *Jacket required* Ⓜ *A, B, C, D, 1 to 59th St./Columbus
Circle* ✛ *5:C6.*

$ ✗**Kefi.** *Kefi* is Greek for the bliss that accompanies a bacchanalia. And
GREEK at Michael Psilakis's Upper West Side eatery—a giant homage to his
grandmother's Greek cooking—it's not hard to achieve such a culinary
state. Among the mezes, the meatballs with roasted garlic, olives, and

tomato is a standout; the flavorful roast chicken, potatoes, red peppers, garlic, and thyme makes for a winning entrée; and the béchamel-rich Kefi mac 'n' cheese is irresistible. Reasonable prices make it easy to stick around for a piece of traditional walnut cake with walnut ice cream. ⑤ *Average main: $15* ⊠ *505 Columbus Ave., between 84th and 85th Sts., Upper West Side* ☎ *212/873–0200* ⊕ *www.kefirestaurant.com* Ⓜ *1 to 86th St.; B, C to 86th St.* ✛ *5:B1.*

$ ╳ **Levain Bakery.** Completely unpretentious and utterly delicious, Levain
BAKERY Bakery's cookies are rich and hefty. In fact, they clock in at 6 ounces
FAMILY each! Choose from the chocolate-chip walnut, dark-chocolate chocolate chip, dark-chocolate peanut-butter chip, or oatmeal raisin. Batches are baked fresh daily, and they taste best when they're warm and melty right out of the oven, so it's definitely worth seeking out this small basement bakery for a cookie craving. Levain's also bakes artisanal breads, including banana chocolate chip and pumpkin ginger spice, sour cream coffee cake, chocolate-chip and cinnamon brioche, sourdough rolls stuffed with Valrhona chocolate, blueberry muffins, a variety of scones, and bomboloncini—their unique jelly doughnuts. ⑤ *Average main: $9* ⊠ *167 W. 74th St., near Amsterdam Ave., Upper West Side* ☎ *212/874–6080* ⊕ *www.levainbakery.com* ⊗ *No dinner* Ⓜ *1, 2, 3 to 72nd St.* ✛ *5:B3.*

$$ ╳ **Nice Matin.** If the Upper West Side and the French Riviera melded
BISTRO into one, it might look a little bit like Nice Matin. This is a longtime
FAMILY neighborhood favorite, particularly in the warm weather months, when regulars plant themselves at sidewalk tables and gawk at passersby while munching on Gallic fare like monkfish wading in sweet potato puree and garlicky mussels, and, of course, steak frites. The novel-size wine list boasts more than 2,000 bottles, so bring your reading glasses. And be sure to dress for the people-watching occasion, particularly at the popular weekend brunch. ⑤ *Average main: $24* ⊠ *201 W. 79th St., at Amsterdam Ave., Upper West Side* ☎ *212/873–6423* ⊕ *www. nicematinnyc.com* Ⓜ *1 to 79th St.* ✛ *5:A2.*

$$$$ ╳ **Per Se.** The New York interpretation of what many consider Amer-
AMERICAN ica's finest restaurant, Napa Valley's French Laundry, Per Se is chef
Fodors Choice Thomas Keller's Broadway stage. The large dining room is understated
★ and elegant, with touches of wood, towering florals, and sweeping windows with views of Central Park. Keller embraces seasonality and a witty playfulness that speaks to his confidence in the kitchen, and some of his dishes are now world renowned, such as the tiny cones of tuna tartare topped with crème fraîche, and the "oysters and pearls"—tiny mollusks suspended in a creamy custard with tapioca. Dessert service is a multicourse celebration of all things sweet, including a choice of 27 house-made chocolates. Service is sublime, as you'd expect. An à la carte "salon" menu is available in the front bar room, but let's face it: if you manage to snag a reservation, there's nothing else to do but submit to the $295 prix fixe. It's best to make reservations at least two months in advance. ⑤ *Average main: $80* ⊠ *Time Warner Center, 10 Columbus Circle, 4th fl., at 60th St., Upper West Side* ☎ *212/823–9335* ⊕ *www. perseny.com* ⌣ *Reservations essential* ⌂ *Jacket required* ⊗ *No lunch Mon.–Thurs.* Ⓜ *A, B, C, D, 1 to 59th St./Columbus Circle* ✛ *5:C6.*

16

$$$$
MEDITERRANEAN

✕ **Picholine.** Terrance Brennan's classic French restaurant has maintained its dignified atmosphere over the years, as well as the emphasis on contemporary Mediterranean cuisine, sourced from artisanal farmers and food producers. The menu is divided into options for a five-course and a twelve-course tasting menu. The duck and foie gras rillette, inventively paired with gingerbread, is particularly tasty. So is the caviar-sprinkled sea urchin panna cotta. But whatever you do, don't miss the famous cheese course, which Brennan practically invented here. The atmosphere is refined but not stuffy. ⑤ *Average main: $45 ⊠ 35 W. 64th St., between Broadway and Central Park W, Upper West Side* ☎ *212/724–8585* ⊕ *www.picholinenyc.com* ⌂ *Reservations essential* ⊘ *No lunch.* Ⓜ *1 to 66th St./Lincoln Center* ✛ *5:C5.*

$$$$
STEAKHOUSE

✕ **Porter House New York.** With clubby interiors by Jeffrey Beers and an adjoining lounge area, Porter House is helmed by veteran chef Michael Lomonaco. Filling the meat-and-potatoes slot in the Time Warner Center's upscale "Restaurant Collection," the masculine throwback highlights American wines and pedigreed super-size meat. The neighborhood, long underserved on the steakhouse front, has warmed to Lomonaco's simple, solid American fare. Begin with his smoky clams casino or rich roasted marrow bones. Steaks are huge and expertly seasoned, and come with the usual battery of à la carte sides—creamed spinach, roasted mushrooms, and truffle mashed potatoes. ⑤ *Average main: $45 ⊠ Time Warner Center, 10 Columbus Circle, 4th floor, at 60th St., Upper West Side* ☎ *212/823–9500* ⊕ *www. porterhousenewyork.com* ⊘ *No lunch weekends* Ⓜ *1, A, B, C, D to 59th St./Columbus Circle* ✛ *5:C6.*

$
ITALIAN

✕ **Salumeria Rosi Parmacotto.** Just up the block from Gray's Papaya is this compact temple to a whole different subset of cured meats. Chef Cesare Casella has created a showcase for dozens of varieties of prosciutto, coppa, mortadella, and more, carved from a professional slicer for consumption on the spot or as indulgent takeout. There's also a more ambitious menu, including salads and a lusty osso buco over creamy mashed potatoes. If you're lucky, you might catch a glimpse of the avuncular chef with his signature rosemary sprig peeking out from his breast pocket. There's a spin-off with a more elaborate menu on the Upper East Side. ⑤ *Average main: $13 ⊠ 283 Amsterdam Ave., between 73rd and 74th Sts., Upper West Side* ☎ *212/877–4800* ⊕ *www. salumeriarosi.com* Ⓜ *1, 2, 3 to 72nd St.* ✛ *5:B3.*

$$
AMERICAN

✕ **Sarabeth's Kitchen.** Lining up for brunch here is as much an Upper West Side tradition as taking a sunny Sunday afternoon stroll in nearby Riverside Park. Locals love the bric-a-brac-filled restaurant for sweet morning-time dishes like lemon ricotta pancakes, as well as for the comforting dinners. The afternoon tea includes buttery scones with Sarabeth's signature jams, savory nibbles, and outstanding baked goods. Dinner entrées include chicken potpie and truffle mac 'n' cheese. There are several other locations around town, including in the Lord & Taylor department store on 5th Avenue at 39th Street. ⑤ *Average main: $18* ⊠ *423 Amsterdam Ave., at 80th St., Upper West Side* ☎ *800/773–7378* ⊕ *www.sarabeth.com* Ⓜ *1 to 79th St.* ✛ *5:B2.*

$$$
AMERICAN
✕ **Telepan.** Chef-owner Bill Telepan's eponymous eatery has brought some much-needed culinary zing to the Upper West Side (and it's a great place to go before Lincoln Center). The greenmarket-driven menu is heavy on the veggies (the seasonal vegetable starter wakes your palate right up), but fish lovers and first-timers should hook into the signature starter, the smoked trout paired with sweet apple sour cream. Anything on the menu that contains eggs, like the "egg-in-a-hole" served with spinach and hen-of-the-woods mushrooms, is worth a try. There's the usual presence of foie gras and pork belly but Telepan does seafood very well (try the scallops). For dessert, a crunchy peanut-butter and gianduja duo with peanut-brittle ice cream is sublime. ⑤ *Average main: $29* ⊠ *72 W. 69th St., between Columbus Ave. and Central Park W, Upper West Side* ☎ *212/580–4300* ⊕ *www. telepan-ny.com* ⊘ *No lunch Mon. and Tues.* Ⓜ *1 to 66th St./Lincoln Center; 1, 2, 3 to 72nd St.; B, C to 72nd St.* ✛ *5:B4.*

HARLEM

Harlem culinary renaissance? Yes, indeed. This historic northern neighborhood has seen an infusion of fantastic restaurants in the last five years or so. Yes, there are still the standby southern/soul food restaurants, but there are also newer arrivals, making your journey northward even more worthwhile.

$$
BISTRO
✕ **Chez Lucienne.** French Harlem? Not exactly, but Chez Lucienne is about as close as you'll get to France without leaving the comfortable confines of this historic neighborhood. And if you can't get into the Red Rooster next door, then grab a seat at the baby blue banquette or relax at an outdoor table where locals come to sip coffee or wine, dogs at their side. The menu looks to Lyon with classics like sauteed foie gras and steak au poivre by a chef who logged time in the kitchen with famed chef Daniel Boulud. ⑤ *Average main: $18* ⊠ *308 Lenox Ave., between 125th and 126th Sts., Harlem* ☎ *212/289–5555* ⊕ *www.chezlucienne. com* Ⓜ *2, 3 to 116th St.* ✛ *6:D1.*

$$$
AMERICAN
✕ **Red Rooster Harlem.** Marcus Samuelsson, who earned his celebrity chefdom at Aquavit in Midtown for his take on Ethiopian-accented Scandinavian cuisine (fusing the food of his birthplace with that of where he grew up), moved way uptown to Harlem in 2010, where he has created a culinary hot spot for the ages. The comfort food menu jumps all over the place, reflecting the ethnic diversity that is modern-day New York City (and the patrons who regularly come here), from plantain-loaded oxtail to fried chicken to the tender meatballs (with lingonberry sauce) that he served at Aquavit. Expect a wait for Sunday brunch, with its gospel music, boozy cocktails, and modern takes on dishes like chicken and waffles. ⑤ *Average main: $26* ⊠ *310 Lenox Ave., between 125th and 126th, Harlem* ☎ *212/792–9001* ⊕ *www. redroosterharlem.com* Ⓜ *2, 3 to 125th St.* ✛ *6:D1.*

$$
SOUTHERN
FAMILY
✕ **Sylvia's.** This Harlem mainstay has been serving soul-food favorites like smothered chicken, barbecue ribs, collard greens, and mashed potatoes to a dedicated crowd of locals, tourists, and college students since 1962. Owner Sylvia Woods may have passed away in the summer of 2012 but her restaurant and the signature sauces that are jarred and sold

online and in the restaurant are more popular than ever. Some say it's overly touristy—and the bus loads attest, but it's still an experience. For the ultimate, come for Sunday gospel brunch. Singing and eating were never a more delicious combination. $ *Average main: $24* ✉ *328 Lenox Ave., near 127th St., Harlem* ☎ *212/996–0660* ⊕ *www.sylviassoulfood. com* Ⓜ *2, 3 to 125th St.* ✚ *6:D1.*

BROOKLYN

BRIGHTON BEACH

The subway trains that shuttle people out to this beachside neighborhood could be nicknamed the "time machine" because strolling the wide boardwalk along the sea feels like you've dropped into another time and space. Odessa in the 1980s comes to mind. After all, it was around that time when a mass migration of Russian immigrants settled in Brighton Beach. Today you'll hear more Slavic than English and you'll most certainly be tempted by the vodka and highly entertaining Russian restaurants that line the boardwalk.

$ ✗ **Tatiana Grill.** It's open year-round, but Tatiana's, right on the board-
RUSSIAN   walk, really bustles in the summer when the outdoor tables fill with Russian-speaking couples and families, as well as day trippers out from Manhattan for a day at the beach. The menu has pages and pages of options that range from sushi to Ukrainian dishes. The excellent Greek salad is a refreshing choice after a day at the beach, and the grilled chicken skewers are simple but good. Order a Russian beer to go with your meal and say "*na zdorovie*," cheers, before taking your first sip. $ *Average main: $15* ✉ *3152 Brighton 6th St. (on boardwalk), Brighton Beach* ☎ *718/891–5151* ⊕ *www.tatianagrill.com* Ⓜ *B, Q to Brighton Beach* ✚ *7:H6.*

BROOKLYN HEIGHTS

Brooklyn may be the place to eat these days, but Brooklyn Heights has always been more pleasing on the eyes than the taste buds. If you know where to look, there are decent neighborhood restaurants, but nearby Carroll Gardens and Cobble Hill are chock full of edible goodness.

$$ ✗ **Henry's End.** At this nearly 40-year-old neighborhood favorite, the
AMERICAN   casual decor belies the quality of the food and wine. Wild game such as elk, kangaroo, and ostrich take center stage in the winter months and during the Wild Game Festival in the late fall; seasonal seafood and foraged vegetables star in the springtime. If duck is your thing, there are usually several preparations on the menu. At the end of Henry Street, the small space still fills up quickly at dinnertime. $ *Average main: $18* ✉ *44 Henry St., near Cranberry St., Brooklyn Heights* ☎ *718/834–1776* ⊕ *www.henrysend.com* ☾ *No lunch* Ⓜ *2, 3 to Clark St.; A, C to High St.* ✚ *7:B3.*

CARROLL GARDENS

If you look closely, you can still see some elements of old Brooklyn in this leafy neighborhood: the older Italian men parked on lawn chairs speaking a southern Italian dialect, the meat market with its archaic sign a relic from the 1950s. But Carroll Gardens is anything but old-fashioned. Walk down Smith or Court Street to find blocks flanked by hip, crowded bars and restaurants good enough to lure even travel-finicky Manhattanites.

$$ ✕ **Buttermilk Channel.** This cozy restaurant is like a spirited slice of down-
AMERICAN home Americana. Locals swear by comfort-food mainstays with empha-
sis on local and organic, especially the all-time fave: buttermilk-fried
chicken with cheddar waffles. Other standouts include the house-made
charcuterie and snacks like handmade mozzarella. Specials include a
Monday night, three-course dinner for $28. It's a bit of a trek if you're
taking the subway but you'll be rewarded with a homey, Brooklyn dining experience. $ *Average main: $20* ✉ *524 Court St., at Huntington
St., Carroll Gardens* ☎ *718/852–8490* ⊕ *www.buttermilkchannelnyc.
com* ⊘ *No lunch weekdays* Ⓜ *F to Carroll St.* ✛ *7:A5.*

$$ ✕ **Char No. 4.** With 300-plus whiskeys to choose from—the focus is
AMERICAN on American labels—Char No. 4 is a connoisseur's dream (the name
refers to barrels in which the golden liquor is aged). Naturally, there
are also plenty of bourbon-accented cocktails (try the Noreaster, with
ginger beer and maple syrup). To complement your tipple, there are
updated dishes from south of the Mason-Dixon line. Many of the appe-
tizers involve bacon; don't miss the thick-cut bacon with peas and car-
rots, lamb pastrami, the BLT, or the cheese curds with pimento sauce.
$ *Average main: $20* ✉ *196 Smith St., between Baltic and Warren Sts.,
Carroll Gardens* ☎ *718/643–2106* ⊕ *www.charno4.com* ⊘ *No lunch
Mon.–Thurs.* Ⓜ *F to Bergen St.* ✛ *7:B4.*

$ ✕ **Pok Pok Ny.** An outpost of the Portland original, this insanely popular
THAI Thai restaurant isn't easy to get to but it's worth the trek—it's in the
Fodor's Choice Columbia Waterfront District on the edge of Carroll Gardens. Chef
★ Andy Ricker has mastered Thai cuisine, or at least made it taste so
good you'll wait for hours to get into this no-reservations restaurant.
The menu floats around the southeast Asian country but seems to stick
around the north longer, with an emphasis on Chiang Mai and Isaan.
Order duck laap (meat salad) and a spicy papaya salad and see if your
taste buds can take more spice. If so, you can't go wrong with the tender
garlic-rubbed pork neck. Put your name in with the host and then wait
it out next door at Ricker's other establishment, Whiskey Soda Lounge.
$ *Average main: $14* ✉ *117 Columbia St., at Kane St., Carroll Gardens*
☎ *718/923–9322* ⊕ *www.pokokny.com* ⚠ *Reservations not accepted*
Ⓜ *F, G to Bergen St.* ✛ *7:A4.*

COBBLE HILL

$ ✕ **Henry Public.** If you're strolling the atmospheric, brownstone-lined
AMERICAN streets of Cobble Hill or Brooklyn Heights, in need of an expertly
crafted cocktail and some tasty victuals, check out this small hipster
tavern. The dark-wood decor and homey touches have an early 20th-
century feel, and the food menu is short but quality. There are several
"hamburger sandwich" variations, the local favorite turkey leg sand-
wich, a daily special or two, and a few small plates. Drinks are updates
on the classics. Prices are moderate compared to Manhattan but note
that it's cash only. $ *Average main: $15* ✉ *329 Henry St., Cobble Hill*
☎ *718/852–8630* ⊕ *www.henrypublic.com/index.html* ▬ *No credit
cards* Ⓜ *F, G to Bergen St.* ✛ *7:B4.*

16

$$ ✕**La Vara.** Chef Alex Raij, who runs the kitchens at Chelsea tapas favor-
SPANISH ites **Txikito** and El Quinto Pino has won over Manhattan foodies with
her flavorful Basque cuisine. At this diminutive, exposed-brick-wall-clad
Cobble Hill restaurant, she turns to new Iberian territory: Moorish and
Jewish-accented Spain. Tender lamb breast topped with a sweet date
jam, saffron-hinted rabbit loin, and intense grilled chicken hearts are
all hits on a menu of snacks, tapas, and larger plates. Pair your grazing
with a well-made gin and tonic or a glass of wine from the affordable
Spanish wine list. $ *Average main: $14* ⊠ *268 Clinton St., near Veran-
dah Pl., Cobble Hill* ☎ *718/422–0065* ⊕ *www.lavarany.com* Ⓜ *F, G to
Bergen St.* ✛ *7:B4.*

CONEY ISLAND

It's no longer an island, but this amusement park on the sea is salt-of-
the-earth paradise. Think pizza and hot dogs and calorie-laden carnival
fare. If you're in town during July 4, a Big Apple must-see is the annual
Nathan's Famous hot dog eating contest where hundreds of people
gather to watch "professional" eaters scarf down tubular meat.

$ ✕**Nathan's Famous.** No visit to Coney Island would be truly complete
AMERICAN without a hot dog from this stand that first opened in 1916. Nathan's
took a hit during Hurricane Sandy in late 2012—it was under six feet
of water, and closed for months. But it's now back and better than
ever. Be sure to order the super crispy fries with your dog. You won't
regret it. On the Fourth of July, thousands come to see their world-
famous hot dog–eating contest; the record stands at 69 in 10 minutes.
$ *Average main: $4* ⊠ *1310 Surf Ave., at Stillwell Ave., Coney Island*
☎ *718/946–2705* ⊕ *www.nathansfamous.com* Ⓜ *D, F, N, Q to Coney
Island–Stillwell Ave.* ✛ *7:G6.*

DOWNTOWN BROOKLYN

Filled with neoclassical courthouse buildings and glass skyscrapers,
there isn't much reason to come to downtown Brooklyn—unless, of
course, you managed to nab a reservation at the borough's only three-
Michelin-starred restaurant, Brooklyn Fare.

$$$$ ✕**Brooklyn Fare.** At Brooklyn's only restaurant with three coveted
ECLECTIC Michelin stars, local star chef César Ramirez and his sous-chefs offer a
culinary performance during three nightly seatings. At each, 20 dainty,
often seafood-focused concoctions are presented to 18 diners seated at
a semicircular steel counter. Dishes might include king salmon parfait
with basil gelée, avocado, maple syrup, and mustard; or fresh tofu and
king crab blended with matsutake mushrooms and dashi sauce. Getting
a reservation is a complicated ordeal so plan in advance. And make sure
you're wearing your best: formal wear is required. $ *Average main:
$250* ⊠ *200 Schermerhorn St., near Hoyt St., Downtown Brooklyn*
☎ *718/243–0050* ⊕ *www.brooklynfare.com* ⚼ *Reservations essential*
☻ *Closed Sun. No lunch* Ⓜ *A, C to Hoyt–Schermerhorn; 2, 3 to Hoyt
St.; 4, 5 to Nevins St.; B, M, Q, R to Dekalb Ave.* ✛ *7:B4.*

DUMBO

Once upon a time, the primary reason for a hungry person to come to DUMBO was to eat pizza at Grimaldi's. The past few years have seen the growing gentrification of the loft-strewn cobblestone streets, though, which are now sprinkled with toothsome eateries and cute boutiques, and now that the Brooklyn waterfront has been fully developed you can walk off your meal with a romantic stroll.

$
PIZZA

✕ **Grimaldi's.** This legendary New York–style parlor serves excellent pizza pies from its coal ovens. Although sometimes inconsistent, when they're good, the thin crisp crust is slightly blackened, and the fresh mozzarella oozes satisfyingly. Grimaldi's is still one of the city's premier pizza spots and, paired with a walk across the Brooklyn Bridge, this is a top-notch New York experience. Grimaldi's popularity allows them to be picky: no slices, no reservations, no credit cards; and there are usually no empty tables so expect a wait. Impatient foodies have been known to phone in a to-go order, swoop past the lines, and then enjoy their pizza in the nearby Brooklyn Bridge Park. Ⓢ *Average main: $15* ✉ *1 Front St., near Water St., DUMBO* ☎ *718/858–4300* ⊕ *www.grimaldis.com* ⌔ *Reservations not accepted* 🖃 *No credit cards* Ⓜ *A, C to High St.; 2, 3 to Clark St.; F to York St.* ✛ *7:B3.*

16

$$$$
MODERN
AMERICAN

✕ **River Café.** Hurricane Sandy left the River Café in bad shape, but after over a year in renovations, the restaurant, which has incredible views of the Manhattan skyline, is back and better than ever. The location and live piano music make it a waterfront favorite for romantic meals, marriage proposals, fancy birthdays, and other special celebrations. The menu offers a contemporary take on local and exotic ingredients. It's fixed price only at dinner; lunch has à la carte options. For the ultimate experience, snag a window seat and try the chef's six-course tasting menu. Gentlemen: jackets are required after 5 pm. Ⓢ *Average main: $100* ✉ *1 Water St., near Old Fulton St., DUMBO* ☎ *718/522–5200* ⊕ *www.rivercafe.com* Ⓜ *F to York St.; A, C to High St.; 2, 3 to Clark St.* ✛ *7:B3.*

$$
MODERN
AMERICAN

✕ **Vinegar Hill House.** In an offbeat enclave on the edge of DUMBO called Vinegar Hill, this intimate eatery has been a hit with Brooklynites since the day it first fired up its burners in 2008. Foodies trek out to the rustic-chic dining room for well-prepared seasonal food, the cozy ambience, and expertly prepared cocktails. Favorites from the small menu include the moist, crispy-skinned cast-iron chicken and the giant pork chop. The homey, vintage-y decor and the clientele are quintessential modern-urban Brooklyn. Brunch is served on the weekends. If you can't get in here, check out Vinegar Hill House's nearby spin-off, Hillside, at 70 Hudson Avenue. Ⓢ *Average main: $25* ✉ *72 Hudson Ave., between Front and Water Sts., DUMBO* ☎ *718/522–1018* ⊕ *www.vinegarhillhouse.com* ⌔ *Reservations not accepted* ⊗ *No lunch weekdays* Ⓜ *F to York St.* ✛ *7:C2.*

FORT GREENE

Fort Greene has become one of the most desirable neighborhoods in Brooklyn, the lovely brownstone apartments attracting young professionals and many of the borough's established writers and artists. It's also a garden of culinary delights with restaurants leading the locavore farm-to-table movement. And who knows? Maybe even a famous director or author will be sitting at the table next to you.

$$
MODERN
AMERICAN

✗ **No. 7.** Perch at the marble-topped bar or lounge at one of the banquettes in the back at this buzzy neighborhood bistro lighted up by Edison bulbs. The frequently changing menu takes American classics and throws them for a global spin. The result is nouveau fusion that pulls in droves of local diners and makes vegetarians happy. Highlights might include anything from crispy eggplant with tofu in a tomato vinaigrette to skirt steak with baked potato, Chinese sausage, and chimichurri sauce. Brunch dishes are similarly innovative but delicious—think fried eggs with nachos and jalapeños, or pork loin with fried eggs, buttermilk pancake, and pineapple maple syrup. On Monday nights, the dining room is closed but the bar is still open. ⓢ *Average main: $20* ✉ *7 Greene Ave., Fort Greene* ☎ *718/522–6370* ⊕ *www.no7restaurant.com* ⊗ *No lunch weekdays; no dinner Mon.* Ⓜ *C to Lafayette Ave.; 2, 3, 4, 5, B, Q to Atlantic Ave.* ✛ *7:C4.*

$$
ITALIAN
Fodor's Choice
★

✗ **Roman's.** When the masterminds behind Marlow & Sons opened this locavore Italian restaurant in Fort Greene, neighborhood foodies rejoiced, and the consistently excellent food, convivial atmosphere, and friendly service still has them clamoring for a table or a spot at the refinished marble bar. The small menu changes nightly and showcases refined interpretations using top of the line produce and proteins. Think appetizers like roasted rabbit loins with lentils; a salad of radishes with anchovy and a boiled egg; innovative pastas; and main courses that might include chicken al diavolo or whole fish. Weekend brunch is a hit—if they're on the menu, don't skip the homemade doughnuts. ⓢ *Average main: $17* ✉ *243 Dekalb Ave., near Vanderbilt Ave., Fort Greene* ☎ *718/622–5300* ⊕ *www.romansnyc. com* ⚐ *Reservations not accepted* ⊗ *No lunch weekdays* Ⓜ *C to Lafayette Ave.* ✛ *7:D4.*

$$
MODERN
AMERICAN

✗ **Stonehome Wine Bar and Restaurant.** Just down the street from BAM, Stonehome is the place to go before or after a show for sophisticated food and wine at reasonable prices. This dimly lighted basement hideaway has excellent tasting flights—three samples for $18—and 38 wines by the glass, perfect to pair with cheese, charcuterie, and housemade pâtés. The small and uncomplicated menu focuses on market-fresh new American fare like pan-roasted chicken with cheddar grits and greens. The back garden is a delight in nice weather. ⓢ *Average main: $19* ✉ *87 Lafayette Ave., at S. Portland Ave., Fort Greene* ☎ *718/624–9443* ⊕ *www.stonehomewinebar.com* ⊗ *No lunch* Ⓜ *C to Lafayette Ave.* ✛ *7:C4.*

PARK SLOPE

Park Slope's reputation precedes it: this handsome, gay-friendly, family neighborhood also happens to be a great place to fill the tummy. Restaurant-crammed 5th Avenue is not for the indecisive: there's everything from Mexican to Italian to Thai and it's all quite good.

$$
ITALIAN
✕ **al di là.** Roughly translated as "the great beyond," al di là has been consistently packed since it first opened back in 1998, and it's easy to understand why: affordable prices, a relaxed and charming environment, and simple yet soulfully comforting dishes from the Veneto region of Italy. Expect to find homemade pastas like black spaghetti with crab or tortellini filled with roasted squash, as well as meaty mains such as braised rabbit, or hanger steak. The dessert fritters are legendary. The no-reservations policy ensures that the place always has a buzz around it from waiting patrons. ⑤ *Average main: $21* ✉ *248 5th Ave., at Carroll St., Park Slope* ☎ *718/783–4565* ⊕ *www.aldilatrattoria.com* ⚲ *Reservations not accepted* Ⓜ *F to 4th Ave.–9th St.; R to Union St.* ✛ *7:C5.*

$
PIZZA
✕ **Franny's.** Though many swear by Grimaldi's for Brooklyn's best pie, this Park Slope pizza shop, which recently moved up Flatbush Avenue to a larger space, has developed a serious following of its own. The crisp, thin-crust pizzas run the gamut from a "naked" pie with olive oil and salt to their justly talked up clam-and-garlic iteration. Many of the toppings are seasonal and locally sourced. And they're creative: clams, 'nduja (spicy, spreadable sausage), chilies, and potatoes may adorn your pies. In the years since Franny's has opened, several other excellent quality artisanal pizza shops have opened in the neighborhood and around, but Franny's still draws lines at dinnertime. ⑤ *Average main: $16* ✉ *348 Flatbush Ave., Park Slope* ☎ *718/230–0221* ⊕ *www.frannysbrooklyn.com* ⚲ *Reservations not accepted* Ⓜ *B, Q to 7th Ave.; 2, 3 to Bergen St.; 4, 5, D, N, R to Atlantic Ave.–Barclays Center* ✛ *7:C5.*

16

$$
ASIAN
✕ **Talde.** Fans of the TV show *Top Chef* will recognize the name of chef Dale Talde (from season 4) but even if you're not familiar with the show it's well worth making a culinary pilgrimage to Park Slope to eat here. Chef Talde churns out an array of impressive dishes that span most of Asia. Standouts on the menu include inventive, fun fare like the sticky kung pao chicken wings, the pretzel pork and chive dumplings, and peanut-sprinkled smoked *char siu* pork. Be sure to save some room for the finale: chocolate pudding with Campari-candied grapefruit rind and Sichuan-spiced peanuts is a real showstopper. ⑤ *Average main: $20* ✉ *369 7th Ave., at 11th St., Park Slope* ☎ *347/916–0031* ⊕ *www.taldebrooklyn.com* ⚲ *Reservations not accepted* Ⓜ *F to 7th Ave.* ✛ *7:C6.*

PROSPECT HEIGHTS

Once referred to as the "new Park Slope," the neighborhood on the other side of Flatbush has come into its own. Leafy, brownstone-laden streets are increasingly filled with great restaurants. If you're hungry, stroll down Vanderbilt or Washington Avenue and you're sure to find a pleasant place to dine.

$$$
AMERICAN

✕ **Saul.** Owner Saul Bolton, who logged time in the kitchens of Le Bernardin and Bouley, was one of the first to include seasonal local ingredients on his plates at his beloved Cobble Hill restaurant. After 14 years, though, the restaurant has moved to a larger space in the Brooklyn Museum. Diners can order à la carte, fixed-price menus, or tasting menus, all based on seasonal ingredients. Saul is particularly good at mixing surf and turf, in dishes like caramelized scallops paired with chorizo and grilled octopus with slow-roasted pork belly—the resulting delights are well-executed without being overly precious. Lunch is served, and there are also more casual brunch and lunch options available at the Counter, the museum's café. ⑤ *Average main: $28* ⊠ *Brooklyn Museum, 200 Eastern Pkwy., at Washington Ave., Prospect Heights* ☎ *718/935–9842* ⊕ *www.saulrestaurant. com* ⊘ *Closed Mon. and Tues.* Ⓜ *2, 3 to Eastern Pkwy.–Brooklyn Museum* ✛ *7:D5.*

$
DINER

✕ **Tom's Restaurant.** Fans of Suzanne Vega may want to make a pilgrimage to this diner, as the crooner supposedly named her most popular song after it (for the record, there's some dispute that this is the place). Whatever the case, for friendly service and great old-school fare—especially the excellent fluffy lemon-ricotta pancakes served with homemade flavored butters—head three blocks north of the Brooklyn Museum to this family-owned restaurant, which opened in 1936. Expect long lines on weekends. ⑤ *Average main: $8* ⊠ *782 Washington Ave., at Sterling Pl., Prospect Heights* ☎ *718/636–9738* ⚎ *Reservations not accepted* ⊟ *No credit cards* ⊘ *No dinner* Ⓜ *2, 3 to Grand Army Plaza* ✛ *7:D5.*

WILLIAMSBURG

Still probably the hippest, happening-est neighborhood in the five boroughs, Williamsburg is also one of the hottest destinations on the culinary landscape. You'll find plenty of decadent twists on farm-to-table cuisine, dressed-up comfort food classics, and killer cocktails.

$$
AMERICAN

✕ **Diner.** Tucked inside a 1927 dining car, this restaurant, which opened in 1999, was at the forefront of the cool culinary landscape that is now Williamsburg. Diner serves simple seasonal fare; the menu changes daily, and your waiter will scrawl it on your paper tablecloth to help you remember. It's more upscale than the name implies but still casual. Expect dishes like a juicy veal chop with butternut squash or braised beef tongue on a baguette. Save room for the intense flourless chocolate cake. ⑤ *Average main: $20* ⊠ *85 Broadway, at Berry St., Williamsburg* ☎ *718/486–3077* ⊕ *www.dinernyc.com* ⚎ *Reservations not accepted* Ⓜ *J, M, Z to Marcy Ave.; L to Bedford Ave.* ✛ *7:D2.*

$$
AMERICAN

✕ **DuMont.** Slide into a candlelight leather booth or sit outside in the charming back garden and peruse the menu of seasonal salads, pasta, and main courses. DuMont has been getting raves from locals (and drawing hungry Manhattanites over the Williamsburg Bridge) since 2001. Why? Inspired cocktails and cuisine in a laid-back atmosphere are the delicious formula here. Classic menu items include juicy brick-oven roasted chicken, a swoon-inducing mac 'n' cheese, and juicy burgers that inspired a second restaurant, Dumont Burger, nearby (314 Bedford

Avenue). $ *Average main: $22* ✉ *432 Union Ave., between Metro-politan Ave. and Devoe St., Williamsburg* ☎ *718/486–7717* ⊕ *www.dumontrestaurant.com* Ⓜ *L to Lorimer St.* ✛ *7:E2.*

$$

FRENCH ✕ **The Elm.** Daring, talented chef Paul Liebrandt, who left two-Michelin-starred Corton in TriBeCa, to man the stoves at this Williamsburg beauty in the summer of 2013 is the real star of the show here. The 70-seat dining room references the neighborhood in subtle ways: the industrial-chic look refers to the neighborhood's past and the vine-clad living green wall is a nod to nearby McCarren Park. The menu is a Gallic-Brooklyn mashup, with British-born Liebrandt using sophisti-cated French cooking techniques on local ingredients, and the results are fantastic. Think beet salad with intensely flavored bacon or *gnudi* (Italian dumplings) wading in a tangy coconut sauce. For a more inti-mate dining experience book a seat at Little Elm, an eight-seat counter inside the restaurant that serves an eight-course meal Wednesday to Sunday. $ *Average main: $18* ✉ *160 N. 12th St., near Bedford Ave., Williamsburg* ☎ *718/218–7500* ⊕ *www.theelmnyc.com* ☉ *No brunch Sat.* Ⓜ *L to Bedford St.* ✛ *7:E1.*

$

AMERICAN ✕ **Fette Sau.** It might seem odd to go to a former auto-body repair shop to eat meat, but the funky building and outside courtyard seem just right for the serious 'cue served here. A huge wood-and-gas smoker delivers well-smoked brisket, sausages, ribs, and even duck, all ordered by the pound. Avoid the disappointing salads and sides, and instead choose from among the more than 40 American whiskeys and 10 microbrews. Come early, as tables fill up quickly, and even with 700 pounds of meat a night, the good stuff sometimes runs out by 9. There's limited indoor seating. $ *Average main: $13* ✉ *354 Metropolitan Ave., between Have-meyer and Roebling Sts., Williamsburg* ☎ *718/963–3404* ⊕ *fettesaubbq.com* ⚐ *Reservations not accepted* ☉ *No lunch Mon.–Thurs.* Ⓜ *L to Lorimer St.* ✛ *7:E2.*

$

MEXICAN ✕ **La Superior.** "Kiss Manhattan's lousy street food goodbye; Brooklyn is taking over," is the restaurant's slogan. And there's something to it—especially here. Serving some of Brooklyn's best Mexican grub this side of the Red Hook ball fields, La Superior is Mexican street food with a Williamsburg ethic. The service is slapdash and the decor is unremark-able, but the food—from beef-tongue tacos to *pescadillas* (fish quesa-dillas)—really delivers. Don't be surprised if your waiter has a seat at your table while discussing the menu. Weekend brunch boasts ample amounts of delightfully sizzling egg concoctions. $ *Average main: $12* ✉ *295 Berry St., Williamsburg* ☎ *718/388–5988* ⊕ *www.lasuperiornyc.com* ⚐ *Reservations not accepted* ▭ *No credit cards* Ⓜ *L to Bedford Ave.; J, M, Z to Marcy Ave.* ✛ *7:D2.*

$$

AMERICAN ✕ **Marlow & Sons.** It may look like a gourmet food store but it's also a buzzy restaurant with a wood-paneled dining room, started by the people behind Diner next door, and Roman's in Fort Greene. Start with oysters or a wedge of delicate tortilla española or choose one of many daily specials. Then move on to entrées like roast cod or the perfectly juicy, crispy brick chicken. The adventurous cocktails are so good they'll almost make you forget about the uncomfortable wooden seating. After dinner, you can shop for delicacies like wildflower honey and aromatic

16

bitters. Stop by in the morning for breakfast—the biscuits with sausage and egg are filling and delicious. $ *Average main: $23* ✉ *81 Broadway, at Berry St., Williamsburg* ☎ *718/384–1441* ⊕ *www.marlowandsons. com* ⌑ *Reservations not accepted* Ⓜ *J, M, Z to Marcy Ave.; L to Bedford Ave.* ✛ *7:D2.*

$$$$
STEAKHOUSE
Fodor'sChoice
★

✕**Peter Luger Steak House.** Long before Brooklyn was chic, even the snobbiest Manhattanites flocked to Peter Luger's, which fired up its grill for the first time in 1887. Other steakhouses have more elegant ambience, bigger wine lists, and less brusque service, but the meat here makes the trip undeniably worth it. Three tips: bring a meat-eating buddy or several (individual steaks are available, but the porterhouse is served only for two, three, or four), make a reservation (prime slots fill up more than a month in advance), and bring lots of cash—Luger's doesn't take plastic. The lunch-only burger is beloved among locals, as is the bacon appetizer, available by the slice. $ *Average main: $50* ✉ *178 Broadway, at Driggs Ave., Williamsburg* ☎ *718/387–7400* ⊕ *www.peterluger.com* ⌑ *Reservations essential* ⊟ *No credit cards* Ⓜ *J, M, Z to Marcy Ave.* ✛ *7:D2.*

$$
MODERN
AMERICAN
Fodor'sChoice
★

✕**Reynards.** In the Wythe Hotel, Reynards opened in 2012 and quickly became part of the increasingly upscale Williamsburg scene, serving sophisticated fare at Manhattan prices to hipsters. The restaurant is from the team who brought Brooklyn the much-lauded Diner and Marlow & Sons, so the pedigree is there and so is the follow through. The high-ceilinged, exposed-brick dining room is a fitting venue for artisanal cocktails and a menu that encapsulates most of the New American food trends of the last couple years—from a kale salad to great grass-fed burgers to intriguing takes on surf and turf (sea urchin and foie gras, anyone?). It's all enough to make you want to sprout a beard and plant a vegetable garden on your roof. $ *Average main: $22* ✉ *Wythe Hotel, 80 Wythe Ave., at N. 11th St., Williamsburg* ☎ *718/460–8004* ⊕ *www. reynardsnyc.com* Ⓜ *L to Bedford Ave.* ✛ *7:D1.*

$$
AMERICAN

✕**Rye.** Delicious bistro classics and creative American fare are on the menu at this dark, moody speakeasy-style hideaway on a little-trodden block. Enter through the unmarked door and you'll find yourself in a world of leather cushions, pressed-tin ceilings, dark wood, mosaic floors, and a 100-year-old oak bar. The signature meatloaf sandwich is daydreamworthy, served with crispy buttermilk onions and horseradish sauce. Cocktails are also excellent; try the Havemayer with overproof rye whiskey. After dinner get a nightcap at the handsome B.B.R (that's Bar Below Rye). $ *Average main: $25* ✉ *247 S. 1st St., at Havemeyer St., Williamsburg* ☎ *718/218–8047* ⊕ *www.ryerestaurant.com* ☽ *No lunch weekdays* Ⓜ *L to Lorimer St.; J, M, Z to Marcy Ave.* ✛ *7:D2.*

GREENPOINT

On the northern edge of Williamsburg, Greenpoint has a number of laid-back neighborhood restaurants, some of which are worth the trek on the G train.

$$$
SCANDINAVIAN

✕**Luksus.** Here's a sophisticated Scandinavian restaurant in historically Polish Greenpoint. The neighborhood sure is changing but when that means dining spots like Luksus (and Torst, the outstanding Scandinavian beer bar at the front of the eatery), we say that's a good thing.

Minimal and low-key, Luksus is a blend of Scandinavian and Brooklyn ethos. The name means "luxury" in Danish and Luksus serves an ever-changing multicourse fixed-price menu five nights a week. Chef Daniel Burns worked as the head pastry chef at Noma in Copenhagen so his pedigree is impressive (although it seems like there are ex-Noma-ites popping all of the place). Expect a blend of sophistication and simplicity on your plate, and bliss on your palate. $ *Average main: $95* ⊠ *615 Manhattan Ave., near Bedford Ave., Greenpoint* ☎ *718/389–6034* ⊕ *www.luksusnyc.com* ⌬ *Reservations essential* ⊗ *No dinner Sun. and Mon.* Ⓜ *G to Nassau Ave.* ✛ *7:E1.*

BUSHWICK

The big draw in Bushwick is Roberta's. The neighbhorhood is still pretty industrial, with funky new restaurants and bars starting to draw the locals.

$$ ✕ **King Noodle.** Is there such a thing as "stoner food"? King Noodle, in burgeoningly hip Bushwick (where hipsters flocked after being priced out of Williamsburg), might be the place to find out. With its Day-Glo seascape drawings on the walls and ceiling, you may think you'll need to be under the influence to enjoy the delights on the menu. Not so. Though when you take your first forkful of kimchi carbonara (sprinkled with bits of Doritos and bacon), you'll might wonder what the chef was smoking when he came up with something so odd and delicious. Other curious but tasty creations include mapo tofu chili fries and spam-fried rice. $ *Average main: $13* ⊠ *1045 Flushing Ave., near Wilson Ave., Bushwick* ☎ *718/456–6543* ⊕ *www.kingnoodlebk.com* Ⓜ *L to Morgan Ave.* ✛ *7:G2.*

$$ ✕ **Roberta's.** Even Manhattan-dwelling food lovers will get on the sub-
ITALIAN way and head out to the buddingly hip neighborhood of Bushwick for
Fodor's Choice Roberta's—and it's worth the trek. The menu, which is something like
★ "Brooklyn Italian" with its emphasis on using very local ingredients (there's a garden on the roof!), changes regularly but expect duck-pro-sciutto pizza, goat-spiked pasta, and variations on the theme of snout-to-tail dining. And, of course, a supercool soundtrack that's music to any hipster's ears. Go in off-hours or the waits can be long. For a more elegant Roberta's experience, check out the adjacent offshoot, Blanca, which serves upscale fixed-price multicourse meals (reservations are necessary and hard to get). $ *Average main: $20* ⊠ *261 Moore St., at Bogart St., Bushwick* ☎ *718/417–1118* ⌬ *Reservations not accepted* Ⓜ *L to Morgan Ave.* ✛ *7:F2.*

QUEENS

ASTORIA

After you're finished with the sights, why head back to Manhattan? End your day with dinner at one of Astoria's legendary Greek restaurants (on or near Broadway), or venture to the Middle Eastern restaurants farther out on Steinway Street.

$ ✕ **Kabab Café.** Middle-Eastern restaurants are a dime a dozen in NYC,
MIDDLE EASTERN but Egyptian-Mediterranean spots are a rarer find, attracting foodies like celebrity chefs/TV personalities Anthony Bourdain and Andrew

16

Zimmern. This charming yet eccentric 16-seat café, which excels at interesting home-style dishes, is a true hidden treasure. The menu changes nightly, but exceedingly tender lamb stuffed with pomegranate is always great. For the super adventurous eater, try the grilled lamb brain or lamb tongue. And, when they have it, the roasted goose in a saffron sauce, is a must. Cash only. ⑤ *Average main: $17* ⊠ *25–12 Steinway St., Astoria* ☎ *718/728–9858* ⌁ *Reservations not accepted* ▭ *No credit cards* ⊘ *Closed Mon.* Ⓜ *N to Astoria–Ditmars Blvd.* ✛ *7:F1.*

$ ✕ **Taverna Kyclades.** The current powerhouse of Hellenic eats in the
GREEK   neighborhood, Taverna Kyclades offers Greek classics at a higher level than you'd expect, given the simple decor and unassuming location. Fried calamari and grilled octopus make appearances at rock-bottom prices, despite their obvious quality, as do more out-of-the-ordinary dishes like "caviar dip" and swordfish kebabs. Lamb chops drip with juice, and grilled sardines are so fresh you'd swear they were just pulled from the sea. Be prepared to wait for a table at peak times, as they don't take reservations. ⑤ *Average main: $14* ⊠ *33–07 Ditmars Blvd., Astoria* ☎ *718/545–8666* ⊕ *www.tavernakyclades.com* ⌁ *Reservations not accepted* Ⓜ *N to Astoria–Ditmars Blvd.* ✛ *7:F1.*

FLUSHING

Manhattan may be known for its fine four-star restaurants, but food lovers know there's one train line to take to some of the best eats in the city. The 7 train snakes its way through the middle of Queens, and conveniently through some of the best eating neighborhoods in New York. At the end of the line is Flushing, home to the second-largest Chinatown in the United States. (First is San Francisco's.) Wide streets have few tourists and many interesting stores and restaurants, making the long trip worth it. A couple tips: bring cash, because not many of these restaurants accept credit cards, and be prepared to encounter language difficulties, as English speakers are in the minority. In Manhattan, catch the 7 train at Times Square or Grand Central Terminal.

$ ✕ **Spicy and Tasty.** Flushing is crammed with quality salt-of-the-earth
CHINESE   Chinese eateries, but Spicy and Tasty is the place to go for standout Chinese, particularly if you're a first-timer to the neighborhood. The restaurant lives up to its name with numbing Szechuan peppercorns and slicks of red chili oil. Tea-smoked duck has crispy skin and smoky, salty meat. Eggplant with garlic sauce tastes of ginger, tomatoes, and red chilies. Cool it all down with a Tsingtao beer. ⑤ *Average main: $10* ⊠ *39–07 Prince St., at 39th Ave., Flushing* ☎ *718/359–1601* ▭ *No credit cards* ⊘ *www.spicyandtasty.com* Ⓜ *7 to Flushing Main St.* ✛ *7:H1.*

LONG ISLAND CITY

Long Island City began attracting people when PS1 MoMa opened up in the 1970s.

$ ✕ **M. Wells Dinette.** When the original version of this beloved and exper-
CANADIAN   imental restaurant in Long Island City lost its lease and had to shut
Fodor'sChoice   down, a swath of New York eaters let out a collective groan. But they
★   didn't have to go too long without their foie gras fix because French-Canadian chef Hugue Dufour reopened the restaurant at MoMA's

PS1. The menu changes depending on the season but diners might find dishes like veal cheek stroganoff, using thick bucatini as the noodles, or bone marrow and escargot. Finish off with a slice of maple pie and a shot of maple bourbon. Then wander the gallery trying to make sense of the art (and your meal). The restaurant currently closes at 6 pm, leaving time for a leisurely lunch but not dinner. $ *Average main: $17* ⊠ *MoMA PS1, 22–25 Jackson Ave., at 46th Ave., Long Island City* ☎ *718/786–1800* ⊕ *www.momaps1.org/about/mwells* ⌕ *Reservations not accepted* ⊙ *Closed Tues. and Wed. No dinner.* Ⓜ *E, M to 23rd St.–Ely Ave.; G to Long Island City–Court Sq.; 7 to 45 Rd.–Court House Sq.* ✛ *7:F1.*

JACKSON HEIGHTS

One of the most ethnically diverse parts of New York City, Jackson Heights is home to a United Nations of cuisine: from outstanding Indian and Pakistani places to surprisingly excellent taco carts. Most recently, Tibetans have been moving into the neighborhood, setting up small shops selling juicy meat-filled *momos* (dumplings).

$ ✕ **Jackson Diner.** Neighborhood folk and Manhattanites alike flock to
INDIAN Jackson Diner for the spicy, authentic fare served in generous portions. Popular choices include chicken tandoori, South Indian lentil dough- nuts in a tangy broth, and any of the curry dishes, as well as the many vegetarian specialties. Check out the daily massive lunch buffet, or stop by in the evening and try a subcontinent-inspired cocktail, like mango juice and vodka. There's now a location in Manhattan at 72 University Place, but it's not quite the same experience as the Jackson Heights orig- inal. $ *Average main: $16* ⊠ *37–47 74th St., between Roosevelt and 37th Aves., Jackson Heights* ☎ *718/672–1232* Ⓜ *A, M, F, R to Jackson Heights/Roosevelt Ave.; 7 to 74th St./Broadway* ✛ *7:F1.*

WOODSIDE

It has long been said that to get great Thai food in the Big Apple, you have to go to Queens. While the Thai dining landscape has improved in other parts of the city, Woodside is still its epicenter. But to only associ- ate Woodside with Thai cuisine is underselling it; you'll find a variety of ethnic eateries here, including Ecuadorian and Italian.

$ ✕ **SriPraPhai.** The main reason foodies flock to Woodside is to go to SriP-
THAI raPhai (pronounced See-PRA-pie). It's widely considered the best Thai restaurant in New York. Don't be overwhelmed by the huge menu—it's hard to go wrong. Crispy watercress salad, *larb* (ground pork salad with mint and lime juice), sauteed chicken with cashews and pineapple, *kao-soy* (curried egg noodles), and roasted duck green curry are a few standouts. If you go with a few people, order the delicately flavored whole steamed fish. There's a large separate menu for vegetarians. But prepare your palate: your mouth might feel like a five-alarm fire by the time you're finished. $ *Average main: $12* ⊠ *64–13 39th Ave., Wood- side* ☎ *718/899–9599* ⊕ *www.sripraphairestaurant.com* ⊙ *Closed Wed.* Ⓜ *7 to 69th St.* ✛ *7:H1.*

16

THE BRONX

People don't really wander into this borough, like they do into Brooklyn and even Queens, hoping to stumble on some gem of an ethnic eatery. But the Bronx actually has a lot going for it, if you know where to look. Dotted around the borough are some great Mexican taquerias, African eateries, and old-school Italian joints. Skip Manhattan's Little Italy and head to the Bronx's Arthur Avenue for a real red-sauce treat; it's a much more authentic Italian-American neighborhood and a great place to carb-load.

$$ ✕ **Antonio's Trattoria.** Antonio's bills itself as "an Italian restaurant serv-
ITALIAN ing simple food," but it's underselling itself. This is fantastic salt-of-
the-earth Italian fare at its best. Start with the mini-meatballs wading in a marinara sauce and move on to baked clams, house-made ravioli, fettuccini carbonara, or the excellent pizzas, which are baked in a brick oven in the Neapolitan manner. It's a bit off the main Arthur Avenue "Little Italy" strip, but worth the trek. And if you haven't eaten enough, expect a server to come by, prodding you with *"Mangia, mangia!"* ⑤ *Average main: $20* ✉ *2370 Belmont Ave., Belmont* ☎ *718/733–6630* ⊕ *www.antoniostrattoria.com* Ⓜ *B, D to 182nd.*

$ ✕ **Zero Otto Nove.** Though insiders who can get a table swear by Rao's
ITALIAN on 114th in Manhattan, Zero Otto Nove chugs along as one of the best Italian restaurants north of 96th Street. The draw? A menu that is a nice balance between authentic Italian fare and good Italian-American classics. Try a wood-oven-fired pizza, perfectly chewy and loaded with buffalo mozzarella. The San Matteo, which adds broccoli rabe to the mix, is just as addictive as the plain-Jane margherita. For those who don't feel like a trek to the Bronx, there's an outpost in Chelsea. ⑤ *Average main: $15* ✉ *2357 Arthur Ave., Belmont* ☎ *718/220–1027* ⊕ *www.roberto089.com* ⌖ *Reservations not accepted* ⊘ *Closed Mon.* Ⓜ *B, D to 182nd.*

NEW YORK CITY DINING AND LODGING ATLAS

KEY

- ☐ Hotels
- ▣ Restaurants
- ▦ Restaurant in Hotel

Ⓜ *1,2,3,A,B,C* — Station
NYC MTA Subway

MORNINGSIDE HEIGHTS

HARLEM

Randalls Island

EAST HARLEM

Riverside Park

Wards Island

6

Hudson River

Central Park

5

UPPER EAST SIDE

Roosevelt Island

QUEENS

UPPER WEST SIDE

MIDTOWN WEST

4

MIDTOWN EAST

East River

Hudson River

MURRAY HILL

CHELSEA

3

GRAMERCY

FLATIRON DISTRICT

GREENWICH VILLAGE

EAST VILLAGE

2

NOLITA

SOHO LITTLE ITALY

LOWER EAST SIDE

TRI-BECA

CHINA-TOWN

NEW JERSEY

LOWER MANHATTAN

1

FINANCIAL DISTRICT

Battery Park

BROOKLYN

Map 5

- Central Park (South)
- Upper E. Side
- Upper W. Side

W. 86th St.

W. 85th St.

Kefi

W. 84th St.

W. 83rd St.

W. 82nd St.

Excelsior

W. 81st St.

Sarabeth's Kitchen

W. 80th St.

The Lucerne   Nice Matin

W. 79th St.

Fishtag

UPPER
WEST SIDE   W. 78th St.

Dovetail

W. 77th St.

NYLO   Isabella's

Big Nick's
Burger Joint &
Pizza Joint

W. 76th St.

Hotel
Beacon   W. 75th St.

Fairway
Café   Levain Bakery   W. 74th St.

Salumeria Rosi
Parmacotto   W. 73rd St.

1, 2, 3   W. 72nd St.

Gray's
Papaya

Café Luxembourg   W. 70th St.

W. 69th St.

Telepan

Lincoln
Towers   W. 67th St.

W. 66th St.   W. 66th St.

1   W. 65th St.

Picholine

W. 64th St.

LINCOLN
CENTER   Bar Boulud   W. 63rd St.   P.J. Clarke's

Damrosch
Park   The Empire Hotel

W. 62nd St.

FORDHAM
UNIVERSITY   W. 61st St.   Jean Georges
Trump International
Hotel and Towers

W. 60th St.   Asiate
Mandarin Oriental

W. 59th St.   Bouchon Bakery   Columbus
Circle   A,B,C,D,1   Central Park South

Per Se   MIDTOWN

W. 58th St.   Porter House   6 Columbus

West End Avenue
Broadway
Amsterdam Avenue
Columbus Avenue
Central Park West

B,C

86th St. Transverse

Jacqueline Kennedy
Onassis Reservoir

Great
Lawn

HAYDEN
PLANETARIUM

Belvedere
Lake

West Dr.

AMERICAN MUSEUM
OF NATURAL HISTORY

B,C

79th St. Transverse

CENTRAL
PARK

The
Lake

B,C

Terrace Dr.

West Dr.

65th St. Transverse

WOLLMAN
RINK

Central Park West

Columbus
Circle

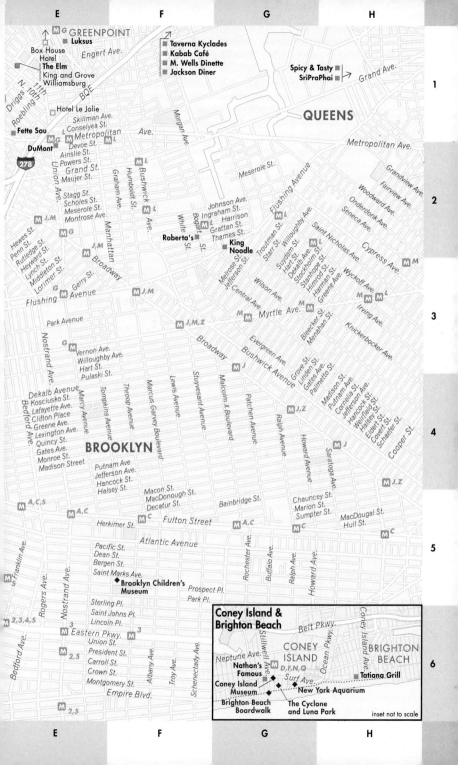

E | F | G | H

GREENPOINT

Luksus

Box House
Hotel
The Elm
King and Grove
Williamsburg

Taverna Kyclades
Kabab Café
M. Wells Dinette
Jackson Diner

Spicy & Tasty
SriPraPhai

Grand Ave.

Engert Ave.

Hotel Le Jolie

Skillman Ave.
Conselyea St.
Fette Sau
Devoe St.
DuMont
Ainslie St.
Metropolitan
Powers St.
Grand St.
Maujer St.

Union Ave.
Stagg St.
Scholes St.
Meserole St.
Montrose Ave.

Hewes St.
Penn St.
Rutledge St.
Heyward St.
Lynch St.
Middleton St.
Lorimer St.

Metropolitan Ave.

QUEENS

278

Meserole St.

Johnson Ave.
Ingraham St.
Harrison
Grattan St.
Thames St.

Roberta's

King
Noodle

Melrose St.
Jefferson St.
Central Ave.
Wilson Ave.

Flushing Avenue

Broadway

Myrtle Ave.

Grandview Ave.
Fairview Ave.
Woodward Ave.
Onderdonk Ave.
Seneca Ave.

Cypress Ave.

Troutman St.
Starr St.
Suydam St.
Hart St.
Willoughby Ave.
Dekalb St.
Stockholm St.
Stanhope St.
Himrod St.
Harman St.
Greene Ave.

Saint Nicholas Ave.
Wyckoff Ave.

Irving Ave.

Knickerbocker Ave.

Park Avenue

Vernon Ave.
Willoughby Ave.
Hart St.
Pulaski St.

Nostrand Avenue

Flushing Avenue

Gerry St.

Manhattan

Graham Avenue

Humboldt St.

Bushwick Ave.

White St.
Bogart St.

Morgan Ave.

Ave.

N. 11th
10th
Driggs
Roebling
BQE

Broadway

Evergreen Ave.

Bushwick Avenue

Grove St.
Linden St.
Gates Ave.
Palmetto St.

Bleecker St.
Menahan St.

Madison St.
Putnam Ave.
Cornelia St.
Jefferson Ave.
Hancock St.
Weirfield St.
Halsey St.
Eldert St.
Covert St.
Schaefer St.

Cooper St.

Dekalb Avenue
Kosciusko St.
Lafayette Ave.
Clifton Place
Greene Ave.
Lexington Ave.
Quincy St.
Gates Ave.
Monroe St.
Madison Street

Bedford Ave.

Marcy Avenue

Tompkins Avenue

Throop Avenue

Marcus Garvey Boulevard

Lewis Avenue

Stuyvesant Avenue

Malcolm x Boulevard

Patchen Avenue

Ralph Avenue

Howard Avenue

Saratoga Ave.

BROOKLYN

Putnam Ave.
Jefferson Ave.
Hancock St.
Halsey St.

Macon St.
MacDonough St.
Decatur St.

Bainbridge St.

Chauncey St.
Marion St.
Sumpter St.

MacDougal St.
Hull St.

Herkimer St.

Fulton Street

Atlantic Avenue

Rochester Ave.

Buffalo Ave.

Ralph Ave.

Howard Ave.

Pacific St.
Dean St.
Bergen St.
Saint Marks Ave.

Franklin Ave.

Rogers Ave.

Nostrand Avenue

Brooklyn Children's
Museum

Prospect Pl.
Park Pl.

Sterling Pl.
Saint Johns Pl.
Lincoln Pl.

Eastern Pkwy.
Union St.
President St.
Carroll St.
Crown St.
Montgomery St.
Empire Blvd.

Bedford Ave.

Albany Ave.

Troy Ave.

Schenectady Ave.

**Coney Island &
Brighton Beach**

Belt Pkwy.

CONEY
ISLAND

BRIGHTON
BEACH

Neptune Ave.

Nathan's
Famous

Coney Island
Museum

Brighton Beach
Boardwalk

Stillwell Ave.

Surf Ave.

D,F,N,Q

New York Aquarium

The Cyclone
and Luna Park

Ocean Pkwy.

Coney Island Ave.

Tatiana Grill

inset not to scale

E | F | G | H

1 | 2 | 3 | 4 | 5 | 6

WHERE TO STAY

Updated by
Jessica Colley

There are more hotel rooms than ever in New York City, as exciting new properties continue to open their doors not only in Manhattan proper but in Brooklyn and the outer boroughs as well. But does that mean that New York is cheap? Well, we wouldn't say *cheap*, but you can still find some deals, especially if you're not set on a specific property or neighborhood, and if you don't mind a few extra minutes of commuting time.

Hotels continue to slash rates based on market sensitivity—especially if you and all of those other Internet-savvy room shoppers are willing to wait until the last minute. That said, if you want to stay in a specific place and the rate seems reasonable, book it—it's just as likely to go up, especially during peak seasons (spring and fall).

And how to choose? The first thing to consider is location (⇨ *Check out our "Where Should I Stay?" chart*). Many New York City visitors insist on staying in the hectic Midtown area—and options are improving there—but other neighborhoods are often just as convenient. Less-touristy areas, such as Gramercy, the Lower East Side, the Upper West Side—even Brooklyn—offer a far more realistic sense of New York life.

Also consider timing: the least expensive months to book rooms in the city are January and February. If you're flexible on dates, ask the reservationist if there's a cheaper time to stay during your preferred traveling month—that way you can avoid peak dates, like Fashion Week and the New York City Marathon. And be sure to ask about possible weekend packages that could include a third night free. (The Financial District in particular can be a discount gold mine on the weekend.)

Another source of bargains? Chain hotels. Many have moved into the city, offering reasonable room rates. In addition to favorites like the Sheraton, Hilton, and Hyatt brands, there are Best Westerns, Days Inns, and Comfort Inns. These rates aren't as low as you'll find outside Manhattan, but they're certainly getting closer.

WHERE SHOULD I STAY?

	NEIGHBORHOOD VIBE	PROS	CONS
Lower Manhattan	Mostly skyscraper hotels in an area that buzzes with activity during weekday hours but can be eerily quiet at night.	Low crime area; easy subway access to uptown sights; great walking paths along the waterfront and in Battery Park.	Construction and congestion near World Trade Center site; limited choice of restaurants and shopping.
SoHo and NoLIta (with Little Italy)	Swanky, high-end hotels with hip restaurants and lounges patronized by New Yorkers and travelers alike.	Scores of upscale clothing boutiques and art galleries nearby; safe area for meandering walks; easy subway access.	Not budget-friendly; streets are crowded on weekends; few major sites nearby.
East Village and the Lower East Side	The epicenter of edgy New York, great for travelers looking to party.	Great low-cost options for young generation. Great restaurants and independent boutiques.	One of the least subway-accessible Manhattan 'hoods; expect late-night noise.
Greenwich Village and the West Village	Hotels in this part of town are few and far between. The ones that are here are small and boutiquey.	Easy subway access to anywhere in town; great shopping, dining, and drinking venues.	Winding streets can be tough to navigate; most hotels are on the pricey side.
Chelsea and the Meatpacking District	More hotels are opening in one of the city's trendiest restaurant and nightlife areas.	See and be seen, and lots of great shopping.	This is a trendy and pricey neighborhood for hotels. Most hotel bars are a real scene.
Union Square, Flatiron District, and Gramercy	A relatively quiet residential area.	Patches of calm respite from the hustle-and-bustle of downtown and midtown; low crime area.	Limited subway access as you move east; Gramercy may be too quiet for some.
Midtown East and West, and Murray Hill	Mostly big-name hotel chains and luxury business suites around Times Square; lots of tourists.	Near Broadway theaters; budget options are available in chain hotels and indies alike.	Streets are often packed with pedestrians; area around Port Authority is gritty. Murray Hill is pretty quiet.
Upper East Side	Well-heeled residential neighborhood near many museums.	Removed from Midtown hustle; near tourist attractions like Central Park.	Streets are quiet after 9 pm; few budget dining options; limited subway access (just the 6 line).
Upper West Side	Hotels in a residential neighborhood near Central Park, Lincoln Center, and some museums.	Lovely tree-lined streets; laid-back neighborhood eateries.	Weekend trains can be slow; most hotels are on the pricey side.
Brooklyn	Brooklyn has a bit of everything so it depends on where you end up. Williamsburg is all about hipsters, while Downtown Brooklyn and around are quite residential.	You'll find generally smaller boutique-style hotels with personalized service and character, and rates worth traveling for. Plus, a whole new borough to explore.	If you're out late in Manhattan, it'll be a subway or a relatively pricey taxi back to Brooklyn.

17

BEST BETS FOR NEW YORK CITY LODGING

Fodor's offers a selective listing of high-quality lodging in every price range. Here we've compiled our top picks by price and experience.

Fodor's Choice★

Ace Hotel, $$, p. 371
Aloft New York Brooklyn, $$, p. 392
Andaz Wall Street, $$, p. 365
The Bowery Hotel, $$$, p. 368
The Carlyle, $$$$, p. 389
The Chatwal, $$$$, p. 381
Crosby Street Hotel, $$$, p. 367
The Greenwich Hotel, $$$, p. 366
Hotel on Rivington, $$, p. 369
Hyatt Union Square, $$, p. 374
The Inn at Irving Place, $$$, p. 374
Inn on 23rd, $, p. 370
James Hotel, $$$, p. 368
Library Hotel, $$, p. 377
The London NYC, $$$, p. 384
Mandarin Oriental, $$$$, p. 384
The Mark, $$$, p. 390
Mondrian Soho, $$, p. 368
NoMad, $$$, p. 373
The Out NYC, $$, p. 385
The Peninsula, $$$$, p. 377

Refinery Hotel, $$$, p. 385
Ritz-Carlton New York, Central Park, $$$$, p. 387
The St. Regis, $$$$, p. 378
The Standard, $$, p. 371
The Wythe Hotel, $$, p. 394

Best by Price

$

Best Western Plus President Hotel, p. 380
Carlton Arms, p. 374
The Herald Square Hotel, p. 379
Hotel Beacon, p. 390
Hotel Metro, p. 382
Inn on 23rd, p. 370
The Jane, p. 370
La Quinta Inn, p. 384
Pod Hotel, p. 377
Pod 39, p. 379
W Hotel New York, p. 379
Yotel, p. 389

$$

Ace Hotel, p. 371
Andaz Wall Street, p. 365

Casablanca Hotel, p. 381
Conrad New York, p. 366
Holiday Inn SoHo, p. 367
Hotel on Rivington, p. 369
The Inn at Irving Place, p. 374
Library Hotel, p. 377
The Mansfield, p. 384
The Maritime Hotel, p. 371
The Michelangelo, p. 384
The Out NYC, p. 385
Room Mate Grace, p. 387
The Standard, p. 371
The Wythe Hotel, p. 394

$$$

Crosby Street Hotel, p. 367
The Greenwich Hotel, p. 366
The James Hotel New York, p. 368
The Mercer, p. 368
Refinery Hotel, p. 385
Thompson LES, p. 369

$$$$

The Carlyle, p. 389
The Chatwal, p. 381
Gramercy Park Hotel, p. 374
Mandarin Oriental, p. 384
The Mark, p. 390
The Peninsula, p. 377
Ritz-Carlton New York, Central Park, p. 387
The St. Regis, p. 378

Best by Experience

BEST BEDS

Four Seasons, p. 376
The Greenwich Hotel, p. 366
Ink48, p. 382
The Inn at Irving Place, p. 374
The Mansfield, p. 384
The Mark, p. 390
The Nolitan Hotel, p. 367
Ritz-Carltons, p. 366, 387

BEST CONCIERGE

Four Seasons, p. 376
Le Parker Meridien, p. 384
The London NYC, p. 384
Mandarin Oriental, p. 384
The Quin, p. 385
Ritz-Carlton New York, Battery Park, p. 366

BEST GYM

The Grand Hyatt New York, p. 376

The James Hotel New York, p. 368

Le Parker Meridien, p. 384

The London NYC, p. 384

The Mark, p. 390

Trump International Hotel and Towers, p. 392

BEST FOR HISTORY BUFFS

The Carlyle, p. 389

The Chatwal, p. 381

The Inn at Irving Place, p. 374

Plaza Hotel, p. 385

The St. Regis, p. 378

BEST HOTEL BAR

Bemelmans Bar at the Carlyle, p. 389

The Biergarten at the Standard, p. 371

Breslin Bar at the Ace Hotel, p. 371

The Gansevoort Park, p. 373

Jimmy at the James Hotel, p. 368

King Cole Bar at St. Regis, p. 378

Lobby Bar at the Bowery Hotel, p. 368

Oak Bar at the Plaza Hotel, p. 385

Print Lounge at Ink48, p. 382

Rose Bar at the Gramercy Park Hotel, p. 374

Winnie's at the Refinery Hotel, p. 385

BEST FOR KIDS

Affinia 50, p. 375

Aloft New York Brooklyn, p. 392

Conrad New York, p. 366

Hotel Beacon, p. 390

Ink48, p. 382

Le Parker Meridien, p. 384

Plaza Hotel, p. 385

BEST-KEPT SECRET

Best Western Plus President, p. 380

Box House Hotel, p. 393

The Franklin, p. 389

The Greenwich Hotel, p. 366

The Inn at Irving Place, p. 374

Inn on 23rd, p. 370

The Lowell, p. 390

BEST LOBBY

Ace Hotel, p. 371

Four Seasons, p. 376

Gramercy Park Hotel, p. 374

Mandarin Oriental, p. 384

The Marlton, p. 369

NYLO, p. 392

The Peninsula, p. 377

The St. Regis, p. 378

BEST NEIGHBORHOOD EXPERIENCE

The Bowery Hotel, p. 368

The Carlyle, p. 389

The Franklin, p. 389

The Greenwich Hotel, p. 366

The Inn at Irving Place, p. 374

The Mark, p. 390

The Standard, p. 371

BEST NEW HOTELS

Aloft New York Brooklyn. P. 392

Hotel Americano, p. 370

The Marlton, p. 369

NYLO, p. 392

The Out NYC, p. 385

Refinery Hotel, p. 385

Union Square Hyatt, p. 374

Yotel, p. 389

BEST POOL

Hotel Gansevoort, p. 373

Mandarin Oriental, p. 384

ONE UN New York, p. 377

The Peninsula, p. 377

Trump International Hotel and Towers, p. 392

BEST SERVICE

The Carlyle, p. 389

The Chatwal, p. 381

Four Seasons, p. 376

The Greenwich Hotel, p. 366

The James Hotel New York, p. 368

The London NYC, p. 384

The Peninsula, p. 377

The Mark, p. 390

Plaza Hotel, p. 385

Ritz-Carlton New York, Battery Park, p. 366

SoHo Grand, p. 368

BEST VIEWS

The Carlyle, p. 389

Mandarin Oriental, p. 384

The Nolitan, p. 367

Ritz Carlton New York, Central Park, p. 387

The Standard East Village, p. 368

The Standard, p. 371

Trump International Hotel and Towers, p. 392

The Wythe, p. 394

MOST ROMANTIC

Andaz Wall Street, p. 365

The Greenwich Hotel, p. 366

The Inn at Irving Place, p. 374

Library Hotel, p. 377

The Lowell, p. 390

The Marlton, p. 369

Ritz-Carlton New York, Battery Park, p. 366

The Standard, p. 371

The Wythe, p. 394

17

PLANNER

STRATEGY

Manhattan has hundreds of hotels, so making a choice may seem daunting. But fret not—our expert writers and editors have done most of the legwork. The 120-plus selections here represent the best this city has to offer—from the best budget motels to the sleekest designer boutiques. Scan "Best Bets" on the previous pages for top recommendations by price and experience. Or find a review quickly in the listings—search by neighborhood, then alphabetically. Happy hunting!

NEED A RESERVATION?

Hotel reservations are an absolute necessity when planning your trip to New York—although rooms are easier to come by these days. Competition for clients also means properties must undergo frequent improvements, especially during July and August, so when booking, ask about any renovations, lest you get a room within earshot of construction. In this ever-changing city travelers can find themselves temporarily, and inconveniently, without commonplace amenities such as room service or spa access if their hotel is upgrading.

SERVICES

Unless otherwise noted in the individual descriptions, all hotels listed have private baths, central heating, air-conditioning, and private phones. Almost all hotels have data ports and phones with voice mail, as well as valet service. Many now have wireless Internet (Wi-Fi) available, though it's not always free. Most large hotels have video or high-speed checkout capability, and many can arrange babysitting. Pools are a rarity, but most properties have gyms or health clubs, and sometimes full-scale spas; hotels without facilities usually have arrangements for guests at nearby gyms, sometimes for a fee.

PARKING

Bringing a car to Manhattan can add significantly to your expenses. Many properties in all price ranges do have parking facilities, but they are often at independent garages that charge $20 or more per day, and valet parking can cost up to $60 a day. The city's exorbitant 18.375% parking tax can turn any car you drive into the Big Apple into a lemon.

FAMILY TRAVEL

New York has gone to great lengths to attract family vacationers, and hotels have followed the family-friendly trend. Some properties provide such diversions as Web TV and in-room video games; others have suites with kitchenettes and foldout sofa beds. Most full-service Manhattan hotels provide rollaway beds, babysitting, and stroller rental, but be sure to make arrangements when booking the room, not when you arrive.

DOES SIZE MATTER?

If room size is important to you, ask the reservationist how many square feet a room has, not just if it's big. A hotel room in New York is considered quite large if it's 500 square feet. Very large rooms, such as those at the Four Seasons, are 600 square feet. To stay anywhere larger you'll have to get a multiroom suite. Small rooms are a tight 150 to 200 square feet, and sometimes even less. Very small rooms are less than 100 square feet; you'll find these at inns and lodges, and they're sold as a single for only one person. There are studio apartments in the city that are 250 square feet and include a kitchen; 1,000 square feet is considered a huge abode in this very compact and crowded urban playland.

PRICES

There's no denying that New York City hotels are expensive, but rates run the full range. For high-end hotels like the Mandarin Oriental at Central Park, prices start at $955 a night for a standard room in high season, which runs from September through December. At the low end of the spending spectrum, a bunk at the Jane starts at $99 for a single. But don't be put off by the prices printed here—many hotels slash their rates significantly for promotions and web-only deals.

Prices in the reviews are the lowest cost of a standard double room in high season.

HOTEL REVIEWS

Listed alphabetically within neighborhoods. Please visit Fodors.com for expanded reviews. Use the coordinate (✛ 1:B2) at the end of each listing to locate a property on the corresponding map preceding this chapter.

LOWER MANHATTAN

17

FINANCIAL DISTRICT

$$ ⊡ **Andaz Wall Street.** If space is a priority, head to the southern tip of

HOTEL Manhattan: this sleek hotel offers generous rooms with large windows,

Fodor'sChoice oak floors, and extra-large bathrooms. **Pros:** free Wi-Fi, bikes, snacks,

★ and nonalcoholic beverages; excellent, intuitive lighting controls; good value. **Cons:** limited choice for restaurants and nightlife in the neighborhood; in-house restaurant not open 7 days a week. ⑤ *Rooms from: $325* ✉ *75 Wall St., Financial District* ☎ *212/590–1234* ⊕ *www. newyork.wallstreet.andaz.hyatt.com* ⮡ *213 rooms, 40 suites* ⱺ *No meals* Ⓜ *2, 3 to Wall St.* ✛ *1:E4.*

$$ ⊡ **Gild Hall.** Captains of Industry, here's a boutique hotel for you: operated

HOTEL by the owners of the several Thompson hotels around the United States and elsewhere, Gild Hall aggressively courts those clientele with a Y chromosome: beds have padded leather headboards and tartan throw blankets. **Pros:** central Financial District location; eye-popping lobby; stylish room design. **Cons:** small rooms for the price; untraditional location. ⑤ *Rooms from: $409* ✉ *15 Gold St., at Platt St., Financial District* ☎ *212/232–7700, 800/268–0700* ⊕ *www.thompsonhotels.com* ⮡ *116 rooms, 10 suites* ⱺ *No meals* Ⓜ *2, 3, 4, 5, 6, A, C to Fulton St./Broadway-Nassau* ✛ *1:E3.*

$$ ⊡ **The W New York Downtown.** In the heart of the Financial District, this

HOTEL W outpost juxtaposes the gritty feel of the Financial District with sleek surfaces. **Pros:** near popular tourist attractions; restaurant offers some surprisingly affordable fare; modern workout room. **Cons:** scaffolding-dense neighborhood; construction of World Trade Center nearby; not family-friendly. ⑤ *Rooms from: $409* ✉ *123 Washington St., at Albany St., Financial District* ☎ *646/826–8600* ⊕ *www.starwoodhotels.com* ⮡ *214 rooms, 3 suites* ⱺ *No meals* Ⓜ *1, N, R to Rector St.* ✛ *1:C4.*

TRIBECA

$$
HOTEL
⌖ **Conrad New York.** A pleasant surprise in a quiet Battery Park City location, this hotel offers many coveted amenities: significant square footage, a breezy rooftop bar, and access to green space in nearby Hudson River Park. **Pros:** spacious rooms; emphasis on art and design; movie theater and restaurants; near downtown attractions. **Cons:** daily fee for Wi-Fi; removed from Midtown attractions; expensive. $ *Rooms from: $359* ✉ *102 North End Ave., between Vesey and Murray Sts., TriBeCa* 🕾 *212/945–0100* ⊕ *www.conradnewyork.com* ↻ *463 suites* �‖*No meals* Ⓜ *1, 2, 3, A, C to Chambers St.; E to World Trade Center* ✛ *1:B3.*

$$
HOTEL
⌖ **The Cosmopolitan Hotel.** For a bargain room in a great downtown neighborhood, it's hard to beat this cost-conscious favorite. **Pros:** friendly staff; great location for power shoppers. **Cons:** sometimes-noisy location; rooms on the small side. $ *Rooms from: $379* ✉ *95 W. Broadway, at Chambers St., TriBeCa* 🕾 *212/566–1900* ⊕ *www.cosmohotel.com* ↻ *129 rooms* �‖*No meals* Ⓜ *1, 2, 3, A, C to Chambers St.* ✛ *1:C2.*

$$
HOTEL
⌖ **Duane Street Hotel.** Amid TriBeCa's historic warehouses and trendy art galleries sits this boutique hotel, a fashionable addition to the neighborhood. **Pros:** great location; free Wi-Fi; stylish rooms; good pick for the allergy conscious. **Cons:** off-site gym; no 24-hour room service. $ *Rooms from: $399* ✉ *130 Duane St., TriBeCa* 🕾 *212/964–4600* ⊕ *www.duanestreethotel.com* ↻ *41 rooms, 2 suites* ❘⊖❘*No meals* Ⓜ *1, 2, 3 to Chambers St.; A, C to Chambers St.* ✛ *1:C1; 2:D6.*

$$$
HOTEL
Fodor's Choice
★
⌖ **The Greenwich Hotel.** This understated, inviting hotel manages to fly under the radar even though Robert De Niro is an owner. **Pros:** fabulous restaurant (Locanda Verde also available for room service); gorgeous pool; excellent service. **Cons:** some plumbing noise; high prices. $ *Rooms from: $550* ✉ *377 Greenwich St., TriBeCa* 🕾 *212/941–8900* ⊕ *www.thegreenwichhotel.com* ↻ *75 rooms, 13 suites* ❘⊖❘*No meals* Ⓜ *1 to Franklin St.* ✛ *1:B1.*

$$$
HOTEL
⌖ **The Ritz-Carlton New York, Battery Park.** If you're staying this far downtown, the Ritz is your top choice. **Pros:** excellent service; best base for downtown exploring; pet- and kid-friendly; Liberty views. **Cons:** removed from Midtown tourist sights; limited nighttime activities; few neighborhood options for dining and entertainment. $ *Rooms from: $545* ✉ *2 West St., at Battery Park, TriBeCa* 🕾 *212/344–0800, 800/241–3333* ⊕ *www.ritzcarlton.com/batterypark* ↻ *259 rooms, 39 suites* ❘⊖❘*No meals* Ⓜ *1, R, J to Rector St.* ✛ *1:C5; 2: C6.*

$$
HOTEL
⌖ **Smyth Tribeca.** Resting almost on top of a convenient subway stop, this thoroughly modern hotel makes TriBeCa a welcoming landing spot for visitors. **Pros:** great service; good restaurant; excellent subway access. **Cons:** Wi-Fi not free; only a frosted glass partition divides bathroom from sleeping area; bathrooms could have better lighting. $ *Rooms from: $299* ✉ *85 W. Broadway, between Chambers and Warren Sts., TriBeCa* 🕾 *212/587–7000* ⊕ *www.thompson hotels.com* ↻ *84 rooms, 16 suites* ❘⊖❘*No meals* Ⓜ *1, 2, 3, A, C to Chambers St.* ✛ *1:C2.*

$$$ 〒 **Tribeca Grand.** Still popular
HOTEL with the glitterati, the scene at the
Tribeca Grand centers on the eight-
story atrium's Church Lounge bar
and café. **Pros:** great dining and
bar scene; central downtown loca-
tion; fun social atrium; pet-friendly.
Cons: rooms get noise from restau-
rant below; bathroom has slightly
cold design. ⑤ *Rooms from: $499*
✉ *2 Ave. of the Americas (6th
Ave.), between Walker and White
Sts., TriBeCa* ☎ *212/519–6600,*
800/965–3000 ⊕ *www.tribecagrand.com* ⤴ *187 rooms, 14 suites*
†◎| *No meals* Ⓜ *A, C, E to Canal St.* ✛ *2:D5.*

SOHO AND NOLITA

NOLITA

$$ 〒 **The Nolitan Hotel.** A welcome addition to an underserved neighbor-
HOTEL hood, the Nolitan combines a hip, slightly gritty feel with some luxe
touches, but don't expect a lot of space to spread out. **Pros:** cool vibe;
fun location convenient to lower Manhattan and Brooklyn; fabulous views from rooftop and some rooms. **Cons:** smallish rooms; gym
access five-minute walk away; some street noise. ⑤ *Rooms from: $409*
✉ *30 Kenmare St., NoLIta* ☎ *212/925–2555* ⊕ *www.nolitanhotel.com*
⤴ *56 rooms, 1 suite* †◎| *No meals* Ⓜ *6 to Spring St.; B, D to Grand
St.* ✛ *2:F4.*

SOHO

$$$$ 〒 **60 Thompson.** This hotel may no longer be the center of the universe
HOTEL scene-wise, but that's a blessing for guests, since the service (and the
staffs' attitudes) have improved. **Pros:** supercentral for SoHo nightlife; good gym; some rooms have balconies. **Cons:** not family-oriented;
no pets allowed. ⑤ *Rooms from: $719* ✉ *60 Thompson St., between
Broome and Spring Sts., SoHo* ☎ *212/431–0400, 877/431–0400*
⊕ *www.thompsonhotels.com* ⤴ *97 rooms, 10 suites* †◎| *No meals* Ⓜ *C,
E to Spring St.* ✛ *2:D4.*

$$$ 〒 **Crosby Street Hotel.** This whimsical boutique hotel, the first branch
HOTEL of a UK chain to open in the U.S., has excellent SoHo views. **Pros:**
Fodor'sChoice unique design; big, bright rooms; great bar. **Cons:** small gym. ⑤ *Rooms*
★ *from: $555* ✉ *79 Crosby St., between Prince and Spring Sts., SoHo*
☎ *212/226–6400* ⊕ *www.firmdalehotels.com* ⤴ *69 rooms, 17 suites*
†◎| *No meals* Ⓜ *6 to Spring St., R to Prince St.* ✛ *2:E3*

$$ 〒 **Holiday Inn SoHo.** "SoHo" and "Holiday Inn" may not sound right
HOTEL together, but here they are. **Pros:** well-priced SoHo solution; well-
trained staff. **Cons:** nothing stylish; closer to Chinatown than to
SoHo. ⑤ *Rooms from: $280* ✉ *138 Lafayette St., near Canal St., SoHo*
☎ *212/966–8898, 800/465–4329* ⊕ *www.hidowntown-nyc.com* ⤴ *215
rooms, 12 suites* †◎| *No meals* Ⓜ *6, M, N, Q, R to Canal St.* ✛ *2:E5.*

17

$$$
HOTEL
FAMILY
Fodor'sChoice
★

The James Hotel New York. This hotel on the edge of SoHo never sacrifices comfort for style, so it's no wonder there's a high percentage of return customers: creative types, businesspeople, fashionistas, and anyone else with deep pockets. **Pros:** stellar service; fabulous views. **Cons:** the upstairs Jimmy bar is expensive and sometimes too-cool-for-school. ⑤ *Rooms from: $549* ✉ *27 Grand St., between Thompson and 6th Ave., SoHo* ☎ *212/465–2000* ⊕ *www.jameshotels.com* ↝ *109 rooms, 5 suites* ⑩*No meals* Ⓜ *A, C, E, 6, J, M, N, Q, R to Canal St.* ✛ *2:D4.*

$$$$
HOTEL

The Mercer. Owner André Balazs has a knack for dating Hollywood starlets and channeling a neighborhood sensibility, and here it's SoHo loft all the way. **Pros:** great location; sophisticated design touches; celebrity sightings in lobby. **Cons:** service inconsistent; some tight rooms. ⑤ *Rooms from: $625* ✉ *147 Mercer St., at Prince St., SoHo* ☎ *212/966–6060, 888/918–6060* ⊕ *www.mercerhotel.com* ↝ *68 rooms, 7 suites* ⑩*No meals* Ⓜ *N, R to Prince St.* ✛ *2:E3.*

$$
HOTEL
Fodor'sChoice
★

Mondrian Soho. Snazzy style and a chic SoHo vibe make the Mondrian a winner for anyone looking for a real downtown New York experience. **Pros:** great design; friendly to electronics addicts. **Cons:** dark elevators; standard rooms are small; charge for Internet. ⑤ *Rooms from: $399* ✉ *9 Crosby St., SoHo* ☎ *212/389–1000* ⊕ *www.mondriansoho.com* ↝ *270 rooms, 43 suites* ⑩*No meals* Ⓜ *A, C, E, 6, J, M, N, Q, R to Canal St.* ✛ *2:E4.*

$$
HOTEL

SoHo Grand. The SoHo Grand defines what SoHo is today—once pioneering, now expensive, and with a vaguely creative vibe. **Pros:** fashionable, laid-back sophistication; great service; surprisingly discreet setting; diverse eating and drinking options. **Cons:** closer to Canal Street than prime SoHo; rooms on small side. ⑤ *Rooms from: $329* ✉ *310 W. Broadway, at Grand St., SoHo* ☎ *212/965–3000, 800/965–3000* ⊕ *www.sohogrand.com* ↝ *341 rooms, 12 suites* ⑩*No meals* Ⓜ *A, C, E, 6, J, M, N, Q, R to Canal St.* ✛ *2:D4.*

EAST VILLAGE AND THE LOWER EAST SIDE

EAST VILLAGE

$$$
HOTEL
Fodor'sChoice
★

The Bowery Hotel. The Bowery Hotel is like an English hunting lodge in Manhattan, warmed by rich tapestries, fireplaces, and chandeliers—and there's no shortage of Brits, who flock to the property; the only thing missing is a trusty hound. **Pros:** quirky, fun location; happening bar and lobby-lounge area; celebrity sightings; interesting views. **Cons:** gritty neighbors; rooms aren't luxurious. ⑤ *Rooms from: $495* ✉ *335 Bowery, at 3rd St., East Village* ☎ *212/505–9100* ⊕ *www.theboweryhotel.com* ↝ *135 rooms, 25 suites* ⑩*No meals* Ⓜ *6 to Bleecker; B, D, F, M to Broadway/Lafayette* ✛ *2:F2.*

$$$
HOTEL

Standard East Village. A jarring, 21-story glass-and-steel finger rising up in the low-rise East Village, this hotel was never going to pass under the radar—and that's guaranteed now that André Balazs and company have taken over. **Pros:** stylish rooms; central location. **Cons:** out of character with the area; restaurant seems constantly in flux. ⑤ *Rooms from: $495* ✉ *25 Cooper Sq., between 5th and 6th Sts.,*

East Village ☎ *212/475–5700* ⊕ *www.standardhotels.com/eastvillage* 🛏️ *145 rooms, 8 suites* ⧈|*No meals* Ⓜ *6 to Astor Pl.; R to 8th. St./ NYU* ✛ *2:F2.*

LOWER EAST SIDE

$$
HOTEL
Fodor'sChoice
★

🏨 **Hotel on Rivington.** A pioneer when it opened back in 2004, this glass-walled hotel on the Lower East Side is still a great choice if you want to be in the thick of the neighborhood's dining and nightlife scene. **Pros:** cool location and vibe; huge windows with wonderful New York views; many rooms have balconies; seriously luxurious bathrooms. **Cons:** feels clubby on weekends; isolated from some subway lines. ⑤ *Rooms from: $380* ⧈ *107 Rivington St., between Ludlow and Essex Sts., Lower East Side* ☎ *212/475–2600, 800/915–1537* ⊕ *www.hotelonrivington.com* 🛏️ *88 rooms, 20 suites* ⧈|*No meals* Ⓜ *F, J, M, Z to Delancey/Essex Sts.* ✛ *2:G3.*

$$$
HOTEL

🏨 **Thompson LES.** This hotel is a great emodiment of the neighborhood inhabitants: hip, but friendly when you get to know it. **Pros:** in the heart of downtown; great views from suites; hip rooftop bar and pool. **Cons:** occasionally snobby staff; rooms stylish but dark. ⑤ *Rooms from: $529* ⧈ *190 Allen St., between Houston and Stanton Sts., Lower East Side* ☎ *212/460–5300* ⊕ *www.thompsonhotels.com* 🛏️ *124 rooms, 17 suites* ⧈|*No meals* Ⓜ *F, J, M, Z to Delancey/Essex Sts.* ✛ *2:G3.*

GREENWICH VILLAGE AND THE WEST VILLAGE

17

GREENWICH VILLAGE

$$
HOTEL

🏨 **The Jade.** Among the ghosts of the literary salons and speakeasies of Greenwich Village is the Jade, a new boutique property on a tree-lined street with an Art Deco sensibility. **Pros:** delivers a true Greenwich Village experience; cozy fireplaces; fresh, brand-new property. **Cons:** small rooms; no connecting rooms. ⑤ *Rooms from: $400* ⧈ *52 W. 13th St., between 5th and 6th Aves., Greenwich Village* ☎ *212/375–1300* ⊕ *www.thejadenyc.com* 🛏️ *109 rooms, 4 suites* ⧈|*No meals* Ⓜ *1, 2, 3, F, M to 14th St.; N, Q, R, L, 4, 5, 6 to Union Square* ✛ *3:E4.*

$
HOTEL

🏨 **The Marlton.** Built in 1900 and once home to Jack Kerouac, this hotel has been remade into a stylish boutique with a residential feel. **Pros:** fresh property with luxurious touches; spacious lobby with coffee bar; great Greenwich Village location; value with style. **Cons:** very small rooms; no work desks; no room service. ⑤ *Rooms from: $275* ⧈ *5 W. 8th St., Greenwich Village* ☎ *212/321–0100* ⊕ *www.marltonhotel. com* 🛏️ *105 rooms, 2 suites* ⧈|*No meals* Ⓜ *A, B, C, D, E, F, M to W. 4th St.* ✛ *3:E5.*

$$
HOTEL

🏨 **Washington Square Hotel.** This low-key hotel in Greenwich Village is popular with visiting New York University parents—the location near Washington Square Park (and just down the street from Mario Batali's Babbo restaurant) is a bonus. **Pros:** parkside location; deluxe rooms are charming; great hotel bar. **Cons:** NYU students everywhere in the neighborhood; rooms are small. ⑤ *Rooms from: $315* ⧈ *103 Waverly Pl., at MacDougal St., Greenwich Village* ☎ *212/777–9515, 800/222–0418* ⊕ *www.washingtonsquarehotel.com* 🛏️ *152 rooms* ⧈|*Breakfast* Ⓜ *A, B, C, D, E, F, M to W. 4th St./Washington Sq.* ✛ *2:D1.*

WEST VILLAGE

$
HOTEL
The Jane. To some, the Jane is impossibly chic; to others, the rooms are reminiscent of Sing Sing. **Pros:** cheap; hot bar scene; amazing decor in lounge; great branch of weekend brunch favorite Café Gitane. **Cons:** tiny standard rooms; shared bathrooms; noise from the bar. ⑤ *Rooms from: $125* ✉ *113 Jane St., at West St., West Village* ☎ *212/924–6700* ⊕ *www.thejanenyc.com* ⤳ *171 rooms* ⑩ *No meals* Ⓜ *A, C, E, L to 14th St. and 8th Ave.* ✛ *3:B5.*

CHELSEA AND THE MEATPACKING DISTRICT

CHELSEA

$
HOTEL
Chelsea Lodge. Popular with Europeans and budget-conscious visitors, the Chelsea Lodge is a great location for guests who don't insist on a lot of amenities. **Pros:** on a gorgeous Chelsea block; residential feel; great bang for the buck. **Cons:** not romantic; shared bathrooms. ⑤ *Rooms from: $144* ✉ *318 W. 20th St., between 8th and 9th Aves., Chelsea* ☎ *212/243–4499* ⊕ *www.chelsealodge.com* ⤳ *22 rooms, 4 suites* ⑩ *No meals* Ⓜ *C, E to 23rd St.; 1 to 18th St.* ✛ *3:C3.*

$$
HOTEL
The GEM Hotel Chelsea. At this stylish, well-priced boutique hotel, the modern rooms are small but designed to make the most of limited space. **Pros:** great Chelsea location; close to several subway lines; coffee-makers in the room. **Cons:** gym and business center, both on the lower level, feel like a work in progress; rooms may be too small for some. ⑤ *Rooms from: $329* ✉ *300 W. 22nd St., Chelsea* ☎ *212/675–1911* ⊕ *www.thegemhotel.com* ⤳ *81 rooms* ⑩ *No meals* Ⓜ *C, E to 23rd St.; 1 to 23rd St.* ✛ *3:C3.*

$
HOTEL
Hilton New York Fashion District. Fashion is the theme at this Hilton, which is in the emerging Fashion District neighborhood (previously known as the Garment District) on the upper edge of Chelsea: the lobby is done in rich textiles with multicolor spools mounted on a white board behind the front desk. **Pros:** reasonable prices for a good location. **Cons:** small closets; trying to be trendier than it is. ⑤ *Rooms from: $249* ✉ *152 W. 26th St., between 6th and 7th Aves., Chelsea* ☎ *212/858–5888* ⊕ *www3.hilton.com* ⤳ *280 rooms* ⑩ *No meals* Ⓜ *1, 2, 3, A, C, E, B, D, F V, N, Q, R, W to 34th St.* ✛ *3:D2.*

$$
HOTEL
Hotel Americano. This boutique property, which overlooks the High Line, captures the artistic and stylist spirit of Chelsea. **Pros:** all-year rooftop pool and bar; views overlooking the High Line; near the thriving gallery scene in Chelsea. **Cons:** low beds; bathrooms lack privacy; some furniture is form over function. ⑤ *Rooms from: $395* ✉ *518 W. 27th St., between 10th and 11th Aves., Chelsea* ☎ *212/216-0000* ⊕ *www.hotel-americano. com* ⤳ *49 rooms, 7 suites* ⑩ *No meals* Ⓜ *C, E to 23rd St.* ✛ *3:A1.*

$
B&B/INN
FAMILY
Fodor's Choice
★
The Inn on 23rd. Friendly innkeepers Annette and Barry Fisherman welcome guests to this five-floor, 19th-century building, which also has its own cat/mascot. **Pros:** charming innkeepers; comfy and relaxed library; affordable, given location. **Cons:** few business services; some older amenities; beware if you have cat allergies. ⑤ *Rooms from: $279* ✉ *131 W. 23rd St., between 6th and 7th Aves., Chelsea* ☎ *212/463–0330* ⊕ *www.innon23rd.com* ⤳ *13 rooms, 1 suite* ⑩ *Breakfast* Ⓜ *F, M to 23rd St.* ✛ *3:D2.*

$$ **The Maritime Hotel.** The former
HOTEL HQ for the National Maritime
Union and the first luxury hotel to
be built in the Chelsea gallery district, the Maritime still feels a bit
nautical: the small rooms resemble
modern ship's cabins, with teak
paneling, sea-blue drapes and bed
accents, and 5-foot "portholes"
that face the Hudson River skyline. **Pros:** fun rooms with big porthole windows; great location near
Chelsea Market and the Chelsea
galleries. **Cons:** street noise; small
rooms. $ *Rooms from: $435* ⊠ *363
W. 16th St., at 9th Ave., Chelsea* ☎ *212/242–4300* ⊕ *www.the
maritimehotel.com* ⤳ *121 rooms,
5 suites* ꙮ *No meals* Ⓜ *A, C, E to
14th St.* ⊹ *3:B4.*

MEATPACKING DISTRICT

$$ **Gansevoort Meatpacking NYC.** Though the nearby Standard New York
HOTEL has stolen some of its thunder, there's plenty to draw guests to this chic
Meatpacking District pioneer, starting with the sleek rooms that overlook the city or the Hudson River and the rooftop deck with a 45-foot
heated pool that remains a draw for locals and tourists alike. **Pros:**
rooftop pool; wonderful art collection; great location for restaurants
and shopping. **Cons:** location can seem too trendy, especially at night;
service can be slipshod. $ *Rooms from: $425* ⊠ *18 9th Ave., at 13th
St., Meatpacking District* ☎ *212/206–6700* ⊕ *www.hotelgansevoort.
com* ⤳ *165 rooms, 21 suites* ꙮ *No meals* Ⓜ *A, C, E, L to 14th St. and
8th Ave.* ⊹ *3:B4.*

$$ **The Standard.** André Balazs's architectural statement on the West Side
HOTEL is still one of New York's hottest hotels. **Pros:** beautiful building; beauFodor'sChoice tiful people; impressive restaurant space. **Cons:** noisy at night; tight
★ rooms; can be too sceney. $ *Rooms from: $395* ⊠ *848 Washington St.,
between 13th and Little W. 12th Sts., Meatpacking District* ☎ *212/645–
4646* ⊕ *www.standardhotels.com* ⤳ *321 rooms, 17 suites* ꙮ *No meals*
Ⓜ *A, C, E, L to 14th St. and 8th Ave.* ⊹ *3:B4.*

UNION SQUARE, FLATIRON DISTRICT, AND GRAMERCY

FLATIRON DISTRICT

$$ **Ace Hotel.** The Ace is not your ordinary boutique hotel. **Pros:** in-
HOTEL house destination restaurants ; supercool but friendly vibe. **Cons:** dark
Fodor'sChoice lobby; caters to a young crowd; may be too sceney for some; neigh-
★ borhood itself isn't the most exciting. $ *Rooms from: $399* ⊠ *20 W.
29th St., at Broadway, Flatiron District* ☎ *212/679–2222* ⊕ *www.
acehotel.com* ⤳ *272 rooms, 8 suites* ꙮ *No meals* Ⓜ *N, R to 28th St.;
1 to 28th St.* ⊹ *3:E1.*

17

CLOSE UP

Hotel Hot Spots

Some of the city's most stylish bars and lounges are in hotels. These boîtes occasionally require crossing a velvet-roped entrance, but most extend automatic entry to hotel guests.

Downtown, the swank bar at the **Mondrian** (⇨ *SoHo*) is a treat, and the Jimmy bar at the **James Hotel** (⇨ *SoHo*) has some of the best views in town. On the Lower East Side, the Lobby Bar in the **Bowery Hotel** (⇨ *Lower East Side*) is a Wes Anderson movie come to life, with worn velvet furniture, Persian rugs, an assortment of taxidermy, and a back patio that harbors some of the most coveted summertime tables in the neighborhood.

Mega-hotelier Ian Schrager's properties are design temples, with chic lounges favored by jet-setters and locals alike. The "haute Bohemian" **Gramercy Park Hotel** (⇨ *Gramercy*) is Schrager's latest offering, with its popular—and pricey—Rose Bar and Jade Bar. The hotel also has a private members-and-guests-only Roof Club. The **Ace Hotel** (⇨ *Flatiron*) is the sweet spot du jour, with one bar in the eclectic lobby and another at the trendy Breslin restaurant. The **Standard** (⇨ *Meatpacking District*) has a happening bar scene at the Standard Grill. It's hard to get in to the 18th-floor lounge but the outdoor beer garden downstairs is more egalitarian and, frankly, more fun—they even have Ping-Pong. It's also open year-round now. At its sister property, the **Standard East Village**, the second-floor bar has a hammered metal bar and tall glass windows—it's one of the nicer spots for daytime libation. Take it outside to one of the cushioned, low-slung settees if weather permits.

In Midtown, the Art Deco–designed **Chatwal** (⇨ *Midtown West*) has a hopping lobby scene with drinks by cocktail guru Sasha Petraske and an elegant second-floor bar decorated with whimsical touches that are a paean to classic New York (look for the shimmering light fixtures shaped like the Chrysler Building). At the **Refinery Hotel**, a new property in an old hat factory, the year-round rooftop has three distinct spaces for imbibing: indoors by the fireplace, outdoors under the Empire State Building, or on the patio with a retractable roof.

Print at the Ink48 (⇨ *Midtown West*) is an elegant place to catch an early bite and a drink—later you can dance to views of the Hudson to the west and the glittering city to the east. **Room Mate Grace** (⇨ *Midtown West*) in Times Square has a bar that's adjacent to its lobby-level pool; you can see all the underwater action through voyeur windows above the bar. Just make sure to pay attention at the end of the evening, or you might be the hotel's next swimming sensation. At the **Mandarin Oriental** on Columbus Circle (⇨ *Midtown West*), the 35th-floor lounge is the place to soak in views of Central Park. Come summertime, **Yotel** (⇨ *Midtown West*) offers one of the city's most expansive outdoor patios, with happening DJs and Latin-inspired cocktails.

$$ ▦ **The Eventi.** This hotel adds a touch of style just below Penn Station
HOTEL in an area desperately in need of new lodging options. **Pros:** great loca-
FAMILY tion; fun dining options; nice gym. **Cons:** crowded lobby; dark rooms.
§ *Rooms from: $350* ⊠ *851 Ave. of the Americas, at 30th St., Flatiron
District* ☎ *212/564–4567* ⊕ *www.eventihotel.com* ⤤ *239 rooms, 53
suites* ⦿ *No meals* Ⓜ *N, R to 28th St.* ✛ *3:D1.*

$$ ▦ **Gansevoort Park Avenue NYC.** A downtown-hip hotel on the edge of
HOTEL lower Midtown, the Gansevoort Park improves upon its hard-living
Meatpacking District sibling by several degrees. **Pros:** happening bar;
location convenient to Union Square; friendly staff. **Cons:** if you want
peace and quiet this hotel is not for you. § *Rooms from: $395* ⊠ *420
Park Ave. S, at 29th St., Flatiron District* ☎ *212/317–2900* ⊕ *www.
gansevoortpark.com* ⤤ *211 rooms, 38 suites* ⦿ *No meals* Ⓜ *6 to 28th
St.* ✛ *3:F1.*

$$$ ▦ **Hotel Giraffe.** A consistent property with friendly service, large rooms,
HOTEL and lots of repeat customers (particularly business travelers) Hotel
Giraffe is often noted for its nightly complimentary wine-and-cheese
reception. **Pros:** rooftop terrace for guests; quiet hotel. **Cons:** street
noise near lower levels; pricey for the quality you get. § *Rooms from:
$449* ⊠ *365 Park Ave. S, at 26th St., Flatiron District* ☎ *212/685–
7700, 877/296–0009* ⊕ *www.hotelgiraffe.com* ⤤ *51 rooms, 21 suites*
⦿ *Breakfast* Ⓜ *6 to 28th St.* ✛ *3:F2.*

$ ▦ **King & Grove.** Convenient to the action without being smack in the
HOTEL middle of it is King & Grove, a sleek new hotel with a sister prop-
erty in Williamsburg, Brooklyn. **Pros:** up and coming neighborhood;
trendy but not over the top; cozy single rooms are a great option for
solo travelers. **Cons:** dark entryway; lower floors lack views and can
feel a bit basement-y. § *Rooms from: $279* ⊠ *29 E. 29th St., between
Park and Madison Aves., Flatiron District* ☎ *212/689–1900* ⊕ *www.
kingandgrove.com* ⤤ *276 rooms* ⦿ *No meals* Ⓜ *6 to 28th St.* ✛ *3:F1.*

$$$ ▦ **The NoMad Hotel.** Named for the emerging "North of Madison" (i.e.,
HOTEL Madison Square Park) neighborhood in which it's located, this upscale-
Fodor'sChoice bohemian property quickly became one of the most buzzed-about hotel
★ openings of 2012. **Pros:** 24-hr room service; free Wi-Fi; rooftop terrace;
central location. **Cons:** those sharing a room with a friend may wish
for more privacy than the exposed bathtubs provide. § *Rooms from:
$485* ⊠ *1170 Broadway, at 28th St., Flatiron District* ☎ *212/796-1500*
⊕ *www.thenomadhotel.com* ⤤ *154 rooms, 14 suites* ⦿ *No meals* Ⓜ *N,
R to 28th St.* ✛ *3:E2.*

$ ▦ **Park South Hotel.** In this beautifully transformed 1906 office build-
HOTEL ing, rooms feel smartly contemporary, though they've retained some
period details; request one that doesn't overlook noisy 27th Street and
isn't too close to the bar on the ground floor—ask instead for a view
of the Chrysler Building. **Pros:** free breakfast and Internet; turndown
service; good value. **Cons:** some noisy rooms; small rooms and bathrooms. § *Rooms from: $299* ⊠ *124 E. 28th St., between Lexington
and Park Aves., Flatiron District* ☎ *212/448–0888, 800/315–4642*
⊕ *www.parksouthhotel.com* ⤤ *128 rooms, 3 suites* ⦿ *Breakfast* Ⓜ *6
to 28th St.* ✛ *3:F2.*

17

$$ ⬚ **The Roger.** A colorful choice in a rather plain neighborhood, the Roger
HOTEL　continues to have a following among repeat visitors to New York, especially since its 2012 redesign. **Pros:** colorful room decor; friendly service; good value. **Cons:** no room service; tiny bathrooms. $ *Rooms from: $350* ⊠ *131 Madison Ave., at 31st St., Flatiron District* ☎ *212/448–7000, 877/847–4444* ⊕ *www.therogernewyork.com* ⇗ *192 rooms, 2 suites* ❁ *No meals* Ⓜ *6 to 33rd St.* ✛ *3:F1.*

GRAMERCY

$ ⬚ **Carlton Arms.** Europeans and students know about the chipper, winning attitude of this friendly, no-frills hotel, where the rooms are painted
HOTEL　by artists on a rotating basis. **Pros:** rock-bottom prices; friendly attitude; quieter residential Murray Hill location. **Cons:** no elevator; many rooms have shared baths. $ *Rooms from: $120* ⊠ *160 E. 25th St., at 3rd Ave., Gramercy* ☎ *212/684–8337, 212/679–0680 for reservations* ⊕ *www.carltonarms.com* ⇗ *54 rooms (20 with bath)* ❁ *No meals* Ⓜ *R to 28th St.* ✛ *3:G2.*

$$$$ ⬚ **Gramercy Park Hotel.** Ian Schrager, boutique hotelier extraordinaire,
HOTEL　decorated this property with contemporary art by the likes of Andy Warhol and Jean-Michel Basquiat. **Pros:** trendy bar scene; opulent rooms; great restaurant; parkside location. **Cons:** inconsistent service; form-over-function rooms; expensive bar. $ *Rooms from: $629* ⊠ *2 Lexington Ave., at Gramercy Park, Gramercy* ☎ *212/920–3300* ⊕ *www.gramercyparkhotel.com* ⇗ *139 rooms, 46 suites* ❁ *No meals* Ⓜ *6 to 23rd St.* ✛ *3:G3.*

$$$ ⬚ **The Inn at Irving Place.** Fantasies of Old New York—Manhattan
HOTEL　straight from the pages of Edith Wharton and Henry James, an era
Fodor'sChoice　of genteel brick town houses and Tiffany lamps—spring to life at this
★　discreet, romantic inn. **Pros:** romantic and charming; big rooms; excellent breakfast and tea service; Mario Batali's Casa Mono is downstairs. **Cons:** rooms aren't flawless, with imperfections like older grouting; some street noise. $ *Rooms from: $449* ⊠ *56 Irving Pl., between 17th and 18th Sts., Gramercy* ☎ *212/533–4600, 800/685–1447* ⊕ *www.innatirving.com* ⇗ *5 rooms, 6 suites* ❁ *Breakfast* Ⓜ *4, 5, 6, L, N, Q, R to 14th St./Union Sq.* ✛ *3:G3.*

$$ ⬚ **Marcel at Gramercy.** The chic, affordable Marcel gives guests both style
HOTEL　and substance in a prime location. **Pros:** outdoor patio has spectacular views of the city; good value. **Cons:** elevators are slow; some rooms are tight on space; decor not to everyone's taste. $ *Rooms from: $299* ⊠ *201 E. 24th St., Gramercy* ☎ *212/696–3800* ⊕ *www.themarcelatgramercy.com* ⇗ *136 rooms* ❁ *No meals* Ⓜ *6 to 23rd St.* ✛ *3:G2.*

UNION SQUARE

$$ ⬚ **Hyatt Union Square New York.** Experiencing a bit of "real" New
HOTEL　York (and getting away from Midtown) got easier when this Hyatt
Fodor'sChoice　opened just south of Union Square in a newly-built tower with three
★　restaurants, an on-site gym, and bikes and scooters to borrow. **Pros:** convenient and vibrant location; buzzy dining and drinking outlets. **Cons:** charge for Internet; some standard rooms are small. $ *Rooms from: $379* ⊠ *134 4th Ave., Union Square* ☎ *212/253-1234* ⊕ *www.unionsquare.hyatt.com* ⇗ *178 rooms and suites* Ⓜ *4, 5, 6, L, N, Q, R to 14th St./Union Sq.* ✛ *3:F4.*

$$$$ 🏨 **W New York Union Square.** The W chain's iconic New York City
HOTEL property continues to attract a mix of trendsetters and tourists,
thanks to the downtown location and its funky style. **Pros:** fashionable location; great restaurant. **Cons:** noisy lobby; expensive Wi-Fi.
⑤ *Rooms from: $650* ✉ *201 Park Ave. S, at 17th St., Union Square*
☎ *212/253–9119, 877/946–8357* ⊕ *www.wnewyorkunionsquare.*
com ⟿ *254 rooms, 16 suites* 🍽 *No meals* Ⓜ *4, 5, 6, L, N, Q, R to*
14th St./Union Sq. ✛ *3:F3.*

MIDTOWN EAST AND MURRAY HILL

MIDTOWN EAST

$$ 🏨 **70 Park Avenue.** A multimillion-dollar refresh in 2012 brought new
HOTEL life to this Midtown business-traveler favorite, infusing the lobby and
rooms with a bright color palette and modern furniture. **Pros:** complimentary evening wine reception; polite service; simple, not overdesigned
rooms and hotel layout. **Cons:** small rooms; decor and art might not suit
all tastes. ⑤ *Rooms from: $299* ✉ *70 Park Ave., at 38th St., Midtown*
East ☎ *212/973–2400, 800/707–2752* ⊕ *www.70parkave.com* ⟿ *202*
rooms, 3 suites 🍽 *No meals* Ⓜ *6 to 33rd St.* ✛ *4:F5.*

$$ 🏨 **Affinia 50.** This popular hotel attracts business travelers but it's also
HOTEL comfortable for families or leisure travelers—especially the studios and
FAMILY suites, which have plenty of space to stretch out in, with full kitchens and a clean, playful design that incorporates oversize chairs and
couches. **Pros:** apartment-style living; large rooms; good value; kid-
and pet-friendly. **Cons:** pricey Wi-Fi. ⑤ *Rooms from: $449* ✉ *155 E.*
50th St., at 3rd Ave., Midtown East ☎ *212/751–5710, 800/637–8483*
⊕ *www.affinia.com* ⟿ *151 rooms, 100 suites* 🍽 *No meals* Ⓜ *6 to 51st*
St./Lexington Ave.; E, M to Lexington–3rd Aves./53rd St. ✛ *4:G3.*

$$$$ 🏨 **Andaz 5th Avenue.** The serene and spacious rooms at this chic, mod-
HOTEL ern property evoke that coveted New York loft feel, with floor-to-ceiling windows that look out over 5th Avenue and the New York Public
Library. **Pros:** spacious and stylish; big, luxurious bathrooms; good
dining and drinking options; suites have outdoors space. **Cons:** pricey;
busy location might not suit all guests. ⑤ *Rooms from: $695* ✉ *485*
5th Ave., Midtown East ☎ *212/601–1234* ⊕ *newyork.5thavenue.*
andaz.hyatt.com ⟿ *137 rooms, 47 suites* 🍽 *No meals* Ⓜ *4, 5, 6 to*
Grand Central ✛ *4:E5.*

$$ 🏨 **The Benjamin.** NYC is often called the City that Never Sleeps, but
HOTEL if a good night's rest is essential for your visit, the Benjamin may be
FAMILY your choice accommodation—with a menu of 12 pillows to choose
from (including buckwheat, water, and Swedish memory varieties),
white-noise machines, and 500-thread-count sheets, they've got it covered. **Pros:** sleep-friendly; great location; gracious staff; kitchenettes
in big rooms; pets stay for free. **Cons:** paid Internet and Wi-Fi; boring
views; dull neighborhood after dark. ⑤ *Rooms from: $359* ✉ *125 E.*
50th St., at Lexington Ave., Midtown East ☎ *212/715–2500* ⊕ *www.*
thebenjamin.com ⟿ *112 rooms, 97 suites* 🍽 *No meals* Ⓜ *6 to 51st St./*
Lexington Ave.; E, M to Lexington–3rd Aves./53rd St. ✛ *4:F3.*

17

$$$$ ⊞ **Four Seasons Hotel.** For better or worse, the Four Seasons remains
HOTEL the blueprint for what a Manhattan luxury hotel should be. **Pros:**
spacious and comfortable rooms; perfect concierge and staff service;
afternoon tea in the lobby lounge. **Cons:** pricey; confusing room
controls; some furniture could use updating. ⑤ *Rooms from: $995*
⊠ *57 E. 57th St., between Park and Madison Aves., Midtown East*
☎ *212/758–5700, 800/487–3769* ⊕ *www.fourseasons.com* ⤴ *300
rooms, 63 suites* ⦿| *No meals* Ⓜ *4, 5, 6, N, Q, R to 59th St./Lexing-
ton Ave.* ⊹ *4:F1.*

$$ ⊞ **The Gotham Hotel.** This sleek hotel has a lot going for it, but a clincher
HOTEL is the fact that every room has an outdoor space. **Pros:** welcoming
staff; central location; every room has a balcony. **Cons:** no on-site
gym. ⑤ *Rooms from: $350* ⊠ *16 E. 46 St., between 5th and 6th Aves.,
Midtown East* ☎ *212/490–8500* ⊕ *www.thegothamhotelny.com* ⤴ *66
rooms* ⦿| *No meals* Ⓜ *B, D, F, M to 47th–50th Sts./Rockefeller Cen-
ter* ⊹ *4:E4.*

$$ ⊞ **Grand Hyatt New York.** This historic hotel has been transformed into
HOTEL sleek and modern central hub. **Pros:** comfy beds, light-filled gym on
a high floor; refreshing modern design; large, well-planned rooms.
Cons: no in-room minibar; Wi-Fi not free. ⑤ *Rooms from: $359*
⊠ *109 E. 42nd St., between Park and Lexington Aves., Midtown East*
☎ *212/883–1234, 800/233–1234* ⊕ *www.grandnewyork.hyatt.com*
⤴ *1,306 rooms, 43 suites* ⦿| *No meals* Ⓜ *4, 5, 6, 7, S to 42nd St./
Grand Central* ⊹ *4:F4.*

$$ ⊞ **Hilton Manhattan East.** This traditional-style, 20-story Tudor City
HOTEL hotel is a stone's throw from the United Nations and Grand Central
Terminal, making it fairly convenient but not very glamorous. **Pros:**
near UN; some balconies; convenient location for getting to major
sights. **Cons:** long walk to subway; unexciting room decor. ⑤ *Rooms
from: $425* ⊠ *304 E. 42nd St., between 1st and 2nd Aves., Midtown
East* ☎ *212/986–8800, 800/879–8836* ⊕ *www3.hilton.com* ⤴ *286
rooms, 14 suites* ⦿| *No meals* Ⓜ *4, 5, 6, 7, S to 42nd St./Grand Cen-
tral* ⊹ *4:G4.*

$$$ ⊞ **Hotel Elysée.** This intimate hotel is a favorite for travelers looking
HOTEL for good value in a desirable midtown location. **Pros:** complimentary
snacks and Wi-Fi; individually decorated rooms; cute library. **Cons:**
underwhelming lobby; slightly outdated decor. ⑤ *Rooms from: $495*
⊠ *60 E. 54th St., between Madison and Park Aves., Midtown East*
☎ *212/753–1066, 800/535–9733* ⊕ *www.elyseehotel.com* ⤴ *87 rooms,
16 suites* ⦿| *Breakfast* Ⓜ *E, M to 5th Ave.* ⊹ *4:F2.*

$$$ ⊞ **The Kitano.** As you might guess from the name, the Kitano imports
HOTEL much of its sensibility from Japan, with touches that include a bilingual
concierge and a high-concept Japanese restaurant—and it also makes
for a notably service-oriented stay. **Pros:** extra soundproofing in guest
rooms; cute mezzanine bar area; good value; excellent live jazz. **Cons:**
lower-floor views are limited; expensive restaurant. ⑤ *Rooms from:
$499* ⊠ *66 Park Ave., at 38th St., Midtown East* ☎ *212/885–7000,
800/548–2666* ⊕ *www.kitano.com* ⤴ *149 rooms, 18 suites* ⦿| *No
meals* Ⓜ *6 to 33rd St.* ⊹ *4:F5.*

$$ ⊞ **Library Hotel Manhattan.** Bookishly handsome, this stately landmark
HOTEL brownstone, built in 1900, is inspired by the nearby New York Public
Fodor's Choice Library—each of its 10 floors is dedicated to one of the 10 categories of
★ the Dewey Decimal System and is stocked with art and books relevant
to a subtopic such as erotica, astronomy, or biography—let your inter-
ests guide your choice. **Pros:** fun rooftop bar; playful book themes; styl-
ish rooms. **Cons:** rooftop sometimes reserved for events; more books in
rooms themselves would be nice. ⑤ *Rooms from: $379* ⊠ *299 Madison
Ave., at 41st Street, Midtown East* ☎ *212/983–4500, 212/983–4500*
⊕ *www.libraryhotel.com* ⤵ *52 rooms, 8 suites* ⦿ *Breakfast* Ⓜ *4, 5, 6,
7, S to 42nd St./Grand Central* ✛ *4:E4.*

$$$$ ⊞ **Loews Regency Hotel.** After a yearlong renovation, this snazzy, spa-
HOTEL cious Park Avenue hotel reopened in early 2014 with state-of-the-
art technology, a new 10,000-square-foot spa, and bright, tastefully
appointed rooms. **Pros:** friendly and helpful staff; fresh, recently
renovated property; huge spa and fitness center. **Cons:** on the expen-
sive side. ⑤ *Rooms from: $799* ⊠ *540 Park Ave., at 61st St., Mid-
town East* ☎ *212/759–4100, 800/233–2356* ⊕ *www.loewshotels.com*
⤵ *321 rooms, 58 suites* ⦿ *No meals* Ⓜ *4, 5, 6, N, Q, R to 59th St./
Lexington Ave.* ✛ *5:F6.*

$$$ ⊞ **New York Palace.** From the moment you enter the gilded gates of these
HOTEL connected mansions, originally built in the 1880s by railroad baron
Henry Villard, you know you're somewhere special; there's a reason
this is called the Palace. **Pros:** fresh property after extensive renovation; great service; unmatched views of St. Patrick's Cathedral. **Cons:**
high prices; harried staff. ⑤ *Rooms from: $599* ⊠ *455 Madison Ave.,
at 50th St., Midtown East* ☎ *212/888–7000, 800/697–2522* ⊕ *www.
newyorkpalace.com* ⤵ *822 rooms, 87 suites* ⦿ *No meals* Ⓜ *6 to 51st
St./Lexington Ave.; E, M to Lexington–3rd Aves./53rd St.* ✛ *4:E3.*

$ ⊞ **One UN New York.** In a sky-high tower near the landmark United
HOTEL Nations building, the One UN New York starts on the 28th floor, offering fabulous views—ask for a room facing west, toward Manhattan's
skyline—and a multilingual staff that caters to a discerning clientele
including heads of state. **Pros:** unbeatable East River and city views;
good value; great front-door and bell staff. **Cons:** a walk to the subway;
pricey Internet access. ⑤ *Rooms from: $220* ⊠ *1 United Nations Plaza,
at 44th St. and 1st Ave., Midtown East* ☎ *212/758–1234, 866/866–
8086* ⊕ *www.millenniumhotels.com* ⤵ *439 rooms, 34 suites* ⦿ *No
meals* Ⓜ *4, 5, 6, 7, S to 42nd St./Grand Central* ✛ *4:H4.*

$$$$ ⊞ **The Peninsula.** Stepping through the Peninsula's Beaux Arts facade
HOTEL onto the grand staircase overhung with a monumental chandelier, you
Fodor's Choice know you're in for a glitzy treat. **Pros:** brilliant service; fabulous rooms
★ with convenient controls; unforgettable rooftop bar. **Cons:** expensive.
⑤ *Rooms from: $1045* ⊠ *700 5th Ave., at 55th St., Midtown East*
☎ *212/956–2888, 800/262–9467* ⊕ *www.peninsula.com* ⤵ *185 rooms,
54 suites* ⦿ *No meals* Ⓜ *E, M to 5th Ave.* ✛ *4:E2.*

$ ⊞ **The Pod Hotel.** If cramped quarters don't bother you, this is one of the
HOTEL best deals in town. **Pros:** great prices; fun design. **Cons:** if you're prone
to claustrophobia, you may want to reconsider; some shared baths.
⑤ *Rooms from: $145* ⊠ *230 E. 51st St., between 2nd and 3rd Aves.,*

17

Midtown East ☎ 212/355–0300, 800/742–5945 ⊕ *www.thepodhotel.
com* ➔ *345 rooms (189 with private bath)* ❶◯❶ *No meals* Ⓜ *6 to 51st St./
Lexington Ave.; E, M to Lexington–3rd Aves./53rd St.* ✛ *4:G2.*

$$ 🏨 **Roger Smith.** This quirky choice is one of the better affordable stays
HOTEL   in the city and the art-filled rooms, matched by the murals in the lobby,
are homey and comfortable, with down pillows and quilts on the beds.
Pros: good location near Grand Central; intimate atmosphere; free
Wi-Fi. **Cons:** street noise; small bathrooms. ⑤ *Rooms from: $379* ⊠ *501
Lexington Ave., between 47th and 48th Sts., Midtown East* ☎ *212/755–
1400, 800/445–0277* ⊕ *www.rogersmith.com* ➔ *102 rooms, 28 suites*
❶◯❶ *No meals* Ⓜ *6 to 51st St./Lexington Ave.; E, M to Lexington–3rd
Aves./53rd St.* ✛ *4:F3.*

$ 🏨 **The Roosevelt Hotel.** Named after Teddy, not Franklin, this Midtown
HOTEL   icon just steps from Grand Central has an ornate lobby with cushy
couches and an old-school bar with heavy wood detailing that makes
the place feel like it's from another time, and it should—the property
dates from 1924. **Pros:** great public areas; big bathrooms; comfort-
able rooftop lounge. **Cons:** dated decor; limited in-room amenities.
⑤ *Rooms from: $299* ⊠ *45 E. 45th St., at Madison Ave., Midtown
East* ☎ *212/661–9600, 888/833–3969* ⊕ *www.theroosevelthotel.com*
➔ *963 rooms, 52 suites* ❶◯❶ *No meals* Ⓜ *4, 5, 6 to Grand Central/42nd
St.* ✛ *4:F4.*

$$$$ 🏨 **The Sherry-Netherland.** The Sherry is a stately part of the New York
HOTEL   landscape so it may come as a surprise to learn that it's essentially a
tall, luxurious apartment building that also has 50 hotel rooms and
suites. **Pros:** gorgeous lobby; commanding, impeccable location; Cipri-
ani access. **Cons:** small check-in area; rooms vary in taste and decor;
nonsuites are on the small side; interior rooms lack views; guests some-
times feel the cold shoulder from the full-time residents. ⑤ *Rooms from:
$649* ⊠ *781 5th Ave., at 59th St., Midtown East* ☎ *212/355–2800,
800/247–4377* ⊕ *www.sherrynetherland.com* ➔ *26 rooms, 24 suites*
❶◯❶ *No meals* Ⓜ *N, R, Q to 5th Ave.* ✛ *5:E6.*

$$$$ 🏨 **The St. Regis.** World-class from head to toe, this 5th Avenue Beaux
HOTEL   Arts landmark comes as close to flawless as any hotel in New York,
Fodor's Choice   with tech-savvy rooms, historic touches, and the iconic King Cole Bar.
★   **Pros:** classic NYC favorite; rooms combine true luxury with helpful
technology; easy-access butler service; superb in-house dining; presti-
gious location. **Cons:** expensive; too serious for families seeking fun.
⑤ *Rooms from: $1495* ⊠ *2 E. 55th St., at 5th Ave., Midtown East*
☎ *212/753–4500, 877/787–3447* ⊕ *www.stregisnewyork.com* ➔ *171
rooms, 67 suites* ❶◯❶ *No meals* Ⓜ *E, M to 5th Ave.* ✛ *4:E2.*

$$ 🏨 **Waldorf-Astoria.** The Waldorf is undeniably historic, and presidents
HOTEL   usually stay here thanks to the security of the drive-in entrance, but
we'd recommend a cocktail at the classic Bull and Bear Bar downstairs
rather than a night in one of the small standard rooms, which can feel
a bit oppressive with their extensive floral patterns. **Pros:** historic Art
Deco building filled with NYC's aristocratic, gangster, and jazz histories; best Waldorf salad in town; knowledgeable doormen. **Cons:** rooms
not up-to-date; more about the name than the experience; in-hotel
Starbucks costs twice as much as ones around the corner. ⑤ *Rooms*

from: $379 ✉ *301 Park Ave., between 49th and 50th Sts., Midtown East* ☎ *212/355–3000, 800/925–3673* ⊕ *www.waldorfnewyork.com* ⤴ *1,183 rooms, 230 suites* ❍❘ *No meals* Ⓜ *6 to 51st St./Lexington Ave.; E, M to Lexington–3rd Aves./53rd St.* ✛ *4:F3.*

$
HOTEL **W Hotel New York.** A hopping bar and sunken lounge in the reception area, funky decor touches like window boxes filled with grass, and guest rooms that hew to the classic brand formula—they're small but they look good—make this a quintessential W property. **Pros:** central location; great-looking rooms; Bliss Spa in hotel. **Cons:** thin walls; small rooms; inconsistent service. ⑤ *Rooms from: $279* ✉ *541 Lexington Ave., between 49th and 50th Sts., Midtown East* ☎ *212/755–1200, 877/946–8357* ⊕ *www.wnewyork.com* ⤴ *629 rooms, 62 suites* ❍❘ *No meals* Ⓜ *6 to 51st St./Lexington Ave.; E, M to Lexington–3rd Aves./53rd St.* ✛ *4:F3.*

MURRAY HILL

$$
HOTEL **The Carlton Hotel.** From the two-story lobby designed by David Rockwell to still-intact, original 1904 Beaux Arts details such as the stained-glass dome (created by workers from the Tiffany glass factory), a 40-foot ceiling in the lobby, and a soaring crystal chandelier, the Carlton is a refurbished gem. **Pros:** spectacular lobby; stylish rooms. **Cons:** expensive bar; small rooms; dimly lit bathrooms. ⑤ *Rooms from: $449* ✉ *88 Madison Ave., between 28th and 29th Sts., Murray Hill* ☎ *212/532–4100, 800/601–8500* ⊕ *www.carltonhotelny.com* ⤴ *294 rooms, 23 suites* ❍❘ *No meals* Ⓜ *6 to 28th St.* ✛ *3:F1.*

$
HOTEL **The Herald Square Hotel.** The sculpted cherubs on the facade and the vintage magazine covers adorning the common areas give good hints that the great value Herald Square Hotel used to be *Life* magazine's headquarters. **Pros:** cheap; centrally located. **Cons:** unattractive lobby; readers report inconsistent service. ⑤ *Rooms from: $199* ✉ *19 W. 31st St., between 5th Ave. and Broadway, Murray Hill* ☎ *212/279–4017, 800/727–1888* ⊕ *www.heraldnyc.com* ⤴ *100 rooms* ❍❘ *No meals* Ⓜ *B, D, F, N, Q, R, M to 34th St./Herald Sq.* ✛ *3:E1.*

$
HOTEL **Pod 39.** This cheap and cheerful sibling of the Pod Hotel on 51st Street offers tight quarters and trendy amenities. **Pros:** quality taco and cocktail spot; big rooftop with gorgeous views; lobby lounge with Ping-Pong table. **Cons:** tight quarters; buzzy lobby and restaurant might not suit all guests. ⑤ *Rooms from: $175* ✉ *145 E. 39th St, Murray Hill* ☎ *212/865–5700* ⊕ *www.thepodhotel.com* ⤴ *366 rooms* ❍❘ *No meals* Ⓜ *4, 5, 6 to Grand Central* ✛ *4:G5.*

$$$
HOTEL
FAMILY **St. Giles New York—The Tuscany.** After a complete gut renovation in 2012, some of the most spacious rooms in New York are back and refreshed at the St. Giles Tuscany. **Pros:** very generous room space for New York; brand-new, fresh decor and furnishings; art installations featuring local artists. **Cons:** on the expensive side. ⑤ *Rooms from: $495* ✉ *120 E. 39th St., between Park and Lexington Aves., Murray Hill* ☎ *212/686–1600* ⊕ *www.tuscany.stgilesnewyork.com* ⤴ *116 rooms, 8 suites* ❍❘ *No meals* Ⓜ *4, 5, 6 to Grand Central* ✛ *4:F5.*

17

MIDTOWN WEST

$ 🏨 **6 Columbus.** This boutique-style hotel nestled in the shadow of the
HOTEL   towering Time Warner center offers the vibe and amenities of downtown lodging with a convenience Midtown location. **Pros:** convenient
location; fun in-hotel restaurant; reasonably priced for neighborhood;
family-friendly. **Cons:** rooms on lower floors facing 58th Street can
be noisy. ⑤ *Rooms from: $295* ⊠ *6 Columbus Circle, on 58th St.
between 8th and 9th Aves., Midtown West* ☎ *212/204–3000* ⊕ *www.
thompsonhotels.com* ⤴ *70 rooms, 18 suites* ⏹ *No meals* Ⓜ *1, A, B, C,
D to 59th St./Columbus Circle* ✛ *4:B1.*

$$$ 🏨 **The Algonquin.** One of Manhattan's most historic properties, the
HOTEL   Algonquin is a landmark of literary history. **Pros:** free Internet; friendly,
knowledgeable staff; central location. **Cons:** some small rooms. ⑤ *Rooms
from: $459* ⊠ *59 W. 44th St., between 5th and 6th Aves., Midtown West*
☎ *212/840–6800, 800/555–8000* ⊕ *www.algonquinhotel.com* ⤴ *156
rooms, 25 suites* ⏹ *No meals* Ⓜ *B, D, F, M to 42nd St.* ✛ *4:D4.*

$$ 🏨 **Belvedere Hotel.** Built during the 1920's, the Belvedere's main draw is
HOTEL   its Times Square/Theater District location; the rooms tend to be dark
and don't stand out design-wise, although they are spacious and have
kitchenettes with a microwave, mini-refrigerator, and coffeemaker.
Pros: good rates available; renovated rooms are good value. **Cons:**
can be loud with street noise; slow elevators; Wi-Fi free in only some
room categories. ⑤ *Rooms from: $329* ⊠ *319 W. 48th St., between
8th and 9th Aves., Midtown West* ☎ *212/245–7000, 888/468–3558*
⊕ *www.belvederehotelnyc.com* ⤴ *345 rooms* ⏹ *No meals* Ⓜ *C, E to
50th St.* ✛ *4:B3.*

$ 🏨 **Best Western Plus President Hotel.** The President is the only politically
HOTEL   themed hotel in the city, starting with the purple color scheme, a combination of Republican red and Democratic blue. **Pros:** sleek rooms for
the price; convenient location; unique theme. **Cons:** cramped lobby;
dark bathrooms; poor views. ⑤ *Rooms from: $249* ⊠ *234 W. 48th
St., between 8th Ave. and Broadway, Midtown West* ☎ *212/246–8800,
800/828–4667* ⊕ *www.bestwestern.com* ⤴ *334 rooms* ⏹ *No meals*
Ⓜ *C, E to 50th St.* ✛ *4:C3.*

$$$ 🏨 **The Blakely New York.** It may be a tried-and-true design motif, but it's
HOTEL   hard to resist the English gentlemen's club when it's done right. **Pros:** all
rooms have kitchenettes; central location; good-size rooms; acclaimed
restaurant. **Cons:** rooms facing 54th Street can be noisy; some rooms
have little natural light; expensive. ⑤ *Rooms from: $529* ⊠ *136 W.
55th St., between 6th and 7th Aves., Midtown West* ☎ *212/245–1800,
800/735–0710* ⊕ *www.blakelynewyork.com* ⤴ *60 rooms, 58 suites*
⏹ *Breakfast* Ⓜ *N, Q, R to 57th St.* ✛ *4:C2.*

$$ 🏨 **Bryant Park Hotel.** A New York landmark that towers over the New
HOTEL   York Public Library and Bryant Park, this sleek hotel is still a Midtown
hot spot. **Pros:** gorgeous building; fashionable crowd and setting; across
from Bryant Park; free Wi-Fi. **Cons:** expensive; Cellar Bar frequently
booked for events. ⑤ *Rooms from: $445* ⊠ *40 W. 40th St., between
5th and 6th Aves., Midtown West* ☎ *212/869–0100, 877/640–9300*
⊕ *www.bryantparkhotel.com* ⤴ *112 rooms, 116 suites* ⏹ *No meals*
Ⓜ *B, D, F, M to 42nd St.; 7 to 5th Ave.* ✛ *4:D5.*

$$ 🏨 **Casablanca Hotel.** A favorite for the comfortable rooms and great
HOTEL location, the Casablanca evokes the sultry Mediterranean. **Pros:** great
access to the Theater District; free continental breakfast and evening
wine/cheese reception; free Wi-Fi. **Cons:** exercise facilities at nearby
New York Sports Club, not on premises; heavy tourist foot traffic.
⑤ *Rooms from: $439* ✉ *147 W. 43rd St., Midtown West* ☎ *212/869–
1212* ⊕ *www.casablancahotel.com* ⤶ *42 rooms, 6 suites* ⑩ *Breakfast*
Ⓜ *1, 2, 3, 7, N, Q, R, S to Times Sq./42nd St.* ✛ *4:C4.*

$$$$ 🏨 **The Chatwal New York.** A lavishly refurbished reincarnation of a classic
HOTEL Manhattan theater club, the Chatwal delivers a stylish, luxury experi-
Fodor'sChoice ence with a matching price tag. **Pros:** gorgeous lobby; state-of-the-art
★ room controls and amenities; excellent service. **Cons:** some visitors may
find the price too high for a Time Square location. ⑤ *Rooms from:
$795* ✉ *130 W. 44th St., between 5th and 6th Aves., Midtown West*
☎ *212/764–6200* ⊕ *www.thechatwalny.com* ⤶ *50 rooms, 26 suites*
⑩ *No meals* Ⓜ *B, D, F, M, 7 to 42nd St./Bryant Park* ✛ *4:D4.*

$$ 🏨 **City Club Hotel.** Ocean-liner-inspired rooms at the City Club are brisk,
HOTEL bright, and masculine: they're also about the same size as a room on
a cruise ship—that means tight quarters, matey, no matter how much
you enjoy sharing space with Jonathan Adler ceramics. **Pros:** free Wi-Fi;
great restaurant; personal service. **Cons:** no gym; occasionally dim lighting; tiny lobby. ⑤ *Rooms from: $400* ✉ *55 W. 44th St., between 5th
and 6th Aves., Midtown West* ☎ *212/921–5500* ⊕ *www.cityclubhotel.
com* ⤶ *62 rooms, 3 suites* ⑩ *No meals* Ⓜ *B, D, F, N, R, M, 1, 2, 3 to
42nd St.; 7 to 5th Ave.* ✛ *4:D4.*

$$ 🏨 **The Distrikt.** Rising high above Port Authority, the Distrikt tries to
HOTEL approximate the boutique hotel experience in an area of town best
known for its bus depot and, for the most part, it succeeds. **Pros:** cen-
tral location; friendly staff; good Midtown views from higher floors.
Cons: on a gritty block right across from Port Authority; noisy on lower
floors. ⑤ *Rooms from: $389* ✉ *342 W. 40th St., between 8th and 9th
Aves., Midtown West* ☎ *212/706–6100* ⊕ *www.distrikthotel.com* ⤶ *155
rooms* ⑩ *No meals* Ⓜ *A, C, E to 42nd St./8th Ave.* ✛ *4:B5.*

$$ 🏨 **DoubleTree Suites by Hilton Hotel New York City–Times Square.** Space is
HOTEL the draw at this 45-story Times Square top dog; every room is a suites,
FAMILY with a separate bedroom and living room (each with a big flat-screen
TV), occupying about 400 square feet overlooking Times Square and
Broadway—an especially desirable location during the New Year's Eve
ball drop. **Pros:** free 24-hour gym and Wi-Fi in public areas; extremely
helpful, informed concierge; convenient to the Theater District; very
quiet considering location. **Cons:** paid Wi-Fi in guest rooms; pricey
for a DoubleTree. ⑤ *Rooms from: $349* ✉ *1568 Broadway, at 47th
St., Midtown West* ☎ *212/719–1600* ⊕ *www.doubletree3.hilton.com*
⤶ *460 suites* ⑩ *No meals* Ⓜ *B, D, F, M to 42nd St.* ✛ *4:C3.*

$ 🏨 **Dream New York.** Part hotel, part Kafkaesque dream, this Midtown
HOTEL spot specializes in style over comfort but is still quite livable, despite
some over-the-top design features—and noise from the scenesters
headed to the rooftop bar. **Pros:** AVA Lounge penthouse bar; large
spa; up-to-the-minute electronics. **Cons:** small rooms; spotty service;
might be too sceney for some. ⑤ *Rooms from: $279* ✉ *210 W. 55th*

17

St., at Broadway, Midtown West ☎ *212/247–2000, 212/247–2000* ⊕ *www.dreamhotels.com* ⬦ *204 rooms, 12 suites* ❤️⊙I *No meals* Ⓜ *N, Q, R to 57th St.* ✛ *4:C2.*

$$$ 🛏 **Hilton Times Square.** A glass-and-steel skyscraper atop a 335,000-square-
HOTEL foot retail complex that includes a movie theater and Madame Tus-
saud's Wax Museum, the Hilton Times Square soars 44 stories above
Manhattan and overlooks New York City's famous skyline and the
Hudson River. **Pros:** great location for Times Square entertainment;
convenient to public transportation; big rooms. **Cons:** impersonal feel;
nickel-and-dime charges and overpriced food and drink, including a
$33 buffet breakfast. Ⓢ *Rooms from: $499* ✉ *234 W. 42nd St., between
7th and 8th Aves., Midtown West* ☎ *212/840–8222, 800/445–8667*
⊕ *www.hilton.com* ⬦ *460 rooms, 2 suites* ❤️⊙I *No meals* Ⓜ *1, 2, 3, 7,
N, Q, R, S to 42nd St./Times Sq.* ✛ *4:C4.*

$ 🛏 **Holiday Inn New York City Midtown.** Business travelers, tourists, and
HOTEL families alike appreciate this good value a stone's throw from Penn
Station, but understand that it's not the most exciting hotel experience
New York has to offer. **Pros:** good value; friendly and efficient ser-
vice; location in the thick of it. **Cons:** small workout room; not much
character. Ⓢ *Rooms from: $219* ✉ *30 W. 31st St., between 5th Ave.
and Broadway, Midtown West* ☎ *212/695–7401* ⊕ *www.holidayinn.
com* ⬦ *120 rooms, 2 suites* ❤️⊙I *No meals* Ⓜ *B, D, F, N, Q, R, M to
34th St./Herald Sq.* ✛ *3:E1.*

$ 🛏 **Hotel Metro.** With mirrored columns and elegant black-and-white
HOTEL photos in the lobby, the Hotel Metro feels distinctively retro. **Pros:**
complimentary coffee and tea 24/7; renovated exercise room has flat-
screen TVs; free Wi-Fi in rooms. **Cons:** noise seeps in from outside;
rooms are tasteful but spartan. Ⓢ *Rooms from: $294* ✉ *45 W. 35th St.,
between 5th and 6th Aves., Midtown West* ☎ *212/947–2500* ⊕ *www.
hotelmetronyc.com* ⬦ *162 rooms, 19 suites* ❤️⊙I *Breakfast* Ⓜ *B, D, F, N,
Q, R, M to 34th St./Herald Sq.* ✛ *4:D6.*

$$ 🛏 **Hudson New York Hotel.** Budget fashionistas are once again drawn
HOTEL to the Hudson after a dramatic renovation of every single room in
2012. **Pros:** fabulous, elegant bar; gorgeous Francesco Clemente fresco
in lobby; breathtaking Sky Terrace. **Cons:** staff can be condescend-
ing; tiny rooms; overpriced cocktails. Ⓢ *Rooms from: $339* ✉ *356 W.
58th St., between 8th and 9th Aves., Midtown West* ☎ *212/554–6000*
⊕ *www.hudsonhotel.com* ⬦ *866 rooms, 69 suites* ❤️⊙I *No meals* Ⓜ *1, A,
B, C, D to 59th St./Columbus Circle* ✛ *4:B1.*

$ 🛏 **Ink48.** If you want to be near Midtown but a bit removed from the
HOTEL hustle and bustle, this Kimpton hotel is a great option. **Pros:** friendly
FAMILY staff; great views; large rooms; beautiful rooftop. **Cons:** out-of-the-way
location; lobby can feel overly quiet at times; street noise in lower-floor
rooms. Ⓢ *Rooms from: $299* ✉ *653 11th Ave., at 48th St., Midtown
West* ☎ *212/757–0088* ⊕ *www.ink48.com* ⬦ *196 rooms, 26 suites*
❤️⊙I *No meals* Ⓜ *C, E to 50th St.* ✛ *4:A3.*

$$$ 🛏 **InterContinental New York Times Square.** A central location mere blocks
HOTEL from the heart of Broadway, Times Square, and restaurant-rich Hell's
Kitchen makes the city's InterContinental a conveniently located draw.
Pros: central for transportation and entertainment; in-house restaurant

Romantic Retreats

As the English explorer Sir Walter Raleigh once wrote, "Romance is a love affair in other than domestic surroundings." Indeed, many high-end hotels seem custom-built for romance, with plush feather beds, silky linens, and ultrasoft robes. But some properties go above and beyond in catering to couples, offering services like bath butlers and in-room massages. Here's our pick of the city's best spots for an intimate getaway.

At the **Ritz-Carlton New York, Battery Park** (⇨ *Lower Manhattan)*, your wish is their command. Take advantage of lower-than-normal weekend rates to book a Liberty Suite, with sweeping views of the Statue of Liberty. With a quick call to the concierge you can arrange to have champagne and strawberries waiting in your room when you arrive. A bath butler can then fill your marble tub with a potion of bath oils and flower petals. If you're here in February, don't miss a trip to the penthouse Chocolate Bar, with its aphrodisiac chocolate-and-champagne buffet.

The **Inn at Irving Place** (⇨ *Union Square/Gramercy)* does romance the old-fashioned way, with four-poster beds, fireplaces, fur throws, and plenty of privacy in an elegant 1800s brownstone. The complimentary breakfast is served on fine bone china either in the cozy sitting room or in bed.

Few things are as romantic as taking a bath, and at the Carlyle (⇨ *Upper East Side)* every room has one. Fill the tub with steaming water and some Kiehl's bubble bath, take a soak, then lounge with your lover in a plush terry robe while looking out at some of the City's best views. The 23,000-square-foot Bliss Spa at **W New York** (⇨ *Midtown East and Upper East Side)*, on Lexington Avenue, is an urban oasis, with men's and women's lounges, a gym, and a full menu of facial and body treatments, massage, waxing, and nail services. Couples can spend a full day being pampered in the spa or unwind in their rooms with an in-room massage, offered 24 hours a day.

All the rooms at the **Library Hotel** (⇨ *Midtown East and Upper East Side)* have an inviting charm that makes them a good choice for a romantic weekend away, but if you're looking for a little mood reading, ask for the Erotic Literature room or the Love Room, curated by Dr. Ruth.

17

helmed by celebrity chef; attentive staff. **Cons:** fee for Internet. ⑤ *Rooms from: $459* ✉ *300 W. 44th St., Midtown West* ☎ *877/331–5888* ⊕ *www. interconny.com* ➷ *578 rooms, 4 suites, 25 studios* ❄ *No meals* Ⓜ *A, C, E to 42nd St./Port Authority Bust Terminal* ✛ *4:B4.*

$$　🖼 **JW Marriott Essex House.** With Central Park views and an Art Deco
HOTEL　masterpiece of a lobby, the JW Marriott Essex House is a comfortable Midtown hotel that is full of character. **Pros:** great service; amazing views; impressive restaurant. **Cons:** overly complex room gadgetry; expensive bar. ⑤ *Rooms from: $399* ✉ *160 Central Park S, between 6th and 7th Aves., Midtown West* ☎ *212/247–0300, 800/937–8461* ⊕ *www.marriott.com* ➷ *509 rooms, 117 suites* ❄ *No meals* Ⓜ *F, N, R, Q to 57th St.* ✛ *4:C1.*

$ 🏨 **La Quinta Inn Manhattan.** Smack in the middle of Koreatown and
HOTEL   close to Penn Station, this budget-friendly hotel in a cheerful old Beaux
Arts building may be one of the best deals in town. **Pros:** self-check-in
machines; gift shop on the premises for necessities; relaxed rooftop bar.
Cons: no room service; no frills. ⑤ *Rooms from: $240* ✉ *17 W. 32nd
St., between 5th Ave. and Broadway, Midtown West* ☎ *212/736–1600*
⊕ *www.lq.com* ⟳ *182 rooms* ❙○❙ *Breakfast* Ⓜ *B, D, F, N, Q, R, M to
34th St./Herald Sq.* ✛ *4:E6.*

$$$ 🏨 **Le Parker Meridien.** The Parker Meridian combines the comforts
HOTEL   of a dependable large hotel with whimsical elements that keep visi-
FAMILY   tors coming back. **Pros:** lively, animated spirit; best hotel gym in the
city; fun dining; tech-friendly rooms. **Cons:** lobby is a public space
and gets crowded at peak times; small bathrooms. ⑤ *Rooms from:
$450* ✉ *119 W. 56th St., between 6th and 7th Aves., Midtown West*
☎ *212/245–5000, 800/543–4300* ⊕ *www.parkermeridien.com* ⟳ *513
rooms, 216 suites* ❙○❙ *No meals* Ⓜ *B, D, E to 7th Ave.; N, Q, R to
57th St.* ✛ *4:D1.*

$$$ 🏨 **The London NYC.** Stylish and sophisticated, the London NYC merges
HOTEL   the flair of both its namesake cities, with the added bonus of Gordon
Fodor's Choice   Ramsay's first stateside restaurant. **Pros:** posh atmosphere without pris-
★   siness; Gordon Ramsay restaurants; great fitness club; generously sized
rooms; free Wi-Fi. **Cons:** no bathtubs in most rooms; expensive dining
options. ⑤ *Rooms from: $599* ✉ *151 W. 54th St., between 6th and
7th Aves., Midtown West* ☎ *866/690–2029, 212/307-5000* ⊕ *www.
thelondonnyc.com* ⟳ *562 suites* ❙○❙ *No meals* Ⓜ *B, D, E to 7th Ave.;
N, Q, R to 57th St.* ✛ *4:C2.*

$$$$ 🏨 **Mandarin Oriental.** The Mandarin's commitment to excess is evident
HOTEL   in the lobby, on the 35th floor of the Time Warner Center, where dra-
Fodor's Choice   matic floor-to-ceiling windows look out over Columbus Circle and
★   Central Park. **Pros:** fantastic views from rooms, lounges, and pool;
all the resources of the Time Warner Center; expansive suites. **Cons:**
Trump hotel blocks some park views; expensive; mall-like surround-
ings. ⑤ *Rooms from: $955* ✉ *80 Columbus Circle, at 60th St., Midtown
West* ☎ *212/805–8800* ⊕ *www.mandarinoriental.com/newyork* ⟳ *198
rooms, 46 suites* ❙○❙ *No meals* Ⓜ *A, B, C, D, 1 to 59th St./Columbus
Circle* ✛ *4:B1; 5:C6.*

$$ 🏨 **The Mansfield.** They sweat the small stuff at the Mansfield: Wi-Fi is
HOTEL   free, bathroom products are from Aveda, and even the key cards are
snazzily embossed with scenes of old-timey New York. **Pros:** compli-
mentary Wi-Fi; business center; 24-hour gym; great bar. **Cons:** small
rooms and bathrooms; air conditioners are window units. ⑤ *Rooms
from: $319* ✉ *12 W. 44th St., between 5th and 6th Aves., Midtown
West* ☎ *212/277–8700, 800/255–5167* ⊕ *www.mansfieldhotel.com*
⟳ *99 rooms, 27 suites* ❙○❙ *No meals* Ⓜ *B, D, F, M to 42nd St.* ✛ *4:E4.*

$$ 🏨 **The Michelangelo.** Italophiles will feel like they've been transported to
HOTEL   the good life in the Mediterranean at this deluxe hotel, where the long,
wide lobby lounge is clad with multihue marble and Veronese-style oil
paintings. **Pros:** good location; spacious rooms. **Cons:** noisy a/c; some
rooms have limited views; small closets; in-room fixtures need some
updating. ⑤ *Rooms from: $399* ✉ *152 W. 51st St., at 7th Ave., Midtown*

West ☎ *212/765–1900, 800/237–0990* ⊕ *www.michelangelohotel.com* 🛏 *123 rooms, 56 suites* ❙❘❙ *Breakfast* Ⓜ *B, D, E to 7th Ave.; 1 to 50th St.; B, D, F, M to 47th–50th Sts./Rockefeller Center* ✛ *4:C3.*

$$ 🏨 **Muse Hotel.** Surrealist prints and busts of Thalia, the muse of comedy,
HOTEL adorn the lobby of this polished Kimpton property, a good pick for
guests looking for a Midtown boutique hotel experience. **Pros:** contemporary interiors; good Midtown location; pet-friendly; complimentary morning coffee and tea. **Cons:** street noise; small gym. Ⓢ *Rooms from: $389* ✉ *130 W. 46th St., between 6th and 7th Aves., Midtown West* ☎ *212/485–2400, 877/692–6873* ⊕ *www.themusehotel.com* 🛏 *181 rooms, 19 suites* ❙❘❙ *No meals* Ⓜ *B, D, F, M to 47th–50th Sts./Rockefeller Center* ✛ *4:C4.*

$$ 🏨 **The Out NYC.** Billed as a straight-friendly "urban resort" in one
HOTEL of New York's most happening gay neighborhoods, the Out is the
Fodor'sChoice incarnation of all things hip and modern. **Pros:** centrally located;
★ affordable; friendly staff. **Cons:** can be noisy at night. Ⓢ *Rooms from: $360* ✉ *510 W. 42nd St., Midtown West* ☎ *212/947-2999* ⊕ *www. theoutnyc.com* 🛏 *87 rooms, 10 suites, 8 quads* ❙❘❙ *No meals* Ⓜ *A, C, E at 42nd St.* ✛ *4:A4.*

$$$$ 🏨 **The Plaza.** Eloise's adopted home on the corner of Central Park, the
HOTEL Plaza is one of New York's most storied hotels, hosting all manner of
Fodor'sChoice dignitaries, moneymakers, and royalty. **Pros:** historic property; lavish
★ rooms. **Cons:** rooms aren't that big for the money. Ⓢ *Rooms from: $895* ✉ *768 5th Ave., at Central Park, Midtown West* ☎ *212/759–3000* ⊕ *www.theplazany.com* 🛏 *180 rooms, 102 suites* ❙❘❙ *No meals* Ⓜ *N, R to 59th St.* ✛ *4:E1.*

$$$ 🏨 **The Quin.** This new luxury hotel just south of Central Park once
HOTEL housed artists like Marc Chagall and Georgia O'Keeffe. **Pros:** new,
fresh property; spacious rooms; close to neighborhood destinations like Carnegie Hall. **Cons:** 57th Street location might be too chaotic for some. Ⓢ *Rooms from: $599* ✉ *101 W. 57th St., Midtown West* ☎ *212/245-7846* ⊕ *www.thequinhotel.com* 🛏 *208 rooms, 28 suites* ❙❘❙ *No meals* Ⓜ *N, Q, R to 57th St./7th Ave.; F to 57th St.* ✛ *4:D1.*

$$$ 🏨 **Refinery Hotel.** This hotel, which occupies a former hat factory, has
HOTEL a gorgeous year-round rooftop, impressively spacious rooms, and sev-
Fodor'sChoice eral buzzing bars and resataurants. **Pros:** lots of character and lovely,
★ detailed design; rooftop. **Cons:** limited dining and nightlife options nearby. Ⓢ *Rooms from: $459* ✉ *63 W. 38th St., Midtown West* ☎ *646/664–0310* ⊕ *www.refineryhotelnewyork.com* 🛏 *197 rooms* ❙❘❙ *No meals* Ⓜ *B, D, F, M to 42nd St./Bryant Park; N, Q, R to 34th St./Herald Sq.* ✛ *4:D5.*

$$$ 🏨 **Renaissance Hotel.** After a shift from all business to a more design-
HOTEL centric approach, the Renaissance is enjoying a renaissance of its own.
Pros: contemporary design; latest in-room technology. **Cons:** rooms can be a bit noisy; high occupancy means rooms can wear out fast. Ⓢ *Rooms from: $539* ✉ *714 7th Ave., between 47th and 48th Sts., Midtown West* ☎ *212/765-7676, 800/628-5222* ⊕ *www.renaissance hotels.com* 🛏 *305 rooms, 5 suites* ❙❘❙ *No meals* Ⓜ *R to 49th St.; 1 to 50th St.* ✛ *4:C3.*

17

Best Hotels with Kids in Tow

Many New York hotels go out of their way to accommodate families, with special amenities and family-size rooms. However, a hotel claiming that it's child-friendly doesn't always translate to true kid-welcoming style. Ask if cribs come with linens, whether there are high chairs and children's menus in the dining room, and if there are in-house babysitters. Some hotels will even clear out the minibar (for bottle or baby-food storage), baby-proof a room, or provide baby-proofing materials. Here are some of the top picks for traveling with kids.

In the Bag. At Aloft hotels in Harlem and Brooklyn, kids receive a sleeping bag, coloring tools, and even popcorn in their own bag. And many rooms at Aloft New York Brooklyn can be conjoined to create family-friendly suites.

Suite Life. Space is at a premium in New York hotels, and if you have more than two people in a standard room, you'll really start to feel the squeeze. The answer? A suite, where you can spread out in style. The **Conrad New York** (⇨ *TriBeCa*) is an all-suite property that's in the same building as a multiplex movie theater and several reasonably priced dining options—including Shake Shack. With renovated, spacious suites, **Affinia 50** (⇨ *Midtown East and Upper East Side*) is the family hotel of choice on the residential East Side. At the **Hotel Beacon** in the calm Upper West Side, all rooms have kitchenettes and comfortable suites are available in one or two bedroom layouts.

Pure Pampering. Just because you have children in tow doesn't mean your dream of a pampering vacation needs to go down the drain. Several top New York hotels go out of their way to accommodate families. The **Mandarin Oriental** (⇨ *Midtown West*) offers complimentary kids' DVDs and video games, and free coloring books and crayons for kids.

Fun Flavor. Room Mate Grace (⇨ *Midtown West*) might make the perfect respite if you have teens in tow. There's a funky lobby pool, a kiosk that stocks sweets with which to fill the in-room refrigerators, and rooms with bunk beds that levitate out of the walls and have their own plasma TVs. At the hip **Hotel on Rivington** (⇨ *East Village and Lower East Side*) a special family suite has two full bedrooms, one with two sets of bunk beds and a big bin of toys, two full baths, and a Japanese tub. Bonus points: the hotel is across from Economy Candy.

Kid Karma. Family-friendly **Le Parker Meridien** (⇨ *Midtown West and Chelsea*) has a large pool, a restaurant that serves decadent breakfast foods such as chocolate French toast until 3 pm, and a casual dining spot, Burger Joint, that serves nothing but burgers and shakes.

Kid-Size. At **70 Park, Eventi,** and **Ink48** (all Kimpton Hotels), kids get their own minisize animal-print robes (also available for purchase) so they can feel just like their grown-up travel companions.

Tea for Two. At the **Plaza,** fanciful children of all ages will revel in dress-up clothes, formal tea service, and film screenings that are all part of the Eloise-theme experiences that seek to re-create the fictional character's time at the iconic hotel.

$$$$ 🏨 **The Ritz-Carlton New York, Central Park.** It's all about the park views
HOTEL   here, though the above-and-beyond service, accommodating to a fault,
FAMILY   makes this renowned property popular with celebs and other demand-
Fodor's Choice   ing guests. **Pros:** great concierge; personalized service; stellar location;
★   views. **Cons:** pricey; limited common areas. $ *Rooms from: $895* ✉ *50*
Central Park S, at 6th Ave., Midtown West ☎ *212/308–9100, 866/671–*
6008 ⊕ *www.ritzcarlton.com* ↻ *259 rooms, 47 suites* ❚⃝❘ *No meals* Ⓜ *F,*
M to 57th St. ✢ *4:D1.*

$$ 🏨 **Room Mate Grace.** A favorite of European visitors and business travel-
HOTEL   ers who work in fashion and entertainment, Grace delivers high-design
FAMILY   lodgings on a budget. **Pros:** cool swimming pool lounge; friendly, help-
ful staff. **Cons:** small rooms; little in-room privacy (no door separating
shower from main room). $ *Rooms from: $319* ✉ *125 W. 45th St.,*
Midtown West ☎ *212/354–2323* ⊕ *www.room-matehotels.com* ↻ *139*
rooms ❚⃝❘ *No meals* Ⓜ *B, D, F, M to 42nd St.* ✢ *4:D4.*

$$ 🏨 **The Royalton.** Back in the 1990s, the Royalton's lobby bar was one of
HOTEL   the prime meeting spots for local A-listers and a redesign now attracts
a new generation of movers and shakers—so be prepared to run the
gauntlet of the buzzing lounge before reaching your room—but the
helpful staff ensures the process goes smoothly. **Pros:** hip lobby scene;
luxurious beds and bathrooms; helpful service. **Cons:** dark hallways;
lighting verges on eye-strainingly dim. $ *Rooms from: $399* ✉ *44 W.*
44th St., between 5th and 6th Aves., Midtown West ☎ *212/869–4400,*
800/697–1791 ⊕ *www.royaltonhotel.com* ↻ *141 rooms, 27 suites*
❚⃝❘ *No meals* Ⓜ *B, D, F, M to 42nd St.* ✢ *4:D4.*

$$ 🏨 **The Shoreham.** In a neighborhood packed with generic hotels, the
HOTEL   Shoreham offers a welcome dose of style, along with proximity to
Midtown's attractions. **Pros:** tech-friendly; pet-friendly attitude; styl-
ish decor. **Cons:** not designed for families; limited space. $ *Rooms from:*
$399 ✉ *33 W. 55th St., between 5th and 6th Aves., Midtown West*
☎ *212/247–6700, 877/847–4444* ⊕ *www.shorehamhotel.com* ↻ *174*
rooms, 37 suites ❚⃝❘ *Breakfast* Ⓜ *E, M to 5th Ave.* ✢ *4:D2.*

$$ 🏨 **Sofitel Luxury Hotel.** With bilingual signage throughout the hotel,
HOTEL   plenty of velvet in the lobby, and European modern design in the
rooms—think blond wood and fresh flowers—the Sofitel brings a
Gallic flair to Midtown West. **Pros:** central location; great beds; some
suites with terraces and views. **Cons:** room views vary. $ *Rooms from:*
$350 ✉ *45 W. 44th St., between 5th and 6th Aves., Midtown West*
☎ *212/354–8844* ⊕ *www.sofitel.com* ↻ *346 rooms, 52 suites* ❚⃝❘ *No*
meals Ⓜ *B, D, F, M to 42nd St.* ✢ *4:E4.*

$ 🏨 **The Time Hotel.** One of the neighborhood's first boutique hotels, this
HOTEL   spot half a block from the din of Times Square tempers trendiness with a
touch of humor. **Pros:** acclaimed and popular Serafina restaurant downstairs; surprisingly quiet for Times Square location; good turndown
service. **Cons:** decor makes the rooms a little dated; service is inconsistent; water pressure is lacking. $ *Rooms from: $275* ✉ *224 W. 49th*
St., between Broadway and 8th Ave., Midtown West ☎ *212/246–5252,*
877/846–3692 ⊕ *www.thetimeny.com* ↻ *164 rooms, 29 suites* ❚⃝❘ *No*
meals Ⓜ *1, C, E to 50th St.* ✢ *4:C3.*

17

$$$ 🏨 **Viceroy New York.** Handsome and finely tailored, this new hotel has

HOTEL   functional, tech-focused rooms and lots of amenities. **Pros:** comfortable, quiet library with "cartender" mixing drinks in late afternoon; generous rooftop space with views of Central Park; appealing restaurant. **Cons:** small, crowded lobby; busy 57th Street location might not suit all guests. ⑤ *Rooms from: $559* ⌧ *120 W. 57th, Midtown West* ☎ *212/830–8000* ⊕ *www.viceroyhotelsandresorts.com/newyork* ⤙ *197 rooms, 43 suites* ⦿| *Breakfast* Ⓜ *N, Q, R to 57th St-7th Ave; F to 57th St.* ✥ *4:D1.*

$$ 🏨 **W Times Square.** Although it opened back in 2001, the W Times

HOTEL   Square still stands out in the the craziness of Times Square, thanks to its iconic, 57-story exterior—and if you want to be in the thick of the action, this is a fun place to stay. **Pros:** bustling nightlife and happy-hour scene; sleek rooms. **Cons:** if you want quiet, head elsewhere; no bathtubs in the smaller rooms. ⑤ *Rooms from: $359* ⌧ *1567 Broadway, at 47th St., Midtown West* ☎ *212/930–7400, 877/946–8357* ⊕ *www. whotels.com* ⤙ *466 rooms, 43 suites* ⦿| *No meals* Ⓜ *1, 2, 3, 7, N, Q, R, S to 42nd St./Times Sq.* ✥ *4:C3.*

$$ 🏨 **Warwick.** This grande dame was built by William Randolph Hearst

HOTEL   in 1926 for his mistress, Hollywood actress Marion Davies, and it's hosted many from Tinseltown since then including Cary Grant in the Presidential Suite for 12 years. **Pros:** excellent restaurant and bar; historic property; spacious suites. **Cons:** some rooms could use a refresh; no a/c in the hallways. ⑤ *Rooms from: $349* ⌧ *65 W. 54th St., at 6th Ave., Midtown West* ☎ *212/247–2700, 800/223–4099* ⊕ *www. warwickhotelny.com* ⤙ *359 rooms, 67 suites* ⦿| *No meals* Ⓜ *E, M to 57th St.; N, Q, R, W to 57th St.* ✥ *4:D2.*

$ 🏨 **Wellington Hotel.** A few blocks south of Central Park and Columbus

HOTEL   Circle, the Wellington is a good base for visitors who want to see the

FAMILY   sights in Midtown and the Upper West Side. **Pros:** central location; chipper, helpful staff; good for big families. **Cons:** dark, often small bathrooms; limited breakfast options. ⑤ *Rooms from: $275* ⌧ *871 7th Ave., at 55th St., Midtown West* ☎ *212/247–3900, 800/652–1212* ⊕ *www. wellingtonhotel.com* ⤙ *515 rooms, 85 suites* ⦿| *No meals* Ⓜ *N, Q, R to 57th St.* ✥ *4:C2.*

$$$ 🏨 **WestHouse.** This new Art Deco–style hotel is designed to feel like a

HOTEL   glamorous private residence. **Pros:** many extras included; fresh, luxurious rooms. **Cons:** guests may have mixed feelings on mandatory daily resident fee; busy Midtown locations lacks quality restaurant and nightlife options nearby. ⑤ *Rooms from: $499* ⌧ *201 W. 55th St., Midtown West* ☎ *212/707–4888* ⊕ *www.westhousehotelnewyork.com* ⤙ *154 rooms, 16 suites* ⦿| *Breakfast* Ⓜ *B, D, E to 7th Ave.; N, Q, R to 57th St./7th Ave.* ✥ *4:C2.*

$$ 🏨 **Westin New York at Times Square.** This giant Midtown hotel has all the

HOTEL   amenities and service you would expect from a reliable brand, at fairly reasonable prices, though without much style. **Pros:** central for Midtown attractions; big rooms; great gym. **Cons:** congested area near the Port Authority; small bathroom sinks; some rooms need to be refreshed. ⑤ *Rooms from: $319* ⌧ *270 W. 43rd St., at 8th Ave., Midtown West* ☎ *212/201–2700, 866/837–4183* ⊕ *www.westinny.com* ⤙ *873 rooms*

○| *No meals* Ⓜ *A, C, E to 42nd St./
Times Sq.* ✚ *4:B4.*

$ ⛫ **Yotel.** Look beyond the gimmicks
HOTEL (a luggage-storing robot, the futuristic white design scheme) you'll
discover one of New York's best-
run, most functional lodgings. **Pros:**
great value; large common outdoor
space; access to West Side piers and
Javits Center. **Cons:** rooms may be
small for some; limited luggage
storage and hanging space; 10th
Avenue is a bit out of the way.
Ⓢ *Rooms from: $149* ✉ *570 10th
Ave., at 42nd St., Midtown West*
☎ *646/449–7700* ⊕ *www.yotelnew
york.com* ⟿ *647 rooms, 22 suites*
○| *Breakfast* Ⓜ *A, C, E to 42nd St./
Times Sq.* ✚ *4:A4.*

UPPER EAST SIDE

$$$$ ⛫ **The Carlyle, A Rosewood Hotel.** On the well-heeled corner of Madison
HOTEL Avenue and 76th Street, the Carlyle's fusion of venerable elegance and
Fodor'sChoice Manhattan swank calls for the aplomb of entering a Chanel boutique:
★ walk in chin-high, wallet out, and ready to be impressed. **Pros:** perhaps
NYC's best Central Park views; refined service; delightful array of din-
ing and bar options; chic shopping in the neighborhood; great bathtubs.
Cons: removed from touristy Manhattan; stuffy vibe may not work for
families; every room is different, limiting consistency. Ⓢ *Rooms from:
$800* ✉ *35 E. 76th St., between Madison and Park Aves., Upper East
Side* ☎ *212/744–1600* ⊕ *www.thecarlyle.com* ⟿ *121 rooms, 66 suites*
○| *No meals* Ⓜ *6 to 77th St.* ✚ *5:F3.*

$ ⛫ **The Franklin.** The best luxury boutique hotel north of 57th Street, the
HOTEL Franklin, in a nine-story town house, is a gem nestled in a decidedly
residential neighborhood. **Pros:** neighborhood-y location; free Wi-Fi
and generous breakfast; pet-friendly. **Cons:** far from many tourist sights
except Museum Mile; small rooms. Ⓢ *Rooms from: $279* ✉ *164 E. 87th
St., between Lexington and 3rd Aves., Upper East Side* ☎ *212/369–
1000, 800/607–4009* ⊕ *www.franklinhotel.com* ⟿ *50 rooms* ○| *Break-
fast* Ⓜ *4, 5, 6 to 86th St.* ✚ *6:G6.*

$$$$ ⛫ **Hôtel Plaza Athénée.** Positioned unobtrusively by Central Park on the
HOTEL Upper East Side, the Plaza Athénée (now related in name only to its Parisian cousin) makes stellar service a priority, with a personal sit-down
check-in off to the side of the lobby, and extravagant in-room dining
service with an old-world feel: white tablecloths, candles, and flowers
are part of the deal. **Pros:** discerning service; fabulous hotel bar. **Cons:**
lobby can feel dark; Wi-Fi costs extra; expensive. Ⓢ *Rooms from: $895*
✉ *37 E. 64th St., at Madison Ave., Upper East Side* ☎ *212/734–9100,
212/606–4600* ⊕ *www.plaza-athenee.com* ⟿ *117 rooms, 25 suites*
○| *No meals* Ⓜ *6 to 68th St./Hunter College* ✚ *5:F5.*

17

$$ ⊞ **Hotel Wales.** A favorite for in-the-know travelers, the Wales is pleas-
HOTEL ant if unassuming in a sedate neighborhood. **Pros:** on-site fitness facili-
FAMILY ties; great neighborhood feel; roof garden. **Cons:** standard rooms are
tight on space; if seeking nightlife go elsewhere. ⑤ *Rooms from: $395*
✉ *1295 Madison Ave., between 92nd and 93rd Sts., Upper East Side*
☎ *212/876–6000, 212/876–6000* ⊕ *www.hotelwalesnyc.com* ⤵ *46
rooms, 43 suites* �‖⊙‖ *No meals* Ⓜ *4, 5, 6 to 86th St.* ✛ *6:F5.*

$$$$ ⊞ **The Lowell.** This old-money refuge was built as an upscale apartment
HOTEL hotel in the 1920s and it still delivers genteel sophistication and pam-
pering service in an unbeatable location. **Pros:** great location; service
with a personal touch; charming decor. **Cons:** cramped lobby; expen-
sive. ⑤ *Rooms from: $775* ✉ *28 E. 63rd St., between Madison and
Park Aves., Upper East Side* ☎ *212/838–1400, 800/221–4444* ⊕ *www.
lowellhotel.com* ⤵ *27 rooms, 47 suites* �‖⊙‖ *No meals* Ⓜ *4, 5, 6, N, R to
59th St./Lexington Ave.; F to 63rd St./Lexington Ave.* ✛ *5:F6.*

$$$$ ⊞ **The Mark.** The Mark is the perfect combo of uptown panache and
HOTEL downtown chic. **Pros:** hip design; cavernous closet space; great ser-
Fodor'sChoice vice; scene-making restaurant and bar. **Cons:** expensive; limited bud-
★ get dining options in neighborhood. ⑤ *Rooms from: $600* ✉ *25 E.
77th St., at Madison Ave., Upper East Side* ☎ *212/744–4300* ⊕ *www.
themarkhotel.com* ⤵ *100 rooms, 50 suites* �‖⊙‖ *No meals* Ⓜ *6 to 77th
St./Lexington Ave.* ✛ *5:F2.*

UPPER WEST SIDE

$$ ⊞ **The Empire Hotel.** In a prime Upper West Side spot, the sophisticated
HOTEL Empire Hotel attracts locals for views from the rooftop pool and lounge
area underneath the hotel's iconic red neon sign, while guests appreciate
the rooms, which are a comfortable and chic escape from the bustle of
the city. **Pros:** great location next to Lincoln Center and blocks from
Central Park; beautiful rooftop pool and bar; nice turndown service.
Cons: rooftop bar brings foot traffic through hotel lobby, plus noise
to some rooms; some rooms could use a refresh; bathrooms are nicely
designed but tiny; pool is quite small. ⑤ *Rooms from: $399* ✉ *44 W.
63rd St., at Columbus Ave., Upper West Side* ☎ *212/265–7400* ⊕ *www.
empirehotelnyc.com* ⤵ *376 rooms, 50 suites* �‖⊙‖ *No meals* Ⓜ *1, A, B, C
to 59th St./Columbus Circle* ✛ *5:C5.*

$$ ⊞ **The Excelsior Hotel.** Directly across the street from the American Museum
HOTEL of Natural History, this well-kept, old-school spot is comfortable but has
occasionally inconsistent staff. **Pros:** excellent neighborhoody Upper West
Side location near Central Park; near foodie mecca Zabar's and popular
burger joint Shake Shack; tranquil environment. **Cons:** spotty front-desk
staff; rooms are inconsistent; Wi-Fi is not free. ⑤ *Rooms from: $329* ✉ *45
W. 81st St., between Central Park W and Columbus Ave., Upper West
Side* ☎ *212/362–9200* ⊕ *www.excelsiorhotelny.com* ⤵ *118 rooms, 80
suites* �‖⊙‖ *No meals* Ⓜ *B, C to 81st St.* ✛ *5:C2.*

$ ⊞ **Hotel Beacon.** A neighborhood favorite for a reason, this Upper West
HOTEL Side hotel is three blocks from Central Park, 10 blocks from Lincoln
Center, and footsteps from great gourmet grocery stores—Zabar's, Fair-
way, and Citarella. **Pros:** kitchenettes; great UWS location; affordable;
great service. **Cons:** though comfortable and spacious, rooms aren't

CLOSE UP

Lodging Alternatives

APARTMENT RENTALS VS. SUITE HOTELS

For your trip to New York, you may want a little more space than the city's typically tiny hotel rooms provide. Some travelers consider apartment rentals, but there are many good reasons to stick to hotel suites instead. Why? First, apartment rentals of less than 30 days are now—with some very limited exceptions—illegal in New York City. Furthermore, apartment-rental scams are prevalent. In some published reports, potential guests have arrived to find that the apartment they rented does not exist, or that they are paying for an illegal sublet. In some cases, travelers have lost their deposit money, or their prepaid rent (note: never wire money to an individual's account).

There are a few reputable providers of short-term rentals, *noted below.* But many Fodorites have turned to suite hotels and bed-and-breakfasts with apartmentlike accommodations to guard themselves from possible scams. We've noted some of their most enthusiastic recommendations.

Local rental agencies that arrange rentals of furnished apartments:

Abode Limited ☎ 212/472-2000, 800/835-8880 ⊕ www.abodenyc.com.

Manhattan Getaways ☎ 212/956-2010 ⊕ www.manhattangetaways.com.

Suite suggestions from **Fodor's Forums** (⊕ www.fodors.com/forums):

"For a week or less, there's no need to risk being scammed or renting something illegal by renting a private apt. There are *loads* of suite hotels and B&Bs at all price levels that will provide the space and convenience of an apartment, many with the amenities of a hotel including the ability to be able to read reviews of them before you book and know what you're getting. **Affinia** (⊕ www. Affinia.com) is a group of seven suite hotels at various prices that's well regarded. **Milburn Hotel** (⊕ www. milburnhotel.com) and the **Salisbury Hotel** (⊕ www.nycsalisbury.com) are some of the more popular independent budget options." —mclaurie

BED-AND-BREAKFASTS

B&Bs booked through a service may be either hosted (you're the guest in someone's quarters) or unhosted (you have full use of someone's vacated apartment, including kitchen privileges). Reservation services:

Bed-and-Breakfast Network of New York ✉ 134 W. 32nd St., Ste. 602, between 6th and 7th Aves. ☎ 212/645-8134, 888/707-4626 ⊕ www.bedandbreakfastnetwork.com.

City Lights Bed-and-Breakfast ☎ 212/737-7049 ⊕ www. citylightsbedandbreakfast.com.

"**West Eleventh** (⊕ www. west-eleventh.com) and **Abingdon Guest House** (⊕ www. abingdonguesthouse.com) are two of many B&Bs in the village with some charm, but are only good for two people." —mclaurie

"Also try **B&B Manhattan** (⊕ www. bandbmanhattan.com) which has very nice studio and 1-bed apartments in Chelsea and GV. A friend stayed with them last year and liked it a lot." —tomassocroccante

17

winning any design awards. $ *Rooms from: $295* ✉ *2130 Broadway, at 75th St., Upper West Side* ☎ *212/787–1100, 800/572–4969* ⊕ *www. beaconhotel.com* ⇱ *138 rooms, 135 suites* ❑No meals Ⓜ *1, 2, 3 to 72nd St.* ✛ *5:A3.*

$$ ❑ **The Lucerne.** Service is the strong suit at this landmark-facaded hotel, HOTEL whose exterior has more pizzazz than the predictable guest rooms decorated with dark-wood reproduction furniture and chintzy bedspreads. **Pros:** free Wi-Fi; clean; great gym; close to Central Park. **Cons:** inconsistent room size; some guests report uncomfortable pillows. $ *Rooms from: $309* ✉ *201 W. 79th St., at Amsterdam Ave., Upper West Side* ☎ *212/875–1000, 800/492–8122* ⊕ *www.thelucernehotel.com* ⇱ *163 rooms, 37 suites* ❑No meals Ⓜ *1 to 79th St.* ✛ *5:A2.*

$ ❑ **NYLO New York City.** Bringing modern style to the sometimes stodgy HOTEL Upper West Side, this new hotel nods to the jazz era—think raucous bar, decadent living room with a fireplace, and tempting restaurants. **Pros:** short walk from Central Park; quiet, safe location; excellent dining and drinking options; rooms with terraces and dynamite views. **Cons:** lobby might be too hectic for some; Upper West Side location removed from some attractions. $ *Rooms from: $259* ✉ *2178 Broadway, Upper West Side* ☎ *212/362–1100* ⊕ *www.nylohotels.com* ⇱ *252 rooms, 33 suites* ❑No meals Ⓜ *1 to 79th St.* ✛ *5:A3.*

$$$$ ❑ **Trump International Hotel and Towers.** This iconic New York property's incomparable views of Central Park has interior design and decor to match, conceived with the help of the Donald's daughter, Ivanka. **Pros:** fine service; stellar views; discerning treatment. **Cons:** expensive. $ *Rooms from: $995* ✉ *1 Central Park W, between 59th and 60th Sts., Upper West Side* ☎ *212/299–1000, 888/448–7867* ⊕ *www. trumphotelcollection.com* ⇱ *33 rooms, 143 suites* ❑No meals Ⓜ *1, A, B, C, D to 59th St./Columbus Circle* ✛ *5:C6.*

HARLEM

$ ❑ **Aloft Harlem.** A reasonably priced option in an increasingly popular HOTEL area of Harlem (Marcus Samuelsson's hot Red Rooster restaurant is nearby), this branch of the Aloft chain delivers with cheerful service and a fun atmosphere, once you get past the confusing front entrance. **Pros:** good room size for the price; convenient to subways; ever-increasing local shopping, and dining options. **Cons:** rooms have minimal space for hanging clothes; rooms get some street noise. $ *Rooms from: $289* ✉ *2296 Frederick Douglass Blvd., between 124th and 125th Sts., Harlem* ☎ *212/749–4000* ⊕ *www.aloftharlem.com* ⇱ *124 rooms* ❑No meals Ⓜ *1, 2, 3, A, B, C, D to 125th St.* ✛ *6:C1.*

BROOKLYN

DOWNTOWN BROOKLYN

$$ ❑ **Aloft New York Brooklyn.** A funky boutique in the heart of Downtown HOTEL Brooklyn, Aloft is a lively yet comfortable space, with world music FAMILY pumping in the lobby lounge and the quality beds Starwood properties are known for in the relatively spacious rooms upstairs. **Pros:** pet- Fodor'sChoice and family-friendly; good subway access; fab rooftop bar; reasonable ★

prices; guests have access to Sheraton's indoor swimming pool and room service. **Cons:** rumored construction at rear of hotel could mean noisy construction in years to come. $ *Rooms from: $359* ✉ *216 Duffield St., between Wiloughby St. and Fulton Mall, Downtown Brooklyn* ☎ *718/256–3833* ⊕ *www.aloftnewyorkbrooklyn.com* ➹ *170 rooms, 6 suites* ❍| *No meals* Ⓜ *B, Q, R to DeKalb Ave.; 2, 3 to Hoyt St.; R to MetroTech* ✛ *7:B4.*

$$ ⬚ **New York Marriott at the Brooklyn Bridge.** You'll find, like many New
HOTEL Yorkers before you, that one virtue of staying in Brooklyn is all the extra space; what Manhattan hotel has room for an Olympic-length lap pool, an 1,100-car garage, and even a dedicated kosher kitchen? **Pros:** near some of New York's hipper neighborhoods; traditional-style full-service hotel. **Cons:** on a busy, trafficky street in Downtown Brooklyn. $ *Rooms from: $369* ✉ *333 Adams St., between Johnson and Willoughby Sts., Downtown Brooklyn* ☎ *718/246–7000* ⊕ *www. marriott.com/nycbk* ➹ *638 rooms, 28 suites* ❍| *No meals* Ⓜ *2, 3, 4, 5 to Borough Hall* ✛ *7:B3.*

COBBLE HILL

$ ⬚ **NU Hotel Brooklyn.** The hip-yet-affordable NU, on one of Brooklyn's
HOTEL main nightlife and shopping streets, is perfect for visitors seeking a manageable taste of outer-borough New York—and the staff is eager to highlight the neighborhood's charms. **Pros:** great Brooklyn launching pad; knowledgeable staff; fitness center open 24 hours. **Cons:** subway or cab ride to anything in Manhattan; bar area can be a little too quiet; limited in-room amenities. $ *Rooms from: $269* ✉ *85 Smith St., Cobble Hill* ☎ *718/852–8585* ⊕ *www.nuhotelbrooklyn.com* ➹ *87 rooms, 6 suites* ❍| *Breakfast* Ⓜ *F to Bergen St.; A, C, G to Hoyt-Schermerhorn* ✛ *7:B4.*

GREENPOINT

$$ ⬚ **Box House Hotel.** Adventurous travelers will be drawn to this all-suite
HOTEL hotel, formerly a door factory, in industrial north Greenpoint. **Pros:** exciting, developing neighborhood; huge suites with kitchens and living rooms; free neighborhood transportation. **Cons:** functional bathrooms not particularly luxurious; no black-out curtains; isolated location in industrial neighborhood isn't for everyone. $ *Rooms from: $379* ✉ *77 Box St., Greenpoint* ☎ *718/383–3800* ⊕ *www.theboxhousehotel.com* ➹ *56 suites* ❍| *No meals* Ⓜ *G to Greenpoint Ave.* ✛ *7:E1.*

WILLIAMSBURG

$ ⬚ **Hotel Le Jolie.** This no-frills favorite has excellent service and is con-
HOTEL venient not only to the arts, culture, and dining scenes that Williamsburg has become known for—but also to several subway lines and the Bronx–Queens Expressway, in case you want to get into the city. **Pros:** good value; free parking on a first-come, first-served basis; convenient part of Brooklyn. **Cons:** location next to highway can mean noise; can feel remote even though convenient to subways. $ *Rooms from: $199* ✉ *235 Meeker Ave., between Lorimer and Union Aves., Williamsburg* ☎ *718/625–2100* ⊕ *www.hotellejolie.com* ➹ *52 rooms* ❍| *Breakfast* Ⓜ *L to Bedford Ave.* ✛ *7:E1.*

17

$$ · HOTEL · ⚏ **King & Grove Williamsburg.** With funky design details like an underfoot, glass-encased river in the lobby (plus a fireplace), and a plum location overlooking Brooklyn's McCarren Park, King & Grove Williamsburg succeeds in scenester savvy. **Pros:** high hip-factor; in-house restaurant-bar, complimentary coffee/tea/water on request; close to main thoroughfare Bedford Avenue. **Cons:** potential for noise from concerts in McCarren Park; some room details like lighting controls could be more user-friendly. ⑤ *Rooms from: $315* ✉ *160 N. 12th St., between Bedford and Berry Sts., Williamsburg* ☎ *718/218–7500* ⊕ *www.kingandgrove.com* ⇆ *60 rooms, 4 suites* ⏃ *No meals* Ⓜ *L to Bedford Ave.* ✛ *7:E1.*

$$ · HOTEL · Fodor'sChoice · ★ · ⚏ **Wythe Hotel.** A former cooperage on the Brooklyn waterfront has found new life as the Wythe Hotel, one of the hottest openings of 2012—and home to stunning Manhattan-skyline views, locally sourced design touches and amenities, and a hip restaurant. **Pros:** unique building history; excellent entry into fun neighborhood; local Brooklyn-based design and environmentally friendly products; fabulous Manhattan skyline views from rooms or rooftop bar; destination-worthy restaurant with wood-fired stove. **Cons:** somewhat isolated from the subway; no room service. ⑤ *Rooms from: $300* ✉ *80 Wythe Ave., at N. 11th St., Williamsburg* ☎ *718/460–8001* ⊕ *www.wythehotel.com* ⇆ *66 rooms, 4 suites* ⏃ *No meals* Ⓜ *L to Bedford Ave.* ✛ *7:D1.*

SHOPPING

Updated by Christina Valhouli

The Big Apple is one of the best shopping destinations in the world, rivaled perhaps only by London, Paris, and Tokyo. Its compact size, convenient subway system, and plentiful cabs (unless it's raining) make it easy to navigate with plenty of bags in tow. But what it really comes down to is the staggering number and variety of stores. If you can't find it in New York, it probably doesn't exist.

If you like elegant flagships and money is no object, head to Midtown, where you'll find international megabrands like Louis Vuitton, Yves Saint Laurent, and Gucci, as well as famed department stores Bergdorf Goodman and Barneys. Nearby Madison Avenue offers couture from Carolina Herrera and Vera Wang, and 5th Avenue is lined with famous jewelry stores like Tiffany, Van Cleef & Arpels, and Harry Winston. This is also the neighborhood to indulge in bespoke goods, such as handmade shoes from John Lobb. If you like designer pieces but can't afford them, don't despair—there are plenty of upscale consignment shops dotted around the city where you can find last season's Chanel suit or a vintage YSL jacket.

The small, independent shops that once lined SoHo have largely been swallowed up by J. Crew and UNIQLO, but if you want to hit the chains, this is a great place to do it, because SoHo also provides high-quality people-watching and superb lunches. If you're craving some of old SoHo's artistic spirit, don't discount the street vendors' stalls, which sell handmade jewelry and simple cotton dresses. You never know—you might buy something from a soon-to-be-famous designer.

The East Village and Lower East Side are hotbeds of creativity and quirky coolness, with little boutiques selling everything from retro furniture to industrial-inspired jewelry tucked among bars and tenement apartments. The Meatpacking District is another great shopping destination, where you'll find chic stores like Diane Von Furstenberg and Catherine Malandrino along with independently owned boutiques.

BEST BETS FOR NYC SHOPPING

With thousands of shops to choose from, how will you decide where to go? Below you'll find some of Fodor's writers and editors favorites to help you get started. You can also search by category within each neighborhood for noteworthy shops.

Fodor'sChoice★

3X1, p. 404
ABC Carpet & Home, p. 428
Aedes de Venustas, p 422
Agent Provocateur, p. 405
Alexander McQueen, p 426
Alexis Bittar, p. 412
Ankasa, p 447
Apple Store, p. 432
Argosy Bookstore, p. 431
Bloomingdale's, p. 433
Calypso St. Barth, p. 443
Century 21, p. 400
Charlotte Olympia, p. 448
Comptoir des Cotonniers, p. 406
Cooper-Hewitt National Design Museum, p. 447
Diane von Furstenberg, p. 426
Dover Street Market, p. 433
Duncan Quinn, p. 415
Dunhill, p. 433

FAO Schwarz Fifth Avenue, p. 436
Fishs Eddy, p. 428
Fivestory, p. 446
Flight 001, p. 424
Fragments, p. 412
Intermix, p. 449
Isabel Marant, p. 407
Issey Miyake, p. 401
Jack Rogers, p. 448
Jacques Torres Chocolates, p. 411
John Varvatos, p. 418
Kidrobot, p. 414
Kiehl's Since 1851, p. 417
La Maison du Chocolat, p. 446
La Petite Coquette, p. 421
Lanvin, p. 443
Leffot, p. 424
Le Labo, p. 414
Louis Vuitton, p. 436
Ludivine, p. 444
Maison Kitsuné, p. 428
Malia Mills, p. 415
Matter, p. 412
Max Brenner: Chocolate by the Bald Man, p. 430

McNally Jackson, p. 414
Opening Ceremony, p. 408
Piperlime, p. 408
Polo Ralph Lauren, p. 445
Shinola, p. 402
Smythson of Bond Street, p. 441
The Strand, p. 430
Tani, p. 450
Tiffany & Co., p. 435
Union Square Wine & Spirits, p. 420
Vosges Haut Chocolat, p. 411
Warm, p. 410
What Goes Around Comes Around, p. 410

BEST CHILDREN'S CLOTHING

A Time for Children, p. 449
Bonpoint, p. 442
Bundle, p. 404
Giggle, p. 404
Les Petits Chapelais, p. 404
Shoofly, p. 400
Space Kiddets, p. 427

BEST DENIM

3X1, p. 404
7 for all Mankind, p. 404
Denim & Supply, p. 421
Madewell, p. 428

BEST DEPARTMENT STORES

Barneys, p. 446
Bergdorf Goodman, p. 438
Bloomingdale's, p. 433
Macy's, p. 439
Saks Fifth Avenue, p. 434

BEST HANDBAGS

Clare V., p. 416
Devi Kroell, p. 448
Fendi, p. 435
Hermès, p. 448
High Way, p. 417
Kate Spade, p. 413
Khirma Eliazov, p. 423
Longchamp, p. 414
Louis Vuitton, p. 436
Lulu Guinness, p. 424
Manhattan Portage/ Token, p. 417
Stuart Weitzman, p. 436

BEST LINGERIE

Aedes de Venustas, p 422
Agent Provocateur, p. 405
Bra Smyth, p. 442

18

LOWER MANHATTAN AND TRIBECA

FINANCIAL DISTRICT

Although it is known primarily as the home of Wall Street, Lower Manhattan—especially TriBeCa—is a hotbed for interesting boutiques and shopping icons. Come here for downtown fixtures, including Century 21 and J&R, the electronics megastore.

BARGAIN SHOPPING

Fodor'sChoice
★
Century 21. For many New Yorkers this downtown fixture—right across the street from the former World Trade Center site—remains the mother lode of discount shopping. Four floors are crammed with everything from Marc Jacobs shoes and half-price cashmere sweaters to Donna Karan sheets, though you'll have to sift through racks and fight the crowds to find the gems. Best bets for men are shoes and designer briefs; the full floor of designer women's wear can yield some dazzling finds, such as a Calvin Klein leather trench coat for less than $600. Don't miss the children's section, either, for brands like Ralph Lauren and Ed Hardy. ■ TIP➔ Since lines for the communal dressing rooms can be prohibitively long, do what the locals do: wear leggings and change discreetly in the aisles. ✉ *22 Cortlandt St., between Broadway and Church St., Lower Manhattan* ☎ *212/227–9092* ⊕ *www.c21stores.com* Ⓜ *R to Cortlandt St.* ✉ *1972 Broadway, between 66th and 67th Sts., Upper West Side* ☎ *212/518–2121* ⊕ *www.c21stores.com/lincoln-square*

CLOTHING

Abercrombie & Fitch. This brand is known for its casual preppy clothes for men, women, and kids—but brace yourself for the thumping club music and dim lighting. ✉ *199 Water St.* ☎ *212/809–9000* ⊕ *www. abercrombie.com.*

GIFTS AND SOUVENIRS

City Store. The official store of NYC sells anything and everything having to do with the city, from books and pamphlets to fun gift ideas. Pick up NYPD T-shirts, taxicab medallions, garbage truck toys, and dishtowels silk-screened with the skyline. The store shuts at 5 pm on weekdays and is closed weekends. ✉ *1 Centre St., at Chambers St., Financial District* ☎ *212/386–0007* ⊕ *a856-citystore.nyc.gov* Ⓜ *4, 5, 6 to City Hall/Brooklyn Bridge.*

TRIBECA

Known for its multimillion-dollar lofts and Hollywood residents, TriBeCa is home to some of the most interesting boutiques in the city. Although there aren't many stores here, specialty shops such as Korin or J. Crew Men's Shop at the Liquor Store are worth a visit.

CHILDREN'S CLOTHING

Shoofly. Children's shoes and accessories imported from all over the world are the name of the game here. Choose from Mary Janes, trendy sneakers, and motorcycle boots along with pom-pom hats, brightly patterned socks, eclectic toys, and jewelry. ✉ *42 Hudson St., between Thomas and Duane Sts., TriBeCa* ☎ *212/406–3270* ⊕ *www.shooflynyc. com* Ⓜ *1 to Franklin St.*

CLOSE UP

Deals and Steals

Everyone loves a bargain—including a temporary New Yorker. Scoring a good deal is a rite of passage, and the city offers everything from low-cost department stores like Century 21 to hawkers of pseudo-Rolex watches and Kate Spade bags stationed at street corners and in Canal Street stalls. And then there are the sample sales.

If a seasonal sale makes New Yorkers' eyes gleam, a sample sale throws shoppers into a frenzy. With so many designer flagships and corporate headquarters in town, merchandise fallout periodically leads to tremendous deals. Although technically the term sample sale refers to stock that's a sample design, a show model, a leftover, or is already discounted, the term is now also used for sales of current-season goods. Location adds a bit of an illicit thrill to the event: sales are held in hotels, warehouses, offices, or loft spaces, where items both incredible and unfortunate jam a motley assortment of racks,

tables, and bins. Generally, there is a makeshift communal dressing room, but mirrors are scarce, so veteran sample-sale shoppers come prepared for wriggling in the aisles; some wear tank tops with tights or leggings for modest quick changes. Two rules of thumb: grab first and inspect later, and call in advance to find out what methods of payment are accepted. One of the ultimate experiences is the Barneys Warehouse Sale, held in February and August in Chelsea. Other luscious sales range from the Vera Wang bridal-gown sale (early winter) to Dwell Studio (spring and late fall).

How to find out about these events? The level of publicity and regularity of sales vary. The print and online versions of *New York* magazine are always worth checking for sample sale tip-offs, as are regular bulletins on Racked (⊕ *www.racked.com*) and Daily Candy (⊕ *www.dailycandy.com*). If you're interested in specific designers, call their shops and inquire—you may get lucky.

18

CLOTHING

Fodor's Choice ★ **Issey Miyake.** This flagship, designed by Frank Gehry, attracts a non-fashion crowd who come just to gawp at his undulating 25-foot high titanium sculpture, *The Tornado*. Miyake's signature style offers clothes that are sleek and slim-fitting, and made from polyester or ultrahigh-tech textiles. This flagship carries the entire runway collection, as well as Pleats Please and Issey Miyake Fete. ⊠ *119 Hudson St., at N. Moore St., TriBeCa* ☎ *212/226–0100* ⊕ *www.tribecaisseymiyake.com* Ⓜ *1 to Franklin St.*

J.Crew Men's Shop at the Liquor Store. It would be easy to walk right past this place and think it's a bar rather than an outpost of J. Crew for men, because it's filled with manly knickknacks like old Jack Kerouac books and vintage photographs. Some of the best finds are the limited-edition suits and cashmere sweaters, as well as non–J. Crew items like Barbour jackets and vintage Timex watches. ⊠ *235 W. Broadway, at White St., TriBeCa* ☎ *212/226–5476* ⊕ *www.jcrew.com* Ⓜ *1 to Franklin St.*

HOME DECOR

Korin. If you're serious about cooking, head to this specialty knife store in Tribeca. Previously only open to the trade, it is one of the best places to shop for top-quality knives imported from Japan. ✉ *57 Warren St., between W. Broadway and Church Sts., TriBeCa* ☎ *212/587–7021* ⊕ *www.korin.com* Ⓜ *1, 2, 3 to Chambers St.*

SHOES, HANDBAGS, AND LEATHER GOODS

Matt Bernson. Thankfully, the footwear at designer Matt Bernson's new TriBeCa store is both beautiful and blister-proof. Though the native New Yorker's comfy, affordable sandals are staples at Bergdorf's, Scoop and Madewell, this shop is his first stand-alone venture. With the help of his father, Bernson renovated the 1820s carriage house he now calls a showroom, giving it an at-home feel with antique furniture he refurbished himself. (Another store fixture is the designer's dog, Abraham, who accompanies him to work every day.) ✉ *20 Harrison St., between Greenwich and Staple Sts., TriBeCa* ☎ *212/941–7634* ⊕ *www.mattbernson.com* Ⓜ *1 to Franklin St.*

Fodor's Choice ★ **Shinola.** World War II–era shoe polish brand Shinola has been relaunched as a company that proudly manufactures its watches, bicycles, and leather goods in Detroit. The Shinola store also sells American-made products from other brands, such as oxford shirts from Gitman Bros. ✉ *177 Franklin St., between Greenwich and Hudson Sts., TriBeCa* ☎ *917/728–3000* ⊕ *www.shinola.com* Ⓜ *1 to Franklin St.*

SOHO AND NOLITA

SOHO

Head to SoHo for both the cheap and the hyperchic. The narrow sidewalks get very busy, especially on the weekends but this is a fun see-and-be-seen neighborhood. You'll see plenty of familiar high-fashion names like Prada, Chanel, and Louis Vuitton and several less expensive chains, like Banana Republic and Sephora, which have made land grabs on Broadway. But you can still hit a few clothing and housewares boutiques you won't find elsewhere in this country. The hottest shopping area runs west from Broadway over to 6th Avenue, between West Houston and Grand streets. Don't overlook a couple of streets east of Broadway: Crosby and Lafayette have several intriguing shops.

BARGAIN SHOPPING

Pearl River Mart. Whether you're looking for a decorative birdcage or a massive bag of jasmine rice, this mega–department store has everything Asian under one roof—at bargain prices. Browse through housewares like bamboo rice steamers and ceramic tea sets, or decorate your apartment with paper lanterns and porcelain stools. On the main floor, under a ceiling festooned with dragon kites and rice-paper parasols, you can buy kimono-style robes, pajamas, and embroidered satin slippers for the whole family. There's also a dry-goods section, where you can load up on ginger candy, jasmine tea, and cellophane noodles. ✉ *477 Broadway, between Broome and Grand Sts., SoHo* ☎ *212/431–4770* ⊕ *www.pearlriver.com* Ⓜ *N, R, Q to Canal St.*

Street Vendor Shopping

If you're looking for original or repro-duced artwork, the two areas to visit for street vendors are the stretch of 5th Avenue in front of the Metropoli-tan Museum of Art (roughly between 81st and 82nd streets) and the SoHo area of West Broadway, between Houston and Broome streets. In both areas you'll find dozens of artists selling original paintings, drawings, and photographs (some lovely, some lurid), as well as photo reproduc-tions of famous New York scenes (the Chrysler building, South Street Seaport). Prices can start as low as $10, but be sure to haggle.

The east–west streets in SoHo are an excellent place to look for handmade crafts: Spring and Prince streets, especially, are jammed with tables full of beaded jewelry, tooled leather belts, cotton sundresses, and homemade hats and purses. These streets are also great places to find deals on art books; several vendors have titles featuring the work of artists from Diego Rivera to Annie Leibovitz, all for about 20% less

than you'd pay at a chain. It's best to know which books you want ahead of time, though; street vendors wrap theirs in clear plastic, and can get testy if you unwrap them but don't wind up buying.

Faux-designer handbags, sunglasses, wallets, and watches are some of the most popular street buys in town—but crackdowns on knockoffs have made them harder to find. The hub used to be Canal Street, roughly between Greene and Lafayette streets, but many vendors there have swept their booths clean of fake Vuitton, Prada, Gucci, and Fendi merchandise. You might have better luck finding a "Faux-lex" near Herald Square or Madison Square Garden, and good old-fashioned fake handbags are still sold by isolated vendors around such shopping areas as Rockefeller Center and the stretch of lower 5th near Union Square. If you're looking for cheap luggage, skip Canal Street, as the bags there might not last beyond the flight home, and instead pick up a bargain at Marshalls, TJ Maxx, or Loehmann's.

18

BEAUTY

MiN. If the selection of grooming products at Duane Reade doesn't cut it for you, head to MiN. This wood-paneled shop is decidedly male-friendly, with leather couches and exposed brick walls. Shop for unusual scents from Santa Maria Novella and L'Artisan Parfumeur, shaving products from Old Bond Street, or quirky items like mustache wax. ✉ *117 Crosby St., between Prince and Houston Sts., SoHo* ☎ *212/206–6366* ⊕ *www.minnewyork.com* Ⓜ *N, R to Prince St.*

BOOKS AND STATIONERY

Scholastic Store. Kids and the young at heart will be delighted by the whimsical design here, including an 11-foot orange dinosaur, a life-size Magic School Bus, and a massive Harry Potter. In addition to the thou-sands of books, kids can amuse themselves with games, toys, DVDs, computers, and arts-and-crafts workshops. It is so kid-friendly that parents will find a separate entrance just for strollers (at 130 Mercer Street). ✉ *557 Broadway, at Prince St., SoHo* ☎ *212/343–6166* ⊕ *www.scholastic.com/sohostore* Ⓜ *R to Prince St.*

CAMERAS AND ELECTRONICS

Apple Store. Branch location at 103 Prince Street, between Greene and Spring streets. *See Midtown East for full review.*

CHILDREN'S CLOTHING

Bundle. This SoHo boutique goes above and beyond selling fashionable onesies by offering a concierge service. If you can't make it to the store to choose a gift, just email them and they'll reply with suggestions. Visit and choose adorable clothes from brands including Kissy Kissy, Baby CZ, and Tea. ✉ *128 Thompson St., between Prince and Houston Sts., SoHo* ☎ *212/982–9465* ⊕ *www.bundlenyc.com* Ⓜ *C, E to Spring St.*

Giggle. This high-end baby store is often crammed with stroller gridlock, but it stocks nearly everything a stylish parent (and baby) could ever need. The Giggle flagship carries all the gear and accessories to build a chic nursery, including Dwell bedding, plush toys, and funky kids' clothing. Basic gear such as highchairs and strollers are also sold, and staff will make sure parents know how to fold that complicated stroller before leaving the store. Additional Giggle outlets are located on the Upper West and Upper East sides. ✉ *120 Wooster St., between Spring and Prince Sts., SoHo* ☎ *212/334–5817* ⊕ *www.giggle.com* Ⓜ *N, R to Prince St.*

J.Crew Crewcuts. If you don't like to dress your child in clothes that are too cute or painfully trendy, head to J.Crew's children's store, Crewcuts. Offering pint-size versions of the preppy classic clothes the brand is famous for, this shop is stocked with cords, cashmere sweaters, and blazers for the junior set. ✉ *99 Prince St., between Greene and Mercer Sts., SoHo* ☎ *212/343–1227* ⊕ *www.jcrew.com* Ⓜ *C, E to Spring St.*

Les Petits Chapelais. Designed and made in France, these kids' clothes (from newborn up to age 12) are cute and stylish but also practical. Corduroy outfits have details like embroidered flowers and contrasting cuffs, and soft, fleecy jackets are reversible. There's also a line of sailor-inspired clothes. ✉ *146 Sullivan St., between Houston and Prince Sts., SoHo* ☎ *212/625–1023* Ⓜ *C, E to Spring St.*

CLOTHING

Fodor's Choice ★ **3X1.** In this huge denim shop, which doubles as a factory, customers can watch their bespoke jeans being made. The walls of the pristine white space are lined with more than 100 bolts of denim. After you select the perfect fabric, jeans are hand cut and sewn by the in-house seamstresses, who work in a glass-enclosed space. Shoppers can also buy off-the-rack jeans; unfinished hems are tailored on the spot (starting at $295). ✉ *15 Mercer St., SoHo* ☎ *212/391–6969* ⊕ *www.3x1.us* Ⓜ *N, R, 4, 6 to Canal St.*

7 for All Mankind. Whether you're hunting for super skinny, high-waisted, or boot-cut jeans in a dark or distressed finish, this temple to denim offers it all. The jeans are a firm celebrity favorite (Cameron Diaz is a fan), but be warned: although they are guaranteed to make your derriere look good, they don't come cheap. You'll also find stylish and sexy dresses here, plus sweaters and jackets for men and women. ✉ *394 W. Broadway, between Broome and Spring Sts., SoHo* ☎ *212/226–8615* ⊕ *www.7forallmankind.com* Ⓜ *A, C, E to Spring St.*

Luxe shops line the streets of SoHo.

A Bathing Ape. Known simply as BAPE to devotees, this exclusive label has a cult following in its native Tokyo. At first it may be hard to see what the fuss is about. A small selection of camouflage gear and limited-edition T-shirts is placed throughout the minimalist space; the real scene stealers are the flashy retro-style sneakers in neon colors. ⊠ *91 Greene St., between Prince and Spring Sts., SoHo* ☎ *212/925–0222* ⊕ *www. bape.com* Ⓜ *R to Prince St.*

Fodor's Choice **Agent Provocateur.** If Victoria's Secret is too tame for you, try this Brit-
★ ish lingerie shop, which has a naughty twist. Showpieces include boned corsets, lace sets with contrast-color trim, bottoms tied with satin ribbons, and a few fetish-type leather ensembles. A great selection of stockings is complemented by the garter belts to secure them. ⊠ *133 Mercer St., between Prince and Spring Sts., SoHo* ☎ *212/965–0229* ⊕ *www. agentprovocateur.com* Ⓜ *R to Prince St.*

Alexander Wang. *Vogue* darling Alexander Wang's boutique is as unfussy—but cool—as his clothes. Shoppers can take a break on a fur hammock in between browsing for perfectly slouchy tank tops, sheath dresses, or edgy ankle boots. ⊠ *103 Grand St., between Greene and Mercer Sts., SoHo* ☎ *212/977–9683* ⊕ *www.alexanderwang.com.*

Allan & Suzi. The duo behind Allan & Suzi have been selling their pristine vintage clothing to celebrities for years—and have also outfitted the cast of *Sex and the City.* Their downtown store offers a mix of new and vintage finds, ranging from the elegant to the wacky. Dig and you may find a Gaultier gown or a Pauline Trigere dress, along with crazy disco gear. ⊠ *237 Centre St., between Grand and Broome Sts., SoHo* ☎ *212/724–7445* ⊕ *www.allanandsuzi.net* Ⓜ *N, R, 4, 6 to Canal St.*

American Two Shot. This boutique offers a carefully curated mix of contemporary designs for men and women, including clothing from Timo Weiland and Jonathan Simkhai, as well as rare vintage finds. The displays are fun and witty (you might see a voodoo doll). The space also functions as an art gallery and includes an outpost of Cafe Integral in case shoppers need a caffeine fix. ⊠ *135 Grand St., between Crosby and Lafayette Sts., SoHo* ☎ *212/925–3403* ⊕ *americantwoshot.com* Ⓜ *R to Canal St.*

Anna Sui. The violet-and-black salon, with its Victorian rock-chick vibe, is the ideal setting for Sui's bohemian and rocker-influenced designs and colorful beauty products. ⊠ *113 Greene St., between Prince and Spring Sts., SoHo* ☎ *212/941–8406* ⊕ *www.annasui.com* Ⓜ *R to Prince St.*

A.P.C. This hip French boutique sells deceptively simple clothes in an equally understated setting. Watch your step on the uneven wooden floorboards while choosing narrow gabardine and corduroy suits or dark denim jeans and jackets. For women, best bets include striped sweaters and skinny jeans. ⊠ *131 Mercer St., between Prince and Spring Sts., SoHo* ☎ *212/966–9685* ⊕ *www.apc.fr* Ⓜ *6 to Spring St.; R to Prince St.*

Bloomingdale's. Branch location at 504 Broadway, between Broome and Spring streets. *See Midtown East for full listing.*

Christopher Fischer. Featherweight cashmere sweaters, wraps, and throws in every hue from Easter-egg pastels to rich jewel tones have made Fischer the darling of the preppy set. His shop also carries leather accessories, home wares such as throw pillows, and baby clothes. ⊠ *80 Wooster St., between Spring and Broome Sts., SoHo* ☎ *212/965–9009* ⊕ *www.christopherfischer.com* Ⓜ *R to Prince St.*

Fodor's Choice   **Comptoir des Cotonniers.** The "cotton counter" angles for multigenera-
★   tional shopping, lining up stylish, comfortable basics for babies, twentysomethings, ladies of a certain age, and everyone in between. There's a subtle Parisian vibe to the understated tunics, dresses, and separates; colors tend to be earthy. The brand's first U.S. branch has a nature-friendly minimalist look, with pale-wood floors and lots of natural light. ⊠ *155 Spring St., at W. Broadway, SoHo* ☎ *212/274–0830* ⊕ *www.comptoirdescotonniers.com* Ⓜ *C, E to Spring St.*

Costume National. Everything about this boutique is sexy and minimalist, with an edge. The clothes—and lighting—are dark. Shoppers will find sharply tailored wool pants for men and silky tops for women in muted shades of black, gray, and charcoal, along with motorcycle boots and leather gloves. ⊠ *150 Greene St., between Prince and Houston Sts., SoHo* ☎ *212/431–1530* ⊕ *www.costumenational.com* Ⓜ *N, R to Prince St.*

C. Wonder. This lifestyle boutique, founded by Tory Burch's ex-husband, offers preppy clothing with a bohemian vibe (think embroidered caftans) as well as home goods, all at surprisingly affordable prices. Just about everything in sight, from tote bags to cuffs and pillows, can be monogrammed on the spot. ⊠ *72 Spring St., at Crosby St., SoHo* ☎ *212/219–3500* ⊕ *www.cwonder.com* Ⓜ *6 to Spring St.*

Emporio Armani. At this middle child of the Armani trio, the clothes are dressy without quite being formal, and are frequently offered in cream, muted blues, and ever-cool shades of taupe. ✉ *410 W. Broadway, at Spring St., SoHo* ☎ *646/613–8099* ⊕ *www.armani.com/us/emporioarmani* Ⓜ *C, E to Spring St.*

Etro. This Italian fashion house is known for its trademark paisleys and bold patterns, which cover everything from suits and dresses to lustrous pillows. Etro's flagship combines the best of Italy with a Soho loft; it boasts high tin ceilings, brightly colored rugs, and industrial lighting. ✉ *89 Greene St., between Spring and Prince Sts., SoHo* ☎ *646/329–6929* ⊕ *www.etro.com* Ⓜ *N, R to Prince St.*

French Connection. This British-owned company stocks an impressive collection of on-trend clothing for men and women at reasonable prices. Some of the best bets are the sharply tailored trench coats and jeans, as well as dresses. For men, try the cashmere sweaters and skinny trousers. ✉ *435 W. Broadway, SoHo* ☎ *212/219–1197* ⊕ *www. frenchconnection.com.*

Fodor's Choice ★ **Isabel Marant.** If you're after that casually glamorous Parisian vibe, look no further than Isabel Marant. Long a favorite of globetrotting fashionistas, this location is the French designer's first U.S. retail store. The tailored jackets, shorts, and flirty dresses are eclectic and sophisticated, with textured, deeply hued fabrics. ✉ *469 Broome St., at Greene St., SoHo* ☎ *212/219–2284* ⊕ *www.isabelmarant.tm.fr* Ⓜ *R to Prince St.*

Kiki de Montparnasse. Named for Man Ray's mistress and muse from the 1940s, this upscale lingerie store serves up decadent styles in a seductive but artistic setting. Shoppers will find exquisitely made corsets and bra and underwear sets, but a large portion of the store is used as a rotating art gallery for erotic art. ✉ *79 Greene St., at Spring St., SoHo* ☎ *212/965–8150* ⊕ *www.kikidm.com* Ⓜ *R to Prince St.*

Kirna Zabête. A heavy-hitting lineup of prestigious designers—Balenciaga, Alexander Wang, Lanvin, Proenza Schouler—is managed with an exceptionally cheerful flair. Step downstairs for dog apparel, coffeetable books, and hip infant gear from Kit and Lili. ✉ *477 Broome St., between Green and Wooster Sts., SoHo* ☎ *212/941–9656* ⊕ *www. kirnazabete.com* Ⓜ *R to Prince St.*

Marc Jacobs. One of Marc Jacobs' various NYC boutiques, this location, housed in a former garage, offers crisply tailored designs for men and women in luxurious fabrics: silk, cashmere, wool bouclé, and tweeds ranging from the demure to the flamboyant. The details, though—oversize buttons, circular patch pockets, and military-style grommet belts—add a sartorial wink. The shoe selection is not to be missed. ✉ *163 Mercer St., between W. Houston and Prince Sts., SoHo* ☎ *212/343–1490* ⊕ *www.marcjacobs.com* Ⓜ *R to Prince St.*

Marni. If you're a fan of the boho chic look, stock up on Consuelo Castiglioni's brightly-colored, happy clothes here. The collection features dresses and jackets in quirky prints and many of the silhouettes are vintage-inspired. Accessories are also eye-popping. ✉ *161 Mercer St., between Houston and Prince Sts., SoHo* ☎ *212/343–3912* ⊕ *www. marni.com* Ⓜ *R to Prince St.*

18

Miu Miu. Prada front woman Miuccia Prada established a secondary line (bearing her childhood nickname, Miu Miu) to showcase her more experimental ideas. Look for Prada-esque styles in more daring colors and cuts, such as high-waist skirts with scalloped edges, Peter Pan–collar dresses in trippy patterns, and patent-leather pumps. ⊠ *100 Prince St., between Mercer and Greene Sts., SoHo* ☎ *212/334–5156* ⊕ *www. miumiu.com* Ⓜ *R to Prince St.*

Moncler. Many New York women swear by Moncler coats to keep them warm but still looking stylish throughout the brutal winters. This store is the Italian brand's first foray into New York. The knee-length puffer is a firm favorite, but there are stylish ski jackets and accessories, along with pieces created in collaboration with designers like Giambattista Valli. ⊠ *90 Prince St., between Mercer St. and Broadway, SoHo* ☎ *646/350–3620* ⊕ *www.moncler.com* Ⓜ *R to Prince St.*

Odin. Men, if you're tired of the corporate look, head to Odin to spruce up your weekend wardrobe. This boutique, which caters only to men, carries separates from cool brands including Rag & Bone, Engineered Garments, and Band Of Outsiders. The cheerful staff will guarantee you will leave looking hip—but not as if you're trying too hard. ⊠ *199 Lafayette St., between Broome and Kenmare Sts., SoHo* ☎ *212/966– 0026* ⊕ *www.odinnewyork.com* Ⓜ *6 to Spring St.*

Fodor'sChoice ★ **Opening Ceremony.** Just like Colette in Paris, Opening Ceremony bills itself as a concept store, which means you never know what you will find. The owners are constantly globetrotting to soak up the style and designers in a foreign country, and bring back the best clothing, products, and vintage items to showcase in their store. Hong Kong, Japan, Brazil, and the United Kingdom have all been represented. There's also a gallery space here. ⊠ *35 Howard St., between Broadway and Lafayette St., SoHo* ☎ *212/219–2688* ⊕ *www.openingceremony. us* Ⓜ *N, R to Canal St.*

Paul Smith. Fans love Paul Smith for his classic-with-a-twist clothes, and his 5,000-square-foot flagship is a temple to his design ethos and inspirations. Victorian mahogany cases complement the dandyish British styles they hold. Embroidered vests; brightly striped socks, scarves, and shirts; and tongue-in-cheek cuff links leaven the classic, double-back-vent suits for men. Women head for the tailored suits and separates, classic outerwear, and dresses. Plus, you'll find furniture and a selection of photography books and ephemera. ⊠ *142 Greene St., between Prince and Houston Sts., SoHo* ☎ *646/613–3060* ⊕ *www. paulsmith.co.uk* Ⓜ *R to Prince St.*

Philosophy di Alberta Ferretti. The designer's eye for delicate detailing and soft, feminine design is evident in the perforated hemlines, embroidered stitching, and sprinkling of beads across gauzy fabrics and knits. ⊠ *452 W. Broadway, between Houston and Prince Sts., SoHo* ☎ *212/460–5500* ⊕ *www.albertaferretti.com* Ⓜ *F, M to Broadway– Lafayette St.*

Fodor'sChoice ★ **Piperlime.** This popular e-tailer now has its first brick and mortar store. The large loft-like space, which is accented with lime green, carries clothing from designers like Rachel Roy and Rebecca Taylor, shoes from Zac Posen, and a multitude of accessories. A smattering of kiosks allows shoppers to purchase items online as well. ⊠ *121 Wooster St., between Prince and Spring Sts., SoHo* ☎ *212/343–4284* ⊕ *www. piperlime.com* Ⓜ *N, R to Prince St.*

Prada. This ultramodern space, designed by Rem Koolhaas, incorporates so many technological innovations that it was written up in *Popular Science.* Dressing room glass walls turn opaque at the touch of a button, and instead of mirrors, shoppers can check themselves out in large video panels. ⊠ *575 Broadway, at Prince St., SoHo* ☎ *212/334– 8888* ⊕ *www.prada.com* Ⓜ *R to Prince St.*

R by 45rpm. Shopping at this Japanese clothing store is a Zen-like experience, thanks to a stone pathway, limestone dressing rooms, and denim dangling from wooden trees. Although it's pricey, fans love the label for its attention to detail, like hand-dyed denim that has been woven on antique looms. The T-shirts are particularly funky. ⊠ *169 Mercer St., between W. Houston and Prince Sts., SoHo* ☎ *917/237–0045* ⊕ *www. rby45rpm.com* Ⓜ *R to Prince St.*

Reiss. Think of Reiss as the Banana Republic of Britain—a go-to place for casual-but-tailored clothes at a relatively gentle price. Kate Middleton is a loyal customer. Standouts for women include cowl-neck sweater dresses and A-line skirts. Men's wool combat trousers are complemented by shrunken blazers, military-inspired peacoats, and trim leather jackets. ⊠ *387 W. Broadway, between Spring and Broome Sts., SoHo* ☎ *212/925–5707* ⊕ *www.reissonline.com* Ⓜ *R to Prince St.*

Sean. This French-pedigreed shop carries classic, understated menswear imported from Europe at reasonable prices. Linen and corduroy painter's coats are best sellers, along with v-neck sweaters and a respectable collection of slim cut suits. ⊠ *199 Prince St., between Sullivan and MacDougal Sts., SoHo* ☎ *212/598–5980* ⊕ *www.seanstore. com* Ⓜ *R to Prince St.*

Seize sur Vingt. Head to this boutique if you're ready to splurge on an exquisitely tailored shirt or suit. Men and women can pick out an off-the-rack item and have it custom tailored in house for a perfect fit, or create a fully bespoke shirt from a mind-boggling array of fabrics (linen, broadcloth oxford, flannel). To complete the look, sweaters, shoes, and accessories are also available. ⊠ *78 Greene St., between Spring and Broome Sts., SoHo* ☎ *212/625–1620* ⊕ *www.16sur20.com* Ⓜ *R to Prince St.*

Stella McCartney. McCartney's flagship store has a luxe look, thanks to parquet flooring and touches of gold found in the art deco sculptures and clothing racks. Her main collection, done mostly in gauzy, muted colors, is on the top floor, while children's, Adidas by Stella McCartney, and lingerie are on the lower level. In keeping with McCartney's vegetarianism, fur and leather are verboten. ⊠ *112 Greene St., between Spring and Prince Sts., SoHo* ☎ *212/255–1556* ⊕ *www.stellamccartney. com* Ⓜ *N, R to Prince St.*

Tess Giberson. This Rhode Island School of Design graduate is making waves for her eponymous women's collection. The boutique has an airy, minimalist feel, with whitewashed walls and rotating art exhibits

18

that perfectly match the clothing's pared down aesthetic. The best bets are floaty silk dresses and draped trousers. ⊠ *97 Crosby St., between Prince and Spring Sts., SoHo* ☎ *212/226–1932* ⊕ *www.tessgiberson. com* Ⓜ *N, R to Prince St.*

Topshop. British cult favorite Topshop, which has only a handful of U.S. stores, is a master at pumping out of-the-minute-fashion at reasonable prices. It can be a madhouse, and items sell quickly, but it's worth fighting the crowds. Slinky dresses are around $130, and jeans and jumpsuits are about $90. Coats and shoes are also standouts. Male stylistas can browse through the ground-level Topman. ⊠ *478 Broadway, between Broome and Grand Sts., SoHo* ☎ *212/966–9555* ⊕ *www.topshop.com* Ⓜ *6 to Spring St.; R to Prince St.*

Vera Wang Mercer. Not content designing just wedding dresses, Wang is also a star at evening wear and casual-but-chic daywear. Her entire ready-to-wear collection is showcased here in this gleaming, all-white store. Choose from clothes ranging from sexy one-shouldered satin gowns to cashmere sweaters and wool pencil skirts. ⊠ *158 Mercer St., between Prince and Houston Sts., SoHo* ☎ *212/382–2184* ⊕ *www. verawang.com* Ⓜ *N, R to Prince St.*

Vivienne Tam. Tam is known for her playful "China chic" take on familiar Asian images. Cold-weather creations in jewel-color silk are embroidered; the warm-weather clothes are floaty and romantic. ⊠ *40 Mercer St., at Grand St., SoHo* ☎ *212/966–2398* ⊕ *www.viviennetam.com* Ⓜ *R to Prince St.*

Fodor's Choice ★ **Warm.** If you want to feel the love, come to this little boutique, owned by lifelong surfer Winnie Beattie. Everything has a sunny, beachy vibe, from leather sandals, bikinis, and bleached sweaters to hand-blown glass vases. There's also a collection of children's books and housewares. ⊠ *181 Mott St., between Kenmare and Broome Sts., SoHo* ☎ *212/925–1200* ⊕ *www.warmny.com* Ⓜ *6 to Spring St.*

Fodor's Choice ★ **What Goes Around Comes Around.** Professional stylists flock here to dig up vintage items like Levi's and Azzedine Alaïa dresses, as well as one-of-a-kind rock-concert T-shirts. WGACA also sells its own line of vintage-inspired clothing, from dresses to coats and tops. The vintage rock tees (think Black Sabbath, Mötley Crüe) are great finds but can set you back an eye-watering $300–$600. ⊠ *351 W. Broadway, between Grand and Broome Sts., SoHo* ☎ *212/343–1225* ⊕ *www.whatgoesaroundnyc.com* Ⓜ *J, M, N, Q, R, Z, 6 to Canal St.*

FOOD AND TREATS

Harney & Sons. Fancy a cuppa? Harney & Sons is famous for producing more than 250 varieties of loose tea, which can be sampled at its store and tea salon in SoHo. The design is sleek and dramatic, with a 24-foot-long tasting bar and floor-to-ceiling shelves stocked with tea. Shoppers will find classic brews like English Breakfast and Oolong, along with interesting herbals (ginger and liquorice, or mint verbena). And no cup of tea would be complete without a scone or two, available at the tea salon. ⊠ *433 Broome St., between Broadway and Crosby St., SoHo* ☎ *212/933–4853* ⊕ *www.harney.com* Ⓜ *4, 6 to Spring St.*

Fodor's Choice
★
Jacques Torres Chocolates. Visit the café and shop here and you'll literally be surrounded by chocolate. The glass-walled downtown space also houses Torres's chocolate factory, so you can watch the goodies being made while you sip a richly spiced cocoa or nibble on a Java Junkie bar. ■TIP➜ Signature taste: the "wicked" chocolate, laced with cinnamon and chili pepper. ⊠ *350 Hudson St., at King St., SoHo* ☎ *212/414–2462* ⊕ *www.mrchocolate.com* Ⓜ *1 to Houston St.*

Kee's Chocolates. Owner Kee Ling Tong whips up delicious truffles and macaroons with unusual, Asian-inspired flavors. Try the ginger peach and rosewater lychee macaroons, or truffles flavored with lemongrass mint and tamarind. ⊠ *80 Thompson St., between Spring and Broome Sts., SoHo* ☎ *212/334–3284* ⊕ *www.keeschocolates.com* Ⓜ *A, C to Spring St.*

MarieBelle. The handmade chocolates here are nothing less than works of art. Square truffles and bonbons—which come in such flavors as Earl Grey, cappuccino, passion fruit, and saffron—are painted with edible dyes (cocoa butter dyed with natural coloring) so each resembles a miniature painting. Relax in the Cacao Bar and Tea Salon while sipping an Aztec hot chocolate, which is made from rich cacao, rather than cocoa powder. ⊠ *484 Broome St., between W. Broadway and Wooster St., SoHo* ☎ *212/925–6999* ⊕ *www.mariebelle.com* Ⓜ *R to Prince St.*

Fodor's Choice
★
Vosges Haut Chocolat. This chandeliered salon lined with apothecary shelves takes a global approach to chocolate. Many of the creations are travel-inspired: the Budapest bonbons combine dark chocolate and Hungarian paprika, and the Black Pearls contain wasabi. Don't miss the best-selling chocolate bacon bars. ⊠ *132 Spring St., SoHo* ☎ *212/625–2929* ⊕ *www.vosgeschocolate.com* Ⓜ *R to Prince St.*

HOME DECOR

de Vera. Owner Federico de Vera crisscrosses the globe searching for unique decorative products, so shoppers will never know what they might find here. Venetian glass vases, Thai Buddhas, and antique rose–cut diamond rings are typical finds. ⊠ *1 Crosby St., at Howard St., SoHo* ☎ *212/625–0838* ⊕ *www.deveraobjects.com* Ⓜ *N, Q, R, 6 to Canal St.*

Jonathan Adler. Everything at this flagship, housed in a former plumbing factory, is fun and happy. Adler funks up midcentury modern designs with his striped, striated, or curvy handmade pottery (ranging from a $30 vase to a chunky $400 lamp) as well as the hand-loomed wool pillow covers, rugs, and throws with bold patterns. Pull up to the Gift Bar if you need inspiration for a present. ⊠ *53 Greene St., between Grand and Broome Sts., SoHo* ☎ *212/941–8950* ⊕ *www.jonathanadler.com* Ⓜ *1 to Canal St.*

Kiosk. Is it a gallery or a boutique? Duck under the neon arrow sign, head up the stairway, and you'll come upon this novelty-shop-cum-art-installation. The owners travel the globe in search of locally unique, interestingly designed or packaged items, then sell their gleanings at this outpost. A new destination is highlighted every few months. As this book was going to press, Kiosk moved to a new location in Union Square. ⊠ *41 Union Square West, #925, Union Square* ☎ *212/226–8601* ⊕ *www.kioskkiosk.com* Ⓜ *4, 5, 6, N, R, Q to Union Sq.*

18

Fodor's Choice
★
Matter. This beautifully curated store will appeal to fans of sleek, modern furniture—if money is no object. How about the iconic Tank armchair by Alvar Aalto for a cool $5,000? Or a smoked-glass coffee table by Established & Sons for $1,400? Even if your budget is limited, Matter is worth a drool for inspiration. ⊠ *405 Broome St., between Centre and Lafayette Sts., SoHo* ☎ *212/343–2600* ⊕ *www.mattermatters.com* Ⓜ *4, 6 to Spring St.*

FAMILY
Pylones. It's hard to beat Pylones for crazily cheerful products. Utilitarian products like toasters and thermoses have been given makeovers of stripes or flowers, hairbrushes have pictures of frogs or ladybugs on their backs, and pepper mills are turned into pirates. ■TIP➡ **There are plenty of fun gifts for less than $20, such as old-fashioned robot toys and candy-color boxes.** ⊠ *69 Spring St., between Crosby and Lafayette Sts., SoHo* ☎ *212/431–3244* ⊕ *www.pylones-usa.com* Ⓜ *6 to Spring St.*

Room & Board. Fans of streamlined, mid-century modern furniture will be in heaven here. This location is stocked with sleek sofas, beds, and children's furniture as well as accessories like rugs and lamps. Design aficionados can choose from iconic pieces like seating cubes from Frank Gehry and Eames molded plywood chairs, or items from up and coming designers. ⊠ *105 Wooster St., between Spring and Prince Sts., SoHo* ☎ *212/334–4343* ⊕ *www.roomandboard.com* Ⓜ *N, R to Prince St.*

JEWELRY AND ACCESSORIES

Fodor's Choice
★
Alexis Bittar. Bittar began selling his first jewelry line, made from Depression-era glass, on a corner in SoHo. Now the Brooklyn-born designer counts A-list celebs and fashion editors among his fans. He makes clean-line, big-statement jewelry from vermeil, colored Lucite, pearls, and vintage glass. The store mirrors this aesthetic with a mix of old and new, like antique-white Victorian-era lion's-claw tables and Plexiglas walls. ⊠ *465 Broome St., between Mercer and Greene Sts., SoHo* ☎ *212/625–8340* ⊕ *www.alexisbittar.com* Ⓜ *R to Prince St.*

Fodor's Choice
★
Fragments. This spot glitters with pieces by emerging designers as well as established ones. Both fine jewelry and lower-priced "fashion" jewelry is available, so there's something for every budget. Try on a chunky blue topaz cocktail ring, or break the bank with a sapphire and diamond collar. ⊠ *116 Prince St., between Greene and Wooster Sts., SoHo* ☎ *212/334–9588* ⊕ *www.fragments.com* Ⓜ *R to Prince St.*

Ivanka Trump. The Donald's daughter would like to see you dripping with her diamonds. Her Soho location has an art deco look, with black-and-white furniture and plenty of glittering chandeliers. But the real bling is the jewelry—drop earrings, tassel lariats, and bold cocktail rings. Don't miss the elegant Bridal Bar for wedding jewelry. ⊠ *109 Mercer St., between Prince and Spring Sts., SoHo* ☎ *212/756–9912* ⊕ *www. ivankatrumpcollection.com* Ⓜ *N, R to Prince St.*

Robert Lee Morris. If you buy into the mantra that bigger is better, make a stop here. Morris designs big, chunky jewelry that is anything but understated. Gold and silver cuffs have a serious weight to them, and necklaces and earrings have dangling hammered disks for a "wind chime" effect. Some pieces incorporate diamonds; others have semiprecious stones like turquoise or citrine. ✉ *400 W. Broadway, between Broome and Spring Sts., SoHo* ☎ *212/431–9405* ⊕ *www.robertleemorris.com* Ⓜ *C, E to Spring St.*

Stuart Moore. Everything about this boutique is minimalist, from the architecture to the jewelry. Most of the designs (from Heinrich + Denzel to Beatrice Mueller) have a streamlined, almost industrial look: diamonds are set in brushed platinum, and gold bangles are impossibly delicate. ✉ *411 W. Broadway, at Spring St., SoHo* ☎ *212/941–1023* ⊕ *www.stuartmoore.com* Ⓜ *C, E to Spring St.*

Swarovski Crystallized. A shrine to all things sparkly, this crystal superstore is a combination boutique and café, and allows shoppers to customize their purchases. Shoppers mix and match pieces from the striking "library of light" to create designs. If you're lacking ideas, there's always ready-made jewelry. Look out for pieces created by top designers like Kenneth Jay Lane and Karen Millen. ✉ *499 Broadway, between Spring and Broome Sts., SoHo* ☎ *212/966–3322* ⊕ *www.swarovski.com* Ⓜ *R to Prince St.; 6 to Spring St.*

Versani. Most of the jewelry here is big, bold, and unisex—and more than a little quirky. Silver teams up with all kinds of materials: leather, denim, and snakeskin, as well as semiprecious stones. There's a good selection of silver rings and pendants under $50. ✉ *152 Mercer St., between Prince and Houston Sts., SoHo* ☎ *212/941–7770* ⊕ *www.versani.com* Ⓜ *R to Prince St.*

SHOES, HANDBAGS, AND LEATHER GOODS

Camper. Urbanites love this Spanish footwear company for its funky but comfortable shoes. The new flagship features an unusual pagoda-style roof made from tubes and inside, there's a vertical garden. All the slip-ons and lace-ups here have generously rounded toes and a springy feel. ✉ *110 Prince St., between Wooster and Green Sts., SoHo* ☎ *212/343–4220* ⊕ *www.camper.com* Ⓜ *N, R to Prince St.*

Frye Boots. This 6,000-square-foot mecca to boots has a Western feel, thanks to the exposed brick walls and reclaimed barn doors. Boots can be tattooed—or hot stamped—with your initials while you wait in the lounge. In addition to Frye's famed boots, shoppers can also pick from flats, oxfords, clogs, and mules. ✉ *113 Spring St., between Mercer and Greene Sts., SoHo* ☎ *212/226–3793* ⊕ *www.thefryecompany.com* Ⓜ *N, R to Prince St.*

Kate Spade. Spade's runaway success with classic kicky, retro-style tote bags has blossomed into a full-fledged lifestyle company. The flagship looks—and feels—like an elegant living room. The totes are still for sale, along with leather handbags, kitten heels, and accessories like eyeglasses and paper. Even the diaper bags are ridiculously stylish. Around the corner you'll find **Jack Spade,** filled with bags, dopp kits, and other men's accessories in a nostalgic setting. ✉ *454 Broome St., between Mercer and Greene Sts., SoHo* ☎ *212/274–1991* ⊕ *www.katespade.com* Ⓜ *C, E to Spring St.*

18

Longchamp. Its Le Pliage foldable nylon bags have become an Upper East Side and Hamptons staple, but don't think this label is stuffy—or all about nylon. There's a wide selection of leather handbags as well as wallets, belts, and shoes. Kate Moss also designs a line for Longchamp. ✉ *132 Spring St., at Elizabeth St., SoHo* ☎ *212/343–7444* ⊕ *www. longchamp.com* Ⓜ *N, R to Prince St.*

TOYS

FAMILY

Fodor's Choice

★

Kidrobot. This shop will appeal to kids, nerds, and the young at heart, who all flock here to stock up on the latest toys from Asian designers. This is a far cry from Mattel—the shelves are stocked with Dunny bunnies, Tokidokis, and Devilrobots. There's also a selection of cool silk-screened T-shirts and hoodies. ✉ *118 Prince St., between Greene and Wooster Sts., SoHo* ☎ *212/966–6688* ⊕ *www.kidrobot.com* Ⓜ *N, R to Prince St.*

NOLITA

NoLIta, short for "North of Little Italy" has become a mecca for shopping, thanks to the abundance of independent boutiques that range from quirky to elegant. Like SoHo, NoLIta has gone from a locals-only, understated area to a crowded weekend magnet, as much about people-watching as it is about shopping. Still, unlike those of its SoHo neighbor, these stores remain largely one-of-a-kind. Running along the parallel north–south spines of Elizabeth, Mott, and Mulberry streets, between East Houston and Kenmare streets, NoLIta's boutiques tend to be small and, as real estate dictates, somewhat pricey.

BEAUTY

Lafco New York. A heavy, iron-barred door leads to a hushed, scented inner sanctum of beauty products. This location is the official retailer of the 600-year-old Santa Maria Novella products from Italy, which include intriguingly archaic colognes, creams, and soaps such as Tooth Cleansing Water and pomegranate soap. Everything is packaged in bottles and jars with antique-style apothecary labels. ✉ *285 Lafayette St., between Houston and Prince Sts., NoLIta* ☎ *212/925–0001* ⊕ *www. lafcony.com* Ⓜ *N, R to Prince St.*

Fodor's Choice

★

Le Labo. If you're bored with department store perfume offerings, come to this tiny boutique that features a rustic industrial vibe and a resident mixologist who will help you create your ideal perfume. After choosing your favorite scents, the perfume is mixed and a personalized label is created for your bottle. ✉ *233 Elizabeth St., between Prince and Houston Sts., NoLIta* ☎ *212/219–2230* ⊕ *www.lelabofragrances.com* Ⓜ *B, D, F, M to Broadway/Lafayette St.*

BOOKS AND STATIONERY

Fodor's Choice

★

McNally Jackson. This cozy, independent bookstore is a bibliophile's dream. The bright two-story space has hardwood floors, a delicious cafe, and plenty of chairs for lounging and curling up with a book. More than 50,000 books are stocked and the literary section is organized geographically. Budding authors can self-print their tomes on a device called the Espresso Machine. ✉ *52 Prince St., between Lafayette and Mulberry Sts., NoLIta* ☎ *212/274–1160* ⊕ *www.mcnallyjackson. com* Ⓜ *R to Prince St.*

CLOTHING

Creatures of Comfort. Owner Jade Lai has brought her popular L.A. outpost to New York. The open, airy boutique offers cool clothes from emerging designers alongside products sourced from around the world. Most of the colors are muted, and brands carried include Acne, MM6, and the house label, Creatures of Comfort. There's a small selection of shoes, plus you never know what you might find for sale on a side table, such as candy and lip gloss from Asia. ⊠ *205 Mulberry St., between Spring and Kenmare Sts., NoLIta* ☎ *212/925–1005* ⊕ *www.creaturesofcomfort.us* Ⓜ *6 to Spring St.*

Dagny & Barstow. College friends Meredith Blank and Emily Titelman have stocked this tiny boutique, sandwiched between restaurant supply stores, with up-and-coming European labels. The high-end store stocks clothing, handbags, and jewelry, and the walls are lined with prints from ArtStar.com. ⊠ *264 Bowery, between Prince and Houston Sts., NoLIta* ☎ *212/675–2346* ⊕ *www.dagnyandbarstow.com* Ⓜ *6 to Bleecker St.*

Fodor's Choice ★ Duncan Quinn. Shooting for nothing less than sartorial splendor, this designer provides everything from chalk-stripe suits to cuff links and croquet shirts, all in a shop not much bigger than its silk pocket squares. Off-the-rack shirts are handmade in England but if you want to splurge, get fitted for a bespoke shirt with mother-of-pearl buttons. ⊠ *70–80 Kenmare St., between Mott and Mulberry Sts., NoLIta* ☎ *212/226–7030* ⊕ *www.duncanquinn.com* Ⓜ *6 to Spring St.*

INA. The clothing at this couture consignment store harks back only one or two seasons, and in some cases, the item has never been worn. Browse through the racks to spot gems from Lanvin, Chanel, and Alexander McQueen. Although there are multiple locations around the city, this flagship also carries menswear. ⊠ *15 Bleecker St., at Elizabeth St., NoLIta* ☎ *212/228–8511* ⊕ *www.inanyc.com* Ⓜ *6 to Bleecker St.*

Jay Kos. There aren't too many boutiques where the owner sometimes whips up a snack for customers in the boutique's custom kitchen, but this designer—famous for dressing Diddy and Johnny Depp—wanted his new boutique to have a homey feel. The clothes veer toward the fabulous: suede shoes, linen suits, and cashmere sweaters, which are displayed in armoires. ⊠ *293 Mott St., at Houston St., NoLIta* ☎ *212* ⊕ *www.jaykos.com* Ⓜ *B, D, F, M to Broadway-Lafayette St.*

Fodor's Choice ★ Malia Mills. Fit fanatics have met their match here—especially those gals who are different sizes on top and bottom (bikini tops go up to a size E). Flattering bikini tops and bottoms are sold separately: halters, bandeaus, and triangle tops, plus boy-cut, side-tie, and low-ride bottoms. There's a collection of one-pieces as well. ⊠ *199 Mulberry St., between Spring and Kenmare Sts., NoLIta* ☎ *212/625–2311* ⊕ *www.maliamills.com* Ⓜ *6 to Spring St.*

Nanette Lepore. "Girly" may well be the description that comes to mind as you browse through this cheerful shop; skirts are pleated and adorned with bows, jackets are enhanced by embroidery and floral appliqués, fur shrugs have tiny sleeves. ⊠ *423 Broome St., between Lafayette and Crosby Sts., NoLIta* ☎ *212/219–8265* ⊕ *www.nanettelepore.com* Ⓜ *6 to Spring St.*

Oak. This boutique looks like an art gallery, thanks to the huge sculpture winding its way though the middle of the store. Most of the clothing is in black and the store carries high-end designers as well as its own line. Come here for skinny jeans, capes, and draped jersey dresses. ✉ *28 Bond St., between Lafayette St. and Bowery, NoLIta* ☎ *212/677–1293* ⊕ *www.oaknyc.com* Ⓜ *6 to Bleecker St.*

Resurrection. If you're serious about vintage—and have deep pockets—Resurrection offers a treasure trove of pristine pieces from Chanel, Gucci, Halston, Alaia, and YSL among others. Kate Moss is a fan, and designers like Marc Jacobs and Anna Sui have sought inspiration among the racks. ✉ *217 Mott St., between Prince and Spring Sts., NoLIta* ☎ *212/625–1374* ⊕ *www.resurrectionvintage.com* Ⓜ *6 to Spring St.*

JEWELRY AND ACCESSORIES

Condor. Owner Loriann Smoak is the consummate world traveler, and she has stocked her serene, white-marbled clothing boutique with plenty of international designers, as well as local ones. Everything from coffee table books to dangly earrings and scarves is available here. ✉ *259 Elizabeth St., between Houston and Prince Sts., NoLIta* ☎ *212/966–4280* ⊕ *www.shopcondor.com.*

Dinosaur Designs. Translucent and colorful, this antipodean work uses an untraditional medium: resin. Some resins look like semiprecious stone, such as onyx or jade. The rest delve into stronger colors like aqua or crimson. Cruise the stacks of chunky bangles and cuffs or rows of rings; prices start at $50. There's some striking tableware, too. ✉ *211 Elizabeth St., between Prince and Houston Sts., NoLIta* ☎ *212/680–3523* ⊕ *www.dinosaurdesigns.com.au* Ⓜ *R to Prince St.*

Erica Weiner. This eponymous designer specializes in vintage-inspired jewelry as well as antiques: delicate art deco earrings, vintage lockets, and necklaces fashioned from antique compasses. The boutique's tile floor and wooden display cabinets reflect Weiner's aesthetic. Prices are surprisingly reasonable. ✉ *173 Elizabeth St., between Kenmare and Spring Sts., NoLIta* ☎ *212/334–6383* ⊕ *www.ericaweiner.com* Ⓜ *4, 6 to Spring St.*

Me&Ro. Minimalist Eastern styling has gained these designers a cult following. The Indian-inspired, hand-finished gold bangles, earrings, and necklaces are covered with tiny dangling rubies, sapphires, or brown diamonds. Although the fine jewelry is expensive, small sterling silver earrings start at around $120. ✉ *241 Elizabeth St., between Prince and Houston Sts., NoLIta* ☎ *917/237–9215* ⊕ *www.meandrojewelry.com* Ⓜ *R to Prince St.*

SHOES, HANDBAGS, AND LEATHER GOODS

Clare V. LA-based designer Clare Vivier's first New York store features her signature simple-but-elegant leather fold-over clutches in every size and color, as well as understated totes and duffels. There are also accessories like iPad cases, and even chic fanny packs. ✉ *239 Elizabeth St., between Prince and Houston Sts., NoLIta* ☎ *646/484–5757* ⊕ *www. clairevivier.com* Ⓜ *N, R to Prince St.*

Dolce Vita. The clothes here are stylish and on-trend but the real show-stoppers are the shoes. Although you won't find big name designers, shoppers can choose from a wide selection of ballet flats, ankle boots, and sexy stilettos, all at affordable prcies. ⊠ *255 Elizabeth St., between Houston and Prince Sts., NoLIta* ☎ *212/226–0635* ⊕ *www.dolcevita. com* Ⓜ *6 to Bleecker St.*

High Way. The bags here marry form and function. Totes and messenger bags come in durable leather and nylon, and some handbags open to disclose a wealth of inner pockets. ⊠ *238 Mott St., between Prince and Spring Sts., NoLIta* ☎ *212/966–4388* ⊕ *www.highwaybuzz.com* Ⓜ *6 to Bleecker St.*

John Fluevog Shoes. The inventor of the Angelic sole (protects against water, acid, "and Satan"), Fluevog designs chunky, funky shoes and boots for men and women. ⊠ *250 Mulberry St., at Prince St., NoLIta* ☎ *212/431–4484* ⊕ *www.fluevog.com* Ⓜ *N, R to Prince St.*

Kathryn Amberleigh. This designer, an FIT grad, has perfected the sexy-but-edgy look in her hand-crafted shoes. There are simple flats and wedges along with peep-toe ankle boots and sky-high heels. Most designs hover around the $250 mark. ⊠ *219 Mott St., between Prince and Spring Sts, NoLIta* ☎ *212/842–2134* ⊕ *www.kathrynamberleigh. com* Ⓜ *6 to Spring St.*

Manhattan Portgage/Token. Pay homage to the store that started the messenger-bag craze. Super-durable bags come in waxed canvas as well as nylon, and the line has expanded to include totes, duffels, and travel bags, all in unadorned, simple styles. ⊠ *258 Elizabeth St., between Houston and Prince Sts., NoLIta* ☎ *212/226–9655* ⊕ *www.tokenbags. com* Ⓜ *R to Prince St.*

18

EAST VILLAGE AND LOWER EAST SIDE

EAST VILLAGE

The East Village is a fabulous hunting ground for independent boutiques.

ANTIQUES AND COLLECTIBLES

Lost City Arts. This sprawling shop is one of the best places to shop for 20th-century-design furniture, lighting, and accessories. Lost City can help you relive the Machine Age with an in-house, retro-modern line of furniture. ⊠ *18 Cooper Sq., at 5th St., East Village* ☎ *212/375–0500* ⊕ *www2.lostcityarts.com* Ⓜ *6 to Astor Pl.*

BEAUTY

Bond No. 9. Created by the same fragrance team as Creed, this line of scents is intended to evoke the New York City experience, with a scent for every neighborhood: Central Park, a men's fragrance, is woodsy and "green," and Park Avenue is discreet but not too sweet. This flagship also carries candles and body creams. ⊠ *9 Bond St., between Lafayette St. and Broadway, East Village* ☎ *212/228–1732* ⊕ *www.bondno9.com* Ⓜ *6 to Bleecker St.*

Fodor's Choice ★ **Kiehl's Since 1851.** At this favored haunt of top models and stylists, white-smocked assistants can help you choose between the lotions and potions, all of which are packaged in simple-looking bottles and jars.

Some of the products, such as the Ultra Facial Cream, Creme with Silk Groom hairstyling aid, and superrich Creme de Corps, have attained near-cult status among fans. ■TIP→ Kiehl's is known for being generous with samples, so be sure to ask for your own bag of take-home testers. ⊠ *109 3rd Ave., at 13th St., East Village* ☎ *212/677–3171* ⊕ *www. kiehls.com* Ⓜ *4, 5, 6, L, N, Q, R to 14th St./Union Sq.*

BOOKS AND STATIONERY

St. Mark's Bookshop. Downtown residents, NYU students, and intellectuals in general spend hours poking through popular and oddball fiction and nonfiction. You'll find a truly eclectic collection of books here, not unlike the salespeople. On the main floor, books on critical theory are right up front, across from new fiction titles—Jacques Derrida facing off against T. C. Boyle. Cultural and art books are up front as well; literature and literary journals fill the back of the store. ■TIP→ It's open daily until midnight. ⊠ *31 3rd Ave., between 8th and 9th Sts., East Village* ☎ *212/260–7853* ⊕ *www.stmarksbookshop.com* Ⓜ *6 to Astor Pl.*

CLOTHING

Cloak & Dagger. Come here if you like refined but on-trend looks. The racks are lined with tulip skirts, belted dresses, and trenches from owner/designer Brookelynn Starnes as well as international labels. ⊠ *441 E 9th St., between Ave. A and 1st Ave., East Village* ⊕ *www. cloakanddaggernyc.com* Ⓜ *6 to Astor Pl.*

Fodor'sChoice
★
John Varvatos. Varvatos has long been inspired by rock and roll. His ad campaigns have starred Franz Ferdinand and Green Day, so it is only fitting that he transformed the former CBGB club into his New York flagship. The space is dotted with vintage pianos and guitars, as well as old vinyl records. And the clothes? The jeans, leather pants, and suede shoes will give you rock star cred, but there are also classic, understated styles for the corporate set. ⊠ *315 Bowery, between 1st and 2nd Sts., East Village* ☎ *212/358–0315* ⊕ *www.johnvarvatos.com* Ⓜ *4, 6 to Bleeker St.*

Pas de Deux. Fashion editors love this little boutique—which looks like it was imported straight from Paris—thanks to the marble checkerboard floor, chandeliers, and fine woodwork. The well-edited selection includes dresses, trench coats, and denim from Isabel Marant, Thakoon, and Alexander Wang. There are also lots of lovely little accessories, like eyeglasses, cardholders, and delicate necklaces. ⊠ *328 E. 11th St., between 1st and 2nd Aves., East Village* ☎ *212/475–0075* ⊕ *www. pasdedeuxny.com* Ⓜ *4, 6 to Astor Pl.*

Patricia Field. If you loved Carrie Bradshaw's wild outfits on *Sex and the City*, this is the place for you. As well as designing costumes for the show, Field has been a longtime purveyor of flamboyant and campy club-kid gear. Her 4,000-square-foot East Village emporium is chockablock with teeny kilts, lamé, marabou, pleather, and vinyl, as well as wigs in every color and stiletto heels in some very large sizes. ⊠ *306 Bowery, between Bleecker and Houston Sts., East Village* ☎ *212/966–4066* ⊕ *www.patriciafield.com* Ⓜ *6 to Bleeker St.*

The Lower East Side is a great area to shop for funky home furnishings.

Screaming Mimi's. Browse through racks bulging with vintage finds from the 1950s through '80s. Retro wear includes everything from dresses to soccer shirts and prom dresses. Although most of the non-designer finds are affordable, Screaming Mimi's also carries vintage designer duds from Valentino, Chloe, and Gaultier. ⊠ *382 Lafayette St., between 4th and Great Jones Sts., East Village* ☎ *212/677-6464* ⊕ *www.screamingmimis.com* Ⓜ *B, D, F, M to Broadway–Lafayette St.*

Tokio 7. Even fashion designers like Alexander Wang have been known to pop into this high-end consignment store to browse. Racks are loaded with goodies from A-list designers such as Gucci, Stella McCartney, DVF, and Philip Lim and the inventory changes almost daily. ⊠ *83 E. 7th St., between 1st and 2nd Aves., East Village* ☎ *212/353-8443* ⊕ *www.tokio7.net* Ⓜ *4, 6 to Astor Pl.–8th St.*

Trash and Vaudeville. This punk mecca is famous for dressing stars like Debbie Harry and the Ramones back in the '70s, and its rock-and-roll vibe lives on. Goths, punks, and pro wrestlers shop here for bondage-inspired pants and skirts, as well as vinyl corsets and minikilts. ⊠ *4 St. Marks Pl., between 2nd and 3rd Aves., East Village* ☎ *212/982-3590* ⊕ *www.trashandvaudeville.com* Ⓜ *6 to Astor Pl.*

HOME DECOR

White Trash. Looking for a midcentury modern Danish desk? This is your place. Owner Stuart Zamsky crams his store with surprisingly afford-able pieces that are mostly from the '40s through '70s, including tables, lamps, and chairs. Some pieces you might find include paper mobiles from the '70s, old fondue sets, and antique medical-office cabinets.

✉ *304 E. 5th St., between 1st and 2nd Aves., East Village* ☎ *212/598–5956* ⊕ *www.whitetrashnyc.com* Ⓜ *4, 6 to Astor Pl./8th St.*

JEWELRY AND ACCESSORIES

Verameat. All the jewelry here is handmade in New York City and none of it is typical. Design motifs include pretzels, dinosaurs, and vampire teeth. Tilda Swinton is a fan. ✉ *315 E. 9th St., between 1st and 2nd Aves., East Village* ☎ *212/388–9045* ⊕ *www.verameat.com* Ⓜ *6 to Astor Place.*

MUSIC STORES

Other Music. DJs and musicians flock here for hard-to-find genres on CD and vinyl, from Japanese electronica and Krautrock to acid folk and Americana. You can buy concert tickets at the in-house box office. ■TIP→ There's also a great selection of used CDs, including seminal punk classics from the Clash and the Stooges. ✉ *15 E. 4th St., between Lafayette St. and Broadway, East Village* ☎ *212/477–8150* ⊕ *www.othermusic.com* Ⓜ *6 to Astor Pl.*

TOYS

Dinosaur Hill. Forget about Elmo and Barbie. This little shop stocks quirky gifts for kids like hand puppets and marionettes from Asia, minibongos, and wooden rattles. Don't miss the medieval themed toys, such as Camelot finger puppets. ✉ *306 E. 9th St., between 1st and 2nd Aves., East Village* ☎ *212/473–5850* ⊕ *www.dinosaurhill.com* Ⓜ *R to 8th St.; 6 to Astor Pl.*

WINE

Astor Wines & Spirits. Stock up on wine, spirits, and sake at this beautiful shop. For unwinding, and learning more about food and wine, there's also a wine library and kitchen for cooking classes. ✉ *399 Lafayette St., at 4th St., East Village* ☎ *212/674–7500* ⊕ *www.astorwines.com* Ⓜ *6 to Astor Pl.*

Fodor's Choice ★ **Union Square Wine & Spirits.** Tastings are easy at this well-stocked store, thanks to Enomatic machines. These card-operated contraptions let you sample dozens of wines. If machines don't do it for you, generous tastings are held most Fridays and Saturdays. ✉ *140 4th Ave., at 13th St., East Village* ☎ *212/675–8100* ⊕ *www.unionsquarewines.com* Ⓜ *L, N, Q, R, 4, 5, 6 to 14th St./Union Sq.*

LOWER EAST SIDE

Head to the Lower East Side for excellent vintage finds. Once home to multitudes of Jewish immigrants from Russia and Eastern Europe, the Lower East Side has traditionally been New York's bargain beat. Today, tiny, no-nonsense clothing stores and scrappy stalls hang on to the past while funky local designers gradually claim more turf. A few cool vintage clothing and furniture spots bridge the two camps. Ludlow Street, one block east of Orchard, has become the main drag for twentysomethings with attitude, its boutiques wedged in between bars and low-key restaurants. Anything too polished is looked on with suspicion—and that goes for you, too. For the full scope of this area, prowl from Allen to Essex streets, south of Houston Street down to Broome Street.

ANTIQUES AND COLLECTIBLES

Las Venus. Step into this kitsch palace and you may feel as though a time machine has zapped you back to the '50s, '60s, or groovy '70s. Look for bubble lamps, lots of brocade, and Knoll knockoffs. Midcentury-modern Danish credenzas are also big here. ⊠ *113 Stanton St., between Essex and Houston Sts., Lower East Side* ☎ *212/982–0608* ⊕ *www.lasvenus.com* Ⓜ *F to 2nd Ave.*

CLOTHING
SHOES, HANDBAGS, AND LEATHER GOODS

Altman Luggage. Having trouble bringing all your purchases home? Altman sells top-of-the-line luggage from Samsonite, Delsey, and Tumi at discount prices. A wide selection of pens is also for sale. ⊠ *135 Orchard St., between Delancey and Rivington Sts., Lower East Side* ☎ *212/254–7275* ⊕ *www.altmanluggage.com* Ⓜ *F, J, M, Z to Delancey St./Essex St.*

GREENWICH VILLAGE AND WEST VILLAGE

GREENWICH VILLAGE

The area around Washington Square and New York University has more than its fair share of touristy souvenir shops, cheap shoe boutiques along 8th Street, and chain stores, but there are also some gems to be found. For a more charming part of the village, head west, to the more residential West Village.

BEAUTY

C. O. Bigelow. Founded in 1838, this is the oldest apothecary-pharmacy in the United States; Mark Twain used to fill prescriptions here. They still fill prescriptions, but the real reason to come is for the hard-to-find-brands like Klorane shampoo and Elgydium toothpaste. Bigelow also has its own line of products, including green-tea lip balm and quince hand lotion. ⊠ *414 6th Ave., between 9th and 10th, Greenwich Village* ☎ *212/533–2700* ⊕ *www.bigelowchemists.com* Ⓜ *A, C, E, B, D, F, M to W. 4th St.*

CLOTHING

Denim & Supply. Owned by Ralph Lauren, this boutique has a rustic, utilitarian look, with distressed wood floors and plenty of Americana. Jeans, denim shirts and jackets are available in every hue along with basics like T-shirts, dresses, and cargo pants. ⊠ *99 University Pl., between 11 and 12th Sts., Greenwich Village* ☎ *212/677–1895* ⊕ *www.ralphlauren.com/shop/index.jsp?categoryId=11757742* Ⓜ *N, Q, R to 14th St./Union Sq.*

Fodor'sChoice
★ **La Petite Coquette.** Everything at this lingerie store is unabashedly sexy, and the helpful staff can find the perfect fit. The store's own line of silk slips, camisoles, and other underpinnings comes in a range of colors. ⊠ *51 University Pl., between 9th and 10th Sts., Greenwich Village* ☎ *212/473–2478* ⊕ *www.thelittleflirt.com* Ⓜ *R to 8th St.*

Personnel of New York. "Lifestyle boutique" is an overused term, but it is the best way to describe this new store, which specializes in men's and women's clothing from New York and LA designers. The boutique also stocks unusual home goods, such as bottle openers by Japanese designer Tadanori Baba, OLO fragrance, and Bellocq teas. ⊠ *9 Greenwich Ave., between Christopher St. and 10th Sts., Greenwich Village* ☎ *212/924–0604* ⊕ *personnelofnewyork.com* Ⓜ *1 to Christopher St.*

18

WEST VILLAGE

It's easy to feel like a local, not a tourist, while shopping in the West Village. Unlike 5th Avenue or SoHo, the pace is slower, the streets are quiet, and the scale is small. This is the place to come for unusual finds rather than global brands (if you don't count Marc Jacobs).

Bleecker Street is a particularly good place to indulge all sorts of shopping appetites. Foodies love the blocks between 6th and 7th avenues for the specialty purveyors like Murray's Cheese (254 Bleecker Street). Fashion foragers prowl the stretch between West 10th Street and 8th Avenue. Hudson Street and Greenwich Avenue are also prime boutique-browsing territory. Christopher Street, true to its connection with the lesbian and gay community, has a handful of rainbow-flag stops. High rents mean there are fewer student-oriented shops around NYU than you might expect.

ANTIQUES AND COLLECTIBLES

Kaas Glassworks. From the outside, this shop is cuter than cute, with its old-fashioned sign and ivy-covered brick façade. The specialty here is decoupage that has been turned into quirky coasters and trays. Owner Carol Kaas uses vintage postcards, maps, and botanical prints in her works. ⊠ *117 Perry St., between Greenwich and Hudson Sts., Greenwich Village* ☎ *212/366–0322* ⊕ *www.kaas.com* Ⓜ *1 to Christopher St./Sheridan Sq.*

BEAUTY

Fodor's Choice
★

Aedes De Venustas. Arguably the best place to buy fragrance in town, this boutique's super-knowledgeable staff will help shoppers find the perfect scent. High-end brands like L'Artisan Parfumeur and Anick Goutal are stocked, along with luxurious skincare products and pricey candles and room diffusers. Their signature giftwrap is as beautiful as what's inside the box. ⊠ *9 Christopher St., between 6th and 7th Aves., Greenwich Village* ☎ *212/206–8674* ⊕ *www.aedes.com* Ⓜ *1 to Christopher St./Sheridan Sq.*

Jo Malone. This crisp black and white boutique offers a serene backdrop to sample tangy scents such as lime blossom and mandarin, or white jasmine and mint. Fragrances can be worn alone or layered. The flagship offers complimentary hand massages and a sampling bar to create a bespoke scent. ⊠ *330 Bleecker St., between 10th and Christopher Sts., West Village* ☎ *212/242–1454* Ⓜ *1 to Christopher St./Sheridan Sq.*

BOOKS AND STATIONERY

bookbook. This small, independent bookstore is crammed with the latest new releases as well as a thoughtful assortment of general nonfiction, guidebooks, and children's books. But the real focus here is the carefully selected sales tables that spill out onto the sidewalk—they have deals on everything from Graham Greene to Chuck Palahniuk. ⊠ *266 Bleecker St., between 6th and 7th Aves., Greenwich Village* ☎ *212/807–8655* ⊕ *www.bookbooknyc.com* Ⓜ *1 to Christopher St./Sheridan Sq.*

Three Lives & Company. Three Lives has one of the city's best book selections. The display tables and counters highlight the latest literary fiction and serious nonfiction, classics, quirky gift books, and gorgeously illustrated tomes. The staff members' literary knowledge is formidable, so don't be afraid to ask them for their own picks. ⊠ *154 W. 10th St., at Waverly Pl., Greenwich Village* ☎ *212/741–2069* ⊕ *www.threelives. com* Ⓜ *1 to Christopher St./Sheridan Sq.*

CLOTHING

Castor & Pollux. The store's interior signals a finely tuned balance of high taste (vintage Bergdorf Goodman display cases) and quirkiness (grass-cloth wall coverings and small horse sculptures). Hard-to-find brands like Hache are mixed with better-known names like Acne and 3.1 Philip Lim. There's also an eye-catching in-house line of jewelry, clutches, and sweaters that are casual but classic. ⊠ *238 W. 10th St., at Hudson St., West Village* ☎ *212/645–6572* ⊕ *www.castorandpolluxstore.com* Ⓜ *1 to Christopher St./Sheridan Sq.*

Cynthia Rowley. Rowley delivers flirty, whimsical dresses that are perfect for cocktail parties. To complete the look, throw on some of her colorful pumps and sharply tailored coats. ⊠ *376 Bleecker St., between Charles and Perry Sts., West Village* ☎ *212/242–3803* ⊕ *cynthiarowley.com* Ⓜ *1 to Christopher St./Sheridan Sq.*

Fisch for the Hip. This high-end consignment store sells carefully edited men's and women's clothing and accessories, from top designers including Tom Ford, Balenciaga, and Lanvin. Hermès bags are a specialty. ⊠ *33 Greenwich Ave., between 10th and Charles Sts., West Village* ☎ *212/633–9053* ⊕ *fischforthehip.com* Ⓜ *1 to Christopher St./Sheridan Sq.*

Hotoveli. This unprepossessing nook stocks some of the most elegant (and expensive) designers in the world, ranging from Alexander McQueen to Vivienne Westwood. If you have to ask how much an item costs, don't try it on. ⊠ *378 Bleecker St., between Charles and Perry Sts., Greenwich Village* ☎ *212/206–7475* ⊕ *www.hotoveli.com* Ⓜ *1 to Christopher St./Sheridan Sq.*

Khirma Eliazov. This former Vogue editor now designs an elegant line of handbags, clutches, and accessories. She uses luxury materials such as python, alligator, crocodile, and stingray skins. ⊠ *102 Charles St., between Hudson and Bleecker Sts., West Village* ☎ *646/998–5240* ⊕ *www.khirmaeliazov.com* Ⓜ *1 to Christopher St./Sheridan Square.*

FOOD AND TREATS

Chocolate Bar. What sets this chocolate emporium apart is its midcentury-modern design, which is also evident in the groovy packaging. Scoop up some retro chocolate bars, whose flavors include salty pretzel, coconut cream pie, and key lime. Or try a salted caramel bonbon and a steaming cup of spicy hot chocolate. ⊠ *19 8th Ave., between Jane and 12th Sts., West Village* ☎ *212/366–1541* ⊕ *www.chocolatebarnyc.com* Ⓜ *A, C, E, to 14th St.*

Li-Lac Chocolates. Li-Lac has been feeding the Village's sweet tooth since 1923. Indulge with almond bark and coconut clusters as well as such specialty items as chocolate-molded Statues of Liberty. Their chocolate-covered pretzels are superior. There's also an outpost in the Grand Central Market. ⊠ *40 8th Ave., at Jane St., Greenwich Village* ☎ *212/924–2280* ⊕ *www.li-lacchocolates.com* Ⓜ *A, C, E to 14th St.*

18

Sockerbit. Who knew Scandinavians were obsessed with candy? There's much more than Swedish fish at this gleaming white candy emporium that stocks hard candies, gummies, licorice, and chocolate. Have fun pronouncing the names of the treats, such as Bumlingar Jordgubb and Zoo Klubba. ⊠ *89 Christopher St., between Bleecker and 4th Sts., West Village* ☎ *212/206–8170* ⊕ *www.sockerbit.com* Ⓜ *1 to Christopher St./ Sheridan Sq.*

SHOES, HANDBAGS, AND LEATHER GOODS

Fodor's Choice ★ **Flight 001.** Frequent flyers can one-stop-shop at this travel-themed store that puts a creative spin on everyday accessories. Shop for bright luggage tags, passport holders, satin sleep masks, and even paper soap. ⊠ *96 Greenwich Ave., between 12th and Jane Sts., Greenwich Village* ☎ *212/989–0001* ⊕ *www.flight001.com* Ⓜ *A, C, E to 14th St.*

Fodor's Choice ★ **Leffot.** This simple, understated store focuses on one thing: selling top-quality men's shoes. Owner Steven Taffel, who previously worked at Prada, has stocked his shop with selections from Church's, Basil Racuk, and Artioli. These shoes are meant to last a lifetime, and many have a price tag to match. Bespoke footwear is also available. ⊠ *10 Christopher St., at Gay St., West Village* ☎ *212/989–4577* ⊕ *www.leffot.com* Ⓜ *1, 2 to Christopher St.*

Lulu Guinness. Hit this black-and-white-stripe salon for cheerfully eccentric accessories such as handbags printed with images of lips, dolls, and cameos. The accessories, including umbrellas and luggage, are equally fun. ⊠ *394 Bleecker St., between 11th and Perry Sts., Greenwich Village* ☎ *212/367–2120* ⊕ *www.luluguinness.com* Ⓜ *1 to Christopher St./Sheridan Sq.*

CHELSEA AND THE MEATPACKING DISTRICT

CHELSEA

Chelsea offers one-stop shopping for some of the biggest retail brands.

BOOKS AND STATIONERY

Books of Wonder. Readers young and old will delight in Manhattan's oldest and largest independent children's bookstore. The friendly, knowledgeable staff can help select gifts for all reading levels. Don't miss the extensive Oz section as well as the collection of old, rare, and collectible children's books and original children's book art. ⊠ *18 W. 18th St., between 5th and 6th Aves., Chelsea* ☎ *212/989–3270* ⊕ *www. booksofwonder.com* Ⓜ *F, M to 14th St.*

Rob Warren Bookseller. Come to this plant-filled shop for out-of-print books in all categories, a large Beat Generation selection, literary first editions, and books on photography and art. ⊠ *51 W. 28th St., between Broadway and 6th Ave., Chelsea* ☎ *212/759–5463* ⊕ *www. robwarrenbookseller.com* Ⓜ *N, R to 28th St.*

CLOTHING

Comme des Garçons. The designs in this stark, white, swoopy space consistently push the fashion envelope with brash patterns, unlikely juxtapositions (tulle and neoprene), and cuts that are meant to be thought-provoking, not flattering. Architecture students come just for the interior design. ⊠ *520 W. 22nd St., between 10th and 11th Aves., Chelsea* ☎ *212/604–9200* ⊕ *www.comme-des-garcons.com* Ⓜ *C, E to 23rd St.*

New York Vintage. Stylists to the stars, TV costumers, and the odd princess descend upon this boutique to browse racks of prime vintage clothing. Everything is high-end, so don't expect any bargains. If money is no object, take your pick from Yves Saint Laurent, Madame Grès, and Thierry Mugler pieces. There's a good selection of handbags and pumps, too. ⊠ *117 W. 25th St., between 6th and 7th Aves., Chelsea* ☎ *212/647–1107* ⊕ *www.newyorkvintage.com* Ⓜ *1 to 28th St.*

GIFTS AND SOUVENIRS

Eleni's. Take a bite out of the Big Apple—in cookie form—with these perfectly decorated treats, shaped like yellow cabs, the Wall Street sign, and the Statue of Liberty. It's not just New York depicted here; the iced cookies come in every design imaginable, from iPhones to shoes and pirates. Cupcakes are also available. ⊠ *Chelsea Market, 75 9th Ave., between 15th and 16th Sts., Chelsea* ☎ *212/255–6804* ⊕ *www.elenis. com* Ⓜ *A, C, E to 14th St.; L to 8th Ave.*

MUSIC STORES AND MEDIA

Jazz Record Center. If you're seeking rare or out-of-print jazz recordings, this is your one-stop shop. Long-lost Ellingtons and other rare pressings come to light here; the jazz-record specialist also stocks collectibles, DVDs, videos, posters, CDs, and LPs. ⊠ *236 W. 26th St., 8th fl., between 7th and 8th Aves., Chelsea* ☎ *212/675–4480* ⊕ *www. jazzrecordcenter.com* Ⓜ *1 to 28th St.*

WINE

Bottlerocket Wine & Spirit. Fun and approachable, this shop puts a new spin on wine shopping. Vintages are organized by quirky factors like their compatibility with Chinese takeout and whom they'd best suit as gifts (ranging from "Someone You Barely Know" to "The Boss"). A reference library, kids' play nook, and doggie area make the space extra welcoming. ⊠ *5 W. 19th St., between 5th and 6th Aves., Chelsea* ☎ *212/929–2323* ⊕ *www.bottlerocketwine.com* Ⓜ *L, N, R, Q, 4, 5, 6 to 14th St.*

MEATPACKING DISTRICT

For nearly a century, this industrial western edge of downtown Manhattan was defined by slaughterhouses and meatpacking plants, blood-splattered cobblestone streets, and men lugging carcasses into warehouses way before dawn.

But in the late 1990s the area bounded by 14th Street, Gansevoort Street, Hudson Street, and 11th Avenue speedily transformed into another kind of meat market. Many of the old warehouses now house ultrachic shops, nightclubs, and restaurants packed with angular fashionistas. Jeffrey, a pint-size department store, was an early arrival, followed by edgy but established brands like Alexander McQueen and a few lofty furniture stores. Despite the influx of a few chains—albeit stylish ones like Scoop—eclectic boutiques keep popping up. The one thing it's hard to find here is a bargain.

18

CAMERAS AND ELECTRONICS

Apple Store. Branch location at 401 West 14th Street. *See Midtown East for full review.*

CLOTHING

Fodor's Choice
★

Alexander McQueen. The late designer's New York flagship is a futuristic, podlike space—an ideal setting for the avant-garde, luxurious clothing. Now under the helm of Sarah Burton, the designs are still theatrical with exquisite tailoring and a touch of softness. ⊠ *417 W. 14th St., between 9th and 10th Aves., Meatpacking District* ☎ *212/645–1797* Ⓜ *A, C, E, L to 14th St.*

Catherine Malandrino. Celebs like Halle Berry love this French-born designer for her sexy-without-trying-too-hard looks. Shop for silk V-neck gowns or one-shouldered ruched wool dresses. ⊠ *652 Hudson St., at 13th St., Meatpacking District* ☎ *212/929–8710* ⊕ *www.catherinemalandrino.com* Ⓜ *A, C, E, L to 14th St.*

Fodor's Choice
★

Diane von Furstenberg. At this light-filled New York flagship, try on the iconic DVF wrap dress in a myriad of patterns. The blouses, shorts, and skirts are equally feminine. ⊠ *874 Washington St., at 14th St., Meatpacking District* ☎ *646/486–4800* ⊕ *www.dvf.com* Ⓜ *A, C, E, L to 14th St.*

Iris. As the Italian shoe manufacturers for stylish brands like John Galliano, Marc Jacobs, Veronique Branquinho, and Chloé, Iris's sole U.S. store is able to carry every style from those lines, including pieces not previously available on our shores. ⊠ *827 Washington St., at Little W. 12th St., Meatpacking District* ☎ *212/645–0950* ⊕ *www.irisnyc.com* Ⓜ *A, C, E, L to 14th St.*

Jeffrey. The Meatpacking District really arrived when this Atlanta-based mini-Barneys opened its doors. You can find an incredible array of designer shoes—Valentino, Lanvin, and red-soled Christian Louboutin are some of the best sellers—plus top labels such as L'Wren Scott, Pucci, and Alaia. ⊠ *449 W. 14th St., between 9th and 10th Aves., Meatpacking District* ☎ *212/206–1272* ⊕ *www.jeffreynewyork.com* Ⓜ *A, C, E, L to 14th St./8th Ave.*

Owen. FIT grad Phillip Salem transformed this space into a whimsical place to shop, thanks to the 25,000 paper bags that line the arched ceiling. This upscale boutique offers men's and womenswear from 70 established and independent designers. Come here for skinny jeans, luxurious sweaters, and dresses from J. Brand, Garter + Derringer, and Roksanda Ilincic. ⊠ *809 Washington St., between Gansevoort and Horatio Sts., Meatpacking District* ☎ *212/524–9770* ⊕ *www.owennyc.com* Ⓜ *A, C, E, L to 14th St./8th Ave.*

Rebecca Taylor. Taylor is known for her soft, feminine designs, which run the gamut from sexy to understated, all with a slightly vintage flair. Her flagship is a serene, spacious environment for browsing racks of silky shirtdresses, embroidered tunics, and ruffled overcoats. Taylor's shoes, handbags, and jewelry are equally romantic. ⊠ *34 Gansevoort St., between Greenwich and Hudson Sts., Meatpacking District* ☎ *212/243–2600* ⊕ *www.rebeccataylor.com* Ⓜ *A, C, E, L to 14 St.*

Tracy Reese. Unabashedly girly but wearable garb is Reese's specialty, as she plays with lush fabrics (silk chiffon is a favorite), quirky color combos, and glamorous touches such as ruffles. The cuts flatter all sorts of figures, often emphasizing the waist. This flagship carries both the ladylike Tracy Reese line and lower-price Plenty label, as well as home accessories. ⊠ *641 Hudson St., between Horatio and Gansevoort Sts., Meatpacking District* ☎ *212/807–0505* ⊕ *www.tracyreese.com* Ⓜ *A, C, E, L to 14th St.*

Trina Turk. Make a bee-line to this boutique if you like bright, happy colors and 70s-influenced clothing. The shop, designed by Jonathan Adler, showcases Turk's ready-to-wear clothing and in a bright, airy setting. Swimwear is a standout, and menswear is also sold here. ⊠ *67 Gansevoort St., between Washington and Greenwich Sts., Meatpacking District* ☎ *212/206–7383* ⊕ *www.trinaturk.com* Ⓜ *A, C, E, L to 14th St.*

JEWELRY AND ACCESSORIES

Ten Thousand Things. You might find yourself wishing for 10,000 things from the showcases in this elegant boutique. Designs run from delicate gold and silver chains to long Peruvian opal earrings. Many shapes are abstract reflections of natural forms, like twigs or seedpods. Prices start around $100. ⊠ *423 W. 14th St., between 9th and 10th Aves., Meatpacking District* ☎ *212/352–1333* ⊕ *www.tenthousandthingsnyc.com* Ⓜ *A, C, E, L to 14th St.*

UNION SQUARE AND THE FLATIRON DISTRICT

FLATIRON DISTRICT

This neighborhood is one of the buzziest in New York, brimming with both large and small stores as well as excellent restaurants and the city's best greenmarket. Come here if you want to shop the big chains minus the midtown tourist crowds.

18

BOOKS AND STATIONERY

Idlewild Books. Named for the pre-1960s JFK Airport, this travel-inspired bookstore groups its goods by destination. It has much more than guidebooks, though; novels, histories, cookbooks, and children's books share each segment, giving you a fascinating look at any given locale. If those chairs look familiar, it may be because you spent a layover in one of them once upon a time in the American Airlines terminal. ⊠ *12 W. 19th St., 2nd fl., at 5th Ave., Flatiron District* ☎ *212/414–8888* ⊕ *www. idlewildbooks.com* Ⓜ *4, 5, 6, L, Q, R to 14th St./Union Sq.*

CHILDREN'S CLOTHING

Space Kiddets. The funky (Elvis-print rompers, CBGB onesies) mixes with the old-school (retro cowboy-print pants, brightly colored clogs, Bruce Lee T-shirts) and the high-end (Lilli Gaufrette, Kenzo, Boo Foo Woo from Japan) at this casual, trendsetting store that is a favorite of Julianne Moore. ⊠ *26 E. 22nd St., between Broadway and Park Ave., Flatiron District* ☎ *212/420–9878* ⊕ *www.spacekiddets.com* Ⓜ *6 to 23rd St.*

CLOTHING

Anthropologie. Bohemian-chic is the aesthetic of this popular women's clothing and home accessories chain. ⊠ *85 Fifth Ave., Flatiron District* ☎ *212/627–5885* ⊕ *www.anthropologie.com.*

Club Monaco. In addition to the brand's signature clothing (think of a hipper Banana Republic), this flagship includes an outpost of Williamsburg favorite Toby's Estate Coffee, as well as a bookstore operated by the Strand. ⊠ *160 5th Ave., between 20 and 21st Sts., Flatiron District* ☎ *212/352–0936* ⊕ *www.clubmonaco.com.*

Madewell. This J.Crew spinoff is ideal for casual women's staples like jeans, t-shirts, and sweaters with a vintage look. The two-story Manhattan flagship has a quirky, homespun design; merchandise is displayed on everything from old mill tables to meat hooks. Don't miss the shoe shop and home goods collection. ⊠ *115 Fifth Ave., between 18th and 19th Sts., Flatiron District* ☎ *212/228–5172* ⊕ *www.madewell.com.*

Fodor'sChoice
★

Maison Kitsuné. This decades-old French fashion and music label recently made its stateside debut. Come to this airy, sunwashed boutique for men's and womenswear classics with a stylish Gallic twist, ranging from cardigans and loafers to blazers and dresses. ⊠ *NoMad Hotel, 1170 Broadway, at 28th St., Flatiron District* ☎ *212/481–6010* ⊕ *www. kitsune.fr* Ⓜ *N, R to 28th St.*

HOME DECOR

Fodor'sChoice
★

ABC Carpet & Home. If you love eclectic goods from around the world, then this is your place. Spread over 10 floors is a superb selection of rugs, antiques, textiles, furniture, and bedding. Shoppers can find sleek sofas or Balinese daybeds. The ground floor is a wonderland of silk pillows and jewelry. To refuel, there's an in-house restaurant from Jean-Georges Vongerichten. More rugs and carpets are unrolled across the street at 881 Broadway. ⊠ *888 Broadway, at 19th St., Flatiron District* ☎ *212/473–3000* ⊕ *www.abchome.com* Ⓜ *L, N, Q, R, 4, 5, 6 to 14th St./Union Sq.*

Fodor'sChoice
★

Fishs Eddy. The dishes, china, and glassware for resale come from all walks of crockery life, from corporate dining rooms to failed restaurants and ocean liners. Fishs Eddy also sells its own line of dishes, which have a classic look, and is a great place to pick up New York–themed gifts, such as mugs and trays. ⊠ *889 Broadway, at 19th St., Flatiron District* ☎ *212/420–9020* ⊕ *www.fishseddy.com* Ⓜ *L, N, Q, R, 4, 5, 6 to 14th St./Union Sq.*

Marimekko. If you love bright, cheerful patterns, make a beeline to the new Marimekko flagship. This 4,000-square-foot store is designed primarily in white, so the colorful merchandise pops. Everything from pot holders and shower curtains to coats and dresses is available here in the signature Marimekko bold prints. If you're feeling crafty, pick up a few yards of fabric to whip up your own creations. ⊠ *200 5th Ave., between 23rd and 24th Sts., Flatiron District* ☎ *212/843–9121* ⊕ *www. marimekko.com* Ⓜ *F, M to 23rd St.*

Holiday Markets

Between Thanksgiving and Christmas, holiday markets—rows of wooden stalls, many with red-and-white-stripe awnings—spring up around town. The gifts and goods vary from year to year, but there are some perennial offerings: colorful handmade knitwear and jewelry; sweet-smelling soaps, candles, and lotions with hand-lettered labels; glittery Christmas ornaments of every stripe; and New York–theme gift items (a group called Gritty City offers T-shirts, coin purses, and undies printed with pictures of taxicabs and manhole covers).

While the holiday market in **Grand Central Terminal's Vanderbilt Hall** is indoors, most vendors set up outside. There's one every year at **Columbus Circle**, near the southwest entrance to Central Park, and another at **Bryant Park**, behind the New York City Public Library. The largest and most popular, however, is at the south end of **Union Square**, where you can go from the greenmarket to the stalls like the downtowners who meet in the afternoon or after work to look for unique or last-minute gifts.

JEWELRY AND ACCESSORIES

Beads of Paradise. Not your ordinary bead store, the baubles here are sourced from around the world. Shoppers can choose silver from Bali and Mexico and ancient glass beads from China, along with semiprecious stones. Sign up for a class to learn how to put it all together. ⊠ *16 E. 17th St., between 5th Ave. and Broadway, Flatiron District* ☎ *212/620–0642* ⊕ *www.beadsofparadisenyc.com* Ⓜ *4, 5, 6, N, Q, R to 14th St./Union Sq.*

TOYS

Kidding Around. This independent shop is piled high with old-fashioned wooden toys, sturdy musical instruments, and plenty of arts-and-crafts materials. The costume racks are rich with dress-up potential. ⊠ *60 W. 15th St., between 5th and 6th Aves., Flatiron District* ☎ *212/645–6337* ⊕ *www.kiddingaroundtoys.com* Ⓜ *L, N, Q, R, 4, 5, 6 to 14th St./Union Sq.*

UNION SQUARE

If you want to browse the big retail chains such as J. Crew, Banana Republic, and Anthropologie without hordes of tourists, come here.

BEAUTY

Fresh. Long a beauty favorite, with ingredients that are good enough to eat (think brown sugar, soy, and black tea), Fresh recently revamped its New York flagship. The boutique has an apothecary-inspired look, with beautifully packaged soaps displayed like pastries in a glass case, and a Sensorial Bar, featuring discontinued perfumes on tap. Pull up at a seat at the communal Kitchen Table to try out a new product. ⊠ *872 Broadway, between 18th and 19th Sts., Union Square* ☎ *212/477–1100* ⊕ *www.fresh.com* Ⓜ *L, N, Q, R, 4, 5, 6 to 14th St./Union Sq.*

18

BOOKS AND STATIONERY

Fodor'sChoice   **The Strand.** Opened in 1927, and still run by the same family, this
★   monstrous book emporium—home to 2 million volumes and "18
Miles of Books"—is a symbol of a bygone era, a mecca for serious
bibliophiles, and a local institution. The store has survived the Great
Depression, World War II, competition from Barnes & Noble, and the
tremendous shift in how readers are consuming literature. The stock
includes both new and secondhand books, plus thousands of collector's items. A separate rare-book room is on the third floor and closes
at 6:20 daily. The basement has discounted, barely touched reviewers'
copies of new books, organized by author. ■TIP➜ If you're looking
for souvenirs, visit the New York section of the bookstore; you'll find
New York–centric literature, poetry, history, photography, and cookbooks, as well as T-shirts, gadgets, and totes. ⊠ *828 Broadway, at
12th St., Union Square* ☎ *212/473–1452* ⊕ *www.strandbooks.com*
◷ *Mon.–Sat. 9:30 am–10:30 pm, Sun. 11–10:30* Ⓜ *L, N, Q, R, 4, 5,
6 to Union Sq./14th St.*

CLOTHING

Beacon's Closet. Brooklyn favorite Beacon's Closet has finally opened a
Big Apple outpost. This simple space, which is lit by multiple chande-
liers, offers a wide selection of gently used modern and vintage clothes.
Comb through the racks and you might find pieces from Christian Dior,
Marc Jacobs, or AllSaints. ⊠ *10 W 13th St., between 5th and 6th Aves.,
Union Square* ☎ *917/261–4863* ⊕ *www.beaconscloset.com* Ⓜ *L, N, Q,
R, 4, 5, 6 to 14th St./Union Square.*

Forever 21. Branch location at 40 East 14th Street. *See Midtown West
for full review.*

J.Crew. The preppy-chic brand that is a staple in so many people's closets continues to push the envelope. Yes, you can still get cardigans,
cords, and tees in every pastel color of the rainbow, but some of the
separates are downright sexy. The leather jackets and sequined skirts
are also perfect for that casual, thrown-together look. This flagship
carries women's, men's, and Crewcuts for children as well as a wedding gown collection. ⊠ *91 5th Avenue, between 15th and 16th Sts.,
Union Square* ☎ *212/255–4848* ⊕ *www.jcrew.com* Ⓜ *N, Q, R to 14th
St./Union Square.* ⊠ *10 Columbus Circle, Upper West Side* ☎ *212/823–
9302* ⊕ *www.jcrew.com.*

FOOD AND TREATS

Fodor'sChoice   **Max Brenner: Chocolate by the Bald Man.** This shop/restaurant is all about
★   a Wonka-ish sense of entertainment. The café encourages the messy
enjoyment of gooey creations like chocolate fondues and chocolate
burgers for kids. Take-away treats include caramelized pralines and tins
of hot-chocolate powder. ⊠ *841 Broadway, between 13th and 14th Sts.,
Union Square* ☎ *646/467–8803* ⊕ *www.maxbrenner.com* Ⓜ *L, N, Q,
R, 4, 5, 6 to 14th St./Union Sq.*

MIDTOWN EAST

If money is no object, put on your shopping shoes and head to Midtown East. Some of the world's most luxurious brands—from Gucci to Christian Dior—have their flagship stores along 5th Avenue.

ANTIQUES AND COLLECTIBLES

The Chinese Porcelain Company. Though the name of this prestigious shop indicates one of its specialties, its stock covers more ground, ranging from lacquerware to Khmer sculpture as well as European decorative arts. ⊠ *475 Park Ave., at 58th St., Midtown East* ☎ *212/838–7744* ⊕ *www.chineseporcelainco.com* Ⓜ *N, R to 5th Ave.*

Flying Cranes Antiques. At this world leader in Japanese antiques, shoppers will find a collection of rare, museum-quality pieces from the Meiji period, the time known as Japan's Golden Age. Items include ceramics, cloisonné, metalwork, baskets, and samurai swords and fittings. ⊠ *Manhattan Art and Antiques Center, 1050 2nd Ave., between 55th and 56th Sts., Midtown East* ☎ *212/223–4600* ⊕ *www.flyingcranesantiques.com* Ⓜ *N, R, 4, 5, 6 to 59th St./Lexington Ave.*

Leo Kaplan Ltd. The impeccable items here include Art Nouveau glass and pottery, porcelain from 18th-century England, antique and modern paperweights, and Russian artwork. ⊠ *114 E. 57th St., between Park and Lexington Aves., Midtown East* ☎ *212/355–7212* ⊕ *www.leokaplan.com* Ⓜ *N, R, 4, 5, 6 to 59th St./Lexington Ave.*

Newel Art Galleries. Housed in a recently renovated six-story building, this huge collection spans the Renaissance through the 20th century. The nonfurniture finds, from figureheads to bell jars, make for prime conversation pieces. Newel is also a major supplier of antiques for Broadway shows, television, and film. ⊠ *425 E. 53rd St., between 1st Ave. and Sutton Pl., Midtown East* ☎ *212/758–1970* ⊕ *www.newel.com* Ⓜ *6 to 51st St./Lexington Ave.; E, M to Lexington–3rd Aves./53rd St.*

18

BOOKS AND STATIONERY

Fodor'sChoice
★

Argosy Bookstore. Family owned since 1925, Argosy keeps a scholarly stock of rare books and autographs. It's also a great place to look for low-price maps and prints that make ideal gifts. ⊠ *116 E. 59th St., between Park and Lexington Aves., Midtown East* ☎ *212/753–4455* ⊕ *www.argosybooks.com* Ⓜ *N, R, 4, 5, 6 to 59th St./Lexington Ave.*

The Complete Traveller Antiquarian Bookstore. Founded in the '80s by two former travel writers, this store specializes in rare and antique voyage-related books, and holds the largest selection of out-of-print Baedeker travel guides. They stock surprisingly affordable vintage maps, unusual tomes with New York City themes, and a full spectrum of books—from history and geography to poetry and fiction—that emphasize travel. ⊠ *199 Madison Ave., at 35th St., Midtown East* ☎ *212/685–9007* ⊕ *www.ctrarebooks.com* Ⓜ *6 to 33rd St.*

Posman Books. One of the last independent book stores in New York City, Posman Books has an outstanding selection of contemporary and classic books across genres. Don't miss the cheeky and serious high-quality greeting cards. ⊠ *9 Grand Central Terminal, at Vanderbilt Ave.*

and 42nd St., Midtown East ☎ *212/983–1111* ⊕ *www.posmanbooks. com* ✉ *30 Rockefeller Plaza, Concourse Level, Midtown West* ☎ *212/489–9100* ⊕ *www.posmanbooks.com* ✉ *Chelsea Market, 75 9th Ave., Chelsea* ☎ *212/627–0304* ⊕ *www.posmanbooks.com.*

CAMERAS AND ELECTRONICS

Fodor's Choice
★

Apple Store. New York's flagship Apple Store features a 32-foot-high glass cube that appears to float over its subterranean entrance. The Apple obsessed will be happy to know this location is open 24/7 every day of the year, and stocks all the latest Apple products. Make an appointment at the Genius Bar if you need tech help. ✉ *767 5th Ave., between 58th and 59th Sts., Midtown East* ☎ *212/336–1440* ⊕ *www. apple.com* Ⓜ *R to 60th St.*

SONY Style. Located on the ground floor of the Sony Building, this sunny space is a wonderland of electronics. You'll find all the latest stereo and entertainment systems, digital cameras, hi-def TVs, and MP3 players on the shelves. ✉ *550 Madison Ave., at 55th St., Midtown East* ☎ *212/833–8800* ⊕ *www.store.sony.com* Ⓜ *E, M, 6 to 51st St./Lexington Ave.*

CLOTHING

Brooks Brothers. The clothes at this classic American haberdasher are, as ever, traditional, comfortable, and fairly priced. Summer seersucker, navy blue blazers, and the peerless oxford shirts have been staples for generations. The women's and boys' selection have variations thereof. ■TIP➜ **Get scanned by a digital tailor for precisely measured custom shirts or suits; appointments are recommended.** ✉ *346 Madison Ave., at 44th St., Midtown East* ☎ *212/682–8800* ⊕ *www.brooksbrothers. com* Ⓜ *4, 5, 6, 7, S to 42nd St./Grand Central.*

Burberry. This six-story glass-and-stone flagship is a temple to all things plaid and British. The iconic trench coat can be made-to-measure here, and the signature plaid can be found on bikinis, scarves, and wallets. For children, there are miniversions of quilted jackets and cozy sweaters. ✉ *9 E. 57th St., between 5th and Madison Aves., Midtown East* ☎ *212/407–7100* ⊕ *www.burberry.com* Ⓜ *N, R to 5th Ave./59th St.*

Chanel. The Midtown flagship has often been compared to a Chanel suit—slim, elegant, and timeless, and decorated in the signature black-and-white colors. Inside, the famed suits themselves await, along with other pillars of Chanel style: chic little black dresses and evening gowns, chain-handled bags, and yards of pearls. There's also a small cosmetics area where you can stock up on the famed scents and nail polish. ✉ *15 E. 57th St., between 5th and Madison Aves., Midtown East* ☎ *212/355– 5050* ⊕ *www.chanel.com* Ⓜ *N, R to 5th Ave./59th St.*

Christian Dior. This very white, very glossy space offers a serene background to showcase the luxe ready-to-wear collection along with handbags and accessories. If you're not in the market for an investment gown or fine jewelry, peruse the latest status bag. The Dior menswear boutique is next door; the rocking cigarette-thin suits are often pilfered by women. ✉ *21 E. 57th St., at Madison Ave., Midtown East* ☎ *212/931–2950* ⊕ *www.dior.com* Ⓜ *E, V to 5th Ave./53rd St.*

Fodor's Choice
★

Dover Street Market. The New York location is the third outpost of Rei Kawakubo's Dover Street Market (the others are in London and Tokyo). It's basically a multilevel fashion-store emporium: each floor has mini boutiques from brands including Prada, Alaïa, and Alexander Want alongside lesser-known designers. The seven-story building is worth a look just for people-watching and the architecture (don't miss the huge sculpture resembling a UFO hovering over the staircase). The in-house Rose Bakery is the perfect spot to refuel with an espresso or iced pound cake. ⊠ *160 Lexington Ave, at 30th, Midtown East* 🖀 *646/837–7750* ⊕ *newyork.doverstreetmarket.com* Ⓜ *6 to 33rd St.*

Fodor's Choice
★

Dunhill. If you're stumped on what to buy the man in your life, head to Dunhill. The menswear is exquisitely tailored; the accessories like wallets and cuff links are slightly more affordable. The walk-in humidor stores top-quality tobacco and cigars. ⊠ *545 Madison Ave., at 55th St., Midtown East* 🖀 *212/753–9292* ⊕ *www.dunhill.com* Ⓜ *F to 57th St.*

Gucci. Located in the Trump Building, this 46,000-square-foot flagship with floor-to-ceiling glass windows is the largest Gucci store in the world. Shoppers will find a special "heritage" department, plus goods exclusive to the store. The clothing is edgy and sexy. Skintight pants might be paired with a luxe leather jacket; silk tops leave a little more to the imagination. The accessories, like wraparound shades or snakeskin shoes, many with signature horsebit detailing, continue to spark consumer frenzies. ⊠ *725 5th Ave., at 56th St., Midtown East* 🖀 *212/826–2600* ⊕ *www.gucci.com* Ⓜ *N, R to 5th Ave./59th St.*

Massimo Dutti. Owned by Zara, think of this brand as its older, more sophisticated sibling. The three-story space specializes in sleek basics that are perfect for work or the weekends, such as blazers, trench coats, and denim. ⊠ *689 5th Ave., between 54th and 55th Sts., Midtown East* 🖀 *212/371–2555* ⊕ *www.massimodutti.com* Ⓜ *E, M to 5th Ave./53rd St.*

18

Tommy Hilfiger. The global flagship oozes old-school Americana, with its dark-wood paneling, shirts displayed on bookshelves, and scattering of antiques. It's filled with tailored suits for men, smart sweater sets and pencil skirts for women, and evening wear along with sportswear, plus a whole floor devoted to denim. ⊠ *681 5th Ave., at 54th St., Midtown East* 🖀 *212/223–1824* Ⓜ *E, M to 53rd St.*

Saint Laurent Paris. This fabled French house is now under the direction of Hedi Slimane, who is revitalizing the brand. Rather than being overtly sexy, the new Saint Laurent nods to the past, with a refined, polished elegance. ⊠ *3 E. 57th St., between 5th and Madison Aves., Midtown East* 🖀 *212/980–2970* ⊕ *www.ysl.com* Ⓜ *N, R to 5th Ave./59th St.*

DEPARTMENT STORES

Fodor's Choice
★

Bloomingdale's. Only a few stores in New York occupy an entire city block; the uptown branch of this New York institution is one of them. The main floor is a crazy, glittery maze of mirrored cosmetic counters and perfume-spraying salespeople. Once you get past this dizzying scene, you can find good buys on designer clothes, bedding, and housewares. ⊠ *1000 3rd Ave., main entrance at 59th St. and Lexington Ave., Midtown East* 🖀 *212/705–2000* ⊕ *bloomingdales.com* Ⓜ *N, R, 4, 5, 6 to 59th St./Lexington Ave.*

Saks Fifth Avenue. Saks sells an astonishing array of clothing. The choice of American and European designers is impressive without being esoteric—the women's selection includes Gucci, Narciso Rodriguez, and Marc Jacobs, plus devastating ball gowns galore. The footwear collections are gratifyingly broad, from Ferragamo to Juicy. In the men's department, sportswear stars such as John Varvatos counterbalance formal wear and current trends. The ground-floor beauty department stocks everything from the classic (Sisley, Lancôme, La Prairie) to the fun and edgy (Nars, M.A.C.). ⊠ *611 5th Ave., between 49th and 50th Sts., Midtown East* 🖀 *212/753–4000* ⊕ *www.saksfifthavenue.com* Ⓜ *E, M to 5th Ave./53rd St.*

GIFTS AND SOUVENIRS

New York City Transit Museum Gift Shop. Located in the symbolic heart of New York City's transit system, the store features an eclectic array of merchandise all linked to the MTA (Metropolitan Transit Authority), from straphanger ties to earrings made from old subway tokens. ⊠ *Grand Central Terminal, Vanderbilt Pl. and 42nd St., Midtown East* 🖀 *212/878–0106* ⊕ *www.transitmuseumstore.com* Ⓜ *4, 5, 6, 7 to 42nd St./Grand Central Terminal.*

HOME DECOR

Armani Casa. In keeping with the Armani aesthetic, the minimalist furniture and homewares have a subdued color scheme (gold, grays, cream, and black). Big-ticket items include luxuriously upholstered sofas and sleek coffee tables. The desk accessories and throw pillows are equally understated. ⊠ *Decoration & Design Building, 979 3rd Ave., Ste. 1424, between 58th and 59th Sts., Midtown East* 🖀 *212/334–1271* ⊕ *www.armanicasa.com* Ⓜ *N, Q, R to Lexington Ave.; 4, 5, 6 to 59th St.*

JEWELRY AND ACCESSORIES

A La Vieille Russie. Antiques dealers since 1851, this shop specializes in European and Russian decorative arts, jewelry, and paintings. Behold bibelots by Fabergé and others, enameled or encrusted with jewels. If money is no object, there are also antique diamond necklaces and pieces of china once owned by Russian nobility. ⊠ *781 5th Ave., at 59th St., Midtown East* 🖀 *212/752–1727* ⊕ *www.alvr.com* Ⓜ *N, R to 5th Ave./59th St.*

Cartier. Pierre Cartier allegedly won the 5th Avenue mansion location by trading two strands of perfectly matched natural pearls with Mrs. Morton Plant. The jewelry is still incredibly persuasive, from such established favorites as the Trinity ring and Tank watches to exquisite cuff links for men. ⊠ *653 5th Ave., at 52nd St., Midtown East* 🖀 *212/753–0111* ⊕ *www.cartier.com* Ⓜ *E, M to 5th Ave./53rd St.*

H. Stern. Sleek designs pose in an equally modern 5th Avenue setting; smooth cabochon-cut stones, most from South America, glow in pale wooden display cases. The designers make notable use of semiprecious stones such as citrine, tourmaline, and topaz. ⊠ *645 5th Ave., between 51st and 52nd Sts., Midtown East* 🖀 *212/655–3910* ⊕ *www.hstern.net* Ⓜ *E, M to 5th Ave./53rd St.*

Department Store Discounts

If you don't have one of these stores in the state where you live, take advantage of special discounts available by showing a state ID card.

Bloomingdale's: Go to the visitor center on the balcony level between the ground and second floors for a 10% discount on all purchases bought that day.

Lord & Taylor: Hit the ground-floor information desk to pick up a coupon for 15% off that day's purchases.

Macy's: Stop by the visitor center on the balcony level between the ground and second floors for a 10% discount voucher. The coupon is valid for five days for U.S. visitors and one month for international visitors.

Fodor's Choice ★ **Tiffany & Co.** The display windows can be soigné, funny, or just plain breathtaking. Alongside the $80,000 platinum-and-diamond bracelets, much here is affordable on a whim (check out the sterling silver floor)—and everything comes wrapped in that unmistakable Tiffany blue box. ⊠ *727 5th Ave., at 57th St., Midtown East* ☎ *212/755–8000* ⊕ *www.tiffany.com* Ⓜ *N, R to 5th Ave./59th St.*

Van Cleef & Arpels. This French jewelry company is considerably more low-key than many of its blingy neighbors, in both the designs and marketing ethos (you won't see them opening a store in your average mall). Their best-known design is the cloverleaf Alhambra, which can be found on rings, necklaces, and earrings. Other designs are just as understated. ⊠ *744 5th Ave., between 57th St. and 58th Sts., Midtown East* ☎ *212/644–9500* ⊕ *www.vancleef-arpels.com* Ⓜ *N, R to 5th Ave./59th St.*

SHOES, HANDBAGS, AND LEATHER GOODS

Bally. If you want to channel your inner princess, you can't go wrong with the ladylike pumps and high-heeled boots here. The accessories and clothing are equally understated. ⊠ *628 Madison Ave., at 59th St., Midtown East* ☎ *212/751–9082* ⊕ *www.bally.com* Ⓜ *N, R, 4, 5, 6 to 59th St./Lexington Ave.*

Bottega Veneta. The signature crosshatch weave graces leather handbags, slouchy satchels, and shoes; the especially satisfying brown shades extend from fawn to deep chocolate. The stylish men's and women's ready-to-wear collection is also sold here. ⊠ *699 5th Ave., between 54th and 55th Sts., Midtown East* ☎ *212/371–5511* ⊕ *www.bottegaveneta.com* Ⓜ *N, R, 4, 5, 6 to 59th St./Lexington Ave.*

Fendi. Once known for its furs, Fendi is now synonymous with decadent handbags. The purses are beaded, embroidered, and fantastically embellished within an inch of their lives. Fancy leathers, ladylike evening dresses, coats, and other accessories are also available. ⊠ *677 5th Ave., between 53rd and 54th Sts., Midtown East* ☎ *212/759–4646* ⊕ *www.fendi.com* Ⓜ *E, F to 5th Ave./53rd St.*

Fratelli Rossetti. Don't come here expecting sexy, skyscraper stilettos. This Italian leather goods company excels at beautiful, classic shoes. Their riding boots are among the most popular items, but there are also pumps, loafers, and slouchy ankle boots. Men can choose from oxfords and boots. There's also a line of leather handbags. ✉ *625 Madison Ave., between 58th and 59th Sts., Midtown East* ☎ *212/888–5107* ⊕ *www.fratellirossetti.com* Ⓜ *N, Q, R to Lexington Ave.; 4, 5, 6 to 59th St.*

Fodor's Choice ★ **Louis Vuitton.** In the mammoth 57th Street store vintage examples of Vuitton's famous monogrammed trunks float above the fray on the ground floor, where shoppers angle for the latest accessories. Joining the initials are the Damier check pattern and colorful striated leathers, plus devastatingly chic clothes and shoes designed by Marc Jacobs. ✉ *1 E. 57th St., at 5th Ave., Midtown East* ☎ *212/758–8877* ⊕ *www. louisvuitton.com* Ⓜ *E, M to 5th Ave./53rd St.*

Salvatore Ferragamo. Elegance and restraint typify these designs, from black-tie patent to weekender ankle boots. The company reworks some of their women's styles from previous decades, like the girlish Audrey (as in Hepburn) ballet flat, released seasonally for limited runs. Don't miss the silk ties for men. ✉ *655 5th Ave., at 52nd St., Midtown East* ☎ *212/759–3822* ⊕ *www.ferragamo.com* Ⓜ *E, M to 53rd St.*

Stuart Weitzman. The broad range of styles, from wing tips to strappy sandals, is enhanced by an even wider range of sizes and widths. Bridal shoes are hugely popular, if pricey. ✉ *625 Madison Ave., between 58th and 59th Sts., Midtown East* ☎ *212/750–2555* ⊕ *www.stuartweitzman. com* Ⓜ *N, Q, R to Lexington Ave.; 4, 5, 6 to 59th St.*

TOYS

American Girl Place. No pink toy convertibles here; instead, the namesake dolls are historically themed, from Felicity of colonial Virginia to Kit of Depression-era Cincinnati. Each character has her own affiliated books, furniture, clothes, and accessories. There's a doll hairdressing station, a café, and a Dress Like Your Doll shop. ✉ *609 5th Ave., at 49th St., Midtown East* ☎ *212/371–2220* ⊕ *www.americangirl.com* Ⓜ *B, D, F, M to 47th–50th Sts./Rockefeller Center.*

Fodor's Choice ★ **FAO Schwarz Fifth Avenue.** A New York classic that's better than ever, this children's paradise more than lives up to the hype. The ground floor is a zoo of extraordinary stuffed animals, from cuddly $20 teddies to towering, life-size elephants and giraffes (with larger-than-life prices to match). FAO Schwartz stocks M&Ms in every color of the rainbow. Upstairs, you can dance on the giant musical floor keyboard, browse through Barbies wearing Armani and Juicy Couture, and take a tour with a Toy Soldier. ✉ *767 5th Ave., at 58th St., Midtown East* ☎ *212/644–9400* Ⓜ *4, 5, 6 to 59th St.*

MIDTOWN WEST

Whether you're window-shopping or have money to burn, Midtown West includes some of the best (and priciest) department stores, including Bergdorf Goodman and Henri Bendel.

CAMERAS AND ELECTRONICS

B&H Photo Video and Pro Audio. As baskets of purchases trundle along on tracks overhead, you can plunge into the excellent selection of imaging, audio, video, and lighting equipment. The staff is generous with advice, and will happily compare merchandise. Low prices, good customer service, and a liberal returns policy make this a favorite with pros and amateurs alike. ■ TIP➔ Be sure to leave a few extra minutes for the checkout procedure; also, keep in mind that the store is closed Saturday. ⊠ *420 9th Ave., between 33rd and 34th Sts., Midtown West* ☎ *212/444–6615* ⊕ *www.bhphotovideo.com* Ⓜ *A, C, E to 34th St.– Penn Station.*

CLOTHING

Banana Republic. Although there are nearly a dozen Banana Republic stores around the city, come to the flagship for the biggest selection of clothing. Don't miss the Heritage collection, or the big clearance racks. ⊠ *Rockefeller Center, 626 5th Ave., at 51st St., Midtown West* ☎ *212/974–2350* ⊕ *www.bananarepublic.gap.com* Ⓜ *B, D, F, M at 47th–50th Sts.–Rockefeller Center.*

Cheap Jack's. Jack's two-floor space may be 12,000 square feet, but it's still jammed with interesting duds—although they are not as cheap as the name would suggest. There's almost everything you could wish for: track suits, bomber jackets, early 1980s madras shirts, old prom dresses, and vintage concert T-shirts with the eau-de-mothball stamp of authenticity. ⊠ *303 5th Ave., at 31st St., Midtown West* ☎ *212/777–9564* ⊕ *www.cheapjacks.com* Ⓜ *N, Q, R to 34th St./ Herald Sq.*

Forever 21. The pounding music, plethora of jeggings, and graffiti-covered NYC taxicab parked inside will appeal to tween shoppers. But even if you are older than 21, you'll still find a reason to shop here. This location, clocking in at a whopping 90,000 square feet, is the biggest Forever 21 on the East Coast. Come for supertrendy clothes that won't break the bank, such as slouchy sweaters, shirtdresses, and pouffy skirts. Menswear and children's clothes are also sold here, and the jewelry is surprisingly well done. There are several other locations in Manhattan, including Union Square. ⊠ *1540 Broadway, between 45th and 46th Sts., Midtown West* ☎ *212/302–0594* ⊕ *www.forever21.com* Ⓜ *B, D, F, M to 47th - 50th St./Rockefeller Ctr.*

Gap. Gap may be as ubiquitous as Starbucks, but it is still a go-to place for classics such as denim, khakis, and sweaters in a rainbow of colors as well as on-trend capsule collections from top designers. This flagship also carries GapBody, GapMaternity, GapKids, and babyGap. ⊠ *60 W. 34th St., at Broadway, Midtown West* ☎ *212/760–1268* ⊕ *www.gap. com* Ⓜ *B, D, F, M to Herald Square.*

18

H&M. Of-the-moment trends are captured for the mass market at this affordable European clothing chain, which has numerous stores in the city. ✉ *640 5th Ave., between 51st and 52nd Sts., Midtown West* ☎ *212/489–0390* ⊕ *www.hm.com* Ⓜ *E, M to 5th Ave./53rd St.* ✉ *435 7th Ave., at 34th St., Chelsea* ☎ *212/643–6955* ⊕ *www.hm.com.*

Joe Fresh. Think of this brand as the Canadian version of H&M crossed with the Gap, offering stylish but classic clothes for men and women at affordable prices. The New York flagship offers everything from sweaters and denim to button-down shirts and shoes in a rainbow of colors. Just about all items are priced under $100. ✉ *510 5th Ave., between 42nd and 43rd Sts., Midtown West* ☎ *212/764–1730* ⊕ *www.joefresh. com* Ⓜ *7 to 5th Ave.*

Norma Kamali. A fashion fixture from the 1980s has a newly modern, though still '80s-influenced, line. Her luminously white store carries graphic bathing suits, Grecian-style draped dresses, and her signature poofy "sleeping-bag coats." The in-house Wellness Café sells olive oil–based beauty products and healthful snacks like kale chips. ✉ *11 W. 56th St., between 5th and 6th Aves., Midtown West* ☎ *212/957–9797* Ⓜ *N, Q, R 5th Ave./59th St.*

UNIQLO. At 89,000 square feet, this location is the biggest Uniqlo in the world (but there are also branches in SoHo and near Macy's). Shoppers can scoop up staples such as sweaters, skinny jeans, and button-down shirts in a rainbow of colors. Don't miss the limited edition collaborations with big name designers and stylists. The Heattech clothing range is always a big hit. ■TIP➔ **Weekday mornings are the best time to avoid long lines for the dressing rooms.** ✉ *666 5th Ave., between 52nd and 53rd Sts., Midtown West* ☎ *877/486–4756* ⊕ *www.uniqlo.com* Ⓜ *E, M to 5th Ave./53rd St.*

Zara. This massive flagship, the biggest Zara store in the U.S., is a haven for cheap and chic fashion. New merchandise arrives twice a week and clothing is arranged throughout the store by color (neutrals on one side, neon on the other). There are also two lounge areas, in case you need a shopping break. ✉ *666 5th Ave., between 52nd and 53rd Sts., Midtown West* ☎ *212/765–0477* Ⓜ *E, M to 5th Ave./53rd St.*

DEPARTMENT STORES

Bergdorf Goodman. This luxury department store is the ultimate shopping destination, offering ladies (and men) who lunch designer clothes, a stellar shoe department, and top-notch service. The fifth floor is where to go for mid-priced lines. The range of products offered in the beauty department is unparalleled—and shoppers can complete their look with highlights at the in-house John Barrett salon. If you need to refuel, grab a bite at the seventh-floor BG Restaurant, with Central Park views. ✉ *754 5th Ave., between 57th and 58th Sts., Midtown West* ☎ *212/753–7300* ⊕ *www.bergdorfgoodman.com* Ⓜ *N, R to 5th Ave.*

Henri Bendel. Behind the graceful Lalique windows you'll discover a mecca of niche boutiques stocking beauty products, accessories, and gifts (but no clothing). Bendel's dedication to the unusual begins in the ground-floor cosmetics area and percolates through the floors of women's lingerie and jewelry, scarves, and sunglasses. If you really want to pamper yourself, the fourth floor is home to Frédéric Fekkai's hair salon. ✉ *712 5th Ave., between 55th and 56th Sts., Midtown West* 🕿 *212/247–1100* ⊕ *www.henribendel.com* Ⓜ *E, M to 5th Ave./53rd St.*

Lord & Taylor. This is not your mother's Lord & Taylor. The department store has been working hard to attract a younger, hipper crowd. Thanks to a recent makeover, the clothing departments are easier to navigate and shoppers will find classic brands like Coach, Donna Karan, and Ralph Lauren. Don't miss the lovely ground floor beauty department. Best of all, it isn't nearly as crowded as competitor Macy's. ✉ *424 5th Ave., between 38th and 39th Sts., Midtown West* 🕿 *212/391–3344* ⊕ *www.lordandtaylor.com* Ⓜ *B, D, F, N, Q, R, M to 34th St./Herald Sq.*

Macy's. Macy's headquarters has more than 1 million square feet of retail space, so expect to lose your bearings at least once. Fashionwise, there's a concentration on the mainstream rather than on the luxe. One strong suit is denim, with everything from Hilfiger and Calvin Klein to Earl Jeans and Paper Denim & Cloth. There's also a reliably good selection of American designs from Ralph Lauren, DKNY, and Sean John. ✉ *Herald Sq., 151 W. 34th St., between 6th and 7th Aves., Midtown West* 🕿 *212/695–4400* ⊕ *www.macys.com* Ⓜ *B, D, F, N, Q, R, M to 34th St./Herald Sq.*

HOME DECOR

Muji. If you're into simple, chic, cheap style, Muji will be your trifecta. The name of this Japanese import translates to "no brand," and indeed, you won't find a logo plastered on the housewares or clothes. Instead, their hallmark is streamlined, often monochromatic design. The whole range of goods, from milky porcelain teapots to wooden toys, is invariably user-friendly. At this branch, you can glimpse the lobby of the *New York Times.* ✉ *620 8th Ave., at 40th St., Midtown West* 🕿 *212/382–2300* ⊕ *www.muji.us* Ⓜ *A, C, E to 42nd St./Port Authority.*

JEWELRY AND ACCESSORIES

Bulgari. This Italian company is certainly not shy about its name, which encircles gems, watch faces, and an ever-growing accessories line. There are beautiful, weighty rings, pieces mixing gold with stainless steel or porcelain, and the brand's signature cabochon multicolored sapphires. Wedding and engagement rings are slightly more subdued. ✉ *730 5th Ave., at 57th St., Midtown West* 🕿 *212/315–9000* ⊕ *www.bulgari.com* Ⓜ *N, R to 5th Ave.*

Harry Winston. These jewels regularly adorn celebs at the Oscars, and you'll need an A-list bank account to shop here. The ice-clear diamonds are of impeccable quality, and are set in everything from emerald-cut solitaire rings to wreath necklaces resembling strings of flowers. No wonder the jeweler was immortalized in the song "Diamonds Are a Girl's Best Friend." ✉ *718 5th Ave., at 56th St., Midtown West* 🕿 *212/399-1000* ⊕ *www.harrywinston.com* Ⓜ *F to 57th St.*

18

Mikimoto. The Japanese originator of the cultured pearl, Mikimoto presents a glowing display of high-luster pearls. Besides the creamy strands from their own pearl farms, check out diamond-and-pearl earrings, bracelets, and rings. ⊠ *730 5th Ave., between 56th and 57th Sts., Midtown West* ☎ *212/457–4600* ⊕ *www.mikimotoamerica.com* Ⓜ *F to 57th St.*

MUSEUM STORES

Museum of Arts and Design. This well-curated gift shop stocks crafts such as beautiful handmade tableware, unusual jewelry, and rugs, often tied in to ongoing exhibits. It's a great place to stock up on gifts. ⊠ *2 Columbus Circle, at 8th Ave., Midtown West* ☎ *212/299–7700* ⊕ *thestore.madmuseum.org* Ⓜ *1, A, B, C, D to 59th St./Columbus Circle.*

Museum of Modern Art Design and Book Store. The redesigned MoMA expanded its in-house shop with a huge selection of art posters and a gorgeous selection of coffee-table books on painting, sculpture, film, and photography. Across the street is the **MoMA Design Store,** where you can find Charles and Ray Eames furniture reproductions, vases designed by Alvar Aalto, and lots of clever trinkets. ⊠ *11 W. 53rd St., between 5th and 6th Aves., Midtown West* ☎ *212/708–9700* ⊕ *www.moma.org/visit/plan/stores* Ⓜ *E, M to 5th Ave./53rd St.*

PERFORMING ARTS MEMORABILIA

Drama Book Shop. If you're looking for a script, be it a lesser-known Russian translation or a Broadway hit, chances are you can find it here. The range of books spans film, music, dance, TV, and biographies. The shop also hosts Q&As with leading playwrights. ⊠ *250 W. 40th St., between 7th and 8th Aves., Midtown West* ☎ *212/944–0595* ⊕ *www.dramabookshop.com* Ⓜ *A, C, E to 42nd St./Port Authority.*

One Shubert Alley. This was the first store to sell Broadway merchandise outside of a theater. Today souvenir posters, tees, and other knickknacks memorializing past and present Broadway hits still reign at this Theater District shop. ⊠ *1 Shubert Alley, between 44th and 45th Sts., Midtown West* ☎ *212/944–4133* Ⓜ *N, Q, R, S, 1, 2, 3 to 42nd St./Times Sq.*

Triton Gallery. Theatrical posters large and small are available, and the selection is democratic, with everything from Marlene Dietrich's *Blue Angel* to recent Broadway shows represented. ⊠ *630 9th Ave., Ste. 808, between 44th and 45th Sts., Midtown West* ☎ *212/765–2472* ⊕ *www.tritongallery.com* Ⓜ *A, E to 42nd St./Port Authority.*

SHOES, HANDBAGS, AND LEATHER GOODS

Cole Haan. This brand is known for its comfortable but hip footwear—many shoes have Nike Air cushioning in the heels. Everything from sandals to boots and pumps is available. ⊠ *620 5th Ave., at Rockefeller Center, Midtown West* ☎ *212/765–9747* ⊕ *www.colehaan.com* Ⓜ *E, M to 5th Ave./53rd St.*

Manolo Blahnik. These sexy status shoes are some of the most expensive on the market. The signature look is a pointy toe with a high, delicate heel, but there are also ballet flats, gladiator sandals, and over-the-knee dominatrix boots that cost nearly $2,000. Pray for a sale. ⊠ *31 W. 54th St., between 5th and 6th Aves., Midtown West* ☎ *212/582–3007* ⊕ *www.manoloblahnik.com* Ⓜ *E, M to 5th Ave./53rd St.*

Cool Local Chains

New Yorkers in the know hit these fabulous local chains for unique frocks and the best of the city's one-stop shopping.

Ricky's. Loud and fun, these drugstores sprinkled around the city attract a young, eclectic crowd who come just as often for the crazy-color wigs as they do for Dove body wash and toothpaste. But if you're feeling spendy, high-end haircare and makeup is also sold here. Every fall the stores turn into Halloween Central, with a huge assortment of costumes referencing everything from Avatar to Jersey Shore. ⊠ *375 Broadway, TriBeCa* ☎ *212/925–5490* ⊕ *www.rickysnyc.com.*

Scoop. If you want to look stylish without trying too hard, come here to stock up on jeans (Levi's, Citizens of Humanity), slinky tops, vintage-looking tees, and cozy knits from designers like Stella McCartney, Theory, and Halston Heritage. Other locations in the city feature menswear. ⊠ *473–475 Broadway, between Broome and Grand Sts., SoHo* ☎ *212/925–3539* ⊕ *www.scoopnyc.com* Ⓜ *6 to Spring St.*

Fodor'sChoice
★
Smythson of Bond Street. Although Smythson still sells stationery fit for a queen—check out the royal warrant from England's HRH—it is also a place to scoop up on-trend handbags, iPad cases, and wallets. The hues range from sedate brown and black to eye-popping tangerine. The softbound leather diaries, address books, and travel accessories make ideal gifts. ⊠ *4 W. 57th St., between 5th and 6th Aves., Midtown West* ☎ *212/265–4573* ⊕ *www.smythson.com* Ⓜ *F to 57th St.*

TOYS

Toys "R" Us. The Times Square megastore is so big that a three-story Ferris wheel—complete with 14 individually themed cars—revolves inside. There's also a life-sized T-Rex that roars and a 4,000-square-foot Barbie dollhouse. With all the movie tie-in merchandise, video games, yo-yos, stuffed animals, and what seems to be the entire Mattel oeuvre, good luck extracting your kids from here. ⊠ *1514 Broadway, at 44th St., Midtown West* ☎ *646/366–8800* ⊕ *www.toysrus.com* Ⓜ *1, N, Q, R to 42nd St./Times Sq.*

THE UPPER EAST SIDE

This neighborhood is known for its antiques shops and high-end designers, such as Carolina Herrera, Oscar de la Renta, and Tom Ford. They are primarily sprinkled along Madison Avenue.

ANTIQUES AND COLLECTIBLES

Florian Papp. Established in 1900, this store has an unassailed reputation among knowledgeable collectors. Expect to find American and European antiques and paintings from the 18th to 20th century. Gilt mirrors and mahogany tables abound. ⊠ *962 Madison Ave., between 75th and 76th Sts., Upper East Side* ☎ *212/288–6770* ⊕ *www.florianpapp.com* Ⓜ *6 to 77th St.*

18

Keno Auctions. Leigh Keno of *Antique Roadshow* fame presides over this auction house, which specializes in Americana. As expected, he has a good eye and an interesting inventory; he's sold silver sauceboats from Paul Revere, paintings, and Chippendale furniture. ⊠ *127 E. 69th St., between Park and Lexington Aves., Upper East Side* ☎ *212/734–2381* ⊕ *www.kenoauctions.com* Ⓜ *6 to 68th St./Hunter College.*

BOOKS AND STATIONERY

Crawford Doyle Booksellers. You're as likely to see an old edition of Wodehouse as a best seller in the window of this shop. Bibliophiles will find a high-quality selection of fiction, nonfiction, and biographies, plus some rare books on the balcony. Salespeople offer their opinions *and* ask for yours. ⊠ *1082 Madison Ave., between 81st and 82nd Sts., Upper East Side* ☎ *212/288–6300* ⊕ *crawforddoyle.com* Ⓜ *4, 5, 6 to 86th St.*

CHILDREN'S CLOTHING

Bonpoint. Celebrities love this French children's boutique for the beautiful designs and impeccable workmanship—think pony-hair baby booties and hand-embroidered jumpers and blouses. Older kids can rock Liberty print dresses and peacoats. ⊠ *1269 Madison Ave., at 91st St., Upper East Side* ☎ *212/722–7720* ⊕ *www.bonpoint.com* Ⓜ *4, 5, 6 to 86th St.*

Infinity. Prep-school girls and their mothers giggle and gossip over the tween clothes (with more than a few moms picking up T-shirts and jeans for themselves) with Les Tout Petits dresses, Juicy Couture jeans, and tees emblazoned with Justin Beiber. ⊠ *1116 Madison Ave., at 83rd St., Upper East Side* ☎ *212/734–0077* Ⓜ *4, 5, 6 to 86th St.*

CLOTHING

Barbour. The signature look here is the company's waxed cotton and quilted jackets, available for men and women. The quilted jackets, tweeds, moleskin pants, lamb's-wool sweaters, and tattersall shirts invariably call up images of country rambles. ⊠ *1047 Madison Ave., at 80th St., Upper East Side* ☎ *212/570–2600* ⊕ *www.barbour.com* Ⓜ *6 to 77th St.*

BCBG Max Azria. If flirtation's your sport, you'll find your sportswear here: fluttering skirts, beaded camisoles, chiffon dresses, and leather pants fill the racks. ⊠ *770 Madison Ave., at 66th St., Upper East Side* ☎ *212/717–4225* ⊕ *www.bcbg.com* Ⓜ *6 to 68th St./Hunter College.*

Belstaff. Nearly a century old, this British brand specializes in motorcycle gear that has quite the pedigree—both Che Guevara and Steve McQueen have worn Belstaff. The relaunched company has expanded its collection to include luxury basics for men and women, including peacoats, waxed jackets, and body hugging dresses with luxury touches like python and crocodile. ⊠ *814 Madison Ave., between 68th and 69th Sts., Upper East Side* ☎ *212/897–1880* ⊕ *www.belstaff.com* Ⓜ *6 to 68th St./Hunter College.*

Bra Smyth. Chic and sweetly sexy French and Canadian underthings in soft cottons and silks line the shelves of this Uptown staple. In addition to the selection of bridal-ready white bustiers and custom-fit swimsuits (made, cleverly, in bra-cup sizes), the store is best known for its knowledgeable staff, many of whom can offer tips on proper fit and size you up on sight. Cup sizes run from AA to J. ✉ *905 Madison Ave., at 73rd St., Upper East Side* ☎ *212/772–9400* ⊕ *www.brasmyth.com* Ⓜ *6 to 68th St./Hunter College.*

Calvin Klein. Though the namesake designer has bowed out, the label keeps channeling his particular style. This stark flagship store emphasizes the luxe end of the clothing line. Men's suits tend to be soft around the edges; women's evening gowns are often a fluid pouring of silk. There are also shoes, accessories, housewares, and makeup. ✉ *654 Madison Ave., at 60th St., Upper East Side* ☎ *212/292–9000* ⊕ *www.calvinklein.com* Ⓜ *N, R, 4, 5, 6 to 59th St./Lexington Ave.*

Fodor'sChoice
★
Calypso St. Barth. Catch an instant island-vacation vibe from Calypso's colorful silk women's wear, dangly jewelry, and boho housewares at the brand's New York flagship, which has a suitably beachy vibe (check out the shell chandeliers). There are multiple branches throughout the city with different themes, including an outlet on Broome Street. ✉ *900 Madison Ave., between 72nd and 73rd Sts., Upper East Side* ☎ *212/535–4100.*

Carolina Herrera. A favorite of the society set (and A-list celebs), Herrera's designs are ladylike and elegant. Her suits, gowns, and cocktail dresses offer luxurious fabrics in timeless silhouettes. ✉ *954 Madison Ave., at 75th St., Upper East Side* ☎ *212/249–6552* Ⓜ *6 to 77th St.*

DKNY. The signature style here is casual sophistication—in other words, a very New York look. Slinky wrap dresses, chunky-knit sweaters, and dark denim are some of the best bets. ✉ *655 Madison Ave., at 60th St., Upper East Side* ☎ *212/223–3569* ⊕ *www.dkny.com* Ⓜ *N, Q, R to Lexington Ave.; 4, 5, 6 to 59th St.*

Dolce & Gabbana. It's easy to feel like an Italian movie star amid these exuberant (in every sense) clothes. Corseted dresses are a favorite; the fabric could be sheer, furred, or leopard-print. Men's suits are slim and sharp. ✉ *825 Madison Ave., between 68th and 69th Sts., Upper East Side* ☎ *212/249–4100* ⊕ *www.dolcegabbana.com* Ⓜ *6 to 68th St./ Hunter College.*

Juliette Longuet. French-born designer Juliette Longuet recently opened her first boutique inside an elegant townhouse. Although the fabrics are produced in Europe, all of the clothing is made in New York. Her designs combine the best of New York and Parisian chic; think leather leggings, chiffon blouses, and little black dresses. ✉ *153 E. 70th St., at Lexington Ave., Upper East Side* ☎ *646/360–3300* ⊕ *www. juliettelonguet.com* Ⓜ *6 to 68th St./Hunter College.*

Fodor'sChoice
★
Lanvin. This French label has been around since 1889, and is the oldest French fashion house still in existence. With Alber Elbaz at the helm, the signature look is fluid and sexy; think one-shouldered cocktail dresses, cigarette pants, and ruffled blouses. This elegant town house is the first U.S. outpost. The interior design itself is a showstopper; the three-story space oozes old money and glamour with its Art Deco chandeliers and soothing gray walls. And the clothes? Just as slinky. ✉ *815 Madison Ave., between 68th and 69th Sts., Upper East Side* ☎ *646/439–0381* ⊕ *www.lanvin.com* Ⓜ *6 to 68th St./Hunter College.*

18

La Perla. If money is no object, shop here for some of the sexiest underthings around. The collection includes lace sets, corsets, and exquisite bridal lingerie. ⊠ *803 Madison Ave., between 67th and 68th Sts., Upper East Side* ☎ *212/570–0050* ⊕ *www.laperla.com* Ⓜ *6 to 68th St./Hunter College.*

Lisa Perry. Perry takes an artist's approach to her clothing designs in this gleaming white space. She has created dresses printed with famous Andy Warhol photographs, such as the image of him drowning in a Campbell's Soup can. Pop art aside, her store is filled with a mix of '60s and '70s vintage clothes as well as her own designs. ⊠ *988 Madison Ave., between 76th and 77th Sts., Upper East Side* ☎ *212/431–7467* ⊕ *www.lisaperrystyle.com* Ⓜ *4, 6 to 77th St./Lexington.*

Fodor's Choice
★ **Ludivine.** Make a beeline for this store if you love French designers. Owner Ludivine Grégoire showcases of-the-moment Gallic (and a few Italian) designers like Vanessa Bruno, Jerome Dreyfuss, and Carvin. ⊠ *1216 Lexington Ave., between 82nd and 83rd Sts., Upper East Side* ☎ *212/249–4053* ⊕ *www.boutiqueludivine.com* Ⓜ *4, 5, 6 to 86th St.*

Marina Rinaldi. If you are a curvy size 10–22 and want to celebrate your figure rather than hide it, shop here. Marina Rinaldi sells form-flattering knit dresses, wool trousers, and coats that are tasteful and luxurious. ⊠ *13 E. 69th St., between Madison and 5th Aves., Upper East Side* ☎ *212/734–4333* ⊕ *www.marinarinaldi.com* Ⓜ *6 to 68th St./Hunter College.*

Max Mara. Think subtle colors and plush fabrics—straight skirts in cashmere or heathered wool, tuxedo-style evening jackets, and several choices of wool and cashmere camel overcoats. The suits are exquisitely tailored. ⊠ *813 Madison Ave., at 68th St., Upper East Side* ☎ *212/879–6100* ⊕ *www.maxmara.com* Ⓜ *6 to 68th St./Hunter College.*

Michael Kors. Michael Kors keeps rolling out boutiques in the city. This location, spread over two levels, showcases his clean-cut, American classic clothing and accessories. If you need fashion inspiration, images from his runway shows are screened on an 18-foot high television. ⊠ *667 Madison Ave., between 60th and 61st Sts., Midtown West* ☎ *212/980–1550* ⊕ *www.michaelkors.com* Ⓜ *N, Q, R to 59th St./5th Ave.*

Milly. These bright, cheerfully patterned clothes look as at home on the Upper East Side as they would in Palm Beach or Marrakech. At designer Michelle Smith's first U.S. flagship, you'll find bold maxi dresses, 1970s-inspired tunics, and slouchy shoulder bags. There is also a small selection of wedding gowns. ⊠ *900 Madison Ave., between 72nd and 73rd Sts., Upper East Side* ☎ *212/395–9100* ⊕ *www.millyny.com* Ⓜ *4, 6 to 77th St.*

Morgane Le Fay. The clothes here have a dreamy, ethereal quality that is decidedly feminine. Silk gowns are fluid and soft; fitted velvet jackets have covered buttons. Her dresses are also popular with brides who want a minimalist look. ⊠ *980 Madison Ave., between 76th and 77th Sts., Upper East Side* ☎ *212/879–9700* ⊕ *www.morganelefay.com* Ⓜ *6 to 68th St./Hunter College.*

Oscar de la Renta. Come here for the ladylike yet lighthearted runway designs of this upper-crust favorite. Skirts swing, ruffles billow, embroidery brightens up tweed, and even a tennis dress looks like something you could go dancing in. ⊠ *772 Madison Ave., at 66th St., Upper East Side* ☎ *212/288–5810* ⊕ *www.oscardelarenta.com* Ⓜ *6 to 68th St./ Hunter College.*

Otte. This store has outposts around the city, but the Upper East Side location has the biggest selection of clothing from on-trend designers such as Alexander Wang, 3.1 Phillip Lim, Thakoon and Isabel Marant. If you want that nonchalant chic look, this is your place. ⊠ *1232 3rd Ave., between 71 and 72nd Sts., Upper East Side* ☎ *212/744–4002* ⊕ *otteny.com.*

Fodor'sChoice
★

Polo Ralph Lauren. Even if you can't afford the clothes, come just to soak up the luxe RL lifestyle. This women's flagship is housed in a 22,000-square-foot building built to look like a historic Beaux Arts mansion (or small palace), complete with a curving marble staircase and stone floors. In addition to the complete women's collection, the brand's lingerie, home wares, and its first fine-jewelry and watch salon are here. The men's collection is just across the street in the Rhinelander Mansion. ⊠ *888 Madison Ave., at 72nd St., Upper East Side* ☎ *212/434–8000* ⊕ *www.ralphlauren.com* Ⓜ *6 to 68th St./Hunter College.*

Reed Krakoff. Coach's president and creative director has branched out to launch his own luxury lifestyle store. The clothing has an edgy look, with little black dresses in heavy wool and massive cuff bracelets. The handbags and shoes, however, lean more toward ladylike. ⊠ *831 Madison Ave., between 69th and 70th Sts., Upper East Side* ☎ *212/988–0560* ⊕ *www.reedkrakoff.com* Ⓜ *6 to 68th St./Hunter College.*

18

Roberto Cavalli. Rock-star style (at rock-star prices) delivers clothing decked out with fur, feathers, and lots of sparkle. Animal prints are big in this temple to the over-the-top. ⊠ *711 Madison Ave., at 63rd St., Upper East Side* ☎ *212/755–7722* ⊕ *www.robertocavalli.com* Ⓜ *N, R to 5th Ave./59th St.*

Tom Ford. Ford is famous for making Gucci supersexy, but the menswear here veers toward the traditional—and is impeccably made. Shirts come in more than 300 hues, and off-the-rack suits start around $3,000. Glide up the ebony staircase for the made-to-measure services, which will customize anything from suits to pajamas. Don't miss the fragrance chamber either. ⊠ *845 Madison Ave., at 70th St., Upper East Side* ☎ *212/359–0300* ⊕ *www.tomford.com* Ⓜ *6 to 68th St./Hunter College.*

Tory Burch. The global flagship of this preppy boho label is housed in an elegantly restored townhouse, so it feels as if you're shopping in a very well-appointed home. The five-story space features Tory Burch's signature orange lacquer walls, purple curtains, and gold hardware. If you already own her iconic ballet flats, browse through the ready-to-wear collection, handbags, shoes, and jewelry. ⊠ *797 Madison Ave., between 67th and 68th Sts., Upper East Side* ☎ *212/510–8371* ⊕ *www. toryburch.com* Ⓜ *6 to 68th St./Hunter College.*

Valentino. The mix here is at once audacious and beautifully cut; the fur or feather trimmings, low necklines, and opulent fabrics are about as close as you can get to celluloid glamour. No one does a better red. ⊠ *747 Madison Ave., at 65th St., Upper East Side* ☎ *212/772–6969* ⊕ *www.valentino.com* Ⓜ *6 to 68th St./Hunter College.*

Vera Wang Bride. This star wedding-dress designer churns out dreamy dresses that are sophisticated without being over-the-top. Choose from A-line and princess styles, and slinky sheaths. If money is no object, bespoke wedding dresses are available. Appointments are essential. ⊠ *991 Madison Ave., at 77th St., Upper East Side* ☎ *212/628–3400* ⊕ *www.verawang.com* Ⓜ *6 to 77th St.*

Vilebrequin. Allow St-Tropez to influence your swimsuit; these striped, floral, and solid-color French-made trunks come in sunny hues. Waterproof pocket inserts keep your essentials safe from beachcombers. Many styles come in boys' sizes, too. ⊠ *1007 Madison Ave., between 77th and 78th Sts., Upper East Side* ☎ *212/650–0353* ⊕ *www. vilebrequinonlinestore.com* Ⓜ *6 to 77th St.*

DEPARTMENT STORES

Barneys New York. Barneys continues to provide fashion-conscious and big-budget shoppers with irresistible items at its uptown flagship store. The extensive menswear selection has a handful of edgier designers, though made-to-measure is always available. The women's department showcases posh designers of all stripes, from the subdued lines of Armani and Nina Ricci to the irrepressible Alaïa and Zac Posen. The shoe selection trots out Prada boots and strappy Blahniks; jewelry runs from the whimsical (Jennifer Meyer) to the classic (Ileana Makri). ⊠ *660 Madison Ave., between 60th and 61st Sts., Upper East Side* ☎ *212/826–8900* ⊕ *www.barneys.com* Ⓜ *N, R, 4, 5, 6 to 59th St./Lexington Ave.*

Fodor's Choice ★ **Fivestory.** This luxurious mini–department store, inside a town house, carries clothing, accessories, shoes, and home decor for men, women, and children in an elegant setting (marble floors and lots of velvet and silk). It specializes in independent designers but also showcases designs from heavy hitters such as Alexander McQueen and Lanvin. ⊠ *18 East 69th St., between 5th and Madison Aves., Upper East Side* ☎ *212/288– 1338* ⊕ *www.fivestoryny.com* Ⓜ *6 to 68th St./Hunter College.*

FOOD AND TREATS

FP Patisserie. French patissier François Payard has multiple boutiques around the city but this is the flagship. Chocolates, pastries, and macarons are displayed like jewels. If you need to calm the sugar rush, a small dining area offers dishes like croque-monsieur. ⊠ *1293 3rd Ave., between 74th and 75th Sts., Upper East Side* ☎ *212/717–5252* ⊕ *www. payard.com* Ⓜ *6 to 77th St.*

Fodor's Choice ★ **La Maison du Chocolat.** Stop in at this chocolatier's small tea salon for a cup of thick, heavenly hot chocolate. The Paris-based outfit sells handmade truffles, chocolates, and pastries that could lull you into a chocolate stupor. ⊠ *1018 Madison Ave., between 78th and 79th Sts., Upper East Side* ☎ *212/744–7117* ⊕ *www.lamaisonduchocolat.com* Ⓜ *6 to 77th St.*

HOME DECOR

Ankasa. Owners Sachin and Babi Ahluwalia used to source textiles for luxury designers like Oscar de la Renta. Now they're using that design sensibility to produce a gorgeous line of housewares and accessories. The embroidery is exquisite. ⊠ *1200 Madison Ave., between 87th and 88th Sts., Upper East Side* ☎ *212/996–5200* ⊕ *www.ankasa.com* Ⓜ *4, 5, 6 to 86th St.*

JEWELRY AND ACCESSORIES

Asprey. Asprey's claim to fame is jewelry; its own eponymous diamond cut has A-shape facets but this British brand caters to all kinds of luxury tastes. Everything from leather goods and rare books to polo equipment and cashmere sweaters is available. ⊠ *853 Madison Ave., between 70th and 71st Sts., Upper East Side* ☎ *212/688–1811* ⊕ *www.asprey.com* Ⓜ *6 to 68th St./Hunter College.*

Fred Leighton. If you're in the market for vintage diamonds, this is the place, whether your taste is for tiaras, Art Deco settings, or sparklers once worn by a Vanderbilt. The skinny, stackable diamond eternity bands are hugely popular. ⊠ *773 Madison St., at 66th St., Upper East Side* ☎ *212/288–1872* ⊕ *www.fredleighton.com* Ⓜ *6 to 68th St./Hunter College.*

MUSEUM STORES

Cooper-Hewitt, National Design Museum. Prowl the shelves here for intriguing urban oddments and ornaments, like sculptural tableware, Alexander Girard dolls, housewares by Alessi and Japanese notebooks by Postalco. ⊠ *2 E. 91st St., at 5th Ave., Upper East Side* ☎ *212/849–8355* ⊕ *www.cooperhewitt.org* Ⓜ *4, 5, 6 to 86th St.*

Metropolitan Museum of Art Shop. This sprawling shop offers a phenomenal book selection, as well as posters, art videos, and computer programs. Reproductions of statuettes and other *objets* fill the gleaming cases in every branch. Don't miss the jewelry selection, with its Byzantine- and Egyptian-inspired baubles. ⊠ *1000 5th Ave., at 82nd St., Upper East Side* ☎ *212/570–3894* ⊕ *store.metmuseum.org* Ⓜ *4, 5, 6 to 86th St.*

Museum of the City of New York. Satisfy your curiosity about New York City's past, present, or future with the terrific selection of books, cards, toys, and photography posters. ⊠ *1220 5th Ave., at 103rd St., Upper East Side* ☎ *212/534–1672* ⊕ *www.mcny.org* Ⓜ *6 to 103rd St.*

Neue Galerie. Like the museum, the in-house bookshop and design store focuses on German, Austrian, and Central European art. Everything from children's toys to accessories and home decor is available here. ⊠ *1048 5th Ave., between 85th and 86th Sts., Upper East Side* ☎ *212/628–6200* ⊕ *www.neuegalerie.org* Ⓜ *4, 5, 6 to 86th St.*

SHOES, HANDBAGS, AND LEATHER GOODS

Anya Hindmarch. Although Anya Hindmarch is arguably most famous for her "I'm Not a Plastic Bag" tote, her real standouts are buttery leather shoulder bags and hobos, which are decidedly understated. Hindmarch's designs run the gamut from cheeky to ladylike. Her new flagship has a bespoke department on the second floor, where leather goods can be embossed with monograms or entire sentences. ⊠ *795 Madison Ave., between 67th and 68th Sts., Upper East Side* ☎ *646/852–6233* ⊕ *us.anyahindmarch.com* Ⓜ *6 to 68th St./Lexington.*

18

Fodor's Choice   **★**   **Charlotte Olympia.** This luxury British shoe brand finally has a store in New York. The art deco-inspired space showcases the very sexy and very expensive stilettos, pumps, and flats. Accessories such as shoulder bags and clutches are also available. ⊠ *22 E. 65th St., at Madison Ave., Upper East Side* ☎ *212/744–1842* ⊕ *www.charlotteolympia.com* Ⓜ *6 to 68th St./Hunter College.*

Christian Louboutin. Lipstick-red soles are the signature of Louboutin's delicately sexy couture slippers and stilettos, and his latest, larger downtown store has carpeting to match. The pointy-toe creations come trimmed with brocade, tassels, buttons, or satin ribbons. ⊠ *965 Madison Ave., between 75th and 76th Sts., Upper East Side* ☎ *212/396–1884* ⊕ *www.christianlouboutin.com* Ⓜ *6 to 77th St.*

Church's English Shoes. Beloved by bankers and lawyers, these shoes are indisputably of quality. You could choose something highly polished for an embassy dinner, a loafer or crepe-sole suede ankle boot for a weekend, or even a black-and-white spectator style worthy of Fred Astaire. ⊠ *689 Madison Ave., at 62nd St., Upper East Side* ☎ *212/758–5200* ⊕ *www.church-footwear.com* Ⓜ *N, R, 4, 5, 6 to 59th St.*

Devi Kroell. You may have spotted her snakeskin hobo on celebs such as Halle Berry and Ashley Olsen. This serene space is a perfect backdrop for the designer's luxury handbags and shoes, which are crafted from premium leather. Roomy shoulder bags come in python and calf leather, and evening bags have a touch of sparkle. There's also a selection of jewelry and scarves. ⊠ *717 Madison Ave., between 63rd and 64th Sts., Upper East Side* ☎ *212/644–4499* ⊕ *www.devikroell.com* Ⓜ *N, Q, R to Lexington Ave.; 4, 5, 6 to 59th St.*

Hermès. This legendary French retailer is best known for its iconic handbags, the Kelly and the Birkin, named for Grace Kelly and Jane Birkin, as well as its silk scarves and neckties. True to its roots, Hermès still stocks saddles and other equestrian items in addition to a line of beautifully simple separates. ⊠ *691 Madison Ave., at 62nd St., Upper East Side* ☎ *212/751–3181* ⊕ *www.hermes.com* Ⓜ *N, Q, R to Lexington Ave.; 4, 5, 6 to 59th St.*

Jimmy Choo. Pointy toes, low vamps, narrow heels, ankle-wrapping straps—these British-made shoes are undeniably vampy, and sometimes more comfortable than they look. ⊠ *716 Madison Ave., between 63rd and 64th Sts., Upper East Side* ☎ *212/759–7078* ⊕ *www.jimmychoo. com* Ⓜ *M to 68th St./Hunter College.*

Fodor's Choice   **★**   **Jack Rogers.** This brand, beloved by prepsters everywhere, is most famous for its Navajo sandal, which was worn by Jackie Onassis. You can still buy the Navajo at the Jack Rogers flagship store, as well as other footwear like ballet pumps, boots, and wedges. ⊠ *1198 Madison Ave., between 87th and 88th Sts., Upper East Side* ☎ *212/259–0588* Ⓜ *4, 5, 6 to 86th St.*

John Lobb. If you truly want to be well heeled, pick up a pair of these luxury shoes, whose prices start at around $1,100. Owned by Hermès, John Lobb offers classic styles such as oxfords, loafers, boots, and slippers. ⊠ *800 Madison Ave., between 67th and 68th Sts., Upper East Side* ☎ *212/888–9797* ⊕ *www.johnlobb.com* Ⓜ *6 to 68th St.*

Robert Clergerie. Although best known for its chunky, comfy wedges, this French brand is not without its sense of fun. The sandal selection includes beaded starfish shapes, and for winter the ankle boots have killer heels but the soles are padded. ⊠ *19 E. 62nd St., between 5th and Madison Aves., Upper East Side* ☎ *212/207–8600* ⊕ *www. robertclergerie.com/en* Ⓜ *N, Q, R to 5th Ave./59th St.*

Tod's. Diego Della Valle's coveted driving moccasins, casual loafers, and boots are the top choice for jet-setters who prefer low-key, logo-free luxury goods. Though most of the women's selection is made up of low-heel or flat styles, an increasing number of high heels are bent on driving sales, rather than cars. The handbags and satchels have the same fine craftsmanship. ⊠ *650 Madison Ave., near 60th St., Upper East Side* ☎ *212/644–5945* ⊕ *www.tods.com* Ⓜ *N, Q, R to 5th Ave./59th St.*

THE UPPER WEST SIDE

Although largely a residential neighborhood, the Upper West Side has some excellent food (Zabar's) as well as smaller boutiques.

BOOKS AND STATIONERY

Westsider Books & Westsider Records. This wonderfully crammed space is a lifesaver on the otherwise sparse Upper West Side. Squeeze in among the stacks of art books and fiction; clamber up the steep stairway and you'll find all sorts of rare books. ⊠ *2246 Broadway, between 80th and 81st Sts., Upper West Side* ☎ *212/362–0706* ⊕ *www.westsiderbooks. com* Ⓜ *1 to 79th St.*

CAMERAS AND ELECTRONICS

Apple Store. Branch location at 1981 Broadway. *See Midtown East for full review.*

CHILDREN'S CLOTHING

A Time for Children. When you shop at this funky boutique, you'll also be doing some good, as 100% of the profits go to the Children's Aid Society. Choose from toys, books, and clothing, which include classics such as Petit Bateau as well as vintage-inspired onesies. ⊠ *506 Amsterdam Ave., between 84th and 85th Sts., Upper West Side* ☎ *212/580–8202* ⊕ *www.atimeforchildren.org* Ⓜ *1 to 86th St.*

CLOTHING

BOC. Who needs to go downtown for cutting-edge designers? This sleek store stocks separates from Rebecca Taylor, Vivienne Westwood, and Alexander Wang, as well as bags, shoes, and jewelry. ⊠ *410 Columbus Ave., between 79th and 80th Sts., Upper West Side* ☎ *212/799-1567* ⊕ *www.bocnyc.com* Ⓜ *1 to 79th St.*

Fodor's Choice ★ **Intermix.** Whether you're looking for the perfect daytime dress, pair of J Brand jeans, or a puffer coat that won't make you look like the Michelin man, Intermix offers a well-edited mix of emerging and established designers. Expect to see designs from DVF, Chloe, and Missoni. There are a number of locations in the city. ⊠ *210 Columbus Ave., between 69th and 70th Sts., Upper West Side* ☎ *212/769–9116* ⊕ *www. intermixonline.com* Ⓜ *1, 2, 3 to 72nd St.*

18

Mint. Trendy dresses that won't break the bank are what Mint is all about. The collection includes Alice & Olivia, Susana Monaco, and Joe's Jeans. The walls are painted, of course, in mint. ⊠ *448 Columbus Ave., between 81st and 82nd Sts., Upper West Side* ☎ *212/362–6250* ⊕ *www.shopmint.com* Ⓜ *1 to 79th St.*

FOOD AND TREATS

Le Palais des Thés. This French owned tea boutique stocks varieties of black and green teas as well as rarer leaves and globally inspired blends, such as a Turkish hammam flavor that references roses and dates. Box sets and canisters make excellent gifts. ⊠ *194 Columbus Ave., at 69th St., Upper West Side* ☎ *646/664–1902* ⊕ *www.palaisdesthes.com* Ⓜ *1 to Lincoln Center.*

Zabar's. When it comes to authentic New York food, it's hard to beat rugelach, bagels, or lox from this specialty food emporium. ⊠ *2245 Broadway, at 80th St., Upper West Side* ☎ *212/787–2000* ⊕ *www. zabars.com.*

SHOES, HANDBAGS, AND LEATHER GOODS

Fodor'sChoice ★ **Tani.** Fashionable Upper West Side ladies love this shoe store for its huge selection and patient staff. Tani's selection is mostly classic-with-a-twist; shoppers will find slightly off-the-radar brands such as Bensimon, Mugumi Ochi, and Butter. ⊠ *2020 Broadway, between 69th and 70th Sts., Upper West Side* ☎ *212/873–4361* ⊕ *www.taninyc.com* Ⓜ *1, 2, 3 to 72nd St.*

NIGHTLIFE

Updated by
Jessica Colley

New Yorkers are fond of the "work hard, play hard" maxim, but the truth is, Gothamites don't need much of an excuse to hit the town. Monday is the new Thursday, which replaced Friday and Saturday, but it doesn't matter: the bottom line is that there's always plenty to do in this 24-hour city. Whether it's raising a glass in a divey 1930s saloon, a gay sports bar, the latest speakeasy-style cocktail den, or a swanky rooftop lounge, it isn't hard for visitors to get a piece of the action.

The nightlife scene still resides largely downtown—in dives in the East Village and Lower East Side, classic jazz joints in the West Village, and the Meatpacking District and Chelsea's see-and-be-seen clubs. Midtown, especially around Hell's Kitchen, has developed a vibrant scene, too, and plenty of preppy hangouts dot the Upper East and Upper West sides. Brooklyn, especially Williamsburg, is the destination for hipsters.

Keep in mind that *when* you go is just as important as *where* you go. A club that is packed at 11 might empty out by midnight, and a bar that raged last night may be completely empty tonight. *Paper* magazine has a good list of roving parties. You can check their online nightlife guide, *PM*, via their website (⊕ *www.papermag.com*). Another streetwise mag, the *L Magazine* (⊕ *www.thelmagazine.com*), lists what's happening at many of the city's lounges and clubs, as well as dance and comedy performances. Scour industry-centric websites, too, like *Eater* and *Grub Street*, which catalog the comings and goings of many a nightlife impresario. The *New York Times* has listings of cabaret and jazz shows, most comprehensively in their Friday and Sunday Arts sections. Bear in mind that a venue's life span is often measured in months, not years. Phone ahead or check online to make sure your target hasn't closed or turned into a polka hall (although you never know—that could be fun, too).

LOWER MANHATTAN

FINANCIAL DISTRICT

Fodor's Choice ★ **The Dead Rabbit.** For exquisite cocktails without the dress code or pretentious door policy typical of some New York cocktail dens, venture to the tip of Manhattan for a night of Irish hospitality in a 19th-century-inspired saloon. The ground-floor taproom serves up craft beers and whiskeys of the world while the upstairs parlor specializes in 72 cocktails revived from history books—along with ragtime music played live on the piano. ⊠ *30 Water St., Financial District* ☏ *646/422–7906* ⊕ *www.deadrabbitnyc.com* Ⓜ *R to Whitehall St.*

TRIBECA

BARS

B-flat. The decor is red-on-red here, and the Asian-style cocktails are particularly groovy (literally—one, with citrusy Japanese yuzu juice and vodka, is dubbed the Groovy) at this Japan-meets-'50s-America lounge. Listen to live jazz while nibbling on American and Japanese-inflected food treats. ⊠ *277 Church St., between Franklin and White Sts., TriBeCa* ☏ *212/219–2970* ⊕ *www.bflat.info* Ⓜ *1 to Franklin St.*

Brandy Library. Alas, the only book in this exquisite, wood-paneled room is the leather-bound menu listing hundreds of brandies and single-malt scotches. The bottles are on gorgeous backlighted "bookshelves," though, and you can learn what makes each of them special by chatting with the spirit sommelier—or by attending the twice-weekly Spirit School tasting classes. ⊠ *25 N. Moore St., between Varick and Hudson Sts., TriBeCa* ☏ *212/226–5545* ⊕ *www.brandylibrary.com* Ⓜ *1 to Franklin St.*

Canal Room. Polished wood floors, potted palms, and stylish chairs give this intimate club an air of glamour. Musicians perform here several times a month, but they also come just to enjoy themselves. The owners' record-business connections, a spectacular sound system, celeb sightings, and DJs with reputations as big as their turntables (size does matter) keep the crowds moving. ⊠ *285 W. Broadway, at Canal St., TriBeCa* ☏ *212/941–8100* ⊕ *www.canalroom.com* Ⓜ *A, C, E to Canal St.*

M1-5. For the more bohemian of TriBeCa pub goers, this lipstick-red, high-ceiling spot is a vast playground (as in pool and darts). A reggae jukebox helps keep it real, as do discounts for local artists on the diverse cocktail menu. Extra points, too, for the bar's name, which cites TriBeCa's warehouse zoning law. ⊠ *52 Walker St., between Broadway and Church St., TriBeCa* ☏ *212/965–1701* ⊕ *www.m1-5.com* Ⓜ *J, M, Z, N, Q, R, 6 to Canal St.*

Smith and Mills. Attractive scenesters frolic at this tiny gem of a gin mill, where mixologists who resemble Daniel Day-Lewis dispense elixirs (and caviar) from a bar hung with pots and pans. There are cozy table-nooks for couples, and an elevator-toilet (yes, you read that correctly) for anyone who feels "nature's call" while heeding "the call of the wild." ⊠ *71 N. Moore St., between Hudson and Greenwich Sts., TriBeCa* ☏ *212/219–8568* ⊕ *www.smithandmills.com* Ⓜ *1 to Franklin St.*

19

Terroir Wine Bar. If the tagline ("the Elitist Wine Bar for Everyone") isn't enough to get you in the door, the extensive wine list—including options by the glass, bottle, or adorable 3-ounce "taste"—should do the trick. This low-lit neighborhood wine bar is easy to walk right by on charming Harrison Street, but once inside you'll find seats at the bar for wine-centric conversations with the sharp staff, or more private nooks for a romantic evening of wine and cheese. ☒ *24 Harrison St., TriBeCa* ☏ *212/625–9463* ⊕ *www.restaurantearth.com/terrior/ Terroir.html* Ⓜ *1 to Franklin St.*

Ward III. You can get a solid Negroni or Manhattan at the exposed-brick-lined watering hole Ward III, but where this bar really shines is with its bespoke cocktails. Fight for a seat at the bar if possible to watch the sharply clad mixologists whip up the house specialties, or simply give them a few descriptive words ("spirit-forward," "something with bourbon," "light and refreshing") and let them create a cocktail on the spot to match your thirst. ☒ *111 Reade St., between W. Broadway and Church St., TriBeCa* ☏ *212/240–9194* ⊕ *www.ward3tribeca.com* Ⓜ *1, 2, 3 to Chambers St.*

DANCE CLUBS AND DJ VENUES

Santos Party House. "Now *this* is what I call a dance club," says Arthur Baker, the legendary DJ (and legendary record producer), about this glorious downtown dance club, where the velvet ropes part for everyone. Co-owned by the rocker Andrew W. K., the bilevel Santos ain't fancy, but that's the point, and the customers are as eclectic (everybody from punks to Upper East Siders) as the DJs, including Mr. Baker, who flies in regularly from London. Hence the musical vibe—underground dance, mostly—is simply kaleidoscopic. ☒ *96 Lafayette St., between White and Walker Sts., TriBeCa* ☏ *212/584–5492* ⊕ *www.santospartyhouse.com* Ⓜ *J, M, Z, N, Q, R, 6 to Canal St.*

CHINATOWN, NOHO, NOLITA, AND SOHO

CHINATOWN

Apotheke. Tucked away down a winding lane deep in Chinatown, this cocktail apothecary is a surprising find in a neighborhood known more for soup dumplings than creative tipples. Influenced by the 19th-century absinthe parlors of Paris, this historically inflected spot is all about drama and presentation. Think more chemistry lab than traditional bar—the results are not only delicious, but a feast for the eyes. ☒ *9 Doyers St., Chinatown* ☏ *212/406–0400* ⊕ *www.apothekenyc.com* Ⓜ *J, M, Q, Z to Canal St.; 4, 5, 6 to Brooklyn Bridge/City Hall.*

NOHO

Madam Geneva. Adjacent to the stylish and packed restaurant Saxon + Parole, this gin den is named after the 18th-century English term for the clear spirit. The brick-lined, dimly lit bar and lounge is a natural spill-over space after dinner next door; you can also nibble on Asian-inspired snacks here (from the same kitchen). The crowd is thirsty, polished, and often on the prowl. There's a DJ on weekends. ☒ *4 Bleecker St., NoHo* ☏ *212/254–0350* ⊕ *www.madamgeneva-nyc.com* Ⓜ *6 to Bleecker St.; F to 2nd Ave.; B, D, F, M to Broadway/Lafayette.*

NOLITA

Sweet and Vicious. The name of this unpretentious butterfly-logo'ed lounge doesn't signify the looks (sweet) and attitude (vicious) of certain downtown pretty things that frequent the bars on this stretch. So what makes this bar in particular so sweet? A lovely back garden that's more private than the sceney bars they might otherwise hit in SoHo and NoLIta. ⊠ *5 Spring St., between the Bowery and Elizabeth St., NoLIta* ☎ *212/334–7915* ⊕ *www.sweetandviciousnyc.com* Ⓜ *6 to Spring St.; J, M to Bowery.*

SOHO

BARS

Broome Street Bar. A local hangout since 1972, the casual yet essential Broome Street Bar still feels like the old SoHo, before trendy boutiques replaced artists' lofts. There's an impressive selection of draft beers and a full menu of burgers and other hearty pub fare. ⊠ *363 W. Broadway, at Broome St., SoHo* ☎ *212/925–2086* ⊕ *broomestreetbar.ypguides. net* Ⓜ *C, E to Spring St.*

Fanelli's. Linger over the *New York Times* at this terrific neighborhood bar and restaurant, which is pretty down-to-earth for a SoHo landmark that's been serving drinks (and solid cuisine—dig those burgers!) since 1847. Check out the hilarious old-timey photos on the walls, too. ⊠ *94 Prince St., at Mercer St., SoHo* ☎ *212/226–9412* Ⓜ *R to Prince St.*

Jimmy. Located on the 18th floor of the trendy James Hotel, Jimmy is a rooftop bar with stellar views. Sit in a corner nook to gaze at the Empire State Building, or head toward the outdoor pool area to survey the bridges over the East River. Cocktails are a highlight, featuring seasonal ingredients and novelties like ice cubes made from cinnamon water. ⊠ *15 Thompson St., at Grand St., SoHo* ☎ *212/465–2000* ⊕ *www. jimmysoho.com* Ⓜ *C, E to Spring St.*

Pegu Club. Modeled after an officers' club in what's now Myanmar, the Pegu manages to feel expansive and calm even when packed. The well dressed and flirtatious come here partly for the exotically lovely surroundings, but primarily for the cocktails, which are innovative, prepared with superlative ingredients, and predictably pricey. ⊠ *77 W. Houston St., 2nd fl., between West Broadway and Wooster St., SoHo* ☎ *212/473–7348* ⊕ *www.peguclub.com* Ⓜ *B, D, F, M to Broadway–Lafayette St.; 6 to Bleecker St.*

Fodor's Choice
★ **Pravda.** This Russian retreat has more than 70 different vodkas, including 10 house-infused flavors, which means your choice of martinis is nearly endless. The speakeasy feel of this underground spot is comfortable enough to spend the entire night, and Russian-inspired nibbles including caviar with blini will provide longevity to try yet another vodka variation, from cucumber-dill to ginger infused flavors. ⊠ *281 Lafayette St., between Prince and Houston Sts., SoHo* ☎ *212/226–4944* ⊕ *www.pravdany.com* Ⓜ *B, D, F, M to Broadway–Lafayette St.; 6 to Bleecker St.*

19

EAST VILLAGE AND LOWER EAST SIDE

EAST VILLAGE

BARS

Beauty Bar. Grab a seat in a barber chair or under a dryer at this made-over hair salon where, during happy hour, the manicurist will do your nails for a fee that includes a drink. (How's that for multitasking?) The DJ spins everything from Britpop to rock—a great soundtrack for primping. ⊠ *231 E. 14th St., between 2nd and 3rd Aves., East Village* ☎ *212/539–1389* ⊕ *www.thebeautybar.com/New_York* Ⓜ *4, 5, 6, L, N, Q, R to 14th St./Union Sq.*

Fodor's Choice ★ **The Bourgeois Pig.** What do you get when you serve all kinds of different fondue concoctions as well as all kinds of inventively delicious cocktails in a velvety yet chilled-out French bordello setting that's smack dab in the middle of the East Village? This keeper of a lounge. ⊠ *111 E. 7th St., between 1st Ave. and Ave. A, East Village* ☎ *212/475–2246* ⊕ *www.bourgeoispigny.com* Ⓜ *F to Lower East Side/2nd Ave.; 6 to Astor Pl.*

Death + Company. It's all about "speakeasy chic" at this sister lounge to the equally imaginative and classy nearby bars Mayahuel and Bourgeois Pig. A hilarious wall mural toward the rear sets the tone for the tongue-in-cheek satanic vibe here, but in the end, it's all about the outlandishly delicious cocktails and accompanying bar bites. ⊠ *433 E. 6th St., between 1st Ave. and Ave. A, East Village* ☎ *212/388–0882* ⊕ *www.deathandcompany.com* Ⓜ *F to Lower East Side/2nd Ave.; 6 to Astor Pl.*

Fodor's Choice ★ **Mayahuel.** The Agave goddess is behind the name of this cocktail den, where all manner of Aztec spirits (raspberry tea–infused tequilas, pineapple-infused mescal) make for the fiendishly rococo concoctions, courtesy of master mixologist Philip Ward. Equally good are snacks such as popcorn with lime, cheese, and chili. The bilevel setting conjures a south-of-the-border bordello feel. ⊠ *304 E. 6th St., between 1st and 2nd Aves., East Village* ☎ *212/253–5888* ⊕ *www.mayahuelny.com* Ⓜ *F to Lower East Side/2nd Ave.; 6 to Astor Pl.; N, R to 8th St.–NYU.*

McSorley's Old Ale House. One of New York's oldest saloons (it claims to have opened in 1854) and immortalized by *New Yorker* writer Joseph Mitchell, McSorley's serves two kinds of brew: McSorley's Light and McSorley's Dark. It's essential for blarney lovers, and much friendlier to women than it was before the '80s (the motto was "Good ale, raw onions, and no ladies"). ⊠ *15 E. 7th St., between 2nd and 3rd Aves., East Village* ☎ *212/473–9148* Ⓜ *6 to Astor Pl.*

Otto's Shrunken Head Tiki Bar & Lounge. Who says NYC doesn't appeal to all tastes? Should you get a sudden urge to visit a tiki bar while in the East Village—and who doesn't sometimes?—Otto's is your ticket. You'll find more than just a bamboo bar: there are fish lamps, a tattooed, punk-rock crowd, cute banquettes, drinking mugs in the form of shrunken heads, and DJs prone to spinning anything from '50s rock to "Soul Gidget" surf music. ⊠ *538 E. 14th St., between Aves. A and B, East Village* ☎ *212/228–2240* ⊕ *www.ottosshrunkenhead.com* Ⓜ *L to 1st Ave.*

Kickin' Karaoke

If you're looking for a venue other than your shower to bust out a rendition of Queen's "Somebody to Love," you're in good company. Otherwise-jaded New Yorkers have become hooked on the goofy, addictive pleasure of karaoke. The K-word means "empty orchestra" in Japanese, and seems to tickle both downtown hipsters (who dig the irony of kitsch) and uptown financiers (who need a good rebel yell at the end of a workday), and everybody in between who loves to flex the golden pipes after a few drinks.

There are three ways of getting your lead-vocalist groove on: doing it in public at a barwide Karaoke Night; reserving a private space at a bar ("karaoke boxes," they're called), where only your friends can hear you scream—er, sing; and bounding up onstage in front of a live band.

The hardcore karaoke places tend to be either grungy or glitzy, with as many as 15 available boxes for rent by the hour or full night (each box includes a music machine, microphones, and bar service), as well as up to 80,000 songs on tap for you to warble. (Don't worry, that figure includes stuff by Journey, REO Speedwagon, Britney Spears, and other grotesquely catchy Top 40 music.) The most popular of this lot include Chinatown's scruffy **Winnie's** (⊠ *104 Bayard St., at Baxter St.* ☎ *212/732–2384*), the East Village's **Sing-Sing** (⊠ *9 St. Marks Pl.* ☎ *212/387–7800*), the triple serving of cheesiness at Midtown's **Pulse** (⊠ *135 W. 41st St., between Broadway and 6th Ave.* ☎ *646/461–7717*), and just about anywhere else in the unofficial Koreatown that sprawls around Herald Square. Try **Karaoke Duet 35** (⊠ *53 W. 35th St., 2nd fl., between 5th and 6th Aves.* ☎ *646/233–2685*).

For live-band karaoke, head to the Lower East Side's hottest sing-fest: Monday-night rock-and-roll karaoke at **Arlene's Grocery** (⊠ *95 Stanton St.* ☎ *212/995–1652*).

19

PDT. Those who crave their cocktails with a little cloak-and-dagger will flip over PDT (it stands for "Please Don't Tell"). Housed beside the unassuming hot-dog joint Crif Dogs, this pseudo-speakeasy can be reached only through a phone booth on the main floor. Patrons with phoned-in reservations are escorted through the phone booth's false back into the cocktail bar, which is decorated with warm wooden beams and tongue-in-cheek taxidermy. ⊠ *113 St. Marks Pl., between 1st Ave. and Ave. A, East Village* ☎ *212/614–0386* ⊕ *www.pdtnyc.com* Ⓜ *6 to Astor Pl.*

Fodor'sChoice ★ **Pouring Ribbons.** This second-floor cocktail bar is named for the way a drink forms iridescent liquid ribbons when it's expertly poured. Bartenders shake or stir your concoction of choice from a grid-based menu that allows you to visualize just how "spirit-forward" or "refreshing" you want your drink to be. There's cheese and charcuterie to accompany your drinks. ⊠ *225 Ave. B, East Village* ☎ *917/656–6788* ⊕ *www. pouringribbons.com* Ⓜ *L to 1st Ave.*

Summit Bar. Manhattan's easternmost cocktail bar, Summit Bar serves high-end sips in a low-key environment. Still, much thought and care is put into the drinks, down to the herbs that come from the Summit's rooftop garden. The menu is split between "classic" and more ambitious "alchemist" sections, the latter boasting drinks with caraway-infused agave and shiso leaf. The snug outdoor patio is ideal for sampling the Summit's surprising take on a margarita in summer. ✉ *133 Ave. C, between 8th and 9th Sts., East Village* ☏ *917/261–7708* ⊕ *www. thesummitbar.net* Ⓜ *L to 1st Ave.*

Temple Bar. Unmarked and famous for its classic cocktails and romantic atmosphere, the Temple is prime first-date territory, especially once you drift past the sleekly wonderful bar to the back, where, swathed in almost complete darkness, you can lounge on a comfy banquette, order an old-fashioned, and do what people on first dates do. ✉ *332 Lafayette St., East Village* ☏ *212/925–4242* ⊕ *www.templebarnyc.com* Ⓜ *B, D, F, M to Broadway–Lafayette St.; 6 to Bleecker St.*

CABARET AND PIANO BARS

Joe's Pub. Wood paneling, red-velvet walls, and comfy sofas make a lush setting for top-notch performers and the A-list celebrities who love them, or pretend to. Named for the Public Theater's near-mythic impresario Joe Papp, and located inside the Public, Joe's doesn't have a bad seat—but if you want to occupy one, buy tickets beforehand and/or arrive at least half an hour early for the Italian-inspired dinner menu. ✉ *425 Lafayette St., between 4th St. and Astor Pl., East Village* ☏ *212/539–8778* ⊕ *www.joespub.com* Ⓜ *6 to Astor Pl.*

ROCK CLUB

Fodor's Choice
★
Lit Lounge. With a rock roster that's included musical forces as diverse as Devendra Banhart and the Hold Steady, Lit is a wonderfully grungy East Village classic. The raucous arty crowd hits not only shows but its charming art gallery Fuse and its theme parties, which cater to fans of specific bands (the White Stripes, Devo, and the Buzzcocks, to name a few). ✉ *93 2nd Ave. #A, East Village* ☏ *212/777–7987* ⊕ *www. litloungenyc.com* Ⓜ *F to Lower East Side/2nd Ave.; 6 to Astor Pl.*

LOWER EAST SIDE
BARS

Fodor's Choice
★
Back Room. The Prohibition-era atmospheric touches here include tin ceilings, velvet wallpaper, mirrored bars, a large fireplace, and a "hidden" outdoor entrance (which you'll find easily enough, though the back-alley walk to the second, indoor entrance puts you in the speakeasy spirit). The music consists of rock CDs rather than a live spinmeister, and the drinks come in old-fashioned teacups or wrapped in paper bags. These, and other quirks, attract a slightly older clientele than many of its rowdy neighbors. ✉ *102 Norfolk St., between Delancey and Rivington Sts., Lower East Side* ☏ *212/228–5098* Ⓜ *F to Delancey St.; J, M, Z to Essex St.*

The Pink Pony. Maintaining a defiantly boho feel on trendy Ludlow Street, this shabby-chic bar-café draws young writers, filmmakers, and designers who come to escape the cacophony from nearby music venues and make conversation over bottles of cheap wine, oysters, French classic dishes, or cup after cup (after cup) of coffee. ✉ *176 Ludlow St., between Houston and Stanton Sts., Lower East Side* ☏ *212/253–1922* ⊕ *www.pinkponynyc.com* Ⓜ *F to 2nd Ave.*

Spitzer's Corner. No, you won't rub shoulders with ex-governor Eliot Spitzer here, but you will find 40 types of beer on tap plus a selection of the bottled variety, good food, floor-to-ceiling windows that pop open in fine weather, and wooden walls supposedly taken from pickle barrels. (Fortunately, the air is free of any scents from the barrel's former contents.) ⊠ *101 Rivington St., at Ludlow St., Lower East Side* ☎ *212/228–0027* ⊕ *www.spitzerscorner.com* Ⓜ *F to Delancey St.; J, M, Z to Essex St.*

LIVE MUSIC VENUES

Arlene's Grocery. On Monday nights, crowds pack into this former Puerto Rican bodega for Rock 'n' Roll Karaoke, where they live out their rockstar dreams by singing favorite punk anthems onstage with a live band. The other six nights of the week are for local bands, and are accordingly hit-or-miss. ⊠ *95 Stanton St., between Ludlow and Orchard Sts., Lower East Side* ☎ *212/358–1633* ⊕ *www.arlenesgrocery. net* Ⓜ *F to 2nd Ave.*

Fodor'sChoice ★ **Bowery Ballroom.** This theater with Art Deco accents is probably the city's top midsize concert venue. Packing in the crowds here is a rite of passage for musicians on the cusp of stardom, including the Gossip, Manic Street Preachers, and the exuberant Go! Team. Grab one of the tables on the balcony (if you can), stand (and thus get sandwiched) on the main floor, or retreat to the comfortable bar in the basement, which really fills up after each show. ⊠ *6 Delancey St., between Bowery and Chrystie St., Lower East Side* ☎ *212/533–2111* ⊕ *www. boweryballroom.com* Ⓜ *J, M, Z to Bowery St.*

Mercury Lounge. You'll have to squeeze past all the sardine-packed hipsters in the front bar to reach the stage, but it's worth it. Not only does this top-quality venue, a "little sister to the Bowery Bar," specialize in cool bands on the indie scene (Holly Golightly, Echo and the Bunnymen, and the Apostle of Hustle, anyone?), but it was where the late great Jeff Buckley used to stop by to do spontaneous solo shows. ⊠ *217 E. Houston St., at Ave. A, Lower East Side* ☎ *212/260–4700* ⊕ *mercury-loungenyc.com* Ⓜ *F to 2nd Ave.*

Piano's. With two venues for live music and DJs—the Showroom downstairs and Lounge upstairs—as well as a full bar that serves food downstairs, there's something for everyone at this Lower East Side staple. It's a blast late nights. ⊠ *158 Ludlow St., just south of Stanton St., Lower East Side* ☎ *212/505–3733* ⊕ *www.pianosnyc.com* Ⓜ *F to Delancey St.*

GREENWICH VILLAGE AND WEST VILLAGE

GREENWICH VILLAGE

BARS

The Dove Parlour. On a colorful block that evokes the Greenwich Village of yore—cigar store, vegetarian cafés, a bootleg music shop, a store specializing in chess—is this wonderful bar whose elegant atmosphere (red velvet wallpaper, white-wood paneling) is belied by the revelry of the very sexy young customers. ⊠ *228 Thompson St., between 3rd and Bleecker Sts., Greenwich Village* ☎ *212/254–1435* ⊕ *www. thedoveparlour.com* Ⓜ *E to Spring St.*

19

Vol de Nuit. Tucked away from the street, the "Belgian Beer Bar" (as everybody calls it) features a European-style, enclosed outdoor courtyard and a cozy interior, all red light and shadows. NYU grad-student types come for the mammoth selection of beers on tap as well as for the fries, which are served with a Belgian flair, in a paper cone with an array of sauces on the side. ⊠ *148 W. 4th St., at 6th Ave., Greenwich Village* ☎ *212/982–3388* ⊕ *www.voldenuitbar.com* Ⓜ *A, B, C, D, E, F, M to W. 4th St./Washington Sq.*

JAZZ VENUES

Fodor'sChoice **Blue Note.** Considered by many (not least its current owners) to be "the
★ jazz capital of the world," the Blue Note was once the stomping ground for such legends as Dizzy Gillespie, and still hosts a varied repertoire from Chris Botti to the Count Basie Orchestra to Boz Scaggs. Expect a steep cover charge except for late shows on weekends, when the music goes from less jazzy to more funky. ⊠ *131 W. 3rd St., near 6th Ave., Greenwich Village* ☎ *212/475–8592* ⊕ *www.bluenote.net* Ⓜ *A, B, C, D, E, F, M to W. 4th St.*

Knickerbocker Bar and Grill. Jazz acts are on the menu on Friday and Saturday nights at this old-fashioned steakhouse, a longtime staple of the city's more intimate music scene. ⊠ *33 University Pl., at 9th St., Greenwich Village* ☎ *212/228–8490* ⊕ *www.knickerbockerbarandgrill. com* Ⓜ *R to 8th St.*

LIVE MUSIC VENUES

(Le) Poisson Rouge. Underneath the site of the late, lamented Village Gate jazz emporium is this cutting-edge jewel of a place, whose name means "the Red Fish" and whose parentheses around Le remain a sacred mystery. Blending just the right mix of posh notes (the lush decor, the fine dining) and brave music programming (jazz, classical, electronic, cabaret, rock, folk—even, with the splendiferous Ralph's World, children's music), the Poisson is quite simply an essential N.Y.C. fixture. ⊠ *158 Bleecker St., at Thompson St., Greenwich Village* ☎ *212/505–3474* ⊕ *www.lepoissonrouge.com* Ⓜ *A, B, C, D, E, F, M to W. 4th St.*

WEST VILLAGE

BARS

Corner Bistro. Opened in 1961, this charming neighborhood saloon serves what many think are the best (and most affordable) hamburgers in town. Once you actually get a seat, the space feels nice and cozy, but until then, be prepared to drink a beer amid loud and hungry patrons. ⊠ *331 W. 4th St., at 8th Ave., West Village* ☎ *212/242–9502* ⊕ *www. cornerbistrony.com* Ⓜ *A, C, E to 14th St.; L to 8th Ave.*

Employees Only. The dapper, white-coated bartenders (many of them impressively mustachio'd) at this Prohibition era–style bar mix delicious, well-thought-out cocktails with debonair aplomb and freshly squeezed mixers. Sip one in the dimly lit bar area and you just might feel like you've stepped back in time—if it weren't for the crush of trendy West Village locals and visitors in the know at your back. Look for the green awning that says EO and the neon "Psychic' sign out front. Dinner is served in the restaurant at the back: it's quality, but pricey. ⊠ *510*

Hudson St., West Village ☎ *212/242–3021* ⊕ *www.employeesonlynyc. com* Ⓜ *1 to Christopher St.; A, B, C, D, E, F, M to West 4th.*

Hudson Bar and Books. Along with its sister branches—Beekman Bar and Books on Beekman Place and Lexington Bar and Books on, yep, Lexington—the Hudson reflects a literary bent on its cocktails with names like the Dewey Decimal, the Cervantes Spritzer, and Alphabet Absinthe (topped off with floating letter-shape sugar cubes). Despite that, it's hardly a hushed library where well-read butlers serve you; no—the atmosphere here is more about book decor than serious literature. It's seriously clubby, with wood paneling and leather banquettes. And it's one of the few places you can still smoke. ⊠ *636 Hudson St., at Horatio St., West Village* ☎ *212/229– 2642* ⊕ *www.barandbooks.cz* Ⓜ *A, C, E to 14th St.; L to 8th Ave.*

Fodor'sChoice **Little Branch.** The owners of the secretive, hard-to-access lounge Milk &
★ Honey created this open-to-everyone cousin with the same high-quality cocktails. The dim lighting and snug booths make it the ideal spot for a con-versation with friends (that you can actually hear) or an intimate date. ⊠ *20 7th Ave., at Leroy St., West Village* ☎ *212/929–4360* Ⓜ *1 to Houston St.*

Otheroom. Ever wish that the bar you're drinking in had something more interesting on its walls than Budweiser signs? Head to the far west Otheroom, art gallery by day, upscale drinking spot by night. The menu is pretty creative, too, with dozens of microbrews as well as American wines available by the glass. ⊠ *143 Perry St., between Greenwich and Washington Sts., West Village* ☎ *212/645–9758* ⊕ *www.theotheroom. com* Ⓜ *1 to Sheridan Sq.–Christopher St.*

White Horse Tavern. According to New York legend, Dylan Thomas drank himself to death in this historic and quintessential West Vil-lage tavern founded in 1880. The Horse remains perpetually popular with literary types, but thankfully it's lacking more death-by-alcohol-poisoning cases of late. When the weather's nice, try to snag a seat at one of the sidewalk tables for prime—and, given the neighborhood, we do mean prime—people-watching. ⊠ *567 Hudson St., at 11th St., West Village* ☎ *212/989–3956* Ⓜ *1 to Christopher St./Sheridan Sq.*

19

Wilfie & Nell. Combine the beloved cozy atmosphere and frothy pints standard at Irish pubs with a well-heeled West Village crowd and you get Wilfie & Nell, a candlelit bar full of communal tables for making new friends. This perpetually crowded neighborhood favorite, with its low ceilings and locally sourced food, is a popular singles spot as well as a good match for night owls: food and brews are served into the wee hours. ⊠ *228 W. 4th St., between 10th St. and 7th Ave. S, West Village* ☎ *212/242–2990* ⊕ *www.wilfieandnell.com.*

CABARET AND PIANO BARS

The Duplex. No matter who's performing, the largely gay audience hoots and hollers in support of the often kitschy performers at this music-scene staple on busy Sheridan Square since 1951. Singers and comedians hold court in the cabaret theater, while those itching to take a shot at open mike head downstairs to the lively piano bar. ⊠ *61 Christopher St., at 7th Ave. S, West Village* ☎ *212/255–5438* ⊕ *www.theduplex. com* Ⓜ *1 to Christopher St.*

GAY NIGHTLIFE

Cubbyhole. Early in the evening the crowd is mixed at this neighborhood institution, where the DJs, the unpretentious decor, and the inexpensive margaritas are popular. Later on, the women take charge. ⊠ *281 W. 12th St., at 4th St., West Village* ☎ *212/243–9041* ⊕ *www. cubbyholebar.com* Ⓜ *A, C, E to 14th St.; L to 8th Ave.*

Fodor's Choice **Henrietta Hudson.** The nightly parties at this laid-back West Village HQ
★ for the Sapphic set attract young professional women, out-of-towners, and longtime regulars. Because the DJ and the pool table quickly create a crowd, though, stake your claim to a spot early, especially on—yup, you guessed it—weekends. ⊠ *438 Hudson St., at Morton St., West Village* ☎ *212/924–3347* ⊕ *www.henriettahudson.com* Ⓜ *1 to Christopher St./Sheridan Sq.*

JAZZ VENUES

Garage Restaurant & Café. Good news for you budget-minded jazzers: there's no cover *and* no minimum at this West Village hot spot, where two jazz groups jam seven nights a week and a fireplace sets the mood upstairs. ⊠ *99 7th Ave. S, between Bleecker and Christopher Sts., West Village* ☎ *212/645–0600* ⊕ *www.garagerest.com* Ⓜ *1 to Christopher St./Sheridan Sq.*

Fodor's Choice **Village Vanguard.** This prototypical jazz club, tucked into a cellar in
★ Greenwich Village since the 1940s, has been the haunt of legends like Thelonious Monk and Barbra Streisand. Today you can hear jams from the jazz-star likes of Bill Charlap and Ravi Coltrane, and on Monday night the sizable resident Vanguard Jazz Orchestra blows its collective heart out. ⊠ *178 7th Ave. S, between 11th and Perry Sts., West Village* ☎ *212/255–4037* ⊕ *www.villagevanguard.com* Ⓜ *1, 2, 3 to 14th St.*

LIVE MUSIC VENUES

SOB's. The initials stand for "Sounds Of Brazil" (no, not what you—and everybody else—might think), and this is *the* place for reggae, African, and Latin music, with some jazz gigs sprinkled in. The late, great Cuban sensation Cachao used to hold court here, as does calypso's Mighty Sparrow when he's up north. Don't miss the Haitian dance parties, the afterwork Latin groove happy hour, or the bossa nova brunches. Dinner is served as well. ⊠ *204 Varick St., West Village* ☎ *212/243–4940* ⊕ *www.sobs.com* Ⓜ *1 to Houston St.*

CHELSEA AND THE MEATPACKING DISTRICT

CHELSEA
BARS

Half King. Writer Sebastian Junger (*The Perfect Storm*) is one of the owners of this would-be literary mecca. We say "would-be" because the ambience can be more pub-like than writerly—but that's fine, since the King draws such a friendly crowd (media types, mostly). We like it best for its frequent readings, gallery exhibits, and Irish-American menu. ⊠ *505 W. 23rd St., between 10th and 11th Aves., Chelsea* ☎ *212/462– 4300* ⊕ *www.thehalfking.com* Ⓜ *C, E to 23rd St.*

COMEDY CLUBS

Fodor's Choice
★

Upright Citizens Brigade Theatre. Raucous sketch comedy, audience-initiated improv, and classic stand-up take turns onstage here at the city's absolute capital for alternative comedy. There are even classes available; the Upright Citizens bill their program as the world's largest improv school, where you can catch indie comic darlings like *SNL*'s Amy Poehler or *Human Giant*'s Rob Huebel. ⊠ *307 W. 26th St., between 8th and 9th Aves., Chelsea* ☎ *212/366–9176* ⊕ *www.ucbtheatre.com* Ⓜ *C, E to 23rd St.*

GAY NIGHTLIFE

Big Apple Ranch. Taking *Brokeback Mountain* style to the dance floor, the Ranch lets you unleash your inner "cowboy dancer" every Saturday night, with half-hour two-step lessons at 8, line dancing at 8:30, and then a down-home country-and-western dance party kicking off at 9. ⊠ *Dance Manhattan, 39 W. 19th St., 5th fl., Chelsea* ☎ *212/358–5752* ⊕ *www.bigappleranch.com* Ⓜ *F, R, M to 23rd St.; 1 to 18th St.*

Gym Sports Bar. At New York's first gay sports bar, the plentiful flat-screen TVs and cheap Budweisers draw athletic enthusiasts of every stripe, from athlete to armchair. Nobly enough, the bar sponsors—and frequently hosts parties for—a number of local gay sports teams. ⊠ *167 8th Ave., at 18th St., Chelsea* ☎ *212/337–2439* ⊕ *www.gymsportsbar. com* Ⓜ *A, C, E to 14th St.; L to 8th Ave.*

THE MEATPACKING DISTRICT

BARS

675 Bar. How can you not love a spot where the bouncer greets you with a grin instead of a scowl, board games abound, a giant black-lacquered horse stands guard next to the pool table, the drinks get amply poured, and each small room along the subterranean stone corridor is decorated in a different creative way? As an ideal spot for both dates (plenty of dark corners) and raucous merriment (bright, big central space), the 675 scores highest for having less attitude than the rest of the neighborhood. ⊠ *675 Hudson St., between Hudson St. and 9th Ave. (enter on 13th St.), Meatpacking District* ☎ *212/699–2410* ⊕ *www.675bar.com* Ⓜ *A, C, E to 14th St.; L to 8th Ave.*

19

Hogs & Heifers. This raucous place is all about the saucy barkeeps using megaphones to berate male customers and bait the females to get up on the bar and dance (and add their bras to the collection on the wall). ⊠ *859 Washington St., at 13th St., Meatpacking District* ☎ *212/929–0655* ⊕ *www.hogsandheifers.com* Ⓜ *A, C, E to 14th St.; L to 8th Ave.*

Plunge. The Gansevoort Hotel's slick rooftop bar would be worth visiting even without its mouthwatering views. The adjectives sleek and glossy could easily be illustrated by Plunge, where the lighting is soft, the furnishings are cool and comfy (at least to a degree), the music isn't too loud, servers of both sexes are sexy, and there is ample space—indoors as well as out. ⊠ *18 9th Ave., at 13th St., Meatpacking District* ☎ *212/660–6766* ⊕ *www.hotelgansevoort.com* Ⓜ *A, C, E to 14th St.; L to 8th Ave.*

The Standard Hotel Biergarten, Grill, and Living Room. Practically the official bar of the High Line park, the Standard Biergarten is a sprawling and riotous space complete with ping pong tables and big steins of beer.

There's also a grill bar and very cool indoor Living Room lounge. As for the chic hot spot on the top floor, unofficially called the Boom Boom Room, it's currently the hardest "door" in town ("hardest," that is, to get through), but given the quality of the accessible fun down below, we'll forgive their snobbery. ⊠ *848 Washington St., at 13th St., Meatpacking District* ☎ *212/645–4646* ⊕ *www.standardhotels.com* Ⓜ *A, C, E, L to 14th St.*

DANCE CLUBS AND DJ VENUES

Cielo. Relatively mature dance club goers (if the word mature can ever be applied to such a crowd) gravitate to this small but sturdy Meatpacking District "music-head" mecca to toss back cocktails, dig the high-quality sound system, groove to top-flight DJs spinning soulful Latin beats and techno, boogie on the sunken dance floor, and smoke in the no-frills garden outside. Monday nights are home to the award-winning Deep Space parties, where resident DJs (as well as guest spinmeisters like Dmitri from Paris) rev up the faithful with everything from dubstep to Stravinsky. ⊠ *18 Little W. 12th St., between 9th Ave. and Washington St., Meatpacking District* ☎ *212/645–5700* ⊕ *www.cieloclub.com* Ⓜ *A, C, E to 14th St.; L to 8th Ave.*

UNION SQUARE, GRAMERCY, AND THE FLATIRON DISTRICT

UNION SQUARE

Rye House. A welcoming bar with slick cocktails and clever takes on comfort food, the Rye House beckons just steps from the chain store overload of Union Square. From boiled peanuts and fried pickles to their own take on a Sazerac, the space is a welcome respite from the hustle and bustle outside. ⊠ *11 W. 17th St., between Broadway and 5th Ave., Union Square* ☎ *212/255–7260* ⊕ *www.ryehousenyc.com* Ⓜ *4, 5, 6, L, N, Q, R to 14th St./Union Sq.*

GRAMERCY

BARS

Old Town Bar. The proudly unpretentious bilevel Old Town is redolent of old New York, and why not—it's been around since 1892. Tavern-style grub, mahogany everywhere, and atmosphere, atmosphere, atmosphere make this a fun stop on any pub crawl. Men, don't miss the giant, person-size urinals. ⊠ *45 E. 18th St., between Broadway and Park Ave. S, Gramercy* ☎ *212/529–6732* ⊕ *www.oldtownbar.com* Ⓜ *4, 5, 6, L, N, Q, R to 14th St./Union Sq.*

Pete's Tavern. This historic landmark (where O. Henry was a loyal customer) claims to be the oldest continuously operating watering hole in the city. Pete's has charm to spare, with its long wooden bar and cozy booths, where locals crowd in for beer and burgers. ⊠ *129 E. 18th St., at Irving Pl., Gramercy* ☎ *212/473–7676* ⊕ *www.petestavern.com* Ⓜ *4, 5, 6, L, N, Q, R to 14th St./Union Sq.*

JAZZ VENUES

Fodor'sChoice ★ **Jazz Standard.** The Standard's sizable underground room draws top names in the business. As a part of Danny Meyer's southern-food restaurant Blue Smoke, it's one of the few spots where you can get dry-rubbed ribs to go with your bebop. Bring the kids for the Jazz Standard Youth Orchestra concerts every Sunday afternoon. ✉ *116 E. 27th St., between Park and Lexington Aves., Gramercy* ☎ *212/576–2232* ⊕ *www.jazzstandard.com* Ⓜ *6 to 28th St.*

LIVE MUSIC VENUES

Fodor's Choice
★

Irving Plaza. This two-story venue is known for its solid rock performances, both indie (DJ Shadow and Sleater-Kinney) and more mainstream (Lenny Kravitz)—even if they can get a little pricey. Red walls and chandeliers add a Gothic touch. And if the main floor gets too cramped, seek sanctuary at the chill bar upstairs. ✉ *17 Irving Pl., at 15th St., Gramercy* ☎ *212/777–6800* ⊕ *www.irvingplaza.com* Ⓜ *4, 5, 6, L, N, Q, R to 14th St./Union Sq.*

FLATIRON DISTRICT

BARS

The Ace Hotel. A hot spot for the digital set, the hotel lobby and adjoining restaurant spaces—the Breslin and the John Dory—have been packed since they opened. If your bearded hipster friend came into some cash, his place would look like the lobby here, with reclaimed wood tables, beer signs, and beautiful folks in oversize eyeglasses drinking coffee by day or a craft brew by night (while a DJ spins in the background). ✉ *20 W. 29th St., between Broadway and 5th Ave., Gramercy* ☎ *212/679–2222* ⊕ *www.acehotel.com* Ⓜ *R to 28th St.*

Flatiron Lounge. Here, resident mixologists rely on the freshest (and sometimes most exotic) ingredients available. The cocktail menu changes often, but if you're stumped, tell the bartenders what you like and they'll happily invent a new concoction on the spot. ✉ *37 W. 19th St., between 5th and 6th Aves., Flatiron* ☎ *212/727–7741* ⊕ *www.flatironlounge.com* Ⓜ *N, R to 23rd St.*

Raines Law Room. There's no phone number or big sign for this cocktail bar; just ring the bell to enter. Wood-burning fireplaces, deep banquettes, and curtains for privacy all contribute to the comfortable, living room–like vibe. An outdoor garden lit by candles is functional, too: herbs grown here are used in the carefully crafted cocktails. ✉ *48 W. 17th St., Flatiron* ⊕ *www.raineslawroom.com* Ⓜ *F, M to 14th St.; 4, 5, 6, N, Q, R to 14th St./Union Sq.*

MIDTOWN EAST

BARS

The Bar Downstairs. The bar without a name in the basement of the Andaz Fifth Avenue may lack a moniker, but it certainly has a pedigree. Alchemy Consulting, a joint venture from Chicago's Violet Hour and New York's Death and Co., designed the cocktails; look for spins on the Negroni and Manhattan in the sleek space. The food menu is similarly upmarket, with a variety of small plates on offer. ✉ *485 5th Ave., at 41st St., Midtown East* ☎ *212/601–1234* Ⓜ *4, 5, 6, 7, S to 42nd St.–Grand Central.*

19

Campbell Apartment. Commuting professionals pack into this Grand Central Terminal bar on their way to catch trains home during the evening rush, but don't let the crush of humanity scare you away—you can have a deeply romantic time here in one of Manhattan's more beautiful rooms. The restored space dates to the 1920s, when it was the private office of an executive named John W. Campbell, and as the exquisite decor suggests, old JWC knew how to live. Sample the good life as you knock back a well-built cocktail from an overstuffed chair. Just try to avoid that weekday evening rush. ⊠ *Grand Central Terminal, 15 Vanderbilt Ave. entrance, Midtown East* ☎ *212/953–0409* ⊕ *www.grandcentralterminal.com* Ⓜ *4, 5, 6, 7, S to 42nd St./Grand Central.*

Galway Pub. This welcoming spot is sought out as one of Midtown's best Irish pubs. Even on a block with a high number of fine drinking establishments, Galway Pub stands out thanks to its gorgeous circular bar, intriguing orange lighting, spirited after-work crowd, and bartenders, some of whom might just actually hail from the Emerald Isle. Snag one of their business cards, too—on the back are words of wisdom from the best Irish writers. ⊠ *7 E. 36th St., between 5th Ave. and Madison Murray Hill, Midtown East* ☎ *212/725–2353* ⊕ *www.galwaypubnyc.com* Ⓜ *6 to 34th St.*

King Cole Bar. A justly beloved Maxfield Parrish mural of "Old King Cole" himself, as well as his psychedelic court, adds to the already considerable elegance at this romantic and essential Midtown meeting place. Try a Bloody Mary—this is where the drink was introduced to Americans. Be warned: prices for a single cocktail are steep. ⊠ *St. Regis Hotel, 2 E. 55th St., between 5th and Madison Aves., Midtown East* ☎ *212/339–6721* ⊕ *www.kingcolebar.com* Ⓜ *E, M to 5th Ave./53rd St.*

Middle Branch. Sasha Petraske's speakeasy-style cocktail bars have expanded into Murray Hill with Middle Branch, a two-story space and former antiques store with no sign outside to announce its presence. Cocktail lovers find the brick townhouse anyway, and inside, linger over small plates, live jazz, and a long list of sophisticated drink options. ⊠ *154 E. 33rd St., Murray Hill* ☎ *212/213–1350* Ⓜ *6 to 33rd St.*

P. J. Clarke's. Mirrors and polished wood and other old-time flair adorn New York's most famous Irish bar, a redbrick brawler of a joint. Steeped in Hollywood lore—Steve McQueen was once a regular, and scenes from the 1945 movie *Lost Weekend* were shot here—Clarke's draws in the after-work crowd that appreciates drinking beer and eating exceptionally juicy burgers around a sense of history. ⊠ *915 Third Ave., at 55th St., Midtown East* ☎ *212/317–1616* ⊕ *www.pjclarkes.com* Ⓜ *4, 5, 6, N, R to 59th St.–Lexington Ave.*

Rodeo Bar. If the honky-tonk music, the bison over the front bar, and peanut shells littering the floor at this neighborhood institution don't clue you in, the rockin' vibe and friendly service will: this is the go-to spot for good times and free live music every night of the week. The Tex Mex food is good (try the Cowboy kisses: shrimp and jalapeños wrapped in bacon) but the real draw is the music. Local bands and touring pros play blues, bluegrass, country, alt-country, rockabilly, and rock 'n' roll. The margaritas are legendary, and the selection of beer includes hard-to-find quaffs like Shiner Bock from Texas. ⊠ *375 3rd Ave., at 27th St., Midtown East* ☎ *212/683–6500* ⊕ *www.rodeobar. com* Ⓜ *6 to 28th St.*

GAY NIGHTLIFE

Evolve Bar and Lounge. Rising from the ashes of a popular gay club on the same site, this glossy, raucous Chelsea-style bar/club gets Midtown East rocking, with its sexy-yet-genial staff and theme nights like Pop-off Thursday, Bulge Friday, and Disco Balls Sunday. ⊠ *221 E. 58th St., between 2nd and 3rd Aves., Midtown East* ☎ *212/355–3395* Ⓜ *4, 5, 6, N, R to 59th St./Lexington Ave.*

Townhouse Bar. It's the elegant yin to the rowdy yang of **Evolve**, which is just across the block at East 58th Street. Distinguished mature men from the Upper East Side meet younger would-be versions of themselves at this "gentlemen's club," which looks like the home of a blueblood with superb taste. The attire is "uptown casual," if not fancier. ⊠ *236 E. 58th St., between 2nd and 3rd Aves., Midtown East* ☎ *212/754–4649* ⊕ *www.townhouseny.com* Ⓜ *4, 5, 6, N, R to 59th St.–Lexington Ave.*

MIDTOWN WEST

BARS

Cellar Bar. Underneath the Bryant Park Hotel—and a tiled, arched ceiling—is one of the more spectacular spaces in Midtown. As a DJ with a taste for classic R&B spins the night away, a fashion-industry crowd gets up to dance—and spills its collective drink. ⊠ *40 W. 40th St., between 5th and 6th Aves., Midtown West* ☎ *212/642–2211* ⊕ *www. cellarbarbryantparkhotel.com* Ⓜ *B, D, F, M to 42nd St.; 7 to 5th Ave.*

Fodor'sChoice ★ **Joe Allen.** Everybody's en route either to or from a show at this "old reliable" on the boisterous Restaurant Row, celebrated in the musical version of *All About Eve*. Chances are you'll even spot a Broadway star at the bar or in the dining room. Still, our favorite thing about Joe's is not the fun show crowd but the hilarious "flop wall," adorned with posters from musicals that bombed, sometimes spectacularly. (Check out the ones for *Paradox Lust*, *Got To Go Disco*, and *Dude*, which was the unfortunate sequel to *Hair*.) ⊠ *326 W. 46th St., between 8th and 9th Aves., Midtown West* ☎ *212/581–6464* ⊕ *www.joeallenrestaurant. com* Ⓜ *A, C, E to 42nd St.*

Russian Vodka Room. Forget **Russian Samovar** across the block—here's where the serious vodka drinking goes down, along with (almost) everything that goes along with serious vodka drinking. The Vodka Room features a glowing, sophisticated front room with nightly piano player (and the superlative Dmitri Kolesnik on Monday, free of charge), a more sumptuous back room, a generous Attitude Adjustment Hour (that's Russki for "Happy Hour"), and more exotically infused vodkas (horseradish! ginger! pepper!) than you can shake a babushka at. For those who crave variety, a vodka tasting menu is available, as are culinary standards like borscht. ⊠ *265 W. 52nd St., between Broadway and 8th Ave., Midtown West* ☎ *212/307–5835* ⊕ *www.russianvodkaroom. com* Ⓜ *C, E, 1 to 50th St.*

19

Salon de Ning. Take a break from 5th Avenue shopping at this glass-lined penthouse bar on the 23rd floor of the ritzy Peninsula Hotel. Drinks are pricey, of course, but what isn't in this neighborhood? The views are worth it, especially from the rooftop terraces. ✉ *Peninsula Hotel, 700 5th Ave., at 55th St., Midtown West* ☎ *212/956–2888* ⊕ *www. salondening.com* Ⓜ *E, M to 5th Ave./53rd St.*

COMEDY CLUBS

Caroline's on Broadway. This high-gloss club presents established names as well as comedians on the edge of stardom. Janeane Garofalo, David Alan Grier, Colin Quinn, and Gilbert Gottfried have all headlined. ✉ *1626 Broadway, between 49th and 50th Sts., Midtown West* ☎ *212/757–4100* ⊕ *www.carolines.com* Ⓜ *N, R to 49th St.; 1 to 50th St.*

Chicago City Limits. This crew touts itself as performing in the longest-running improv show in the city. Heavy on audience participation, the improv shows take place Friday and Saturday (with stand-up comics taking the stage the rest of the week) and seldom fail to whip visitors into what the comics might call a "phun phrenzy." ✉ *318 W. 53rd St., between 8th and 9th Aves., Midtown West* ☎ *212/888–5233* ⊕ *www. chicagocitylimits.com* Ⓜ *C, E to 50th St.*

DANCE CLUBS AND DJ VENUES

Pacha. Maybe you've been to the exclusive Pacha clubs in Buenos Aires, Ibiza, and London. But the jewel in the crown of the Pacha empire may well be here. Assuming you pass muster to enter, you'll find four stories' worth of high-tech fittings (blinding lights, go-go girls, humungous sound), plus celeb DJs and celeb customers. ✉ *618 W. 46th St., between 11th and 12th Aves., Midtown West* ☎ *212/209–7500* ⊕ *www. pachanyc.com* Ⓜ *C, E to 50th St.*

GAY NIGHTLIFE

Posh. Lest you think that Hell's Kitchen has no fine gay lounges, Posh has walls covered in canvases by local artists, trophies over the bar, ample room for kibitzing and dancing, plenty of neon decor, and hours that are "4 pm to 4 am GUARANTEED." Who says nothing is certain anymore in these confusing times? ✉ *405 W. 51st St., at 9th Ave., Midtown West* ☎ *212/957–2222* ⊕ *www.poshbarnyc.com* Ⓜ *C, E to 50th St.*

JAZZ VENUES

Birdland. This place gets its name from saxophone great Charlie "Yardbird" (or just "Bird") Parker, so expect serious musicians such as John Pizzarelli, the Dave Holland Sextet, and Chico O'Farrill's Afro-Cuban Jazz Orchestra (on Sunday night). The dining room serves moderately priced American fare with a Cajun accent. ✉ *315 W. 44th St., between 8th and 9th Aves., Midtown West* ☎ *212/581–3080* ⊕ *www. birdlandjazz.com* Ⓜ *A, C, E to 42nd St./Port Authority.*

Iridium. This cozy, top-drawer club is a sure bet for big-name talent like the David Murray Black Saint Quartet and Michael Wolff. The sight lines are good, and the sound system was designed with the help of Les Paul, the inventor of the solid-body electric guitar, who used to play here every Monday night. The rest of the week sees a mix of artists like Chuck Mangione and the Eddie Daniels Band. ✉ *1650 Broadway, at 51st St., Midtown West* ☎ *212/582–2121* ⊕ *www.theiridium.com* Ⓜ *1 to 50th St.; N, R to 49th St.*

LIVE MUSIC VENUES

B. B. King Blues Club & Grill. This lavish Times Square club is vast and shiny and host to a range of musicians, from the Harlem Gospel Choir to George Clinton and the P-Funk All-Stars. It's also where surviving rock legends like Little Richard, Chuck Berry, and, yes, the still-relentlessly-touring owner play as well. (If you happen to meet Mr. King here, give our regards to Lucille, his guitar.) ⊠ *237 W. 42nd St., between 7th and 8th Aves., Midtown West* ☎ *212/997–4144* ⊕ *www.bbkingblues. com* Ⓜ *1, 2, 3, 7, A, C, E, N, Q, R, S to 42nd St./Port Authority.*

UPPER EAST SIDE

BARS

American Trash. You might tell from the name that this isn't exactly your granddad's UES drinking establishment. Bicycle tires, golf clubs, and other castoffs cover the walls and ceiling, ensuring that the 20-year-old Trash, a sanctum of sleaze, merits its descriptive name. Eight plasma TVs, three video games, a defiantly rock 'n' roll jukebox, and a pool table keep the neighborhood crowd (as well as stray bikers who hate them) busy. Some nights, local bands play classic rock. ⊠ *1471 1st Ave., between 76th and 77th Sts., Upper East Side* ☎ *212/988–9008* ⊕ *www. americantrashnyc.com* Ⓜ *6 to 77th St.*

Fodor'sChoice ★ **Auction House.** This Victorian lounge brings a touch of downtown chic to the sometimes suburban-feeling Upper East Side with candlelit tables, high tin ceilings, and velvet couches. Rap and hip-hop fans should look elsewhere (the only tunes coming out of this joint are alternative and rock), and baseball caps and sneakers are strictly forbidden, as are—at the other end of the spectrum—fur coats. ⊠ *300 E. 89th St., between 1st and 2nd Aves., Upper East Side* ☎ *212/427–4458* ⊕ *www. auctionhousenyc.com* Ⓜ *4, 5, 6 to 86th St.*

Bar Pleiades. The cocktail bar companion to Café Boulud, also in the Surrey Hotel, Bar Pleiades is a livelier alternative to the more staid atmosphere at the Carlyle's Bemelmans Bar. The decor is classic to a fault, employing a black-and-white theme that's positively Audrey Hepburn–esque. Drinks rotate seasonally, and there are tasty nibbles from the café kitchen. Though it doesn't have the same drink menu, the rooftop bar is a cozy aerie good for people- (and skyscraper-) watching. ⊠ *Surrey Hotel, 20 E. 76th St., between 5th and Madison Aves., Upper East Side* ☎ *212/772–2600* ⊕ *www.barpleiades.com* Ⓜ *4, 5, 6 to 77th St.*

Opia. The motto for this upscale-yet-unpretentious bar–restaurant— "If you like us, tell your friends, and if you don't, tell your enemies!"— isn't necessary, given its manifold charms: a drop-dead-gorgeous design, plenty of space for canoodling and cavorting, a romantic balcony (though 57th Street isn't exactly a scenic beach), plus live jazz on Tuesday and Saturday nights. Opia is ideal for couples in full-on infatuation or spouses hoping to remember the wine-and-roses days before the kids. ⊠ *130 E. 57th St., between Lexington and 3rd Aves., Upper East Side* ☎ *212/688–3939* ⊕ *www.opiarestaurant.com* Ⓜ *N, R, 6, to 59th St.*

19

CABARET AND PIANO BARS

Fodor's Choice ★ **The Carlyle.** The hotel's discreetly sophisticated Café Carlyle hosts such top cabaret and jazz performers as Christine Ebersole, John Pizzarelli, and Steve Tyrell. Stop by on a Monday night and take in Woody Allen, who swings on the clarinet with the Eddy Davis New Orleans Jazz Band. The less fancy-schmancy (though still pricey) **Bemelmans Bar,** with a mural by the author of the *Madeline* books, features a rotating cast of pianist-singers. ⊠ *35 E. 76th St., between Madison and Park Aves., Upper East Side* ☎ *212/744–1600* ⊕ *www.thecarlyle. com* Ⓜ *6 to 77th St.*

GAY NIGHTLIFE

Fodor's Choice ★ **Brandy's Piano Bar.** A singing waitstaff warms up the mixed crowd at this delightful and intimate Upper East Side lounge, getting everyone in the mood to belt out their favorite tunes. In fact, the Brandy's scene is so cheerful that some patrons have used this as a musical Prozac, keeping depression at bay. ⊠ *235 E. 84th St., between 2nd and 3rd Aves., Upper East Side* ☎ *212/744–4949* ⊕ *www.brandyspianobar.com* Ⓜ *4, 5, 6 to 86th St.*

UPPER WEST SIDE

BARS

Ding Dong Lounge. "Gabba gabba hey," kids—the CBGB's punk ethos is most alive and well not downtown but way up near Columbia University, at this out-and-out rock 'n' roll bar. All manner of music posters (along with punk chanteuse Patti Smith's actual birth certificate) adorn the walls; the bathrooms are wallpapered entirely with do-it-yourself concert fliers. An exuberant young student crowd swills the many beers on tap, and candles at every table do little to dispel the near-total darkness. Just wear night-vision goggles—and maybe a crash helmet, given how often the DJs really shake up the joint. ⊠ *929 Columbus Ave., between 105th and 106th Sts., Upper West Side* ☎ *212/663–2600* ⊕ *www.dingdonglounge.com* Ⓜ *B, C to 103rd St.*

The Empire Hotel Rooftop Bar. The only thing better than hanging out in Lincoln Center on a lovely night is hanging out a dozen stories above Lincoln Center. Thanks to the radically refurbished Empire Hotel's sprawling new rooftop bar, you can enjoy that pleasure even on nights that are less than lovely. We're talking thousands of square feet here, most of it outdoors, and heated in winter. ⊠ *44 W. 63rd St., between Broadway and Columbus Ave., Upper West Side* ☎ *212/265–7400* ⊕ *www.empirehotelnyc.com* Ⓜ *1 to 66th St./Lincoln Center.*

JAZZ VENUES

Smoke. If you can't wait until sunset to get your riffs on, head uptown to this lounge near Columbia University, where the music starts as early as 6 pm. Performers include some of the top names in the business, including turban-wearing organist Dr. Lonnie Smith and the drummer Jimmy Cobb (who laid down the beat on Miles Davis's seminal album *Kind of Blue*). ⊠ *2751 Broadway, between 105th and 106th Sts., Upper West Side* ☎ *212/864–6662* ⊕ *www.smokejazz.com* Ⓜ *1 to 103rd St.*

HARLEM

BARS

Corner Social. With nearly 20 beers on tap, sports on big screens, and bar food that's anything but boring, it's no surprise that this neighborhood favorite is packed on weekends. In warm weather an outdoor patio gives you a front-row seat to the scene on Lenox Avenue. ✉ *321 Lenox Ave., at 126th St., Harlem* ☎ *212/510–8552* ⊕ *www.cornersocialnyc. com* Ⓜ *2, 3 to 125th St.*

Fodor'sChoice
★

Ginny's Supperclub. Head downstairs from Marcus Samuelsson's renowned Red Rooster restaurant and you'll find yourself in what amounts to a glamorous lounge that seems right out of the 1920s. The cocktails are classic with a modern flair and there is live music and/or DJs most Saturday evenings and some weeknights, as well as a gospel brunch. ✉ *310 Lenox Ave., at 125th St., Harlem* ☎ *212/421–3821* ⊕ *www.ginnyssupperclub.com* Ⓜ *2, 3 to 125th St.*

Harlem Public. A juicy burger, live music, and more than a dozen craft beers on tap makes this the type of neighborhood watering hole every New Yorker wants on their corner. Plenty of stools fill the exposed brick space, along with a scattering of tables on the sidewalk during warm weather. It's an unfussy spot to raise a glass after a day of exploring vibrant Harlem. ✉ *3612 Broadway, at 149th St., Harlem* ☎ *212/939–9404* ⊕ *www.harlempublic.com.*

JAZZ VENUES

Minton's. Welcome back. The jazz institution that once featured big-name performers such as Dizzy Gillespie and Duke Ellington has reopened as a sophisticated supper club with a roster of house band jazz performers and featured musicians. The southern revival food is garnering acclaim (the kitchen is shared with the Cecil restaurant next door). It's not a cheap night out but worth the splurge. Jackets are required for men. ✉ *206 W. 118 St., near Adam Clayton Powell Jr. Blvd., Harlem* ☎ *212/243–2222* ⊕ *www.mintonsharlem.com* Ⓜ *B, C to 116th St.*

19

BROOKLYN

COBBLE HILL

BARS

Clover Club. When the end of the day calls for a stiff drink, you want to be in close proximity to this cocktail parlor. A long, brick-lined bar with leather stools is manned by mixologists with expert opinions on what you should be drinking. Trust their instincts and retreat to a table or fireside couch to happily sip away an evening. ✉ *210 Smith St., Cobble Hill* ☎ *718/855–7939* ⊕ *www.cloverclubny.com* Ⓜ *F, G to Bergen St.*

DUMBO

BARS

reBar. Occupying several rooms inside a former factory, this cavernous industrial space does multiple duty as bar, lounge, indie movie theater, gastropub, and supper club. Sample one of the many beers and enjoy the dungeony vibe under terra-cotta ceilings and antique chandeliers. ⊠ *147 Front St., DUMBO* ☎ *718/766–9110* ⊕ *www.rebarnyc.com* Ⓜ *F to York St.; A, C to High St.*

Superfine. The huge orange pool table is a focal point (it's free) at the front of this sprawling restaurant and bar at the base of the Manhattan Bridge. Rotating artwork, exposed-brick walls lined with tall windows, sunken secondhand chairs, and mellow music (including a bluegrass brunch on Sunday) make this a fun, neighborhoody place to hang out. ⊠ *126 Front St., between Jay and Pearl Sts., DUMBO* ☎ *718/243–9005* ⊗ *Closed Mon.* Ⓜ *F to York St.*

PERFORMANCE SPACE

Galapagos Art Space. Performances here almost take a backseat to the unique architecture of supper-club red banquettes floating above a huge lagoon of water (hold on to your purse!). Thankfully, the theater, music, and performance art is dynamic enough to keep your attention. ⊠ *16 Main St., DUMBO* ☎ *718/222–8500* ⊕ *www.galapagosartspace.com* ⊗ *Hrs vary* Ⓜ *F to York St.; A, C to High St.*

WILLIAMSBURG

BARS

Barcade. Like Chuck E. Cheese for grown-up hipsters, Barcade invites you to stop reminiscing about your arcade-loving youth and start playing the more than 30 vintage arcade games. You'll find everything from familiar favorites like Ms. Pacman to rarities like Rampage. And it's not just about the games; there's also a full menu of small-label beers to choose from. ⊠ *388 Union Ave., near Ainslie St., Williamsburg* ☎ *718/302–6464* ⊕ *www.barcadebrooklyn.com* Ⓜ *L to Lorimer St.*

Bembe. This steamy bilevel lounge is Williamsburg's answer to Miami clubbing, except it's constructed of found items from all over New York, including the old redwood front door from a winery. The crowd is as eclectic as the DJ-spun beats, from reggae to Brazilian, often accompanied by live drumming. The tropical bar menu gives it proper Latin cred. ⊠ *81 South 6th St., at Berry St., Williamsburg* ☎ *718/387–5389* ⊕ *www.bembe.us* ⊗ *Mon.–Thurs. 7:30–4; Fri.–Sun. 7–4.*

Brooklyn Bowl. This former ironworks foundry packs in 16 bowling lanes, a cocktail bar, a music stage, and a restaurant—the food is conjured up by the team behind Blue Ribbon and includes Louisiana-style southern specialties like po' boy sandwiches, Cajun catfish, and excellent signature fried chicken. Hipster crowds congregate over local brews on tap. Weekends means crowds so it can take a while to get a bowling lane but you'll have a blast while you wait. ⊠ *61 Wythe Ave., at N. 11th St., Williamsburg* ☎ *718/963–3369* ⊕ *www.brooklynbowl.com* 🖃 *$20 per lane for 30 min* ⊗ *Weekdays 6 pm–2 am; weekends noon–2 am* Ⓜ *L to Bedford Ave.*

Brooklyn Brewery. Brooklyn was once known as America's brewing capital: at the turn of the 20th century Williamsburg alone was home to nearly 60 breweries. The originals are mostly gone, but this relative newcomer has been bringing hops back to the 'hood since it opened in 1996. Friday-evening happy hour means $5 beers—the Brooklyn Lager is popular, as is the Belgian-inspired Local 1, and there are usually seasonal brews, too. Beer buffs can join a free guided tour on Saturday or Sunday afternoon; other tours are by reservation only. ⊠ *79 N. 11th St., between Berry St. and Wythe Ave., Williamsburg* ☎ *718/486–7422* ⊕ *www.brooklynbrewery.com* ☉ *Fri. 6–11 pm, weekends noon–6* Ⓜ *L to Bedford Ave.*

Pete's Candy Store. A retro feel, friendly crowd, and cheerful bartenders make this a perennial favorite, slightly off the Willamsburg beaten path. The back room, smaller than a subway car, hosts intimate music performances nightly. Hipsters come out for spelling bees, bingo, and the infamous quiz-off contest every Wednesday night. There's a short menu of sandwiches and cocktails but no actual candy. Pete's is also home to one of Brooklyn's preeminent reading series, held on alternate Thursday evenings. ⊠ *709 Lorimer St., between Frost and Richardson Sts., Williamsburg* ☎ *718/302–3770* ⊕ *www.petescandystore.com* Ⓜ *L to Lorimer St.*

Radegast Hall & Biergarten. The perfect alternative if you don't want to trek out to Queens for al fresco Slavic beers, Radegast Hall & Biergarten serves Central European suds and hearty eats under a retractable roof. Schnitzel, goulash, and pretzels are authentic complements to the beer, along with live music on most nights. ⊠ *113 N. 3rd St., Williamsburg* ☎ *718/963–3973* ⊕ *www.radegasthall.com* Ⓜ *L to Bedford Ave.*

Spuyten Duyvil. Only the geekiest of beer geeks will recognize the obscure names of the more than 100 imported microbrews available here. Fortunately for the rest of us, the friendly connoisseurs behind the bar are more than happy to offer detailed descriptions and make recommendations. ⊠ *359 Metropolitan Ave., near Havermeyer St., Williamsburg* ☎ *718/963–4140* ⊕ *www.spuytenduyvilnyc.com* Ⓜ *L to Lorimer St.*

Union Pool. This former pool-supply store is a funky warehouse-like venue complete with a corrugated-tin-backed bar, a photo booth, a small stage for live music, and cheap PBR. The back patio has a taco truck and a fire pit, all part of the hipster-paradise package. ⊠ *484 Union Ave., near Meeker Ave., Williamsburg* ☎ *718/609–0484* ⊕ *www.unionpool.com* ☉ *Weekdays 5–4; weekends 1 pm–4 am* Ⓜ *L to Lorimer St.*

LIVE MUSIC VENUES

Knitting Factory. This concert venue for rock, indie, and underground hip-hop does double duty as a neighborhood watering hole, with a dimly lit bar up front and a small stage behind a glass wall. There are 10 beers on tap, including Brooklyn Brewery's Pennant Ale. ⊠ *361 Metropolitan Ave., at Havemeyer St., Williamsburg* ☎ *347/529–6696* ⊕ *bk.knittingfactory.com* ⊴ *$8–$35* ☉ *Bar daily 5–4* Ⓜ *L to Lorimer St.*

Music Hall of Williamsburg. This former mayonnaise factory is Brooklyn's answer to the Bowery Ballroom and, indeed, it's run by the same bookers as Bowery Presents. The three-level venue with balcony seating has rounded ceilings and walls, which makes for excellent acoustics; no surprise that it draws die-hard live-music hawks. ⊠ *66 N. 6th St., near Wythe Ave., Williamsburg* ☎ *718/486–5400* ⊕ *www.musichallofwilliamsburg.com* ⊴ *$10–$35* Ⓜ *L to Lorimer St.*

19

PARK SLOPE
BARS
Barbès. It's not *quite* like stepping into the funky Parisian neighborhood of the same name, but this cozy bar does have French-accented bartenders, pressed-tin ceilings, and a red-tinted back room. Diverse events range from the energetic Slavic Soul Party performance to classical music concerts. ⊠ *376 9th St., at 6th Ave., Park Slope* ☎ *347/422–0248* ⊕ *www.barbesbrooklyn.com* Ⓜ *F to 7th Ave.*

Union Hall. Comfortably hip is the name of the game at this Brooklyn hangout. Grab a beer in the "library" area up front, cozy up around the fireplace in winter, or if you're up for a little sport, join the friendly locals in a game of bocce ball. In the basement, check out some rising indie rock stars on stage. ⊠ *702 Union St., at 5th Ave., Park Slope* ☎ *718/638–4400* ⊕ *www.unionhallny.com* Ⓜ *R to Union St.*

LIVE MUSIC VENUES
The Bell House. A 1920's Brooklyn warehouse has found new life as the Bell House, a live music venue and events space with vintage details, a dozen beers on draft, and a reasonably priced cocktail list. Expect everything from live bands or DJs to comedy acts to take the stage on any given night; check the online events calendar for details on upcoming shows. ⊠ *149 7th St.* ☎ *718/643–6510* ⊕ *www.thebellhouseny.com* Ⓜ *F, G to 4th Ave.; R to 9th St.*

QUEENS

ASTORIA
Bohemian Hall & Beer Garden. Warm summer nights and cold beers have been savored by locals for over 100 years at the Bohemian Hall & Beer Garden. With pitchers of beer, picnic tables, live music, and Czech dishes from the kitchen, this sunny garden is an ideal spot for getting together with old friends—or making new ones over big mugs of Staropramen and Pilsner Urquell. ⊠ *29-19 24th Ave., Astoria* ☎ *718/274–4925* ⊕ *www.bohemianhall.com* Ⓜ *N, Q to Astoria/Ditmars Blvd.*

LONG ISLAND CITY
Dutch Kills. The dark bar and cozy wooden booths at Dutch Kills—a cocktail den with a nod to the neighborhood's historic roots—serves up finely crafted drinks at a few dollars cheaper than similar Manhattan watering holes. Expect precisely chiseled chunks of ice and skilled bartenders that, with a few queries into your preferences and curiosities, can create a concoction just to your taste. ⊠ *27–24 Jackson Ave., Long Island City* ☎ *718/383–2724* ⊕ *www.dutchkillsbar.com* Ⓜ *E, M, R to Queens Plaza.*

PERFORMING ARTS

Updated by
John Rambow

"Where do you wait tables?" is the not-so-ironic question New York performers get when they say they're in the arts. But even more telling is that most of these toughened artists won't miss a beat when they respond with the restaurant's name. Fact is, if you're an aspiring performer here, you'd better be tough and competitive. There is a constant influx of artists from around the globe, and all these actors, singers, dancers, and musicians striving for their big break infuse the city with a crackling creative energy.

Just as tough are the audiences. Although rising ticket prices have made attending a Broadway show a less common outing for even the most devout theater-loving New Yorkers, that's not true of many other kinds of performances. Whether the audiences are primarily local or not, it's their discernment that helps drive the arts scene, whether they are flocking to a concert hall to hear a world-class soprano deliver a flawless performance, or crowding into a cramped café to support fledgling writers reading their own prose.

New York has somewhere between 200 and 250 "legitimate" theaters (meaning those with theatrical performances, not movies), and many more ad hoc venues—parks, churches, lofts, galleries, rooftops, even parking lots. The city is also a revolving door of special events: summer jazz, one-act-play marathons, film festivals, and music and dance celebrations from the classical to the avant-garde, to name just a few. It's this unrivaled wealth of culture and art that many New Yorkers cite as the reason they're here, and the reason why many millions more come to pay a visit.

PLANNING

DANCE, OPERA, MUSIC . . .

In addition to theater, New York is one of the premier cities in the world for ballet and contemporary dance, opera, and classical music. Start your search by a visit to the websites for the three biggest performing-arts centers: Lincoln Center (⊕ *www.lincolncenter.org*), Carnegie Hall (⊕ *www.carnegiehall.org*), and the Brooklyn Academy of Music (⊕ *www.bam.org*). They all have detailed calendars that are organized by month and season; their listings will give you a good sense of the sheer depth of great performances available in New York. It's also helpful to consider the time you're visiting. Many arts groups schedule their local performances from September through May, with special holiday events planned in November and December. Although the number of performances in many venues taper off in the dog days of summer, the period also brings lots of festivals and outdoor performances, many of them inexpensive or free. Finally, it's smart to also check out the websites of any museums you think you might want to visit while in town. The Frick, for instance, has been hosting world-class classical-music concerts in its 175-seat Music Room since 1939; The Metropolitan Museum periodically stages concerts on its rooftop, or near the Egyptian Temple of Dendur, or in its enviable gallery of musical instruments.

WHAT'S ON?

The *New York Times* (⊕ *www.nytimes.com/events*) listings are probably the single best place to find out what's happening in the city. The *New Yorker* (⊕ *www.newyorker.com*) is more selective; its "Goings On" app lets you filter performances and other events by their location near you. *New York* magazine (⊕ *www.nymag.com*) gives a slightly more opinionated spin on the performing arts. All three publish preview issues listing the major events that will be coming in the season up ahead. The sites ⊕ *www.broadway.com,* ⊕ *playbill.com,* ⊕ *www.theatermania.com,* and ⊕ *offoffonline.com* (for Off-Off-Broadway) provide synopses, accessibility info, run times, seating charts, and links to buy theater tickets.

BROADWAY AND OFF-BROADWAY— WHAT'S THE DIFFERENCE?

There are roughly 40 Broadway theaters in New York, and although you might expect their shows to be the best ones in town, the definition depends on theater capacity, not quality. Per the Actors' Equity union, which determines such matters, a Broadway theater must have at least 500 seats, though most have at least 1,000. Nearly all are within a few blocks of Times Square. A show must be performed in a Broadway theater to be eligible for a Tony Award. Off-Broadway theaters, which are scattered throughout Manhattan, have 100 to 499 seats; Off-Off-Broadway venues seat fewer than 100.

20

BUYING TICKETS AT FULL PRICE

What do tickets sell for, anyway? The average price paid for a Broadway show is hovering around $100; and not counting the limited "premium seat" category (or discount deals), the top ticket price for Broadway musicals is now an astounding $299 (that's for the megahit *Book of Mormon*). The low end for musicals is in the $50–$75 range. Nonmusical comedies and dramas start at about $60 and top out at about $120. Off-Broadway show tickets average $60–$90, and Off-Off-Broadway shows can run as low as $15–$25, or even less if you find a deal. Tickets to an opera start at about $25 for nosebleed seats and can soar over $400 for prime locations. Classical music concerts go for $20 to $100 or more, depending on the venue. Dance performances are usually in the $15 to $60 range, but expect seats for the ballet in choice spots to cost more.

Scoring tickets is fairly easy, especially if you have some flexibility. Always start with the website of the venue or theater company to see what deals and prices are available. If timing or cost is critical, the only way to ensure you'll get the seats you want is to make your purchase in advance—and that might be months ahead for a hit show. In general, tickets for Saturday evening and for weekend matinees are the toughest to secure, and the priciest.

For smaller performing-arts companies, and especially for Off-Broadway shows, try **Ticket Central,** which is right in the center of Theatre Row; service charges are nominal here. **SmartTix** is a reliable resource for (usually) smaller performing-arts companies, including dance and music; their service charges are nominal as well.

Sure bets for Broadway (and some other big-hall events) are the box office or either **Telecharge** or **Ticketmaster.** Virtually all larger shows are listed with one service or the other, but never both; specifying "premium" will help you get elusive—and expensive (sometimes topping $500)—seats. A broker or your hotel concierge should be able to procure last-minute tickets, but prices may even exceed "premium" rates. Be prepared to pay steep add-on fees (per ticket *and* per order) for all ticketing services.

■ TIP→ Although online ticket services provide seating maps to help you choose, the advantage of going to the box office is twofold: there are no add-on service fees, and a ticket seller can personally advise you about sight lines—and knee room—for the seat location you are considering. Broadway box offices do not usually have direct phone lines; their walk-in hours are generally 10 am until curtain.

BUYING DISCOUNT TICKETS

The cheapest—though chanciest—ticket opportunities are found at participating theater box offices on the day of the performance. These rush tickets, usually about $25–$40, may be distributed by lottery and are usually for front-row (possibly neck-craning) seats, though it can vary by theater. Check the comprehensive planner on ⊕ *www.nytix.com,* or go to the box office of the show you are interested in to discover whether they have such an offer and how to pursue it. Obstructed-view seats or those in the very rear balcony are sometimes available for advance purchase; the price point on these is usually in the $35–$40 range.

But for advanced discount purchases, the best seating is likely available by using a discount code. Procure these codes, good for 20% to 50% off, online. (You will need to register on each website.) The excellent no-subscription-required ⊕ *www.broadwaybox.com* is comprehensive and posts all discount codes currently available for Broadway shows. As with all discount codes offered through online subscriber services—**TheaterMania, Playbill,** and **Best of Off Broadway** among them—to avoid service charges, you must bring a printout of the offer to the box office, and make your purchase there.

For seats at 25% to 50% off the usual price, go to one of the **TKTS booths** (⊕ *www.tdf.org*): there's one in Times Square, another at South Street Seaport, and another in Downtown Brooklyn. Although they do tack on a $4-per-ticket service charge, and not all shows are predictably available, the broad choices and ease of selection—and, of course, the solid discount—make TKTS the go-to source for the flexible theatergoer. You can browse available shows for that day online or via a TKTS app, or check the electronic listings board near the ticket windows to mull over your options while you're in line. At the Times Square location (look for the red glass staircase), there is a separate "Play Express" window (for nonmusical events) to further simplify—and speed—things. Times Square hours are: Monday and Wednesday–Saturday 3–8, and Tuesday 2–8 for evening performances; for Wednesday and Saturday matinees 10–2; for Sunday matinees 11–3; and for Sunday evening shows, from 3 until 7. The South Street Seaport location, at the corner of Front and John streets, is open Monday–Saturday 11–6 and Sunday 11–4. Brooklyn hours are Tuesday–Saturday 11–3 and 3:30–6. All shows offered are for that same day (one exception: the Brooklyn location's matinee tickets are for next-day performances only). Credit cards, cash, or traveler's checks are accepted at all locations. ■ TIP➔ Ticket-booth hours may vary over holiday periods.

CONTACTS
Best of Off Broadway ⊕ *www.bestofoffbroadway.com.*

Playbill ⊕ *www.playbill.com.*

SmartTix ⊕ *www.smarttix.com.*

Telecharge ☎ *212/239-6200, 800/447-7400* ⊕ *wwww.telecharge.com.*

TheaterMania ⊕ *www.theatermania.com.*

Ticket Central ✉ *416 W. 42nd St., between 9th and 10th Aves., Midtown West* ☎ *212/279-4200* ⊕ *www.ticketcentral.com* ⊗ *Daily noon-8* Ⓜ *1, 2, 3, 7, N, Q, R, S to Times Sq.-42nd St.; A, C, E to 42nd St.-Port Authority.*

Ticketmaster ☎ *866/448-7849 for automated service, 800/745-3000* ⊕ *www. ticketmaster.com.*

TKTS ✉ *Duffy Sq., W. 47th St. and BroadwayMidtown West* ⊕ *www.tdf.org* Ⓜ *1, 2, 3, 7, N, Q, R, S, to 42nd St./Times Sq.; N, Q, R, to 49th St.; 1 to 50th St.* ✉ *1 Metrotech Center, between Myrtle St. Promenade and Jay St., Downtown Brooklyn* Ⓜ *A, C, F to Jay St.-MetroTech; 2, 3, 4, 5, to Court St.-Borough Hall* ✉ *John and Front Sts., South Street Seaport* Ⓜ *J, Z, 2, 3, 4, 5 to Fulton St; A, C to Broadway-Nassau St..*

20

Best Tips for Broadway

Whether you're handing over hundreds of dollars for a top seat or shoestringing it in with a standing-room ticket, you'll have better Broadway experiences to brag about if you take our advice.

Do your homework. Remember—your friend's "must-see" may not be yours. Subscribe to online newsletters ahead of your trip; you'll get access to show synopses, special ticket offers, and more. If it's a classic play or opera, you might enjoy it more if you've read a synopsis before you go.

Reserve ahead. The TKTS booth is great if you're up for what the fates make available, but for must-sees, book early. While you're at it, ask whether the regular cast is expected. (An in-person stop at the box office is the most reliable way to score this information, but don't hold them to it unless it's the day of performance. If there is a change then—and the replacement cast is not acceptable to you—you may get a refund.) For musicals, live music will always add a special zing; confirm when ticketing to avoid surprises on the rare occasion when recorded music is used.

Check theater seating charts. Front mezzanine is a great option; with seats that overhang the orchestra section, they can be better (though not always less expensive) than many orchestra seats. Book with a seating chart at hand (available online and at the box office). Check accessibility, especially at older theaters with multiple flights of stairs and scarce elevators.

Know when to go. Typically, Broadways shows give eight performances a week. There are nightly performances from Tuesday through Saturday night, and matinees at 2 pm on Wednesday and Saturday and 3 pm on Sunday (on Monday most theaters are closed, or "dark"). Saturday nights and Wednesday matinees are the most difficult. Weeknights are popular with locals. Tuesday is especially promising, and typically an earlier curtain—7 or 7:30 instead of the usual 8 pm—helps ensure that you'll get a good night's sleep for your next day of touring.

Dress right. You can throw on jeans to go to the theater these days, but personally we feel shorts and sneakers have no place on Broadway (at least in the audience). Bring binoculars if your seats are up high, leave behind the heavy coat (coat checks are *not* the norm), and drop bags and packages off at your hotel room in advance—theater seats tend to be narrow, with little leg room.

Travel smart. Trying to get to the show on time? Unless you don't mind watching the meter run up while you're stuck in traffic, avoid cabs into or out of Times Square. Walk, especially if you're within 10 blocks of the theater. Otherwise, take the subway.

Dine off Broadway. Dining well on a budget and doing Broadway right are not mutually exclusive. The key is avoiding eating in Times Square itself—even the national chains are overpriced. Consider instead eating earlier, in whatever neighborhood you're visiting that day. Or, if you're already in midtown, head west to 9th or 10th Avenue. That's where many actors and other theater folk live, and you never know who you'll see on the street or at the next table. Prix-fixe deals and ethnic eateries are plentiful.

THE PERFORMING ARTS IN NEW YORK CITY

Listings are alphabetical by neighborhood.

LOWER MANHATTAN

FINANCIAL DISTRICT

MUSIC

Brookfield Place Winter Garden. Count on this office complex's events programming for inspired musical performances, which have included jazz, gospel, avant-garde, and site-specific sound installations—and a little theater, dance, and film as well. Events are presented within Brookfield Place's spectacular 10-story glass-covered Winter Garden atrium, or on its outdoor plaza, overlooking the Hudson. ⊠ *World Financial Center, West St. between Vesey and Liberty Sts., Financial District* ⊕ *www.brookfieldplaceny.com/EventsCalendar* Ⓜ *E to World Trade Center; 1 to Rector St.*

TRIBECA

MUSIC

FAMILY **Tribeca Performing Arts Center.** This center celebrates theater (with a clever children's series) and dance, but more so, jazz in all its forms. Highlights in Jazz and Lost Jazz Shrines are two of its special series. ⊠ *199 Chambers St., at Greenwich St., TriBeCa* ☎ *212/220–1459* ⊕ *www.tribecapac.org* Ⓜ *1, 2, 3 to Chambers St.*

READINGS AND LECTURES

Poets House. Situated in a bright and airy building near the Hudson River, Poets House has a setting that rises to its theme: it is an open resource for all ages, one that offers a 50,000-volume library and readings and other poetry-centric events. ⊠ *10 River Terr., at Murray St., Battery Park City, TriBeCa* ☎ *212/431–7920* ⊕ *www.poetshouse.org* Ⓜ *E to World Trade Center; 1, 2, 3, A, C to Chambers St.*

SOHO

READINGS AND LECTURES

Housing Works Bookstore Cafe. Amid its collection of roughly 25,000 titles for sale, Housing Works hosts a wide range of literary and cultural events, including quirky readings, sometimes with unannounced surprise guests; journal and book launches; and storytelling or music nights. This cozy store is staffed largely by volunteers, and all profits go toward fighting homelessness and HIV/AIDS. ⊠ *126 Crosby St., between Houston and Prince Sts., SoHo* ☎ *212/334–3324* ⊕ *www.housingworks.org/events* Ⓜ *N, R to Prince St.; B, D, F, M to Broadway–Lafayette St.; 6 to Bleecker St.*

The Jerome L. Greene Performance Space (The Greene Space). New York Public Radio invites the public into its intimate (125 seats), technologically forward-thinking studio for live shows featuring classical, rock, and jazz music; audio theater; and conversation and interviews. It's a great place to get up-close with writers, newsmakers, and musicians and actors who might be playing Carnegie Hall, Broadway, or the Met Opera a few days later. ⊠ *44 Charlton St., at Varick St., SoHo* ☎ *646/829–4000* ⊕ *www.thegreenespace.org* Ⓜ *C, E to Spring St.; 1 to Houston St. or Canal St.*

20

THEATER

HERE. Celebrating all manner of contemporary, genre-bending productions, the original home of Eve Ensler's *Vagina Monologues* and Basil Twist's *Symphonie Fantastique* also houses art exhibitions and a café. ⊠ *145 6th Ave., between Spring and Broome Sts., SoHo* ☎ *212/352–3101 for tickets* ⊕ *www.here.org* Ⓜ *C, E to Spring St.*

EAST VILLAGE AND LOWER EAST SIDE

EAST VILLAGE

FILM

Anthology Film Archives. Dedicated to preserving and exhibiting independent and avant-garde film, Anthology Film Archives is made up of two screening rooms that seat 187 and 75 as well as a film repository, all inside a renovated redbrick courthouse. Cofounded in the 1960s by the downtown legend and filmmaker Jonas Mekas, Anthology remains a major destination for adventurous and unusual movies, new as well as old. The Essential Cinema series delves into the works of canonized, groundbreaking directors; the frequent festivals are more eclectic and may cover under-recognized auteurs, such as a series devoted to the director Edgar G. Ulmer, as well as unappreciated or hard-to-see films of all types. ■TIP➔ This is an experience for film lovers, not casual moviegoers—screening rooms can be hot or cold depending on the outside temperature, and there are no standard movie theater amenities. ⊠ *32 2nd Ave., at 2nd St., East Village* ☎ *212/505–5181* ⊕ *www.anthologyfilmarchives.org* Ⓜ *F to 2nd Ave.*

MUSIC

SubCulture. With its exposed brick, structural pillars, theater-style seating, and an industrial-chic bar, this intimate concert hall beneath the Lynn Redgrave Theater could just as easily be an alternative comedy club as a venue for classical, jazz, and new music. Partnerships in place with established uptown institutions, including the New York Philharmonic and the 92nd Street Y, mean that the pool of musicians is much deeper than it might otherwise be for a new venue. The eclectic performance calendar also finds room for singer-songwriters, world music, and, yes, comedy. ⊠ *Downstairs, 45 Bleecker St., between Bowery and Lafayette St., East Village* ☎ *212/533–5470* ⊕ *www.subculturenewyork.com* Ⓜ *6 to Bleecker St.; B, D, F, or M to Broadway–Lafayette St.; N or R to Prince St.*

READINGS AND LECTURES

Nuyorican Poets Cafe. The reigning arbiter of poetry slams, the Nuyorican Poets Cafe schedules open-mic events and hosts the influential granddaddy (b. 1989) of the spoken-word scene, the Friday Night Poetry Slam. Other performances, including hip-hop open mic nights, jazz acts, and theatrical performances, round out the schedule. ■TIP➔ Line up early for the Friday Night Poetry Slam and the Monday night open mikes; the small venue gets packed quickly. ⊠ *236 E. 3rd St., between Aves. B and C, East Village* ☎ *212/780–9386* ⊕ *www.nuyorican.org* Ⓜ *F to 2nd Ave.*

The Poetry Project. Launched in 1966, the Poetry Project has been a source of sustenance for poets (and their audiences) ever since. This is where Allen Ginsberg, Amiri Baraka, and Sam Shepard first found their voices, and at current readings you might find artists of the same caliber today. Prime times: Monday, Wednesday, and Friday. ⊠ *St. Mark's Church-in-the-Bowery, 131 E. 10th St., at 2nd Ave., East Village* ☎ *212/674–0910* ⊕ *www.poetryproject.org* Ⓜ *6 to Astor Pl.*

THEATER

Classic Stage Company. At the CSC's cozy 178-seat theater you can see excellent revivals—such as Chekhov's *Three Sisters* or Shakespeare's *Romeo and Juliet*—often with a modern spin, reigning theatrical stars, and new scores. ⊠ *136 E. 13th St., between 3rd and 4th Aves., East Village* ☎ *212/677–4210* ⊕ *www.classicstage.org* Ⓜ *4, 5, 6, L, N, Q, R to Union Sq.*

La MaMa E.T.C. Ellen Stewart (1919–2011) founded La MaMa E.T.C. in 1961 in a small Manhattan basement. Since that time, the Experimental Theatre Club has grown continuously, all the while taking risks on unknown works that cross cultures and performance disciplines. ⊠ *74A E. 4th St., between Bowery and 2nd Ave., East Village* ☎ *212/475–7710 tickets* ⊕ *www.lamama.org* Ⓜ *F to 2nd Ave.; B, D, F, M to Broadway–Lafayette St.; 6 to Bleecker St.*

New York Theatre Workshop (NYTW). Works by new and established playwrights anchor this theater's repertoire. Jonathan Larson's *Rent* got its start here before going to Broadway, as did the hit musical *Once*. Works by Tony Kushner (*Homebody/Kabul*), Caryl Churchill, Amy Herzog, and Paul Rudnick have also been staged here. Hit the box office for Sunday night CheapTix; those seats are $20—in cash—as available (advance purchase is recommended). ⊠ *79 E. 4th St., between Bowery and 2nd Ave., East Village* ☎ *212/460–5475 for tickets* ⊕ *www.nytw.org* Ⓜ *F to 2nd Ave.; B, D, F, M to Broadway–Lafayette St.; 6 to Astor Pl.*

The Public Theater. Fresh theater, such as *Here Lies Love*, David Byrne's and Fatboy Slim's "poperetta" about Imelda Marcos, keep people talking about the Public Theater. Many noted productions that began here (*Hair, A Chorus Line*) went on to Broadway. Some shows offer limited-availability $20 rush standby tickets at the box office one hour before curtain (two tickets max; cash only). Check online for available performances. ⊠ *425 Lafayette St., south of Astor Pl., East Village* ☎ *212/539–8500, 212/967–7555 for tickets* ⊕ *www.publictheater.org* Ⓜ *6 to Astor Pl.; N, R to 8th St.*

Theater for the New City. This four-theater cultural complex stages three- or four-weeks runs of new shows by emerging and mid-career American playwrights. The socially conscious group also runs a free summer program of street theater, performed in all five boroughs of New York. ⊠ *155 1st Ave., between 9th and 10th Sts., East Village* ☎ *212/254–1109* ⊕ *www.theaterforthenewcity.net* Ⓜ *6 to Astor Pl.; L to 1st Ave.*

20

LOWER EAST SIDE

FILM

Sunshine Cinema. Talk about busy: according to a *Village Voice* article, this building, which supposedly dates back to 1844, has served as "a church, an immigrant meeting hall, a boxing venue, a nickelodeon, a Yiddish vaudeville house, a hardware warehouse, a graffiti showcase, and an indie-rock playroom." Since 2001, it's been a great neighborhood theater showing a mix of art-house and smaller-release mainstream independent films on five decent-size screens. Great midnight movies, too. ⊠ *143 E. Houston St., between 1st and 2nd Aves., Lower East Side* ☎ *212/260–7289* ⊕ *www.landmarktheatres.com* Ⓜ *F to 2nd Ave.*

THEATER

Dixon Place. Founded back in the rough-and-ready 1980s, this downstairs black-box theater continues to feature worthy, and frequently wacked-out and hilarious, performances. One recent hit was the monologuist and writer Mike Albo's account of what led to his getting fired by a certain very prestigious local newspaper. Dixon Place's popular HOT! Festival of Queer Performance, held in July, is the longest-running LGBTQ festival in the world. Whatever you're seeing, the Lounge, Dixon Place's cheerful bar on the ground floor, is a great place to meet up before the show. ⊠ *161A Chrystie St., between Rivington and Delancey Sts., Lower East Side* ☎ *212/219–0736* ⊕ *www.dixonplace. org* Ⓜ *J to Bowery; F to 2nd Ave.; B, D to Grand St.*

GREENWICH VILLAGE AND WEST VILLAGE

GREENWICH VILLAGE

FILM

Angelika Film Center. Foreign, independent, and, some mainstream films are screened at the Angelika Film Center. Despite its (six) tunnel-like theaters, small screens, and the occasionally audible subway rumble below, it's usually packed; get a snack at the café while you wait for your movie to be called. ⊠ *18 W. Houston St., at Mercer St., Greenwich Village* ☎ *212/995–2570* ⊕ *www.angelikafilmcenter.com* Ⓜ *B, D, F, M to Broadway–Lafayette St.; 6 to Bleecker St.*

IFC Center. Sharing the same owner as the IFC cable channel, the IFC Center shows a mix of repertory as well as first-run independent, art-house, shorts, and foreign movies. Despite the wire-mesh facade, there are still clues that this was once the much-beloved Waverly Theater. ⊠ *323 6th Ave., at 3rd St., Greenwich Village* ☎ *212/924–7771* ⊕ *www. ifccenter.com* Ⓜ *A, B, C, D, E, F, M to West 4th St./Washington Sq.*

READINGS AND LECTURES

Center for Architecture. This contemporary glass-faced gallery hosts lively discussions (which may be accompanied by films or other visuals) on topics like radical architecture in Mexico City or what to expect when you renovate an apartment. ⊠ *536 LaGuardia Pl., between 3rd and Bleecker Sts., Greenwich Village* ☎ *212/683–0023* ⊕ *www.aiany.org* Ⓜ *A, B, C, D, E, F, M to W. 4th St./Washington Sq.*

The New School. In addition to panels that pull in heavy hitters from a variety of trades and disciplines, the New School also hosts readings and films. The results are often incisive and thought provoking, whether the subject is philosophy, economics, fashion, or design. Jazz and chamber music performances are also part of the New School's lineup. ⊠ *66 W. 12th St., between 5th and 6th Aves., Greenwich Village* ☎ *212/229–5600* ⊕ *www.newschool.edu/events* Ⓜ *1, 2, 3, F, M to 14th St.; L to 6th Ave.*

New York Studio School. The venerable New York Studio School hosts two—always free, almost always on Tuesday and Wednesday—evening lecture series on contemporary issues in art. Hear from both emerging and established artists, as well as some of the biggest names in art history and criticism. The school building served as the original location of the Whitney Museum. ⊠ *8 W. 8th St., between 5th and 6th Aves., Greenwich Village* ☎ *212/673–6466* ⊕ *www.nyss.org* Ⓜ *A, B, C, D, E, F, M to W. 4th St./Washington Sq.*

THEATER

Skirball Center for the Performing Arts. This pristine, wood-lined theater on the NYU campus supports emerging artists, with interesting dance, music, and theater events, often in collaboration with other esteemed companies. Conferences and even a circus or two round out the calendar. ⊠ *566 LaGuardia Pl., at Washington Sq. S, Greenwich Village* ☎ *212/998–4941 for tickets* ⊕ *www.nyuskirball.org* Ⓜ *A, B, C, D, E, F, M to W. 4th St./Washington Sq.*

WEST VILLAGE

Fodor's Choice ★ **Film Forum.** In addition to premiering new international features and documentaries that are otherwise hard to catch on the big screen, this nonprofit theater with three small screening rooms hosts movies by canonized directors such as Hitchcock, Godard, and Bertolucci; in-depth film series devoted to particular actors or genres; and newly restored prints of classic works. The small café in the lobby serves tasty cakes and freshly popped popcorn. ■TIP→ This is no megaplex; be prepared for small seats and screens and a cash-only box office (though credit cards can be used to purchase tickets online in advance). ⊠ *209 W. Houston St., between 6th Ave. and Varick St., West Village* ☎ *212/727–8110* ⊕ *www.filmforum.org* Ⓜ *1 to Houston St.*

20

CHELSEA

DANCE

Fodor's Choice ★ **Joyce Theater.** In a former Art Deco movie house in Chelsea, the 472-seat Joyce Theater has superb sight lines and presents a full spectrum of contemporary dance. **Garth Fagan Dance** (⊕ *www.garthfagandance. org*), **Ballet Hispanico** (⊕ *www.ballethispanico.org*), and taut and athletic **Parsons Dance** (⊕ *www.parsonsdance.org*) are regulars on the Joyce's always rewarding lineup. ⊠ *175 8th Ave., at 19th St., Chelsea* ☎ *212/691–9740, 212/242–0800 for tickets* ⊕ *www.joyce.org* Ⓜ *A, C, E to 14th St.; L to 8th Ave.*

New York Live Arts. Formerly the Dance Theater Workshop, this Chelsea space teamed up with the Bill T. Jones/Arnie Zane Dance Company in 2011 and now serves as the home stage for the innovative dance troupe. New York Live Arts also continues to act as a laboratory for new choreographers and artists in residence, and hosts non-choreographed events such as panel discussions. ⊠ *219 W. 19th St., between 7th and 8th Aves., Chelsea* ☎ *212/691–6500* ⊕ *www.newyorklivearts.org* Ⓜ *1 to 18th St.; A, C, E, L to 14th St.–8th Ave.*

THEATER

The Kitchen. Formed in 1971 and housed in its current location, a former ice factory, since 1986, the Kitchen has long been a leading light for interdisciplinary performance art. Expect works by such experimental artist as Charles Atlas, Kiki Smith, Philip Glass, and Elizabeth Streb. Music, visual arts, and dance are represented as well as theater. Literary events are often free; most others can be seen for $10–$15. ⊠ *512 W. 19th St., between 10th and 11th Aves., Chelsea* ☎ *212/255–5793* ⊕ *www.thekitchen.org* Ⓜ *A, C, E, L to 14th St.; L to 8th Ave.*

FAMILY **TADA!.** Vibrant musical theater pieces for kids are performed by all-kid casts. Most shows are on weekends, and children's tickets start at $8. ⊠ *15 W. 28th St., between Broadway and 5th Ave., Chelsea* ☎ *212/252–1619* ⊕ *www.tadatheater.com* Ⓜ *1, 6, N, R to 28th St.*

MIDTOWN WEST

DANCE

Baryshnikov Arts Center (BAC). Famed dancer, actor, and choreographer Mikhail Baryshnikov's longtime vision came to fruition in this modern venue for contemporary performance. Works here are dedicated to movement, which can be as much about theater as it is about dance. The center hosts a range of resident artists, including dancers and musical groups, as well as productions by boundary-breaking international choreographers. The vibrant programming is presented in the center's 238-seat Jerome Robbins Theater and the 136-seat Howard Gilman Performance Space. ⊠ *450 W. 37 St., between 9th and 10th Aves., Midtown* ☎ *646/731–3200* ⊕ *www.bacnyc.org* Ⓜ *A, C, E, to 34th St./Penn Station.*

FILM

Museum of Modern Art (MoMA) films. You'll find some of the most engaging international film repertory around at MoMA's Roy and Niuta Titus Theaters 1 and 2. Many of the films tie in with current art exhibitions upstairs; the Contenders series, which starts each fall, is a chance to catch up on the past year's releases that are likely to win awards, or at least stand the test of time. Movie tickets are available at the museum for same-day screenings (a limited number are released up to one week in advance for an extra fee); they're free if you have purchased museum admission ($25); otherwise they cost $12. ⊠ *11 W. 53rd St., between 5th and 6th Aves., Midtown West* ☎ *212/708–9400* ⊕ *www.moma.org* Ⓜ *E, M to 5th Ave./53rd St.; B, D, F, M to 47th–50th Sts./Rockefeller Center.*

20

The Paris. Across from the Plaza Hotel stands the Paris—a rare stately remnant of the single-screen era. Opened in 1948, it retains its wide screen (and its balcony) and is a fine showcase for new movies, often foreign and with a limited release. ⊠ *4 W. 58th St., between 5th and 6th Aves., Midtown West* ☏ *212/688–3800* ⊕ *www.theparistheatre.com* Ⓜ *N, Q, R to 5th Ave./59th St.; F to 57th St.*

Ziegfeld Theatre. Its vintage is late 1960s, but the Ziegfeld Theatre is as close as you'll come to a movie-palace experience in New York today. Its chandeliers and crimson decor, raised balcony, wide screen, some 1,100 seats, good sight lines, and solid sound system make the Ziegfeld a special place to view anything it serves up. Grand-opening red-carpet galas often take place here as well. ⊠ *141 W. 54th St., between 6th and 7th Aves., Midtown West* ☏ *212/765–7600 for showtimes* ⊕ *www. clearviewcinemas.com* Ⓜ *F to 57th St./6th Ave.; N, Q, R to 57th St./7th Ave.; B, D, E to 7th Ave.*

MUSIC

FAMILY

Fodor'sChoice

★

Carnegie Hall. Carnegie Hall is, of course, one of the world's most famous concert halls. Its incomparable acoustics make it one of the best venues in the world to hear classical music, but it's also strong in jazz, pop, cabaret, and folk music. Since the opening-night concert on May 5, 1891, which Tchaikovsky conducted, virtually every important musician the world has known has performed in this Italian Renaissance–style building. Leonard Bernstein had his debut here; Vladimir Horowitz made his historic return to the concert stage here. The world's top orchestras perform in the grand and fabulously steep 2,804-seat **Isaac Stern Auditorium,** the 268-seat **Weill Recital Hall** often features young talents making their New York debuts, and the subterranean 599-seat **Judy and Arthur Zankel Hall** attracts big-name artists such as the Kronos Quartet and Milton Nascimento to its modern and stylish space. A noted roster of family concerts is also part of Carnegie's programming. ■TIP➔ The Carnegie box office offers $10 rush tickets for some shows on the day of performance, or you may buy partial-view seating in advance at 50% off the full ticket price. ⊠ *881 7th Ave., at 57th St., Midtown West* ☏ *212/247–7800* ⊕ *www.carnegiehall.org* Ⓜ *N, Q, R to 57th St.; B, D, E to 7th Ave.*

The Town Hall. Garrison Keillor's *A Prairie Home Companion* radio show sometimes broadcasts from this historic venue, which was founded by suffragists and built in 1921 by McKim, Mead, and White. Winston Churchill, Theodore Roosevelt, and Bob Dylan have all appeared on stage here; these days it hosts programs that include jazz, gospel, blues, folk, show tunes, political humor, theater, dance, world music, and more. ⊠ *123 W. 43rd St., between 6th and 7th Aves., Midtown West* ☏ *212/840–2824, 800/982–2787 for Ticketmaster* ⊕ *thetownhall.org* Ⓜ *1, 2, 3, 7, N, Q, R, S to 42nd St./Times Sq.*

OPERA

Gotham Chamber Opera. This opera company presents lesser known chamber works as well as new ones in inspired productions, many of them mounted in surprising New York locations, such as St. Paul's Chapel and the Metropolitan Museum. Recent standout works have included a production of Nico Muhly's 2011 work *Dark Sisters*, as well as Marc-Antoine Charpentier's baroque opera *La descente d'Orphée aux enfers*, written in 1686 and never before performed in New York. ✉ *410 W. 42nd St., between 9th and 10th Aves., Midtown West* ☎ *212/868–4460* ⊕ *www.gothamchamberopera.org* Ⓜ *A, C, E to 42nd St./Port Authority.*

PERFORMANCE CENTERS

New York City Center. Pause as you enter this neo-Moorish building, built in 1923 for the Shriners (cousins of the Freemasons), and admire the beautifully ornate tile work that plasters the lobby. City Center's 2,200-seat main stage is perfectly suited for dance and special theatrical events. The very popular Encores! series, held in spring, revisits musicals of the past in a concert format—an event that has led to shows returning to Broadway. Tickets for City Center's annual Fall for Dance festival sell out quickly. ✉ *131 W. 55th St., between 6th and 7th Aves., Midtown West* ☎ *212/581–1212 for CityTix* ⊕ *www.nycitycenter.org* Ⓜ *N, Q, R to 57th St./7th Ave.; F to 57th St./6th Ave.*

Radio City Music Hall. This icon of New York City was built to shortly after the stock market crash of 1929; John D. Rockefeller wanted to create a symbol of hope in what was a sad, broke city. He partnered with the Radio Corporation of America to build a grand theater. When it opened, some said Radio City Music Hall was so grand that there was no need for performances, because people would get more than their money's worth simply by sitting there and enjoying the space. Despite being the largest indoor theater in the world with its city-block-long marquee, it feels warm and intimate. One-hour "Stage Door" walking tours run year-round, but avoid taking the tour during show times, as access is limited. Day-of tour tickets are sold at the Radio City Avenue Store; advance tickets are available by phone or through the website.

Although there are music concerts and other events here year-round, more than a million visitors every year come to see the Radio City Christmas Spectacular, starring the iconic Rockettes. Make reservations as early as possible, especially if you want to attend on a day near Christmas or on weekends. The shows do sell out, but you can usually find tickets until mid-October. Tickets cost a hefty $35–$299 per person for the 90-minute show, although there are often promotions and deals available, especially for nonpeak times. ✉ *1260 6th Ave., between 50th and 51st Sts., Midtown West* ☎ *212/247–4777, 866/858–0007 for tickets* ⊕ *www.radiocity.com* Ⓜ *B, D, F to 47th–50th/Rockefeller Center; N, Q, R to 49th St.*

READINGS AND LECTURES

LIVE from the NYPL. The New York Public Library's discussion series features a rich program of lectures and reading events from the biggest names in books. Most programs are held at the famous main library. ✉ *Stephen A. Schwarzman Building, W. 42nd St. at 5th Ave., Midtown West* ☎ *212/930–0855* ⊕ *www.nypl.org/events/live-nypl* Ⓜ *B, D, F, M to 42nd St./Bryant Park.*

20

THEATER

Roundabout Theatre Company. This nonprofit theatrical company is known for its revivals of classic musicals and plays, including *Anything Goes* and *The Importance of Being Earnest.* Its main stage, the American Airlines Theatre, is the former Selwyn—the venerable home to the works of Coward, Kaufman, and Porter in their heyday. The Roundabout's other Broadway venues are Studio 54, the longtime home of its successful *Cabaret* revival, and the Stephen Sondheim Theatre. The two Off-Broadway stages at the Harold and Miriam Steinberg Center for Theatre show a mix of classics and works from up-and-coming playwrights. ⊠ *American Airlines Theatre, 227 W. 42nd St., between 7th and 8th Aves., Midtown West* ☎ *212/719–1300 for tickets* ⊕ *www. roundabouttheatre.org* Ⓜ *1, 2, 3, 7, N, Q, R, S to 42nd St./Times Sq.; A, C, E to 42nd St./Port Authority.*

New Amsterdam Theater. In 1997 Disney refurbished the elaborate 1903 Art Nouveau New Amsterdam Theater, where Bob Hope, Jack Benny, Fred Astaire, and the Ziegfeld Follies once drew crowds. *The Lion King* ruled here for the first nine years of its run, followed by *Mary Poppins* and then *Aladdin* in 2014. ⊠ *214 W. 42nd St., between 7th and 8th Aves., Midtown West* ☎ *212/282–2907* ⊕ *www.disneyonbroadway.com* Ⓜ *1, 2, 3, 7, N, Q, R, S to 42nd St./Times Sq.; A, C, E to 42nd St./ Port Authority.*

FAMILY

Fodor'sChoice

★

The New Victory Theater. In a magnificently restored space from 1900, The New Victory Theater presents an international roster of supremely kid-pleasing plays, music, and dance performances. Children and their parents can also learn more about the theater process, from playwriting to set design to acting, through the organization's workshops and exhibits. Count on reasonable ticket prices ($14 and up), high-energy and high-class productions, and the opportunity for kids to chat with the artists after many performances. ⊠ *209 W. 42nd St., between 7th and 8th Aves., Midtown West* ☎ *646/223–3010* ⊕ *www.newvictory. org* Ⓜ *1, 2, 3, 7, N, Q, R, S to 42nd St./Times Sq.; A, C, E to 42nd St.–Port Authority.*

Playwrights Horizons. Known for its support of new work by American playwrights, this off-Broadway theater was the first home for eventual Broadway hits such as *Grey Gardens* and Wendy Wasserstein's *Heidi Chronicles.* ⊠ *416 W. 42nd St., between 9th and 10th Aves., Midtown West* ☎ *212/564–1235, 212/279–4200 for tickets* ⊕ *www.phnyc.org* Ⓜ *A, C, E to 42nd St./Port Authority.*

Signature Theatre Company. Designed by the architect Frank Gehry and completed in 2012, the company's Pershing Square Signature Center houses three theater spaces. All tickets are $25 for a show's initially announced run. A central space with a café and bookstore connects the theaters, so come early, or stay late; the café is open until midnight Tuesday through Sunday. ⊠ *Pershing Square Signature Center, 480 W. 42nd St., between 9th and 10th Aves., Midtown West* ☎ *212/244–7529* ⊕ *www.signaturetheatre.org* Ⓜ *A, C, E to 42nd St./Port Authority.*

UPPER EAST SIDE

PERFORMANCE CENTER

FAMILY **92nd Street Y.** Well-known soloists, jazz musicians, show-tune stylists, and chamber music groups perform in the 92Y's 905-seat **Kaufmann Concert Hall.** But the programming is hardly limited to music—its online calendar bristles with popular lectures-and-readings series featuring big-name authors, poets, playwrights, political pundits, and media bigwigs. Also worth the Upper East Side trek here are the Harkness Dance Festival, film programs, and many family-friendly events. ⊠ *1395 Lexington Ave., at 92nd St., Upper East Side* ☎ *212/415–5500 for tickets* ⊕ *www.92y.org* Ⓜ *6 to 96th St.*

READINGS AND LECTURES

Works & Process. Insight into the creative process is what the Works & Process program is all about. Often drawing on dance and theater works-in-progress, the live performances are complemented with illuminating discussions with their choreographers, playwrights, and directors. ⊠ *Guggenheim Museum, 1071 5th Ave., at 89th St., Upper East Side* ☎ *212/423–3587* ⊕ *www.worksandprocess.org* Ⓜ *4, 5, 6 to 86th St.*

UPPER WEST SIDE

MUSIC

Great Music in a Great Space. This organ and choral concert series is aptly named St. John the Divine's massive and massively atmospheric Gothic space. Any music you come to hear at St. John the Divine will likely be an unforgettable experience, but the Christmastime programming of the **Early Music New York** (⊕ *www.earlymusicny.org*) ensemble is especially moving in this space. ⊠ *The Cathedral Church of St. John the Divine, 1047 Amsterdam Ave., at 112th St., Upper West Side* ☎ *212/316–7540* ⊕ *www.stjohndivine.org* Ⓜ *1 to 110th St./Broadway; B, C to 110th St./Cathedral Pkwy.*

Jazz at Lincoln Center. A few blocks south of Lincoln Center itself, this Columbus Circle venue is almost completely devoted to jazz, with a sprinkling of other genres mixed in. Stages in Rafael Viñoly's crisply modern **Frederick P. Rose Hall** feature the 1,200-seat **Rose Theater** (where a worthy Jazz for Young People series joins the buoyant adult programming a few times each year). Also here is the **Allen Room,** an elegant theater with a glass wall overlooking Columbus Circle, and the smaller **Dizzy's Club Coca-Cola,** where there are two sets nightly. It's known for its late-night concerts, and there's also a full bar and restaurant here. ⊠ *Time Warner Center, Broadway at 60th St., 5th fl., Upper West Side* ☎ *212/258–9800* ⊕ *www.jalc.org* Ⓜ *1, A, B, C, D to 59th St./Columbus Circle.*

Merkin Concert Hall at Kaufman Music Center. A destination for both classical and cutting-edge musical performances, this concert hall around the corner from Lincoln Center is a lovely, acoustically advanced 450-seater that presents chamber pieces. It's also a fine spot for jazz, world, and new music. ⊠ *129 W. 67th St., between Broadway and Amsterdam Ave., Upper West Side* ☎ *212/501–3300* ⊕ *www.kaufmanmusiccenter. org/mch* Ⓜ *1 to 66th St./Lincoln Center.*

20

Miller Theatre. Adventurous programming of jazz, classical, early and modern music, and dance makes up the calendar at this university theater. A well-designed 688-seater, this is a hall that rewards serious listeners. ⊠ *Columbia University, 2960 Broadway, at 116th St., Morningside Heights* 🕾 *212/854–1633, 212/854–7799 for box office* ⊕ *www. millertheatre.com* Ⓜ *1 to 116th St.*

PERFORMANCE CENTERS

Fodor's Choice **Lincoln Center for the Performing Arts.** This massive and somewhat fortresslike white travertine-clad complex contains 23 theaters, as well as the Juilliard School, the New York City Ballet, the Film Center of Lincoln Center, and a branch of the New York Public Library, making it one of the most concentrated places for the performing arts in the nation. Its 16-acre campus, planned by the master architect Philip Johnson and built as part of an urban-renewal effort, arose over the course of several years from 1962 to 1969; some 40 years later, it was given a thorough remodel to better integrate it with the neighborhood.

To get oriented, start across the street, on Broadway between 62nd and 63rd streets, at the David Rubinstein Atrium. There you'll find free Wi-Fi, tables, a café, free concerts Thursday at 7:30 pm, and that rarest of NYC commodities, a public restroom. The daily guided backstage tours of Lincoln Center ($18) leave from the atrium; reservations are recommended. In addition, discounted day-of-show tickets for many Lincoln Center venues may be purchased in person here; there is a limit of four tickets per customer, and the amount of discount depends on the performance. ■TIP➜ **Because the box office is closed on Monday, any available tickets for Monday performances are sold on Sunday.**

After its recent renovation, the acoustics in **Alice Tully Hall** are considered to be as wonderful as a concert hall's can be; the hall's primary resident is the Chamber Music Society of Lincoln Center (⊕ *www. chambermusicsociety.org*). **Avery Fisher Hall** is home to the New York Philharmonic (⊕ *www.nyphil.org*); the season is late September to late June. Orchestra rehearsals are open to the public on selected weekday mornings (usually Wednesday or Thursday; $20). A popular Young People's Concert series is offered on Saturday afternoon, four times throughout the season.

The largest hall, the **Metropolitan Opera House** is notable for its dramatic arched entrance as well as its lobby's immense Swarovski crystal chandeliers and Marc Chagall paintings, both of which can be seen from outside later in the day. The titan of American opera companies and an institution since its founding in 1883, the Metropolitan Opera (⊕ *www.metfamilyopera.org*) brings the world's leading singers to the vast stage here from September to May. All performances, including those sung in English, are subtitled on small screens on the back of the seat in front of you. Also resident at the Met is the American Ballet Theatre (⊕ *www.abt.org*), renowned for its gorgeous full-program renditions of the 19th-century classics (*Swan Lake, Giselle, The Sleeping Beauty*) with choreography reenvisioned by 20th-century or

The fountain in front of Lincoln Center is particularly lovely in the evening.

contemporary masters. ABT has two New York seasons: eight weeks of performances begin in May here at the Met, and during the holiday season their Nutcracker is staged at the Brooklyn Academy of Music (BAM). ■TIP→ Check the Met box office Monday to Thursday two hours before performance for a limited number of same-day $20 rush orchestra seats.

The **David H. Koch Theater** is the home of the formidable New York City Ballet (⊕ *www.nycballet.com*), and has an unmatched repertoire of 20th-century works, predominantly by George Balanchine, Jerome Robbins, and Peter Martins. The company particularly excels at short-form programs. Its fall season starts in September and early October, then returns in late November through December for their beloved annual production of Balanchine's *The Nutcracker*. Its winter repertory program runs in January and February, and a spring season runs from April into May. Sharing the theater is a mix of other internationally famous dance troupes.

The **Lincoln Center Theater** complex houses the Vivian Beaumont Theater, the smaller Mitzi E. Newhouse Theater, and the rooftop Claire Tow Theater, which has 131 seats and a small outdoor terrace.

The auditorium of the **Walter Reade Theater** (⊕ *www.filmlinc.com*) shows film series devoted to "the best in world cinema," including silents, documentaries, retrospectives and recent releases, often on the same theme or from the same country. The Elinor Bunin Munroe Film Center has two small screening rooms, a café, and an amphitheater that hosts lectures and panel discussions.

In addition to extensive musical and theatrical holding, the **New York Public Library for the Performing Arts** mounts periodic exhibitions related to major artists and composers. At the library's free *Silent Clowns* series (⊕ *www.silentclowns.com*), held Sunday afternoon in its auditorium from September to May, rarely seen prints of the silent era's comedy masters are paired with live piano music.

Tours of Lincoln Center, including the Met take place daily (✉ *$15* ☎ *212/769–7028*). They do not include backstage areas but do sometimes include parts of the auditoriums. Back stage tours of the Met (✉ *$22* ☎ *212/769–7028*) are held during the performance season. Call or visit the Lincoln Center website for more information. ✉ *62nd to 66th Sts. from Broadway/Columbus Ave. to Amsterdam Ave., Upper West Side* ☎ *212/875–5000, 212/721–6500 for CenterCharge* ⊕ *www. lincolncenter.org* ☉ *Box Office: Tues.–Sat. noon–7:45, Sun. noon–5:45. David Rubinstein Atrium: weekdays 8 am–10 pm, weekends 9 am–10 pm* Ⓜ *1 to 66th St./Lincoln Center.*

FAMILY **Symphony Space.** Although Symphony Space runs an energetic roster of classical, jazz, international, and many other kinds of music, it also excels with many other kinds of art programming. On the literary front, its two halls—the **Peter Jay Sharp Theatre** and the **Leonard Nimoy Thalia**—host a celebrated roster of literary events, including Bloomsday on Broadway, the Thalia Book Club, and the famed Selected Shorts series: stories read by prominent actors and broadcast live on National Public Radio. Plays, films, and Thalia Docs on Sunday (usually a true-to-its-roots art-house screening) round out the adult programming. For the family, turn to their hugely popular **Just Kidding** lineup for a nonstop parade of zany plays, sing-alongs, midday Saturday (and sometimes Sunday) movies, and animation. ✉ *2537 Broadway, at 95th St., Upper West Side* ☎ *212/864–5400* ⊕ *www.symphonyspace.org* Ⓜ *1, 2, 3 to 96th St.*

THEATER

Shakespeare in the Park. Some of the best things in New York are, indeed, free—including this summer festival presented by the Public Theater and performed at an open-air stage in Central Park. The casts are often studded with Hollywood stars—Meryl Streep, Michelle Pfeiffer, Christopher Walken, Helen Hunt, Morgan Freeman, and Kevin Kline among them. The tickets are given out (limit two per person) starting at 1 pm on the day of each show, and always sell out. What you save in money, you make up for in time and tedium—lines are *long*. Plan to line up by midmorning or earlier if there have been good reviews. The easiest way to score these scarce tickets is to register via an online lottery between midnight and noon on the day you'd like to attend; an email response after noon confirms (or denies) success. Making a donation to the Public Theater is one way to avoid the lines and be sure you get a ticket. ✉ *Delacorte Theater, Central Park, midpark near W. 81st St., Upper West Side* ☎ *212/539–8500* ⊕ *www.shakespeareinthepark.org* Ⓜ *6 to 77th St.; B, C to 81st St.*

FILM SERIES AND REVIVALS

Although many of the screens listed here also show first-run releases, old favorites and rarities are the heart of their programming. These gems—which include just about every kind of film, from silent and noir to the most *au courant* experimental work—frequently screen at museums, cultural societies, and other institutions, such as the **French Institute** (☎ 212/355–6100 ⊕ www.fiaf.org), **Scandinavia House** (☎ 212/779–3587 ⊕ www.scandinaviahouse.org), **Instituto Cervantes** (☎ 212/308–7720 ⊕ nyork.cervantes.es), and major branches of the **New York Public Library** (⊕ www.nypl.org). Harlem's **Maysles Cinema** (⊕ www.maysles.org), under the aegis of legendary documentary filmmaker Albert Maysles, is, no surprise, the place for doc screenings, old and new. A reliably creative range of repertory screenings can always be found at **Anthology Film Archives** (☎ 212/505–5181 ⊕ www.anthologyfilmarchives.org), **Film Forum** (☎ 212/727–8110 ⊕ www.filmforum.org), the **Museum of Modern Art (MoMA)** (☎ 212/708–9400 ⊕ www.moma.org), the **Museum of the Moving Image** (☎ 718/784–0077 ⊕ www.movingimage.us), the **Brooklyn Academy of Music** (☎ 718/636–4100 ⊕ www.bam.org), and Lincoln Center's **Walter Reade Theater** (☎ 212/875–5600 ⊕ www.filmlinc.com).

HARLEM

Apollo Theater. Michael Jackson, Ella Fitzgerald, and James Brown are just a few of the world-class black performers who have appeared on this equally famed stage, which first opened back in 1934 and is Harlem's oldest surviving stage. If the Apollo's Amateur Night doesn't get you off the couch, consider its more intimate Apollo Music Café events on Friday and Saturday nights, featuring a variety of underground jazz, pop, hip-hop, and rock performers. In May the Apollo teams up with Harlem Stage and JazzMobile to present the weeklong Harlem Jazz Shrines festival, with performances in venerable nearby venues such as Lenox Lounge, Minton's Playhouse, and Showman's Cafe. ✉ 253 W. 125th St., at Frederick Douglass Blvd., Harlem ☎ 212/531–5300, 800/745–3000 for Ticketmaster ⊕ www.apollotheater.org Ⓜ A, B, C, 2, 3, 4, 5, 6 to 125th St.

BROOKLYN

BROOKLYN HEIGHTS

Bargemusic. Bargemusic keeps chamber music groups busy year-round on a renovated harbor barge that has a fabulous view of the Manhattan skyline from its spot on a Brooklyn ferry landing. Since you really are on the water, you'll probably want to skip this if you're susceptible to seasickness. ✉ Fulton Ferry Landing, Old Fulton and Furman Sts., Brooklyn Heights ☎ 718/624–4924 ⊕ www.bargemusic.org Ⓜ A, C to High St.; F to York St.; 2, 3 to Clark St.

New York's Film Festivals

New York's extreme diversity is what makes it a cinephile's heaven: you'll find dozens of festivals for niche interests and for those just wanting to be at the front end of what's out there. New releases and premieres dominate the festival scene, but the city has its share of retrospective events, especially in summer.

The city's preeminent film event is the annual **New York Film Festival** (⊕ *www.filmlinc.com*), sponsored by the **Film Society of Lincoln Center,** from late September into October. Screenings are announced more than a month in advance and often sell out quickly. Film venues are usually Lincoln Center's Alice Tully Hall and Walter Reade Theater. In January, the Film Society joins forces with the Jewish Museum to produce the **New York Jewish Film Festival** (⊕ *www. nyjff.org*); in March it joins with MoMA to present **New Directors/New Films** (⊕ *www.newdirectors.org*), and June brings its collaboration with the **Human Rights Watch Film Festival** (⊕ *ff.hrw.org*).

The **Tribeca Film Festival** (⊕ *www. tribecafilm.com/festival*) takes place in mostly downtown venues for about two weeks starting mid-April, and features mainstream premieres along with indie flicks, as well as a **Family Festival,** which attracts big crowds for its street fair and movies for all ages.

Fans also flock to other noteworthy annuals like the **Asian American International Film Festival** (⊕ *www.asiancinevision.org*) from late July to early August (usually at the Clearview Chelsea Cinemas); and the **Margaret Mead Film Festival** (⊕ *www.amnh.org/explore/ margaret-mead-film-festival*) and **DOC NYC** (⊕ *www.docnyc.net*), two November festivals that both focus on documentaries for all over.

And for kids, the year-round programs of the **New York International Children's Film Festival (NYICFF)** (⊕ *www.gkids.com*) peak in March with an extravaganza of about 100 new films and videos for ages 3–18.

Summer in New York sees a bonanza of alfresco film; screenings are usually free (but arrive early to secure a space; screenings begin at dusk). The **HBO Bryant Park Summer Film Festival** (☎ *212/512–5700* ⊕ *www.bryantpark.org*) has classic films at sundown on Monday, June–August. The Hudson River Park RiverFlicks (⊕ *www.riverflicks. org*) series in July and August has movies for grown-ups on Wednesday evening on Pier 63; RiverFlicks for kids are at Pier 46 on Friday. The Upper West Side has Summer on the Hudson (⊕ *www.nycgovparks. org*) with Wednesday night screenings on Pier 1. **Rooftop Films'** (⊕ *www.rooftopfilms.com*) Underground Movies Outdoors is more eclectic than most other film series, with shows outdoors in summer on rooftops in all five boroughs. Check their schedule for off-season screenings as well. Summer Thursday nights, check out **Movies with a View** in Brooklyn Bridge Park (⊕ *www.brooklynbridgepark.org*).

DOWNTOWN BROOKLYN
PERFORMANCE CENTERS

Fodor's Choice ★ **Brooklyn Academy of Music (BAM).** BAM presented its first show in 1861, making it the nation's first performing-arts center. Today it has a much-deserved reputation for the unusual and the unexpected, presented in grand-scale stagings. Contemporary dance, theater, music, opera, and cross-media productions mingle here with an array of classics. BAM has three primary performance spaces: the 2,090-seat **Howard Gilman Opera House,** inside a restored Renaissance Revival palace built in 1908; the 834-seat **Harvey Theater,** an updated 1904 theater a block away, at 651 Fulton Street; and the **BAM Fisher,** at 321 Ashland Place, which includes the 250-seat Fishman Space and the Hillman Studio. Every fall the Next Wave Festival fills the house with a global mix of renowned and up-and-coming artists. Every spring brings a top-notch roster of international theater (such as works performed by the Royal Shakespeare Company). Year-round you can catch a movie at the four-screen **BAM Rose Cinemas,** which screens classic films as well as first-run indies, documentaries, and international films. Or, hit the industrial-glam **BAMcafé** for the Eat, Drink & Be Literary series on select Wednesday nights, and free music on Friday and Saturday nights with the BAMcafé Live series. ⊠ *Peter Jay Sharp Bldg., 30 Lafayette Ave., between Ashland Pl. and St. Felix St., Fort Greene* 🕾 *718/636–4100* ⊕ *www.bam.org* Ⓜ *2, 3, 4, 5, B, D, N, Q, R to Atlantic Ave.–Barclays Ctr.; G to Fulton St.; C to Lafayette Ave. (2, 3, 4, 5 to Nevins St. for Harvey Theater).*

THEATER

FAMILY **Puppetworks.** Finely detailed wooden marionettes and hand puppets are on the bill at Puppetworks. Kid-friendly performances like *The Prince and the Magic Flute* come to life on weekends in this 75-seat neighborhood theater. Reservations are required; credit cards are not accepted. ⊠ *338 6th Ave., at 4th St., Park Slope* 🕾 *718/965–3391* ⊕ *www. puppetworks.org* Ⓜ *F, G to 7th Ave.*

DUMBO
THEATER

Fodor's Choice ★ **St. Ann's Warehouse.** This innovative Brooklyn performance space hosts boundary-stretching and imaginative works from all over; past hits have included the National Theatre of Scotland's *Black Watch,* a play about soldiers in the Iraq War; a woman-only production of Shakespeare's *Julius Caesar* set in prison; a song cycle starring Karen O of the Yeah Yeah Yeahs; Noël Coward's *Brief Encounter*; and *Mies Julie,* an adaptation of Strindberg's *Miss Julie* set in postapartheid South Africa. ⊠ *29 Jay St., at Plymouth St., DUMBO* 🕾 *718/254–8779 for box office* ⊕ *www.stannswarehouse.org* Ⓜ *A, C to High St.; F to York St.*

20

QUEENS

FILM

FAMILY   **Museum of the Moving Image Films.** Video art, digital screenings, live musical collaborations, and in-person appearances by moviemaker luminaries join retrospectives and themed repertory such as an Alain Resnais series, Recovered Treasures (from world archives), or Avant-Garde Masters. Daily short films are screened in Tut's Fever Movie Palace, a fab Red Grooms and Lysiane Luong–designed installation. Weekend Family Film matinees make this museum a great choice for kids. ✉ *3601 35th Ave., at 37th St., Astoria* ☎ *718/777–6888* ⊕ *www.movingimage. us* Ⓜ *R, M to Steinway St.; N to 36th Ave.*

TRAVEL SMART
NEW YORK CITY

GETTING HERE AND AROUND

New York City packs a staggering range of sights and activities into the 322 square miles of its five boroughs. You'll probably want to focus most of your visit in Manhattan, but with more time, taking a trip to Brooklyn or one of the other "outer" boroughs (Queens, the Bronx, or Staten Island) is worthwhile.

If you're flying into one of the three major airports that service New York—John F. Kennedy (JFK), LaGuardia, or Newark, which is in New Jersey—pick your mode of transportation for getting to Manhattan before your plane lands. The route tourists typically take is to hire a car or wait in the taxi line, but those aren't necessarily the best choices, especially if arriving during rush hour. Public transportation is inexpensive and should be considered, especially if you are traveling light and without young children. Keep in mind that it's particularly expensive to take a cab from Newark, making the AirTrain or another form of public transportation a better deal.

Once you're in Manhattan, getting around can be a breeze when you get the hang of the subway system. When you're not in a rush and the weather's cooperating, just walk—it's the best way to discover the true New York. Not quite sure where you are or how to get where you're headed? Ask a local. You may be surprised at how friendly the city's inhabitants are, debunking their reputation for rudeness. In the same getting-there-is-half-the-fun spirit, there are water, land, and air journeys that let you see the city from a whole new perspective.

▌ AIR TRAVEL

Generally, international flights go in and out of John F. Kennedy or Newark airport, while domestic flights go in and out of both of these, as well as LaGuardia Airport.

Airlines and Airports Airline and Airport Links.com (⊕ www.airlineandairportlinks.com) has links to many of the world's airlines and airports.

Airline Security Issues The Transportation Security Administration (⊕ www.tsa.gov) has answers for almost every question that might come up.

AIRPORTS

The major air gateways to New York City are LaGuardia Airport (LGA) and JFK International Airport (JFK) in the borough of Queens, and Newark Liberty International Airport (EWR) in New Jersey. ■TIP➔ **Long layovers don't have to be only about sitting around or shopping. These days they can be about burning off vacation calories. Check out** ⊕ *www.air-portgyms.com* **for lists of health clubs that are in or near many U.S. and Canadian airports.**

Airport Information JFK International Airport (*JFK*). ☎ 718/244–4444 ⊕ *www.jfkairport.com.* **LaGuardia Airport** (*LGA*). ☎ 718/533–3400 ⊕ *www. laguardiaairport.com.* **Newark Liberty International Airport** (*EWR*). ☎ 973/961–6000, 888/397–4636 ⊕ *www.newarkairport.com.*

TRANSFERS—CAR SERVICES

Car services can be a great convenience because the driver will often meet you in the baggage-claim area and help you with your luggage. The flat rates are often comparable to taxi fares, but some car services will charge for parking and waiting time at the airport. To eliminate these expenses, other car services require that you telephone their dispatcher when you land so they can send the next available car to pick you up. New York City Taxi and Limousine Commission rules require that all car services be licensed and pick up riders only by prior arrangement; if possible, call 24 hours in advance for reservations, or at least a half day before your flight's departure.

Drivers of nonlicensed vehicles ("gypsy cabs") often solicit fares outside the terminal in baggage-claim areas. Don't take them: you run the risk of an unsafe ride, and you'll definitely pay more than the going rate.

⇨ *For phone numbers, see Taxi Travel.*

TRANSFERS—TAXIS AND SHUTTLES

Outside the baggage-claim area at each of New York's major airports are taxi stands where a uniformed dispatcher helps passengers find taxis (⇨ *Taxi Travel*). Cabs are not permitted to pick up fares anywhere else in the arrivals area, so if you want a taxi, take your place in line. Shuttle services generally pick up passengers from a designated spot along the curb.

New York Airport Service, NYC Airporter, and SuperShuttle run vans and some buses between the JFK, Newark, and LaGuardia airports to Grand Central Terminal, the Port Authority Bus Terminal, and Penn Station, and hotels in Manhattan. Fares cost about $15–$18 one-way and $33–$38 round-trip; those rates are significantly cheaper than taking a taxi if you're on your own, but are probably not worth it if there's two or more of you traveling together. If you choose to use such services, keep in mind that customers' satisfaction with them is very mixed; online reviews often complain of rude employees and significant waits for vans to both arrive and to reach their destinations. In any case, allow lots of time for the shuttle's other pick-ups and drop-offs along the way.

Shuttle Service New York Airport Service
☎ 718/875-8200 ⊕ www.nyairportservice.com.
NYC Airporter ☎ 855/269-2247
⊕ www.nycairporter.com. **SuperShuttle**
☎ 800/258-3826 ⊕ www.supershuttle.com.

TRANSFERS FROM JFK INTERNATIONAL AIRPORT

The rate for traveling between JFK and Manhattan by yellow cab in either direction is a flat fee of $52.50 plus tolls (which may be as much as $6.50). The trip takes 35–60 minutes. Prices are roughly $25–$55 for trips to most other locations in New York City. You should also tip the driver.

JFK's AirTrain ($5) connects JFK Airport to the New York City Subway (A, E, J, and Z trains) and the Long Island Railroad (LIRR)—both of which will take you to Manhattan or Brooklyn. The monorail system runs 24 hours. ■TIP➡ Not sure which train to take? Check ⊕ *Hopstop.com* and ⊕ *Citymapper.com* (or their corresponding apps) for the best route to your destination. Subway travel between JFK and Manhattan takes less than an hour and costs $3.50 in subway fare (including $1 to buy a MetroCard) plus $5 for the AirTrain. The LIRR travels between JFK's AirTrain stop (Jamaica Station) and Penn Station in around 30 minutes, for about $17, including the AirTrain fee. When traveling *from* Manhattan to the Howard Beach station, be sure to take the A train marked "Far Rockaway" or "Rockaway Park," not "Lefferts Boulevard."

JFK Transfer Information AirTrain JFK
☎ 718/244-4444 ⊕ www.airtrainjfk.com.
Long Island Railroad ☎ 718/217-5477
⊕ www.mta.info/lirr.

TRANSFERS FROM LAGUARDIA AIRPORT

Taxis cost $30–$50 plus tip and tolls (which may be as high as $6.50) to most destinations in New York City, and take at least 20–40 minutes.

For $2.50 (pay with a MetroCard or exact change in coins, no pennies) you can ride the Q70 bus to the Jackson Heights–Roosevelt Avenue subway station, where you can transfer to the E, F, M, R, and 7 trains and reach many points in Manhattan and Brooklyn. Another option is to take the M60 public bus to 106th Street and Broadway on Manhattan's Upper West Side, with connections en route to several New York City Subway lines (N, Q, 2, 3, 4, 5, 6, A, B, C, D trains). Allow at least 90 minutes for the entire trip to Midtown, and perhaps a bit more during heavy traffic or rain.

TRANSFERS FROM NEWARK AIRPORT

Taxis to Manhattan cost $50–$70 plus tolls and tip and take 20–45 minutes. "Share and Save" group rates are available for up to four passengers between 8 am and midnight—make arrangements with the airport's taxi dispatcher. If you're heading to the airport from Manhattan, there's a $17.50 surcharge on top of the normal taxi rate.

AirTrain Newark, an elevated light rail system, can take you from the airline terminal to the Newark Liberty International Airport Station. From here you can take New Jersey Transit (or, for a much higher price, Amtrak) trains heading to New York City's Penn Station. It's an efficient and low-cost way to get to New York City, particularly if you don't have many in your group and aren't carrying massive amounts of luggage. Total travel time to New York Penn Station via a New Jersey Transit train is approximately 30 minutes and costs $12.50. In contrast, a similar, slightly faster trip on an Amtrak train costs roughly $35. The AirTrain runs every 3 minutes from 5 am to midnight and every 15 minutes from midnight to 5 am. Note that New Jersey Transit trains first make a stop at the confusingly named Newark Penn Station before they reach New York City's Penn Station, their final stop. If you're not sure when to get off the train, ask a conductor or a fellow passenger.

Coach USA with Olympia Trails buses leave for Manhattan stops at the Port Authority, Bryant Park (at 42nd Street and 5th Avenue), and Grand Central Terminal about every 15 to 30 minutes until midnight. The trip takes roughly 45 minutes, and the fare is $16. Headed from near the Grand Central, Bryant Park, and the Port Authority, to Newark, buses run every 20 to 30 minutes. The trip takes 55 to 65 minutes.

Newark Airport Information
AirTrain Newark ☎ *888/397-4636*
⊕ *www.airtrainnewark.com.* **Coach USA**
☎ *877/863-9275* ⊕ *www.coachusa.com.*

TRANSFERS BETWEEN AIRPORTS

There are several transportation options for connecting to and from area airports, including shuttles, AirTrain and mass transportation, and car service or taxi. New York Airport Service and NYC Airporter run vans and buses between Newark, JFK, and LaGuardia airports. AirTrain provides detailed, up-to-the-minute recorded information on how to reach your destination from any of New York's airports. Note that if you arrive after midnight at any airport, you may wait a long time for a taxi. Consider calling a car service, as there is no shuttle service at that time.

Contacts AirTrain ☎ *800/247-7433*
⊕ *www.panynj.gov/airtrain.*

▌ BOAT TRAVEL

The Staten Island Ferry runs across New York Harbor between Whitehall Street next to Battery Park in Lower Manhattan and St. George terminal in Staten Island. The free 25-minute ride gives you a view of the Financial District skyscrapers, the Statue of Liberty, and Ellis Island.

New York Water Taxi, in addition to serving commuters, shuttles tourists to the city's many waterfront attractions between the West and East sides and Lower Manhattan (including the 9/11 Memorial), the South Street Seaport, and Brooklyn's waterfront parks.

An all-day pass to the water taxi is $30; a similar pass that also allows passengers to visit the 9/11 Memorial as part of their sightseeing package is $32. Another package includes an eight-hour bike rental for $54.

Information New York Water Taxi (*NYWT*).
☎ *212/742-1969* ⊕ *www.nywatertaxi.com.*
Staten Island Ferry ⊕ *www.siferry.com.*

BUS TRAVEL

Most city buses in Manhattan follow easy-to-understand routes along the island's street grid. Routes go up or down the north–south avenues, or east and west on the major two-way cross-town streets: 96th, 86th, 79th, 72nd, 66th, 57th, 42nd, 34th, 23rd, and 14th. Usually bus routes operate 24 hours, but service is infrequent late at night. Traffic jams can make rides maddeningly slow, especially along 5th Avenue in Midtown and on the Upper East Side. Certain bus routes provide "limited-stop service" during weekday rush hours, which saves travel time by stopping only at major cross streets and transfer points. A sign posted at the front of the bus indicates that it has limited service; ask the driver whether the bus stops near where you want to go before boarding.

To find a bus stop, look for a light-blue sign (green for a limited bus) on a green pole; bus numbers and routes are listed, with the stop's name underneath.

Bus fare is the same as subway fare: $2.50. Pay fare when you board, with exact change in coins (no pennies, and no change is given) or with a MetroCard. MetroCards (⇨ *Public Transportation*) allow you one free transfer between buses or from bus to subway; when using coins on the bus, you can ask the driver for a free transfer coupon, good for one change to an intersecting route. Legal transfer points are listed on the back of the slip. Transfers generally have time limits of two hours.

Several routes in the city now have so-called Select Bus Service (SBS) rather than limited-stop service. These routes include those along 1st and 2nd Avenues and 34th Street in Manhattan; the M60, which travels between LaGuardia Airport and 125th Street in Harlem, is due to get SBS service in 2014. The buses, which are distinguished from normal city buses by flashing blue lights on their front, make fewer stops. In addition, riders must pay for their rides before boarding with either a MetroCard or coins at a machine mounted on the street. The machine prints out a receipt. This receipt is the only proof that you have paid, so be sure to hold onto it for your entire SBS trip or risk a ticket for fare evasion.

Bus route maps and schedules are posted at many bus stops in Manhattan, at major stops throughout the other boroughs, and at ⊕ *MTA.info*. Each of the five boroughs of New York has a separate bus map; they're available from some station booths, but rarely on buses. The best places to obtain them are the MTA booth in the Times Square Information Center, the information kiosks in Grand Central Terminal and Penn Station, and the MTA's website.

Most buses that travel outside the city depart from the Port Authority Bus Terminal, on 8th Avenue between 40th and 42nd streets. You must purchase your ticket at a ticket counter, not from the bus driver, so give yourself enough time to wait in a line. Several bus lines serving northern New Jersey and Rockland County, New York, make daily stops at the George Washington Bridge Bus Station from 5 am to 1 am. The station is connected to the 175th Street Station on the A line of the subway, which travels down the West Side of Manhattan.

A variety of discount bus services, including BoltBus and Megabus, offer direct routes from cities such as Philadelphia, Boston, and Washington, D.C., with the majority of destinations along the East Coast. These budget options, priced from about $20 one-way, depart from locations throughout the city and can be more convenient than more traditional bus services.

Buses in New York Metropolitan Transportation Authority (MTA) Travel Information Line ☎ 511 ⊕ *www.mta.info*.

Buses to New York Academy Bus Lines ☎ 201/420–7000, 800/442–7272 ⊕ www.academybus.com. **Adirondack, Pine Hill & New York Trailways** ☎ 800/225–6815 ⊕ www.trailways.com. **BoltBus** ☎ 877/265–8287 ⊕ www.boltbus.com. **Coach** ☎ 800/631–8405 ⊕ www.coachusa.com. **Greyhound Lines Inc.** ☎ 800/231–2222 ⊕ www.greyhound.com. **Megabus** ☎ 877/462–6342 ⊕ us.megabus.com. **New Jersey Transit** ☎ 973/275–5555 ⊕ www.njtransit.com. **Vamoose Bus** ☎ 212/695–6766 ⊕ www.vamoosebus.com.

Bus Stations George Washington Bridge Bus Station ⊠ 4211 Broadway, between 178th and 179th Sts., Washington Heights ☎ 800/221–9903 ⊕ www.panynj.gov. **Port Authority Bus Terminal** ⊠ 625 8th Ave., at 42nd St., Midtown West ☎ 212/564–8484 ⊕ www.panynj.gov.

▪ CAR TRAVEL

If you plan to drive into Manhattan, try to avoid the morning and evening rush hours and lunch hour. The deterioration of the bridges to Manhattan, especially those spanning the East River, means that repairs will be ongoing for the next few years. Tune in to traffic reports online or on the radio (i.e., WCBS 880 or 1010 WINS on the AM radio dial) before you set off, and don't be surprised if a bridge is partially closed or entirely blocked with traffic.

Driving within Manhattan can be a nightmare of gridlocked streets, obnoxious drivers and bicyclists, and seemingly suicidal jaywalkers and bike riders. Narrow and one-way streets are common, particularly downtown, and can make driving even more difficult. The most congested streets of the city lie between 14th and 59th streets and 3rd and 8th avenues. In addition, portions of Broadway near Times Square (from 42nd to 47th Street) and Herald Square (33rd to 35th) are closed to motorized traffic. This can create gridlock and confusion in nearby streets.

GASOLINE

Gas stations are few and far between in Manhattan. If you can, fill up at stations outside the city, where prices are 10¢ to 50¢ cheaper per gallon. In Manhattan, you can refuel at stations along the West Side Highway and 11th Avenue south of West 57th Street and along East Houston Street. Some gas stations in New York require you to pump your own gas; others provide attendants. Across the river in New Jersey, all gas stations are required to offer full service only; turn off the engine and wait for the attendant to help you.

PARKING

Free parking is difficult to find in Midtown, and on weekday evenings and weekends in other neighborhoods. If you find a spot on the street, check parking signs carefully, and scour the curb for a faded yellow line, the bane of every driver's existence. Violators may be towed away or ticketed literally within minutes. If you do drive, use your car sparingly in Manhattan. Instead, park it in a guarded parking garage for at least several hours; hourly rates (which can be as much as $23 for two hours) decrease somewhat if a car is left for a significant amount of time. ▪TIP➔ Best Parking (⊕ nyc.bestparking.com) will help you find the cheapest parking-lot options for your visit; search by neighborhood, address, or attraction.

RULES OF THE ROAD

On city streets the speed limit is 30 mph, unless otherwise posted. No right turns on red are allowed within city limits, unless otherwise posted. Be alert for one-way streets and "no left turn" intersections.

The law requires that front-seat passengers wear seat belts at all times. Children under 16 must wear seat belts in both the front and back seats. Always strap children under age four into approved child-safety seats. It is illegal to use a handheld cell phone while driving in New York State. Police will immediately seize the car of anyone arrested for DWI (driving while intoxicated) in New York City.

CAR RENTALS

When you reserve a car, ask about cancellation penalties, taxes, drop-off charges (if you're planning to pick up the car in one city and leave it in another), and surcharges (for being under or over a certain age, for additional drivers, or for driving across state or country borders or beyond a specific distance from your point of rental). All these things can add substantially to your costs. Request car seats and extras such as GPS when you book.

Rates are sometimes—but not always—better if you book in advance or reserve through a rental agency's website. There are other reasons to book ahead, though: for popular destinations, during busy times of the year, or to ensure that you get certain types of cars (vans, SUVs, exotic sports cars).

■TIP➔ Make sure that a confirmed reservation guarantees you a car. Agencies sometimes overbook, particularly for busy weekends and holiday periods.

Rates in New York City are around $50–$110 a day and $250–$425 a week for an economy car with air-conditioning, automatic transmission, and unlimited mileage. This includes the state tax on car rentals, which is 19.87%. Rental costs are lower just outside New York City, specifically in such places as Hoboken, New Jersey, and Yonkers, New York. If you already have a membership with Zipcar or a similar short-term car-rental service, then consider using them for your car needs in the city.

CAR-RENTAL INSURANCE

If you own a car and carry comprehensive car insurance for both collision and liability, your personal auto insurance will probably cover a rental, but read your policy's fine print to be sure. If you don't have auto insurance, then you should probably buy the collision- or loss-damage waiver (CDW or LDW) from the rental company. This eliminates your liability for damage to the car. Some credit cards offer CDW coverage, but it's usually supplemental to your own insurance and rarely covers SUVs,

minivans, luxury models, and the like. If your coverage is secondary, you may still be liable for loss-of-use costs from the car-rental company (again, read the fine print). But no credit-card insurance is valid unless you use that card for *all* transactions, from reserving to paying the final bill.

■TIP➔ Diners Club offers primary CDW coverage on all rentals reserved and paid for with the card. This means that Diners Club's company—not your own car insurance—pays in case of an accident. It doesn't mean that your car-insurance company won't raise your rates once it discovers you had an accident.

You may also be offered supplemental liability coverage. The car-rental company is required to carry a minimal level of liability coverage insuring all renters, but it's rarely enough to cover claims in a really serious accident if you're at fault. Your own auto-insurance policy will protect you if you own a car; if you don't, you have to decide whether you are willing to take the risk.

U.S. rental companies sell CDWs and LDWs for about $20 to $40 a day; supplemental liability is usually more than $10 a day. The car-rental company may offer you all sorts of other policies, but they're rarely worth the cost. Personal accident insurance, which is basic hospitalization coverage, is an especially egregious rip-off if you already have health insurance.

■TIP➔ You can decline the insurance from the rental company and purchase it through a third-party provider such as Travel Guard (⊕ *www.travelguard. com*)—$9 per day for $35,000 of coverage. That's sometimes just under half the price of the CDW offered by some car-rental companies.

▌ PUBLIC TRANSPORTATION

When it comes to getting around New York, you have your pick of transportation in almost every neighborhood. The subway and bus networks are extensive, especially in Manhattan, although getting across town can take some extra maneuvering. If you're not pressed for time, consider taking a public bus (⇨ *Bus Travel*); they generally are slower than subways, but you can also see the city as you travel. Yellow cabs (⇨ *Taxi Travel*) are abundant, except during the evening rush hour, when many drivers' shifts change, and in bad weather, when they get snapped up quickly. Like a taxi ride, the subway (⇨ *Subway Travel*) is a true New York City experience; it's also often the quickest way to get around. But New York (especially Manhattan) is really a walking town, and depending on the time of day, the weather, and your destination, hoofing it could be the easiest and most enjoyable option.

During weekday rush hours (from 7:30 am to 9:30 am and 5 pm to 7 pm) avoid Midtown if you can—subways and streets will be jammed, and travel time on buses and taxis can easily double.

Subway and bus fares are $2.75 for a single-ride ticket, or $2.50 per ride if you buy a MetroCard for two or more rides or pay with coins on the bus. Reduced fares are available for senior citizens and people with disabilities during nonrush hours.

You pay for mass transit with a Metro-Card, a plastic card with a magnetic strip, which costs $1 but can be refilled. As you swipe the card through a subway turnstile or insert it in a bus's card reader, the cost of the fare is automatically deducted. With the MetroCard, you can transfer free from bus to subway, subway to bus, or bus to bus, within a two-hour period.

MetroCards are sold at all subway stations and at some stores—look for an "Authorized Sales Agent" sign. The MTA sells two kinds of MetroCards: unlimited-ride and pay-per-ride. Seven-day unlimited-ride MetroCards ($30) allow bus and subway travel for a week. If you will ride more than 11 times, this is the card to get.

Unlike unlimited-ride cards, pay-per-ride MetroCards can be shared between riders. (Unlimited-ride MetroCards can be used only once at the same station or bus route in an 18-minute period.)

You can buy or add money to an existing MetroCard at a MetroCard vending machine, available at most subway station entrances (usually near the station booth). The machines accept major credit cards and ATM or debit cards. Many also accept cash, but note that the maximum amount of change they will return is $6, which will be doled out in dollar coins

Schedule and Route Information Metropolitan Transportation Authority (MTA) Travel Information Line ☎ 511 ⊕ www.mta.info.

▌ SUBWAY TRAVEL

The subway system operates on more than 840 miles of track 24 hours a day and serves nearly all the places you're likely to visit. It's cheaper than a cab, and during the workweek it's often faster than either taxis or buses. The trains are well lighted and air-conditioned. Still, the New York subway is hardly problem-free. Many trains are crowded, the older ones are noisy, the air-conditioning can break, and platforms can be dingy and damp. Homeless people sometimes take refuge from the elements by riding the trains, and panhandlers head there for a captive audience. Although trains usually run frequently, especially during rush hours, you never know when some incident somewhere on the line may stall traffic. In addition, subway construction sometimes causes delays or limitation of service, especially on weekends.

Most subway entrances are at street corners and are marked by lampposts with an illuminated Metropolitan Transportation Authority (MTA) logo or globe-shape green or red lights—green means the station is open 24 hours and red means the station closes at night (though the colors don't always correspond to reality). Subway lines are designated by numbers and letters, such as the 3 line or the A line. Some lines run "express" and skip stops, and others are "local" and make all stops. Each station entrance has a sign indicating the lines that run through the station. Some entrances are also marked "uptown only" or "downtown only." Before entering subway stations, read the signs carefully. One of the most frequent mistakes visitors make is taking the train in the wrong direction. Maps of the full subway system are posted in every train car and usually on the subway platform (though these are sometimes out of date). You can usually pick up free maps at station booths.

For the most up-to-date information on subway lines, call the MTA's Travel Information Center or visit its website. The Hopstop and Citymapper apps and websites are a good source for figuring out the best line to take to reach your destination, as are Google Maps. Alternatively, ask a station agent.

You can transfer between subway lines an unlimited number of times at any of the numerous stations where lines intersect. If you use a MetroCard (⇨ *Public Transportation*) to pay your fare, you can also transfer to intersecting MTA bus routes for free. Such transfers generally have time limits of two hours.

Pay your subway fare at the turnstile, using a MetroCard bought from a vending machine.

Subway Information **Citymapper.** Android and iOS apps are available. ⊕ *www.citymapper. com*. **HopStop.** A related app is available for iOS devices. ⊕ *www.hopstop.com*. **Metropolitan Transportation Authority (MTA) Travel Information Line** ☎ *511* ⊕ *www.mta.info*.

▌TAXI TRAVEL

Yellow cabs are in abundance almost everywhere in Manhattan, cruising the streets looking for fares. They are usually easy to hail on the street or from a cabstand in front of major hotels, though finding one at rush hour or in the rain can take some time (and assertiveness). Even if you're stuck in a downpour or at the airport, do not accept a ride from a "gypsy cab." If a cab is not yellow and

does not have a numbered aqua-color plastic medallion riveted to the hood, you could be putting yourself (or at least your wallet) in danger by getting into the car.

You can see whether a taxi is available by checking its rooftop light. If the center panel is lit and the side panels are dark, the driver is ready to take passengers—he is required to take passengers to any location in New York City as well as Newark Airport and two adjoining counties, although only NYC and Newark locations are metered. Once the meter is engaged (and if it isn't, alert your driver; you'll seldom benefit from negotiating an off-the-record ride), the fare is $2.50 just for entering the vehicle and 50¢ for each unit thereafter. A unit is defined as either   mile when the cab's cruising at 6 mph or faster or as 60 seconds when the cab is either not moving or moving at less than 6 mph. New York State adds 50¢ to each cab ride. There's also a 50¢ night surcharge added between 8 pm and 6 am, and a much-maligned $1 weekday surcharge is tacked on between 4 pm and 8 pm. All taxi drivers are required to accept credit cards as payment. Occasionally, some who would prefer cash choose to claim that their machines are broken when that isn't actually the case. If a driver waits until the end of the ride to mention a broken machine and you want to pay by credit card, you may wish to ask the driver to turn off the meter and drive you to an ATM to see if this extra hassle is worth it to him.

One taxi can hold a maximum of four passengers (an additional passenger under the age of seven is allowed if the child sits on someone's lap). You must pay any bridge or tunnel tolls incurred during your trip (a driver will usually pay the toll himself to keep moving quickly, but the amount will be added to the final fare). Taxi drivers expect a 15% to 20% tip.

To avoid unhappy taxi experiences, try to know where you want to go and how to get there before you hail a cab.

■TIP→ Know the cross streets of your destination (for instance, "5th Avenue and 42nd Street") before you enter a cab; a quick call to your destination will give you cross-street information, as will a glance at a map. Also, speak simply and clearly to make sure the driver has heard you correctly—few are native English-speakers, so it never hurts to make sure you've been understood. When you leave the cab, remember to take your receipt. It includes the cab's medallion number, which can help you track the cabbie down in the event that you've left your possessions in the cab or if, you want to report an unpleasant ride. Any charges, such as those for bridges, are itemized on the receipt; you can double-check to make sure you were charged correctly.

Yellow taxis can be difficult (if not impossible) to find in parts of Brooklyn, Queens, the Bronx, and Staten Island. To help with this issue, in 2013 the city of New York allowed car-service companies to convert their vehicles to apple-green Boro Taxis, which act like yellow taxis: they charge the same metered rates, they accept credit cards, and they must take you to any location within the city of New York. The major difference is that green taxis are only allowed to pick up fares in non-Manhattan boroughs and in Manhattan locations above 96th Street.

If you're outside Manhattan and you can't find a yellow or green taxi, you may have no choice but to call a car service. Locals and staff at restaurants and other public places can often recommend a reliable company. Always determine the fee beforehand when using a car service sedan; a 10%–15% tip is customary above that.

Another option is booking a car through Uber, a startup with an app and website that can be used to summon normal taxi cabs, but whose main business is in matching passengers with potential car-service drivers. After booking a car through Uber's app, you can trace its journey to you via GPS, and you get a text message once it has arrived. For this service, you're likely to pay more than for a taxi or a traditional car service—probably at least 20% more, and sometime much more than that, especially during rainy nights and other high-demand times. The app does let you get an estimate on rates before you book, so that you can see if the convenience is worth it. Payment (which includes a tip) is also done via the Uber app.

Car-Service Companies Boro Taxi information ⊕ www.borotaxis.org. **Carey Driving Sucess** ☎ 800/336–4646 ⊕ www.carey. com. **Carmel Car Service** ☎ 212/666–6666, 866/666–6666 ⊕ www.carmelcarservice.com. **Dial 7 Car Service** ☎ 212/777–7777 ⊕ www. dial7.com. **London Towncars** ✉ Long Island City ☎ 212/988–9700, 800/221–4009 ⊕ www. londontowncars.com. **Uber** ⊕ www.uber.com.

▌TRAIN TRAVEL

⇨ For information about the subway, see Subway Travel.

Metro-North Railroad trains take passengers from Grand Central Terminal to points north of New York City, both in New York State and Connecticut. Amtrak trains from across the United States arrive at Penn Station. For trains from New York City to Long Island and New Jersey, take the Long Island Railroad and New Jersey Transit, respectively; both operate from Penn Station. The PATH trains offer service to Newark, Jersey City, and Hoboken. All of these trains generally run on schedule, although occasional delays occur.

Information Amtrak ☎ 800/872–7245 ⊕ www.amtrak.com. **Long Island Rail Road** ☎ 511 ⊕ www.mta.info/lirr. **Metro-North Railroad** ☎ 212/532–4900, 511 ⊕ www.mta. info/mnr. **New Jersey Transit** ☎ 973/275–5555 ⊕ www.njtransit.com. **PATH** ☎ 800/234–7284 ⊕ www.pathrail.com.

Train Stations Grand Central Terminal ✉ 87 E. 42nd St., at Park Ave., Midtown East ⊕ www.grandcentralterminal.com. **Penn Station** ✉ W. 31st to W. 33rd Sts., between 7th and 8th Aves., Midtown West.

ESSENTIALS

■ COMMUNICATIONS

INTERNET

You can check your email or surf the Internet at all public libraries, many cafés and public parks, and most hotels. The organization NYCwireless keeps track of free Wi-Fi hot spots in the New York area, while the JiWire website and apps can help you find Wi-Fi hot spots in cafés, hotels, libraries, parks, and other locations throughout the city.

Contacts JiWire. The same company also makes the apps WiFi Finder (for Android devices) and Free Wi-Fi Finder (for iOS). ⊕ *v4.jiwire.com/search-hotspot-locations.htm.* **NYCwireless** ⊕ *www.nycwireless.net.*

■ DISABILITIES AND ACCESSIBILITY

New York has come a long way in making life easier for people with disabilities. At most street corners, curb cuts allow wheelchairs to roll along unimpeded. Many restaurants, shops, and movie theaters with step-up entrances have wheelchair ramps. And though some New Yorkers may rush past those in need of assistance, you'll find plenty of people who are more than happy to help you get around.

NYC & Company's website (⊕ *www. nycgo.com*) has information on the accessibility of many landmarks and attractions, as well as a downloadable guide. Big Apple Greeter's Access Program offers tours of New York City tailored to visitors' personal preferences. If you need to rent a wheelchair or a scooter while you are in New York, Scootaround will deliver it to your hotel or another location, and reservations can be made up to a year in advance.

Local Resources Big Apple Greeter ☎ *212/669-8159* ⊕ *www.bigapplegreeter. org.* **NYC & Company** ⊕ *www.nycgo.com/ accessibility.* **Scootaround** ☎ *888/441-7575* ⊕ *www.scootaround.com/rentals/n/newyork.*

LODGING

Despite the Americans with Disabilities Act, the definition of accessibility seems to differ from hotel to hotel. Some properties may be accessible by ADA standards for people with mobility problems but not for people with hearing or vision impairments, for example.

If you have mobility problems, ask for the lowest floor on which accessible services are offered. If you have a hearing impairment, check whether the hotel has devices to alert you visually to the ring of the telephone, a knock at the door, and a fire/emergency alarm. Some hotels provide these devices without charge. Discuss your needs with hotel personnel if this equipment isn't available, so that a staff member can personally alert you in the event of an emergency.

If you're bringing a guide dog, get authorization ahead of time and write down the name of the person with whom you spoke.

RESERVATIONS

When discussing accessibility with an operator or reservations agent, ask hard questions. Are there any stairs, inside *or* out? Are there grab bars next to the toilet *and* in the shower/tub? How wide is the doorway to the room? To the bathroom? For the most extensive facilities meeting the latest legal specifications, opt for newer accommodations. If you reserve through a toll-free number, consider also calling the hotel's local number to confirm the information from the central reservations office. Get confirmation in writing when you can.

SIGHTS AND ATTRACTIONS

Most public facilities in New York City, whether museums, parks, or theaters, are wheelchair-accessible. Some attractions have tours or programs for people with mobility, sight, or hearing impairments.

TRANSPORTATION

Although the city is working to retrofit stations to comply with the ADA, not all stations are accessible and they are unlikely to be in the near future. Accessible stations are clearly marked on subway and rail maps. Visitors in wheelchairs will have better success with public buses, all of which have wheelchair lifts and "kneelers" at the front to facilitate getting on and off. Bus drivers will provide assistance.

Reduced fares are available to disabled passengers; if you're paying with cash, you will need to present a Medicare card or Paratransit card. You may also apply for a Temporary Reduced Fare Metro-Card in advance of your visit. Visitors to the city are also eligible for the same Access-a-Ride program benefits as New York City residents. Drivers with disabilities may use windshield cards from their own state or Canadian province to park in designated handicapped spaces.

The U.S. Department of Transportation Aviation Consumer Protection Division's online publication *New Horizons: Information for the Air Traveler with a Disability* offers advice for travelers with a disability, and outlines basic rights. Visit ⊕ *www.disability.gov* for general information.

Information and Complaints
Reduced Fare MetroCard ☎ 511 ⊕ www.mta. info/accessibility/transit.htm. **U.S. Department of Transportation Aviation Consumer and Protection** ⊕ airconsumer.dot.gov/ publications/horizons.htm.

▌ GAY AND LESBIAN TRAVEL

Attitudes toward same-sex couples are very tolerant in Manhattan and most other parts of the city. Hell's Kitchen, Chelsea, and (to a lesser degree) Greenwich Village are the most prominently gay neighborhoods, but gay men and lesbians feel right at home almost everywhere. The world's oldest gay-pride parade takes place on 5th Avenue the last Sunday in June.

PUBLICATIONS

For listings of gay events and places, check out *Next*, which is online and also distributed in many gay bars throughout Manhattan. The magazines *New York, Paper,* and *Time Out New York* have a gay-friendly take on what's happening in the city, as do most other local publications.

Gay Publications
Gay City News ⊕ www.gaycitynews.com. *Next* ⊕ www.nextmagazine.com.

Local Information Lesbian, Gay, Bisexual & Transgender Community Center (*The Center*). ✉ 208 W. 13th St., between 7th and 8th Aves., Greenwich Village ☎ 212/620-7310 ⊕ www.gaycenter.org.

▌ KIDS IN NEW YORK

For listings of children's events, consult *New York* magazine and other local media. The Friday *New York Times* Arts section also includes children's activities. Other good sources on happenings for youngsters are the websites NYMetroParents and New York Family (and their respective magazines). If you have access to cable television, check the local all-news channel New York 1, where you'll find a spot aired several times daily that covers current and noteworthy children's events. *Fodor's Around New York City with Kids* (available in bookstores everywhere) can help you plan your days together.

New York magazine ⊕ nymag.com/ family/kids. **NY Metro Parents** ⊕ www. nymetroparents.com. **Time Out New York** ⊕ www.timeout.com/new-york-kids.

LODGING

Before you consider using a cot or fold-out couch for your child, ask just how large your hotel room is—New York City rooms are usually small. Most hotels in New York allow children under a certain age to stay in their parents' room at no extra charge, but others charge for them as extra adults; be sure to find out the cutoff age for children's discounts.

PUBLIC TRANSPORTATION

Children shorter than 44 inches (about 1.1 meters) ride for free on MTA buses and subways. If you're pushing a stroller, don't struggle through a subway turnstile; ask the station agent to buzz you through the gate (the attendant will ask you to swipe your MetroCard through the turnstile nearest the gate). Keep a sharp eye on young ones while in the subway; at some stations there is a gap between the train doors and the platform.

▌ MONEY

In New York, it's easy to get swept up in a debt-inducing cyclone of $60-per-person dinners, $120 theater tickets, $20 nightclub covers, and $300 hotel rooms. But one of the good things about the city is that you can spend in some areas and save in others. Within Manhattan, a cup of coffee can cost from 75¢ to $4, a pint of beer from $5 to $8, and a sandwich from $7 to $10. Generally, prices in the outer boroughs are lower than those in Manhattan.

The most generously bequeathed treasure of the city is the arts. The stated admission fee at the Metropolitan Museum of Art is a suggestion; you can donate a lesser amount and not be snubbed. Many other museums in town have special times during which admission is free. The Museum of Modern Art, for instance, is free on Friday from 4 to 8. In summer a handful of free music, theater, and dance performances, as well as films (usually screened outdoors), fill the calendar each day.

Prices throughout this guide are given for adults. Substantially reduced fees are typically available for children, students, and senior citizens.

CREDIT CARDS

Record all your credit card numbers—as well as the phone numbers to call if your cards are lost or stolen—in a safe place, so you're prepared should something go wrong. Both MasterCard and Visa have general numbers you can call if your card is lost, but you're better off calling the number of your issuing bank, since MasterCard and Visa usually just transfer you anyway. Your bank's number is typically printed on your card.

Reporting Lost Cards
American Express ☎ 800/528-4800 in U.S. ⊕ www.americanexpress.com. **Diners Club** ☎ 800/234-6377 ⊕ www.dinersclub.com. **Discover** ☎ 800/347-2683 in U.S. ⊕ www.discovercard.com. **MasterCard** ☎ 800/627-8372 ⊕ www.mastercard.com. **Visa** ☎ 800/847-2911 ⊕ www.visa.com.

▌ RESTROOMS

Public restrooms in New York are few and far between. If you find yourself in need of a restroom, head for Midtown department stores, museums, or the lobbies of large hotels to find the cleanest bathrooms. Public atriums, such as those at the Citicorp Center and Trump Tower, also provide good public facilities, as do Bryant Park and the many Starbucks coffee shops in the city. If you're in the area, the Times Square Information Center, on Broadway between 46th and 47th streets, can be a godsend.

Restaurants usually allow only patrons to use their restrooms, but if you're dressed well and look as if you belong, you can often just sail right in. And if you're too self-conscious for this brand of nonchalance, just ask the host or hostess nicely. Be aware that cinemas, Broadway theaters, and concert halls have limited amenities, and there are often long lines before performances and during intermissions.

Find a Loo The Bathroom Diaries. This website is flush with unsanitized info on restrooms the world over—each one located, reviewed, and rated. ⊕ www.thebathroomdiaries.com.

▌ SAFETY

New York City is one of the safest large cities in the country. However, do not let yourself be lulled into a false sense of security. As in any large city, travelers in New York remain particularly easy marks for pickpockets and hustlers.

After the September 11, 2001, terrorist attacks security was heightened throughout the city. Never leave any bags unattended, and expect to have yourself and your possessions inspected thoroughly in such places as airports, sports stadiums, museums, city buildings, and sometimes even subway stations.

Ignore the panhandlers on the streets and subways, people who offer to hail you a cab (they often appear at Penn Station, the Port Authority, and Grand Central), and limousine and gypsy-cab drivers who (illegally) offer you a ride.

Keep jewelry out of sight on the street; better yet, leave valuables at home. Don't carry wallets, smartphones, or other gadgets in your back pockets, and make sure bags and purses stay closed.

Avoid deserted blocks in unfamiliar neighborhoods. A brisk, purposeful pace helps deter trouble wherever you go.

The subway runs around the clock and is generally well trafficked until midnight (and until at least 2 am on Friday and Saturday nights), and overall it is very safe. If you do take the subway late at night, ride in the center car, with the conductor. Watch out for unsavory characters lurking around the inside or outside of stations.

When waiting for a train, head to the center of the platform, and stand far away from its edge, especially when trains are entering or leaving the station. Once the train pulls into the station, avoid empty cars. While on the train, don't engage in verbal exchanges with aggressive riders. If a fellow passenger makes you nervous while on the train, trust your instincts and change cars. When disembarking, stick with the crowd until you reach the street.

THE FODORS.COM CONNECTION

Before your trip, be sure to check out what fellow travelers are saying in Talk on ⊕ www.fodors.com.

Travelers Aid International helps crime victims, stranded travelers, and wayward children, and works closely with the police.

▌TIP➔ Distribute your cash, credit cards, IDs, and other valuables between a deep front pocket, an inside jacket or vest pocket, and a hidden money pouch. Don't reach for the money pouch once you're in public.

Information Travelers Aid International ✉ JFK International Airport, Terminal 4, Queens ☎ 718/656–4870 ⊕ jfk.travelersaid.org ✉ Newark International Airport, Newark, New Jersey ☎ 973/623–5052 ⊕ www.travelersaid.org.

▌ SENIOR-CITIZEN TRAVEL

The Metropolitan Transportation Authority (MTA) offers lower fares for passengers 65 and over.

To qualify for age-related discounts, mention your senior-citizen status up front when booking hotel reservations (not when checking out). Be sure to have identification on hand. When renting a car, ask about promotional car-rental discounts, which can be cheaper than senior-citizen rates.

▌ SPORTS AND THE OUTDOORS

The City of New York's Parks & Recreation division lists all of the recreational facilities and activities available through New York's Parks Department. The *New York Times*'s sports section lists upcoming events, times, dates, and ticket information.

Contact Information Department of Parks & Recreation ☎ 311 in New York City, 212/639–9675 ⊕ www.nycgovparks.org.

BASEBALL

The subway will get you directly to the stadiums of both New York–area major-league teams: the New York Mets play at Citi Field, at the next-to-last stop on the 7 train in Queens, while the Yankees defend their turf at Yankee Stadium in the Bronx, accessible via the B, D, or 4 trains. Affiliated with the Mets, the minor-league Brooklyn Cyclones are named for Coney Island's famous wooden roller coaster. They play 38 home games at KeySpan Park, next to the boardwalk, with views of the Atlantic over the right-field wall and views of historic Astroland over the left-field wall. Most people make a day of it, with time at the beach and amusement rides before an evening game. Take the D, F, or Q subway to the end of the line, and walk one block to the right of the original Nathan's Famous hot dog stand.

For another fun, family-oriented experience, check out the Staten Island Yankees, one of New York's minor-league teams, which warms up many future New York Yankees players. The stadium, a five-minute walk from the Staten Island Ferry terminal, has magnificent views of Lower Manhattan and the Statue of Liberty.

Contact Information Brooklyn Cyclones
✉ *MCU Park, 1904 Surf Ave., at 19th St., Coney Island, Brooklyn* ☎ *718/449–8497* ⊕ *www. brooklyncyclones.com* Ⓜ *D, F, N, Q to Stillwell Ave.* **New York Mets** ✉ *123–01 Roosevelt Ave., off Grand Central Pkwy., Flushing, Queens* ☎ *718/507–8499* ⊕ *www.mets.com* Ⓜ *7 to Mets/Willets Pt.* **New York Yankees** ✉ *Yankee Stadium, 1 E. 161st St., at River Ave., Bronx* ☎ *718/293–6000* ⊕ *www.yankees.com* Ⓜ *B, D, 4 to 161st St.–Yankee Stadium, or some Metro-North Hudson Line trains.* **Staten Island Yankees** ✉ *Richmond County Bank Ballpark, 75 Richmond Terr., St. George, Staten Island* ☎ *718/720–9265* ⊕ *www.siyanks.com.*

BASKETBALL

The New York Knicks arouse intense hometown passions, which means tickets for home games at Madison Square Garden are hard to come by. Try StubHub to score tickets. The Brooklyn Nets are across the river, in the swanky Barclays Center. The stadium is easily reachable by nine different subway lines. The men's basketball season runs from late October through April. The New York Liberty, a member of the Women's NBA, had its first season in 1997. The season runs from mid-May through August, with home games played once again at Madison Square Garden after several years of being in New Jersey.

If the professional games are sold out, try to attend a college game, where New York stalwarts Fordham, Hofstra, and St. John's compete against national top 25 teams during invitational tournaments.

Contact Information Brooklyn Nets
✉ *Barclays Center, 620 Atlantic Ave., at Flatbush Ave., Prospect Heights, Brooklyn* ☎ *917/618–6700 for box office* ⊕ *www.nba. com/nets* Ⓜ *2, 3, 4, 5, B, D, N, Q, R to Atlantic Avenue–Barclays Center.* **Madison Square Garden** ✉ *4 Pennsylvania Plaza, near W. 32nd St. and 6th Ave.* ☎ *212/465–6741* ⊕ *www.msg. com* Ⓜ *1, 2, 3 to 34th St.–Penn Station.* **New York Knicks** ☎ *212/465–5867* ⊕ *www.nba. com/knicks.* **New York Liberty** ☎ *212/465–6766 for tickets, 212/564–9622 for fan hotline* ⊕ *www.wnba.com/liberty.*

BICYCLING

In the past couple years, bicycling the streets of Manhattan and many parts of Brooklyn has become more and more mainstream, and much less the sole province of bike messengers and zealots. The city government and biking organizations have both helped make it safer than it had been for decades, and drivers and pedestrians are more aware that bikes are likely to be on the road, too. Check the Department of Transportation's website for a cycling map that maps the best routes, including roads with designated bike lanes, as well as local road rules, including rules for taking a bike on public transit.

For biking under more controlled conditions, head to New York's major parks. Central Park has a 6-mile circular drive with a couple of decent climbs. It's closed to car traffic from 10 am to 3 pm (except the southeast portion between 6th Avenue and East 72nd Street) and 7 pm to 7 am on weekdays, and from 7 pm Friday to 7 am Monday. On holidays it's closed to car traffic from 7 pm the night before until 7 am the day after.

The bike lane along the Hudson River Park's esplanade parallels the waterfront from West 59th Street south to the esplanade of Battery Park City. The lane also heads north, connecting with the bike path in Riverside Park and the promenade between West 72nd and West 110th streets, and continuing all the way to the George Washington Bridge. A two-way bike lane runs along the park's Terrace Drive, a popular route across the park at 72nd Street. From Battery Park it's a quick ride to the Wall Street area, which is deserted on weekends, and over to South Street and a bike lane along the East River.

The 3.3-mile circular drive in Brooklyn's Prospect Park is closed to cars year-round except from 7 am to 9 am (on the northbound East Drive) and 5 pm to 7 pm (on the southbound West Drive) on weekdays. It has a long, gradual hill that tops off near the Grand Army Plaza entrance.

Bike Rentals Bicycles NYC ✉ *1400 3rd Ave., between 79th and 80th Sts., Upper East Side* ☎ *212/794–2929* ⊕ *www.bicyclesnyc.com* Ⓜ *4, 5, 6 to 86th St.* **Bicycle Rentals at Loeb Boathouse** ✉ *Midpark near E. 74th St., Central Park* ☎ *212/517–2233* ⊕ *www.centralparknyc. org* ☾ *Apr.–Nov., weekdays 10–6, weekends 9–6* Ⓜ *6 to 68th St./Hunter College.* **Pedal Pusher Bike Shop** ✉ *1306 2nd Ave., at 69th St., Upper East Side* ☎ *212/288–5592* ⊕ *www. pedalpusherbikeshop.com* Ⓜ *6 to 68th St./ Hunter College.* **Toga Bike Shop** ✉ *110 West End Ave., at 64th St., Upper West Side* ☎ *212/799–9625* ⊕ *togabikes.wix.com/toga* Ⓜ *1 to 66th St.*

CITI BIKE BICYCLING SHARE

New York's bike-sharing program debuted in 2013 with hundreds of stations, the majority in Manhattan south of Central Park, and some others scattered in a few neighborhoods in Brooklyn and Queens. The three-speed, 40-pound, bright-blue bikes, which are either charming or clunky depending on your perspective, are outfitted with lights and bungee cords to secure small bags and other items. They don't come with helmets, though: wearing one is recommended but not mandatory.

After buying a Citi Bike pass, you are able to borrow an unlimited number of the bikes for either 24 hours ($9.95) or 7 days ($25). What is limited is your time with a particular bike—the time between unlocking a bike at one station at returning it to another must be 30 minutes or under, or you'll face additional charges, and these overtime charges add up quickly (all the way to $1,200 for never returning a bike at all). As soon as you return one bike, you're free to get another—even one from the same location.

Before you pull a bike from one of the bays and start the 30-minute clock running, spend a little time planning your route. City Bike's apps are helpful with this, because they show which of the computerized outdoor stations have bikes available, and—just as important—which have empty bays available for when it's time to return your bike.

Contact Information Citi Bike. The Citi Bike website and apps, for Android and iOS operating systems, will help you locate nearby bike stations and the best route to reach destinations. ☎ *855/2453–311 for customer service* ⊕ *www.citibikenyc.com.*

GROUP BIKE RIDES

Bike New York runs a 40-mile, five-borough bike ride the first Sunday in May. The Five Borough Bicycle Club organizes day and weekend rides. The New York Cycle Club sponsors weekend rides for every level of ability. Time's Up!, a nonprofit advocacy group, leads free recreational rides at least twice a month for cyclists as well as skaters; the Central Park Moonlight Ride, departing from Columbus Circle at 10 pm the first Friday of every month, is a favorite.

Contact Information Bike New York ☎ 212/870–2080 ⊕ www.bikenewyork.org. **Five Borough Bike Club** ☎ 347/688–2925 ⊕ www.5bbc.org. **New York Cycle Club** ⊕ www.nycc.org. **Time's Up!** ☎ 212/802–8222 ⊕ www.times-up.org.

BOATING AND KAYAKING

Central Park has rowboats (plus one Venetian gondola for glides in the moonlight) on the 22-acre Central Park Lake. Rent your rowboat, which holds up to four people, at Loeb Boathouse, near East 74th Street, from April through November ($12 an hour); gondola rides are available only in summer and can be reserved ($30 per half hour); they hold up to six people.

In summer at the Pier 96 Boathouse in Midtown West, you can take a sturdy kayak out for a paddle for free on weekends and weekday evenings from mid-May through mid-October. Pier 40, in the West Village, and the pier at West 72nd Street have similar schedules. Beginners learn to paddle close to shore until they feel ready to venture farther out into open water. More experienced kayakers can partake in the three-hour trips conducted every weekend and on holiday mornings. Because of high demand, there is a lottery to determine who gets to go out each morning; to be entered, you must be at the pier to sign up before 8 am. No reservations are taken in advance. Manhattan Kayak Company gives kayak and stand-up paddleboard (aka SUP) lessons for all levels and runs trips on the Hudson River between May and late September, including a fun New York After Dark tour for $80.

Contact Information
Loeb Boathouse ✉ Midpark near E. 74th St., Central Park ☎ 212/517–2233 ⊕ www. thecentralparkboathouse.com/boats.php Ⓜ 6 to 68th St./Hunter College. **Manhattan Kayak Company** ✉ The Boathouse, Pier 66,

W. 26th St. at 12th Ave., Chelsea ☎ 212/924–1788 ⊕ www.manhattankayak.com Ⓜ C, E to 23rd St. **Pier 96 Boathouse** ✉ 56th St. at the Hudson River, Midtown West ⊕ www. downtownboathouse.org Ⓜ 1, A, C, E to 59th St.

FOOTBALL

The football season runs from September through December. The enormously popular New York Giants play at MetLife Stadium in East Rutherford, New Jersey. Most seats for Giants games are sold on a season-ticket basis—and there's a long waiting list for those. However, single tickets are occasionally available at the stadium box office or on ticket resale sites like StubHub. The New York Jets also play at MetLife Stadium. Although Jets tickets are not as scarce as those for the Giants, most are snapped up by fans before the season opener.

Contact Information New York Giants ☎ 201/935–8222 for tickets ⊕ www.giants. com. **New York Jets** ☎ 800/469–5387 for tickets ⊕ www.newyorkjets.com.

ICE-SKATING

The outdoor rink in Rockefeller Center, open from October through early April, is much smaller in real life than it appears on TV and in movies—though it *is* as beautiful, especially when Rock Center's enormous Christmas tree towers above it. Tickets are first come, first served, so be prepared to wait—especially around the holidays. And be prepared to pay, too: skating rates are $27 for adults, which doesn't include skate rental ($12), and that only pays for admission during a single 90-minute skating session. The city's outdoor rinks, open from roughly November through March, all have their own character. Central Park's beautifully situated Wollman Rink offers skating until long after dark beneath the lights of the city. Be prepared for daytime crowds on weekends. The Lasker Rink, at the north end of Central Park, is smaller and usually less crowded than Wollman. Chelsea Piers' Sky Rink has two year-round indoor rinks overlooking the Hudson. Skate rentals are available at all rinks. The skating rink at the Winter Village at Bryant Park offers "free" skating, although this doesn't include skate rental ($15–$19) or the likely fee you'll pay to either buy a lock for a locker or have bags checked ($9–$10). Winter Village's rink is open from November through early March, from 8 am to 10 pm Sunday through Thursday and from 8 am to midnight Friday and Saturday. A FastPass (available online, includes skate rental and bag check) allows you to skip the line; it costs $22–$28. ■TIP➜ Every winter the trendy Standard Hotel, in the Meatpacking District, makes its own tiny ice rink. Skate tickets are $12 and skate rental is $3; the rink, at 848 Washington Street at 13th Street, is open from noon to midnight on weekdays and 9 am to 1 am on weekends. When you're done, cocktails and doughnuts are both ready to take the edge off any chill.

Contact Information Winter Village at Bryant Park ⊠ *1065 6th Ave., between 40th and 42nd Sts., Midtown West* ☎ *212/661-6640* ⊕ *wintervillage.org* Ⓜ *B, D, F, M to 42nd St.* **Lasker Rink** ⊠ *Midpark near E. 106th St., Central Park* ⊕ *www.laskerrink.com* Ⓜ *B, C to Cathedral Parkway (110th St.)–Central Park West; 2, 3 to Central Park North (110th St.).* **Rockefeller Center** ⊠ *Lower plaza, 50th St. at 5th Ave.,Midtown West* ☎ *212/332-7654* ⊕ *www.therinkatrockcenter.com* Ⓜ *B, D, F to 47th–50th Sts./Rockefeller Center; E, M to 5th Ave.–53rd St.* **Sky Rink** ⊠ *Pier 61, W. 23rd St. & the Hudson River, Chelsea* ☎ *212/336-6100* ⊕ *www.chelseapiers.com/sr* Ⓜ *C, E to 23rd St.* **Trump Wollman Skating Rink** ⊠ *North of 6th Ave. and Central Park S entrance, between 62nd and 63rd Sts.* ⊕ *www. wollmanskatingrink.com* Ⓜ *A, B, C, D, 1 to 59th St./Columbus Circle.*

JOGGING

All kinds of New Yorkers jog, some with dogs or babies in tow, so you'll always have company on the regular jogging routes. What's not recommended is setting out on a lonely park path at dusk. Go running when and where everybody else does. On Manhattan streets, roughly 20 north–south blocks make a mile.

In Manhattan, Central Park is the busiest spot, specifically along the 1.6-mile path circling the Jacqueline Kennedy Onassis Reservoir, where you jog in a counterclockwise direction. A runners' lane has been designated along the park roads; the entire loop road is a hilly 6 miles. A good 1.75-mile route starts at the Tavern on the Green along the West Drive, heads south around the bottom of the park to the East Drive, and circles back west on the 72nd Street park road to your starting point. Riverside Park, along the Hudson River bank in Manhattan, is glorious at sunset. You can cover 4.5 miles by running from West 72nd to 116th Street and back, and the Greenbelt trail extends 4 more miles north to the George Washington Bridge at 181st Street. Other favorite Manhattan circuits are the Battery Park City esplanade (about 2 miles), which connects to the Hudson River Park (about 1.5 miles), and the East River Esplanade (just over 3 miles from East 63rd to East 125th streets).

▌ STUDENTS IN NEW YORK

New York is home to Columbia University, New York University, Fordham University, and the City College of New York. With other colleges scattered throughout the five boroughs, and a huge population of public and private high-schoolers, it's no wonder the city is rife with student discounts. Wherever you go, especially museums, sightseeing attractions, and performances, identify yourself as a student and ask if a discount is available, but be prepared to show your ID.

High 5 for the Arts is a great program for teens 13 and 18 (or anyone in middle or high school). Tickets to a wide variety of performances (though only rarely Broadway shows) are sold for $5 online or by phone. Check the website to find out about upcoming events.

IDs and Services **High 5 for the Arts**
☎ *212/750–0555* ⊕ *www.highfivetix.org.*
STA Travel ✉ *722 Broadway, between
Washington Pl. and Waverly Pl.* ☎ *212/627–
3111, 800/781–4040 for 24-hr service center*
⊕ *www.sta.com.*

▌TAXES

A sales tax of 8.875% applies to almost
everything you can buy retail, including restaurant meals. However, prescription drugs
and nonprepared food bought in grocery
stores are exempt. Clothing and footwear
costing less than $110 are also exempt.

▌TIPPING

The customary tipping rate for taxi drivers is 15%–20%, with a minimum of $2;
bellhops are usually given $2 per bag
in luxury hotels, $1 per bag elsewhere.
Hotel maids should be tipped $2 per day
of your stay. A doorman who hails or
helps you into a cab can be tipped $1–$2.
You should also tip your hotel concierge
for services rendered; the size of the tip
depends on the difficulty of your request,
as well as the quality of the concierge's
work. Waiters should be tipped 15%–
20%, though at higher-end restaurants, a
solid 20% is more the norm. Tip $1 or $2
per drink you order at the bar.

▌VISITOR INFORMATION

The Grand Central Partnership (a busi-
ness-improvement district) has installed
a number of information booths in and
around Grand Central Terminal (there's
one near Vanderbilt Avenue and 43rd
Street). They're loaded with maps and
helpful brochures on attractions throughout the city and staffed by friendly, knowledgeable, multilingual New Yorkers.

NYC & Company's Times Square Visitors
Center (at 7th Avenue and 46th Street) is
decked out with lots of fun and helpful
tools like multilingual kiosks. The bureau
also has a Midtown visitor center on 7th
Avenue (near 52nd Street) and runs kiosks
in Lower Manhattan at City Hall Park
and in Chinatown, at the triangle where
Canal, Walker, and Baxter streets meet.

The Downtown Alliance has information
on the area encompassing City Hall south
to Battery Park, and from the East River
to West Street. For a free booklet listing
New York City attractions and tour packages, contact the New York State Division
of Tourism.

CONTACTS
City Information Downtown Alliance
☎ *212/566–6700* ⊕ *www.downtownny.com.*
Grand Central Partnership ☎ *212/883–2420*
⊕ *www.grandcentralpartnership.org.* **NYC &
Company Convention & Visitors Bureau**
✉ *Midtown Information Center, 810 7th
Ave., between 52nd and 53rd Sts., Midtown
West* ☎ *212/484–1222* ⊕ *www.nycgo.com.*
Times Square Visitors Center ✉ *1560
Broadway, entrance at 7th Ave. and 46th St.,
Midtown West* ☎ *212/452–5283* ⊕ *www.
timessquarenyc.org* Ⓜ *N, Q, R, S, 1, 2, 3, 7 to
42nd St./Times Square.*

**Statewide Information New York State
Division of Tourism** ☎ *800/225–5697*
⊕ *www.iloveny.com.*

INDEX

PHOTO CREDITS

Front cover: Stockelements/Shutterstock and Rockefellercenter.com. [Description: Atlas at Rockefeller Center]. Back cover (from left to right): Tomas Fano/Flickr (CC BY-SA 2.0); Thomas Schauer; Dave Winer/Flickr (CC BY-SA 2.0). Spine: AlexGul/Shutterstock. 1, Songquan Deng/Shutterstock. 2, Kord. com/age fotostock. 5, Liberty Helicopters, Inc. Chapter 1: Experience New York City: 8-9, Rudy Sulgan/age fotostock. 10, Luc Novovitch/age Fotostock. 11, Oote Boe Photography/Alamy. 14, Ace Stock Limited/Alamy. 16, Alija/iStockphoto. 18 (left), Rome and Greece gallery by Xuan Che http://www. flickr.com/photos/rosemania/2157661526/Attribution License. 18 (top center), Kord.com/age fotostock. 18 (top right), New York. MoMA by Tomas Fano http://www.flickr.com/photos/tomas fano/2713778452/Attribution-ShareAlike License. 18 (bottom), Doug Scott/age fotostock.19 (top left), SuperStock/age fotostock. 19 (bottom left), Craig Chesek/AMNH. 19 (right), Picture-Quest. 20, Black Star/Alamy. 21 (left), David H. Wells/age fotostock. 21 (right), Richard Levine/Alamy. 24, Brooklyn Bridge Park Etienne Frossard/www.brooklynbridgeparknyc.org. 25 (left), Frances M. Roberts/Alamy. 25 (right), Union Square by adactio http://www.flickr.com/photos/adactio/3817931108/Attribution-License. 29 (left), David Berkowitz/Flickr. 29 (right), emilydickinsonridesabmx/Flickr. 31, Jeff Greenberg/Alamy. 33, Adriano Castelli/Shutterstock, 36, Corbis. 37, Photodisc. 39 (top), Liberty Helicopters, Inc. 39 (bottom), Joshua Haviv/shutterstock. 41 (top), Library of Congress Prints and Photographs Division. 41 (bottom), Library of Congress Prints and Photographs Division. Chapter 2: Lower Manhattan: 43, Bill Grove/iStockphoto. 45, Heeb Christian/age fotostock. 46, Chuck Pefley/Alamy. 50, Silverstein Properties. 51 (top), White House Photo/Alamy. 51 (bottom), Sondra Paulson/iStockphoto. 52 (top left), Fireball erupting in the South Tower by Robert http://www.flickr.com/photos/themachine stops/88181088/Attribution-ShareAlike License. 52 (top right), Jim Watson/CHINFO, Navy Visual News Service (Public Domain), via Wikimedia Commons. 52 (bottom), RodneyRamsey/Flickr. 53 (left), Jim Watson/CHINFO, Navy Visual News Service (Public Domain), via Wikimedia Commons. 53 (center), Peter Comitini/Flickr. 53 (right), Denise Gould (Public Domain), via Wikimedia Commons. 54-55 (top), Silverstein Properties. 54 (bottom), Silverstein Properties. 55 (bottom left), meunierd/Shutterstock. 55 (bottom right), Joe Woolhead/Silverstein Properties. 56 (top left), Luca Cepparo/iStockphoto. 56 (top right), FaceMePLS/Flickr. 56 (bottom left), p_c_w/Flickr. 56 (bottom right), cytech/Flickr. 60-61, kropic1/Shutterstock. 63, Estormiz/Wikimedia Commons. Chapter 3: SoHo, NoLIta, Little Italy, and Chinatown: 65, Art Kowalsky/Alamy. 67, Ambient Images Inc./Alamy. 68, Yadid Levy/Alamy. 70-71, Renault Philippe/age fotostock. 73, OK Harris Works of Art. 74, Philip Lange/Shutterstock. Chapter 4: The East Village and the Lower East Side: 77, Jeff Greenberg/Alamy. 79, peyri/Flickr. 80, New York. East Village. Stop the Violence. E 12TH St by http://www.flickr.com/photos/tomas fano/2710315445/Attribution-ShareAlike License. Chapter 5: Greenwich Village and the West Village: 87, wdstock/iStockphoto.89, Tenement Houses Overlooking Washington Square Park, New York City by http://www.flickr. com/photos/43533334@ N07/5139725894/Attribution License. 90, wdstock/iStockphoto. 91, Ambient Images Inc./Alamy. 94, PCL/Alamy. Chapter 6: Chelsea and the Meatpacking District: 97, David Berkowitz/Flickr. 99, Black Star/Alamy. 100, By Gryffindor [CC-BY-SA-3.0 (www. creativecommons.org/licenses/by-sa/3.0)], via Wikimedia Commons. 102-103, Kord.com/age fotostock. 105, Kokyat Choong/Alamy. Chapter 7: Union Square, the Flatiron District, and Gramercy Park: 111, David Shankbone/Wikipedia.org. 113, Kord.com/age fotostock. 114, Yadid Levy/Alamy. 115, Russell Kord/Alamy. 117, naphtalina/iStockphoto. 118, IMG_0776 by Jan-Erik Finnberg http://www. flickr.com/photos/wheany/2233336954/Attribution-NonCommercial License. Chapter 8: Midtown East: 121, Kord.com. 123, Jaap Hart/iStockphoto. 124, svlumagraphica/iStockphoto. 126, Rudy Sulgan/age fotostock. 129, Stuart Monk/iStockphoto/Thinkstock. 131, Empire State Sunset by Eric E Yang http://www.flickr.com/photos/midweekpost/142493669/Attribution License. 133, Sylvain Grandadam/ age fotostock. Chapter 9: Midtown West: 135, Times Square - New York by C.line http://www.flickr. com/photos/pepsiline/4247882387/Attribution-ShareAlike License. 137, Bruno Perousse/age fotostock. 138, (c) Mirceanil Dreamstime.com. 141, New York. Radio City Music Hall by Tomas Fano http:// www.flickr.com/ tomasfano/2738549430/Attribution-ShareAlike License. 143, overnap/ iStockphoto. 146, New York. MoMA by Tomas Fano http://www. flickr.com/photos/tomas fano/2713778452/Attribution-ShareAlike License. Chapter 10: The Upper East Side: 149, Nicholas Pitt/Alamy. 151, JayLazarin/iStockphoto. 152, Janine Wiedel Photolibrary/Alamy. 155, Doug Scott/age fotostock. 156, Geoffrey Clements. 158, Brooks Walker. 159, Renaud Visage/age fotostock. 160 (top), Renaud Visage/age fotostock. 160 (center), Metropolitan Museum of Art. 160 (bottom), An East Greek Late Archaic Alabastron in the Form of a Kore by http://www.flickr.com/photos/antiquities project/5515795335/Attribution License. 162 (top), the new American wing by Kristen Bonardi Rapp http://www.flickr.com/photos/gezellig girl/3835837758/Attribution-ShareAlike License. 162 (bottom), Metropolitan Museum of Art. 163, Wild Bill Studio/Metropolitan Museum of Art. 164 (top and bot-